# foundations of
# MARKETING

# foundations of
# MARKETING

eighth canadian edition

M. Dale Beckman
**UNIVERSITY OF VICTORIA**

John M. Rigby
**UNIVERSITY OF SASKATCHEWAN**

THOMSON

NELSON

Australia   Canada   Mexico   Singapore   Spain   United Kingdom   United States

**THOMSON**

**NELSON**

**Foundations of Marketing**
Eighth Canadian Edition

by M. Dale Beckman and John M. Rigby

**Editorial Director and Publisher:**
Evelyn Veitch

**Acquisitions Editor:**
Veronica Visentin

**Developmental Editor:**
Shefali Mehta

**Marketing Manager:**
Bram Sepers

**Managing Production Editor:**
Susan Calvert

**Production Coordinator:**
Hedy Sellers

**Copy Editor/Proofreader:**
Gail Marsden

**Creative Director:**
Angela Cluer

**Interior Design:**
Peter Papayanakis

**Cover Design:**
Peter Papayanakis

**Cover Image:**
Tim Flach/Stone

**Compositor:**
Gerry Dunn

**Indexer:**
Andrew Little

**Printer:**
Transcontinental Printing Inc.

Statistics Canada information is used with the permission of Statistics Canada. Information on the availability of the wide range of data from Statistics Canada can be obtained from Statistics Canada's Regional Offices, its World Wide Web site at http://www.statcan.ca, and its toll-free access number 1-800-263-1136.

Every effort has been made to trace ownership of all copyrighted material and to secure permission from copyright holders. In the event of any question arising as to the use of any material, we will be pleased to make the necessary corrections in future printings.

**National Library of Canada Cataloguing in Publication Data**

Beckman, M. Dale, 1934-
 Foundations of marketing / M. Dale Beckman, John M. Rigby.— 8th Canadian ed.

ISBN 0-17-622465-3

1. Marketing. I. Rigby, John M. (John Mark), 1957- II. Title

HF5415.B56 2003    658.8
C2002-906156-3

To Bobby and Wendy, with thanks for constant encouragement

# Brief Contents

# Table of Contents

## PART 4: The Visible Marketing Plan: Product Management

# PART 4: The Visible Marketing Plan: Pricing

## PART 4:   The Visible Marketing Plan: Distribution

*Foundations of Marketing* has maintained a leadership role among Canadian marketing textbooks for over twenty-five years. Faculty and students have returned to this respected book again and again.

### It is up-to-date.

This edition features a new and creative model in Chapter 1 depicting the entire marketing process and entitled *Marketing from the Inside Out*. This text has contemporary coverage of topics such as lifetime-customer value and relationship marketing. It looks at the possibilities as well as the challenges of e-commerce and direct marketing. It has an expanded discussion of branding and supply chain management. *Foundations of Marketing* reflects contemporary academic thinking and business practices.

### It has a proven record of providing the "foundation" for future study and careers promised in the book title.

The book presents a sound and complete introduction to the subject of marketing. Professors and students can be assured of finding an excellent and full introduction to marketing. It fully prepares students for more advanced study of marketing but also provides considerable substance in its own right for those students who will not be taking further marketing courses. *Foundations of Marketing*, Eighth Canadian Edition, is completely updated but maintains its established focus on the key issues of marketing practice and theory.

### Students like to read and study the book.

*Foundations of Marketing* has been acclaimed for its interesting and lively style. Past students have commented that the reading/studying experience is facilitated by the engaging writing and readability and this continues to be a hallmark of this edition. Throughout the book, many interesting photos and advertisements provide further excitement to the textual material. Previous editions have been lauded for their excellent design and layout. The Eighth Canadian Edition upholds that high standard.

## Special Interest Boxes

To help students more easily connect principles to practice, six feature boxes are interspersed throughout the text:

| | |
|---|---|
| **INTERNET IMPACT** | showcases the importance and impact of the Internet on marketing. |
| **THE PRACTISING MARKETER** | demonstrates practical applications of marketing concepts. |
| **THE CANADIAN MARKETPLACE** | contains interesting statistics, marketing trivia, and quotations. |
| **THE ETHICAL MARKETER** | presents various ethical issues, such as campus monopolies, marketing to children, and telephone advertising. |
| **THE INFORMED CONSUMER** | provides information to help make readers more knowledgeable consumers and more aware of their legal rights. |
| **THE ROOTS OF MARKETING** | features anecdotes and quotations that provide a historical perspective on marketing. |

The special interest boxes include discussion questions to guide the students as they apply the concepts covered in the chapter.

## Pedagogical Features

The marketing concept is presented as the central theme connecting marketing strategy and the entire marketing program and process. Diagrams and tables highlighting key strategic issues are reiterated throughout the text to aid learning.

Each chapter begins with a list of **Chapter Objectives** and concludes with a **Summary**. In addition, chapters contain **Web links** and a list of **Key Terms**. **Marginal definitions** of key terms are also highlighted as they are explained in the text.

A unique feature is the **Interactive Summary** and **Discussion Questions** section. These questions are specially designed to ensure understanding and facilitate student learning. In this section, portions of chapter material are summarized and the student is asked to answer thought-provoking questions that require *more than just reciting textual material*—the questions challenge the student to demonstrate mastery of the chapter concepts. Furthermore, an Internet-based discussion question has been included with every chapter.

For additional marketing resources and a list of further readings for each chapter, students may refer to the *Foundations of Marketing* Web site at www.beckmanmarketing8e.nelson.com.

## Special Chapters

Some specialized marketing applications present very meaningful and unique issues for the manager. While integrating many special topics throughout the text, *Foundations of Marketing* recognizes this unique material. It provides more depth than many other texts through the inclusion of the following chapters:

- **Ensuring Total Customer Satisfaction and Managing Customer Relationships**
- **Supply Chain and Logistics Management**
- **Not-for-Profit Marketing**
- **Global Marketing.** International marketing is also integrated into every chapter throughout the book. However, the separate chapter allows a greater coverage of many special international topics not easily incorporated into standard textual material.
- **Marketing Research Chapter Appendix.** This popular feature has been totally updated. It has been found to be so valuable that other marketing research books have included it.

# NEW TO THIS EDITION

## Cases

Each chapter now has a case that follows the question section. In addition, a collection of shorter and comprehensive cases is included at the end of the book. Realizing that global competition is increasing, a number of these cases illustrate marketing situations in international settings.

## Major Chapter Revisions

- Pricing has been reorganized to better distinguish pricing theory from pricing management and application.
- Product chapters have been reorganized around the total product concept with an increased emphasis on branding and brand management.
- Significant revisions have been made to the introductory and segmentation chapters.
- The introductory chapter includes *Marketing from the Inside Out* with accompanying diagram. There is also a useful new diagram illustrating different organizational orientations.
- Segmentation has been updated. It now includes a discussion of the popular VALS™ psychographic profiles while retaining the Canadian example of the Environics profiles.
- The channels and retailing chapters are streamlined, and the retailing chapter has a newly written section on the present and future prospects for e-tailing.

- The global marketing chapter not only sets the scene for an understanding of international marketing but provides a stronger emphasis on strategies for entering the global market, as well as including a good discussion on cultural differences and the Internet and international business.

## Coverage of the Internet, Technology, and e-Commerce

After the first burst of enthusiasm for electronic commerce, businesses have come to realize that there are great possibilities, but also challenges to its use. The book provides a realistic look at these issues. The role of technology has been woven in throughout the book, beginning with an overview of the issues in Chapter 2, The Environment for Marketing Decisions. E-commerce—retailing and advertising on the Internet—is discussed extensively.

Special coverage is provided in the discussion of relationship marketing, business-to-business marketing, retailing, marketing communications, and global marketing. Web site addresses (URLs) are provided for many of the companies mentioned in the text. The instructor or the student can then easily follow up on the current situation of these companies. In addition, readers can consult the *Foundations of Marketing* Web site. The marketing research chapter Appendix, which lists and describes marketing research data sources, includes both print and Internet sources.

*Foundations of Marketing* pays special attention to the marketing concept and marketing strategy. These topics introduce marketing planning and the marketing mix in a manner that is consistent, clear, and pedagogically appropriate. The text uses the terms strategy, marketing planning, and marketing mix in such a way that their meaning is consistent and unclouded. We avoid using these terms until they can be introduced and developed properly. The overall strategy of a firm, of which marketing strategy is an essential component, is shown to be paramount. A marketing plan is required to implement the marketing strategy, and the marketing mix is part of the marketing plan. By introducing the marketing mix a little later in the course, students are more likely to comprehend the power and usefulness of this concept, rather than viewing the "P's" of the mix as a simple formula that can be understood superficially and treated in a trivial way.

We believe *Foundations of Marketing*, Eighth Canadian Edition, will be a strong pedagogical support for marketing instructors and an interesting introduction to the exciting and varied world of marketing for students. We wish you all the best as you explore this world together.

# THE *FOUNDATIONS OF MARKETING* PACKAGE

A full educational package is also available to complete *Foundations of Marketing*, Eighth Canadian Edition:

- **Computerized Test Bank** The updated and revised Computerized Test Bank contains more than 2200 multiple-choice, true/false, matching, and fill in the blank questions. Instructors are able to preview and edit test questions as well as add their own. Answers are provided, as well as scoring and grade-recording management.

- **Instructor's Manual** The Instructor's Manual contains chapter overviews, chapter objectives, lecture outlines, answers to end-of-chapter questions, questions and answers to video cases, and teaching notes to accompany the cases.

- **Instructor's CD-ROM** This CD-ROM includes resources designed specifically for instructors: PowerPoint® slides, Instructor's Manual, and Computerized Test Bank.

- **PowerPoint® Presentation Software** This collection of PowerPoint® slides covers all the essential topics presented in each chapter of the book and also includes figures, tables, graphs, and other examples to reinforce major concepts and issues. Instructors are able to custom design their own multimedia classroom presentations by adapting or adding slides.

www.beckmanmarketing8e.
nelson.com

**CBC**

- **Study Guide** This new learning tool is designed to enhance students' understanding of marketing practices by bringing marketing concepts and theories to life. The workbook contains numerous types of exercises that deal with real-life marketing issues and events. Each chapter highlights the content discussed in the corresponding textbook chapter.

- *Foundations of Marketing* **Web Site** Students and instructors who are interested in acquiring additional information on the study of marketing will find links to current marketing information, a variety of marketing-related sites, and other useful learning tools. The site also offers on-line marketing resources, hot new topics, and case resources.

- **CBC Video Cases** This collection of segments from CBC illustrates real-life cases related to major topics discussed in the text. Suggestions for use are provided in the Instructor's Manual.

- **Overhead Transparencies** The approximately 160 full-colour transparencies in this package are described in detail in the notes included with the package.

# ACKNOWLEDGEMENTS

Any textbook represents the work and thinking of countless scholars. We recognize and appreciate the stream of knowledge-creating activities of our colleagues from around the world.

This book naturally builds upon the seven previous editions, and thus reflects the comments and suggestions of reviewers over the years. It also reflects the work of previous editors, copy editors, and researchers.

We are also grateful for the time, attention, and suggestions of the following reviewers. We have considered their recommendations carefully and tried to respond to them. This is a better book because of their input.

Morie Shacker,
*BCIT*

Linda Donville,
*Centennial College*

Robert Soroka,
*Dawson College*

Steve Janisse,
*St. Clair College*

Jayne Van Dusen,
*Algonquin College*

N. Garth Maguire,
*Okanagan University College*

Case writing is a special calling and skill. Those who write cases provide exceptional opportunities for instructors and students to develop understanding through their work in solving case problems together. We acknowledge with thanks their participation in the cases that appear at the end of this book.

We also acknowledge the diligent efforts of the Nelson publishing team. Special thanks go to Shefali Mehta for her willing support and patient understanding of sometimes impossible academic schedules. We would also like to thank Susan Calvert, Evelyn Veitch, Veronica Visentin, and Gail Marsden.

The sales team deserves specific mention. We recognize that your intelligent and faithful work is a key to the success of this book. We know that you will continue your dependable achievements.

Most importantly, we give thanks to our families. We appreciate their willingness to forgo numerous activities, and even our presence, while we spent the hours necessary to complete this project.

*M. Dale Beckman*
University of Victoria

*John M. Rigby*
University of Saskatchewan

# foundations of

# MARKETING

Fall 2002 National Campaign

Summer 2002 New Market Launch Campaign

TELUS's complete marketing program, including its whimsical nature ads, has resulted in strong gains in the Canadian telecommunications market.

## Chapter 1

# THE NATURE OF MARKETING

## CHAPTER OBJECTIVES

After reading and studying this chapter, you should be able to

1. Define marketing and describe its primary nature.
2. Show how marketing bridges the gap between producer and consumer.
3. Outline the functions of marketing.
4. Demonstrate the scope of marketing.
5. Contrast activities in each of the three orientations of business in the marketing domain.
6. Position marketing as one of the basic business functions.

Canada's telecommunications sector has been the scene of some spectacular, headline-making setbacks in the last few years. We sometimes forget, though, that there have also been some spectacular successes.

TELUS clearly belongs in the "success" category. Thanks to award-winning national marketing and an aggressive sustainable growth strategy, it has undergone a startling transformation.

Until the late 1980s, TELUS was Alberta's provincial telephone company, called Alberta Government Telephones. In 1990, AGT was privatized in what was then the biggest public offering in Canadian history. From that beginning, the company moved to establish itself as Western Canada's biggest telecommunications company. A 1998 merger with BC Tel, British Columbia's telephone service provider, was a key component of its growth.

In 2000, TELUS moved to the national stage with multiple acquisitions of communications companies across Canada, including QuébecTel and national wireless operator Clearnet.

Along with its acquisitions TELUS has launched an innovative marketing campaign based on whimsical nature themes. The Telus brand has been promoted and the Telus message of consistent high-quality service has been matched by customers' experiences.

TELUS is now a true national telecommunications company with more than $7 billion dollars in annual revenue. In a relatively short time, TELUS has gone from being a regional telephone company to being a national success story—thanks in no small part to its unique approach to marketing.

www.telus.ca

# INTRODUCTION

Marketing has changed the face of Western civilization in the past 50 years. Many consumer products are available in the most remote parts of the globe—and products can be found on Canadian shelves that come from the most remote parts of the globe. We are exposed to thousands of marketing messages on any given day. It is hard to imagine what our world would look like if all marketing activity were to suddenly stop.

The practice of marketing has itself changed a great deal and seems destined to continue to evolve rapidly. Today you can apply for a mortgage, buy insurance, order books—or any number of other products or services—over the Internet without ever leaving your home. Marketers are increasingly forming a sort of relationship with their customers based on information gleaned from extensive databases. For example, retailers can and do track your shopping history and custom-design promotional offerings just for you and other people with your shopping habits and tastes. Even a few years ago such possibilities were only dreamed of at futurist conferences.

Even though the practice of marketing is changing at a dizzying speed, the basic, and deceptively simple, underlying principles of marketing are remarkably stable. Against that backdrop of rapid and exciting change, this book is intended to help you learn and understand basic marketing principles and to illustrate and help you learn how the principles can be applied.

Many people think that marketing is really just a synonym for advertising or selling. In fact, marketing is a much broader concept, although advertising and selling can certainly be part of the marketing process. In the most general sense, marketing is all about matching producers' output to customers' activities. As a consumer, you know that sometimes this is done very well and other times not. Generally, this matching process results in a continuous flow of goods and services for consumers, and the economic activity that maintains profitable business and employment.

The idea of matching producers' output to customers' activities sounds less complicated than it really is. There are many product and even company failures, and often people cannot seem to find the product that really satisfies their needs. Poor marketing frequently causes these problems. The cause of poor marketing is usually a lack of focus on customers.

FedEx strives for 100 percent customer satisfaction.

# THE ROOTS OF MARKETING

If we want to know what a business is we have to start with its purpose. And its purpose must lie outside the business itself. In fact, it must lie in society since a business enterprise is an organ of society. There is one valid definition of business purpose: to create a customer.[1]

Peter F. Drucker is recognized as one of the most influential management thinkers of the modern era. He has written extensively and is quoted widely. In a salute to his contribution, he has been awarded nineteen honorary

www.drucker.com

doctorates by different universities around the world. He is particularly interested in non-profit organizations and serves as Honorary Chairman of the Peter F. Drucker Foundation for Nonprofit Management, New York, NY.

To learn more about Peter F. Drucker, visit the Peter F. Drucker Canadian Foundation for Nonprofit Innovation Web site.

Serving the needs of customers is what business should be all about. A good example is the well-known philosophy of FedEx, which is to strive for 100 percent customer satisfaction and time-certain delivery. This philosophy has made FedEx the leader in its field. Marketing is the business function that interprets customer needs to the rest of the organization and brings the resulting offerings of the firm to the consumer.

www.fedex.com/ca/ca_english

Even with excellent customer focus, meeting customer needs can be difficult. It is as if there is a gap between producers and consumers that marketing must bridge. Many things can contribute to this gap. The most common are consumer perceptions, lack of information, attitudes, time constraints, cost constraints, and space or location. Consider the gap between Cheryl, a university student whose current stereo works, but not very well, and a stereo manufacturer, say Sony, that would like to sell her a new stereo.

- *Consumer perceptions.* Cheryl may not realize that her stereo is poor quality and may perceive the sound it produces to be acceptable.
- *Lack of information.* Cheryl does not realize that Sony makes mid-priced stereo systems, not only high-end equipment.
- *Attitudes.* Cheryl's friend had problems with his Sony stereo, so Cheryl suspects that the brand is over-rated.
- *Time constraints.* Cheryl is a second-year commerce student and doesn't have a lot of time to shop for and compare stereos.
- *Cost constraints.* Because she's a student, Cheryl does not have much extra cash right now, so even a mid-priced stereo system would stretch her resources.
- *Space or location.* Sony manufactures its stereos in Japan (and other countries), but Cheryl wants hers in Lethbridge.

www.sony.com

A careful study of customer needs allows marketing and the rest of the organization to bridge the gap between producer and consumer. This bridge is built through eight **marketing functions**: buying, selling, transporting, storing, grading, financing, risk taking, and information collecting and disseminating.

**marketing functions**
Buying, selling, transporting, storing, grading, financing, risk taking, and information collecting and disseminating.

One or more of the contributors to the gap between Cheryl and Sony can be addressed by each of the marketing functions. These functions are a part of all marketing transactions, to a greater or lesser degree. They may be shifted to various members of the retail or wholesale trade, or even to the customer, but they cannot be eliminated. The marketing functions are discussed further in Chapter 15.

Performing the marketing functions reduces the size of the gap between the organization and the consumer. As we shall see, a reduction in the gap implies an increase in the utility consumers associate with a product or service. The result is that consumers are more likely to enter into an exchange relationship with the marketing organization. Let's first consider the notion of exchange, and then we'll examine how it relates to utility.

# MARKETING IS ABOUT EXCHANGE

**exchange process**

The means by which two or more parties give something of value to one another to satisfy felt needs.

The essence of marketing is the **exchange process**. This is the means by which two or more parties give something of value to one another to satisfy felt needs.[2] In many cases, the item is a tangible good, such as a newspaper, a calculator, or a pair of shoes. In other cases, intangible services, such as a car wash, transportation, or a concert performance, are exchanged for money. In still other instances, funds or time donations may be offered to political candidates, a Red Cross office, or a church or synagogue.

cell phone (to call friends):
$180

pda (to beam friends):
$200

internet setup (to IM friends):
$50

actually being with friends:
priceless

MasterCard® is accepted most everywhere, for everything from cell phones to marshmallows.
For more information, go to mastercard.com

there are some things money can't buy. *MasterCard* for everything else there's MasterCard.™

**MasterCard's "priceless" campaign recognizes that MasterCard provides many different types of utility for its customers.**

The marketing function is both simple and direct in subsistence-level economies. For example, assume that a primitive society consists solely of George and Elaine. Assume also that the only elements of their standard of living are food, clothing, and shelter. The two live in adjoining caves on a mountainside. They weave their own clothes and tend their own fields independently. They are able to subsist even though their standard of living is minimal.

George is an excellent weaver but a poor farmer, while Elaine is an excellent farmer but a poor weaver. In this situation, it would be wise for each to specialize in the line of work that he or she does best. The net result would then be a greater total production of both clothing and food. In other words, specialization and division of labour will lead to a production surplus. But neither George nor Elaine is any better off until they trade the products of their individual labour, thereby creating the exchange process.

Exchange is the origin of marketing activity. In fact, marketing has been described as "the process of creating and resolving exchange relationships."[3] When there is a need to exchange goods, the natural result is marketing effort on the part of the people involved.

The cave-dweller example is simplistic, and our society has a more complicated exchange process. Nonetheless, the basic concept is the same: production is not meaningful until a system of marketing has been established. As Wroe Alderson observes in the Roots of Marketing box, without the possibility of exchange, the world as we know it would not exist.

## Marketing Defined

Ask five people to define marketing, and you will likely get five different definitions. Most of them will be too limited, and wrong. As we mentioned, because of the visibility of personal selling and advertising, many people will say that marketing is selling or that marketing is advertising. But marketing is much more comprehensive than these narrow perspectives.

Marketing can be defined from a macro (or societal) or from a micro (or organizational level) perspective. At the macro level, marketing is defined as the development of systems that direct an economy's flow of goods and services from producers to consumers. This definition shows that, when added up, all marketing activities produce a flow of goods and services that are distributed throughout society. In a sense, at a macro level, marketing is the fuel that drives the engines of the economy.

This book will mostly look at marketing from a micro level. When defined at a micro level, we can think of marketing as everything that an organization does to stay in tune with its customers or clients in order to ensure that the organization's products or services continue to effectively meet the customer's needs. More formally, the definition of **marketing** is "the process of planning and executing the conception, pricing, promotion, and distribution of ideas, goods, and services to create exchanges that satisfy individual and organization objectives."[5]

This definition implies much more than you may at first think. The rest of this book is required to elaborate it. The definition applies to not-for-profit as well as business organizations. Note also that the definition is specific in pointing out that exchanges created by marketing activities must satisfy individual (customer) objectives and organizational objectives.

It is important to realize that effective marketing does not happen accidentally—careful planning is part of the definition. Professional marketers have found that success comes about much more easily when planning starts with a thorough analysis of customers and their needs. This is such an important idea, with so many ramifications, that we will spend the next section elaborating it.

## The Successful Organization

The successful organization is geared toward making desired exchanges more likely to occur—that is, closing the gap discussed earlier between the organization and the consumer. Organizations increase the likelihood of desired exchanges taking place through production and marketing. These organizational functions increase **utility**, which can be defined as the want-satisfying power of a product or service. The higher the levels of utility a product possesses, the more attractive it is to a customer. There are four basic kinds of utility: form, time, place, and ownership.

Form utility is created when the firm converts raw materials and components into finished products and services. Ford Motor Company converts glass, steel, fabrics, rubber, and other components into a new Mustang or Taurus. Tommy Hilfiger converts fabric, thread, and buttons into clothes. Symphony Nova Scotia converts sheet music, musical instruments, musicians, a conductor, and the Rebecca Cohn Auditorium into a performance. Although marketing inputs may be important in specifying consumer and audience preferences, actually creating form utility is the responsibility of the production function of the organization.

Marketing directly creates the other utilities: time, place, and ownership. Time utility is created when products and services are available to the consumer when she or he wants to purchase them.

### THE ROOTS OF MARKETING

It seems altogether reasonable to describe the development of exchange as a great invention which helped to start primitive man on the road to civilization.[4]

Professor Wroe Alderson published *Marketing Behavior and Executive Action* in 1957. It has been an extremely influential book, informing and anticipating much of the subsequent theoretical writings in marketing.

**marketing**
The process of planning and executing the conception, pricing, promotion, and distribution of ideas, goods, and services to create exchanges that satisfy individual and organizational objectives.

**utility**
The want-satisfying power of a product or service.

www.tommypr.com

Coca-Cola, for example, is available 24 hours a day at 7 Eleven, Mac's, or vending machines. Place utility is created when the product is available at a convenient location, such as a movie theatre in Coca-Cola's case. Ownership utility is created when facilities are available whereby title to the product or service may be transferred at the time of purchase. For low-value goods, such as Coca-Cola, there is an implied contract when the customer purchases the product. For high-value products, such as a car, there is a literal contract that transfers ownership from the car dealership to the purchaser.

## Three Types of Business Orientation

Most companies have an orientation that fits one of the following three categories: product-oriented, sales-oriented, or market-oriented.[6] That is, most companies act as if organizational success is achieved either through their product design, through intensive sales efforts, or through integrated marketing activities. Marketers argue that the surest route to organizational success is by following the marketing concept (see Figure 1.1). Let's look at each orientation in turn.

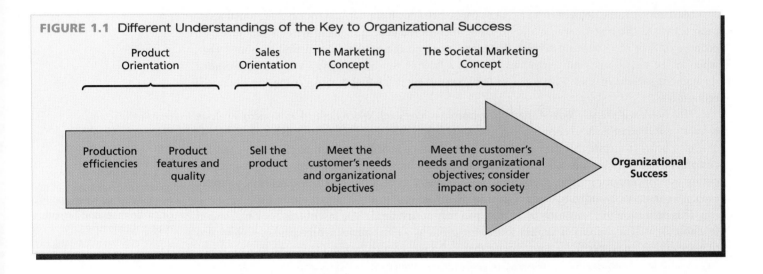

**FIGURE 1.1** Different Understandings of the Key to Organizational Success

### Product or Production Orientation

**product orientation**
A focus on the product itself rather than on the consumer's needs.

In firms with a **product orientation**, the emphasis is on the product itself rather than on the consumer's needs. For the production-oriented firm, the dominant considerations in product design are those of ease or cheapness of production. In either case, market considerations are ignored or de-emphasized. Firms stress production of goods or services,[7] then look for people to purchase them. The prevailing attitude of this type of firm is that a good product will sell itself. Beginning entrepreneurs often take this approach, convinced that their product idea is a sure-fire winner. Such a strategy is very limiting, for it assumes that the producer's tastes and values are the same as those of the market. Often a firm does not consider changing from this narrow approach until it runs into trouble.

### Sales Orientation

**sales orientation**
A focus on developing a strong sales force to convince consumers to buy whatever the firm produces.

A **sales orientation** is an improvement on a product orientation. The firm is still quite product-oriented, but it recognizes that the world will not beat a path to its door to purchase its products. Therefore, the firm focuses its marketing efforts on developing a strong sales force to convince consumers to buy. "Get the customer to fit the company's offerings" could be a motto of such a sales-oriented strategy. From this perspective, to be successful, what you really need is an aggressive, high-powered sales organization and advertising program.

As you are watching TV some evening (with your marketing text in your lap), try to identify some ads with a pure sales orientation. For some reason, furniture retailers often use this approach.

# S+ARCK™

Not all furniture retailers are stuck in a sales orientation. Starck Furniture takes a tongue-in-cheek approach to showing customer reactions to great value.

## THE INFORMED CONSUMER

### BAIT AND SWITCH

Bait and switch is a high-pressure sales approach that is considered unethical and, in certain circumstances, is illegal. Consumers are often baited with advertisements of a particular item. Once they get to the store, the salesperson will not sell the item because he or she says it is inferior or they have sold out. The salesperson then uses high-pressure sales tactics to sell the consumer a more expensive item.

A 14" colour TV is advertised for only $200 at Scam Stereo Sales and Service. Pat heads down at opening time to be sure to get one. However, David, the salesperson, tells Pat that several customers have complained about that particular set (that's why it is on sale); it is not guaranteed; and

the manufacturer is out of business (so there are no spare parts available). David just knows Pat (a person David has never met before) will not be satisfied with the sale set, but there are other sets in the store that are fully guaranteed, are very popular, and only sell for $399. (Pat should head for the nearest exit when this happens.)

Always find a dealer with a good reputation when making major purchases of any kind. Sellers must have reasonable quantities of products they advertise at bargain prices (*The Competition Act*).

Source: Adapted from *Consumer Wisdom: A Guide for Making Informed Consumer Decisions* (Saskatoon: Public Legal Education Association of Saskatchewan, Inc., 2002, version 1.1), p. 8.

Clearly, good, persuasive communication is an important part of a marketing plan. However, selling is only one component of marketing. As marketing expert Theodore Levitt has pointed out, "Marketing is as different from selling as chemistry is from alchemy, astronomy from astrology, chess from checkers."[8]

## Market Orientation

**market orientation**

A focus on understanding customer needs and objectives, then making the business serve the interests of the customer rather than trying to make the customer buy what the business wants to produce.

Many firms have discovered that the product and sales orientations are quite limiting. They have found that it makes a great deal of sense to pay careful attention to understanding customer needs and objectives and then make the business serve the interests of the customer rather than trying to make the customer buy what the business wants to produce. A primary task under a **market orientation**, then, is to develop ways to research and understand various aspects of the market.

A market-oriented strategy can produce any of the benefits of the other two orientations, but it avoids their drawbacks. In addition, it can identify new opportunities and avoid nasty surprises as changes occur in the market.

In a market-oriented firm, the marketing function is not tagged on at the end of the process. It takes a primary role right from the beginning of the planning process. A marketing orientation represents a set of processes that touch on all aspects of the company. It involves much more than just understanding the customer. Three characteristics make a company market-driven:

- *Intelligence generation.* The market-oriented firm generates intelligence in three major areas: customers' current needs, customers' emerging needs, and competitive activity. Understanding the current needs of customers is a relatively straightforward matter that involves formal and

TIME ON YOUR HANDS? WHY NOT DO YOUR BANKING?

**imagine** doing your banking whenever you want, wherever you are. Now you can, with Scotiabank wireless banking and brokerage, available with your Rogers™ AT&T® wireless service. Pay your bills, check your account balance, transfer funds, get real-time stock updates, buy and sell equities and much more. It's a better way to manage your money. And your time.

TO REGISTER FOR SCOTIABANK'S WIRELESS BANKING SERVICE, SIMPLY CALL 1-800-4-SCOTIA (472-6842)
™Scotiabank is a trademark of the Bank of Nova Scotia. ™Rogers Communications Inc. Used under License. ®AT&T Corp. Used under License.

**Scotiabank and Rogers AT&T explicitly highlight the time utility of using their product.**

informal dialogue with target customers. The formal dialogue can take the form of customer surveys and other types of marketing research. The market-oriented firm is not satisfied with simply trying to understand customers' present situation and needs—it also looks to the future to anticipate customers' unfolding needs. Such anticipation usually involves monitoring the environment for legal, technical, or other developments that might influence customers' requirements. Market-oriented computer manufacturers, for example, are monitoring the development and refinement of voice-recognition software, because it represents a potentially superior method of inputting computer data for their customers. The third area of intelligence generation focuses on competitive activity. Companies must have an accurate understanding of what competitors are doing to ensure that their own products or services are not left behind, and to evaluate the attractiveness of different markets.

■ *Intelligence dissemination.* Market-oriented firms not only gather intelligence, they make it available throughout the organization. Customer information must reach all areas of the organization, including research and development, engineering, manufacturing, and accounting.

■ *Responsiveness.* Up-to-the-minute information that is widely available within the organization serves no purpose unless the organization actually adjusts its products or processes based on

# THE PRACTISING MARKETER

## CONSUMERS WANT BENEFITS NOT FEATURES

From coffee makers to computer software, home consumer products seem to have been designed by engineers with little thought given to the people who will ultimately use them. In the age of convergence, the electronics industry promises home entertainment mega-devices: televisions combined with computers; digital video discs that hold movies and data; telephones with screens that can access the Internet. Although such appliances will run on digital systems much like computers, manufacturers expect them to also appeal to a mass audience that computers do not reach.

"But first these devices are going to have to work for people," Dr. Kim Vicente warns. The University of Toronto professor of mechanical and industrial engineering adds, "Manufacturers do what's possible, technologically. Whether it's easy to use is secondary. It should be the other way around."

The result is what technology experts call the 80-20 rule. People use 20 percent of the functions in devices such as computers 80 percent of the time, and the other 80 percent just 20 percent of the time.

A product from Toshiba Crop., the Infinia 7220, includes a computer, television, telephone, fax machine, pager, digital video disc player, and surround-sound movie and game centre. The question is how many of these features will all but the most dedicated technology devotees learn and use. Even options included in today's appliances are rarely used, such as picture-within-picture features in TVs and CD players that can be programmed to play selected tracks.

Don Norman, the author of a book called *The Design of Everyday Things*, questions the whole drive to build a convergence appliance that takes in myriad functions. "You can guarantee that it doesn't fit any individual," he says, because people have different needs and abilities.

The electronics industry appears to be listening. Electronics manufacturers attending the 1998 Consumer Electronics Show in Las Vegas, the world's largest showcase for gadgets of the future, acknowledged that their products are too complicated.

Michael Bloomberg, president of Bloomberg Financial Markets, says that people coming home from work want to relax, not "write a term paper on Mesopotamia" or pay bills on-line.

"The real challenge we face is going to be finding out, what does the consumer want, and satisfying that," he says. "If you don't , you are going to get chewed up."

Still, Dr. Vicente hopes that, one day, consumers aware of the issues will reach a critical mass and lead a revolt for simplicity.

"They should ask how easy a product is to use, to put together, and how good is the support once they have it," Dr. Vicente says. "If people demand ease of use, that's going to make companies pay attention, because they won't make money."

**What orientation are the manufacturers of consumer electronic products displaying? What changes in orientation would you recommend?**

Source: Adapted from Mary Gooderham, "Baffled Consumers Plead for Simplicity," *The Globe and Mail* (December 8, 1998), pp. C1, C10. Reprinted with permission of the author.

that information. A remarkable number of organizations are fully aware that customers are unhappy with some aspect of their product or service delivery—long waits at an automotive service desk, for example—but make no attempt to address the problem. The market-oriented firm does not just understand its customer and its environment, it acts on that understanding.[9]

# The Marketing Concept: A Guiding Philosophy for Marketing

**marketing concept**

An organization-wide philosophy that holds that the best route to organizational success is to find an unserved or underserved need in society and meet that need better than anyone else, while still meeting long-term organization objectives.

The discussion of market orientation is primarily focused on how firms behave: what actions they take to achieve marketing success. Underlying those actions is a particular attitude or philosophy known as the **marketing concept**. The marketing concept is an organization-wide philosophy that holds that the best route to organizational success is to find an unserved or underserved need in society and meet that need better than anyone else, while still meeting long-term organizational objectives.

The marketing concept requires careful analysis and monitoring of competitors' actions. A company that practises the marketing concept holds basic assumptions in relation to its competitors. Management believes that the firm has the capacity to compete, that it is not at the mercy of its competitors and is a force of its own. At the same time, it recognizes that the firm has to be up-to-date on its competitors' actions to make sure that it does not lose its competitive edge. An organization that views itself as dominated by others is incapable of taking new initiatives, even if it identifies major unsatisfied customer needs.[10]

## Ethics and Marketing

The marketing concept is a useful way to think about individual organizations, their missions, and the role they play in meeting the needs of individuals. Sometimes, though, the success of the organization and the satisfaction of the organization's customers can be at odds with the interests of society as a whole. "Lucky" Luciano, the notorious New York City mobster of the 1920s and 1930s, used many modern management techniques and presumably had at least some satisfied customers.[11] Nonetheless, most people would applaud neither his goals nor his outcomes. Similarly, the tobacco industry as a whole has come under severe attack for using masterful marketing techniques to sell a product everyone but members of the tobacco industry considers addictive and dangerous. More subtly, perhaps, how is one to judge a legitimate enterprise, such as a steel mill, that makes a necessary, quality product for satisfied customers but in the process contributes inordinately to the deterioration of air quality?

**societal marketing concept**

An organization-wide philosophy that holds that the best route to organizational success is to find an unserved or underserved need in society and meet that need better than anyone else, while still meeting long-term organizational objectives and also considering the long-term impact on society.

One approach to dealing with these types of concerns is to broaden the marketing concept from its focus on organizations and customers to explicitly include consideration of the long-term benefit of society as a whole. This broader approach is called the **societal marketing concept**. It can be defined as an organization-wide philosophy that holds that the best route to organizational success is to find an unserved or underserved need in society and meet that need better than anyone else, while still meeting long-term organizational objectives and also considering the long-term impact on society.

The societal marketing concept is a useful perspective, but it does not instantly and easily solve every possible moral dilemma marketers encounter. Companies that operate in more than one country sometimes face particularly thorny issues. Depending on the country, executives can find themselves trying to deal with institutionalized discrimination, systemic corruption (is it ever acceptable to offer a bribe?), or even powerful criminal pressures. The unanswered question of the societal marketing concept that international dealings uncover is "Whose society are we concerned about?" Increasingly, the answer will have to be "The world as a whole."

Even if marketers are committed to operating on the general principles implied by the societal marketing concept, individual decisions can still be bewildering. One of the simplest and most practical approaches to considering moral dilemmas is the TV test. In the TV test, the marketer simply asks, "Would I be able to justify what I'm doing on the 6 o'clock news?" A positive answer suggests that the marketer is at least operating within the ethical norms of society. This approach leaves open the question of whether the norms of society are themselves ethical. An eighteenth-century landowner would have had no difficulty justifying the use of slave labour using the TV test (except, of course, to figure out what a TV was).

Delving deeply into the philosophical and religious perspectives behind the study of ethics is well beyond the scope of this text. What we will do is periodically highlight ethical issues related to different topic areas in marketing. We will invite you to consider the issues and come to conclusions about the ethical acceptability of different marketing actions. We encourage you to grapple with the examples and use them to examine and perhaps further articulate your own value system. It is much easier to come to conclusions about "the right thing to do" when you are considering textbook examples than when you are facing similar issues for the first time in the workplace.

## The Importance of Marketing

Marketing is a core business discipline. It is important to people, companies, and the economy.

- *Importance to people.* Each of us responds to marketing every time we buy a product. Marketing efforts attempt to match goods and services to our needs. An infinite variety of offerings is available, and marketers try to tell us about these offerings. Marketing communications permeate the media and, sometimes, our consciousness. Marketing costs amount to between 40 and 60 percent of everything we buy. From a personal standpoint, studying marketing can make us better-equipped to react to the endless marketing efforts directed toward us.

  Jobs in marketing are also numerous. Marketing-related occupations account for 25 to 33 percent of the jobs in our country—a good reason to study marketing. Starting salaries rank high, and marketing positions often lead to the most senior company posts. Marketers can be found in virtually every sector of the economy, including government, not-for-profit organizations such as the United Way, financial service providers such as the Bank of Montreal, or large multinationals such as Procter & Gamble.

- *Importance to companies.* As the main revenue-producing function, marketing is essential to a firm. Without sales, the firm dies. As sales increase, fixed costs are spread over more units. This increases profitability and enables firms to compete through lower prices.

- *Importance to the economy.* The benefits brought to people and firms make marketing a vital component of the economy. The more efficient the marketing process, the higher a nation's standard of living.

www.pg.com

The study of marketing is therefore truly relevant for students. Furthermore, working in marketing is fascinating because it requires considerable initiative and creativity. Many find great satisfaction in such work. It is little wonder that marketing is now a popular field of academic study.

## Marketing in Not-for-Profit Organizations

Most marketing activity is meant to generate a profit for the firm, but nonbusiness public organizations like public art galleries, churches, and charities have also found that they can benefit from applying marketing principles. For instance, the Canadian government is one of Canada's leading advertisers, spending approximately $44 million annually on advertising. World Vision and other charitable

---

### THE ETHICAL MARKETER

**MARKETING TO CHILDREN**

**Billboards to Pop Up on Calgary Students' Computers**
Elementary school students in Calgary will soon be bombarded by advertisements for Burger King, Pepsi, Kellogg's, and other brands when they turn on their computers. The Calgary public school board has agreed to allow the screen-saver ads in a deal with Screen Ad Billboards Inc. of Brampton, Ont., *Marketing* magazine reports. The pilot program in eight to ten schools could generate about $300 000 for the board if it is expanded to all 11 000 of its computers.

**Is this an ethical marketing approach? Does the use that the revenues are put to affect your answer? If you think this example is unethical, do you think it is ever ethical to target marketing activity at children?**

Source: Excerpted from "Ad Lib, Marketing Shorts," *The Globe and Mail* (October 14, 1998), p. B29. Reprinted with permission from *The Globe and Mail*.

groups have developed considerable marketing expertise, some police departments have used marketing-inspired strategies to improve their image with the public, and we are all familiar with the marketing efforts employed in political campaigns. Most arts organizations now employ a director of marketing. Chapter 21 discusses marketing in not-for-profit settings more fully.

# MARKETING FROM THE INSIDE OUT

This textbook is organized around two themes: the marketing concept and marketing planning. Figure 1.2 illustrates how these central issues guide the practice of marketing, and the organization of this textbook. The marketing concept suggests that our organization's goal must be to serve our customers extremely well while meeting our own long-term objectives. We need marketing planning because "serving customers extremely well" does not happen accidentally but is the conscious outcome of careful thought and consideration.

To consciously serve customers' needs, we must understand what opportunities are available and what difficulties we might encounter. In short, we have to understand the marketing context in which our organization exists. Chapter 2 discusses important concepts within the marketing envi-

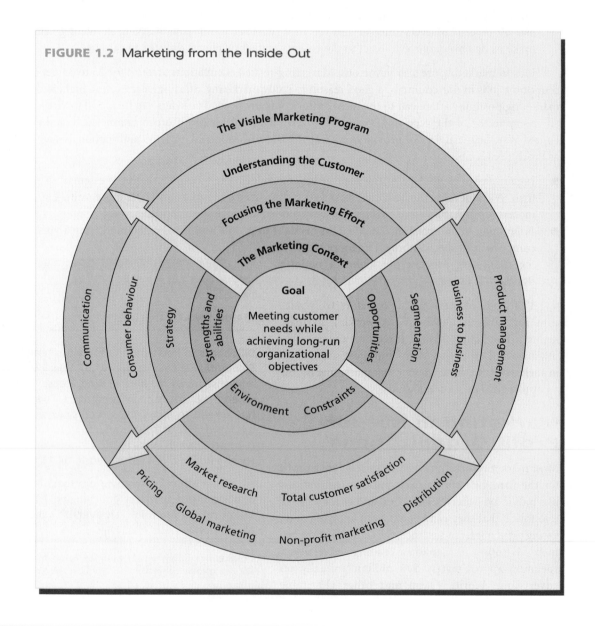

**FIGURE 1.2** Marketing from the Inside Out

ronment and presents a framework to help you organize and understand information about this environment.

Part 2 of the text highlights the fact that the marketing concept will force us to focus the marketing effort. If our goal is to serve a particular group of customers extremely well, it follows that there is simply too much diversity in the marketplace to serve everyone's needs equally well. We must select a subgroup of customers, or market segment, and focus on meeting that subgroup's needs better than anyone else. Chapters 3 and 4 highlight the need for and process of market segmentation. Once we have basic information about the environment and have chosen our segments we have to begin to consciously form a plan of action. Chapter 5 highlights the process of developing a marketing strategy and marketing plan.

Another obvious implication of the marketing concept is that if we are planning to meet our chosen customers' needs extremely well, we must know something about those customers and their needs. Part 3 looks at different ways of understanding our customers. Chapter 6 revisits the issue of serving customer needs and presents in far greater detail what that implies and how it can be accomplished. Chapter 7 introduces the marketing research process. In addition to detailed information about our specific customers, a great deal is known about customers in general. As further background for the marketing plan, Chapters 8 and 9 outline consumer behaviour and business-to-business relations in general, highlighting information that is particularly useful as we try to serve our specific customer groups.

The analysis of the environment, organizational goals and objectives, and customers is complete by the end of Chapter 9. The text then examines the visible marketing program, frequently called the marketing mix. Chapters 10 through 19 consider designing and managing a product or service so that it meets customer needs, pricing the product so that it is attractive to the customer, distributing the product so that it is available to customers when needed, and communicating with customers and potential customers the benefits that the organization is offering. The marketing mix is frequently referred to as the "Four P's" of marketing for Price, Product, Promotion (communication) and Place (distribution). The text concludes with the unique issues facing global marketers (Chapter 20) and not-for-profit marketers (Chapter 21).

Throughout the textbook you will find six different types of interest boxes. The Practising Marketer addresses some of the theoretical concepts of marketing. The Ethical Marketer presents possible ethical dilemmas to consider. Internet Impact boxes showcase the importance of the Internet and the impact that it has had—and continues to have—on marketing. The Canadian Marketplace gives interesting facts, figures, and quotations about marketing in Canada. The Informed Consumer highlights issues that you may find useful in your role as a Canadian consumer. The Roots of Marketing points out historical trends or issues in marketing.

## SUMMARY

Marketing is a dynamic force in our society. One way to think about marketing is the bridge that closes the gap between customers and producers. That gap can consist of consumer perceptions, lack of information, attitudes, time constraints, cost constraints, and space or location.

The formal definition of marketing indicates that it is really about managing exchange processes between customers and producers. Marketing is defined as "the process of planning and executing the conception, pricing, promotion, and distribution of ideas, goods, and services to create exchanges that satisfy individual and organizational objectives." [12]

Companies can take three common orientations in their business practices. A product or production orientation emphasizes the product itself rather than the customer's needs. A sales orientation emphasizes convincing the customer that the product offered should be purchased. A market orientation tries to understand the customer's needs and organize the company in such a way that those needs are met.

Ethical considerations are becoming an important part of marketing planning. The societal marketing concept is an organization-wide philosophy that holds that the best route to organizational success is to find an unserved or underserved need in society and meet that need better than anyone else, while still meeting long-term organizational objectives and also considering the long-term impact on society.

## KEY TERMS

exchange process, p. 6
market orientation, p. 10
marketing, p. 7
marketing concept, p. 12
marketing functions, p. 5

product orientation, p. 8
sales orientation, p. 8
societal marketing concept, p. 12
utility, p. 7

## INTERACTIVE SUMMARY AND DISCUSSION QUESTIONS

1. The gap between producer and consumer has the following components: consumer perceptions, lack of information, attitudes, time constraints, cost constraints, and space or location. Choose a product, and explain how marketing could be said to be the force that bridges the gap between producer and consumer.

2. The marketing gap components are satisfied by one or more of the marketing functions. Match functions with gap components in the columns that follow.

| | |
|---|---|
| buying | consumer perceptions |
| selling | lack of information |
| transporting | attitudes |
| storing | time constraints |
| grading | cost constraints |
| financing | space or location |
| risk taking | information collecting and disseminating |

3. The exchange process is the means by which two or more parties give something of value to one another to satisfy felt needs. Explain how this is the core of all marketing activity.

4. Marketing is "the process of planning and executing the conception, pricing, promotion, and distribution of ideas, goods, and services to create exchanges that satisfy individual and organizational objectives." Explain why the definition mentions ideas, goods, and services.

5. In a product-oriented firm, the emphasis is on the product itself rather than on the consumer's needs. Give an example of such a firm, and explain the limitations of this approach.

6. A sales-oriented firm is still quite product-oriented, but it focuses its marketing efforts on developing a strong sales force to convince consumers to buy. Is this what most companies need? Why or why not?

7. A market-oriented firm tries to understand customer needs and then makes the business serve the interests of the customer. How can such an approach be a practical way of making money?

8. Relate the definition of marketing to the concept of the exchange process.

9. Identify the product and the consumer market in the following:
   a. local cable television firm
   b. Vancouver Canucks hockey team
   c. Planned Parenthood
   d. annual boat and sports equipment show in local city auditorium
   e. regional shopping mall

10. Explain the effect of a market orientation on products offered to the market, and on marketing planning.

11. Check the Web sites of three major companies. Do they have statements of guiding principles to assist ethical decision making? If so, how do you think the stated principles will actually affect company actions and employee behaviour?

# Case

## Alzheimer's Coffee Breaks

Sylvia Mitchell is expecting a few friends to drop in to Middleton Baptist Church for coffee. Actually, if things work out, about 150 local residents will come by, and each one will leave a few dollars in the collection box and pick up some pamphlets about Alzheimer's disease.

Mrs. Mitchell, whose 47-year-old husband, Steve, is suffering from the grave neurological disease, is hosting one of 12 000 Alzheimer's Coffee Breaks being held in Canada.

The fundraiser is a prototype for successful charitable events, striking proof that it is still possible to carve out a niche in the highly competitive $10-billion-a-year fundraising field.

The idea underlying Coffee Break is devilishly simple: Sponsors, either individuals or corporations, invite people for coffee and ask for a small donation in return.

"The secret of our success, I think, is that we have been able to transform an ordinary ritual into a significant gesture," said Andrea Olson, director of marketing, development, and communications at the Alzheimer Society of Canada.

A simple habit, such as buying a cup of coffee, becomes a charitable act. And because most Coffee Breaks have an educational component, the event raises awareness not only of the Alzheimer Society but of a disease whose prevalence is increasing at an alarming rate.

For Terry Smethurst, whose mother-in-law is one of 250 000 Canadians with Alzheimer's, there is also powerful symbolism in drinking coffee, because people affected by the disease first lose their rituals and then their ability to communicate, things that most people take for granted.

"To me, it's a super idea because when you sit down for coffee, everybody talks about their problems," said Ms. Smethurst, who is hosting a Coffee Break at the Royal Canadian Legion Hall in Watrous, Saskatchewan.

"When you get talking, you realize how many people are affected, and maybe you can help them. That's probably more important than the money."

Last year, that Coffee Break raised $770, part of the $630 000 collected across the country. But, more important, it was one of 32 such events in the pharmacies, hair salons, fire halls, and churches of the small town, making Watrous the biggest per-capita fundraiser in the country.

At a time when many charities are abandoning long-time special events because they are being crowded out or their revenues are failing, Coffee Break has not only growth potential but the likelihood of a long life span. If every coffee drinker got into the habit of giving a loonie, to Coffee Break, for example, it would raise millions of dollars annually.

Like many fundraising events, it also has a corporate component. For example, National Public Relations Inc.—because one of the company's executives has a mother with Alzheimer's—provides hundreds of hours of high-priced marketing help gratis. All the printing and publicity also comes in the form of in-kind donations.

www.alzheimer.ca

The Alzheimer Society has two corporate sponsors who make big cash donations and host king-size Coffee Breaks. Pfizer Canada Inc. of Kirkland, Quebec, makes the only drug available to treat the symptoms of Alzheimer's, and Imperial Life Financial (Desjardins-Laurentian Life Assurance in Quebec), as a big insurance company, knows the financial impact of a disease that is a $4-billion-a-year economic drain.

At Imperial Life, for example, most representatives will host a Coffee Break, and the celebration at corporate headquarters in Toronto will raise several thousand dollars.

Restaurants, big and small, are also coming on board quickly. McDonald's restaurants in Quebec will add their marketing muscle to the cause. In Manitoba, the provincial restaurant association has enticed restaurants into giving a fixed percentage of their day's receipts to the charity.

Another staple of modern fundraising events is a celebrity spokesperson, and the Alzheimer Society has a powerful one in hockey star Brendan Shanahan.

The Detroit Red Wings player was 21 when he lost his father, Donal, to Alzheimer's, and he has lent his time and name to the cause in his honour because "I'm dedicated to continuing his fight." Mr. Shanahan is a big giver himself and will probably be passing the hat at the team's training camp.

For Mrs. Mitchell, who had never been involved in a fundraising event before hosting her Coffee Break, it is also about doing her part against a disease that devastates individuals and their families.

"Three years ago, I didn't know what I was getting into. I just said: 'I'm going to do it. I'm going to do it for Steve,'" she said.

The first year, she raised $700, the next $1100. In 1998, Mrs. Mitchell was joined by about 25 volunteers and her 6 children. (Her husband's illness is so advanced that he is in a nursing home.) She is also participating in a handful of other Coffee Breaks in the Annapolis Valley.

"The way I look at it, if we raise $100 or $1000, it will be more than we had the day before. That money will go to research and it will go to helping families. All those cups of coffee, it adds up."

### You Be the Marketer

1. How is the Alzheimer's Society applying marketing principles in this case?

2. Is this an illustration of the marketing concept in action? Why or why not?

Source: Adapted from André Picard, "Charity Made Easy," *The Globe and Mail* (September 24, 1998), pp. A1 and A4. Reprinted with permission from *The Globe and Mail*.

Changes in Canada's demographic profile create new opportunities and challenges for marketers.

## Chapter 2

# THE ENVIRONMENT FOR MARKETING DECISIONS

**CHAPTER OBJECTIVES**

After reading and studying this chapter, you should be able to

1. Identify the environmental factors that affect marketing decisions.
2. Identify three categories of competition faced by marketers, and outline the issues to consider in developing a competitive strategy.
3. Illustrate the association between marketing plans and the technological environment.
4. Demonstrate how the sociocultural environment influences marketing decisions.
5. Show how the economic environment has a bearing on marketing planning.
6. Explain the major legislative framework that regulates marketing activities.

**B**ess Lokach's vision loss was sudden. "Sunday night, my eyes weren't right," the Toronto retiree recalls, "and Monday morning, when I woke up, they were very dark and cloudy." That was last November. Ms. Lokach has ischemic optic neuropathy, a condition that usually strikes after the age of 40. It affects relatively few people—most people's vision deteriorates far more gradually and to a lesser degree.

Such problems can only grow as the population ages and as even more seniors use computers. But technology to help overcome them is proliferating. For instance, Ms. Lokach, who doesn't expect to recover full vision, can now use a computer well enough to help out part-time in her son and daughter-in-law's store. Software that enlarges print on the screen lets her use word-processing, accounting, and payroll programs. "When I first saw the letters come up on the screen, I could have kissed the computer," she says.

If enlarging the display isn't enough, software is available that can read aloud the contents of a computer screen.

As the first generation to grow up with computers reaches its bifocal years, it's natural that technology vendors are working to keep their products accessible to a growing group of customers. The sad thing, Ms. Lokach says, is that too few people know about the aids already available.

Health Canada projects Canada's population of seniors will grow from about 3.7 million or 12.3 percent of Canadians in 1998 to 5.9 million or 15.9 percent by 2016.

Source: Excerpted from Grant Buckler, "For an Aging Population, Technology Help Is at Hand," *The Globe and Mail*, May 31, 2002, p. T5. Reprinted with permission of the author.

# INTRODUCTION

Organizations operate in an environment that is constantly shifting and changing. Assumptions that held yesterday may no longer be valid today. Opportunities that are pursued enthusiastically today may disappear tomorrow, while new opportunities, unthought of today, may occupy a major portion of the manager's time in the future. Manufacturers of computers and input devices are able to take advantage of opportunities arising from a convergence of changes in the technological environment—increasingly sophisticated and subtle input devices; and the socio-cultural environment—an aging but technically sophisticated population that demands continuing access to information technology.

As dramatic as these changes and resulting opportunities are, they represent only two aspects of the environment that face technology firms and all other organizations.

# ENVIRONMENTAL SCANNING

**environmental scanning**
The process by which the marketing manager gathers and sorts information about the marketing environment.

The marketing environment seems to be in a state of constant flux. If marketing managers are to make informed, intelligent decisions, they must develop methods of monitoring environmental changes. **Environmental scanning** is the process by which the marketing manager gathers and sorts information about the marketing environment.

Information can come from formal or informal sources. It can be gathered periodically, in the form of major focused market research projects, or it can be gathered continuously, by systematic ongoing market research, by tracking trade publications, commercially available reports, the general media, information made public by competitors, government press releases, internal company records, and even conversations with people both inside and outside the company.[1]

Simply gathering information, of course, is not enough: the information must be analyzed and acted upon in some way. The smaller the company, the more likely action will be taken to try to recognize and adjust to new environmental realities. Environmental changes can also be positive from an individual company's perspective, and they can represent significant opportunities for growth or competitive advantage.

If an issue arises that affects an industry as a whole, sometimes industry players will cooperate to try to shape or manage environmental realities. Air bags in cars were developed jointly by car manufacturers in response to government pressure to make cars safer. Kellogg's and Quaker have cooperated to try to have restrictions on health claims of food products eased. Even modest shifts in one or more of the environmental elements can alter the results of marketing decisions. In the next few years VHS video tapes will likely disappear from the marketplace, replaced by DVD. This shift will result in lost business for some companies and huge opportunities for others.

The environment for marketing decisions may be classified into five components: the competitive environment, the technological environment, the sociocultural environment, the economic environment, and the political–legal environment. This is the structure upon which marketing decisions are made, as well as the starting point for marketing planning. Figure 2.1 illustrates this relationship. The remainder of this chapter looks at the different components of the environment in more detail.

# THE COMPETITIVE ENVIRONMENT

**competitive environment**
The interactive process that occurs in the marketplace in which different organizations seek to satisfy similar markets.

The interactive process that occurs in the marketplace in which different organizations seek to satisfy similar markets is known as the **competitive environment**. Marketing decisions by an individual firm influence consumer responses in the marketplace; they also affect the marketing strategies of competitors. As a consequence, marketers must continually monitor and adjust to the

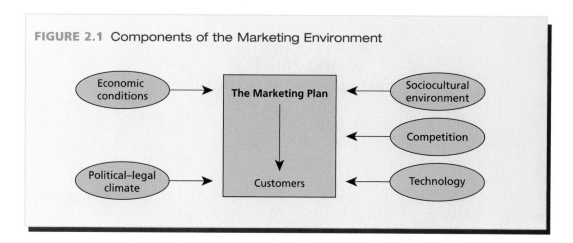

**FIGURE 2.1** Components of the Marketing Environment

marketing activities of competitors—their products, channels of distribution, prices, and communication efforts.

In a few instances, organizations enjoy a monopoly position in the marketplace. Utilities, such as natural gas, electricity, water, and cable television service, accept considerable regulation from government in such marketing-related activities as rates, service levels, and geographic coverage in exchange for exclusive rights to serve a particular group of consumers. However, such instances are relatively rare. In addition, portions of such traditional monopoly industries as telephone service have been deregulated in recent years, and telephone companies currently face competition in such areas as selling telephone receivers, providing some long-distance services, and installing and maintaining telephone systems in larger commercial and industrial firms.

In many industries, the competition among firms is fierce. For example, consider the retail food industry. For supermarkets, the profit margin on most items is quite low. Therefore, to make an adequate return on investment, a store must generate a high volume of sales. Supermarkets are thus very sensitive to fluctuations in sales caused by the actions of competitors. If one competitor advertises a sale on certain products, another will be inclined to match those sale prices. Or if a new store format (such as Loblaws superstores) is developed, it will be countered (as was done with Safeway's Food for Less outlets).

## Types of Competition

Marketers face three types of competition. The most direct form is inter-product or direct competition, which is among marketers of similar products. Xerox photocopiers compete with models offered by Canon, Sharp, and Olivetti. Estée Lauder cosmetics face competition from Lancôme and Revlon. Competitors are as likely to be from abroad as from the local market.

A second type of competition is product-substitute or indirect competition, which is among products that can be substituted for one another. In the construction industry and in manufacturing, steel products by Stelco may compete with similar products made of aluminum by Alcan. Paper bags compete with plastic bags. In circumstances where a change such as a price increase or an improvement in the quality of a product occurs, demand for substitute products is directly affected.

The final type of competition is alternative-gratification, sometimes called total-dollar, competition. This involves all organizations that compete for the consumer's purchases. Traditional economic analysis views competition as a battle among companies in the same industry or among substitutable products and services. Marketers, however, accept the argument that all firms are competing for a limited amount of discretionary buying power. The Ford Focus competes with a vacation in the Bahamas; the local live theatre centre competes with pay television and the Leafs, Blue Bombers, or Expos for the consumer's entertainment dollars.

Changes in the competitive environment can wipe out a product, or an entire business, in short order. Marketers must, therefore, continually assess the marketing strategies of competitors, as well as monitor international business developments.

We won't argue with Ivory's claim to mildness. We'll leave that to the dermatologists.

13% of dermatologists surveyed recommend Ivory.

87% of dermatologists surveyed recommend Dove.

When asked which bars they recommended for mildness on skin, most dermatologists named Dove. Why are they so enthusiastic? Try it yourself and see.

*Dove*

Unilever Canada, the maker of Dove, is emphasizing mildness to challenge Procter and Gamble's Ivory. Dove and Ivory are direct competitors.

New product offerings with technological advances, price reductions, special promotions, or other competitive actions must be monitored in order to adjust the firm's marketing program in the light of such changes. Among the first purchasers of any new product are the product's competitors. Carefully analyzing the product—its physical components, performance attributes, packaging, retail price, service requirements, and estimated production and marketing costs—allows competitors to forecast its likely competitive impact. If necessary, current marketing procedures may be adjusted as a result of the new market entry. The competitive environment is a fact of life for most marketers. They ignore it at their peril! Competitive analysis is discussed in more detail in Chapter 5.

# THE TECHNOLOGICAL ENVIRONMENT

**technological environment**

The applications of knowledge based on scientific discoveries, inventions, and innovations.

The **technological environment** consists of the applications of knowledge based on scientific discoveries, inventions, and innovations. Technology, especially computer technology and the Internet, is reshaping the face of marketing. Virtually every aspect of the marketing program has been affected.

Existing products have been redesigned. Everything from cars to hearing aids to toasters incorporates computer technology. The performance of many products has improved, while size and cost have often fallen. Some products we see everywhere today, such as palm-sized computers, didn't even exist a few years ago.

Today manufacturers are planning to incorporate night-vision technology from the military in cars, and some models already have satellite-based on-board navigation systems as an option.[2] Some appliance manufacturers are musing about smart appliances that are directly wired to the Internet.

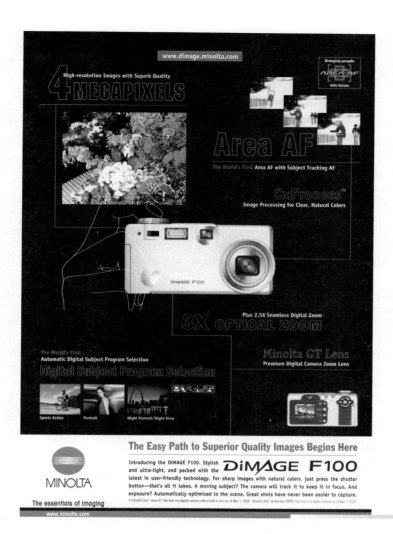

Changes in the technological environment can change entire industries, as the development of digital photography seems to be doing to cameras.

Frigidaire has developed a refrigerator that can keep a running inventory of its contents and automatically order fresh groceries as required (if only it would also identify the container full of green fuzzy things on the back shelf).

Service design is also changing. The Internet has simultaneously become a huge communication device and a global shopping mall. Some storefronts exist only in cyberspace. Probably the best known of these "e-tailers" is Amazon.com, which recently launched an all-Canadian site: Amazon.ca. (There is, of course, considerable irony in the fact that one of the Internet's earliest and largest retailers sells books!) Internet-based businesses, or e-businesses, are attracting a great deal of interest both from the media and from investors. It's worth noting, though, that virtually none of them has turned a profit— although that may just be a matter of time.

Less visibly, advances in computing and communications technology have allowed marketers to maintain more detailed records and to access those records in more useful ways. This in turn allows them to identify and track major accounts and regional and customer sales figures in depth and more quickly. The Royal Bank of Canada used improved databases to divide its clients into A-, B-, and C-level clients based on profitability. The bank assigned the A-level customers to account managers who now call these customers several times a year to discuss specific products. In a two-year period, the average profit per A client increased 292 percent.[3]

Advances in technology have also helped in inventory management by reducing the level of inventory necessary while avoiding stock-outs and automating the reorder process. Many of these topics are discussed in more detail in Chapter 16.

Marketers should take note of several points when analyzing technological changes in their environment. The first is not to be left behind by these changes—marketers must keep abreast of devel-

## NEW ON-LINE COMPETITION FOR CANADIAN BOOK RETAILERS

In the early summer of 2002, Amazon.com Inc. launched its Canadian on-line site.

Jeff Bezos, chief executive officer of the world's biggest Internet retailer, unveiled his plans for Canada at a Toronto press conference and at a cocktail reception for members of the industry.

The long-rumoured arrival of the on-line giant was applauded by some Canadian publishers who have felt the squeeze of operating in a market dominated by one major player—Indigo Books & Music Inc.

Many publishers also have been hurt by the financial troubles of struggling distributor General Publishing Co. Ltd., which is currently in creditor protection and owes publishers millions of dollars.

Tim Inkster, president of Porcupine's Quill, Inc. in Erin, Ont., northwest of Toronto, is one publisher who made the drive to Toronto to hear what Mr. Bezos has to offer with Amazon.ca.

"I'm going to be there," Mr. Inkster said. "I'm very hopeful about what this will mean."

Mr. Inkster, whose press has published early works by well-known writers such as Jane Urquhart and Russell Smith, said he welcomes the new distribution channel that Amazon.com's arrival in Canada will give him.

Mr. Inkster has sold books through Amazon.com's special program for small publishers out of its U.S. site and said he is impressed with the results.

"I'm not a big fan of large companies, particularly large American companies, but Amazon has treated Porcupine's Quill with kid gloves in the U.S.," he said.

Canadian booksellers are less excited about the news.

Before Amazon's entry into Canada, the Canadian Booksellers Association called on Ottawa to review Amazon.com's plans, saying the Seattle-based retailer was violating federal foreign investment rules for the industry.

Federal cultural investment regulations require that a majority of any bookseller be Canadian-owned.

Amazon.com appears set to get around the foreign ownership restrictions by using Canada Post Corp.'s warehouse in Mississauga, as its new fulfillment centre to ship books from large distributors, industry sources have said.

It would also use wholesaler BookExpress, owned by Vancouver-based Raincoast Book Distribution, sources said.

E-commerce consultant and author Rick Broadhead said the arrival of Amazon.ca will likely put instant pressure on the Chapters/Indigo e-commerce site.

"Indigo probably can't afford to compete," he said.

But he said for consumers, the event is good news. "Canadians deserve to have the best retailers to shop at and Amazon is the undisputed king of on-line retailing," he said.

**Update this news story. Has Amazon.ca run into regulatory problems with the Canadian government? What moves has Indigo made to counter Amazon's presence?**

www.amazon.ca

www.chapters.indigo.com

Source: Excerpted from Elizabeth Church, "Amazon.ca Set to Go Today," *The Globe and Mail*, June 25, 2002, p. B6. Reprinted with permission from *The Globe and Mail*.

opments that might affect their business and be willing to adjust to those developments. The other side of the story, though, is that marketers should not be seduced by technology. Technological change and innovation should be driven by customer needs. Adopting new technology will not be successful if it works only to the benefit of the company while ignoring the customer.

Any time of significant change represents tremendous opportunity for those companies that anticipate and correctly adjust to and incorporate the change. It can be a time of catastrophe for those who do not. In the next ten years, new forms of business organizations will probably appear. Undoubtedly, some established businesses will disappear. What will be most interesting to watch, and what will require the greatest managerial skill and vision, are established businesses that are able to embrace the environmental change and be transformed into new and exciting marketing organizations.

# THE SOCIOCULTURAL ENVIRONMENT

A probation officer and his wife have found a novel way of marrying people who do not belong to an organized religion or who prefer not to get married in a church. Edward and Ruth Simmons have formed a company called Weddings and have opened chapels in Hamilton and Burlington, Ontario. Weddings offers five different ceremonies: four religious and one secular. The rituals are open to change, at clients' request.

Edward Simmons says that he came up with the idea when he saw couples being married in the courts. "They would go in happy and come out with a stunned look on their faces. I don't think they realized the abruptness of the proceedings. That really bothered me," he says. "Religion doesn't always meet the needs of a secular society," he adds. "In many cases, a place of worship won't marry couples who don't belong to it, people who have been divorced, couples that have been living together, and those who have crossed religious barriers."[4]

A few years ago, the success of the Simmons' company would have been doubtful. However, changes in the sociocultural fabric of Canada now make this type of business quite viable. This example illustrates the importance of understanding and assessing the relevant social and cultural components when making marketing decisions. The **sociocultural environment** is the mosaic of societal and cultural components that are relevant to the organization's business decisions. Obviously, many different aspects are significant. One important category is the general readiness of society to accept a marketing idea; this aspect was important in the Simmons' decision.

Another important category involves the trust and confidence of the public in business as a whole. Such relationships have been on the decline since the mid-1960s. Opinion polls suggest that people have lost confidence in major companies (although they maintain faith in the private-enterprise system). These declines should, however, be viewed in perspective. All institutions have lost public confidence to some degree. In fact, some would argue that governments and labour unions are even less popular than business.

**sociocultural environment**
The mosaic of societal and cultural components that are relevant to the organization's business decisions.

## THE CANADIAN MARKETPLACE

### FEEDING A NEED TO EAT ON THE RUN

Hungry but starved for time? Has your get-up-and-go got up and gone? If so, you're the prime target for a group of products whose recent sales growth has been nothing short of phenomenal—energy bars and drinks.

They come with names like Powerbar, Ensure Plus, and Boost, and Canadians bought $1.72-millon worth of them at food stores and pharmacies in 1996. In 1997, however, we spent $3.46-million on them, an increase of just over 100 percent. Sales in 1998 look set to post a 70-percent leap over 1997.

"It's a lifestyle thing," said Peter Elgersma, a business manager with the market-research firm A.C. Nielsen. "Life is fast and you often need an energy lift."

Raminder Bindra, brand manager for Mead Johnson Nutritionals, says his company's Boost drinks are intended more as a breakfast food, while the bars are designed for snacks during the day for people on the run who want something more than a candy bar.

The energy bars are dense and chewy but pleasantly flavoured. And they contain a few things you won't find in a Mars bar: phosphorus, magnesium, iron, zinc, copper, manganese, and chromium.

**What changes in the sociocultural environment are contributing to the success of energy bars?**

Source: Adapted from Philip Jackman, "Feeding a Need to Eat on the Run," *The Globe and Mail* (December 3, 1998), p. A30. Reprinted with permission from *The Globe and Mail*.

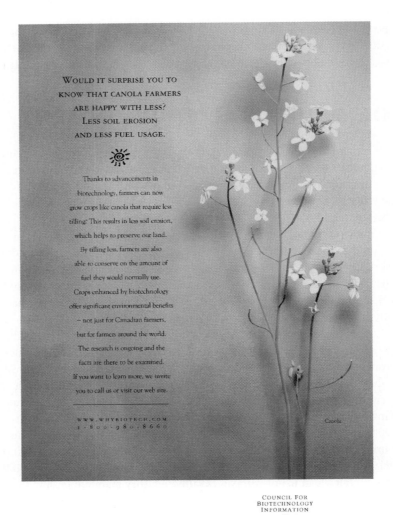

Many marketers predict that it will soon be very difficult to sell a product that is not environmentally friendly.

The sociocultural environment for marketing decisions has both expanded in scope and increased in importance. Today, no marketer can initiate a strategy without taking the social context into account. Marketers must be aware of the way in which this context affects their decisions. The constant flux of social issues requires that marketing managers place more emphasis on solving these questions as part of the marketing decision process. Some firms have created a new position—manager of public policy research—to study the changing social environment's future impact on the company.

One question facing contemporary marketing is how to measure the accomplishment of socially oriented objectives. A firm that is attuned to its social environment must develop new ways of evaluating its performance. Traditional income statements and balance sheets are no longer adequate. This issue is one of the most important problems facing contemporary marketing.

Many marketers recognize societal differences among countries, but assume that a homogeneous social environment exists at home. Nothing could be further from the truth! Canada is a mixed society composed of varied submarkets that can be classified by age, place of residence, gender, ethnic background, and many other determinants. For example, the Quebec market segment has enough distinctive characteristics that separate marketing programs are sometimes developed for that province.

Gender is another increasingly important social factor. The feminist movement has had a decided effect on marketing, particularly promotion. Television commercials now feature women in less stereotyped roles than in previous years.

Since social variables change constantly, marketers must continually evaluate this dynamic environment. What appears to be out-of-bounds today may be tomorrow's greatest market opportunity. Consider the way that previously taboo subjects, such as condoms, are now commonly advertised.

The social variables must be recognized by modern business executives, since these variables affect the way consumers react to different products and marketing practices. One of the most serious—and avoidable—of all marketing mistakes is failing to appreciate social differences within our own domestic market.

The rise of consumerism can be partly traced to the growing public concern with making business more responsible to its constituents. Consumerism is an evolving aspect of marketing's social environment. Certainly the advent of this movement has influenced the move toward more direct protection of consumer rights in such areas as product safety and false and misleading advertising. These concerns will undoubtedly be amplified and expanded in the years ahead.

# THE ECONOMIC ENVIRONMENT

Marketers must understand economic conditions and their impact on the organization. An economy with growing monetary resources, high employment, and productive power is likely to create strong demand for goods and services.

In a deteriorating **economic environment**, on the other hand, many firms experience a decline. However, such conditions may represent good news for other companies. As inflation and unemployment go up and production declines, consumer buying patterns shift. Flour millers note that flour sales go up. Automobile repairs and home improvements also increase. Greeting card firms report that consumers buy fewer gifts but more expensive cards. Hardware stores show higher sales. The economic environment considerably affects the way marketers operate.

**economic environment**
The factors in a region or country that affect the production, distribution, and consumption of its wealth. Key elements are monetary resources, inflation, employment, and productive capacity.

## Stages of the Business Cycle

Within the economic environment, there are fluctuations that tend to follow a cyclical pattern comprising three or four stages:

1. recession (sometimes involving such factors as inflation and unemployment)
2. depression[5]
3. recovery
4. prosperity

No marketer can ignore the economic climate in which a business functions, because the type, direction, and intensity of a firm's marketing strategy depend on it. In addition, the marketer must be aware of the economy's relative position in the business cycle and how it will affect the position of the particular firm. This requires the marketer to study forecasts of future economic activity.

Of necessity, marketing activity differs with each stage of the business cycle. During prosperous times, consumers are usually more willing to buy than when they feel economically threatened. For example, during a recent recession, personal savings climbed to high levels as consumers (fearing possible layoffs and other workforce reductions) cut back their expenditures for many products they considered nonessential. Marketers must pay close attention to the consumer's relative willingness to buy. The aggressiveness of one's marketing strategy and tactics often depends on current buying intentions. More aggressive marketing may be called for in periods of lessened buying interest, as when automakers use cash rebate schemes to move inventories. Such activities, however, are unlikely to fully counteract cyclical periods of low demand.

While sales figures may experience cyclical variations, the successful firm has a rising sales trend line. Achieving this depends on management's ability to foresee, correctly define, and reach new market opportunities. Effective forecasting and research is only a partial solution. Marketers must also develop an intuitive awareness of potential markets. This requires them to be able to correctly identify opportunities.[6]

Besides recession, two other economic subjects have been of major concern to marketers in recent years: inflation and unemployment.

## Inflation

**Inflation**, which can occur during any stage in the business cycle, critically influences marketing strategy. Inflation is a rising price level that results in reduced purchasing power for the consumer. A person's money is devalued in terms of what it can buy. Traditionally, inflation has been more prevalent in countries outside North America. However, in the late 1970s and early 1980s, Canada experienced double-digit inflation, an inflation rate higher than 10 percent a year. Although the rate of inflation has declined considerably since then, experiences of inflation's effects have led to widespread concern over political approaches to controlling interest rates and stabilizing price levels, and over ways in which the individual can adjust to such reductions in the spending power of the dollar.

**Stagflation** is a word that has been coined to describe a peculiar brand of inflation that Canada experienced in the 1970s, an economy with high unemployment and a rising price level at the same time. Formulating effective strategies is particularly difficult under these circumstances.

## Unemployment

Another significant economic problem that has affected the marketing environment in recent years is unemployment. The ranks of the unemployed—officially defined as people actively looking for work who do not have jobs—fluctuate as a result of the business cycle. Since 1966, the unemployment rate in Canada has ranged from 4.4 percent to 12.4 percent.

In the severe recession of the early 1980s, numerous businesses failed, production slowed, many factories ceased operation entirely, and thousands of workers found themselves out of work. The consequences of reduced income and uncertainty about future income were reflected in the marketplace in many ways. Similar conditions were experienced in Canada during some of the 1990s.

### Government Tools for Combatting Inflation and Unemployment

The government can attempt to deal with the twin economic problems of inflation and unemployment by using two basic approaches: fiscal policy and monetary policy. **Fiscal policy** concerns the receipts and expenditures of government. To combat inflation, an economy can reduce government expenditures, raise its revenue (primarily through taxes), or both. It could also use direct controls such as wage and price controls. **Monetary policy** refers to the manipulation of the money supply and market rates of interest. In periods of rising prices, the government may take actions to decrease the money supply and raise interest rates, thus restraining purchasing power.

Both fiscal and monetary policy have been used in our battles against inflation and unemployment. Their marketing implications are numerous and varied. Higher taxes mean less consumer purchasing power, which usually results in declining sales for nonessential goods and services. However, some taxes that have been collected may find their way into various job-creation programs. Income earned from these tends to be spent on basic goods and services. Lower federal spending levels make the government a less attractive customer for many industries. A lowered money supply means that less liquidity is available for potential conversion to purchasing power. High interest rates often lead to a significant slump in the construction and housing industries.

Both unemployment and inflation affect marketing by modifying consumer behaviour. Unless employment insurance, personal savings, and union supplementary unemployment benefits are sufficient to offset lost earnings, unemployed individuals have less income to spend in the marketplace. Even if individuals are completely compensated for lost earnings, their buying behaviour is likely to be affected. As consumers become more conscious of inflation, they are likely to become more price-conscious in general. This can lead to three possible outcomes that are important to marketers. Consumers can (1) elect to buy now in the belief that prices will be higher later (car dealers often use this argument in their commercial messages), (2) decide to alter their purchasing patterns, or (3) postpone certain purchases.

## Demarketing—Dealing with Shortages

Shortages—temporary or permanent—can be caused by several factors. A brisk demand may exceed manufacturing capacity or outpace the response time required to gear up a production line. Shortages may also be caused by a lack of raw materials, component parts, energy, or labour. Regardless of the cause, shortages require marketers to reorient their thinking.[7]

**Demarketing**, a term that has come into general use in recent years, refers to the process of cutting consumer demand for a product, because the demand exceeds the level that can reasonably be supplied by the firm or because doing so will create a more favourable corporate image. Some oil companies, for example, have publicized tips on how to cut gasoline consumption as a result of the gradual depletion of oil reserves. Utility companies have encouraged homeowners to install more insulation to lower heating bills. And growing environmental concerns have resulted in companies' discouraging demand for plastic packaging for their products.

Shortages sometimes force marketers to be allocators of limited supplies. This is in sharp contrast to marketing's traditional objective of expanding sales volume. Shortages require marketers to decide whether to spread a limited supply over all customers so that none are satisfied, or to backorder some customers so that others may be completely supplied. Shortages certainly present marketers with a unique set of marketing problems.

**demarketing**
The process of cutting consumer demand for a product, because the demand exceeds the level that can reasonably be supplied by the firm or because doing so will create a more favourable corporate image.

---

# THE INFORMED CONSUMER

## WHEN 'SALE-PRICED' IS NOT A BARGAIN

If I gave you the choice between paying the regular price for something and paying half-price for the same product, what would you choose? A no brainer, right? The half-price deal. But what if the regular price at Store A was lower than the half-price deal at Store B? Suddenly, the item on sale wouldn't look like much of a bargain anymore.

This begs the question: What, exactly, is the meaning of a word like "sale" or "discounted" or "reduced?" How do I know when I walk into a store to buy, say, a piece of jewellery, that the store hasn't inflated the original price, then slapped on a new sticker showing a "deep discount"? And why do some things—like mattresses and appliances—appear to be on sale all the time?

There is a law in Canada that spells out when a retailer can advertise it's selling something at a discount. That law is called The Competition Act—and it says storeowners can't run around slapping "sale" stickers on things just because they figure it's smart for business.

In order to say it's been "discounted," a retailer should have been selling the product at the regular price for a long period of time (about six months)—or should have sold at least half their stock at the regular price before putting it on sale.

A retailer who doesn't follow those rules can be hauled before the Competition Tribunal and slapped with a fine as high as $200 000.

### Advertising Dos and Don'ts for Businesses
But since 1999, when the government passed its last amendments to the Competition Act, not a single company has appeared before the Competition Tribunal for misleading consumers with the word "sale."

To be fair, the Competition Bureau doesn't have to take legal action on most complaints because a good wrist-slapping does the trick.

The wrist-slapping can't hurt—but how about a few hefty fines, if only to send a message? "Don't be playing loosey-goosey with the price tags to make us think we're getting a good deal when we're not."

So don't be duped by the word "sale." If you know about a store that's been playing fast and loose, take action, blow the whistle and always be sure to shop around.

**Check closely two or three sales flyers. Do any seem to be misusing the word "sale"? What about comparison prices? Are any making comparisons you think are suspect?**

Source: Adapted from Talin Vartanian, "When 'Sale-priced' Is Not a Bargain" broadcast on *This Morning*, CBC Radio, March 20, 2002. Copyright ©Canadian Broadcasting Corporation. http://www.cbc.ca/consumers/citizentalin/talin_sales.html#

---

# THE POLITICAL–LEGAL ENVIRONMENT

It would be absurd to start playing a new game without first understanding the rules, yet some businesspeople exhibit a remarkable lack of knowledge about marketing's **political–legal environment**—the laws and interpretation of laws that require firms to operate under competitive conditions and to protect consumer rights. Ignorance of laws, ordinances, and regulations can result in fines, embarrassing negative publicity, and possible lawsuits.

It requires considerable diligence to develop an understanding of the legal framework of marketing. Numerous laws, often vague and legislated by a multitude of different authorities, characterize the legal environment for marketing decisions. Regulations affecting marketing have been enacted at the federal, provincial, and local levels as well as by independent regulatory agencies. Our existing legal framework was constructed on a piecemeal basis, often in response to a concern over current issues.

Canada has tended to follow a public policy of promoting a competitive marketing system. To maintain such a system, competitive practices within the system have been regulated. Traditionally, pricing and promotion have received the most legislative attention.

## Society's Expectations Create the Framework

We live in and want a "free-enterprise society"—or do we? The concept of free enterprise is not clear and has been gradually changing. At the turn of the century, the prevalent attitude was to let business act quite freely. It was expected that new products and jobs would be created as a result and the economy would develop and prosper. Currently, the former communist countries are trying to make free enterprise develop their chaotic economies.

In North America, an uncontrolled approach provided great freedom for the honest and the dishonest. Although many businesses sought to serve their target markets in an equitable fashion, abuses did occur. Figure 2.2 shows an example of dishonest marketing practices. Such advertisements were not unusual in the late 1800s and early 1900s. Advancing technology led to the creation of many products in many fields. Often the buying public did not have the expertise needed to choose among them.

With the increasing complexity of products, the growth of big, impersonal business, and the unfair or careless treatment of consumers by some firms, society's values changed. "Government should regulate business more closely," we said. Over time, governments at the federal and provincial levels have responded to this shift: many laws have been passed to protect consumers, and to attempt to maintain a competitive environment for business. Large bureaucracies have grown with this increase in market regulation.

A significant development in the legal environment at the federal level was the consolidation in 1967 of consumer and business regulation programs into Consumer and Corporate Affairs Canada (now called the Competition Bureau of Industry Canada), and the appointment of a cabinet minister to represent these interests at the highest level. Previously these functions had been scattered among several different government departments. Following the lead of the federal government, most provinces have established consumer and corporate affairs branches and have generally streamlined the regulation of these sectors.

strategis.ic.gc.ca/SSG/
ct01254e.html

## The Competition Act Sets the Standards

The Competition Act (formerly the Combines Investigation Act) has the most significance in the legal environment for marketing decisions. The Act dates back to 1889, when it was enacted to protect the public interest in free competition. Since then, various revisions have occurred in response to changes in social values and business practices.

**FIGURE 2.2** An Example of Dishonest Advertising

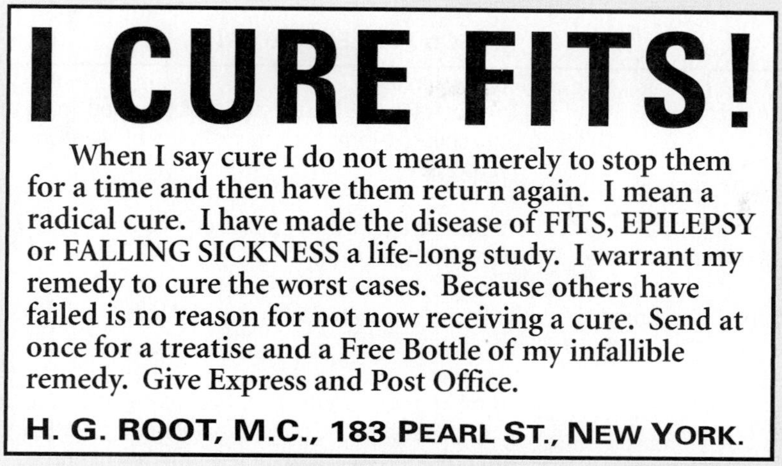

# I CURE FITS!

When I say cure I do not mean merely to stop them for a time and then have them return again. I mean a radical cure. I have made the disease of FITS, EPILEPSY or FALLING SICKNESS a life-long study. I warrant my remedy to cure the worst cases. Because others have failed is no reason for not now receiving a cure. Send at once for a treatise and a Free Bottle of my infallible remedy. Give Express and Post Office.

**H. G. ROOT, M.C., 183 PEARL ST., NEW YORK.**

Source: Excerpt from *Advertising: Its Role in Modern Marketing*, 5th ed. by S. Watson Dunn and Arnold M. Barban, page 84. Copyright ©1982. Reprinted with permission of South-Western, a division of Thomson Learning: www.thomsonrights.com. Fax 800-730-2215

The Act prohibits rather than regulates. That is, it does not spell out in detail the activities that industry may undertake, but greatly discourages certain activities through the threat of penal consequences.

The provisions of the Act fall into three main classes. Generally, they prohibit the following:

1. combinations that prevent, or lessen unduly, competition in the production, purchase, sale, storage, rental, transportation, or supply of commodities, or in the price of insurance
2. mergers, monopolies, or abuses of dominant market position that may operate to the detriment of the public
3. deceptive trade practices, including
   - price discrimination
   - predatory pricing
   - certain promotional allowances
   - false or misleading representations, by any means, to promote the sale of a product or to promote a business
   - unsubstantiated claims of performance
   - misleading warranties or guarantees
   - misrepresentation of the ordinary price
   - misleading testimonials for a product or service
   - double ticketing
   - pyramid sales
   - referral selling
   - nonavailability of advertised specials
   - sale above advertised price
   - promotional contests

Despite the long history of the Combines Investigation Act, it proved remarkably powerless for prosecuting those who appeared to contravene either of the first two categories. The passage of the Competition Act to replace the Combines Investigation Act in June 1986 was an important change. Classified as civil law, it corrected many problems in the strictly criminal, proof-beyond-a-reasonable-doubt approach of the old Act. The new Competition Act also created a quasi-judicial body, known as the Competition Tribunal, to deal with matters via the civil route and to make certain rules.

| DATE | LEGISLATION | REASON FOR LEGISLATION |
|------|-------------|------------------------|
| 1888 | Combines Investigation Commission | To protect small businesses that suffered from monopolistic and collusive practices in restraint of trade by large manufacturers. |
| 1889 | Act for the Prevention and Suppression of Combinations Formed in Restraint of Trade | To declare illegal monopolies and combinations in restraint of trade. |
| 1892 | Above Act incorporated into the Criminal Code as Section 502 | To make the above a criminal offence. |
| 1900 | Above Act amended | To make the Act effective, because as it stood, an individual would first have to commit an illegal act within the meaning of common law. Now, any undue restriction of competition became a criminal offence. |
| 1910 | Additional legislation passed to complement the Criminal Code and assist in the application of the Act | To stop a recent rush of mergers that had involved some 58 firms. |
| 1919 | Combines and Fair Prices Act | To prohibit undue stockpiling of the "necessities of life" and prohibit the realization of exaggerated profits through "unreasonable prices." |
| 1923 | Combines Investigation Act | To consolidate combines legislation. |
| 1952, 1960 | Amendments to the above | |
| 1976 | Bill C-2; amendments | To include the service industry within the Act, to prohibit additional deceptive practices, to give persons the right to recover damages, and to protect the rights of small businesses. |
| 1986 | Competition Act replaces Combines Investigation Act | To facilitate prosecutions of illegal combinations, mergers, and monopolies. |

## Combines and Restraint of Trade

It is an offence to conspire, combine, agree, or arrange with another person to prevent or lessen competition unduly. The most common types of combination relate to price fixing, bid rigging, market sharing, and group boycotting of competitors, suppliers, or customers.

While the list covers much territory, it should be noted that in the following circumstances agreements between businesspeople are lawful:

- exchanging statistics
- defining product standards
- exchanging credit information
- defining trade terms
- cooperating in research and development
- restricting advertising

Consequently, it is permissible to report statistics centrally for the purpose of analyzing factors relating to industrial operation and marketing, as long as competition is not lessened unduly.

## Mergers

Until the passage of the Competition Act in 1986, the law regarding mergers was largely ineffective. Important provisions in the new Act changed the situation. The Competition Tribunal has the power to stop mergers that substantially lessen competition without offering offsetting efficiency gains. Furthermore, the Tribunal must be notified in advance of large mergers (transactions larger than $35 million in sales or assets, and/or companies with combined revenues or assets of more than $400 million). This enables the review and modification of large, complex mergers that are difficult to reverse once consummated. Four of Canada's chartered banks ran afoul of this legislation when they were refused permission to merge into two very large banks in 1999.

## Deceptive Trade Practices

This is an extremely important section for marketing decision makers, as it contains a number of directly related provisions. There are real teeth in the legislation, which the marketer should be aware of. Many successful prosecutions have been made under this section.

### Misleading Advertising

False statements of every kind (even in the picture on a package) made to the public about products or services are prohibited. For example, in 1998 The Bay was fined $600 000 for misrepresenting how long sale prices would be in effect.

Often carelessness has been seen as responsible for the offence, and over the years, numerous advertisers have been prosecuted under the misleading-advertising provisions of the Combines Investigation Act. The fines meted out have been surprisingly small. The Bay's fine was quite large by comparison.

## THE ROOTS OF MARKETING

### FIRST ANTIMONOPOLY CASE AFTER PASSAGE OF COMPETITION ACT

The first antimonopoly case after the new Competition Act was passed in 1986 was laid in 1989. NutraSweet Co., a subsidiary of U.S. chemical giant Monsanto, was charged with "abuse of dominance" (monopoly) in the Canadian market for aspartame, an artificial sweetener. The Bureau of Competition Policy said in a statement that NutraSweet, the sole supplier of aspartame in the United States, had captured more than 95 percent of the Canadian market. It claimed that NutraSweet demanded contracts with customers that precluded them from buying aspartame from anyone other than NutraSweet. Where exclusive contracts were not made, it claimed, NutraSweet insisted that customers give the company a chance to match the lowest price charged by a competitor. The Bureau also charged NutraSweet with selling aspartame in Canada at a price below its acquisition cost or below its long-run average cost, with the result of substantially lessening competition.

NutraSweet issued a statement disagreeing with the Bureau's charges and believed that the issue would be decided in its favour.[8] However, a few months later, in a precedent-setting decision, the Competition Tribunal ruled that NutraSweet had effectively maintained monopolistic powers over the $25 million domestic aspartame market at the expense of potential competitors.

NutraSweet invented aspartame in the 1960s, but health testing delayed its introduction in many countries, including Canada, until the early 1980s. Soon afterward, NutraSweet's patents on the product began running out. In Canada, that took place in 1987. But in preparation, NutraSweet tied up its customers in exclusive contracts. Under the Tribunal's order, NutraSweet can no longer enforce existing contracts or sign new ones that make it the exclusive aspartame supplier. Nor can NutraSweet sign contracts that give it the right to match, in the future, a competing bid from another aspartame producer. As well, it has been prohibited from giving financial inducements on the sale of aspartame to companies that display NutraSweet's swirl insignia on their products. The director of the Bureau of Competition Policy called the Tribunal's ruling a significant sign that anticompetitive behaviour by companies will not be tolerated.[9]

It is an offence to make unsubstantiated claims. Therefore, claims for a product are expected to be based on an adequate and proper test. Significantly, the onus is on whoever is making the claim to prove its efficacy, rather than on someone else to prove that the product is not as claimed. This reverse onus has been challenged before the courts under the Charter of Rights as being unconstitutional, because it purports to put the onus on the accused to prove innocence, but the section was upheld. One example, and there are many, concerns Professional Technology of Canada, which was convicted in Edmonton on May 27, 1986, for promoting a gas-saving device that claimed to offer 10 to 35 percent better mileage for cars. The company was fined $12 500.[10]

Another important fact of the misleading-advertising legislation concerns pricing. Many businesses seem to be unaware that much care needs to be taken when advertising comparative prices. It is, for example, considered misleading for a retailer to advertise a television set as follows:

| Manufacturer's suggested list price | $680 |
| On sale for | $500 |

if the manufacturer's suggested list price is not normally followed in this retail trading area, and the usual price is less, for example, around $600. Although the retailer is offering a bargain, the magnitude of the saving is not indicated accurately.

Retailers may try to get around this provision by choosing different comparative expressions, such as "regular price," "ordinarily $ ...," "list price," "hundreds sold at," "compare with," "regular value," and the like. But such tactics may nevertheless be problematic. For example, in Moncton, Best for Less (a division of Dominion Stores Ltd.) compared its price with a "why pay up to" price on in-store signs, and depicted the savings. It was established that items were available from competitors at lower prices than the "why pay up to" prices, and the firm was convicted and fined $7650.[11]

The businessperson who genuinely seeks to comply with this provision should ask two questions:

1. Would a reasonable shopper draw the conclusion from the expression used that the figure named by way of comparison is a price at which goods have been, are, or will ordinarily be sold?
2. If the answer is yes, would such a representation be true?

## Pricing Practices

It is an offence for a supplier to make a practice of discriminating in price among purchasers who are in competition with one another and who are purchasing like quantities of goods. Selling above the advertised price is also prohibited. Furthermore, the lowest of two or more prices must be used in the case of double-ticketed products. This latter provision has led to the development of easy-tear-off, two-price stickers, so that the sale price can readily be removed after a sale.

If you are a ski manufacturer and wish all ski shops to sell your skis at your suggested list price, can you force them to do so? No; it is an offence under the Act to deny supplies to an outlet that refuses to maintain the resale price. Thus, resale price maintenance is illegal, and a reseller is generally free to set whatever price is considered appropriate.

The Competition Act includes several other prohibitions, including ones against bait-and-switch selling, pyramid selling, and some types of referral selling and promotional contests.

## Other Provisions of the Competition Act

### Protection Against Extraterritorial Laws and Directives

Foreign companies that do business in Canada have sometimes been constrained by laws or judgements in their home country to the detriment of competition in Canada, or of opportunities for Canadian international trade. For example, Canadian subsidiaries of American companies have felt constrained by American laws against doing business with countries the United States is having disputes with. This is theoretically no longer the case, because the Restrictive Trade Practices Commission (established under the anticombines provisions of the Competition Act) has been given power to rule against such interference in Canadian affairs. In practical terms, companies can still face strong external government pressures. For example, in 1996 the United States demanded that any foreign company that wished to do business with the United States must stop trading with Cuba. Wal-Mart Canada Ltd., which at the time sold Cuban-made pyjamas, found itself having to choose between violating U.S. law by selling the pyjamas or violating Canadian law by pulling them because they were made in Cuba. The company pulled them.[12]

### Civil Damages

In some situations, people have the right to recover damages incurred as a result of a violation by others. This has profound implications. In some jurisdictions, not only can an individual sue for damages, but if he or she wins, that judgement will apparently serve as evidence for anyone else who has experienced a similar loss. Would this mean that a company could face the possibility of virtually every purchaser of a product claiming damages? Consider the millions of dollars involved for an automobile manufacturer, for example. To our knowledge, there have been no such cases in Canada.

## Regulation, Regulation, and . . . More Regulation

So far, only some of the provisions from the federal Competition Act have been cited. Provincial governments are also very active in this area. Fortunately, each marketer need not be aware of all provisions, for many are specific to the situation, time, place, and products.

In addition, provincial and municipal governments have other laws and by-laws that must be considered when developing marketing plans. For example, regulations vary from province to province concerning the amount and nature of advertising directed at children. Some other significant laws or regulations relate to bilingual specifications for packaging and labelling; there are special language requirements in Quebec.

From a broad point of view, the legal framework for relations between business and consumers is designed to encourage a competitive marketing system that employs fair business practices. In many respects, various laws have resulted in more effective competition, although many feel that business is overregulated and others think that more regulations are needed. There is little doubt that consumers in Canada are protected as well as or better than consumers in any other country in their dealings with sellers, especially regarding truth in advertising. It is clear that governments will continue to act in response to society's expectations of a fair and honest marketplace.

## SUMMARY

Marketers must understand and monitor the five aspects of their environment. The competitive environment is the interactive process that occurs in the marketplace in which different organizations seek to satisfy similar markets. Competition occurs on three levels: similar products, substitutable products, and all organizations that compete for the consumer's purchases.

The technological environment consists of the applications of knowledge based on scientific discoveries, inventions, and innovations. Computer-based innovations, particularly the Internet, are having a tremendous impact on the practice of marketing.

The sociocultural environment is the mosaic of societal and cultural components that are relevant to the organization's business decisions.

The economic environment—the general national and global economic conditions—sets the framework for developing marketing plans.

The political–legal environment consists of the laws and the interpretation of laws that require firms to operate under competitive conditions and to protect consumer rights.

## KEY TERMS

competitive environment, p. 22
demarketing, p. 31
economic environment, p. 29
environmental scanning, p. 22
fiscal policy, p. 30
inflation, p. 30

monetary policy, p. 30
political–legal environment, p. 32
sociocultural environment, p. 27
stagflation, p. 30
technological environment, p. 24

## INTERACTIVE SUMMARY AND DISCUSSION QUESTIONS

1. The competitive environment is the interactive process that occurs in the marketplace in which competing organizations seek to satisfy markets. Give an example of how the competitive environment might be viewed for the following firms:
   a. McCain Foods
   b. local aerobics exercise centre
   c. Swiss Chalet franchise
   d. Avon products
   e. Sears catalogue department
   f. local television station
2. Marketers face three types of competition: similar products, products that can be substituted for one another, and all organizations that compete for the consumers' purchases. Give an example of each for three different organizations that you are familiar with.
3. The technological environment consists of the applications of knowledge based on scientific discoveries, inventions, and innovations. Discuss the relevance of the technological environment for the firms listed in question 1.
4. Identify some aspects of the sociocultural environment that would likely be of specific relevance to the firms listed in question 1.
5. Where are we now in the business cycle? Give examples of how the economic environment currently could be affecting the marketing practices of the firms listed in question 1.
6. The political–legal environment consists of the laws and the interpretation of laws that require firms to operate under competitive conditions and to protect consumer rights. Give examples of how the political–legal environment might apply to the six firms listed in question 1.
7. Explain how the expectations of society can be said to create the legal framework for business practice.
8. Can the consumerism movement be viewed as a rejection of the competitive marketing system? Defend your answer.
9. The Competition Act has the most significance in the legal environment for marketing decisions. In which areas has the Act had little effect, and for what types of business practices has it been productive?
10. Would a gas station that sold gasoline to a city's police department for one cent a litre less than its price for other customers be in violation of the Competition Act? Why or why not?
11. Visit the home page of the Competition Bureau, and follow the links to the section on deceptive telemarketing (http://strategis.ic.gc.ca/SSG/ct01067e.html). How might the restrictions outlined affect legitimate telemarketers? As a consumer, do you think that a company that follows the Competition Bureau's guidelines would make telemarketing more acceptable to you? Explain your answer.

www.strategis.ic.gc.ca/SSG
/ct01067e.html

## WestJet Offers $3 Fares

Flying from Hamilton to Ottawa or Calgary to Edmonton cost a measly $3 on June 30, 2002 but customers needed to be careful to read the fine print.

In WestJet's promotion entitled: Ridiculous fares, ridiculous fees, the no-frills airline basically gave away flights for one day on the two heavy-traffic short-haul routes.

But throw in the NavCanada fees, insurance, airport improvement charges, new air traveller security surtax, and GST, and the return flight actually cost $83.92 for the Alberta route and $81.78 for the Ottawa jaunt.

And that didn't even include an extra fuel surtax. Competitor Air Canada charges customers $15 per flight to help pay for volatile jet fuel costs.

"We continue to hear from our guests their frustration over the ridiculous rise in taxes and fees associated with air travel," explained Bill Lamberton, WestJet's vice president of marketing.

"By offering this ridiculous $3 one-way fare, we want to clearly show the impact these extra charges have on the wallets of Canadians."

Calgary-based WestJet is well known for its promotional larks, including Prime Minister's day, where John Turner and his friend Mackenzie King could fly for free because they have the same names as past Canadian leaders. Or its Halloween special where anyone with the last name Black, Jack, or Orange gets a free trip.

But the airline says this one has more than a tinge of seriousness to it. Short-haul flights especially are disproportionately impacted by all the various add-on fees and continue to see declining traffic.

"It is a very serious issue," says spokeswoman Siobhan Vinish.

"And it's a growing concern to the travel industry as a whole and not just airlines," she said.

The Calgary–Edmonton, Ottawa–Hamilton routes were chosen for the promotion since those routes have the lowest daily fares and are the most impacted by all the add-on fees, said Vinish.

"Because people are making decisions not to travel due to higher taxes and fees and it impacts car rentals and hotels and tourism in many areas and it is a serious issue that we feel is important to keep in front of Canadians."

In April 2002, WestJet announced it was cutting 13 flights per week between Calgary and Edmonton, blaming the reduction on the new $12 airport security fee, which it said was deterring travellers.

### You Be the Marketer

1. What aspect of the environment is WestJet reacting to in this case?

2. What is the serious point that Ms. Vinish is trying to make with this promotion?

3. What would you predict the outcome will be?

Source: James Stevenson, "WestJet Offers $3 for Fares But The Actual Price Came to $81.78 When All Taxes Were Added," Canadian Press, http://www.canoe.ca/CNEWS/westjet_jun20-cp.html. Reprinted with permission of The Canadian Press.

## 訪努納伏特區不足三小時

# 英女王感動恩律人

星島日報
SING TAO DAILY

2002年10月5日
星期六第6223號
今日出紙5疊20頁每份75¢ 連稅

**英**女王在細雪紛飛天色微暗的周五展開為期十二日的加國之行,首先踏足位於北極凍原的努納伏特區,由於她對愿律族人的文化和奮鬥史相當了解,令當地人士印象深刻。

**加通社努納伏特區伊桂魯四日電**

英女王在努納伏特區省議會歡迎詞時,首先讚賀加國創造新成立省額原民,羅西向權土進省政客和嘉賓表示,努納伏特區居民的努力和信相當無限,其成立締造了歷史,顯示了特區居民的努力和信相無限。

英女王是次親風遊涂離族不足三小時,但已令當地居民深受感動,因為據說她對恩律族人在爭取成立加國第三個地區的無數挑戰和抨扎,明白他們的文化。

### 讚揚與自然環境協調

她在致詞中形容土著是加國建國的重要支柱,從愿律族的土地可以明知道律族人的祖先是加國最早一批的公民。愿律族人者於對自然環境調小時不同,使率年專機照相伊桂魯伊(IQALUIT)發許申請作一直陌作無限。

### 長老石硫點火

在前往上用海索,在伊桂魯伊地區接受南名女童軍上海海教奔著的乾花,瓶達省議會時,王夫,邊理克菲特和邊督低冰枝唱出英國國歌,再由統中一名長老在一個石碗中點大以示歡迎。

---

## 葛利衡:無需要推翻薩達姆

**加通社滿地可四日電**

外交部長葛利衡周五說,他與美國的想法不同,不部局有否要推伊拉克總統薩達姆下台。

葛利衡說,最理想解決問題的方法是,讓達姆接受國安全,無條件接受武器檢查員進入,國。

他又表示,這種做法可以避免...

---

## 曼里:續行降低國債政策

**經濟社滿地可四日電**

財政部長曼里表示,加國經濟在未來一年將持續增長,政府同時須繼續實行降低國債的政策。

曼里周五於多倫多麥基爾大學(MCGILL UNIVERSITY)學生作會見發表講話...

---

## 強風夜探多市

**星報透訊社四日電**

颶風莉莉和Lili的威脅力周五夜夜橫掃多倫多地區...

夾道歡迎　　　飛抵維市

英女王抵努納伏特區伊桂魯伊時,居民夾道歡迎。　加通社

英女王依爾從努納伏特區抵卑詩省省會市。　加通社

警助疏散

多倫多市中心周五年間發生氣體洩漏事件,警方到場協助附近上班人士疏散。　加通社

經濟出色

副總理是黑墨積改造經濟基本狀況出色。　加通社

---

## 氣體洩漏上班族疏散

**加通社多倫多四日電**

ADELAIDE STREET 與央街(YONGE STREET)附近周五下午一時半左右發生氣體洩漏事件,數以千計寫字樓職員須疏散處理。事件中無人受傷。

救援人員將氣體洩漏事件中輕傷警員送院治理。　攝影 MICHAEL STUPARYK

---

### 要聞提示

美西封港 勞資未達成協議　A16

成龍留名星光大道　A24

[欄目標題]　B1

中國女乒終嚐敗績　B21

第14屆亞運會獎牌榜

| 國家 | 金 | 銀 | 銅 | 總 |
|---|---|---|---|---|
| 中國 | 71 | 34 | 21 | 126 |
| 南韓 | 24 | 30 | 36 | 87 |
| 日本 | 23 | 25 | 32 | 81 |
| 哈薩克 | 6 | 5 | 10 | 21 |
| 泰國 | 4 | 5 | 5 | 14 |
| 台北 | 4 | 6 | 6 | 16 |
| 印度 | 3 | 5 | 7 | 15 |
| 伊朗 | 3 | 1 | 2 | 6 |
| 香港 | 2 | 2 | 2 | 6 |
| 馬來西亞 | 2 | 2 | 4 | 8 |

SUPER 7 中獎號碼
7 9 12 22 24 40 41
14

六合彩 658128

### 重要資訊版面索引

|  |  |
|---|---|
| 要聞 | A1 |
| 加國重要新聞 | A3 |
| 加拿大新聞 | A7 |
| 社論新聞 | A9,11 |
| 工商新聞 | A13 |
| 影視新聞 | A14 |
| 家庭生活 | A15 |
| 世界新聞 | A16 |
| 世界新聞 | A21,23,24 |
| 財經新聞 | C1 |
| 加拿大地產 | C4 |
| 多倫多旅行情報 | C5,6 |
| 分類廣告 | C7,8 |
| 香港新聞 | C13,17,21,24 |

訂報部　(416)861-8168 EXT 5
傳真　(416)861-8169
電郵　singtao@singtao.ca
廣告部　(416)596-8140
　　　(905)513-6968
　　　(416)599-9980
　　　(905)513-6973
發行　(416)596-8140
零售　(416)572-9946

75 CENTS/COPY (GST INCLUDED)

Dundas Street West, Toronto, Ontario M5T 1G6 Tel:(416)596-8140　Fax:(416)599-6688 Markham Office Tel:(905)513-6968　Fax:(905)513-6973　http://www.singtao.ca

# MARKET SEGMENTATION: FINDING A BASE TO START

## CHAPTER OBJECTIVES

After reading and studying this chapter, you should be able to

1. Explain the concept of the marketing plan.
2. Define market segmentation.
3. Discuss and apply five types of market segmentation in consumer markets.
4. Illustrate some aspects of the Canadian market in terms of the five types of consumer market segmentation.
5. Discuss and apply the main types of segmentation in industrial markets.

In the busy Toronto newsroom of *Sing Tao Daily*, there's the usual linguistic chaos. Staffers at *Sing Tao* are facing one of their biggest competitive tests to date. The challenge: beat out their rivals, *Ming Pao Daily* and *World Journal*, in covering the announcement of which city will host the 2008 Olympic Summer Games, an event that's of huge interest to the roughly one million Canadians who are of Chinese descent. Already, a group of younger newsroom employees, many of them recent immigrants from the People's Republic of China (PRC), are at work on a story about the Beijing bid. They talk amongst themselves in their native Mandarin, a language that the senior editors—old-timers from Hong Kong and the Canton region who have lived in Canada for decades and who speak mainly Cantonese—have trouble understanding. The language difficulties get even worse whenever *Sing Tao* chairman Andrew Go, who was born in the Philippines, is in the newsroom. He can follow Cantonese, but usually talks to staff in English or Mandarin. There's confusion, and often things have to be repeated. But editors, reporters, and the chairman find ways to bridge the language divisions—an ability that bodes well for the paper's long-term prosperity.

When word arrives of the International Olympic Committee's decision, staffers mobilize. They're well aware of the deep split among Chinese-Canadians over the Olympics. Some favour Toronto, while others are rooting for Beijing out of a sense of ethnic pride. *Sing Tao*'s headline the next morning is intended to speak to both camps. Those of their rivals do not. *Ming Pao*'s front page screams: "Olympic Success: Beijing celebrates through the night." The *World Journal* exclaims: "On second attempt, a dream come true for Beijing." *Sing Tao*, however, deftly bridges the divisions. Its headline reads: "Beijing's dream fulfilled; Toronto heartbroken."

Welcome to Canada's other newspaper war, a war that has many similarities to its English-language counterpart—and one key difference. Like the *National Post*, *The Globe and Mail* and, in Toronto, the *Star* and the *Sun*, Canada's three Chinese-language dailies, with a combined readership of almost a half a million people per week, fight it out on the obvious battlegrounds: editorial stance, circulation methods, and advertiser appeal.

**The Chinese language newspapers are using market segmentation analysis as the basis of their marketing plan. Markets are not usually homogeneous. They consist of many different groups of people from many geographical locations, with a multitude of differing lifestyles, needs, and economic realities. The newspapers have identified a segment of potential customers, which is currently being ignored by other newspapers. In order to reach this segment, managers have made decisions specifying an appropriate product and service package, an affordable price, methods of communicating the availability of the service to poential customers, and details on how the product will actually be distributed to the customers. In combination, these decisions are known as the marketing plan. Truly effective marketing plans always flow from consideration of market segments.**

Source: Excerpted from Michael Szonyi, "Paper Tigers," *National Post Business*, July 2002. http://www.nationalpost business.com/home.asp?include=9&section=9&articleid =362. Downloaded July 11, 2002. Reprinted with permission of the author.

www.singtao.ca

# INTRODUCTION

Developing the marketing plan is one step of the strategic marketing planning process, a process that involves the consideration of many factors. Two of these factors, customer needs and environmental analysis, have already been introduced in Chapters 1 and 2. Those chapters provide an important base for the rest of this book. We now want to begin building on that base by introducing the strategic marketing planning process, and seeing the role of market segmentation within that process.

If you have a product to market, a decision must be made about the *target market*; that is, to whom will you market the product? In most cases, you will achieve greater success by focusing on part of the entire market. Therefore, an analysis of appropriate target market segments is necessary. Other aspects of strategic marketing planning include taking a careful look at what competitors are doing and at your own firm's situation and resources. Marketing research is also required. A marketing manager and his or her staff take all these elements into consideration in forecasting sales and developing a unique marketing plan that will enable the organization to compete successfully in the marketplace.

Figure 3.1 shows a model of the strategic marketing planning process. It will provide a preliminary perspective on the role each of Part 2's chapter topics plays in the marketing planning process.

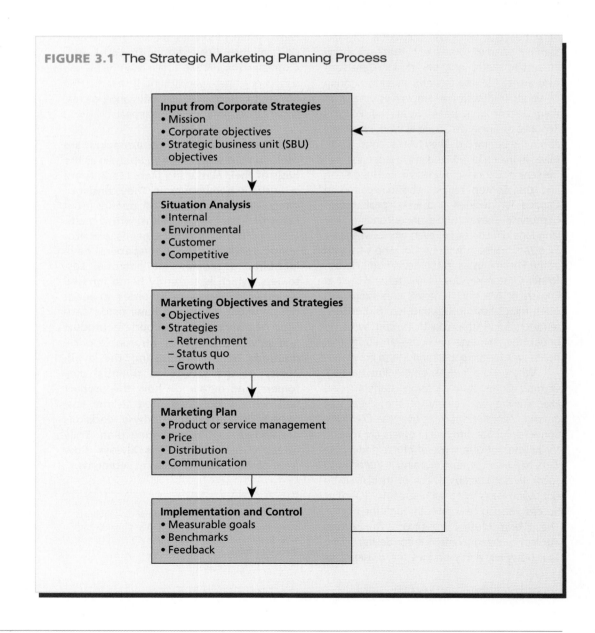

**FIGURE 3.1** The Strategic Marketing Planning Process

An expanded discussion of the model is included in Chapter 5. We will start the discussion of marketing planning with the topic of market segmentation.

# DEVELOPING A STRATEGIC MARKETING PLAN

Although marketers may face hundreds of decisions in developing an effective plan for achieving organization objectives, these decisions may be summarized as two fundamental tasks:

- Marketers must identify, evaluate, and ultimately select a target market.
- Once the target market has been selected, marketers must develop and implement a marketing program that is designed to satisfy the chosen target group.

These two tasks reflect the philosophy of customer orientation in action. The choice of a target market is based on recognizing differences among consumers and organizations within a heterogeneous market. The starting point is to understand what is meant by a *market*.

## What Is a Market?

A market is *people*. It is also business, not-for-profit organizations, and government—local, provincial, and federal purchasing agents who buy for their "firms." But people alone do not make a market. The local dealer for foreign cars is unimpressed by news that 60 percent of the marketing class raise their hands in response to the question "Who wants to buy a new BMW?" The next question is, "How many of them are waving cheques in their outstretched hands?" A **market** consists of people with the willingness, purchasing power, and authority to buy.

One of the first rules that the successful salesperson learns is to determine who in the organization or household has the authority to make particular purchasing decisions. Much time can be wasted convincing the wrong person that a product or service should be bought.

**market**
People with the willingness, purchasing power, and authority to buy.

## Types of Markets

Products may be classified as consumer or industrial goods. **Consumer goods** are those products and services purchased by the ultimate consumer for personal use. **Industrial goods** are those products purchased to be used, either directly or indirectly, in the production of other goods or for resale. Most of the products you buy—books, clothes, milk—are consumer goods. Refined nickel is an industrial good for the mint; rubber is a raw material for Michelin. It is important to make the distinction, because often the motivations and buying process in each case are quite different. The marketing of industrial goods is often called business-to-business marketing.

Sometimes the same product is destined for different uses. The new set of tires purchased by your neighbour are clearly consumer goods, yet when they are bought by General Motors Corporation to become part of a new Malibu, they are classified as industrial goods, since they become part of another good that is destined for resale. The key to the proper classification of goods lies in the purchaser and in *the reasons for buying the good*.

**consumer goods**
Those products and services purchased by the ultimate consumer for personal use.

**industrial goods**
Those products purchased to be used, either directly or indirectly, in the production of other goods or for resale.

# MARKET SEGMENTATION

A country is too large and filled with too many diverse people and firms for any single marketing plan to satisfy everyone. Unless the product is an item such as an unbranded commodity, trying to satisfy everyone may doom the marketer to failure. Even a seemingly functional product like hand soap is aimed at a specific market segment. Ivory positions itself as a pure, wholesome product; Dove emphasizes moisturizing qualities; while Dial focuses on deodorizing.

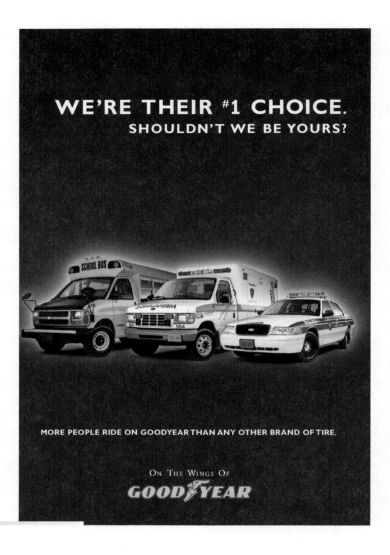

Goodyear tires purchased by fleet operators, such as police or other emergency departments, are classified as industrial goods. Similar Goodyear tires purchased by a motorist to install on her own car are classified as consumer goods.

The auto manufacturer who decides to produce and market a single car model to satisfy everyone will encounter seemingly endless decisions to be made about such variables as the number of doors, type of transmission, colour, styling, and engine size. In its attempt to satisfy everyone, the firm may be forced to compromise in each of these areas and, as a result, may discover that it does not satisfy anyone very well. Other firms that appeal to particular segments—the youth market, the high-fuel-economy market, the large-family market, and so on—may capture most of the total market by satisfying the specific needs of these smaller, more homogeneous target markets. Although everyone is different, we can group people according to their similarity in one or more dimensions related to a particular product category. This aggregation process is called **market segmentation**.

Once a specific market segment has been identified, the marketer can design an appropriate marketing approach to match its needs, improving the chance of sales to that segment. Market segmentation can be used by both profit-oriented and not-for-profit organizations.[1]

**market segmentation**
Grouping people according to their similarity in one or more dimensions related to a particular product category.

## SEGMENTING CONSUMER MARKETS

Market segmentation results from determining the factors that distinguish a certain group of consumers from the overall market. These characteristics—such as age, gender, geographic location, income and expenditure patterns, and population size and mobility, among others—are vital factors in the success of the overall marketing strategy. A toy manufacturer such as Mattel studies not only birthrate trends, but also shifts in income and expenditure patterns. Colleges and universities are affected by such factors as the number of high-school graduates, changing attitudes toward the value of college educations, and increasing enrolment of older adults. Figure 3.2 identifies five commonly used bases for segmenting consumer markets. The first two are descriptive, while the next three are behavioural approaches.

**Geographic segmentation**, dividing an overall market into homogeneous groups based on population location, has been used for hundreds of years. The second basis for segmenting markets is **demographic segmentation**—dividing an overall market on the basis of characteristics such as age, gender, and income level. Demographic segmentation is the easiest way of subdividing total markets, and is therefore often used.

The third and fourth bases require more sophisticated techniques to implement. **Psychographic segmentation** uses behavioural profiles developed from analyses of the activities, opinions, interests, and lifestyles of consumers in identifying market segments. **Benefit segmentation** depends on advanced marketing research techniques that focus on benefits the consumer expects to derive from a product. Product attributes can then be designed to provide desired benefits. These segmentation bases can be important to marketing strategies provided they are significantly related to differences in buying behaviour. The final segmentation base, **usage rate**, divides the market by the amount of product consumed, and/or the degree of brand loyalty.

# GEOGRAPHIC SEGMENTATION

A logical starting point in market segmentation is to find out where buyers are. It is not surprising, therefore, that one of the first bases for segmentation to be considered is geographic. Country and regional variations in consumer tastes often exist. In Japan, for example, consumers are much more particular about the type of rice they use and the way it is cooked than most Canadians. In Canada, per capita consumption of seafood is higher in the Maritimes than in Alberta. Brick and stone construction, a mainstay in many homes in Ontario, is much less common in the West.

**geographic segmentation**
Dividing an overall market into homogeneous groups based on population location.

**demographic segmentation**
Dividing an overall market on the basis of characteristics such as age, gender, and income level.

**psychographic segmentation**
Uses behavioural profiles developed from analyses of the activities, opinions, interests, and lifestyles of consumers in identifying market segments.

**benefit segmentation**
Depends on advanced marketing research techniques that focus on benefits the consumer expects to derive from a product.

**usage rate**
Divides the market by the amount of product consumed, and/or the degree of brand loyalty.

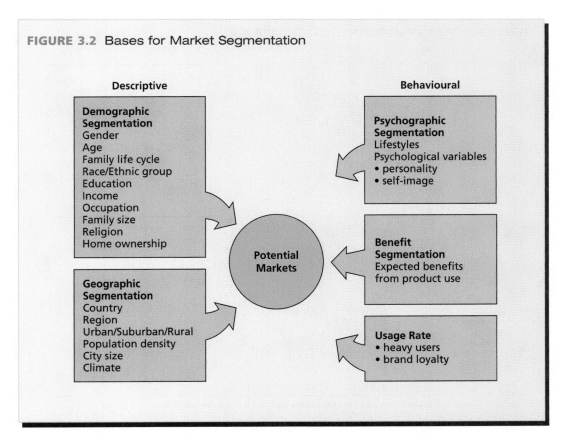

FIGURE 3.2 Bases for Market Segmentation

# Geographic Location of the Canadian Population

Canada's population has grown from 3 million in 1867 to about 31 million in 2002.[2] The Canadian population, like that of the rest of the world, is not distributed evenly. In fact, it is extremely uneven; large portions of this country are uninhabited.[3]

In Canada, about 7 percent of the land surface is occupied farmland.[4] The inhabited space in Canada is depicted in Figure 3.3. This map shows dramatically that a relatively small strip along the American border is the land area most heavily settled and utilized. Business and social activities therefore must operate in an east–west manner, over tremendous distances. It is thus not surprising to see the emergence of various distinct market segments, such as Central Canada (Ontario and/or Quebec), the Maritimes, the Prairies, and British Columbia.

Not only do provinces vary widely in total population (see Figure 3.4 and Table 3.1), but pronounced shifts also occur. People tend to move where work and opportunities exist. Thus, Ontario and British Columbia have been continuously attractive to those on the move. In the late 1970s, Alberta experienced large population influxes because of the oil-induced prosperity there. Many left during the recession of the early 1980s. More recently, Alberta has again been seen as a province with attractive possibilities.

Natural factors and immigration also influence population. Growth has occurred as a result of natural increase (births minus deaths) and net migration (immigration minus emigration). Overall, the rate of natural increase has been somewhat higher than that of net migration.[5] In fact, the Atlantic provinces and Saskatchewan depend on natural increase to restore population levels lost by emigration. On the other hand, Ontario, British Columbia, and Alberta have shown significant total population increases because on balance they have received migration flows plus a natural increase. In recent years natural increases have been declining.

Immigration has had a tremendous impact on Canadian society. The injection of a steady stream of British immigrants and short bursts of Central, Eastern, and Southern Europeans and

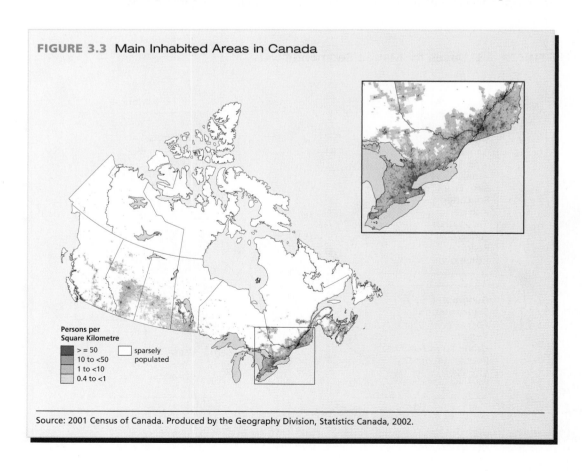

**FIGURE 3.3** Main Inhabited Areas in Canada

Persons per Square Kilometre
- >= 50
- 10 to <50
- 1 to <10
- 0.4 to <1
- sparsely populated

Source: 2001 Census of Canada. Produced by the Geography Division, Statistics Canada, 2002.

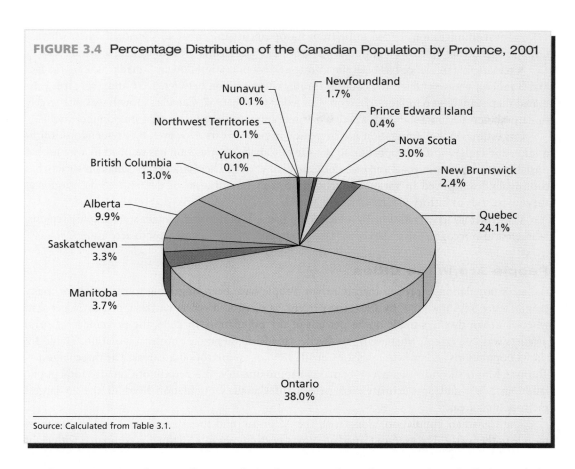

**FIGURE 3.4** Percentage Distribution of the Canadian Population by Province, 2001

Nunavut
0.1%

Newfoundland
1.7%

Northwest Territories
0.1%

Prince Edward Island
0.4%

Yukon
0.1%

Nova Scotia
3.0%

British Columbia
13.0%

New Brunswick
2.4%

Alberta
9.9%

Quebec
24.1%

Saskatchewan
3.3%

Manitoba
3.7%

Ontario
38.0%

Source: Calculated from Table 3.1.

Southeast Asians into the Canadian population have created social pressures in assimilation and citizenship. Some areas have attracted much more immigration. In fact, Ontario contains 54.8 percent of Canada's living foreign-born people.[6] The western provinces contain the greatest percentages of foreign-born "old-timers" (people who immigrated before 1946).

**TABLE 3.1** Provincial and Territorial Populations, 1981, 1991, 2001

| | POPULATION (THOUSANDS) | | |
|---|---|---|---|
| **Region** | **1981** | **1991** | **2001** |
| Newfoundland | 568 | 568 | 513 |
| Prince Edward Island | 123 | 130 | 135 |
| Nova Scotia | 847 | 900 | 908 |
| New Brunswick | 696 | 724 | 729 |
| Quebec | 6 438 | 6 896 | 7 237 |
| Ontario | 8 625 | 10 085 | 11 410 |
| Manitoba | 1 026 | 1 092 | 1 120 |
| Saskatchewan | 968 | 989 | 979 |
| Alberta | 2 238 | 2 546 | 2 975 |
| British Columbia | 2 744 | 3 282 | 3 908 |
| Yukon | 23 | 28 | 29 |
| Northwest Territories | 46 | 36 | 37 |
| Nunavut | n/a | 21 | 27 |
| Canada | 24 343 | 27 297 | 30 007 |

Source: "Provincial and Territorial Populations, 1981, 1991, 2001" adapted from the Statistics Canada Website http://geodepot.ca/English/Pgdb/People/Population/demo05.htm. Reprinted with permission of the Minister of Industry Canada.

Postwar immigration tended to be from European urban centres to Canadian cities, whereas immigration before World War II was largely from European rural areas to Canadian rural areas.

A remarkable influence has been the immigration–emigration flow in Canada. Despite the fact that 8 million people entered the country through immigration between 1851 and 1961, it is estimated that more than 6 million *left*. From Confederation to 1967, Canada's growth was due largely to natural increase (14.5 million), whereas net migration produced only a 2.4 million increase.[7]

It is estimated that emigration has decreased in recent years. However, the tremendous immigration and emigration in proportion to the size of Canada's population has resulted in a somewhat unstable set of common goals and ends for Canadian society. The character of Canadian society has continually been pulled in various directions through the infusion of different ethnic groups at varying periods of history via immigration.

These factors have traditionally affected the political outlook of Canada's geographic regions. Marketers also recognize that they must take geographic market segments into account.

## People Are in the Cities

Canada's population is predominantly urban. People have been migrating to the cities for many years. Figure 3.5 shows that by 1991, the percentage of rural dwellers had dropped to 26 percent, whereas urban dwellers made up 74 percent of the population. In 2001, the percentage of rural dwellers was 20 percent, whereas urban dwellers made up 80 percent of the population.[8] Table 3.2 shows populations and growth rates for Canada's 25 largest metropolitan areas. The three largest—Toronto, Montreal, and Vancouver—contained approximately 33.8 percent of Canada's total population in 2001, and approximately 63 percent of Canada's population lived in the 25 largest metropolitan areas.[9]

The Canadian population, along with the American and the Australian, is one of the most mobile in the world. The average Canadian moves twelve times in a lifetime, as compared with eight times for the average English citizen and five for the typical Japanese.[10] However, this trend may be

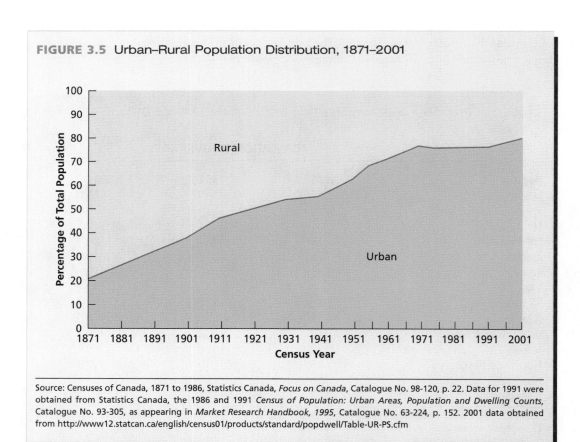

**FIGURE 3.5** Urban–Rural Population Distribution, 1871–2001

Source: Censuses of Canada, 1871 to 1986, Statistics Canada, *Focus on Canada*, Catalogue No. 98-120, p. 22. Data for 1991 were obtained from Statistics Canada, the 1986 and 1991 *Census of Population: Urban Areas, Population and Dwelling Counts*, Catalogue No. 93-305, as appearing in *Market Research Handbook, 1995*, Catalogue No. 63-224, p. 152. 2001 data obtained from http://www12.statcan.ca/english/census01/products/standard/popdwell/Table-UR-PS.cfm

**TABLE 3.2** The 25 Largest Metropolitan Areas in Canada, 1996, 2001

| Area | 1996 Population (Thousands) | 2001 Population (Thousands) |
| --- | --- | --- |
| Toronto | 4445 | 4881 |
| Montreal | 3359 | 3512 |
| Vancouver | 1891 | 2079 |
| Ottawa–Hull | 1031 | 1107 |
| Calgary | 852 | 972 |
| Edmonton | 892 | 957 |
| Quebec | 698 | 693 |
| Winnipeg | 677 | 685 |
| Hamilton | 650 | 681 |
| London | 416 | 426 |
| Kitchener | 403 | 432 |
| St. Catharines–Niagara | 390 | 393 |
| Halifax | 347 | 359 |
| Victoria | 313 | 319 |
| Windsor | 292 | 314 |
| Oshawa | 281 | 305 |
| Saskatoon | 222 | 231 |
| Regina | 199 | 198 |
| St. John's | 178 | 176 |
| Chicoutimi–Jonquière | 167 | 159 |
| Sudbury | 166 | 157 |
| Sherbrooke | 150 | 155 |
| Trois-Rivières | 144 | 142 |
| Saint John | 129 | 128 |
| Thunder Bay | 131 | 125 |

Source: Adapted from the Statistics Canada publication *Canada Year Book 1999*, Catalogue No. 11-402, page 94 and from the Statistics Canada Website http://www.statcan.ca/english/Pgdb/People/Population/demo05.htm. Reprinted with permission of the Minister of Industry Canada.

waning. The slowdown may be due to a number of factors: poor job prospects elsewhere, the tendency of wage earners in two-income families to refuse transfers, an aging population, and a heightened concern about the quality of life.

## Using Geographic Segmentation

There are many instances where markets for goods and services may be segmented on a geographic basis. Country and regional variations in taste often exist. Breakfast in Germany normally includes bread, cheese, and cold meat. In countries with large Chinese populations, this segment will eat rice porridge and other "nonbreakfast" items (by Canadian standards). Quebec has long been known for its interest in fine and varied foods.

Residence location within a geographic area is another important geographic variable. Urban dwellers may eat more meals in restaurants than their suburban and rural counterparts, while suburban dwellers spend proportionally more on lawn and garden care than do people in rural or urban areas. Both rural and suburban dwellers may spend more of their household income on gasoline and automobile needs than do urban households.

Climate is another important factor. Snow blowers, snowmobiles, and sleds are popular products in many parts of Canada. Residents of southwestern British Columbia may spend proportionately less of their total income on heating and heating equipment than other Canadians. Climate also affects patterns of clothing purchases.

Geographic segmentation influences decisions about which sales regions to enter, where sales force offices are located, and where retail outlets are located.

Geographic segmentation is useful only when true differences in preference and purchase patterns for a product emerge along regional lines. Geographic subdivisions of the overall market tend to be rather large and often too heterogeneous for effective segmentation for many products without carefully considering additional factors. In such cases, it may be necessary to use other segmentation variables as well.

# DEMOGRAPHIC SEGMENTATION

The most common approach to market segmentation is to group consumers according to demographic variables. These variables—age, gender, income, occupation, education, household size, and others—are typically used to identify market segments and to develop appropriate market mixes. Demographic variables are often used in market segmentation for three reasons:

- They are easy to identify and measure.
- They are associated with the sale of many products and services.
- They are typically referred to in describing the audiences of advertising media, so that media buyers and others can easily pinpoint the desired target market.[11]

Vast quantities of data are available to assist the marketing planner in segmenting potential markets on a demographic basis. Gender is an obvious variable for segmenting many markets, since many products are gender-specific. Electric-razor manufacturers have used gender as a variable in successfully marketing such brands as Lady Remington. Diet soft drinks have often been aimed at female markets. Even deodorants are targeted at males or females.

Age, stage in the family life cycle, household size, and income and expenditure patterns are important factors in determining buying decisions. The often distinct differences in purchase patterns based on such demographic factors justify their frequent use as a basis for segmentation.

## Segmenting by Age

The population of Canada is expected to grow by 10 percent between 1999 and 2006, but this growth will be concentrated in persons aged 45 and older. This group represents two potentially profitable target markets.

The older and senior middle-aged adult segment (45–64) includes households where the children have grown up and most have left home. For many, housing costs are lower because mortgages are paid off. In general, this group finds itself with substantial disposable income because it is in a peak earning period, and many basic purchases for everyday living have been completed. This disposable income is often used for luxury goods, new furniture, and travel. While this segment currently represents 20.8 percent of the Canadian population, it will account for 65 percent of the growth in population between 1999 and 2006.

Not so many years ago, there was no such thing as a senior-citizen market, since few people reached old age. Now, however, some 12.3 percent of the total population is 65 or older.[12] Not only is it comforting for this year's retiree to learn that at age 60 her or his average life expectancy is at least another 22.2 years,[13] but the trend also creates a unique and potentially profitable segment for the marketing manager. The manager of course will not ignore the youth segment, which will decline in proportion to the whole population but remain large. Figure 3.6 shows the changing profile of the Canadian population.

Each of the age groups in Figure 3.6 represents different consumption patterns, and each serves as the target market for particular firms. For instance, Gerber Products Company has been extremely successful in aiming at the parents-of-infants market, and prepackaged tours appeal to older consumers. Table 3.3 lists some of the types of merchandise often purchased by the various age groups.

# Segmenting by Family Life Cycle

The **family life cycle** is the process of family formation, development, and dissolution. Using this concept, the marketing planner combines the family characteristics of age, marital status, presence or absence of children, and ages of children in developing the marketing strategy. Patrick E. Murphy

**family life cycle**
The process of family formation, development, and dissolution.

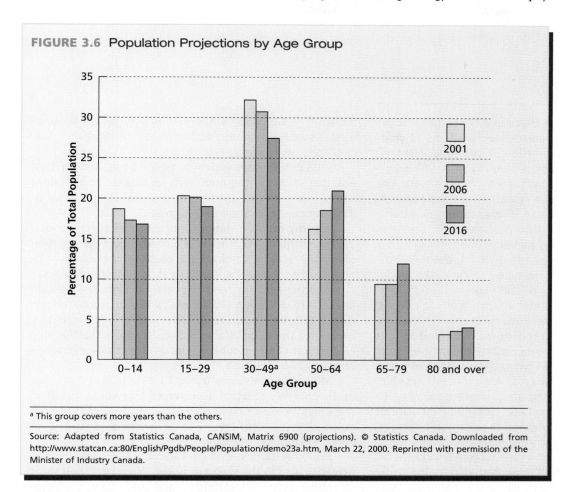

**FIGURE 3.6** Population Projections by Age Group

*Percentage of Total Population* (vertical axis)
*Age Group* (horizontal axis): 0–14, 15–29, 30–49ᵃ, 50–64, 65–79, 80 and over

Legend: 2001, 2006, 2016

ᵃ This group covers more years than the others.

Source: Adapted from Statistics Canada, CANSIM, Matrix 6900 (projections). © Statistics Canada. Downloaded from http://www.statcan.ca:80/English/Pgdb/People/Population/demo23a.htm, March 22, 2000. Reprinted with permission of the Minister of Industry Canada.

**TABLE 3.3** Buying Patterns for Different Age Groups

| AGE | NAME OF AGE GROUP | MERCHANDISE |
|---|---|---|
| 0–5 | Young children | Baby food, toys, nursery furniture, children's wear |
| 6–19 | Schoolchildren (including teenagers) | Clothing, sports equipment, records, school supplies, food, cosmetics, used cars |
| 20–34 | Young adults | Cars, furniture, houses, clothing, recreational equipment, purchases for younger age groups |
| 35–49 | Younger middle-aged adults | Larger homes, better cars, second cars, new furniture, recreational equipment |
| 50–64 | Older middle-aged adults | Recreational items, purchases for young marrieds and infants |
| 65+ | Senior adults | Medical services, travel, drugs, purchases for younger age groups |

Market Segmentation: Finding a Base to Start
Chapter 3  **51**

and William A. Staples have proposed a six-stage family life cycle with several subcategories. These stages are shown in Table 3.4.

The behavioural characteristics and buying patterns of people in each life-cycle stage often vary considerably. Young singles have relatively few financial burdens, tend to be early purchasers of new fashion items, are recreation-oriented, and make purchases of basic kitchen equipment, cars, and

## THE CANADIAN MARKETPLACE

### CATERING TO THE TWEENS

While Britney Spears laments that she is "not a girl, not yet a woman," 2.4 million Canadian tweens—8- to 12-year-olds—could write their own version of that tune. After all, they are not children, but not yet teenagers.

Nowadays, mature, sophisticated "tweens" are the "it" demographic. They have honed street-and-pop culture radars, are knowledgeable of brands and designers, and are old enough to make their own decisions. They also have $1.4 billion in spending power, influencing $196 billion annually in household spending, doling out their outspoken tweens' opinions on the type of food to the model and style of car their parents should buy.

Smart retailers are now catering specifically to tweens. Established vendors such as Pottery Barn and William Sonoma have recently launched stores dedicated to this segment. West Elm, a catalogue collection with cool stuff for tweens, and c2b, a Web site/store with a tween twist, both opened their doors recently for business. Retailers such as Urban Outfitters and Anthropologie (a romantic/nostalgic-styled retailer owned by Urban Outfitters) are all trying to expand their tween offerings, looking to cash in on this lucrative market.

"The boom and interest in the tweeny market is all but teeny," says designer Karim Rashid, who recently designed Bozart toys, a rubbery chess set, and Kapsule, a storage chair for tweens. He is perhaps best-known, however, for his Umbra Garbo trash can, which was a hit with tweens due to shape, size, and bright colours.

"It is a massive market because this new, super-young, hip generation is living in the moment and our visual world is becoming very sophisticated, yet there is not enough commodity in their market that reflects the present," Mr. Rashid says.

What is appealing to fickle tweens?

"Widget-things are items that aren't necessary to life, but [they are] fun," says Betty Kahn, in public relations at Crate & Barrel, whose widgets include a Slinky CD wall holder (US$39.95), the Boom Bag (US$54.95), a bag with built-in speakers, and the Pop-Up, an expandable trash bin (US$12.95–$15.95).

"[Tweens] normally go for the novelty items like the Kung Fu Hamster—a motorized hamster ($24) that sings Kung Fu Fighting while boogeying and swinging his numchucks, or the Dancing James Brown ($45), that lip-syncs the song "I Got You" while swinging his hips back-and-forth," says Hal Winnick, a 25-year-old manager at Urban Outfitters on Yonge Street.

High design does appeal to tweens, too, and the best example of this is the popularity of mid-century modern chairs—not that such tags are of importance or interest to this younger generation of design aficionados.

It turns out the design is economical to reproduce: Urban Outfitters sells numerous butterfly chairs (frame, $44; cover, $32–$38) "It's one of our best-sellers because of its casual, urban, laid-back, student-y look," Mr. Winnick says.

Another enduring and appealing design: the Herman Miller DCM, or Dining Chair Metal, which is a moulded plywood, tubular, metal-based chair designed by seating icons Ray Eames and Charles Eames. Its new and affordable incarnation can be found at cb2 as the ergonomic wood Tamago Chair (US$149).

More companies are trying to develop products that touch on every facet of a person's life, tweens included. The only difference these days is that tweens are the ones doing the purchasing (with allowance, birthday or Christmas money) instead of their parents.

Everyday items sold in packages are fast, easy, and no-fuss and cater to the speed of tweens' lives and their short attention spans. Anthropologie and Urban Outfitters supplement their clothing collections with disposable, cheap chic furniture and décor accessories for tweens.

If you wear Anthropologie's Adriana patchwork clogs (US$158), you can snuggle up in the Anna patchwork quilt (US$148) or adorn your windows with the Patch Lace Curtain (US$84). Tweens wearing Urban Outfitters' Buddha Tee ($32) might also be interested in hanging the spiral, paper Bohemian Lanterns ($54) in their rooms.

It seems for tweens that matching belts and shoes is not as important as matching the contents of their closets to the contents of their rooms.

**What other types of products might be of interest to tweens? Do you see any ethical issues in targeting this group?**

Source: Susan Chong, "Catering to the Tweens," *The National Post*, August 3, 2002. http://www.nationalpost.com/specialreports/postdecor/20020803/story.html?id={ACAD6F87-E083-42CC-B89B-F9AE33270E82}. Reprinted with permission of the author.

La Coupe is using two bases of segmentation: age and benefits sought.

**TABLE 3.4 Family Life-Cycle Stages**

1. Young Single
2. Young Married without Children
3. Other Young
   a. Young divorced without children
   b. Young married with children
   c. Young divorced with children
4. Middle-Aged
   a. Middle-aged married without children
   b. Middle-aged divorced without children
   c. Middle-aged married with children
   d. Middle-aged divorced with children
   e. Middle-aged married without dependent children
   f. Middle-aged divorced without dependent children
5. Older
   a. Older married
   b. Older unmarried (divorced, widowed)
6. Other
   All adults and children not accounted for by family life-cycle stages

Source: Adapted from Patrick E. Murphy and William A. Staples, "A Modernized Family Life," *Journal of Consumer Research* (June 1979), p. 16, published by the University of Chicago Press. Reprinted with permission.

vacations. By contrast, young marrieds with young children tend to be heavy purchasers of baby products, homes, television sets, toys, and washers and dryers. Their liquid assets tend to be relatively low, and they are more likely to watch television than young singles or young marrieds without children. The empty-nest households in the middle-aged and older categories with no dependent children are more likely to have more disposable income; more time for recreation, self-education, and travel; and more than one member in the labour force than their full-nest counterparts with younger children. Similar differences in behavioural and buying patterns are evident in the other stages of the family life cycle.[14]

Analyzing life-cycle stages often gives better results than relying on single variables, such as age. The buying patterns of a 25-year-old bachelor are very different from those of a father of the same age. The family of five headed by parents in their 40s is a more likely prospect for a Ford Windstar minivan than the childless 40-year-old divorced person.

Marketing planners can use published data such as census reports to divide their markets into more homogeneous segments than would be possible if they were analyzing single variables. Such data are available for each classification of the family life cycle.

## Segmenting by Household Size

Half the households in Canada are composed of only one or two persons, and the average household size is three persons. This development is in marked contrast to households that averaged more than four persons before World War II. Married couples still form the largest segment of households, but in relative terms their numbers are decreasing.

There are several reasons for the trend toward smaller households. Among them are lower fertility rates, the tendency of young people to postpone marriage, the increasing desire among younger couples to limit the number of children, the ease and frequency of divorce, and the ability and desire of many young single adults and elderly people to live alone.

Over 2.6 million people live alone according to the 1996 Census.[15] The single-person household has emerged as an important market segment with a special title: **SSWD** (single, separated, widowed, or divorced). SSWDs buy approximately 25 percent of all passenger cars, but a much higher proportion of specialty cars. They are also customers for single-serving food products, such as Campbell's Soup-for-One and Green Giant's single-serving casseroles.

## Segmenting by Income and Expenditure Patterns

Earlier, markets were defined as people and purchasing power. A very common method of segmenting consumer markets is on the basis of income. For example, fashionable specialty shops that stock designer-label clothing obtain most of their sales from high-income shoppers.

A household's expenditures may be divided into two categories: (1) basic purchases of essential household needs, and (2) other purchases that can be made at the discretion of the household members once the necessities have been purchased (disposable income). Total Canadian disposable income is estimated to have tripled in constant dollars since 1961,[16] a substantial increase.

## Engel's Laws

How do expenditure patterns vary with increased income? More than 100 years ago a German statistician named Ernst Engel published three general statements—**Engel's Laws**—based on his studies of spending behaviour. According to Engel, as family income increases:

1. A smaller percentage of expenditures goes for food.
2. The percentage spent on housing and household operations and clothing will remain constant.
3. The percentage spent on other items (such as recreation, education, etc.) will increase.

Are Engel's Laws still valid today? Figure 3.7 supplies the answers. A small decline in the percentage of total income spent for food occurs from low to high incomes. Note the emphasis on the

www.ford.com

**SSWDs**

Single, separated, widowed, or divorced people

www.campbellsoup.ca

www.greengiant.com

**Engel's Laws**

As family income increases, (1) a smaller percentage goes for food, (2) the percentage spent on housing and household operations and clothing will remain constant, and (3) the percentage spent on other items will increase.

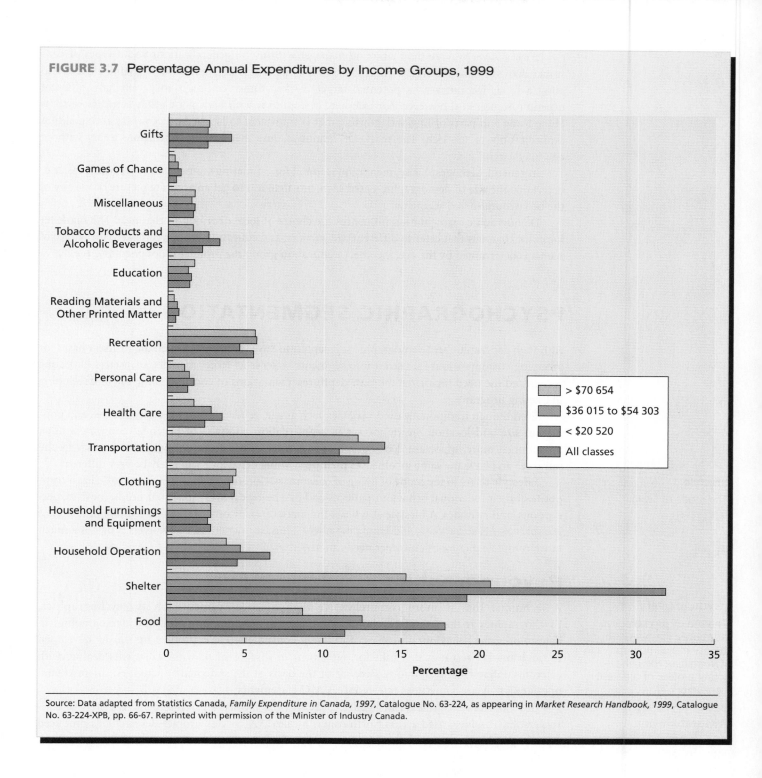

**FIGURE 3.7 Percentage Annual Expenditures by Income Groups, 1999**

Legend:
- > $70 654
- $36 015 to $54 303
- < $20 520
- All classes

X-axis: Percentage (0, 5, 10, 15, 20, 25, 30, 35)

Categories (top to bottom): Gifts, Games of Chance, Miscellaneous, Tobacco Products and Alcoholic Beverages, Education, Reading Materials and Other Printed Matter, Recreation, Personal Care, Health Care, Transportation, Clothing, Household Furnishings and Equipment, Household Operation, Shelter, Food

Source: Data adapted from Statistics Canada, *Family Expenditure in Canada, 1997*, Catalogue No. 63-224, as appearing in *Market Research Handbook, 1999*, Catalogue No. 63-224-XPB, pp. 66-67. Reprinted with permission of the Minister of Industry Canada.

word *percentage*. The high-income families will spend a greater absolute amount on food purchases, but their purchases will represent a smaller percentage of their total expenditures than will be true of low-income households.

With respect to Engel's second law, expenditures for shelter decline rather than remain constant. However, as predicted, there is relatively little change in the percentage of income spent on household operations and in household furnishings and equipment, as well as on clothing.

The third law is also true with respect to recreation and education. However, there are notable exceptions to the original generalization, such as transportation. It has become a much greater part of family expenditures than Engel might have dreamed.

Engel's Laws provide the marketing manager with useful generalizations about types of consumer demand that will evolve with increased income. These laws may also be useful when evaluating a foreign country as a potential target market. Other countries may well have different expenditure patterns, however. For example, in countries with high population densities, such as Hong Kong and parts of England, housing that is equivalent to North American size and quality is available only to the rich. The marketer cannot assume that Engel's conclusions apply without checking carefully.

In general, demographic segmentation is useful for estimating segment size—it's much easier to determine the size of demographic-based segments than it is to get an accurate picture of the size of the behavioural-based segments.

Demographic segmentation influences the choice of local distribution channels. The marketer looks for channels that cater to different age, income, and education groups. Similarly, the choice of media is determined by the age, income, or education group the product is designed to serve.

# PSYCHOGRAPHIC SEGMENTATION

Although geographic and demographic segmentation have traditionally been the primary bases for grouping customers and industries into segments to serve as target markets, marketers have long recognized the need for richer, more in-depth representations of consumers for use in developing marketing programs.

Even though traditionally used variables such as age, gender, family life cycle, income, and population size and location are important in segmentation, lifestyles of potential consumers often prove much more important. Demographically, a truck driver and a college professor may be the same age and have the same income, yet their purchasing behaviour will likely be very different.

**lifestyle**
The mode of living.

**Lifestyle** refers to the mode of living of consumers. Consumers' lifestyles are regarded as a composite of their individual behaviour patterns and psychological makeup—their needs, motives, perceptions, and attitudes. A lifestyle also bears the mark of many other influences—those of reference groups, culture, social class, and family members. Thus, segmentation by lifestyles provides a much more complete picture of customer needs and wants.

## Psychographics

**psychographics**
The use of psychological attributes, lifestyles, attitudes, and demographics in determining the behavioural profiles of different consumers.

A technique that is more comprehensive than lifestyle segmentation is **psychographics**. Psychographics is the use of psychological attributes, lifestyles, attitudes, and demographics in determining the behavioural profiles of different consumers. These profiles are usually developed through market research that asks for agreement or disagreement with statements dealing with activities, interests, and opinions. Because of the basis of the statements (activities, interests, and opinions), they are sometimes referred to as **AIO statements**.

**AIO statements**
Statements about activities, interests, and opinions that are used in developing psychographic profiles.

SRI Consulting Business Intelligence (SRIC-BI) has created a psychographic typology of consumers that is widely used across North America called VALS™. Environics Research has produced a psychographic grouping of the Canadian market. Their findings are somewhat different, but both provide some interesting insights into the marketplace.

The SRIC-BI segments are created by mapping consumers on what the firm refers to as "self-orientation" and "resources." Self-orientation refers to the pattern of attitudes and activities that help people reinforce, sustain, or modify their social identities. A consumer's self-orientation can be towards either principle, status, or action. Resources is a holistic measure intended to capture everything from financial ability to an individual's energy levels. Taken together these dimensions yield eight psychographic groupings.

### ACTUALIZERS

Actualizers are successful, sophisticated, active, "take-charge" people with high self-esteem and abundant resources. They are interested in growth and seek to develop, explore, and express them-

## FIGURE 3.8 VALS™ Network

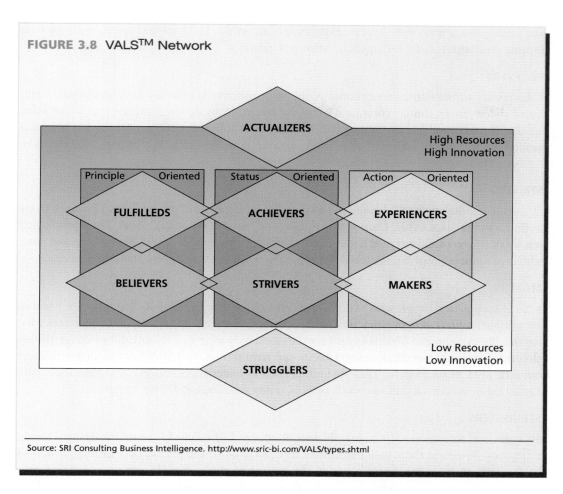

Source: SRI Consulting Business Intelligence. http://www.sric-bi.com/VALS/types.shtml

selves in a variety of ways—sometimes guided by principle, and sometimes by a desire to have an effect, to make a change. Image is important to Actualizers as an expression of their taste, independence, and character.

### FULFILLEDS

Fulfilleds are mature, satisfied, comfortable, reflective people who value order, knowledge, and responsibility. Most are well educated and in (or recently retired from) professional occupations. They are well informed about world and national events and are alert to opportunities to broaden their knowledge. Content with their career, families, and station in life, their leisure activities tend to centre around the home. Fulfilleds are conservative, practical consumers; they look for durability, functionality, and value in the products they buy.

### ACHIEVERS

Achievers are successful career and work-oriented people who like to, and generally do, feel in control of their lives. They value consensus, predictability, and stability over risk, intimacy, and self-discovery. They are deeply committed to work and family. Work provides them with a sense of duty, material rewards, and prestige. Their social lives reflect this focus and are structured around family, church, and career. Achievers favour established, prestige products and services that demonstrate success to their peers.

### EXPERIENCERS

Experiencers are young, vital, enthusiastic, impulsive, and rebellious. They seek variety and excitement, savoring the new, the offbeat, and the risky. Still in the process of formulating life values and patterns of behaviour, they quickly become enthusiastic about new possibilities but are equally quick to cool. At this stage in their lives, they are politically uncommitted, uninformed, and highly ambivalent about what they believe. Experiencers are avid consumers and spend much of their income on clothing, fast food, music, movies, and videos.

## BELIEVERS

Believers are conservative, conventional people with concrete beliefs based on traditional, established codes: family, church, community, and the nation. Many Believers express moral codes that are deeply rooted and literally interpreted. They follow established routines, organized in large part around home, family, and social or religious organizations to which they belong. As consumers, Believers are conservative and predictable.

## STRIVERS

Strivers seek motivation, self-definition, and approval from the world around them. They are striving to find a secure place in life. Unsure of themselves and low on economic, social, and psychological resources, Strivers are concerned about the opinions and approval of others. Strivers emulate those who own more impressive possessions, but what they wish to obtain is often beyond their reach.

## MAKERS

Makers are practical people who have constructive skills and value self-sufficiency. They live within a traditional context of family, practical work, and physical recreation and have little interest in what lies outside that context. Makers experience the world by working on it—building a house, raising children, fixing a car, or canning vegetables—and have enough skill, income, and energy to carry out their projects successfully. They are unimpressed by material possessions other than those with a practical or functional purpose (such as tools, utility vehicles, and fishing equipment.)

## STRUGGLERS

Struggler lives are constricted. Chronically poor, ill-educated, low-skilled, without strong social bonds, elderly and concerned about their health, they are often resigned and passive. Because they are limited by the need to meet the urgent needs of the present moment, they do not show a strong self-orientation. Their chief concerns are for security and safety. Strugglers are cautious consumers. They represent a very modest market for most products and services, but are loyal to favourite brands.

## The Environics Segments[17]

Environics has produced a slightly more complicated scheme than VALS. Two key dimensions underly the Environics approach: traditional to modern and social to individual. The dimensions are applied in a two-stage process. First, the population is divided into three main age groups: the Elders (pre-boomers), the Boomers, and Generation X (post-boomers). Each age group is then subdivided into various psychographic segments as follows:

www.erg.environics.net/
surveys

## ELDERS

- *Rational Traditionalists* (15 percent of total population, 54 percent of Elders) are motivated to achieve and preserve financial independence, stability, and security. Key values include religiosity and primacy of reason.

- *Extroverted Traditionalists* (7 percent of total population, 26 percent of Elders) are motivated by traditional community, institutions, and social status. Key values include religiosity and family.

- *Cosmopolitan Modernists* (6 percent of total population, 20 percent of Elders) are motivated by traditional institutions and experience seeking. Their key values include a global world-view, respect for education, and desire for innovation.

## BOOMERS

- *Autonomous Rebels* (10 percent of total population, 25 percent of Boomers) are motivated by personal autonomy and self-fulfillment. They have a strong belief in human rights, are skeptical toward traditional institutions, and are suspicious of authority. They also value freedom, individuality, and education.

- *Anxious Communitarians* (9 percent of total population, 20 percent of Boomers) are motivated by traditional community, institutions, and social status. They value family, community, and duty and need respect.

- *Connected Enthusiasts* (6 percent of total population, 14 percent of Boomers) are motivated by both traditional and new communities and are experience seekers. They value family, community, hedonism, and immediate gratification.

- *Disengaged Darwinists* (18 percent of total population, 41 percent of Boomers) seek financial independence, stability, and security. They are nostalgic about the past.

**GENERATION X**

- *Aimless Dependents* (8 percent of total population, 27 percent of Gen Xers) are motivated to achieve financial independence, stability, and security. They desire independence.

- *Thrill-Seeking Materialists* (7 percent of total population, 25 percent of Gen Xers) are motivated by traditional communities, social status, and experience seeking. They desire money and material possessions, recognition, respect, and admiration.

- *New Aquarians* (4 percent of total population, 13 percent of Gen Xers) are experience seekers interested in new communities. They value egalitarianism, ecology, and hedonism.

- *Autonomous Postmaterialists* (6 percent of total population, 20 percent of Gen Xers) are motivated to achieve personal autonomy and self-fulfillment. They value freedom and respect for human rights.

- *Social Hedonists* (4 percent of total population, 15 percent of Gen Xers) are experience seekers interested in new communities. They value aesthetics, hedonism, sexual permissiveness, and immediate gratification.

Environics has a Web site where you can see which profile you best match.

What can be done with such segment analyses? Each segment can be related to product preference and use. There are many possibilities. For example, using the Environics segments, the "Disengaged Darwinists" are an obvious target for mutual funds and for high quality, long-lasting consumer durables. On the other hand, "Thrill-Seeking Materialists" are the natural target for high performance sports gear.

Such information is extremely useful for marketers planning a communication campaign because they know what types of messages and products to feature on different television and radio programs and in other media. The insights developed by such a process go far beyond demographic segmentation and influence product positioning (see Chapter 4), advertising themes, and media choice.

Psychographic segmentation is often part of an overall segmentation strategy in which markets are also segmented on the basis of demographic/geographic variables. These more traditional bases provide the marketer with accessibility to consumer segments through orthodox communications channels such as newspapers, radio and television advertising, and other promotional outlets. Psychographic studies may then be implemented to develop lifelike, three-dimensional profiles of the lifestyles of the firm's target market. When combined with demographic/geographic characteristics, psychographics emerges as an important tool for understanding the behaviour of present and potential target markets.[18]

# BENEFIT SEGMENTATION

Benefit segmentation is based on the attributes of products as seen by the customer. Segments are developed by asking consumers about the benefits they perceive in a good or service. Since many

The yogurt market can be segmented by benefits sought.

people perceive and use the same product differently, those who perceive benefits that are similar are clustered into groups. Each group then constitutes a market segment.

Many marketers now consider benefit segmentation one of the most useful methods of classifying markets. One analysis of 34 segmentation studies indicated that benefit analysis provided the best predictor of brand use, level of consumption, and product type selected in 51 percent of the cases. In a pioneering benefit segmentation investigation, Daniel Yankelovich revealed that much of the watch industry operated with little understanding of the benefits watch buyers expect in their purchases. At the time of the study, most watch companies were marketing relatively expensive models through jewellery stores and using prestige appeals. However, Yankelovich's research revealed

## THE ETHICAL MARKETER

### PROBLEMS WITH HEAVY USERS

For most products and services there is no particular ethical problem with targeting and attempting to increase the heavy user segment. But what if your product tends to lead to physical addiction, psychological compulsion, negative health outcomes, or all three?

Tobacco marketers and, to a somewhat lesser degree, alcohol marketers have faced this situation for decades. It is also one of the principal arguments made by opponents to legalized gambling. The fear is that a very large proportion of gambling revenues will come from a small number of gamblers who likely cannot afford the losses.

**What do you think? Are there ethical options for the marketers of such products?**

that less than one-third of the market was purchasing a watch as a status symbol. In fact, 23 percent of his respondents reported they purchased the lowest-price watch, and another 46 percent focused on durability and overall product quality. The Timex Company decided to focus its product benefits on those two categories and market its watches in drugstores, variety stores, and discount houses. The rest is history. Within a few years of adopting the new segmentation approach, it became the largest watch company in the world.[19]

Table 3.5 illustrates how benefit segmentation might be applied to the yogurt market. The table reveals that some consumers are primarily concerned with spending the least amount, some with providing choice for their family members, others are looking for taste and quality, while still others are searching for various health benefits. These different "benefit seekers" could be grouped together and marketing programs developed to appeal to each group.

**TABLE 3.5** Benefit Segmentation Applied to Yogurt

| BENEFITS SOUGHT FROM YOGURT | ATTRIBUTES OF YOGURT | | | | | | | |
|---|---|---|---|---|---|---|---|---|
| | Individually packaged | With fruit | High-priced | Mild | Organic | Contains bio-bifidus | Low fat | Low-priced |
| Provides choice for family members | X | X | | | | | | |
| Convenient to use | X | | | | | | | |
| Tastes good | | X | | X | | | | |
| Good quality | | X | X | X | X | | | |
| Healthy | | X | | X | X | X | | |
| Helps digestion | | | | | | | X | |
| Helps diet | | | | | | | X | |
| Spend less money | | | | | | | | X |

Source: Adapted from Marco Vriens and Ter Hofstede, "Linking Attributes, Benefits, and Consumer Values," *Marketing Research*, Chicago, Fall 2000, V. 12(3) pp. 4–10. Reprinted with permission by the American Marketing Association.

# PRODUCT USAGE RATE SEGMENTATION

A final common way of segmenting consumer markets is by product usage rate. Marketers are especially interested in identifying and serving the heavy user of a particular product. Many markets follow a rule of thumb known as the 80/20 rule. That is, about 80 percent of a company's sales will tend to come from 20 percent of its customers. The 80/20 rule is not always a rigid literal relationship; the real point is that a disproportionate amount of sales tend to come from a relatively small group of customers. It only makes sense, then, to try to identify and cultivate that small group.

Brand loyalty is also an important issue. Someone who drinks five or six cans of Coca-Cola—and only Coca-Cola—a day, is a far more valuable customer to The Coca-Cola Company than is the person who only drinks one or two cans of cola a month and doesn't much care if they're drinking Coca-Cola, Pepsi, or President's Choice. Again, identifying and cultivating the brand-loyal heavy user can be extremely profitable for the marketer.

To attract heavy users, companies may create different product size offerings, promotions that reward frequent purchasers, or special financing terms for heavy users.

www.coca-cola.com

www.pepsiworld.com

Table 3.6 summarizes the different methods of segmentation and some of the marketing decisions that are affected by those choices.

---

**TABLE 3.6** Consumer Marketing Decisions Affected by Segmentation Choices

| SEGMENTATION BASIS | DECISIONS AFFECTED |
|---|---|
| Geographic | • Choice of sales region<br>• Sales force location<br>• Retail location |
| Demographic | • Estimates of segment size<br>• Choice of local distribution channels or channels that cater to different age, income, and education groups<br>• Choice of media that serve different age, income, and education groups |
| Psychographic | • Product/service positioning<br>• Advertising themes<br>• Choice of media |
| Benefit | • Product/service design—different models with different features<br>• Advertising themes<br>• Sales training |
| Product Usage Rate | • Special products (sizes and quality)<br>• Special services<br>• Frequent-user promotions<br>• Special financial terms |

Source: Adapted from *Marketing Management*, 2nd ed. by Peter R. Dickson, p. 187. Copyright © 1997. Reprinted with permission of South-Western, a division of Thomson Learning: www.thomsonrights.com. Fax 800-730-2215.

---

# SEGMENTING BUSINESS-TO-BUSINESS MARKETS

While the bulk of market segmentation research has concentrated on consumer markets, the concept can also be applied to business-to-business marketing. The overall process is similar. Four industrial market segmentation approaches have been identified: geographic segmentation, product segmentation, end-use application segmentation, and account size and potential segmentation.

## Geographic Segmentation

Geographic segmentation is useful in industries where the bulk of the customers are concentrated in specific geographical locations. This approach can be used in such instances as the automobile industry, concentrated in the central Ontario area, or the lumber industry, centred in British Columbia and Quebec. It might also be used in cases where the markets are limited to just a few locations. The oil-field equipment market, for example, is largely concentrated in cities like Calgary and Edmonton. Geographic segmentation is especially helpful when organizing a sales force and making sales management decisions.

## Product Segmentation

It is possible to segment some business-to-business markets in terms of their need for specialized products. Industrial users tend to have much more precise product specifications than do ultimate consumers, and such products often fit very narrow market segments. For example, special rivets for bridge-building might be a market segment. Therefore, the design of an industrial good or service and the development of an associated marketing plan to meet specific buyer requirements is a form of market segmentation.

The **North American Industrial Classification System (NAICS)** formerly the Standard Industrial Classification, or SIC—is a coding system used to categorize different types of businesses and products. The NAICS codes are the business-to-business equivalent of demographic and psychographic consumer information and can be used in much the same way.[20] Chapter 9 discusses NAICS codes in more detail.

**North American Industrial Classification System (NAICS)**

A coding system used to categorize different types of businesses and products (formerly the Standard Industrial Classification, or SIC).

www.census.gov/epcd/

www/naics.html

## End-Use Application Segmentation

A third segmentation base is end-use applications—that is, precisely how the industrial purchaser will use the product. (This is similar to benefit segmentation in consumer markets.) A manufacturer of, say, printing equipment may serve markets ranging from a local utility to a bicycle manufacturer to Agriculture Canada. Each end use may dictate unique specifications of performance, design, and price. The market for desktop computers provides a good example: IBM has several computers for different market sizes. Caterpillar has equipment designed for road construction as well as for other industrial applications. End-use segmentation affects product design, sales force training, and advertising and communications emphasis.

## Account Size and Potential Segmentation

A final way to segment business-to-business customers is by account size and growth potential.[21] Using this segmentation base is similar to segmenting on the usage rate in consumer markets. The benefits to the marketer are also similar in that this technique allows the marketer to concentrate resources where they will have the biggest payoff.

Business-to-business segmentation choices and the marketing decisions affected are summarized in Table 3.7. Regardless of how it is done, market segmentation is as vital to industrial marketing as it is in consumer markets.

---

**TABLE 3.7** Business-to-Business Marketing Decisions Affected by Segmentation Choices

| SEGMENTATION BASIS | DECISIONS AFFECTED |
|---|---|
| Geographic | • Choice of sales region<br>• Sales force organization |
| Product (including NAICS) | • Product design<br>• Media choices<br>• Trade show choices |
| End-Use Application | • Product design<br>• Sales force training<br>• Advertising emphasis |
| Account Size and Growth Potential | • Account and relationship management |

Source: Adapted from *Marketing Management*, 2nd ed. by Peter R. Dickson, p. 187. Copyright © 1997. Reprinted with permission of South-Western, a division of Thomson Learning: www.thomsonrights.com. Fax 800-730-2215.

---

This chapter has introduced the concept of market segmentation and has explained the main bases for segmenting both consumer and industrial markets. Some segmentation procedures are quite simple; others require the use of advanced research techniques. The next chapter examines how segmentation concepts may be applied to market segmentation strategies.

## SUMMARY

It is impossible to serve all possible customers equally well. Therefore, in developing a marketing plan, managers must select a target market segment and then develop and implement a marketing program for that segment.

A market consists of people with the willingness, purchasing power, and authority to buy. Products are classified as consumer products or industrial products based on their end use. Some products can be classified as both consumer and industrial products. Market segmentation is the grouping of people according to their similarity in one or more dimensions related to a particular product category.

Five commonly used bases for segmenting consumer markets are geographic, demographic, psychographic, benefit, and usage rate. Commonly used bases for segmenting industrial markets are geographic, product, end-use application, and account size and potential.

## KEY TERMS

AIO statements, p. 56
benefit segmentation, p. 45
consumer goods, p. 43
demographic segmentation, p. 45
Engel's Laws, p. 54
family life cycle, p. 51
geographic segmentation, p. 45
industrial goods, p. 43
lifestyle, p. 56

market, p. 43
market segmentation, p. 44
North American Industrial
    Classification System (NAICS), p. 63
psychographic segmentation, p. 45
psychographics, p. 56
SSWDs, p. 54
usage rate, p. 45

## INTERACTIVE SUMMARY AND DISCUSSION QUESTIONS

1. In developing a marketing plan, managers must select a target market, then develop and implement a marketing program for that segment. Explain how these tasks reflect the philosophy of consumer orientation in action.
2. A market consists of people with the willingness, purchasing power, and authority to buy. Illustrate the application of this concept in the case of a salesperson for a photocopier company who is trying to make a sale to the Royal Bank.
3. Illustrate how some products can be classified as both consumer and industrial products. Why is it important to make a distinction between the two?
4. Market segmentation is the grouping of people according to their similarity in one or more dimensions related to a particular product category. Show how segmentation might be advantageous in developing a marketing plan for the following products:
   a. textbooks
   b. women's clothing
   c. chain saws
   d. life insurance

**5.** Five commonly used bases for segmenting consumer markets are geographic, demographic, psychographic, benefit, and usage rate. Suggest one descriptive segmentation approach and one behavioural segmentation approach for each item in the list in question 4. Give as detailed an example as possible.

**6.** Suggest two different types of geographic segmentation approaches that could be used in each of the following markets:

a. Canada

b. United States

c. Mexico

d. Germany

e. Japan

f. Italy

g. Hong Kong

**7.** Canadian census data reveal that a significant number of Canadians have a mother tongue other than English or French (mother tongue is defined as the language first learned and still understood). Some of the larger language groups are Italian (approximately 484 500 people), German (approximately 450 140 people), Chinese (approximately 715 640 people), and Ukrainian (approximately 162 695 people).[22] How could a marketer use this demographic information? How could a behavioural segmentation approach enhance the demographic segmentation?

**8.** Industrial market segmentation methods are geographic segmentation, product segmentation, end-use application segmentation, and account size and potential segmentation. Give an example of how Xerox Corporation might use each segmentation method.

**9.** Explain and describe the use of AIO questions.

**10.** How might a fast-food marketer such as Harvey's respond to the changing age-group projections shown in Figure 3.6?

**11.** Visit the SRIC-BI Web site and the Environics Web site, and complete your psychographic profile. Which approach do you think best captures who you are? Which would be most useful to marketers? Explain.

w w w
www.sric-bi.com/VALS/
types.shtml

w w w
erg.environics.net/surveys

# Case

## Shifting Customer Segments in Canadian Banking

The number of Canadians who bank primarily through the Internet has doubled in the past two years to 16 percent, a poll by the Canadian Bankers Association says.

The national survey by Strategic Counsel, a market research and polling company, found 16 percent saying the Internet is the primary means through which they conduct most of their financial transactions, compared with 8 percent in a similar CBA poll two years ago. The survey found about one-third of respondents now do at least some of their banking on-line and 56 percent expect to be banking over the Internet within two to three years, compared with 46 percent in 2000.

About 40 percent of Canadians now bank primarily through automated banking machines, while 8 percent bank mainly by phone and 30 percent bank mainly in person.

"What these figures tell us is that Canadians have an ever-increasing appetite for new technology," said Raymond Protti, chief executive officer of the Canadian Bankers Association.

"In our view, what makes Canadian banking so successful as an e-commerce enterprise is a combination of substantial investments in new technology and the steady growth of a system which offers people choice and convenience in how, when and where they handle their financial affairs."

### You Be the Marketer

1. If you were managing a Canadian bank, what possible segments would you see in the bank market?
2. How would you reach those segments?

www.strategiccounsel.com

Source: Anonymous, "More Canadians Do Their Banking On-line," *The Globe and Mail*, July 11, 2002, p. B11. Reprinted with the permission of The Canadian Press.

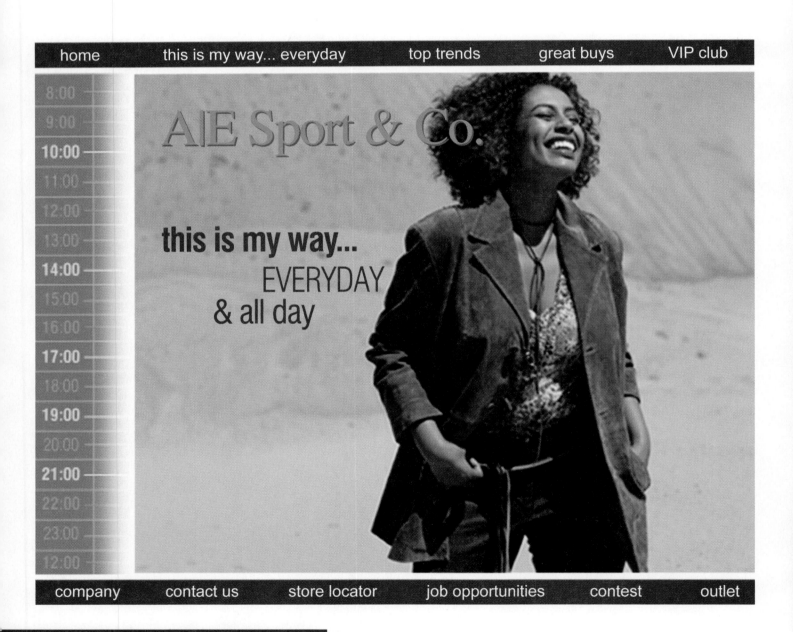

Emerging market segments create whole new opportunities for Canadian clothing retailers.

## Chapter 4

# THE MARKET SEGMENTATION PROCESS

It has been a sluggish time for apparel sales but one notable exception has been the robust market for plus-size clothing, a burgeoning sector that retail watchers describe as radically underserved.

According to market researcher Trendex North America, women's apparel sales in Canada increased just 2.6 percent in 2001 to $9.3 billion. Sales of clothing sized 14 and over—which account for 20–25 percent of the overall women's market—soared 8.3 percent.

"It's possible that the market is even larger, but I won't speculate," said Trendex president Randy Harris. "Plus-size is defined differently by different retailers. If a company sells an extra-large sweatshirt, should that be considered a plus-size sale?"

Industry watchers say the plus-size segment is dramatically under-represented at the retail level relative to statistical and sociocultural trends.

The majority of fashion-conscious specialty retailers carry fashions in sizes zero to 12, even though about 30 percent of Canadian women wear size 14 and over. Just 5 percent of retail space is devoted to larger clothing sizes.

"It gets frustrating," said shopper Kristen McKenzie, 44, who was recently perusing the size-20 offerings at an Addition-Elle boutique in Toronto. "There still aren't a lot of choices out there, compared to what you can get if you're a smaller woman."

Things began to improve in the 1990s, she said, with the rise of specialty retailers such as Penningtons and Addition-Elle. Ms. McKenzie no longer buys men's casual button-down shirts for herself because she is generally satisfied with the offerings made for women.

"The off-the-rack styles have improved— you don't have just the ugly tent dresses anymore." The trend is clearly paying off for specialty retailers of plus-size clothing, which account for 47 percent of all large-size women's sales.

Cotton Ginny Ltd., which sells plus-size apparel at its name brand and Tabi International stores, has seen its share of the plus-size market increase to 3.7 percent in 2001 from 2.3 percent in 1999, according to Trendex.

Montreal-based Shirmax Fashions Ltd., which operates 195 stores for larger women under the banners Addition-Elle and A/E Sport & Co., saw its share under those banners grow to 6.8 percent in 2001 from 4 percent in 1999.

Daniel Langevin, vice-president of marketing at Shirmax, said plus-size clothing sales are increasing as baby boomers age. "As we get older we don't necessarily get slimmer," he noted.

But despite a growing population of heavier people, few retailers know what plus-size customers are looking for. Trend spotters say apparel retailers should consider getting acquainted with those customers if they want to improve flagging sales.

**Even in a market as long established as clothing sales, opportunities can be found to grow established businesses or develop new ones. The trick is to see the market with new eyes—perhaps to identify unseen potential or to see opportunities in the form of market segments that may not be profitable for other companies to pursue but that you can serve profitably. Once these segments are identified and an appropriate product is developed, the rest of the marketing plan, including price, communication, and distribution, must be developed. In fact, developing the marketing plan, at least in outline, is a necessary part of deciding whether the segment is viable.**

Source: Adapted from Hollie Shaw, "Plus-size Clothing Market Is Expanding," *The Financial Post*, March 19, 2002, p. FP1. Reprinted with permission.

## CHAPTER OBJECTIVES

After reading and studying this chapter, you should be able to

1. Explain the factors underlying market segmentation strategy choices.
2. Outline the stages in the market segmentation process.
3. Explain the concept of positioning within market segments.
4. Show how target market decision analysis can be used in market segmentation.
5. Show how target market decision analysis can be used to assess the assortment of products offered to the market.

www.addition-elle.com

www.cottonginnyltd.com

# INTRODUCTION

This chapter continues the discussion of market segmentation. Chapter 3 discussed the role of market segmentation in developing a marketing strategy, and the bases for segmenting the consumer market (geographic, demographic, psychographic, usage rates, and benefit segmentation). In this chapter, the emphasis shifts to the process of market segmentation.

We will consider the rationale and process of matching product offerings to specific market segments. As we will see, selecting an appropriate strategy depends on a variety of internal and external variables facing the firm.

# ALTERNATIVE MARKET MATCHING STRATEGIES

Market segmentation may take many forms, ranging from treating the entire market as a single homogeneous entity to subdividing it into several segments and providing a separate marketing plan for each segment.

The very core of the firm's strategy is to match product offerings with the needs of particular market segments. To do so successfully, the firm must take the following factors into consideration:

- *Company resources.* These must be adequate to cover product development and other marketing costs.
- *Differentiability of products.* Some products can be easily differentiated from others. Some can be produced in versions designed specially for individual segments.
- *Stage in the product life cycle.* As a product matures, different marketing emphases are required to fit market needs. (Product life cycles are discussed in detail in Chapter 10.)
- *Competitors' strategies.* Strategies and product offerings must be continually adjusted in order to be competitive.
- *Size of segment.* The potential segment must be large enough to make it worthwhile to develop.

Essentially, the firm makes a number of goods/services offerings to the market in view of these determinants. Figure 4.1 summarizes the segmentation strategies available to a firm.

One firm may decide on a **single-offer strategy**. This is the attempt to satisfy a large or a small market with one product and a single marketing program. Such a strategy may be adopted for different reasons. A small manufacturer of wheelbarrows might concentrate on marketing one product to retailers in only one city because it does not have the resources to serve a mass market. A large producer of drafting equipment might offer a single product line with a marketing program aimed at draftspersons because it believes that only this limited segment would be interested in the product.

**single-offer strategy**

The attempt to satisfy a large or a small market with one product and a single marketing program.

FIGURE 4.1 Segmentation Strategies

| MARKET STRATEGY | SMALL OR FOCUSED MARKET | LARGE MARKET |
|---|---|---|
| Multi-offer (Many products) | High value niche e.g., Custom home builders | Differentiated e.g., Ford Motor Company |
| Single-offer (One product) | Concentrated e.g., Jolt Cola | Mass marketing (Undifferentiated) e.g., Magic® Baking Powder |

A single-offer strategy focused on one segment is often called *concentrated marketing*. Jolt Cola is practising concentrated marketing. When aimed at mass markets a single-offering approach is often call *undifferentiated* or *mass marketing*. For close to 100 years, until the early 1980s, the marketing of Coca-Cola was an example of the latter. Recent examples of true undifferentiated marketing are difficult to find as competitive forces tend to force segmentation over time. Magic® Baking Powder, or other near commodities, tend to offer one product in an undifferentiated way.

On the other hand, another company with greater resources may recognize that several segments of the market would respond well to specifically designed products and marketing programs. It adopts a **multi-offer strategy**. This is the attempt to satisfy several segments of the market very well with specialized products and unique marketing programs aimed at each segment. A bank designs particular services to fit the unique needs of different consumer and commercial market segments. A multi-offer strategy, aimed at a large market, is also called *differentiated marketing*. Since about 1982 the Coca-Cola Company has gradually moved to a multi-offer strategy by marketing Coke II, Diet Coke, Cherry Coke, Diet Cherry Coke, and Coca-Cola Classic. All of the large automakers practice differentiated marketing.

When these determinants are combined with markets segmented on the dimensions discussed in Chapter 3, the firm is able to develop a market matching strategy. A successful match of products

**multi-offer strategy**
The attempt to satisfy several segments of the market very well with specialized products and unique marketing programs aimed at each segment.

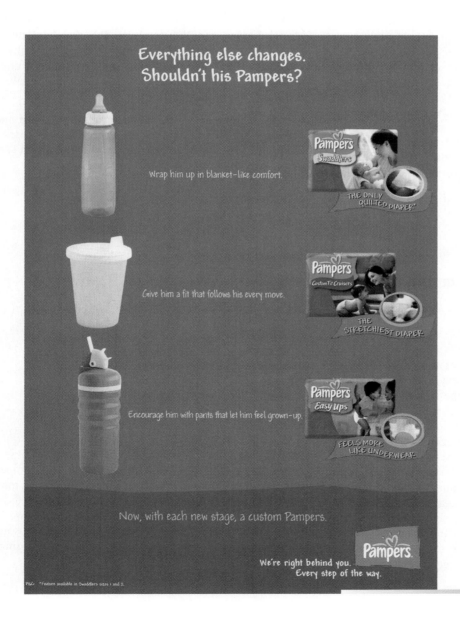

Pampers® uses a multi-offer strategy by providing a specialized product for each stage — from newborn to toddler.

## SINGLE- VERSUS MULTI-OFFER STRATEGIES

### A Single-Offer Strategy—Ford Motor Company in 1908

In 1908, Henry Ford introduced the Model T and revolutionized the automobile business around the world. Until the late 1920s, he sold only the Model T car and Model T truck. Ford's strategy was based on the belief that if he could get the price of a serviceable, utilitarian car low enough, he could develop a large mass market. His competitors were several hundred manufacturers who were producing vehicles that were virtually custom-built, with short production runs and high costs. Ford's strategy generated unprecedented sales. A dealership organization evolved that carried spare parts and service facilities to users across North America and through much of Europe. The marketing program, including an excellent service network, quickly made Henry Ford a multimillionaire and contributed to economic development by improving the transportation system.

Some dangers are inherent in a single-offer strategy, however. A firm that attempts to satisfy a very wide market with a single product of service fairly well is vulnerable to competition from those who choose to develop more specialized products that appeal to and serve segments of the larger market very well. Over time, General Motors and Chrysler developed a wider variety of models, price ranges, styles, and colour options. What worked

superbly in 1908 faltered in the 1920s, and Ford had to move to a multi-offer strategy. The firm developed the Model A and the Model B, offering them with various options. The company differentiated the product line further in the 1930s by introducing the first mass-produced V-8 engine, which was a company hallmark for years.

www.ford.com

### An Extensive Multi-Offer Strategy—Ford Motor Company in the Early 2000s

The market matching strategy of the Ford Motor Company today is quite different from that of 1908. It has evolved with the changing environment that faces the automobile industry. Ford's product line is much expanded from the Model T days, but the company still does not produce products for all markets. Instead, it serves those markets where its resources, marketing skills, product strengths, and competitive offerings can best be exploited. Table 4.1 compares the product lines then and now.

**Can a firm use a single-offer strategy today? Using one or more of the five segmentation approaches discussed in Chapter 3, write a short description of the segment served by each of the Ford cars listed in Table 4.1.**

## SEGMENTATION STRATEGIES REFLECT OTHER COMPETITIVE CONSIDERATIONS

### A Single-Offer Strategy for Different Reasons—Audi/Volkswagen/Porsche in 1955

When Volkswagen decided to enter the North American market, it chose to do so with only the "Beetle" for a variety of reasons. First, the company was strapped for funds and could not expand its production facilities, which were stretched to the limit in trying to supply automobile-short postwar Europe. It also recognized that a dealer-support system and spare-parts inventory had to be developed from scratch if it was to compete successfully in North America. With these constraints in mind, Volkswagen marketers determined that the serviceable Beetle was the answer. The Beetle was relatively low-priced, was supported by an imaginative promotional campaign, and became an immediate success with those who wanted a small, relatively basic car. Volkswagen sold a much wider

variety of products in Europe (and continued to introduce new products in that market much earlier than in North America). It deliberately chose to make a single offer to the North American market.

www.vw.com

### A Strategic Move to a Multi-Offer Strategy—Audi/Volkswagen/Porsche in the Early 2000s

Today, products under the Volkswagen parent company's control compete for a much broader number of market segments than did the Beetle. The changes are indicative of a major change in the segmentation strategies. The company has not only the products but also the resources and the marketing infrastructure to serve more segments.

**TABLE 4.1** Market Matching Strategies

| MARKET SEGMENT | PRODUCT OFFERINGS | | | |
|---|---|---|---|---|
| | Ford Motor Company | | Audi/Volkswagen/Porsche | |
| | 1908 Single-Offer Strategy | Early 2000s Multi-Offer Strategy | 1955 Single-Offer Strategy | Early 2000s Multi-Offer Strategy |
| **General-Purpose Cars** | | | | |
| Small | Model T | Focus | Beetle | Golf |
| Medium | Model T | Taurus | | Jetta |
| | | | | Passat |
| Large | | Crown Victoria | | |
| **Sporty Cars** | | | | |
| Low-priced | | ZX2 Escort | | new Beetle |
| | | | | GTI |
| Medium-priced | | Cougar | | Cabrio |
| | | Mustang | | Audi TT |
| | | | | Porsche Boxster |
| High-priced | | Jaguar XK8 | | Porsche 911 |
| | | Aston Martin DB7 | | |
| **Luxury Cars** | | | | |
| Medium-priced | | Lincoln Continental | | Audi A4 |
| | | Lincoln Town Car | | |
| High-priced | | Jaguar S-Type | | Audi A6 |
| | | | | Audi A8 |
| **Vans** | | | | |
| | | Windstar | | EuroVan |
| | | Econoline | | |
| **Trucks** | | | | |
| Small | Model T (truck) | Ford Ranger | | |
| Medium | | Ford "F" series | | |
| **Sport Utility Vehicles (SUVs)** | | | | |
| | | Explorer | | |
| | | Expedition | | |
| | | Excursion | | |
| | | Lincoln Navigator | | |

to segments through developing a marketing program with the appropriate product design, pricing strategy, distribution strategy, and communication strategy is vital to the market success of the firm.

The other possible segmentation strategy is a multi-offer approach in a small or focused market. In order for this strategy to be successful, the marketer must identify a high value niche in which customers can afford to pay for small production runs or, in some instances, customized products. Custom home builders are practising this approach to the market.

Many firms, large and small, practise a multi-offer strategy in today's environment. Procter & Gamble markets Tide, Dash, Duz, Cheer, Bold, Gain, Oxydol, and Bonus, among other detergents, to meet the desires of specific groups of detergent buyers. IBM offers huge mainframe computers, mid-range size tailored for medium-sized organizations, and computers designed for the home market.

www.can.ibm.com

Generally speaking, the company with a multi-offer marketing strategy should produce more sales by providing higher satisfaction for each of several target markets than would be possible with only a single-offer strategy. However, whether a firm should choose a single- or a multi-offer strategy depends on management's goals, as well as on the economics of the situation—whether the company has the resources, and whether greater profits can be expected from the additional expense of a multi-offer strategy.

# THE STAGES OF MARKET SEGMENTATION

The marketer has a number of potential bases for determining the most appropriate market matching strategy. Geographic, demographic, psychographic, usage rate, and benefit bases are often used in converting heterogeneous markets into specific segments that serve as target markets for the consumer-oriented marketer. The industrial marketer segments geographically, by product, by end-use application, or by account size and potential. In either case, a systematic five-stage decision process is followed. This framework for market segmentation is shown in Figure 4.2.

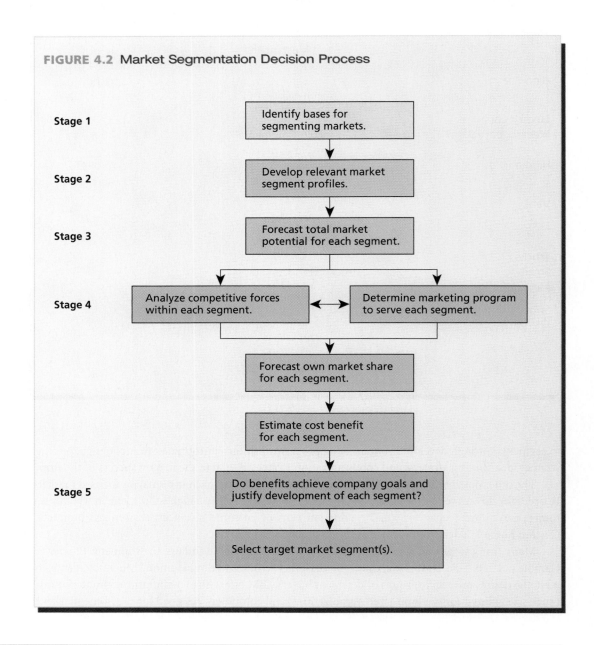

**FIGURE 4.2** Market Segmentation Decision Process

Stage 1 — Identify bases for segmenting markets.

Stage 2 — Develop relevant market segment profiles.

Stage 3 — Forecast total market potential for each segment.

Stage 4 — Analyze competitive forces within each segment. ↔ Determine marketing program to serve each segment.

Forecast own market share for each segment.

Estimate cost benefit for each segment.

Stage 5 — Do benefits achieve company goals and justify development of each segment?

Select target market segment(s).

No single basis for segmentation is necessarily the best, so the firm should segment the market in a way that most suits the situation. For example, demographic segmentation may be used in planning an advertising campaign that uses print media, because magazines are normally aimed at specific demographic segments. The marketer thus often experiments with segmenting markets in several ways in the process of discovering which of the marketing elements can be changed for greatest effect. (Similarly, marketing opportunities are sometimes discovered by rating how well competitors have served segments differentiated on a particular dimension.) This is part of the interactive process of analysis. The systematic five-stage decision process shown in Figure 4.2 lends form to what are otherwise often complex and unstructured problems.[1]

## Stage 1: Identify Market Segmentation Bases

The decision process begins when a firm identifies characteristics of potential buyers as bases that will allow the marketer to classify them into market segments. For example, IBM might segment on the basis of computer usage (accounting firms) or by company size. Segmentation bases should be selected so that each segment contains customers who have similar needs, so that specific marketing programs can be designed to satisfy those needs. For example, before Procter & Gamble decides to market Crest to a segment made up of large families, management should be confident that most large families are interested in preventing tooth decay and thus receptive to the Crest marketing offer. In some cases, this objective is difficult to achieve. Consider the marketer trying to reach the

www.pg.com

"Peer pressure is the best selling tool you could possibly have," said Adam Starr, president of Gearwerx, a Montreal-based youth marketing agency that has used undercover campaigns for more than a year to promote such products as cellphones, beverages, and health and beauty items.

"It's basically marketing to somebody without them knowing they're being marketed to," he said, adding that the companies involved do not want to be identified because that would blow their cover with consumers.

In one technique used by Gearwerx, two actors board a crowded bus during the morning commute and begin discussing what they ostensibly did the night before. The scripted conversation includes liberal mentions of the product being plugged so that everyone nearby can hear.

Practitioners of undercover marketing also refer to it as "roach bait marketing." The unsuspecting consumers are the roaches, and they take the bait and spread it to friends and family members.

**One defence of the undercover approach to marketing is that the chosen target market is too difficult to communicate with through conventional marketing communication approaches. What do you think? Does difficultly in reaching your target market justify this approach? How would you feel if you discovered that the friendly fellow tourist was actually a marketing representative trying to pique your interest in a product?**

Source: Excerpted from "Beware Tourists with Talking Cameras" by John Heinzl, *The Globe and Mail*, Aug. 1, 2002, p. A1. http://www.globeandmail.com/servlet/ArticleNews/front/RTGAM/20020801/wxsnap/Front/homeBN/breakingnews. Reprinted with permission of *The Globe and Mail*.

consumer segment that is over 50 years of age. Saturday-evening television commercials can reach this group, but much of the expenditure may be wasted since the other major viewer group at that time consists of teenagers.

## Stage 2: Develop Relevant Profiles for Each Segment

Once segments have been identified, marketers should develop a profile of the relevant customer needs and behaviours in each segment.

Segmentation bases provide some insight into the nature of customers, but typically not enough for the kinds of decisions that marketing managers must make. Managers need precise descriptions of customers in order to match marketing offers to their needs. In other words, the task at this stage is to develop profiles of the typical customer in each segment with regard to lifestyle patterns, attitudes toward product attributes and brands, brand preferences, product-use habits, geographic location, demographic characteristics, and so on. For example, one regional retail chain surveyed female customers and identified the following profile: ages 25–55, 147–160 cm tall, 38–55 kg, career-oriented, and having a household income of $20 000 or higher. The retailer used this profile to set up separate "petites" sections[2]. In contrast, the opening vignette of this chapter points out the attractiveness of the plus-size clothing segment. And that's the point: different segments are attractive and profitable for different marketers depending on the resources and abilities of those marketers.

## Stage 3: Forecast Market Potentials

In the third stage, market segmentation and market opportunity analysis are used together to produce a forecast of market potential within each segment. Market potential is the upper limit on the demand that can be expected from a segment and, combined with data on the firm's market share, sales potential.

This stage is management's preliminary go or no-go decision point as to whether the sales potential in a segment is sufficient to justify further analysis. Some segments will be screened out because they represent insufficient potential demand; others will be sufficiently attractive for the analysis to continue.

Consider the segments of the CD market. A producer must think carefully about whether it will be profitable to enter the jazz segment, for example, given total sales in the segment are already relatively small.

## Stage 4: Forecast Probable Market Share

Even when the segment is large enough, a firm may not be able to compete in it successfully. Therefore, once market potential has been estimated, the share of that market that can be captured by the firm must be determined. This requires analyzing competitors' positions in target segments. At the same time, the specific marketing strategy and tactics should be designed for these segments. These two activities should lead to an analysis of the costs of tapping the potential demand in each segment.

Procter & Gamble once outsold Colgate nearly two to one in dishwashing liquids. Colgate also ran behind in heavy-duty detergents and soaps. A realistic assessment indicated that for most directly competitive products, Colgate had little chance of overtaking P&G. So Colgate diversified its product line. Today, many of the firm's offerings do not face a directly competitive Procter & Gamble product, and those that do compete effectively.

## Stage 5: Select Specific Market Segments (Target Markets)

Finally, the accumulated information, analyses, and forecasts allow management to assess the potential for achieving company goals and justify developing one or more market segments. The market segment that the company chooses to serve is known as the **target market**. Demand forecasts combined with cost projections are used to determine the profit and return on investment that can be expected from each segment. Analyses of marketing strategy and tactics will determine the degree of consistency with corporate image and reputation goals, as well as with unique corporate capabilities that may be achieved by serving a segment. These assessments will, in turn, determine management's selection of specific segments as target markets.

**target market**
A market segment that a company chooses to serve.

At this point of the analysis, the costs and benefits to be weighed are not just monetary, but also include many difficult-to-measure but critical organizational and environmental factors. For example, the firm may not have enough experienced personnel to launch a successful attack on a segment that has the potential to be an almost certain monetary success. Similarly, a firm with a product that is suitable for export may choose one country over another because management likes that country better. A public utility may decide not to encourage higher electricity consumption because of possible environmental and political repercussions. Assessing both financial and nonfinancial factors is a vital and final stage in the decision process.

There is not, and should not be, any simple answer to the market segmentation decision. The marketing concept's prescription to serve the customer's needs and to meet organization goals while doing so implies that the marketer has to evaluate each possible marketing program on how it achieves this goal in the marketplace. By performing the detailed analysis outlined in Figure 4.2, the marketing manager can increase the probability of success in profitably serving consumers' needs.

# OVERALL EVALUATION OF MARKET SEGMENTS

In general, attractive market segments share five traits: uniqueness, responsiveness, actionability, stability, and profitability.[3]

Uniqueness implies that there are real differences between the segment and the rest of the population. There is no point, for example, in designing a plastic food wrap specifically for second- and third-generation Ukrainians living in the Prairie provinces if there is no difference in how that group uses plastic food wrap compared with the rest of the population.

Responsiveness means that the identified segment will actually be influenced by marketing activity. For example, there is a segment of homeowners who, one could charitably say, are somewhat disinterested in yard care. The marketer of easy-to-use yard care products may have difficulty targeting this group, because they are so disinterested that they will ignore even easy-to-use products.

An actionable segment is one that the marketing manager can actually direct marketing activity toward. Sometimes behaviourally based segments, in particular, are difficult to address if the marketing manager is unable to match the behaviour with classification (demographic) variables.

A stable segment will exist for a reasonable period. The Practising Marketer box illustrates that teenagers are becoming an attractive market segment after having been somewhat ignored for a while because there were too few of them. On the other hand, during the last part of 1998 and 1999, a segment emerged that might be labelled "millennium worriers." This group was a bit of a windfall for manufacturers of generators and staple foods. Obviously though, these people do not represent a viable long-term segmentation opportunity.

Finally, the chosen segment must be sufficiently profitable to be worth the effort. What constitutes "sufficiently profitable" varies from one company to the next.

# THE PRACTISING MARKETER

## TEENS ARE A VIABLE SEGMENT

The resounding power of the Echo Generation seems to be a North American phenomenon. Europe did not have the same baby boom that North America experienced, so there is not the accompanying "boomlet." In the United States, however, the Echo market is staggering; Teenage Research Unlimited, a Northbrook, Illinois-based demographics firm, says there are 26 million teens who last year spent $141 billion (U.S.)—almost twice as much as a decade ago. That has U.S. companies battling for a slice of that pie, and their products spill over into Canada. *Teen People* boasts 10 million readers each issue. Launched in 1998, its circulation has grown from 500 000 to 1.2 million, making it one of the fastest-growing magazines in American publishing history. "It wasn't cool to be a teen in the '70s or '80s," says managing editor Christina Ferrari. "The teenage population hasn't taken centre stage like this since the '50s and '60s."

Where does all their money come from? Studies show that while the popularity of after-school jobs is important it is not the source of the vast majority of kids' cash. A recent report by the Canadian Council on Social Development showed the youth labour market is actually at its lowest point in 25 years—fewer than half of 15- to 19-year-old students worked in 1997, down from two-thirds in 1989. The big money instead comes from family sources. Economics professor David Foot calls teens "six-pocket kids" who get money from mom, dad, grandparents, and often step-parents. Family money gets divided up into bigger chunks by fewer siblings, since Canadians are having smaller families (on average 1.7 children each).

**How useful is this information? What differences would you expect between marketing to teens in Canada and marketing to teens in Europe?**

Source: Excerpted from Andrew Clark, "How Teens Got the Power," *Maclean's* (March 22, 1999), p. 43. Reprinted with permission of *Maclean's Magazine*.

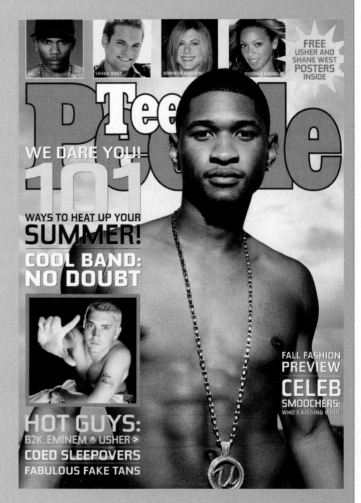

Teenagers comprise an important market segment for many marketers. From television shows to clothes to magazines, the many products aimed at teens indicate the significance of this group's buying power.

# TARGET MARKET DECISION ANALYSIS

Identifying specific target markets is an important aspect of overall marketing strategy. Clearly delineated target markets allow management to effectively employ marketing efforts like product development, distribution, pricing, and advertising to serve these markets.

**Target market decision analysis**, the evaluation of potential market segments, is a useful tool in the market segmentation process. Targets are chosen by segmenting the total market on the basis of any given characteristics (as described in Chapter 3). The example that follows illustrates how target market decision analysis can be applied.[4]

**target market decision analysis**
The evaluation of potential market segments.

## A Useful Method of Identifying Target Markets

Sometimes marketers fail to take all potential market segments into consideration. A useful process is the "divide-the-box" procedure (Figure 4.3). Visualize the entire market for the product category as a single box. Then divide this total market box into realistic boxes or cells, with each cell representing a potential target segment. How the cells are defined is up to you. They can be based on consumer benefits desired; on geographic, demographic, and psychographic characteristics; or on some combination of these. While this concept is simple, it can be extremely complex in practice, and it requires creativity.

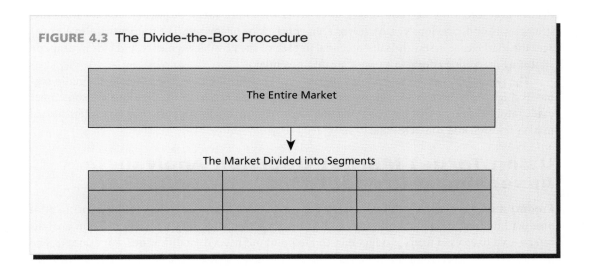

**FIGURE 4.3 The Divide-the-Box Procedure**

The Entire Market

The Market Divided into Segments

Let's apply the divide-the-box technique to an imaginary example of a radio station. The station manager is considering changing to a new format from the current Country/Punk fusion. Figure 4.4 illustrates the move from thinking of the radio listening audience (the market) as one undifferentiated group to dividing the audience into segments and potential targets. In our imaginary example, the manager has divided the market by benefits sought and age groups.

After some careful thought the station manager decides to explore the Middle Adult segment further. The divide-the-box process isn't finished though, because clearly, "Middle Adult" is a very broad category. Accordingly, in Figure 4.5, the manager looks more carefully at middle adults and divides them into four sub-categories by occupation. Figure 4.5 seems to imply that the manager should consider information radio. "Information" is also a very broad category so the manager divides that into seven sub-categories shown in Figure 4.6. Based on this final grid, the manager concludes that she needs to explore targeting Professionals and Business Owners with the new format, which will focus on breaking news, and political and financial market commentary. Having identified her station's potential target market, the manager now needs to assess the potential profitability of that target market.

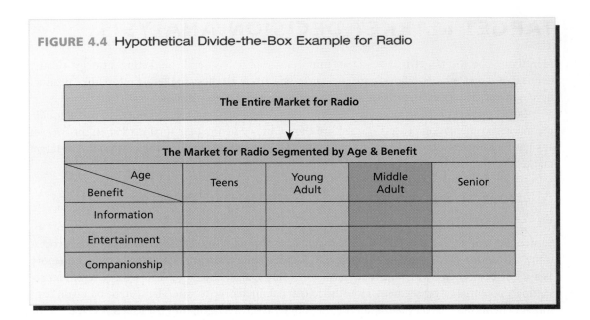

FIGURE 4.4 Hypothetical Divide-the-Box Example for Radio

| The Entire Market for Radio | | | | |
|---|---|---|---|---|

| The Market for Radio Segmented by Age & Benefit | | | | |
|---|---|---|---|---|
| Age / Benefit | Teens | Young Adult | Middle Adult | Senior |
| Information | | | | |
| Entertainment | | | | |
| Companionship | | | | |

The divide-the-box approach can be quite useful. It enables the company to match the possible types of service offerings with various customer classifications. The process of developing the target market grid forces the decision maker to consider the entire range of possible market matching strategies. New or previously underserved segments may be uncovered. The framework also encourages the marketer to assess the sales potential in each of the possible segments, and aids in properly allocating marketing efforts to areas of greatest potential.

The potential bases for segmenting markets are virtually limitless. For example, the radio segments might have been based on psychographic data or on gender. Such divisions are sometimes made intuitively in the first place, but the final decisions are usually supported by very sophisticated market research and concrete data.

## Using Target Market Decision Analysis in Assessing a Product Mix

**product mix**

The assortment of product lines and individual offerings available from a company.

**Product mix**, a concept we will take a detailed look at in Chapter 11, refers to the assortment of product lines and individual offerings available from a company. Target market decision analysis can be used to assess a firm's product mix and to point out needed modifications. For example, one

FIGURE 4.5 Hypothetical *Middle Adult* Segment for Radio

| | | Middle Adults | | | |
|---|---|---|---|---|---|
| | | Early Retiree | Professional | Hourly Employee | Business Owner |
| Desired Benefit | Information | X | X | | X |
| | Entertainment | X | | X | |
| | Companionship | X | | | |

**FIGURE 4.6** Hypothetical *Middle Adult* Segment for *Information* Radio

| | | Middle Adults | | | |
|---|---|---|---|---|---|
| | | Early Retiree | Professional | Hourly Employee | Business Owner |
| **Desired Information Focus** | Breaking news | | X | | X |
| | Political commentary | | X | | X |
| | Financial market commentary | X | X | | X |
| | Advice | X | | X | |
| | Weather | X | | X | |
| | Call-in | X | | | |
| | Gossip | X | | | |

telephone company has used the concept to evaluate its product offerings.[5] The company segments the total market by psychographic categories as shown in Figure 4.7. Two of these categories are "belongers" and "achievers." Belongers were defined in this instance as those who are motivated by emotional and group influences. Achievers were defined as those whose dominant characteristic is the need to get ahead.

The telephone company's rule was to offer two—and only two—types of telephones in a given market segment in order not to have too complicated a market offering. Belongers were thus offered a regular phone and a romantic-type phone to appeal to their sentiments. Achievers were offered the regular phone plus one designed to suggest efficiency and character. This analysis helped to select a product from the assortment shown in Figure 4.7.

Target market decision analysis can go beyond merely identifying target markets. It can play a crucial role in actually developing marketing strategies such as product mixes.

**FIGURE 4.7** Using Target Market Decision Analysis to Evaluate a Product Mix

| Product Offering | Psychographic Category | | |
|---|---|---|---|
| | Belongers | Achievers | Etc. |
| Romantic | Phone M Phone A Phone C | | |
| Character | | Phone R Phone Y | |
| Contemporary | | | |

Source: "Properly Applied Psychographics Add Marketing Luster," *Marketing News* (November 12, 1982), p. 10. Reprinted with permission by the American Marketing Association.

# PRODUCT POSITIONING

positioning

Shaping the product and developing a marketing program in such a way that the product is perceived to be (and actually is) different from competitors' products.

After a target market has been selected, the task has just begun. Your firm will naturally find others competing in that segment. The challenge is to develop a marketing plan that will enable your product to compete effectively against them. It is unlikely that success will be achieved with a marketing program that is virtually identical to competitors', for they already have attained a place in the minds of individuals in the target market and have developed brand loyalty. Since people have a variety of needs and tastes, market acceptance is more easily achieved by **positioning**—shaping the product and developing a marketing program in such a way that the product is perceived to be (and actually is) different from competitors' products.

When done properly, positioning is very research dependent. That is because a product's position really is determined by customer perceptions. In order to manage and effect positioning, the marketing manager has to understand those perceptions.

The first step in successful positioning is to determine what attributes of your product or service your chosen target market care about, and how your customers perceive your product on those attributes. Returning to our earlier radio example, suppose the manager of the radio station wants to carry out a positioning study and, for ease of discussion, let's say the various programs on CBC radio are her main competition. What the manager might discover is that radio listeners key on two dimensions when they are categorizing radio stations, and in this instance, individual radio programs. Those dimensions might be whether the station carries entertaining or challenging programs versus whether it's dominated by music or by informational programs. Figure 4.8 shows where several CBC programs are positioned on those dimensions and where most commercial radio is positioned. Figure 4.8 is called a perceptual map, or sometimes a positioning map. It is a pictorial representation of how customers perceive related products on key attributes. Our radio station manager would want to study the perceptual map in Figure 4.8 carefully to decide if there is a viable position that her reformatted radio station could occupy.

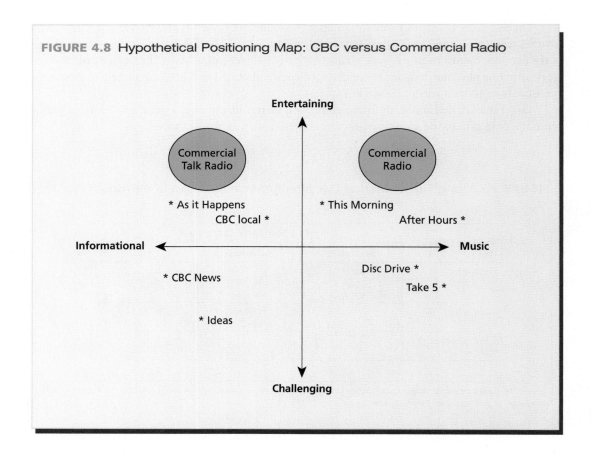

**FIGURE 4.8** Hypothetical Positioning Map: CBC versus Commercial Radio

For a second example consider a simple positioning map of the cola market (see Figure 4.9). By plotting brands on a price-reputation/quality matrix the relative positions of the brands listed can be determined. The perceptual map shows the positions of Pepsi and Coca-Cola being threatened by brands such as Cott and President's Choice. Many consumers position the quality of the newer brands near Pepsi and Coca-Cola, and are quite aware that they cost less. If you were a potential newcomer to the cola market segment, a positioning analysis such as this would be essential. Where would you position a new brand of cola?

The positioning process requires a careful analysis of the features and strengths of competitive offerings, as well as a good understanding of the needs and wants of the target market. From comparing the two, the marketer tries to find a niche of significant size that is currently poorly served, and to develop an offering to fit that opportunity. In products where very little natural differentiation exists, such as the cola market we just looked at, positioning can sometimes be accomplished by using advertising to differentiate a product.

7-Up used promotion as the sole element in positioning. The firm discovered that its product was missing the primary market for soft drinks—children, teenagers, and young adults—because of 7-Up's image as a mixer for older people's drinks. The firm used its now well-known "uncola" campaign to reposition 7-Up by first identifying the product as a soft drink and then positioning it as an alternative to colas in the soft-drink market. Since then the company has continued its focus on advertising that emphasizes youth and action.

Another classic positioning campaign was that used by Avis to position itself against Hertz with the theme "Avis is only number two, why go with us? Because we try harder." In this case, the service was also adjusted to make the claim true.

A total marketing program is often dictated to secure position. An example is the establishment of CFM Inc. In 1987, Colin Adamson and Heinz Rieger were senior managers for a wood-burning fireplace maker. In the fireplace market, they saw an opportunity to develop a product to position against wood-burning and gas fireplaces, so they formed their own company and began to develop a product. They positioned their product away from the more traditional style of gas fireplace—a row of uniform, nonflickering blue flames coming from a steel pipe decorated, perhaps, with a poor imitation of a log. Instead, Adamson and Rieger developed a way to produce dancing yellow flames that simulate a wood fire, and surrounded them with natural-looking logs. The product could then be positioned as a realistic-looking alternative to wood.

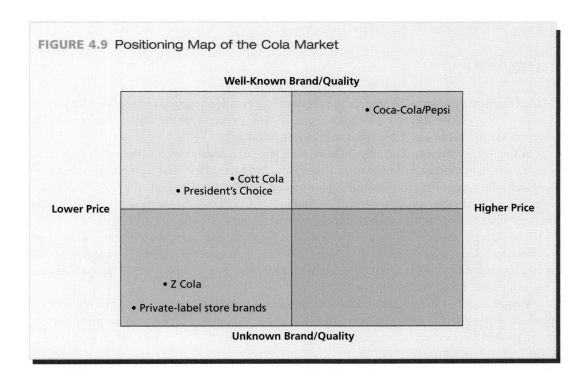

FIGURE 4.9 Positioning Map of the Cola Market

The Market Segmentation Process          Chapter 4

**Where does Vanilla Coke™ fit on the cola positioning map?**

"Coke", the Distinctive Bottle and the Wave Design are registered and "Vanilla Coke" is a trademark of Coca-Cola Ltd.

CFM has now developed a range of products to enhance its gas fireplace position. Colin Adamson says, "A lot of people make things and then try to sell the market on them, [but] success comes from making what people want."[6] The firm has developed a loyal group of dealers, and therefore has the distribution system necessary to move its products from manufacturer to consumer. In product development, CFM pays much attention to regional tastes in materials, trims, and sizes. CFM's positioning strategy enabled the company to focus on developing product and marketing plans that led to achieving a sales volume of over $416 million by 2001.[7]

Using product positioning to evaluate and develop marketing strategies in the light of competitive offerings in the market is a valuable and basic concept. It should follow naturally from the market segmentation decision.

## SUMMARY

Market segmentation ranges from treating the entire market as one segment to subdividing it into a number of segments. No single basis for segmentation is necessarily the best, so the firm should segment the market in a way that most suits the situation.

A single-offer strategy is an attempt to satisfy a large or a small market with one product and a single marketing program. A multi-offer strategy is a bid to satisfy several segments of the market very well with specialized products and unique marketing programs aimed at each segment. Because of resource constraints or management inclination, a firm may choose to adopt a single-offer strategy in a market that has several obvious market segments.

The stages of the market segmentation process are as follows: (1) identify segmentation bases, (2) develop relevant profiles for each segment, (3) forecast market potentials, (4) forecast probable market share, and (5) select specific market segments. Attractive segments will be unique, responsive, actionable, stable, and profitable.

Positioning is shaping the product and developing a marketing program in such a way that the product is perceived to be different from competitors' products. Positioning can sometimes be accomplished through advertising alone, and sometimes requires a total marketing program.

# KEY TERMS

multi-offer strategy, p. 71
positioning, p. 82
product mix, p. 80

single-offer strategy, p. 70
target market, p. 77
target market decision analysis, p. 79

# INTERACTIVE SUMMARY AND DISCUSSION QUESTIONS

1. Market segmentation ranges from treating the market as one to subdividing it into a number of portions. Give examples of firms that have adopted each of the two alternatives. In your opinion, have these firms made the correct decision?

2. A single-offer strategy is an attempt to satisfy a large or a small market with one product and a single marketing program. Give an example of where this seems to be working well for a company, as well as an example of where this strategy may not be so beneficial to the company.

3. A multi-offer strategy is a bid to satisfy several segments of the market very well with specialized products and unique marketing programs aimed at each segment. Explain how a company that is marketing in Canada and Europe might manage this.

4. A firm may choose to adopt a single-offer strategy in a market that has several obvious market segments. Explain why.

5. Give an example of how a not-for-profit organization might apply a multi-offer segmentation strategy.

6. "No single base for segmentation is necessarily the best, therefore the firm should segment the market in a way that most suits the situation." Explain.

7. The stages of the market segmentation process are (1) identify segmentation bases, (2) develop relevant profiles for each segment, (3) forecast market potentials, (4) forecast probable market share, and (5) select specific target markets. Explain how each of these steps would apply to a marina and to a radio station.

8. Assume you are a manufacturer of computers and related hardware. Using the divide-the-box procedure, identify the various target markets among college students.

9. Positioning is shaping the product and developing a marketing program in such a way that the product is perceived to be different from competitors' products. Draw a positioning matrix for a product category that you are familiar with.

10. Positioning can sometimes be accomplished through advertising alone, and sometimes requires a total marketing program. Give an example of each situation.

11. Visit The Coca-Cola Company's and Pepsi-Cola's Web sites. Compare them with Jones Soda's Web site. How has Jones Soda differentiated itself from Coca-Cola and Pepsi?

www.coca-cola.com

www.pepsiworld.com

www.jonessoda.com

# Case

## CanWest Gets Radio Licence in Winnipeg

CanWest Global Communications Corp. has won approval for an all-jazz FM radio station in its home base of Winnipeg, the company's first foray into the Canadian radio market.

The as-yet unnamed station is expected to launch in early 2003 with a staple of Canadian and Western-Canadian-based jazz—serving a city that does not offer a competing radio format.

In its application to the federal broadcast regulator, CanWest also committed $2.5 million for development of Canadian talent over the seven-year licence period.

CanWest spokesman Geoffrey Elliot noted the firm's founder and chairman Izzy Asper is a fervent lover of jazz, a factor that clearly influenced the decision to seek approval for a jazz station.

He also noted that the station is not expected to turn a profit over the licence period, though he said its losses will not be steep enough to have a material impact on the company's bottom line.

Canada's largest newspaper company and second-biggest private TV broadcaster, CanWest said the acquisition plays into its multimedia strategy, adding that it may move to expand its presence in the radio medium as opportunities arise, and as the regulator allows.

Mr. Elliot, CanWest's vice-president of corporate affairs, said the station could collaborate with CanWest's local TV station to offer advertisers a bundled media platform.

CanWest chief executive Leonard Asper called the approval an important step into Canadian radio.

"We hope this new licence heralds the eventual creation of a national radio system just as we entered the TV industry 25 years ago with a single TV station in Winnipeg, which became part of the Global Television Network."

The company owns the Southam chain of newspapers, including *National Post*, *The Vancouver Sun*, *Ottawa Citizen*, and *The Gazette* in Montreal, and operates Global TV, Canada's largest private broadcaster after CTV Inc.

The new Winnipeg outlet will accompany another CanWest entry into music programming, with the firm already granted a licence for a digital specialty channel, COOL TV. No date for launch has been announced.

### You Be the Marketer

1. What segmentation approach is CanWest using in the radio market?
2. How successful do you expect this new radio station to be?
3. What other purposes seem to be motivating CanWest management?
4. Check the Internet to see what else you can find out about this radio station—how is it doing today?

---

Source: Excerpted from Michael Lewis, "CanWest Gets Radio Licence in Winnipeg," *National Post*, August 9, 2002. http://www.nationalpost.com/search/site/story.asp?id=1895C91D-5AD8-4EE5-8750-0A45D37957B0. Reprinted with permission.

Now boarding the world

Air Canada voted Best Airline based in North America
Aeroplan® voted Best Frequent Flyer Program in the world

aircanada.ca

**AIR CANADA** ✺

A STAR ALLIANCE MEMBER ✺

Will Air Canada's new multiple brand strategy be successful?

# MARKETING STRATEGY AND THE MARKETING PLAN

In a market littered with struggling or failing airline companies, Air Canada reported a second-quarter profit of $30 million in 2002. That's not a lot, especially for a business of Air Canada's size. But it was more than enough to make Mr. Milton, Air Canada's CEO, in relative terms, seem like either extremely lucky or extremely smart. Air Canada became one of the few big carriers in the world to make a profit. The only other significant airline in North America to make money was Dallas-based Southwest, the discount carrier. In the second quarter, the rest of the U.S. airline industry lost $1.5 billion (U.S.). There, bankruptcies and mergers seemed virtually certain as airlines failed to adapt quickly enough to a world of skittish travelers, fairly high fuel prices, and business-class passengers unwilling to pay thousands of dollars to fly hundreds of kilometres.

The company's product strategy is what sets it apart from the others. The company chose to break itself up into a family of low-cost, stand-alone brands. Tango is the airline's first no-frills domestic brand. Zip is the second cheapie carrier; it will take on WestJet in the West. Jetz is a charter service for pro athletes and Jazz is the new name for the old feeder services, which now operate as one airline. More brands are due to add to the clutter.

The problem with discount brands launched by big, traditional airlines is that they rarely work. British Airways and Continental Airlines are just two carriers whose cheapie offshoot experiments failed. The discount brands tend to cannibalize the main carrier. It's also hard to reduce their costs in a meaningful way. The planes and the fuel cost the same, as do the unionized labour and airport fees. Air Canada said unit costs at Tango, whose chief features are a different paint job and less leg room, were 12 percent lower than the main airline's in the second quarter. In the long run, 12 percent may not be worth the effort. At a consistent 20 percent, you're getting somewhere.

Nonetheless, Mr. Milton's effort to turn Air Canada into a flying version of Marriott International, whose all-things-to-all-people brands include Fairfield Inns and Renaissance Hotels, is starting to capture the attention of airline chiefs. It's bold, it's risky and, if Mr. Milton pulls it off, it may revolutionize the industry in the same way that Southwest did. At the time of writing it was simply too early to tell, though, whether the concept would work where so many others haven't.

But that's not the only big risk that Mr. Milton faces. Air Canada, at least in the federal government's eyes, is not a true private sector company. They are not keen on the notion that Air Canada, with 80 percent of the domestic market, may take out successful competitors such as WestJet. If Mr. Milton's strategy works, government might react.

Right now, Mr. Milton looks good. In a year, he could be a true hero or yet another executive who got it all horribly wrong at shareholders' expense.

Source: Eric Reguly, "Milton's Armour Shines Amid CEO Tarnish, For Now," *The Globe and Mail,* Saturday, August 3, 2002, p. B7, http://www.globeandmail.com/servlet/ ArticleNews/PEstory/TGAM/20020803/RERIC/Columnists/ columnists/columnistsBusiness_temp/2/2/4/. Reprinted with permission from *The Globe and Mail.*

www.aircanada.com

# INTRODUCTION

Long-term organizational success is never accidental. It results from managers being committed to providing benefits that customers need and want—or being market-oriented, as we discussed in Chapter 1. In Chapter 2 we saw that long-term success also implies that managers understand the environment in which the organization operates and are adapting to that environment. Chapters 3 and 4 pointed out that customer needs are too complex for any one product to satisfactorily meet everyone's needs, so the successful organization segments its markets.

Market orientation, sensitivity to the operating environment, segmentation, and market information are not in and of themselves sufficient to assure organizational success. These factors must be thoughtfully combined into a marketing strategy and plan that guide the organization.

Two main aspects of strategy formulation will be discussed in this chapter: strategy for the organization as a whole (corporate strategy), and marketing strategy. After marketing strategy has been established, the marketing plan can be developed (see Figure 5.1). You will find that discussing these concepts is relatively simple, but practitioners know that implementing them is extremely difficult.

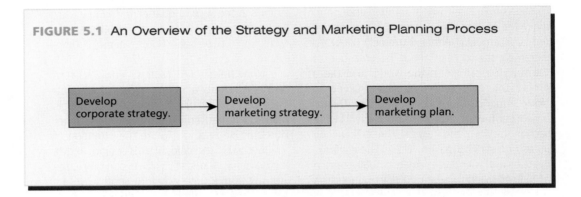

**FIGURE 5.1** An Overview of the Strategy and Marketing Planning Process

# STRATEGY FOR THE ORGANIZATION AS A WHOLE

**corporate strategy**

The overall purpose and direction of the organization that is established in the light of the challenges and opportunities found in the environment, as well as available organizational resources.

Strategy is the overall purpose and direction of the organization that is established in the light of the challenges and opportunities found in the environment, as well as available organizational resources. This is often referred to as **corporate strategy**. The process of developing a corporate strategy starts with analyzing market and environmental opportunities and threats facing the company as a whole. Simultaneously, the company undertakes an analysis of its own strengths and weaknesses. From this external and internal examination, the organization generates a list of *possible* alternative courses of action and objectives that could be followed. The next step involves evaluating and selecting the *most appropriate* alternative options for the organization. Finally, implementation and control programs must be planned for the strategy that has been developed. Figure 5.2 shows all five stages of the corporate strategy process.

Developing the corporate strategy is the responsibility of the head of the organization, and requires input from all the functional areas of the company (for example, finance, production, and marketing). The corporate strategy, in turn, gives direction in the form of objectives and intended resource allocation to the subunits of the corporation. These subgroups are often set up as distinct profit centres within the corporation and are usually referred to as strategic business units, or SBUs.

The strategy chosen is often expressed in a *mission statement*. This formal statement channels all of the organization's activities. From the mission statement, all individuals can determine which activities are appropriate to engage in and which are not. This keeps activities within the scope considered most suitable for the company. An example of a mission statement can be found in Table 5.1.

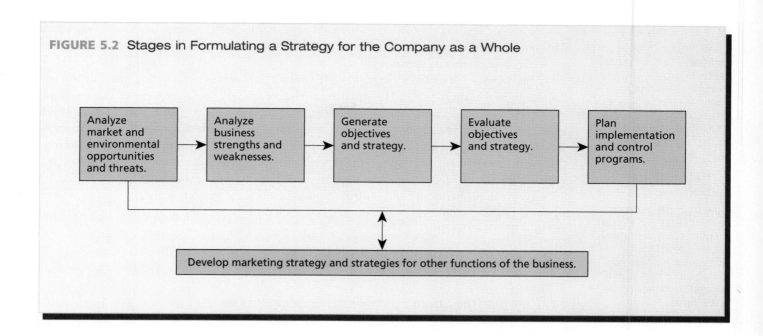

**FIGURE 5.2** Stages in Formulating a Strategy for the Company as a Whole

| Analyze market and environmental opportunities and threats. | → | Analyze business strengths and weaknesses. | → | Generate objectives and strategy. | → | Evaluate objectives and strategy. | → | Plan implementation and control programs. |

Develop marketing strategy and strategies for other functions of the business.

**TABLE 5.1** Example of an Organizational Mission Statement

The Gillette Company is a globally focused consumer products marketer that seeks competitive advantage in quality, value-added personal care and personal use products. We are committed to building shareholder value through sustained profitable growth.

www.gillette.com

**Our vision**
The Gillette Company's Vision is to build Total Brand Value by innovating to deliver consumer value and customer leadership faster, better and more completely than our competition. This Vision is supported by two fundamental principles that provide the foundation for all of our activities: Organizational Excellence and Core Values.

Source: Used with permission from the Gillette Web site, "Our Vision" page (http://www.gillette.com/company/ourvision.asp). Downloaded November 8, 2002.

# MARKETING STRATEGY

**Marketing strategy**, which is based on the strategy set for the company as a whole, focuses on developing a unique long-run competitive position in the market by assessing consumer needs and the firm's potential for gaining competitive advantage.[1] Day and Wensley add that "[marketing] strategy is about seeking new edges in a market while slowing the erosion of present advantages.[2]

Knowing everything there is to know about the customer is not enough. To succeed, marketers must know the customer in a context that includes the competition, government policy and regulation, and the broader economic, social, and political macroforces that shape the evolution of markets. In other words, a strategic approach is necessary.

**marketing strategy**
A strategy that focuses on developing a unique long-run competitive position in the market by assessing consumer needs and the firm's potential for gaining competitive advantage.

Figure 5.3 illustrates a marketing-oriented approach to strategy formulation and evaluation. This model extends the corporate strategy model depicted in Figure 5.2 and shows the important components of marketing strategy.

After receiving input from corporate-level strategies, the strategic marketing planning process unfolds in four main steps. (1) The **situation analysis** considers the internal circumstances of the organization or product, the external environment, competitive activity, and characteristics of the customer that may be relevant to the marketing plan. (2) The **marketing objectives and strategy** flow from the situation analysis. They are a statement of what the organization intends to accomplish with its marketing program and the general strategic approach it will take. (3) The **marketing plan** is a specific detailed statement of how the marketing mix will be used to realize the marketing strategy. (4) **Implementation and control** consist of putting the marketing plan into action as well as doing ongoing monitoring and gathering feedback on how well the plan is accomplishing the stated marketing objectives.

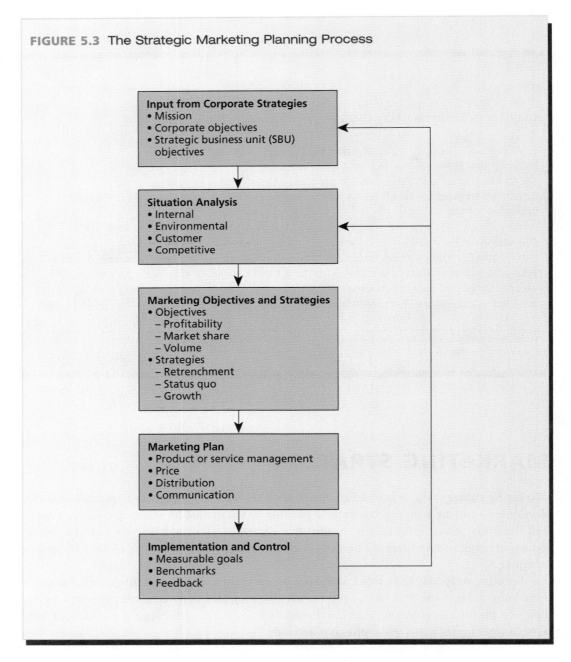

**FIGURE 5.3** The Strategic Marketing Planning Process

# SITUATION ANALYSIS

## Internal Analysis

A situation analysis begins with an internal analysis. Managers consider both the nature of the organization itself as well as the specific product or service being marketed. A key question managers will consider is whether the organization has, or can create, a *sustainable competitive advantage,* or SCA. An SCA is some aspect of the product that will give it value in the marketplace that cannot be easily duplicated by other companies. McDonald's has an SCA of consistency in its restaurants and product offerings. Harley-Davidson, on the other hand, builds on its SCA of legendary mystique. WestJet, mentioned in the opening vignette of this chapter, created an SCA of friendly, no frills, consistently lower price, air travel service.

A realistic assessment of company resources is an important part of an internal analysis. Managers decide whether the organization has the financial resources to pursue certain strategies. Production, managerial, and human resources must also be considered. Sheldon Birney, the founder of Reliance, a Winnipeg company that manufactures plastic water jugs, related his mixed feelings when, early in the company's history, he received an extremely large order from a well-known department store chain. Convinced that he could not successfully service the order and unwilling to risk his fledgling company's reputation, he politely declined and set about building his production and sales capacity. Today, many years later, Reliance products can be found all over the world — including in that department store.[3] Many companies without Mr. Birney's managerial insight and discipline have outgrown their resource base by overly rapid expansion only to collapse back in on themselves.

In addition to SCAs and available resources, managers should review the past market performance and reputation of a product. Products that have performed well and have strong reputations

www.mcdonalds.com

www.harleycanada.com

Fresh, good-tasting coffee is an important part of Tim Hortons' product portfolio.

**product portfolio**
The complete collection of products or services that a company produces.

**BCG growth-share matrix**
Plots market share relative to the market share of the largest competitor, against market growth rate.

can be used as a basis for further market gains. Procter & Gamble has built on the original success of its Head and Shoulders dandruff shampoo to create a full line of dandruff-related shampoos that share the same brand name. In contrast, poor-performing products with poor reputations must be supported in other ways or even discontinued. General Motors stopped producing the Corvair in the 1960s after the car's safety record was attacked.

A final important issue that must be considered when analyzing a company's internal situation is the product portfolio. The **product portfolio** is the complete collection of products or services that a company produces. Portfolio analysis is a very useful tool to apply when reviewing a firm's overall product mix.

A particularly well-known approach to portfolio analysis was developed by the Boston Consulting Group (BCG). The **BCG growth-share matrix**, shown in Figure 5.4, plots market share relative to the market share of the largest competitor, against market growth rate. All of a firm's various businesses or products can be plotted in one of the four quadrants. The resulting quadrants are labelled Cash Cows, Stars, Dogs, and Question Marks, and BCG suggests a unique marketing strategy for each one.

■ *Cash Cows* (dominant market share in a market with low growth): Cash Cows are the main source of earnings and cash to support growth areas. Marketing planners want to maintain this situation for as long as possible, since it produces a strong cash flow. The objective is to maximize cash flow while maintaining market share.

■ *Stars* (dominant market share in a market with high growth): While this type of business produces profits, it requires heavy cash consumption to maintain a leading market position. If this share can be maintained until growth of the market slows, Stars may become high dollar

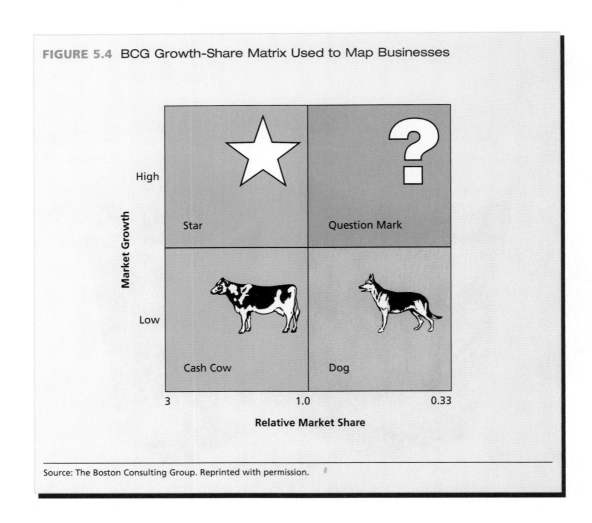

**FIGURE 5.4** BCG Growth-Share Matrix Used to Map Businesses

Source: The Boston Consulting Group. Reprinted with permission.

earners. In the meantime, Stars may even produce a negative cash flow. Such products require considerable management attention.

- *Dogs* (small market share in a market with low growth): This type of business generally consumes too much management attention. Usually, the company should minimize its position in this market area, pulling investment from it and withdrawing completely if possible.

- *Question Marks* (small market share in a market with high growth): Question Mark enterprises must achieve a dominant position before growth slows, or they will be frozen in a marginal position and become Dogs. Because they demand a heavy commitment from limited financial and management resources, their number in the portfolio should be restricted. These situations require that marketers make a basic go–no go decision. Unless Question Marks can be converted to Stars, the firm should pull out of these markets.

The BCG matrix highlights the importance of creating a mix that works to the best advantage of the firm. It emphasizes the importance of having common agreed-upon goals for all products in the firm's portfolio. Many variations of this basic approach are now in use.

There are some difficulties with the matrix. Many so-called Dogs can be, and are, extremely profitable. Further, whether a product is labelled a Dog or a Cash Cow depends on how the product's market is defined. If we look at the market for cars, for example, a Lamborghini is a Dog; if we define our market as luxury sport cars valued at $200 000 or higher, it's a Cash Cow.

More seriously, critics of the BCG approach argue that the health of Cash Cows can be seriously damaged if resources are constantly being drained without appropriate levels of reinvestment. As with all management models, the insights gained by applying the BCG matrix should not be used as a substitute for managerial ability.

An alternative to the market growth–market share approach to portfolio analysis was developed by General Electric. Usually referred to as the **GE business screen**, it is a 3 x 3 matrix that considers business strengths and industry attractiveness. The basic premise of the model is that businesses should be concentrating on opportunities in which they are strong and the industry is attractive. If either or both of those factors are merely average, a company should monitor the situation, accept earnings that it may be enjoying, but be cautious of new investment. If either or both factors are poor, the company should avoid new investment. If the company is already involved in the area, it should attempt to withdraw. The GE business screen is shown in Figure 5.5. The business screen is a useful planning tool, because it provides an effective method of evaluating SBUs at the corporate level and individual product opportunities at the SBU, or marketing, level. In actual practice, applying the screen is an extremely sophisticated matter that involves the careful quantitative analysis and rating of up to twelve different factors for each axis.

When the various aspects of the internal situation have been considered, the internal analysis is usually summarized as a list of strengths and weaknesses. Strengths are any internal factor, such as a well-known and respected brand name, that a company can use to contribute to future success. Weaknesses are any internal shortcomings, such as a poorly trained sales force, that must be overcome before the company can achieve success.

**GE business screen**

A process using a 3 x 3 matrix that considers business strengths and industry attractiveness.

www.ge.com

## Environmental Analysis

When the internal examination of the company is complete, the situation analysis continues with an environmental analysis. Chapter 2 discussed the importance of the environment in detail. From a marketing planning perspective, the understanding of the environment should be distilled into major issues, events, or trends that could affect, positively or negatively, an organization's success in the marketplace. This distillation of issues is often presented under the headings of opportunities and threats. Opportunities are environmental issues or trends that a company can use to its advantage. Threats are issues or trends that may interfere with an organization's ability to thrive. Sometimes the same factor can be an opportunity for one company but a threat for another. For example, the demographic trend of an aging population is an opportunity for developers of retirement communities, for manufacturers of products traditionally used by an older population such as Geritol, or even for funeral homes. On the other hand, it could be perceived as a threat by Fisher-

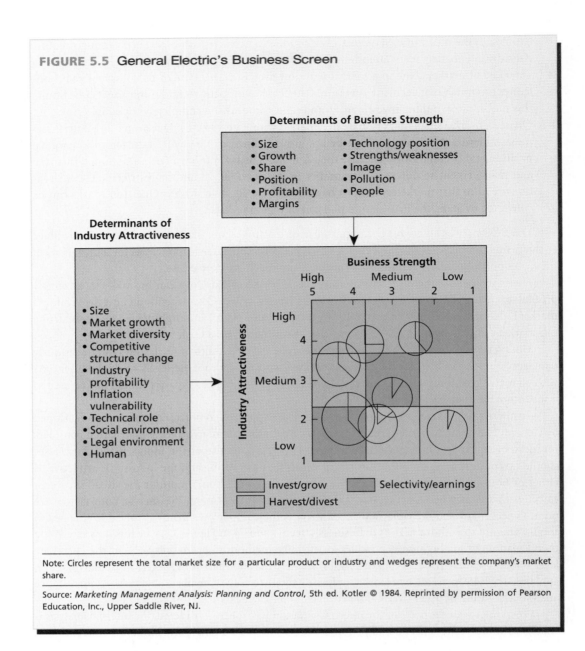

**FIGURE 5.5** General Electric's Business Screen

**Determinants of Business Strength**

- Size
- Growth
- Share
- Position
- Profitability
- Margins
- Technology position
- Strengths/weaknesses
- Image
- Pollution
- People

**Determinants of Industry Attractiveness**

- Size
- Market growth
- Market diversity
- Competitive structure change
- Industry profitability
- Inflation vulnerability
- Technical role
- Social environment
- Legal environment
- Human

**Business Strength**

| | High | Medium | Low |
|---|---|---|---|
| | 5    4 | 3 | 2    1 |

Industry Attractiveness

High — 4
Medium — 3
Low — 1

Invest/grow    Selectivity/earnings
Harvest/divest

Note: Circles represent the total market size for a particular product or industry and wedges represent the company's market share.

Source: *Marketing Management Analysis: Planning and Control*, 5th ed. Kotler © 1984. Reprinted by permission of Pearson Education, Inc., Upper Saddle River, NJ.

Price or Gerber baby food company, both of whom depend on a growing base of young children and babies for success.

The combined summary of the internal analysis and the environmental analysis is widely abbreviated as a **SWOT analysis**, which stands for *strengths, weaknesses, opportunities,* and *threats.* Examining the first two boxes of Figure 5.2 reveals that corporate planners have already gone through a parallel exercise. Although the description of the process is similar for large corporations, these steps imply very different levels of analysis. A corporate planner at The Coca-Cola Company, for example, might consider "thirst quenchers" as the relevant competition, and based on that analysis, give input to the Minute Maid, Powerade, and Diet Coke units of the company. In contrast, a market planner within the Diet Coke unit would probably concentrate on Diet Pepsi as the primary competition while also monitoring the actions of store brands of diet cola. In a similar way, all of the strategic analysis undertaken at the corporate level of large organizations tends to be at a higher level of abstraction than at the product, or marketing, level. At the same time, for smaller organizations, there is often little practical difference between strategic marketing planning and strategic corporate planning, with the one flowing seamlessly into the other.

**SWOT analysis**

The combined summary of the internal analysis and the environmental analysis. Stands for *strengths, weaknesses, opportunities,* and *threats*.

www.coca-cola.com

# Customer Analysis

We have emphasized repeatedly that understanding and being in tune with the customer's needs is the very heart of successful marketing. Customer analysis has an important role to play in developing marketing strategy. In customer analysis, both market segmentation, discussed in Chapters 3 and 4, and market research, discussed in Chapter 7, have a role to play. In general, there are seven questions marketers should ask about their customers:

1. Who are our actual and potential customers?
2. Why do they buy our product?
3. Why do noncustomers *not* buy our product?
4. Where do our customers buy our product?
5. How do they buy it?
6. When do they buy it?
7. What do they do with our product?[4]

With the seven customer usage questions answered, plus additional input from market research, the marketer can then consider the issue of segmentation.

Each segment must first be subjected to a **positioning analysis**. This means that the competing companies and brands in each segment are identified, and their positioning in the segment is indicated. For example, in the business microcomputer segment, Compaq (now merged with Hewlett Packard), IBM, Apple, and a number of other manufacturers compete. IBM and Compaq position themselves as the firms with leading-edge technology and high quality. Apple is positioned as providing the most user-friendly and versatile quality computer. Several clones also compete in this segment, and will be positioned as providing various combinations of features at a low price (see Figure 5.6). IBM and Compaq are adopting a head-to-head positioning strategy—directly taking each other on in the microcomputer market. On the other hand, Apple with its iMac has chosen to follow a differentiation strategy—distinguishing itself from IBM and Compaq on user-friendliness. In some of its advertisements, Apple used its multicoloured computer casings as an indicator, or cue, of that difference.

The result of this analysis is the identification of certain segments and positions that are deemed worthy of further consideration. Many different reasons could lead to the decision to consider a seg-

**positioning analysis**
Identifying brands in each segment and how they differ from each other.

www.compaq.ca/English/atcompaq/atcompaq.htm

www.can.ibm.com

www.apple.com

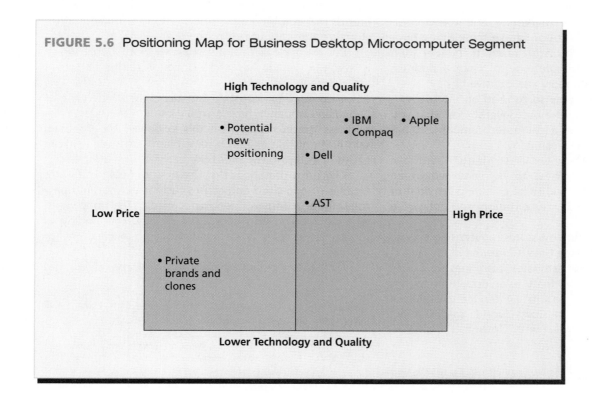

**FIGURE 5.6  Positioning Map for Business Desktop Microcomputer Segment**

High Technology and Quality

• Potential new positioning

• IBM     • Apple
• Compaq

• Dell

• AST

Low Price                    High Price

• Private brands and clones

Lower Technology and Quality

ment further—for example, size of market, an opportunity to position a product where there is little competition, or evidence that existing competition can be overcome.

Next, as Chapter 4 discusses, a more thorough analysis of the selected segments is undertaken. One method of doing this is by conducting a more focused SWOT analysis to develop a picture of the situation faced by a business. For example, within the above-mentioned microcomputer segment, a firm might have a unique product (a strength), but limited additional funds for advertising (a weakness). This strongly affects the type of marketing program that can be developed.

Following this, the positioning analysis shown in Figure 5.6 makes it possible to clearly identify areas of opportunity. In our example, the upper left quadrant has no other direct competitors. If the size of that market is significant, the company might design a product to match that segment.

It is also necessary to have a realistic assessment of the current or potential threats faced within the market segment. For example, companies with two closely positioned products, such as Compaq and IBM, can see that there are threats posed by each other, as well as by other companies that might be trying to move in for a share of their position. Management should carefully select the most desirable bases for segmentation and positioning to encompass all of the firm's current and potential offerings.

## INTERNET IMPACT "PLUS"

### USING E-BUSINESS LEADERSHIP AS AN OVERALL STRATEGY

IBM Canada is using "winning the game" as a theme in a new e-business ad campaign in newspapers, magazines, and television.

The campaign, part of a sweeping global effort, is directed primarily at medium-sized business firms with 100 to 999 employees.

IBM's counsel to the business community is that "e-business is a game they need to play to win," said Keyvan Cohanim, vice-president of marketing and communications with IBM Canada. "A lot of people think that e-business is just e-commerce. It's actually much broader than that. It's about tools and solutions to make a business more efficient, to make it more competitive."

IBM, in fact, has become so focused on Internet-oriented technologies during the past several years that you might say it is no longer a computer company. It has morphed into an e-business company.

"E-business is IBM's overall strategy," said Mr. Cohanim. The company strives to be perceived as an e-business thought leader and to be a leading provider of hardware and software implementation and follow-up services, he said.

IBM introduced its first e-business advertising several years ago at about the same time it unveiled its stylized e-business symbol. The new campaign continues to display the iconic symbol, but it also features an updated slogan— "e-business is a game. Play to win"—intended to highlight a basic truth about the business world, said Graham Calderwood, senior partner with Toronto's Ogilvy & Mather.

"Business is a competition. We come into the office every day looking to beat the other guy."

www.ibm.com

In a major coup last month, IBM Canada beat out Montreal's CGI Corp. for a lucrative $850 million outsourcing contract from Manulife Financial Corp. The deal will see IBM's services consulting branch manage Manulife's information technology infrastructure throughout North America.

But major deals of this sort are in short supply, which is why IBM Canada has set its sights on raising its profile among medium-sized business.

According to Statistics Canada, only 29 percent of Canadian companies have a Web presence, much less an e-business strategy. Based on this evidence, Mr. Cohanim said IBM anticipates it will have plenty of work if it can excite mid-sized firms about the benefits of e-business.

The print component of the new campaign features profiles of mid-sized enterprises such as eBay.ca and payroll-solution company Ceridian Canada. The concept of winning is conveyed through the depiction of employees raising their arms over their heads in expressions of triumph.

Mr. Cohanim said the campaign will appear in eight countries.

**Two strategies are described in this article. What are they? What is your evaluation of them?**

Source: Excerpted from Patrick Allossery, "Big Blue Playing to Win," *Financial Post*, May 13, 2002, p. FP8. Reprinted by permission of the author.

# Competitive Analysis

A major objective in strategic planning is to create and sustain competitive advantage. Therefore, along with customer analysis, competitor analysis is fundamental. In addition to identifying the relative positions of competitors, an effective strategy for dealing with competitors is essential. For example, if you should develop a new soft drink that is as good as or better than Pepsi, you would be foolish to develop a plan for marketing it without taking into consideration the competitive response of Pepsi if that company thought you might threaten its market share.

Competitor assessment leads some firms to specialize in particular market segments. Others with greater resources compete in a broad range of product markets in several areas of the world. Determining a competitive strategy involves answering five questions:

1. Who are our competitors, and what are their strengths and weaknesses?
2. What is our competitors' strategy, and what will be their likely response to our competitive moves?
3. Should we compete?
4. If so, in what markets should we compete?
5. How should we compete?

The first question, "Who are our competitors?" focuses attention on the various potential challenges to be faced to gain a share of the market. Firms sometimes enter a market with an inadequate understanding of the extent of the competition. Or, if they are already established, firms sometimes respond poorly to the entrance of a new and powerful competitor. In Canadian retailing, the responses of various firms to the entrance of the powerful Wal-Mart chain is a good example. Zellers and Canadian Tire anticipated that they would be some of the most affected retailers. Each studied the Wal-Mart operation carefully and made adjustments to its pricing and advertising to compete. As discussed in Chapter 2, two types of competition must be clearly identified: inter-product, and product-substitute competition.

## How to Assess Competitive Advantage

Peter Chandler suggests two steps for thinking strategically about gaining competitive advantage:

1. Think through your own organization's strategic capabilities, and also how you can link these business processes to serve customer needs in a way that is superior to your competitors.
2. Read everything you can about how other organizations in other industries and countries are gaining competitive advantage. "To be ignorant of how others are succeeding is a bit like fighting set piece trench warfare as occurred in World War I. The smart commander will be looking outside the square to see what new forces or approaches can be brought to bear."[5]

The second question, "What is our competitors' strategy?" points out that a marketing strategy cannot be developed in a vacuum. It must be at least as good as, more effective than, or different from that of competitors. Often a great deal of creativity is required to come up with a winning plan.

The third question, "Should we compete?" should be answered based on the resources and objectives of the firm and the expected profit potential for the firm. In some instances, potentially successful ventures are not considered due to a lack of a match between the venture and the overall organizational objectives. For example, a clothing manufacturer may reject an opportunity to diversify through purchasing a profitable chain of retail clothing stores. Or a producer of industrial chemicals might refrain from entering the consumer market and instead sell chemicals to another firm that is familiar with serving consumers at the retail level.

In other cases, a critical issue is expected profit potential. If the expected profits are insufficient to pay an adequate return on the required investment, then the firm should consider other lines of business. Many organizations have switched from less profitable ventures quite efficiently. This decision should be subject to continual re-evaluation so that the firm avoids being tied to traditional markets with declining profit margins. It is also important to anticipate competitive responses.

"In what markets should we compete?" Whatever decision is made acknowledges that the firm has limited resources (engineering and productive capabilities, sales personnel, advertising budgets, research and development, and the like) and that these resources must be allocated to the areas of

Bringing out our **true** colours

Want to get your shopping done quicker
**and easier than ever before?**
Our associates in GREY shirts create a pleasant shopping
environment every day! Got a question? Need direction?
Our associates in RED shirts are happy to help you
**Introducing** our brand new service team,
ready to help busy moms like you!

**Zellers' competitive strategy to make shopping more pleasant and efficient.**

greatest opportunity. Too many firms have taken a "shotgun" approach to market selection and thus do an ineffective job in many markets rather than a good one in selected markets.

"How should we compete?" is the fifth question. It requires the firm's marketers to make the decisions involved in setting up a comprehensive marketing strategy.

## MARKETING OBJECTIVES AND STRATEGY

Profit-oriented firms usually state objectives in terms of desired market share, or sales or profitability targets. Frequently, more than one issue will be considered simultaneously. For example, a firm might set an objective of a 15 percent return on investment, subject to market share remaining at or above 22 percent. In other words, the firm's objectives imply that executives might be willing to sacrifice profits in the short term in order to protect market share.

Not-for-profit organizations more often express their objectives in terms of level of services provided, number of clients served, and funds raised. Each year, the United Way establishes a national objective and then a city-by-city objective for fundraising. Once objectives are established, strategies must be developed to achieve the objectives.

At the level of the marketplace—what you see as you watch commercials, check out flyers, and walk around retail outlets—there is an endless variety of marketing strategies and accompanying tactics. When reduced to their most basic level, though, there are really three strategies that a firm can pursue: retrenchment, status quo, or growth.

Firms can choose to pull back from the marketplace by following a *retrenchment* strategy. Retrenchment implies that a company has narrowed its product line, reduced its geographic scope by closing some locations, or tried to cut costs in some significant way. More often, retrenchment involves all three activities. Major retrenchment signals a retreat from the marketplace and is usually only pursued in times of crisis. Eaton's went through a retrenchment in the late 1990s by closing more than twenty unprofitable stores and shedding some low-margin, high-cost product lines such as major appliances. By the end of 1999 it was clear that even these actions would not save the venerable retailer, and it was forced into bankruptcy. Kmart, another retailer, was also forced to take drastic retrenchment measures. A few years after Wal-Mart entered the Canadian retailing scene, Kmart sold its Canadian operations to Zellers and retreated to its U.S. base.

*Status quo* strategies are an attempt to maintain competitive equilibrium in a market. A firm that uses this strategy defends its position in a market but does not aggressively pursue increased market share. Some would argue that the entire Canadian retail sector was pursuing a status quo strategy before the appearance of Wal-Mart and the big-box stores such as Home Depot and Costco. A status quo strategy tends to leave a firm open to attack by aggressive competitors, as happened to Canadian retailers, and as a result it is rarely a marketer's conscious choice. In practice, most firms are pursuing a growth strategy.

The product–market growth matrix, illustrated in Figure 5.7, is a convenient way to think about growth opportunities. The matrix is based on the observation that growth must come from some combination of existing or new products and existing or new markets. Growth strategies can take four forms.

*Growth* that comes from selling existing products in existing markets is penetration. It implies that current customers are buying more of the product. The dairy industry, with its many milk advertisements, pursues a penetration strategy. Growth through new products in existing markets is called product development. When General Mills produced Honey Nut, Frosted, and Apple Cinnamon Cheerios, it was following a product development strategy. Selling existing products in new markets is called market development. The strategy involves either appealing to buyers in a different geographical area or appealing to a different segment in a served area. Finally, creating new products for new markets is called diversification.

Within each of the three broad strategies and each of the growth strategies that a firm can follow, several more specific strategies can be considered: focus, niche, low-cost, and differentiation.

Microsoft is a very large company, but it became large by pursuing a very focused strategy and market—high-volume microcomputer software. Most other companies of Microsoft's size are widely diversified across many different markets. Focused strategies concentrate on single, but large, markets.

www.walmart.com

www.zellers.ca

www.generalmills.com

---

**FIGURE 5.7  Product–Market Growth Matrix**

| MARKET / PRODUCT | Present | New |
|---|---|---|
| Present | Penetration | Product development |
| New | Market development | Diversification |

The freshness of the seasons. The strength of Mr. Clean.

Mr. Clean now brings you Seasons' Freshness. An antibacterial cleaner with four great scents.
Spring Garden, Summer Citrus, Sparkling Apple and Invigorating Breeze.
They'll remind you of your favourite season. Any time of the year.

One differentiation strategy for Mr. Clean is to offer the product in four different scents.

Netscape, in contrast to Microsoft, has been following a niche strategy, concentrating on Web browser software. Niche strategies pursue smaller subsegments of large markets. Tag Heuer, a manufacturer of upscale watches, is another example of a firm pursuing a niche strategy.

Low-cost strategies are difficult to accomplish but extremely powerful if achieved. Wal-Mart is feared by other retailers because it has persistently and aggressively reduced its costs until they are lower than competitors'. That implies that Wal-Mart can set prices in a range that severely squeezes, or eliminates altogether, other retailers' profit margins while still making a profit for itself. (Note the distinction between a low-cost strategy and low prices—it's easy to lower prices but very difficult to lower costs.)

Finally, a differentiation strategy seeks to create a point of distinction between a product or service and that of competitors. Differentiation is the foundation of most successful marketing campaigns. Dr. Pepper has cheerfully pursued a differentiation strategy for years. Differentiation is the strategy behind product positioning and market segmentation discussed in Chapters 3 and 4.

Each of these strategies has different implications for the total marketing program put together by the organization. Those implications must be systematically considered and accommodated in the marketing plan.

## THE MARKETING PLAN

The marketing plan is a detailed statement of how the marketing mix will be used to realize the marketing strategy. In marketing planning, the first question to be addressed is "What should be

An example of a market development strategy for a niche market.

included in the plan?" How can the planner have confidence that the marketing plan developed accomplishes the strategy that has been set out and includes the appropriate planning elements? The criterion for a marketing plan should be that it leads to organization effectiveness.

How does a manager know whether the plans made will be effective or not? Contingency theory, which originated in the organizational behaviour literature, provides some excellent guidance. This theory argues that managerial decisions are not right or wrong per se. They must be made and assessed in the light of the circumstances surrounding the decisions. For example, if profits are falling because of declining sales, a decision to reduce or increase advertising might depend on whether the drop is caused by lack of awareness of the product or adverse economic conditions (people know about the product but have no money). Therefore, a marketing plan should be based on a careful analysis of the key factors in the business environment. In a generic sense, most firms face the following conditions. Since the importance of each condition varies according to the individual firm's situation, it is impossible to present an exhaustive set.

## Increasing Competition

The current environment is characterized by intense and increasing competitiveness. Some authors have argued that marketing strategy should be based on a competitive rather than a marketing orientation.[6] This is an extreme position. However, increased competition can be observed in several ways:

- *Intertype competition.* Firms readily cross industry lines to compete if they think they can apply their technology to another field (for example, agricultural companies may begin producing recreational vehicles, or computer software firms may play a leading role in producing machine tools and industrial robots).
- *International competition.* A fundamental strategy of most countries today is to increase exports. Alert companies are responding. Consequently, domestic firms are finding aggressive new competitors facing them in traditional domestic markets.

# THE ETHICAL MARKETER

## THE DARK SIDE OF HOCKEY CARDS

There's a hidden danger lurking in the harmless activity of collecting hockey cards, a California law firm claims.

Every time a child buys a pack of cards, they're being lured into an illegal and exploitative racket, says the firm Milberg Weiss Bershad Hynes & Lerach. It has begun a class-action lawsuit against the National Hockey League, the NHL Players' Association, and six other professional sports organizations, claiming sports cards are a kind of lottery with the odds stacked against collectors.

Kids buy the cards in the hopes of finding valuable "chase cards" randomly inserted into the packages. Buyers stand only a small chance of getting those coveted cards, such as the rare Wayne Gretzky card that contains small patches of a jersey he wore during a game.

As these are worth $500 or more to collectors, consumers are manipulated to keep buying until they find a package with one of the "artificially scarce" cards, the suit claims. This creates a "chase mania" and keeps kids spending until they hit a winner, it says.

The plaintiffs contend that sports card marketing satisfies the criteria for a lottery because consumers pay for a chance by buying the card package, have certain odds of receiving a chase card, and, if they're lucky, receive a prize with a cash value in the form of a chase card.

"Major league sports claim they're anti-gambling, and they're out there encouraging kids to gamble," said lawyer Kevin Roddy, who leads the litigation.

Mr. Roddy has assembled statements from addiction experts who will testify that "chase mania" is a form of gambling.

www.nhl.com/nhlhq

"What is particularly scary to the experts is that, whatever it is that makes certain adults get addicted to gambling, it's four times stronger in kids," he said. "They are less able to resist."

The NHL disagrees. "We do not believe that this case has any merit, and we intend to defend it vigorously," said Frank Brown, vice-president for media relations. The defendants have moved to dismiss the claim.

**From the NHL's perspective, the organization is practising market penetration—encouraging its current customers to buy more of its products. Do you feel that the approach the NHL has taken is ethical, or do you agree with Mr. Roddy? If you feel that the NHL is not behaving ethically, is it possible to have an ethical penetration strategy when marketing a product that will be purchased primarily by children? Explain.**

Source: Excerpted from Glen McGregor, "Sports Cards Denounced as Gambling Racket: Lawsuit Targets Valuable 'Chase Cards'," *The Ottawa Citizen* (February 1, 1999). Reprinted with permission.

---

■ *More demanding economic conditions.* As a result of the economic decline in the early 1980s, virtually all firms had to become more efficient and aggressive in order to survive. Many continued this posture as the economy turned around. Through the business cycles of the 1990s, it was clear that a prolonged period of intense domestic and worldwide competition had turned into the norm for business.

To take account of these conditions, a marketing plan should have a realistic assessment of the competitive domestic and worldwide industry environment. It should also include a statement of current market share, and a recognition of the shares and strategies of leading competitors. The plan should include an analysis of competitive strengths and weaknesses, and a forecast of market demand.

## Dynamic Consumer Society

Today's marketplace is characterized by fragmented, rapidly changing, sophisticated consumers. More products have emerged to more precisely meet tastes and higher consumer expectations. International travel and world communication have added to this sophistication. A marketing plan must include a thorough analysis of current customer motivations and trends.

## Hi-Tech Environment

Computers have revolutionized products and services. The inherent nature of many products, as well as their design and production, has changed. For example, the microchips now commonly built into such products as telephones and tools enable functions unheard of a few years ago. Many services are similarly affected.

## Social Consciousness

An acute sensitivity to ecological issues continues to grow. The marketplace is showing evidence of the desire for a clean environment, as well as environmentally friendly products. In a related development, the requirements for socially responsible business behaviour continue to increase. If changes do not happen voluntarily, governmental regulation and legislation may be expected.

A comprehensive marketing plan should explicitly take such factors into consideration. Failing this, contingency theory suggests that it would be more difficult for the organization to be effective and competitive, and that the firm will sooner or later fall out of phase with its competitors and the environment.

## Planning Process Requirements

For every marketing plan statement, a system for expeditiously developing a complete plan is necessary. Possible elements of such a system include identifying problems and opportunities, conducting a post-mortem of previous plans, stating alternative strategies considered, identifying risk factors, stating objectives, stating an action plan, and developing contingency plans.

## Operational Organizational Requirements

In order to make it operational, each plan should also include a statement of objectives, a budget statement, a section identifying those responsible for executing the plan, and specific timetables and controls for the new plan.

---

## THE PRACTISING MARKETER

### WILL VANILLA COKE FLY?

Coca-Cola has finally confirmed one of the world's worst-kept corporate secrets by formally announcing the launch of a new flavour, Vanilla Coke.

The new drink, which appeared in the United States and Canada on May 15, 2002 reportedly tastes just like the old, "with a hint of natural vanilla."

Normally such a story would not spark international interest, but this is the iconographic company that 17 years ago almost throttled itself on the eve of its centenary by replacing its flagship drink with New Coke.

Back then Coca-Cola was spooked by the growing success of Pepsi, which argued that blind tests showed Joe Bloggs preferred Pepsi to Coke. So Coke ditched its original sharp soda and replaced it with a sweeter one.

The change sparked outrage in middle America, which for generations had been bombarded with advertising convincing them Coke was an integral part of their life, up there with apple pie and handguns.

The decision was reversed, and Americans returned to the original product in droves.

Coke has introduced new flavours before.

Diet Coke came in 1982, Cherry Coke was launched in the U.S. in 1985, and last year Diet Coke with lemon hit the U.S. streets.

An analyst with ABN Amro, David Cook, said the launch of a new line was standard marketing practice. "I'd be very surprised if any financial analysts were reading into [the launch that] the classic Coke is failing; it's just a way of keeping themselves in the public eye."

Other Coca-Cola products under different brands, such as new Fanta flavours, are selling well, and dairy producers have been on edge over rumours that Coke will break into the flavoured-milk market.

Vanilla flavouring is hardly a new idea—back before Coke became the first bottled soda drink, Coke with vanilla was a favourite at the soda fountains of Main Street.

**Is this a major strategic move for Coke? What do you think of this decision?**

www.coca-cola.com

Source: Adapted from Nick O'Malley, "Vanilla Coke—The Secret's Out," April 17, 2002 from *The Sydney Morning Herald*. Reprinted with permission. http://www.smh.com.au/articles/2002/04/17/1018333551674.html

---

Table 5.2 presents a model of how these important environmental features might be identified. It also shows the corresponding marketing planning activities required to operate effectively in the environment. This model can serve as a comprehensive guide for marketing planning.

When this model is used as a base for developing a marketing plan, decisions about whether to include a component of the plan are contingent on the conditions found in the environment. Following a contingency approach enables a firm to be more relevant in its planning. Because the process begins with a careful analysis of the environment, current conditions that are of direct significance as well as long-term trends can be identified and responded to. This process should also lead to a more comprehensive plan, as outlined in the right-hand column of the table.

What, then, should be included in a marketing plan? The answer can be determined from Table 5.2. The left-hand column shows the environmental conditions that must be addressed. The marketing plan should meet these new conditions. The right-hand column outlines the marketing plan components that are required to meet the conditions in the illustration. Obviously, as conditions change, different marketing plan components will be included, excluded, or emphasized.

Identifying key elements of the environment that must be responded to ensures that the marketing plan is focused on the right things. A further important advantage of this approach is that the marketing plan is not focused solely on current conditions. To properly understand the environment requires taking long-term trends into consideration. Providing that the organization's reward structure is not excessively focused on short-term results, a marketing plan based on current environmental conditions, as well as the forces behind them, will have a longer-term perspective. A more common description of a process for developing a marketing plan is shown in Figure 5.8. (It should in fact look familiar—we saw a less detailed version early in Chapter 3.)

# THE MARKETING MIX

Marketing plans address four main elements: product or service management, pricing, distribution, and communication. Each is an essential part of the marketing mix.

**Product management** includes decisions about what kind of product is needed, its uses, package design, branding, trademarks, warranties, guarantees, product life cycles, and new product development. The marketer's concept of product takes into account the satisfaction of all consumer needs in relation to a good or service.

**Pricing** involves decisions concerning the methods of setting competitive, profitable, and justified prices. Most prices are freely set in Canada. However, some prices, such as those for public utilities and housing rentals, are regulated to some degree, and are therefore subject to public scrutiny.

**Distribution** decisions involve the selection and management of marketing channels and the physical distribution of goods. **Marketing channels** are the steps or handling organizations that a good or service goes through from producer to final consumer. Channel decision making entails selecting and working with the institutional structure that handles the firm's goods or services. This includes wholesalers, retailers, and other intermediaries.

**Communication** includes personal selling, advertising, sales promotion, and publicity. The marketing manager has many decisions to make concerning when, where, and how to use these elements of communication so that potential buyers will learn about and be persuaded to try the company's products.

The marketing mix is sometimes called the "four P's" for ease of remembering: product, price, place, promotion. The rest of this book will be devoted largely to explaining these four marketing elements. The elements of the marketing mix are shown in Figure 5.9.

Starting with a careful evaluation of the market—using market segmentation—every marketing plan must take into consideration the appropriate product for a particular segment, the price that should be charged for it, and the appropriate outlet in which it ought to be sold. All of this information must be effectively communicated to the target market.

A quick examination of various companies' marketing programs shows that, even though they each have all the marketing variables, no two programs use them in exactly the same way. The

**product management**

Decisions about what kind of product is needed, its uses, package design, branding, trademarks, warranties, guarantees, product life cycles, and new product development.

**pricing**

The methods of setting competitive, profitable, and justified prices.

**distribution**

The selection and management of marketing channels and the physical distribution of goods.

**marketing channels**

The steps or handling organizations that a good or service goes through from producer to final consumer.

**communication**

Personal selling, advertising, sales promotion, and publicity.

**TABLE 5.2** Marketing Planning Model Based on Environmental Antecedents

| ENVIRONMENTAL ANTECEDENTS | MARKETING PLAN REQUIREMENTS |
|---|---|
| **Increasing Competition**<br><br>• Intertype competition<br>• Increasing complexity of economic conditions<br>• International competition | • Statement of market share<br>• Recognition of shares and strengths of leading competitors<br>• Analysis of competitive strengths and weaknesses<br>• Forecast of market demand |
| **Dynamic Consumer/Buyer Society**<br><br>• Rapid changes in tastes and behaviour<br>• High customer expectations<br>• Exposure to varied domestic and international mass media<br>• Highly fragmented customer groups<br>• Increasing customer sophistication | • Consideration of the changing needs of customers<br>• Product life-cycle analysis<br>• Market segmentation analysis<br>• Product portfolio position analysis |
| **Hi-Tech Environment**<br><br>• Effect of technology on<br>  –product design<br>  –product performance<br>  –price<br>• Automation of production | • Technological trends statement |
| **Social Consciousness**<br><br>• Health and safety issues<br>• Clean/pure environment issues<br>• Increasing expectations for responsible business behaviour<br>• Expectations for proactive governmental regulation/legislation | • Environmental issues statement<br>• Consideration of government regulatory issues |
| **Planning Process Requirements**<br><br>• Existence of a system for expeditiously developing a complete plan | • Identification of problems and opportunities<br>• Post-mortem of previous plan<br>• Statement of alternative strategies considered<br>• Identification of risk factors<br>• Statement of objectives<br>• Statement of action plan<br>• Development of contingency plans |
| **Operational Organizational Requirements**<br><br>• Guidance<br>• Control<br>• Financial responsibility<br>• Efficiency | • Statement of objectives<br>• Budget statement of proposed plan<br>• Responsibility for execution pinpointed<br>• Timetables and controls for the new plan specified |

*emphasis* and *use* of each can vary markedly. For example, the target market for McDonald's might be families with children. The company's products are standardized and reliable, but not considered to match the same calibre as those of Dubrovnik's, a famous Winnipeg restaurant that one might visit on an evening out. Dubrovnik's target market would be couples celebrating a special event or

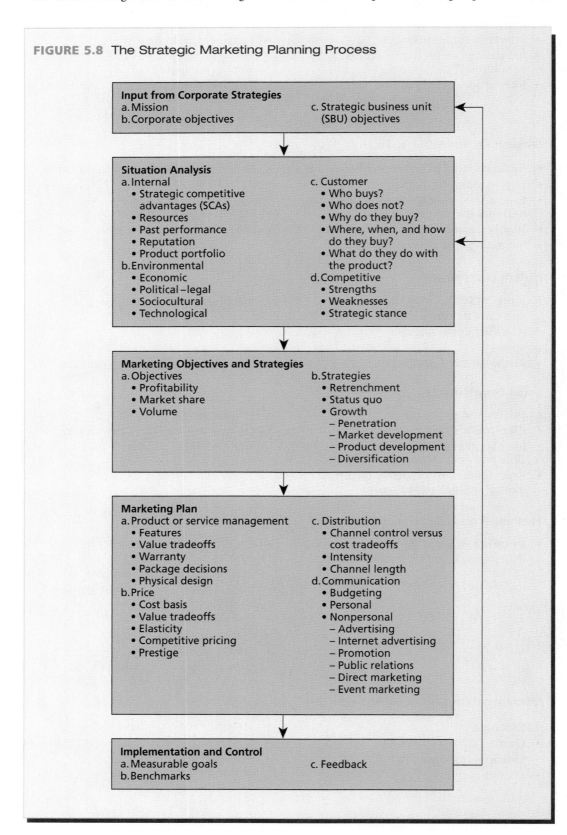

FIGURE 5.8 The Strategic Marketing Planning Process

**Input from Corporate Strategies**
a. Mission
b. Corporate objectives
c. Strategic business unit (SBU) objectives

**Situation Analysis**
a. Internal
  • Strategic competitive advantages (SCAs)
  • Resources
  • Past performance
  • Reputation
  • Product portfolio
b. Environmental
  • Economic
  • Political–legal
  • Sociocultural
  • Technological
c. Customer
  • Who buys?
  • Who does not?
  • Why do they buy?
  • Where, when, and how do they buy?
  • What do they do with the product?
d. Competitive
  • Strengths
  • Weaknesses
  • Strategic stance

**Marketing Objectives and Strategies**
a. Objectives
  • Profitability
  • Market share
  • Volume
b. Strategies
  • Retrenchment
  • Status quo
  • Growth
    – Penetration
    – Market development
    – Product development
    – Diversification

**Marketing Plan**
a. Product or service management
  • Features
  • Value tradeoffs
  • Warranty
  • Package decisions
  • Physical design
b. Price
  • Cost basis
  • Value tradeoffs
  • Elasticity
  • Competitive pricing
  • Prestige
c. Distribution
  • Channel control versus cost tradeoffs
  • Intensity
  • Channel length
d. Communication
  • Budgeting
  • Personal
  • Nonpersonal
    – Advertising
    – Internet advertising
    – Promotion
    – Public relations
    – Direct marketing
    – Event marketing

**Implementation and Control**
a. Measurable goals
b. Benchmarks
c. Feedback

## FIGURE 5.9 The Marketing Mix

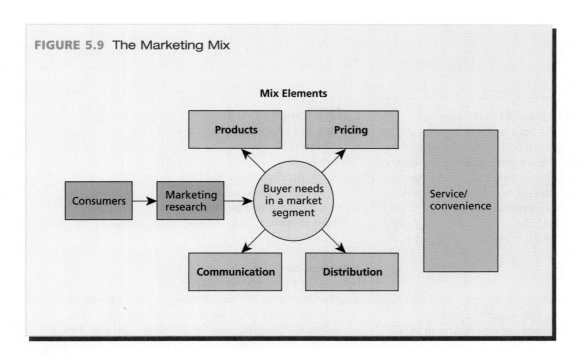

businesspeople entertaining their clients. Prices at McDonald's are low compared with those at the fine restaurant. In terms of distribution, it is important for McDonald's to have outlets at many locations, because consumers are not prepared to drive great distances to visit them. In contrast, people are fully prepared to drive downtown to the one Dubrovnik's location. McDonald's employs a communication program that involves extensive television advertising. Dubrovnik's counts on favourable word-of-mouth publicity, and purchases only a limited number of advertisements in local magazines and theatre guides.

# THE ROOTS OF MARKETING

## INTERACTION WITHIN THE MARKETING MIX

Since the notion of the marketing mix was first popularized by Neil H. Borden, many other writers have elaborated on it. In 1985 Benson P. Shapiro pointed out how important it is that the individual elements of the marketing mix fit together. His argument is summarized below.

The marketing mix concept emphasizes the fit of the various pieces and the quality and size of their interaction. There are three degrees of interaction. The least demanding is *consistency*—a logical and useful fit between two or more elements. It would seem generally inconsistent, for example, to sell a high-quality product through a low-quality retailer. It can be done, but the consumer must understand the reason for the inconsistency and respond favourably to it. Even more difficult is maintaining such an apparent inconsistency for a long time.

The second level of positive relationship among elements of the mix is *integration*. While consistency involves only a coherent fit, integration requires an active, harmonious interaction among the elements of the mix. For example, heavy advertising is sometimes harmonious with a high selling price because the added margin from the premium price pays for the advertising, and the heavy advertising creates the brand differentiation that justifies the high price. National brands of consumer packaged goods such as Tide laundry detergent, Campbell soup, and Colgate toothpaste use this approach. This does *not* mean, however, that heavy advertising and high product pricing are always harmonious.

The third—and most sophisticated—form of relationship is *synergy*, whereby each element is used to the best advantage in support of the total mix and results in effects greater than the sum of the parts.

**Explain how an intelligent application of these concepts will provide customer satisfaction.**

Source: Adapted from Benson P. Shapiro, "Getting Things Done: Rejuvenating the Marketing Mix," *Harvard Business Review* (September–October 1985), p. 29. Copyright © 1985 by the President and Fellows of Harvard College; all rights reserved.

## THE FIRST MARKETING MIX LIST

### Elements of the Marketing Mix of Manufacturers

While we normally talk of the four main categories of the mix, it should be clearly understood that each of the mix elements can, and should, be divided into many subcategories when developing a marketing plan. For example, *communication* includes decisions about advertising, selling, and point-of-purchase promotion, to name a few. Neil Borden, who first coined the term "marketing mix," used to use the following much more extensive list in his teaching and consulting:

### 1. Product Planning
Policies and procedures relating to
a.  Product lines to be offered—qualities, design, etc.
b.  Markets to sell—whom, where, when, and in what quantity.
c.  New-product policy—R & D program.

### 2. Pricing
Policies and procedures relating to
a.  Price level to adopt.
b.  Specific prices to adopt—odd–even, etc.
c.  Price policy—one price or varying price, price maintenance, use of list prices, etc.
d.  Margins to adopt—for company, for the trade.

### 3. Branding
Policies and procedures relating to
a.  Selection of trademarks.
b.  Brand policy—individualized or family brand.
c.  Sale under private label or unbranded.

### 4. Channels of Distribution
Policies and procedures relating to
a.  Channels to use between plant and consumer.
b.  Degree of selectivity among wholesalers and retailers.
c.  Efforts to gain cooperation of the trade.

### 5. Personal Selling
Policies and procedures relating to
a.  Burden to be placed on personal selling and the methods to be employed in:
    • Manufacturer's organization.
    • Wholesale segment of the trade.
    • Retail segment of the trade.

### 6. Advertising
Policies and procedures relating to
a.  Amount to spend—i.e., burden to be placed on advertising.
b.  Copy platform to adopt:
    • Product image desired.
    • Corporate image desired.
c.  Mix of advertising—to the trade, through the trade, to consumers.

### 7. Promotions
Policies and procedures relating to
a.  Burden to be placed on special selling plans or devices directed at or through the trade.
b.  Form of these devices for consumer promotions, for trade promotions.

### 8. Packaging
Policies and procedures relating to
a.  Formulation of package and label.

### 9. Display
Policies and procedures relating to
a.  Burden to be put on display to help effect sale.
b.  Methods to adopt to secure display.

### 10. Servicing
Policies and procedures relating to
a.  Providing service needed.

### 11. Physical Handling
Policies and procedures relating to
a.  Warehousing.
b.  Transportation.
c.  Inventories.

### 12. Fact-Finding and Analysis
Policies and procedures relating to
a.  Securing, analyzing, and using facts in marketing operations.

Source: The twelve elements are from Neil H. Borden, "The Concept of the Marketing Mix," *Journal of Advertising Research* (June 1964), pp. 2–7. Reprinted by permission of the Advertising Research Foundation.

The point is that each firm uses the elements of marketing differently—the marketing elements are harmonized in a unique way to form the main aspects of the marketing plan. This blending of the four elements of marketing to satisfy chosen consumer segments is known as the **marketing mix**. The marketing mix concept is one of the most powerful ever developed for marketers. It is now the main organizing concept for countless marketing plans. It gives executives a way to ensure that all elements of their program are considered in a simple yet disciplined fashion.[7]

The marketing planner must actually make wise decisions about *many* sub-elements of the marketing mix. This takes much skill and attention.

**marketing mix**
The blending of the four elements of marketing to satisfy chosen consumer segments.

# THE ROLE OF THE MARKETING MANAGER

To conclude our examination of marketing strategy and the marketing plan, Figure 5.10 illustrates some aspects of the role of the marketing manager in the process of developing a marketing plan. The responsibility of developing and implementing the marketing plan falls on the marketing manager. In the light of the opportunities and constraints perceived in the environmental framework, appropriate market segments are selected.

Based on the strategy, objectives, and resources of the firm, the manager and his or her team establishes marketing strategy and then develops a competitive marketing plan. Products or services, pricing, distribution, and communication are blended in a unique way to make up the marketing mix. The result wins customers, sales, and profits for the firm.

This is the essence of the first five chapters of this text. Chapter 6 introduces the important concept of total customer satisfaction and customer relationship management. Total customer satisfaction is becoming the overarching objective of all informed marketing activity. Its principles and

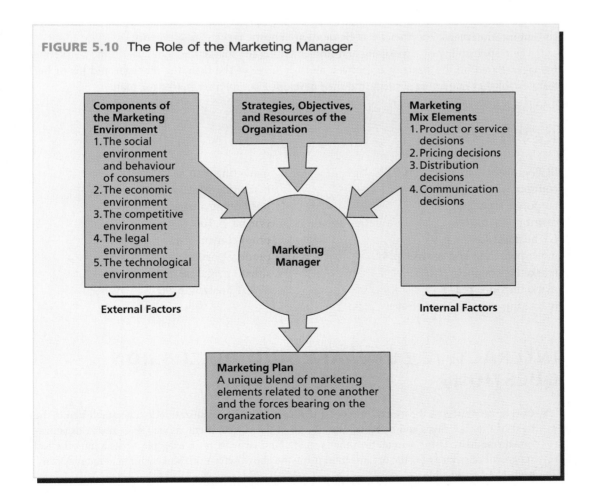

**FIGURE 5.10** The Role of the Marketing Manager

philosophies have broad implications for the implementation of the marketing plan, including the types of feedback and control systems employed. Customer relationship management is a critical part of this process, and it also opens new and significant marketing opportunities.

The rest of the book will elaborate on the many considerations involved in formulating and implementing marketing strategy and subsequent marketing plans, as well as managing the elements of the marketing mix.

## SUMMARY

Long-term organizational success is never accidental. It results from managers being committed to providing benefits that customers need and want or being market-oriented. Long-term success also implies that managers understand the environment in which the organization operates and are adapting to that environment. Corporate strategy is the overall purpose and direction of the organization that is established in the light of the challenges and opportunities found in the environment, as well as available organizational resources.

Corporate strategy gives input to marketing strategy. Setting marketing strategy begins with a situation analysis, which consists of analyzing internal, environmental, customer, and competitive issues. Marketing objectives can include profitability objectives, market share, or volume objectives. Most companies pursue growth strategies, which can include penetration, market development, product development, and diversification.

The strategic marketing planning process thus unfolds in four main steps. (1) Undertake a situation analysis. (2) Establish marketing objectives and strategy. (3) Develop a marketing plan—a specific detailed statement of how the marketing mix will be used to realize the marketing strategy. (4) Develop a system to implement and control the plan.

The four main elements of the marketing plan are product or service, price, distribution, and communication plans. Together, these elements are known as the marketing mix.

The responsibility of developing and implementing the marketing plan falls on the marketing manager. Based on the strategy, objectives, and resources of the firm, the manager and his or her team establishes marketing strategy and then develops a competitive marketing plan.

## KEY TERMS

BCG growth-share matrix, p. 94
communication, p. 106
corporate strategy, p. 90
distribution, p. 106
GE business screen, p. 95
implementation and control, p. 92
marketing channels, p. 106
marketing mix, p. 111
marketing objectives and strategy, p. 92

marketing plan, p. 92
marketing strategy, p. 91
positioning analysis, p. 97
pricing, p. 106
product management, p. 106
product portfolio, p. 94
situation analysis, p. 92
SWOT analysis, p. 96

## INTERACTIVE SUMMARY AND DISCUSSION QUESTIONS

1. Corporate strategy is the overall purpose and direction of the organization that is established in the light of the challenges and opportunities found in the environment, as well as available organizational resources. Using a small firm that you are familiar with as an example, write a hypothetical statement of strategy for the organization using the above definition. Make your statement as comprehensive as possible.

2. Marketing strategy is based on the strategy set for the company as a whole, and focuses on developing a unique long-run competitive position in the market by assessing consumer needs and the firm's potential for gaining competitive advantage. Explain, using an example, the relation between corporate strategy and marketing strategy.

3. The marketing plan is a program of activities that lead to the accomplishment of the marketing strategy. Using the text discussion as a base, explain how the manager can make sure that the plan includes the appropriate elements for the conditions facing the enterprise.

4. A marketing plan must take into consideration six major factors: increasing competition, dynamic consumer society, hi-tech environment, social consciousness, planning process requirements, and operational organizational requirements. Using the following organizations as examples, specify key elements that a marketing plan should include under each of the above headings:
   a. Canadian Tire store
   b. exporter of apples to Japan

5. Marketing plans consist of four main elements: product or service, pricing, distribution, and communication. Describe the marketing mix for the following:
   a. Canadian Tire store
   b. Clearly Canadian mineral water
   c. Royal Bank mortgage service
   d. Tide detergent

6. "The 'mix' concept is very important in marketing." Discuss.

7. In marketing planning, it is helpful to think of a broader list of subelements of the marketing mix. Explain.

8. Illustrate why it is important for the marketing planner to base the plan on a competitive analysis as well as on a consumer analysis.

9. Figure 5.10 illustrates some aspects of the role of the marketing manager in the process of developing a marketing plan. Translate this into an example based on the job of the marketing manager of a city transit system.

10. Visit the Web sites for Tide and Cheer, both Procter & Gamble brands. How are the marketing strategies for the brands similar? How are they different? Who are the brands targeting? What competitive advantage do the products seem to be emphasizing?

www.tide.com

www.cheer.com

# Case

## PerfectBook

Jeff Marsh of St. Louis, a former car engineer, has developed a machine that draws on the same high-tech source as e-books, but harnesses it to a fancy, industrial-strength photocopier.

To demonstrate, Marsh placed an order on the Internet for the first print-on-demand book in history. Twelve minutes later *Mistress Ruby Ties It Together*, a sado-masochist novel made available by its publisher, Random House, slid down the chute of Marsh's PerfectBook machine. With economies of scale, Marsh figures his system, which is about the size of an industrial photocopier, could sell for as little as $30 000, making it affordable to everything from bookstores and photocopy shops to convenience stores and gas stations. The technology is simple: electronic files of books would be stored on publishers' Internet sites. Once paid for and downloaded, the PerfectBook laser-prints the cover and double-sided pages, glue-binds the two parts, and trims and finishes them to paperback size. The cost of digital printing would mean the books would be priced about the same as a retail paperback, but Marsh figures convenience will be its selling point: retail outlets, particularly bookstores, would no longer have to devote so much of their capital to inventory.

Marsh feels that the machine's potential is large. The beleaguered book industry in North America is awash in waste, with retailers returning as much as 50 percent of their unsold inventory for full credit, costing publishers billions. The industry produces about 50 000 new titles each year, and without a precise metric for calculating demand, publishers must guess how many of each to print. Sometimes they guess wrong.

With something like Marsh's machine sitting in copy shops and bookstores across the land, customers could order a book over the Internet and pick it up within minutes. The need for overstock would be eliminated, the cost of shipping and warehousing drastically reduced. It is estimated that the price of a trade paperback could drop by 20 percent. The most esoteric taste could, in theory, be satisfied anywhere and anytime: Running to catch the 6 a.m. flight to Calgary, you could stop at an airport kiosk and buy a title as obscure as Thomas Merton's *The New Man* just as easily as you now pick up a copy of Stephen King's *Dreamcatcher*.

Marsh, it seems, has devised a way to realize most of the advantages of digitized book catalogues, while neatly avoiding many of the problems—real and imagined—of electronic publishing. Piracy, for example, goes away almost magically, since the network is closed and files are designated for printing, not for viewing on a handheld device or PC. That realness also dispatches the other nagging worry about e-books—the inconvenient fact that, so far, no one really enjoys reading from a screen.

The average hardcover book is priced from about $24.95 to $39.95. Here's a breakdown of some rough costs associated with a typical $29.95 hardcover (around 256 to 288 pages) with a print run of 10 000 copies. Amount to writer: $2.99. To retailer: $13.48. To various suppliers, such as the printer, the designer, etc.: $5.40 (figures include $1500 for a four-colour jacket design, another $1500 for a no-frills interior design). To marketing: $1.00 or less. (The formula hovers around $1.00 per book.) To publisher's overhead: $5.78. To bottom line: $1.30.

### The Canadian Market

In 2000, the most recent year for which numbers are available, publishers and bookstores in Canada had about 50 000 books on offer. Of that total, 6175 were new trade books (those sold in retail stores) and 1690 children's books (a separate category), plus 4017 reprinted books (those which had sold out their first print runs), of which there were 2745 trade and 1272 children's books. Joining them were about 38 000 of what are known as backlist books. In all, buyers spent approximately $1 billion in 2000 choosing from among 41 078 trade books and 9933 children's books.

### Buyers

Nearly seven out of ten adult Canadians are "book buyers" (people who purchase one or more books every six months). The market is divided in three. Infrequent buyers (40%) do the statistically possible but retail impossible: purchase less than one book per month—usually nonfiction in trade paperback. Frequent buyers (30 percent) purchase 70 percent of all books sold, picking up two or more books per month, usually fiction in mass-market paperback (Danielle Steel is a favourite). Occasional buyers (30 percent) purchase one to two books per month, primarily hardcover and children's books. Book buyers are most likely to be women aged 25 to 39, earning $60 000 or more per household and living in cities. Those who rarely buy books are most likely to be rural men over 60, earning less than $20 000.

This dream requires at least one thing that Marsh cannot supply: a vast digital catalogue of titles. Though virtually every book published since the late 1980s was typeset by computer and presumably exists in digital file format, the vast majority of books ever published were not and do not. While some publishers have begun to digitize their back catalogues, it's a forbiddingly expensive enterprise, and the industry's enthusiasm is tempered by rights questions, as well as other clouds hanging on the e-book horizon. And the publishing industry has never been known for a readiness to innovate. Furthermore, the traditional time-honoured models by which publishers make money are in trouble, so it's difficult to free up capital for investment in this kind of digital content.

The PerfectBook Web site (http://www.marshtechinc.com/) includes the following questions and answers:

**Q:** How many technicians does it take to make books using the PerfectBook system?

**A:** One!

**Q:** What is the skill level required to operate the system?

**A:** See photo!

## You Be the Marketer

1. What are the strengths, weaknesses, and opportunities for PerfectBook?
2. Develop a marketing plan for the PerfectBook Machine.

**Zack Sheets, age 12, just ran a 250 book run for the United Nations**

Source: http://www.marshtechinc.com/q&a.htm

Source: Adapted from David Hayes, "Book Markers: In the Beginning, Gutenberg Printed the Bible," National Post Business, August, 2002; John McCloskey, "The PerfectBook Machine," *Business2*, July 2001 Issue, http://www.business2.com/articles/mag/0,14849,FF.html; and Marsh Technologies Web site, www.marshtechinc.com/ q&a.htm.

Paying careful attention to the customer has resulted in a solid market position for Hard Rock.

## Chapter 6

# ENSURING TOTAL CUSTOMER SATISFACTION AND MANAGING CUSTOMER RELATIONSHIPS

## CHAPTER OBJECTIVES

After reading and studying this chapter, you should be able to

1. Explain the importance of striving for total customer satisfaction in marketing planning and implementation.
2. Explain the concept of value and the importance of creating value for customers.
3. Illustrate the concept of Lifetime-Customer Value.
4. Outline and explain the value-adding chain.
5. Explain the concept of benchmarking and its application in producing customer satisfaction and company competitiveness.
6. Explain the important features of customer relationship marketing and how it is applied.
7. Explain the concept of performance gap analysis.
8. Outline the steps involved in a marketing effectiveness audit.

**W**ith more than 100 cafés in 36 countries and over 28 million guests each year, Hard Rock Café offers high-quality North American fare and great service in rock 'n' roll-theme restaurants. Since its founding in 1971, Hard Rock has built an impressive following while other members of the theme-dining space have faltered. Not content to simply amass a large following, however, Hard Rock set out to better understand and interact with its dedicated customer base.

Hard Rock knew that it had a loyal customer base, but it lacked the means to collect and analyze the data needed to fully understand its customers. How did the firm really relate to dedicated customers worldwide? "We didn't know about the different types of customers we had, nor did we fully grasp their preferences and tastes," says Kelly Maddern, the Director of Loyalty and Customer Relationship Marketing (CRM) at Hard Rock.

Hard Rock also needed to streamline its customer-service efforts. "In the past, we didn't really have a central way for customers to reach us," says Maddern. "We had a series of administrative assistants within our corporate headquarters trying to process an average of 3000 e-mails per week. Issuing a response could take anywhere from a week to ten days—we knew we could be more efficient in responding to our customers."

The company decided that the solution was to find, and adopt, a Customer Relationship analysis system that would enable them to analyze their database of customer information. In this way they would deepen their understanding of their customers and be able to serve them better.

Hard Rock reviewed a full selection of CRM software vendors before choosing a system called "E.piphany." Hard Rock found the system fast and easy to deploy. With E.piphany in place as the foundation of its CRM efforts, Hard Rock has gained a single view of the customer, launched a loyalty program, personalized its marketing campaigns, and dramatically improved the efficiency of its customer service.

Hard Rock is excited about the possibility of further extending its CRM capabilities and strengthening its loyalty program. "E.piphany is helping us transform into a really dynamic one-to-one marketing company," says Maddern. "The program permits us to engage a dialogue with our customers and provide offers that are relevant to what they want. The more we know about our customers, the more we're able to show them what Hard Rock has to offer."

**This example is only one illustration of the growing importance leading firms place on providing total customer satisfaction. Other companies ignore this trend at their peril.**

Source: Excerpted from http://www.epiphany.com/customers/detail_hardrock.html, May 21, 2002. Reprinted with permission.

www.hardrockcafe.ca

# INTRODUCTION

This book is about finding and serving customers profitably. In discussing the issue, we have developed an understanding of the many elements involved in the marketing planning process. As shown in the previous chapter, the final aspect of the marketing planning process is *control*—determining whether the objective of achieving consumer satisfaction has been met and marketing plans realized. Achieving these goals leads to accomplishing the objective of obtaining competitive advantage and profits for the firm.

**total customer satisfaction**

Providing a good or service that fully and without reservation conforms to the customer's requirements.

The criterion for assessing success in this area should be more than satisfaction—it must be *total* customer satisfaction. **Total customer satisfaction** means that a good or service fully and without reservation conforms to the customer's requirements. For example, when asked by a waiter, "How was your meal?" how many times have you said, "Fine," even though you were not really satisfied? Our objective must be to create "raving fans" if we are to assume a position of leadership and profitability in the market in which we have chosen to compete. Only by systematically reviewing the outcome of the process can improvements be made in the marketing plan. Note that this approach recognizes that goods and services must be designed for specific target markets. It is difficult, if not impossible, to meet everyone's needs.

Consider the following scenario:

"How is your company performing?" William Brand asked. "Sales and profits are up," the president replied. "In fact, our financial people tell me this year we will have one of our best 'bottom lines' ever!"

Mr. Brand was reviewing with the president the recent accomplishment of a manufacturer of computer components as they prepared to set the stage for planning the company's strategy for next year.

"Today's financial results measure the outcomes of strategic initiatives taken in the past. Are you monitoring the critical factors that will create success in the future?" Brand challenged.

"What do you mean? Aren't strong financial controls the proper measuring tools to monitor business performance?" the president said, somewhat taken aback.

Financial measures, used alone, are like driving a car while watching the rear-view mirror. They tell a company where it has been. A manager also needs a forward-looking view toward building success in the areas that lead to a long-run competitive advantage. The key success factors include product quality, after-sale service, corporate flexibility, and employee innovativeness.[1]

In a study of the marketing planning practices of the top 500 Canadian firms, this author found that only 57.8 percent of firms developed a written marketing plan. Furthermore, only 25.4 percent included a post-mortem of the past year's results in their current marketing plan. How could such performance lead to total customer satisfaction?

Marketers need to concentrate on relevant measures that bear on whether or not customer satisfaction has been achieved. What is customer satisfaction, really? Here are some answers given by managers:[2]

■ "You have to start with the definition of customer satisfaction and quality from the customer perspective. Do the diagnostic work. What are the key factors that drive the customer on the good or service?"

■ "The customer doesn't care about your system. The customer cares about satisfaction; having problems handled."

■ "The customer doesn't care how you track his order. What the customer thinks is, 'I need the answer as to what the status of my shipment is, within the hour.' They don't care about how you execute, only that you do. They care about the *results*."

There is a common thread in the above responses: customer satisfaction comes down to the ability to better serve your customers. As the managers' comments imply, organizations have to get beyond the lip service paid to satisfaction. One way they are doing this is by going into the marketplace and measuring satisfaction regularly.

While most companies try to differentiate themselves by providing a succession of new product features, Hewlett-Packard is a company that has chosen not to rely solely on product features to create differentiation. Its European division decided to use customer satisfaction as an additional explicit method of differentiation. Its stated goal is to keep customers forever, and the company has created a new position called "customer satisfaction executive" to help ensure that it achieves this goal.

H-P has also established a customer satisfaction program. The three components of the program are customer feedback input, customer satisfaction surveys, and total quality control. The company carefully monitors and documents customers' complaints as well as compliments. H-P has recognized that it should not always focus on the negative comments but explicitly consider the positive feedback that is received as well. The company administers worldwide "relationship" surveys every eighteen months. These focus on asking how satisfied the customer is with the company as a whole, and how H-P rates against its competition. As well, some product questions are asked. By collecting this information on a regular basis, the company can evaluate whether it is making progress in its goal of providing customer satisfaction from year to year. The third aspect of the customer satisfaction program is a program of total quality control in production and service. With such a comprehensive program, it is not surprising that the worldwide relationship surveys show a steady improvement in customer satisfaction.[3]

Many companies are still behind in the trend toward making customer service number one. They haven't quite realized that customer service is a critically important marketing tool.

Customer satisfaction must be defined from an external, customer-based viewpoint. Marketing executives must lead their organizations to a better understanding of customer satisfaction that is defined in customer terms. Products may be perfectly manufactured, but they will fail if they do not meet market requirements.

For example, when informed consumers see ads proclaiming high-quality service provided by an airline, they are likely to think, "Why waste the money on hype when I can't get through on the phone to make an inquiry?" Furthermore, staff who see the ads will say, "Why put all that money into marketing and nothing into providing us with the means of improving the quality of customer treatment?"

Reassuring the public that the company cares and provides high-quality service is a sound way to build a customer base and profitability, but only if such claims are undeniably true. Total customer satisfaction must be a constant byword of managing every facet of the marketing program. Total customer satisfaction means that a good or service totally conforms to the customer's requirements. This, of course, cannot be done without an active program of monitoring customer satisfaction.

# LIFETIME-CUSTOMER VALUE (LCV)

Total customer satisfaction is more than just an intangible concept. There are very sound, quantifiable business reasons that affirm the benefit of providing total customer satisfaction. Reorganizing the company around the customer has become a competitive mandate, not an option. Total customer satisfaction leads to customer loyalty and a focus on existing customer loyalty can generate spectacular gains.

## The Value of Customers

InfoQuest Customer Relationship marketing undertook a detailed study of 20 000 of its customer surveys from around the world in order to understand the true value of a customer. The results of the study were as follows:[4]

- A Totally Satisfied Customer contributes 2.6 times as much revenue to a company as a Somewhat Satisfied Customer.
- A Totally Satisfied Customer contributes 14 times as much revenue as a Somewhat Dissatisfied Customer.

When you begin with a dream you believe in, there's no telling where you'll end up. Good luck to all of our athletes at the XVII Commonwealth Games.

- A Totally Dissatisfied Customer actually decreases revenue at a rate equal to 1.8 times what a Totally Satisfied Customer contributes to a business.

This last finding is particularly worrying since it means that even with twice as many totally satisfied as completely dissatisfied customers, the business would be doing little better than standing still.

## Increased Sales

Some firms operate their business from the perspective of treating each customer transaction as a single event that has little or no connection with future transactions. They pay limited attention to the long-term relationship a firm has with its customers, or at least they do not explicitly recognize the long-term *value* of this relationship. This is a dangerous strategy in today's age. The advent of the Internet and the availability of technology has reduced time and distance to almost zero. Thus customers are much more aware, and their expectations have increased accordingly. Consequently, the balance of power in the buyer–seller relationship is shifting to the buyer.

Another way of thinking about customers is to recognize that a relationship developed with a customer can provide long-term value to the firm as well as the customer. With every additional interchange between company and customer, trust in the company and its product grows. Thus, it takes progressively fewer resources to make additional sales. Customers put the company high on their list. The benefit to the firm is called the **lifetime-customer value (LCV)**. Lifetime-customer value is the sum of all future-customer revenue streams minus product and servicing costs, acquisition costs, and remarketing costs. The sum of the value of a firm's customers and prospects (total LCV) is *customer equity*. Customer equity measures the total-asset value of a company's customers.

Let's use a more simplified example to illustrate. An average driver buys ten cars in a lifetime. If you sell a young woman her first car and if you make an average profit of $2000 on each car sold, the LCV of that customer is potentially $20 000. Furthermore, assume that a loyal customer will recommend your business to five others. The combined LCV now could be 5 times $20 000 = $100 000. Conversely, when you lose a customer due to poor service you lose a lot more than his/her next transaction. Thus, whatever you sell you should appreciate that looking after your existing customers is

**lifetime-customer value (LCV)**

The sum of all future-customer revenue streams minus product and servicing costs, acquisition costs, and remarketing costs.

at least as important as looking for new ones. Customer loyalty is being recognized as a path to long-term profitability.

It is expensive to acquire new customers. The costs include advertising, selling, setting up new accounts, and the customer learning process. There is also a cost of retention. The cost of retention is lower than the cost of acquiring new customers. These costs include ongoing service and communication, which often decrease over time. The lifetime value of retained customers increases with the years of retention. The concept of Lifetime-Customer Value Development is shown in Figure 6.1.

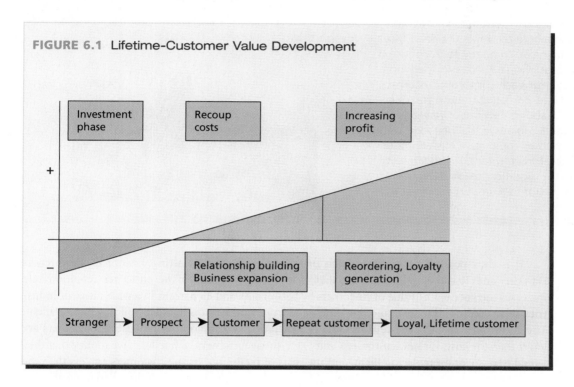

**FIGURE 6.1** Lifetime-Customer Value Development

Saturn's customer-oriented philosophy was aptly demonstrated in this popular television commercial. In the commercial, a young woman purchases her first car—a Saturn. When she loses her job, she must return the car. At the end of the commercial she has a new job and returns to buy another Saturn.

## USING A DATABASE TO CALCULATE LIFETIME-CUSTOMER VALUE

By comparing the difference in the aggregate lifetime value of customers from year to year, companies have a better measure of performance than simply comparing gross sales revenues. An example of this is the Shell Fleet Card. Shell was the first major oil company to introduce a vehicle fleet card for corporations. The card provided more detailed billing information for each corporate customer.

For Shell, it provided the perfect database for calculating lifetime value, by tracking retention year-to-year and litres of fuel purchased. However, if Shell had only looked at total cards in use, they could have missed important information about customer retention and loyalty. They could have missed the significance of defection in cardholders over time. Defections mean that customer sat-

isfaction is low. This also means lost revenue and higher costs for acquiring new customers. With the database, Shell was able to use a customer retention program to reverse this.

It is thus possible to increase profit primarily by retaining existing customers. Researchers Dawkins and Reichheld[5] have shown that a 5 percent increase in the customer retention rate increases the net present value of customers by between 25 and 85 percent in a wide range of industries, from credit card to insurance brokerage and from auto services to office building management. The reasons are that (1) the relative costs of generating cash inflows from existing customers are lower than the costs for new customers, and (2) as these customers stay, sellers save money that they would have spent on replacing them, and the costs of retaining existing customers are less than the costs of generating new ones.[6] Furthermore, loyal customers can positively influence new customers.

Focusing on LCV can change the marketing strategy of a company. As can be seen in Figure 6.2, the marketing management function is divided into two primary activities: customer management

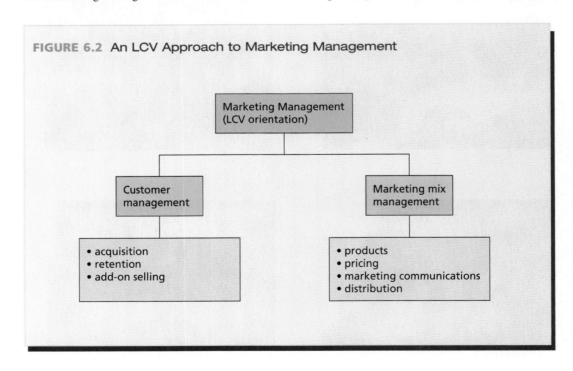

FIGURE 6.2  An LCV Approach to Marketing Management

and marketing mix management. Customer management concentrates on determining how to acquire customers, retain them, and sell them additional products and services (add-on selling). Marketing mix management focuses on products, pricing, marketing communications, and distribution.[7] There is a strong link between the two, but it helps to analyze these functions separately. Companies with such an orientation work very hard to provide total customer satisfaction and build relationships to maximize the lifetime value of each customer.

Focusing on LCV concentrates an organization on managing customers as critical assets of the firm. Customers are no longer transactions but relationships. It is important to develop a good database to achieve these results (a later section will discuss this further). Furthermore, financial measures such as quarterly sales and profits should be enhanced by other measures, such as retention levels, add-on selling, cost of customer acquisition versus long-term lifetime value, and changes in total LCV. For example, Sears believes the cost of making the first sale to a new customer is twenty times greater than a sale to a regular customer. Office Depot estimates the lifetime value of a customer at $10 000.

Figure 6.3 provides a perspective of the importance of concentrating on customer satisfaction. Customer satisfaction leads to increasing levels of trust in the organization. The stock of trust that is built in turn enhances the image of the company in the customer's view, and results in company and brand loyalty. This positive image and company loyalty are related to company reputation, and the customer may develop a strong relationship with the company. All of this leads to increased profits and market share.

www.sears.com

www.officedepot.com

## The Value Vision

Most managers have been taught to manage *activity* rather than *value*. Strategic plans for production, sales, and administration of business units are often focused on short-term gross volume improvements rather than on long-term value-building. These plans reward on the basis of quantity rather than value added, which skews performance toward activity and short-term gain.[8]

The vision of an organization should be to add value for customers and employees. Without a clear understanding of value, all marketing activity is in danger of falling into the activity trap. *Activity is the process by which value is created.* Value should be the heart of organizational purpose.

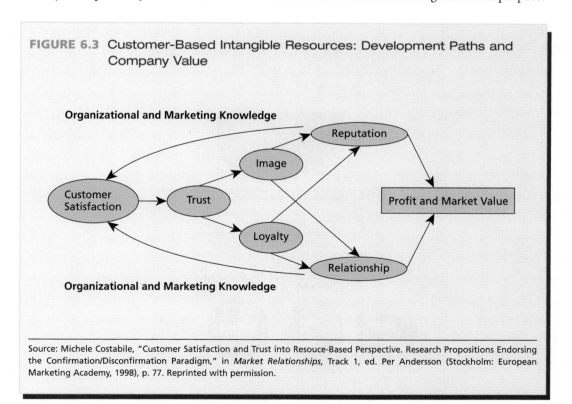

**FIGURE 6.3  Customer-Based Intangible Resources: Development Paths and Company Value**

Source: Michele Costabile, "Customer Satisfaction and Trust into Resouce-Based Perspective. Research Propositions Endorsing the Confirmation/Disconfirmation Paradigm," in *Market Relationships*, Track 1, ed. Per Andersson (Stockholm: European Marketing Academy, 1998), p. 77. Reprinted with permission.

**value**

A subjective term that is defined by the customer; part of customer expectations, which are a combination of cost, time, quantity, quality, and human factors.

www.pepsiworld.com

What is value? **Value** is a subjective term, and is defined by the customer. Each customer defines it somewhat differently. It is too simplistic to say that value is synonymous with customer satisfaction. Value is part of customer expectations. These are often complex and sometimes hidden, and they change. Expectations are a combination of cost, time, quantity, quality, and human factors.

Pepsi-Cola is an example of a company that diligently seeks out customer values. It surveyed 10 000 customers to develop sixteen priorities for its total quality effort. For example, it found that customers wanted improved deliveries. Two years later, it followed up with a survey of 2000 customers to see how it was doing.

Johnson & Johnson's McNeil Consumer Products subsidiary, which manufacturers the Tylenol product line, found that it had become too inwardly focused. It set up a special booth in its plant for workers who previously had had no opportunity to interact with customers. In this booth, they can now hear queries and complaints from the outside world that come in on an 800 line.[9]

Intel's continuous technological development creates value for different types of customers.

If a company wants to build value, it has to recognize that value starts with the customer. However, there is a problem with simply asking customers what they want: they often cannot define their wants clearly. There are two main reasons for this. First, when technology is involved, laypeople are unqualified to judge a product and to specify what they want. Second, customers are focused on their problem, not on the supplier's good or service. The supplier is only a means to helping customers reach their goals.

In spite of this, the marketer must find out which values to offer. Some key questions to ask customers: "What are you trying to achieve?" "What other forces are at work on you?" "What are your problems and opportunities?" "Who is pressuring you?"

## Market Challenges

In this context, three significant market challenges[10] highlight the importance of concentrating on providing value: (1) escalating customer expectations, (2) competitive forces, and (3) cost pressures.

### Escalating Customer Expectations

Customers expect firms to deliver better value, satisfy fragmenting markets, achieve closer relationships with them, and respond faster to their needs.

#### BETTER VALUE

The global marketplace provides many options, so providing better value as perceived by the customer is essential. For example, because of competition from Japan and Europe, North American car companies have been forced to produce better engineered and more customer-friendly cars. The competition to provide more customer value is intense.

#### SATISFY FRAGMENTING MARKETS

With a growing number of products, customers expect to find products that serve their particular tastes and needs more precisely. Thus businesses need to be more in tune with market needs in order to identify and serve appropriate market segments.

---

## THE PRACTISING MARKETER

**CREATING AN ENVIRONMENT CUSTOMERS WANT TO RETURN TO**

Every business believes the one element that sets it apart from the competition is great customer service. But very few companies deliver this level of quality.

The objective is to create an environment where customers want to return and buy again. A consumer will tell at least ten people about a bad service experience, but the same person will only tell three people about a great one.

It takes continuous vigilance to ensure your business provides a positive experience time after time. Here is part of a process you can use to determine whether you have great customer service.

1. Start by surveying your existing customers to determine why they are buying from your company.
2. Set up a continuing process of measuring the perceived service your business provides to customers.

3. Understand the service level expectation in your industry and make sure your company exceeds it.
4. Make sure that customer service permeates the organization.
5. Recognize that employee attitudes are the best indicator of how your business views its customers.
6. Sit down with key customers to discuss their plans over the next few years.
7. Recognize that when you treat a customer badly, it is an opportunity to shine.

**Explain the logic behind each of these steps.**

Source: Adapted from Larry Ginsberg, "Customer Service Requires Vigilance," *The Globe and Mail* (July 20, 1998), p. B11. This article also appears in *Mind Your Own Business: Ginsberg's Guide to Entrepreneurial Success*, published by CCH. Reprinted with permission.

---

## ACHIEVE CLOSER RELATIONSHIPS WITH CUSTOMERS

As firms tune in to customer needs more precisely, they can establish closer links with individual customers by using sophisticated databases. This is known as relationship marketing, and will be dealt with in more detail later in this chapter.

## RESPOND FASTER

Competition and technological developments have also led to rising expectations for rapid responses to consumer needs.

## Competitive Forces and Cost Pressures

Competition leads to pressures to lower prices or to increase value. Much of the easy cost cutting has already been achieved; nevertheless, firms are pushed to continue to seek economies. There is a continuing urgency to do more. This leads to employee layoffs and such activities as requiring customers to provide more input into the transaction, such as self-serve banking and expecting them to endure automated telephone answering systems. Responding to cost pressures while increasing customer satisfaction is a significant challenge.

## The Value-Adding Chain

Building value is a function of a five-link chain, as shown in Figure 6.4. This chain links the corporate vision and its human and material assets to the customer's requirements. Any weak link in the value-adding chain breaks the bond between the business and the customer.

The *culture* of the organization must be right. Cultural factors spur people to design systems that fit the culture. When a corporation's vision and culture are out of sync, a fatal flaw is exposed and the organization experiences problems. For example, when Jan Carlzon took over the Linjeflyg airline in Sweden (before it was merged into Scandinavian Airlines System in 1993), he started by calling all employees into an empty airplane hangar and asking them for their ideas and help in resurrecting the airline. The result was that Linjeflyg changed from offering high-priced travel that only businesses could afford to offering real travel value to a great number of other customers by dra-

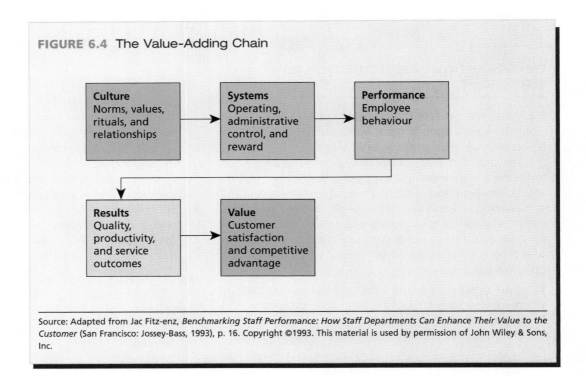

FIGURE 6.4 The Value-Adding Chain

Source: Adapted from Jac Fitz-enz, *Benchmarking Staff Performance: How Staff Departments Can Enhance Their Value to the Customer* (San Francisco: Jossey-Bass, 1993), p. 16. Copyright ©1993. This material is used by permission of John Wiley & Sons, Inc.

matically lowering prices. This vision brought about a great change in the culture of the organization. Within two years, the company was profitable.

*Systems* form the second link in the value-adding chain. They direct employee and management behaviour in the desired direction. Systems are inherently powerful—like a river, they flow along taking everything in their path in one direction. However, like rivers, some systems are lazy, winding, uncertain, and slow. Other rivers are more direct, deep, and strong. When these are flowing in the right direction, they establish a force of tremendously effective power in the marketplace.

The integration of culture and systems affects *performance,* or employee behaviour. This performance produces operating *results,* such as quality, productivity, and service outcomes. The final link, *value,* achieves customer satisfaction and competitive advantage. Every link in the chain should be observed for its impact on customer value.

## Quality or Value?

*Quality* is an overworked management term that is used to describe too many things. Quality is just one type of outcome from operations. The other two are productivity and service. Organizations do not survive and prosper because they provide quality. Collectively, quality, productivity, and service should comprise value. Table 6.1 illustrates that customers assess value leaders by considering operational excellence, performance superiority, and customer responsiveness.

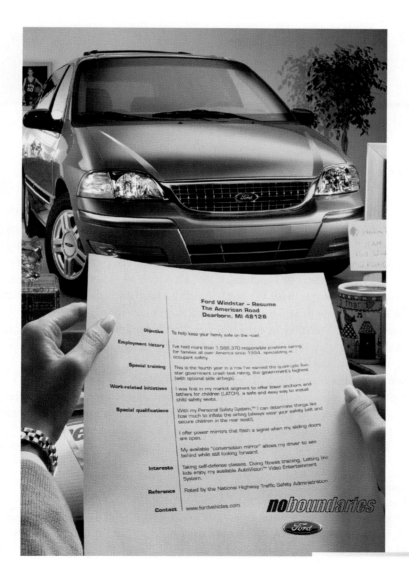

Ford Windstar: the end of a value-adding chain.

## TABLE 6.1 Customer's Views of Value Leaders

**Operational Excellence**

"They provide a great deal"
- excellent/attractive price
- minimum acquisition cost and hassle
- lowest overall cost of ownership

"A no-hassles firm"
- convenient
- consistent quality

**Performance Superiority**

"They're the most innovative"
"Constantly renewing and creative"
"Always at the leading edge"

**Customer Responsiveness**

"Exactly what I need"
- customized products
- personalized communication

"They're very responsive"
- handling of exceptions
- inducing/building relationships

Source: George Day, adapted from "CSC Index" presentation at ASAC Conference, Lake Louise, May 1993. Reprinted with permission.

# BENCHMARKING

The core issue of the marketing plan is how to add value. One way of achieving this is through benchmarking. The computer industry has used the term *benchmarking* for many years to compare the characteristics of computers. A standard software program is run on each computer being tested, and various aspects of their performance are measured. The best performance on each characteristic becomes the standard, or benchmark, against which all others are compared.

The concept of *comparison with the best* is much better than merely setting objectives. It is of little value for one company to set an objective for its computer to increase the number of calculations per second from 500 to 700 when the benchmark rate for another computer is 1100. The only way to be competitive is to meet or beat the benchmark. The Japanese have a word for this concept—*dantotsu*—striving to be "the best of the best."

**benchmarking**

The comparison of performance with industry best practices.

**Benchmarking** is the comparison of performance with industry best practices. It is now applied to organizational performance, such as marketing programs. The advantages of using benchmarking are that managers are forced to seek out the best practices in the external environment, and must strive to incorporate these best practices in company marketing planning.

There are four fundamental requirements for using benchmarking as a tool to provide value to customers:[11]

1. *Know your operation.* It is fundamental for a company to develop a good understanding of the strength and weaknesses of its internal operation.
2. *Know the industry leaders and competitors.* Only a comparison with the best practices of leaders and competitors will provide the correct benchmarks to strive for. In addition, knowing their key strengths and weaknesses will lead to good decisions for differentiating products.

3. *Incorporate the best.* As a company finds out the strengths in others, it should not hesitate to learn from them, and copy, modify, or incorporate these strengths into its own operation.

4. *Develop superiority.* As the company's marketing planning and implementation respond by meeting and improving upon the benchmarks set by others, it will be on the right track for providing total customer satisfaction in marketing. Being the best of the best in dimensions that consumers value brings an organization closest to the goal of providing total customer satisfaction.

## The Benchmarking Process

Benchmarking comprises five stages: planning, analysis, integration, actions, and maturity. Within these stages there are ten distinct steps.

### Planning

The process starts with *identifying what is to be benchmarked.* For example, if consumers value competent, friendly service, this should be measured. Other examples might be excellent after-sale service, clear and interesting advertising, or high-quality products.

*Identifying leading companies and competitors* is the next step. These are the companies that are now doing the best job on these characteristics. Careful attention should be paid to international competitors, as the leaders need to set the standard no matter where they are found. Note that some companies might be better on some benchmark characteristics than others. Therefore, the comparison could be with more than one firm.

*Collecting data* includes using sound marketing research methodology and the many marketing research techniques. At this stage, it is important to derive quantifiable goals as well as to search out and document the best industry practices.

### Analysis

The next step is *determining the current performance gap.* The **performance gap** is the difference between the company's performance and that of the best of the best. This gap can be positive, negative, or nonexistent. Is the benchmarking partner better? Why is it better? By how much? How can its practices be incorporated or adapted for implementation? See Figure 6.5.

Step 5 of the benchmarking process is *projecting future performance levels.* It is also important to project whether current performance, for the benchmark partner as well, is improving or not. Such projections might show that the gap is narrowing or that the gap will be even wider in the competitor's favour in two to five years.

**performance gap**
The difference between the company's performance and that of the best of the best.

### Integration

Once the findings are established, it is critical to *communicate the benchmark findings and gain acceptance from the rest of the organization.* The organization must have faith in the methodology, and understand and accept the findings, if change is to occur.

Following this, *functional goals must be established.* This is a critical part of the process, as it involves converting benchmark findings into a statement of operational principles. To make the necessary changes, the organization must subscribe to these principles. They will be the criteria upon which the organization will focus in order to provide the value that will lead to customer satisfaction.

### Action

Implementing these principles involves *developing action plans, implementing specific actions and monitoring progress,* and *recalibrating benchmarks.* Recalibration is necessary over time, as the external environment is constantly changing.

### Maturity

Maturity is reached when the plans have been implemented, and a position of leadership has occurred in each of the benchmarked conditions.

This is the necessary process that will lead to total customer satisfaction. The benchmarking process steps are shown in Table 6.2.

A graphic way of showing how a benchmarking exercise can help a company find where it is positioned is shown in the performance gap chart in Figure 6.5. This shows that the company's historic performance in providing marketing information in comparison with a benchmark competitor is poor, and is likely to get worse if it doesn't adjust.

A similar analysis can be done for each of the salient characteristics that contribute to total value, as perceived by the customer. For example, Pepsi-Cola could undertake such an analysis for each of its sixteen priorities.

## Taking Total Customer Satisfaction from Slogan to Substance

www.pillsbury.com

It is important to do more than talk about providing total satisfaction for customers. Companies must also develop methods to measure whether those goals are being met. Pillsbury is one company that has made a commitment to measuring how well it is serving customer needs. "For Pillsbury, it's been a revolution. In the past, we only measured performance on cost, but we have found it's no longer adequate. The problem is that if you don't measure it, you can't improve it," said one executive.[12]

To take total customer satisfaction from slogan to substance, management should follow these guidelines:

1. Identify customer segments and the characteristics that they consider most important for the good or service.
2. Identify specific requirements for each target market.
3. Develop an information system that includes a database of customers, including past purchase behaviour and other relevant data for individual communication and interaction.

---

**TABLE 6.2  The Benchmarking Process**

**Planning**
  1. Identify what is to be benchmarked.
  2. Identify comparative companies.
  3. Determine data collection method and collect data.

**Analysis**
  4. Determine current "performance gap."
  5. Project future performance levels.

**Integration**
  6. Communicate benchmark findings and gain acceptance.
  7. Establish functional goals.

**Action**
  8. Develop action plans.
  9. Implement specific actions and monitor progress.
  10. Recalibrate benchmarks.

**Maturity**
• Leadership position attained.
• Practices fully integrated into processes.

Source: Robert C. Camp, *Benchmarking: The Search for Industry Best Practices That Lead to Superior Performance* (Milwaukee, WI: ASQC Quality Press, 1989), p. 17. Reprinted with permission.

---

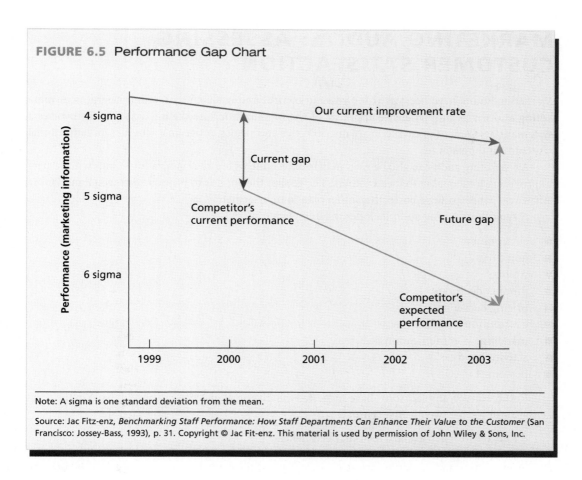

**FIGURE 6.5** Performance Gap Chart

Performance (marketing information)

4 sigma

5 sigma

6 sigma

Our current improvement rate

Current gap

Competitor's
current performance

Future gap

Competitor's
expected
performance

1999   2000   2001   2002   2003

Note: A sigma is one standard deviation from the mean.

Source: Jac Fitz-enz, *Benchmarking Staff Performance: How Staff Departments Can Enhance Their Value to the Customer* (San Francisco: Jossey-Bass, 1993), p. 31. Copyright © Jac Fit-enz. This material is used by permission of John Wiley & Sons, Inc.

4. Translate resolved customer requirements into objectives and specifications for the marketing plan.
5. Identify the steps in the implementation process.
6. Determine the capability of the process to meet the requirements.
7. Select measurements for critical process steps.
8. Implement the program—fulfill customer values relating to the good or service. This must be the overriding goal for every department in the organization. Every service must be measured against the same standard, and every employee should be working toward 100 percent satisfaction of each value attribute.
   ■ Communicate these goals and standards to all employees, whether or not they communicate with the public. The best salespeople cannot make a company popular and profitable if other aspects of the organization are inefficient or error-prone.
   ■ Train all employees in a voluntary, cooperative atmosphere. It is woefully inadequate for a vice president or chief executive officer to announce that "all employees should do their best" without universal training in what that means and how to achieve it.
   ■ Give rewards, financial and otherwise, to those employees whose involvement leads to improvements in customer satisfaction and real cost savings.
9. Evaluate the results of the process, and identify steps for improvement.

As an example, the Royal Bank of Canada has an active program of assessing customer satisfaction and loyalty whereby customer feedback is obtained through a telephone interview. In doing so, the company uses a carefully designed nine-page questionnaire. It is designed to determine:

■ Customer's experiences with the Royal Bank overall.
■ Its overall reputation as a financial institution compared to other financial institutions.
■ The type and quality of customer service received from each branch.
■ The amount and quality of financial planning and advice received.
■ Problem resolution—how well problems that arose have been resolved.

# MARKETING AUDITS: ASSESSING CUSTOMER SATISFACTION

**marketing audit**

A comprehensive appraisal of the organization's marketing activities. It involves a systematic assessment of marketing plans, objectives, strategies, programs, activities, organizational structure, and personnel.

Marketing audits have been used for years to control and evaluate marketing programs. A **marketing audit** is a comprehensive appraisal of the organization's marketing activities. It involves a systematic assessment of marketing plans, objectives, strategies, programs, activities, organizational structure, and personnel.

A marketing audit can also be used to help determine where an organization stands with respect to providing total quality to its customers. The goal of the audit is to improve the overall marketing efficiency by presenting a corrective action plan to management.

A typical marketing audit includes the following topics:

- environment
- objectives
- strategy
- product decisions
- pricing decisions
- distribution decisions
- marketing communication decisions
- activities and tasks
- personnel

Rothe, Harvey, and Jackson[13] have suggested that five areas also need to be addressed in the marketing audit for the twenty-first century:

1. the degree to which a global focus has been taken
2. support for having a marketing controller position in the organization
3. incorporating and measuring the ecological efforts of the marketing programs in the organization
4. integrating the periodic and continuous marketing control efforts to provide a seamless control mechanism
5. broadening the marketing audit concept to focus on resource management and control

We would suggest a sixth item:

6. broadening the marketing audit concept to focus on and measure total customer satisfaction, which should also include assessing the use of lifetime customer value principles.

In conclusion, the marketing audit, which has traditionally been used to assess marketing effectiveness in the management of the marketing mix, can be broadened to assess how well the firm is doing in managing consumer relationships and providing total customer satisfaction.

# CUSTOMER RELATIONSHIP MANAGEMENT: SERVING GOOD CUSTOMERS BETTER

**customer relationship marketing (CRM)**

Identifying and establishing, maintaining and enhancing, and, when necessary, also terminating relationships with customers and other stakeholders so that the objectives of all parties involved are met, through a mutual exchange and fulfillment of promises.

Chapter 1 introduced the marketing concept. An ongoing theme of successful marketing is customer orientation—seeking out customer needs and trying to fill them. This chapter takes the concept further by suggesting that the job is not done until the work of the company results in total customer satisfaction.

An important component of this is the determination to develop a long-term relationship with individual customers through generating a base of knowledge about them and tailoring goods, services, and communications to specific needs. This is known as **customer relationship marketing (CRM)**. More specifically, relationship marketing involves identifying and establishing, maintaining and enhancing, and, when necessary, terminating relationships with customers and other stakeholders so that the objectives of all parties involved are met, through a mutual exchange and fulfillment of promises. These tasks rely on relational processes such as trust, commitment, and satisfaction.[14]

In one sense, the local general store manager practised this in Grandma's day. He knew her needs and catered to them. However, as companies grew to serve customers across the country and globally, this became much more difficult. Database technology now makes possible the development of meaningful relationships with customers. It enables customer information to be stored and retrieved, and it allows more efficient communication between the company and its clientele.

It is important to differentiate between three related, but different concepts: customer satisfaction management (CSM), customer relationship marketing (CRM), and mass customization. A clear understanding of these terms will help managers select the most appropriate program for their situation.

A **customer satisfaction management (CSM)** program focuses on identifying key performance areas where the average customer's expectations must be met or exceeded. "Average customer" is significant here. Most CSM programs are based on serving the average customer in their target market. This means that *individual* customer identity is of less interest to such programs. Having this type of a focus has worked well for many companies. Firms have been able to identify improvement initiatives for various customer segments, and customers have responded positively to such approaches.

Consider the following story: A gentleman checked into a luxury hotel, ordered a glass of white wine and requested a cube of ice in it. Six months later, he checked into another property of the same lodging company, halfway across the world, called room service to order a glass of white wine and—lo and behold—was asked if he would like a cube of ice in the wine. The customer was amazed and, yes, delighted. The hotel earned the customer's loyalty for a lifetime, and he and many others have narrated the story many times over. The hotel chain was able to manage this because it had a customer relationship marketing program. If it had had a CSM program it would have known that business customers in general want comfortable beds, telephone ports for their laptop computers, and other similar, and important amenities, but not specific information about the wants of a single individual.

CRM programs also focus on earning customer goodwill by matching or exceeding customer requirements, but they go even farther. First, the focus of CRM programs is more specific. It is on *individual* customers of the firm. Rather than basing plans on "average customers," the focus might shift to a "Ms. Jan Martin who is a regular purchaser on Indigo.ca."

The second difference is that while CSM programs often measure customer perceptions and behaviour at a single point in time, CRM programs measure customer perceptions and behaviour at multiple points in time. For instance, all the transactional information of Ms. Jan Martin over the last year might be used to gauge the strength and nature of her relationship with the firm.

Before undertaking a CRM program ask the question, "Would such individual customer-level information make the firm more successful?" For example, in marketing to other businesses the size of the sale is likely to be large, and understanding the past history would be very helpful. On the other hand, in the case of cell phone subscribers or grocery shoppers, detailed information might be more than what is required.

If management believes that individual customer-level information is important, such data is easy to organize into meaningful and useful formats. Good software CRM packages are available which enable management to make productive use of the masses of data that a firm might collect on individual behaviour. The analysis of Jan Martin's last eight transactions should lead to some distinctive pattern across these transactions. For example, knowing the type of books she buys can lead the firm to offer her other books of the same type. The next marketing approach to her can be enhanced even more if past purchase data is combined with demographic data such as age, gender, and income. Such an analysis can provide management with useful information on ways to please Ms. Martin on her next encounter with the firm.

The CRM process begins by determining how your customers relate to your product. For example, what do they like and dislike about it, and how do they use it? This information can be used to improve weaknesses, and to maintain and accentuate positive features that can lead to total customer satisfaction.

**customer satisfaction management (CSM)**
A program that focuses on identifying key performance areas to meet or exceed the average customer's expectations.

The next step is to determine what your customer base really looks like. A profile of customers in the database is essential. Especially important is the identification of key customers—those who are heavy users. Knowing these profiles you can find other people like them to market to. One company found that 4 percent of its customers accounted for 45 percent of its sales. It developed a profile of this important customer base, and then developed a marketing program to reach other potential customers with the same profile. As mentioned earlier this information is obtained using database technology. Therefore, this process is sometimes referred to as **database marketing**. Examples of popular CRM systems are E.Piphany, Siebel, and Pivotal.

A good example of database marketing is the Delta Hotels CRM program. The company has 37 properties across Canada, and thus has a large customer base. From this database of customers they used **CRM software** from Pivotal Corp., to analyze its best customers—including profiles and purchase history. Delta found that it could segment its best customers into three classes: those who want to participate in a loyalty Delta program (designated as green); those who stay five or more times in a calendar year (gold); and those who stay 15 or more times in a calendar year (platinum).

Delta then developed a direct mail campaign designed to move customers from the lower loyalty segments into the next higher class. One objective was to improve lifetime-customer value (LCV). Customers in the "green" category were encouraged to stay with them three more times in a five-month period in order to be moved into the gold class. Gold members were invited to stay three

## PEOPLE WHO SPEND THEIR LIVES

# TRAVELLING ON BUSINESS

### DESERVE TO BE SENT TO THEIR ROOMS IMMEDIATELY.

The road takes so much out of you. When it feels like you practically live there, we know you'll appreciate our exclusive one-minute check-in guarantee. It's part of our Delta

**DELTA**
HOTELS

Privilege program for frequent travellers, and we know it'll take a little sting out of having to travel so much. Call 1-800-268-1133, or visit us online at deltahotels.com

Your room is ready

more times to be moved into the platinum class. Customers moving to the new category would receive all the benefits that go with that class.

The result was that Delta upgraded about 9000 customers into gold from green—an increase of 2000 more than expected.[15] Delta thus increased repeat business by using CRM tools to segment and target customers with an above-average interest in the offer. Database marketing can be a powerful tool to deliver the right message to the right customer.

Relationship marketing involves five categories of activities: (1) listening to customers, (2) customizing marketing communication, (3) performing "customer care" activities, (4) customizing products, and (5) rewarding loyal customers.[16]

With respect to *listening* to customers, the focus is on gaining information from individual existing customers. *Customizing marketing communication* implies more individualized communications. *Customer care* activities may also be communication-related. They sometimes involve messages of the "we-care-about-you" type; follow-up messages from car dealers, and Christmas and other greetings are examples. *Customizing products* has often been done in the case of offering services. Flexible manufacturing has also enabled products to be customized. For example, Levi jeans offered made-to-order jeans (since discontinued because it wasn't really what was most important to the customer.)

The fifth category of relationship marketing is *rewarding loyal customers*. Hilton Hotels developed a special "Honors Program" for key customers. The company found that the amount of business generated from these top customers accounted for about 33 percent of its revenue.[17] Loyalty programs such as frequent flier or frequent buyer programs are often used to help build databases as well as to generate repeat business.

However, it should be noted that rewards are only one aspect of relationship marketing. Some people are confused by this category and tend to think of it as the main part of relationship marketing. A solid relationship marketing program goes beyond these specific activities. Table 6.3 contrasts an earlier transactional view of marketing with a relationship perspective. Note that the objective of the relationship perspective is to satisfy existing customers by delivering superior value.

**TABLE 6.3** A Relationship View of Marketing

| TRANSACTIONAL VIEW | RELATIONSHIP VIEW |
|---|---|
| • Purpose of marketing is to make a sale | • Purpose of marketing is to create a customer |
| • Sale is a result and the measure of success | • Sale is beginning of relationship; profit is measure of success |
| • Business is defined by its products and factories | • Business is defined by its customer relationships |
| • Price is determined by competitive market forces; price is an input | • Price is determined by negotiation and joint decision making; price is an outcome |
| • Communications are aimed at aggregates of customers | • Communications are targeted and tailored to individuals |
| • Marketer is valued for its products and prices | • Marketer is valued for its present and future problem-solving capability |
| • Objective is to make the next sale and/or find the next customer | • Objective is to satisfy the customer you have by delivering superior value |

Source: Presentation by Frederick E. Webster, Jr., at Special Session on "Relationship Marketing," American Marketing Association Educators' Conference (August 1993), Boston, MA. In Michael D. Hutt and Thomas W. Speh, *Business Marketing Management*, 6th ed. (Fort Worth, TX: Dryden Press, 1998), p. 16. Reprinted with permission by the American Marketing Association.

Affinity cards such as these provide direct benefits to customers. Information from use of these cards can help companies build a database for more accurately serving customers and marketing to them.

One of the keys to success in relationship marketing is information and how you use it. Before technological developments like the Web and the availability of electronic databases, it was not possible to do sophisticated relationship marketing on a large scale. Now, by using the Web and other direct marketing methods, it is possible to deliver personalized messages. Because of this, there is a trend away from mass market communication to more relationship building and one-to-one communication with customers and prospects. Because of technology we are smarter and can create customized ads and newsletters and have direct dialogue with individual customers. Again, it is important to recognize that using databases is only *one* tool in relationship marketing.

The benefits of relationship marketing cannot be realized without securing and maintaining a quality database. It is the database's quality—the information itself and how it is used and acquired—that drives the program, targets customers, and enables the firm to provide the kind of customer satisfaction needed to build long-term relationships.

## Flexibility: Facilitating Relationship Marketing and Customer Service

Leading companies have created new possibilities for customers by providing more choices and better response times. They have accomplished this by pushing their operations to perform much more flexibly. Instead of running a production line to produce one specific product for a week, companies are organizing to change production from one product to another within hours. This is known as **mass customization**. The purpose is to maximize the flexibility of the whole company's response to demand.[18]

For example, product life cycles for low-end computers are measured within months these days, so flexible production lines allow the company to guard against running short of a hot model or overproducing one whose sales have slowed.

**mass customization**

Organizing to make production of products more flexible to meet specifically stated customer requirements.

Kao Corp., Japan's biggest soap and cosmetics company, has developed incredible flexibility in distribution. The company and its wholly owned wholesalers can deliver goods within 24 hours to any of 280 000 shops, whose average order is for just seven items. The key is a sophisticated information system. Brand managers see daily sales, stock, and production figures. Within a day, they can learn whether a competitor is running a sale. This network virtually eliminates the lag between an event in the market (e.g., Mrs. Takada buys a bar of soap) and the arrival of the news at the company.

www.kao.co.jp

A flexible factory is useless if a company doesn't know what is selling, and it doesn't help to know the market cold if the company can't react to it back at the plant. Building flexibility into an organization enables a firm to add value for customers in several ways. It can provide enhanced product features for specific market segments, lower product prices, rapid change of the product mix, introduction of many new products, and excellent customer response time. Thus, incorporating flexibility into production and marketing can greatly enhance customer satisfaction, and make such organizations extremely competitive in the marketplace.

Ensuring total customer satisfaction is a major challenge to an organization. However, the firm that understands lifetime-customer value will recognize that implementing the philosophy of customer satisfaction brings great satisfaction and rewards to the firm.

## SUMMARY

Total customer satisfaction means that a good or service fully and without reservation conforms to the customer's requirements. This approach leads to developing long-term relationships with customers and generating lifetime-customer value (LCV). LCV is the sum of all future customer revenue streams minus product and servicing costs, acquisition costs, and remarketing costs. Focusing on LCV can change the marketing strategy of a company.

Some firms make the mistake of relying solely on traditional financial analysis to determine how they are doing. Financial analysis measures the outcomes of strategic initiatives taken in the past. A manager also needs a forward-looking perspective toward building success in the future as well as calculation of LCV. An emphasis on assessing the amount that total customer satisfaction provides is an important means of accomplishing future success.

Activity is the process by which value is created. Managers have to be careful not to focus on activity rather than value. Value should be the focus of marketing activity, but it is a subjective term and is defined by the customer. Thus a marketing program that tries to provide total customer satisfaction must research the values of target customers.

Building value is the function of a five-link chain composed of culture, systems, performance, and results, which lead to the provision of value. Total quality is a popular management goal, but value is more fundamental.

Benchmarking is the comparison of performance with industry best practices. The concept of "comparison with the best" provides better standards for control of a marketing plan than setting objectives. There are four fundamental requirements to using benchmarking as a tool to provide value to customers: know your operation, know the industry leaders and competitors, incorporate the best practices, and develop superiority.

The performance gap is the difference between a company's performance and that of the best of the best. It is important not only to determine the current performance gap, but to project the future gap as well. This provides a basis on which to develop marketing plans.

How do you know whether your firm is providing total customer satisfaction? Research is the key. This can be done through regular surveys of customers as well as through a marketing audit that includes a customer satisfaction assessment.

Relationship marketing consists of identifying and establishing, maintaining and enhancing, and when necessary, terminating relationships with customers and other stakeholders, at a profit, so that the objectives of all parties involved are met through a mutual exchange and fulfillment of promises. This helps the company to fulfill the mandate of the marketing concept as discussed in Chapter 1. An emphasis on flexibility in production and marketing is a competitive thrust that can provide significant customer value and enable the development of long-term relationships with customers. This is particularly important in a mass marketing situation.

## KEY TERMS

benchmarking, p. 128
CRM software, p. 134
customer relationship marketing (CRM), p. 132
customer satisfaction management (CSM), p. 133
database marketing, p. 134
lifetime-customer value (LCV), p. 120

marketing audit, p. 132
mass customization, p. 136
performance gap, p. 129
total customer satisfaction, p. 118
value, p. 124

## INTERACTIVE SUMMARY AND DISCUSSION QUESTIONS

1. Financial results measure the outcomes of strategic initiatives taken in the past. A manager also needs a forward-looking view toward building success in the future. Explain how an emphasis on total customer satisfaction can assist in directing the company's activities.
2. Activity is the process by which value is created. Why are managers often programmed to manage activity rather than value?
3. Value should be the focus of marketing activity. However, value is a subjective term and is defined by the customer. How, then, can a marketing program that tries to provide total customer satisfaction determine customer values?
4. Building value is a function of a five-link chain composed of culture, systems, performance, and results, which lead to the provision of value. Explain how this chain works.
5. Total quality is a popular management goal, but value is more fundamental. Explain.

6. Benchmarking is the comparison of performance with industry best practices. The concept of "comparison with the best" provides better standards for control of a marketing plan than setting objectives. Give an example to illustrate this concept.

7. There are four fundamental requirements in using benchmarking as a tool to provide value to customers: know your operation, know the industry leaders and competitors, incorporate the best practices, and develop superiority. Using a small business that you are familiar with as an example, explain how these requirements might be explained or applied in terms of that business.

8. The performance gap is the difference between a company's performance and that of the best of the best. Why is it important not only to determine the current performance gap but to project the future gap as well?

9. Review the benchmarking process in Table 6.2. Apply it to two or three marketing features of a local bookstore.

10. Relationship marketing can help to provide total customer satisfaction. Explain how such a program can be implemented for a mass marketer.

11. An emphasis on flexibility is a competitive thrust that can provide significant customer value. Explain how this necessarily involves most aspects of the organization.

12. A marketing audit is based on five variables: customer philosophy, integrated marketing organization, adequate marketing information, strategic orientation, and operational efficiency. Outline the probable steps in a marketing audit for a local dry-cleaning company.

13. In detail, describe how the total customer satisfaction concept could be applied to the marketing management system of a company you are familiar with.

14. Go to the Web site of ten companies of your choice. Determine the degree to which the concept of total customer satisfaction is reflected in the information they provide.

# Case

## Levi Strauss

"We need to be talking more to customers and finding out what their needs are and servicing those needs."
(Glenn Sato, Levi Strauss's Manager of Retail Operations for Canada, April 1997)

Two years later, Levi Strauss & Co.'s foray into mass customization came to an end in Canada. The San Francisco–based jean maker, which has been reeling from slumping sales, pulled the plug last week on its Personal Pair program that allowed women to order jeans personally sized for them.

The program, which operated out of 30 stores in Canada and about a dozen in the United States, was praised by industry watchers who see mass customization—the ability to produce goods on a large scale, but with personalized features—as a winning formula for today's economy.

Among them was U.S. marketing guru Donald Peppers, who used the Levi Strauss example to illustrate how a large corporation could deploy technology to offer personalized service to its customers and heighten brand loyalty by providing a unique product.

But that's not exactly what happened. Shelley Nandkeolyar, the director of consumer relationships for Levi Strauss & Co. (Canada) Inc., says the company found that the program did not offer women the variety they wanted. "It was targeted at fit and what we realized quickly was that fit was not what the consumer was really looking for. The consumer was looking more and more for style variations."

The Personal Pair system did not technically provide women with made-to-measure jeans. Instead, a pair of "personalized" pants was produced by using a combination of set pattern pieces.

For example, a woman would be measured by staff in a Levi's store and would try on some of the 440 sample pairs each participating store stocked. From that, she would be offered two choices of leg cut, a limited variety of colours, and various size combinations that may not be available off the shelf.

The theory was that a woman with a small waist, long legs, or large hips would finally be able to buy a pair of jeans that fit her unique body type.

But what often happened, Mr. Nandkeolyar says, is that after a customer was measured, the clerk would be able to find a pair of jeans that fit her from Levi's standard inventory. The pair cost $10 less and came without the one-to-three-week wait that a Personal Pair required. "People don't realize the extent of the styles and fits that are available with Levis and the variety that we offer and all the different styles and models."

www.levistrauss.com

But that lack of awareness is part of Levi Strauss's problem, as it battles to regain some of the market share it has lost in recent years to designer labels and retailers such as Gap Inc.

The jean maker, which is a private company owned by the descendants of founder Levi Strauss, does not report detailed financial statistics, but disclosed that sales were down 13 percent.

Although Levi Strauss has ended the Personal Pair offering, Mr. Nandkeolyar says that the company still firmly believes in the benefits of mass customization. While there is no replacement program in Canada, in the fall of 1998 the company introduced a new mass customization effort in the United States called Original Spin. Mr. Nandkeolyar says it tries to respond to customers' demand for more style variations and, unlike Personal Pair, is also available to men. That program is now being tested in about 15 U.S. stores, he says, and could be expanded to Canada if it proves successful.

As for Personal Pair, like many corporate ventures that have come and gone, Mr. Nandkeolyar now describes it as an educational experience. "It was one of the green shoots that the company put out to learn from," he says.

### You Be the Marketer

1. Did the company make a marketing mistake in starting the mass customization program?
2. What else might have been done to make the program a success?
3. Look at the U.S. Levi Strauss Web site and compare and evaluate their "Original Spin" program.

Source: Adapted from Elizabeth Church, "Personal Pair Didn't Fit into Levi Strauss's Plans," *The Globe and Mail*, May 27, 1999, p. B13. Reprinted with permission from *The Globe and Mail*.

# Tony the Tiger ™

## From the Beginning...

In 1952, Tony™ and three other characters where developed as part of a contest for packages of Kellogg's Sugar Frosted Flakes of Corn. The other 3 characters were Katy the Kangaroo, Elmo the Elephant and Newt the Gnu. Tony™ rapidly proved to be the most popular with consumers and all of the other characters were removed from the packaging.

In 1953, Kellogg's advertising agency developed the first four-color ad with Tony the Tiger™, and was published in the August issue of Life Magazine. Since then, his career has been the envy of any human star with many appearances on TV, in magazines, newspapers, radio and at stores across the country.

Tony™ was created especially for children, but his lifetime characteristics make him popular with consumers of all ages. His fans call him friendly, lovable, talented, boastful and almost human.

We are all very proud of Tony™, and we think he does an outstanding job representing the Kellogg Company and Kellogg's Frosted Flakes®. That is why we all love to sing the "Hey Tony" jingle.

The new Tony the Tiger reflects extensive research of the target market.

## Chapter 7

# OBTAINING DATA FOR MARKETING DECISIONS

## CHAPTER OBJECTIVES

After reading and studying this chapter, you should be able to

1. Describe the development and current status of the marketing research functions.
2. Present the steps of the marketing research process.
3. Discuss the nature and sources of primary and secondary data.
4. Outline the methods of collecting survey data.
5. Discuss the nature of marketing information systems, and relate them to the marketing research function.

K ellogg's has flourished through skilful marketing of good products. Using a multiple branding strategy, each product within the range is given its own clear identity, but is marketed using the Kellogg's name as an umbrella.

Segmentation and targeting are key factors in creating these brand identities. For example, in Britain the main segment for Frosties (known as Frosted Flakes in Canada) consists of children under the age of 12 years. Tony the Tiger has been used to create characteristics and brand values for Frosties that appeal to children.

As markets change over time Kellogg's of Britain undertook a large strategic market research study of its target market to gain insights about the brand, its icon Tony the Tiger, and the current position of Frosties within its product life cycle.

## Research Results

Qualitative research finds out about the opinions, views, and thoughts of consumers. The Frosties qualitative research showed that Tony, while 'cool,' was losing relevance for some kids, which resulted in Frosties not having the 'playground credibility' like some other kids' brands.

Quantitative research identifies factors that are measurable; it creates numbers that can be analyzed. This research showed that the Frosties brand was nearing the end of the growth phase in its life cycle and was moving towards maturity as more competition entered the market. Children no longer considered Tony to be as 'cool' as other cereal characters.

The company considered whether to try to extend the life of the brand, or to develop new, replacement products or brands. The decision was to try to extend the Frosties life cycle by modernizing Tony in the hope that Tony would again become the favourite cereal character of consumers in the targeted age range.

## Modernizing Tony the Tiger

Market research showed that although Tony the Tiger's new role should rely heavily upon the image and activities associated with Tony's past, his role should be updated and linked with current and futuristic activities. Their agency developed and modernized Tony's role, basing it on the term 'Action Hero.'

After much discussion, it was decided to go beyond TV cartoon animation, as used with *Tom and Jerry* and to create a 3D Tony as used in *Toy Story* and to use him not only in standard advertising media but also in new media such as the Internet.

## Evaluating the Success of the Campaign

Quantitative research after the launch showed that, although not all targets were achieved immediately, the advertising had moved Tony forward and had met many of the concerns highlighted by the previous research. In the short term, following the launch, Frosties achieved an increase in market penetration, consumption, brand share, and sales.

In the highly competitive market for cereals, the sales performance of Frosties relates directly to the positive images projected by Tony. Giving Tony a new injection of life was seen as a vital contribution towards improving the competitiveness of the brand and prolonging its useful life.

**This is a good example of the importance of marketing research. Without it, management would not have been able to do such a thorough analysis of the situation, and to make the marketing decisions that it did.**

www.kelloggs.com

# INTRODUCTION

The quality of all marketing planning decisions depends on the quality of the information on which they are based. A variety of sources of marketing information are available to the marketing decision maker. Some involve the regular information flow that occurs in a company—for example, sales-force reports, accounting data, and other internal statistics. Sophisticated firms apply the power of computers to analyze such internal data, and to simulate the effects of changes in strategy.

Another important source of information is **marketing research**. Marketing research is the systematic gathering, recording, and analyzing of data about problems relating to the marketing of goods and services. This is the function that links the consumer to the company through information that is used to identify and define marketing opportunities and problems; to generate, refine, and evaluate marketing actions; to monitor marketing performance; and to improve understanding of marketing as a process.

Marketing research specifies the information required to address these issues, designs the method for collecting information, manages and implements the data collection process, analyzes the results, and communicates the findings and their implications.[1]

The critical task of the marketing manager is decision making. Managers earn their salaries by making effective decisions that enable their firms to plan marketing programs and to solve problems as they arise, and by anticipating and preventing the occurrence of future problems. Many times, though, they must make decisions with limited information that is of uncertain accuracy. If the decision maker undertakes some marketing research, much valuable additional information can be gained to help with the decision. Although the marketing research does not *make* the decision, it does make it easier for the manager to do so.

marketing research
The systematic gathering, recording, and analyzing of data about problems relating to the marketing of goods and services.

## THE ROOTS OF MARKETING

### THE FIRST FULL-TIME RESEARCHER

Marketing research in Canada may be said to have existed since there first were buyers and sellers. However, the day on which marketing research became a full-time profession was January 2, 1929. On that day, Henry King became the first full-time marketing researcher in Canada. His employer was an advertising agency, Cockfield Brown.[2]

In 1932, through the encouragement of Cockfield Brown, the first independent research company—Ethel Fulford and Associates—was founded in Toronto. In 1937, the Fulford company became known as Canadian Facts. Marketing research firms are now found in most major centres.

Most of the market segmentation procedures outlined in Chapters 3 and 4 are based on information collected through marketing research. There is a growing use of marketing research for developing marketing plans. Its regular use is now considered indispensable by most successful companies.

Marketing research studies generate data that may serve many purposes, for example, developing sales forecasts, determining market and sales potential, designing new products and packages, analyzing sales and marketing costs, evaluating the effectiveness of a firm's advertising, and determining consumer motives for buying products.

Many companies do not have their own marketing research departments. The function is often at least partly contracted out to specialists, because the research skill and activity levels are quite variable for different projects. Even large firms typically rely on outside agencies to conduct interviews. Such agencies have a large number of trained interviewers and the appropriate systems in place to conduct the studies.

There are two basic types of marketing research organizations that a firm may use. The first can be categorized as a *full-* or *partial-service research supplier*. Full-service firms handle all aspects of the research and provide a final report to management, whereas those offering partial service specialize in some activity, such as conducting field interviews. An example of a full-service research supplier is NFO CF group, one of Canada's largest marketing and social research firms.

The second type of external research organization is known as a *syndicated service*. A syndicated service provides a standardized set of data on a regular basis to all who wish to buy it. Normally, such research firms specialize in providing information on a small number of industries. For example, the Consumer Panel of Canada regularly gathers information on consumer purchases of food and other household items from 7000 households. These data inform marketers about brand preferences, brand-switching, and the effects of various promotional activities. Since all major products in the category are reported, a purchaser of this information can see how competitors are doing as well. Employing essentially the same households through time, CPC is able to track market trends and analyze market place dynamics.

Research is likely to be contracted to outside groups when

www.ipsos-npd.com/
canada/consumer_panel_of
_canada.htm

- Problem areas can be defined in terms of specific research projects that can easily be delegated.
- There is a need for specialized know-how or equipment.
- Intellectual detachment is important.[3]

The Gillette Company is a world leader in developing and marketing shaving systems and other products. Marketing research is a key element of the company's strategy. Gathering many kinds of information enables Gillette to analyze customer needs, test products, and advertise successfully to a large global market. The types of marketing research studies conducted by Gillette are a good example of how well-run companies rely on marketing research information:[4]

www.gillette.com

- *Annual National Consumer Studies* The objectives of these annual studies are to determine what brand of razor and blade was used for the respondents' last shave, to collect demographic data, and to examine consumer attitudes toward the various blade and razor manufacturers. These studies rely on personal interviews with national panels of male and female respondents, who are selected by using probability sampling methods.
- *National Brand Tracking Studies* The purpose of these studies is to track the use of razors and blades to monitor brand loyalty and brand switching tendencies over time. These studies are also conducted annually and use panels of male and female shavers. However, the information for them is collected via mail questionnaires.
- *Annual Brand Awareness Studies* These studies are aimed at determining the "share of mind" Gillette products have. This information is collected by annual telephone surveys that employ unaided as well as aided recall of brand names and advertising campaigns.
- *Consumer Use Tests* The key objectives of the use-testing studies are to ensure that "Gillette remains state of the art in the competitive arena, that our products are up to their desired performance standards, and that no claims in our advertising, packaging, or display materials are made without substantiation." At least two consumer use tests are conducted each month by Gillette. In these tests, consumers are asked to use a single variation of a product for an extended period of time, at the end of which their evaluation of the product is obtained.
- *Continuous Retail Audits* The purpose of the retail audits is to provide top management with monthly market share data, along with information regarding distribution, out-of-stock, and inventory levels of the various Gillette products. This information is purchased from the commercial information services providing syndicated retail audit data. The information is supplemented by special retail audits, which Gillette conducts itself, that look at product displays and the extent to which Gillette blades and razors are featured in retailer advertisements.
- *Laboratory Research Studies* These studies are designed to test the performance of existing Gillette products and to help in the design of new products. They include having people shave with Gillette and competitor products and measuring the results, as well as determining the number of whiskers on a man's face, how fast whiskers grow, and how many shaves a man can get from a single blade.

Marketing research-generated information helps to define target markets. It also helps managers understand consumer needs and responses to product offerings in those target markets. The process of generating, analyzing, and transmitting that information is a core part of the marketing research approach.

A Gillette product that has benefited by much past and ongoing marketing research.

# THE MARKETING RESEARCH PROCESS

## Marketing Research in Action

Infotech, a provincially based organization, was intrigued by the possibilities of stimulating in the province a computer software industry that would specialize in producing software for use in schools (known as "courseware"). Such an industry could be on the leading edge in the rapidly growing computer sector and thus could stimulate much economic growth in the province. In order to know whether such a strategy was worthwhile, Infotech commissioned a marketing research study. It wanted to know (a) the size of the courseware market in North America, (b) the trends in courseware for education usage, (c) what channels of distribution exist in the courseware industry and what it costs to use them, and (d) the marketing and financial aspects of courseware development. Be sure to follow the progress of the Infotech case throughout this chapter.

Given the need for information, how is marketing research actually conducted? Normally, there are five basic steps in the marketing research process: (1) formulate the problem, (2) develop the research design, (3) determine the data collection method, (4) collect the data, and (5) analyze, interpret, and present the information.

Figure 7.1 diagrams the marketing research process from the information need to the research-based decision.

## Formulate the Problem

Problems are barriers that prevent the accomplishment of organizational goals. A clearly defined problem helps the researcher to focus the research process on securing data that are necessary to solve the problem. Someone once remarked that well-defined problems are half solved.

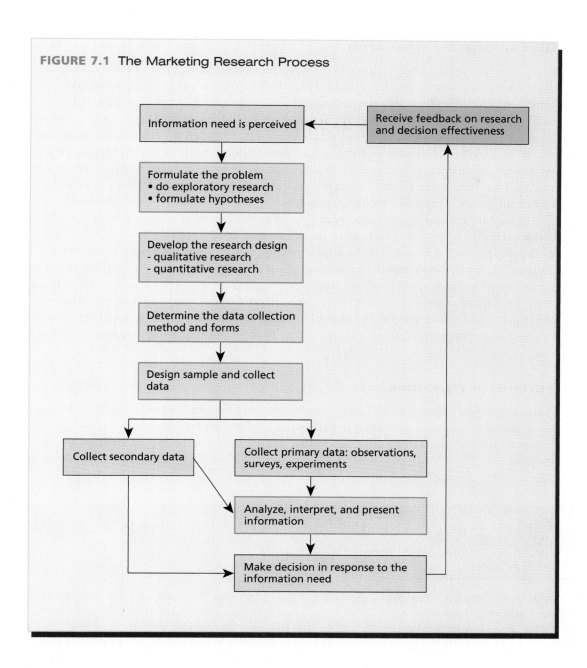

FIGURE 7.1 The Marketing Research Process

Defining the problem is not always easy. Suppose a tennis player with a sore knee and other symptoms goes to the doctor for treatment. His "problem," he tells the doctor, is a sore knee. However, on further investigation, it is discovered that the knee pain is merely a symptom of the real problem: damage to an Achilles tendon. Sometimes it is easy to pinpoint the business problem that requires research information to solve. However, it is often difficult to determine the specific problem, since what the researcher is confronted with may be only symptoms of the real underlying problem. To focus research properly, the research must look beyond the symptoms. This is done through exploratory research. Typical questions that are addressed at this stage are:

- What is the purpose of the study? to solve a problem? identify an opportunity?
- Is additional background information necessary?
- What information is needed to make the decision at hand?
- How will the information be used?
- Should research be conducted?

## Do Exploratory Research

**exploratory research**

Learning about the problem area and beginning to focus on specific areas of study by discussing the problem with informed sources within the firm (a process often called situation analysis) and with knowledgeable others outside the firm (the informal investigation).

Exploratory research can help to formulate the problem. In searching for the cause of a problem, the researcher will learn about the problem area and begin to focus on specific areas for study. This search, often called **exploratory research**, consists of discussing the problem with informed sources within the firm and with wholesalers, retailers, customers, and others outside the firm, and examining secondary sources of information. Marketing researchers often refer to internal data collection as *situation analysis* and to exploratory interviews with informed persons outside the firm as *informal investigation*. Exploratory research also involves evaluating company records, such as sales and profit analyses of its own and its competitors' products. Table 7.1 provides a checklist of topics that might be considered in an exploratory analysis.

In the Infotech case, exploratory research was done through a review of the literature about courseware; then in-person and telephone interviews were undertaken with knowledgeable people in departments of education and the school systems. Before a specific research plan could be designed, the researchers needed to know more about the subject and about the existing trends in the industry. Only then was it possible to begin planning a more complete research program. It was determined that the next steps should be (1) to systemically explore every current article written on the subject, and (2) to develop a plan to obtain information directly from different market groups. In some research projects, the next step might have been formulating hypotheses, but this did not seem appropriate in the Infotech situation.

## Formulate Hypotheses

**hypothesis**

A tentative explanation about the relationship between variables as a starting point for further testing.

After the problem has been defined and an exploratory investigation has been conducted, the marketer should be able to formulate a **hypothesis**, a tentative explanation about the relationship between variables as a starting point for further testing. In effect, the hypothesis is an educated guess.

# THE PRACTISING MARKETER

### RESEARCHING CUSTOMER SATISFACTION

Customer satisfaction or service quality research can help define the attributes that your customer associates with good service and determine areas of weakness that undermine your competitive edge.

Customer satisfaction research can evaluate everything from after-market service and responsiveness to complaints to convenience of hotel check-in and timeliness and accuracy of courier services.

Often designed as tracking studies, customer satisfaction research can be conducted at regular intervals against a benchmark to reflect trends and changes in service performance. Here is an example situation:

**Issue:** An automobile manufacturer has had many complaints about the quality of CD player installed as a factory option in its cars, particularly the sporty models favoured by young adults. Apparently it eats CDs and eventually stops altogether. Although the manufacturer honours its warranty on these items and replaces them promptly, dealerships report that customers who have had the problem players continue to complain. What is going on here?

**Solution:** It turns out that the manufacturer is replacing the defective CD players with the same brand and model that causes the problem in the first place. These customers travel with their music loud and fear that if they have had operating problems once with this player, they will probably recur. Service quality research among both customers and service reps at the dealerships would reveal that although the manufacturer is honouring the letter of the warranty, the customers believe that it is half-hearted compliance. Indeed they believe that a stockpile of defective players exists and that's all they'll get until the supply has been exhausted. Many have indicated that they will not purchase that brand of automobile again.

**Can you think of other products for which customer satisfaction studies would be helpful?**

Source: Adapted from the NFO CF Group Web site (www.nfocfgroup.com/services/custom_customer.html) May 26, 2002. Reprinted with permission.

**TABLE 7.1** Topics for the Exploratory Analysis

| The Company and Industry | • Company objectives<br>• The companies in the industry (size, financial power) and the industry trends<br>• Geographic locations of the industry<br>• The company's market share as compared with the competitor's<br>• Marketing policies of competitors |
| --- | --- |
| The Market | • Geographic location<br>• Demographic characteristics of the market<br>• Purchase motivations<br>• Product-use patterns<br>• Nature of demand |
| Products | • Physical characteristics<br>• Consumer acceptance—strengths and weaknesses<br>• Package as a container and as a promotional device<br>• Manufacturing processes, production capacity<br>• Closeness and availability of substitute products |
| Marketing Channels | • Channels employed and recent trends<br>• Channel policy<br>• Margins for resellers |
| Sales Organization | • Market coverage<br>• Sales analysis by number of accounts per salesperson, size of account, type of account, etc.<br>• Expense ratios for various territories, types of product, size of accounts, etc.<br>• Control procedures<br>• Compensation methods |
| Pricing | • Elasticity<br>• Season or special promotional price cuts<br>• Profit margins of resellers<br>• Legal restrictions<br>• Price lines |
| Advertising and Sales Promotion | • Media employed<br>• Dollar expenditures as compared with competitors'<br>• Timing of advertising<br>• Sales promotional materials provided for resellers<br>• Results from previous advertising and sales promotional campaigns |

A marketer of industrial products might formulate the following hypothesis: "Failure to provide 36-hour delivery service will reduce our sales by 20 percent." Such a statement may prove correct or incorrect. Formulating a hypothesis does, however, provide a basis for investigation and an eventual determination of its accuracy. It also allows the researcher to move to the next step: developing the research design.

## Develop the Research Design

**research design**
A series of advance decisions that, taken together, make up a master plan or model for conducting the investigation.

The research design should be a comprehensive plan for testing the hypotheses formulated about the problem. **Research design** refers to a series of advance decisions that, taken together, make up a master plan or model for conducting the investigation. Developing such a plan allows the researcher to control each step of the research process.

The research design for Infotech was quite complicated. No fewer than five individual data collection procedures were planned. These included surveys of (1) departments of education across Canada and in selected American states, (2) principal textbook and software publishers, (3) key hardware and software manufacturers in Canada, and (4) a sampling of the teacher population.

Typical questions to be addressed in developing the research design are:

- How much is already known?
- Can a hypothesis be formulated?
- What types of questions need to be answered?
- What type of study will best address the research question

## Determine the Data Collection Method

Data can be obtained in many ways. These include finding existing statistics and information, as well as collecting new data through surveys and experiments. These topics are covered in greater detail later in this chapter. There is a great deal of science, as well as art, in choosing the best data collection method. As always, these decisions are affected by the importance of the decision and the budget available. Significant issues to be dealt with here are:

- Can existing data be used to advantage?
- What is to be measured? How?
- What is the source of the data to be collected?
- Are there any cultural factors that need to be taken into account in designing the data collection method? If so, what are they?
- Are there any legal restrictions on the collection methods? If so, what are they?
- Can objective answers be obtained by asking people?
- How should people be questioned?
- Should the questionnaires be administered in person, over the phone, or through the mail?
- Should electronic or mechanical means be used to make the observations?
- What specific behaviours should the observers record?
- Should structured or unstructured items be used to collect the data?
- Should the purpose of the study be made known to the respondents?
- Should rating scales be used in the questionnaires?

## Collect the Data

**primary data**
Data being collected for the first time.

After the research design has determined what data are needed, the data must then be collected. Collecting data is a major part of the marketing research project. Two types of data are typically obtained: primary data and secondary data. **Primary data** refer to data being collected for the first time during a study. Primary data are normally the *last* to be collected. This stage of the research can be guided by considering:

- Who is the target population?
- Is a list of population elements available?
- Is a sample necessary?
- Is a probability sample desirable?
- How large should the sample be?
- How should the sample be selected?
- Who will gather the data?

- How long will the data gathering take?
- How much supervision is needed?
- What operational procedures will be followed?
- What methods will be used to ensure the quality of the data collected?

**Secondary data** are previously published matter. They serve as an extremely important source of information for the marketing researcher. Secondary data are collected and reviewed first.

**secondary data**
Previously published matter.

## Collect Secondary Data

Not only are secondary data important, they are also abundant in many areas that the marketing researcher may need to investigate. In fact, the overwhelming quantity of secondary data available at little or no cost often challenges the researcher, who wants to select only pertinent information.

Secondary data consists of two types: internal and external. *Internal secondary data* include company records of sales, product performances, sales-force activities, and marketing costs. *External data* are obtained from a variety of sources. Governments—local, provincial, and federal—provide a wide variety of secondary data. Private sources also supply secondary data for the marketing decision maker. The appendix at the end of this chapter describes a wide range of secondary data sources.

### GOVERNMENT SOURCES

The federal government provides the country's most important sources of marketing data, the most frequently used being census data. Although the government spends millions of dollars in conducting the various censuses of Canada, the information obtained thereby is available at no charge at local libraries and Statistics Canada offices, or it can be purchased at a nominal charge in various electronic forms for instant access. In fact, Statistics Canada produces several different censuses. Table 7.2 briefly describes the main ones. In addition, there are monthly and annual surveys of important economic sectors, such as manufacturing.

www.statcan.ca

The current data are so detailed for large cities that breakdowns of population characteristics are available for areas comprising only a few city blocks (census tracts) or by postal code. Thus local retailers or shopping-centre developers can easily gather detailed information about the immediate neighbourhoods that will constitute their customer bases without spending time or money conducting a comprehensive survey.

So much data are produced by the federal government that the marketing researcher often purchases summaries such as the *Canada Year Book* or *Market Research Handbook* or subscribes to *Statistics Canada Daily.* The latter is the vehicle for first (official) release of statistical data and publications produced by Statistics Canada. It provides highlights of newly released data with source information for more detailed facts, contains weekly and monthly schedules of upcoming major news releases, and announces new nonprint products and new services.

The Official Release Unit also produces *Infomat,* a weekly review of Canadian economic and social trends (also available electronically at order@statcan.ca). Or it can be found, along with many other resources, in the nearest Statistics Canada Regional Reference Centre.

The other main Statistics Canada publications are

- *CANSIM.* The Canadian Socio-Economic Information Management System (CANSIM) is a time series database containing more than 650 000 items. CANSIM can be accessed through the Internet at http://www.statcan.ca/English/CANSIM.
- *Canadian Social Trends.* This on-line quarterly publication that discusses the social, economic, and demographic changes affecting the lives of Canadians contains the latest figures for major social indicators.

A number of other Statistics Canada publications can be found on its Web site at http://www.statcan.ca. Many statistics are also available on CD-ROM.

Provincial and city governments are other important sources of information on employment, production, and sales activities.

**TABLE 7.2** Major Statistics Collected by Statistics Canada

**Census of Canada**
Conducted once each decade, with certain categories checked every five years. It provides a count of all residents of Canada by province, city or town, country, or other suitable division, and, in large cities, by census tract. Particularly useful to marketers are the data provided by economic rather than political boundaries, such as greater metropolitan areas. Data are also gathered on age, gender, race, citizenship, education level, occupation, employment status, income, and family status of inhabitants. A less detailed census is conducted at the halfway point in the decade.

**The Economy—The Latest Indicators**
Key monthly and quarterly measures of economic performance for Canada and each province.

**The Economy in Detail**
Annual data covering most aspects of Canada's economy.

**The Land**
Statistics on Canada's land area, plant and animal life, and environment.

**The People**
Statistics on Canada's population traits and trends, plus education, culture, and health.

**The State**
Statistics on government finances and employment, justice, and elections.
Web sites associated with the above data can readily be accessed on the Internet at http://www.canada.gc.ca.

www.nationalpost.com

www.acnielsen.com

## PRIVATE SOURCES

Numerous private organizations provide information for the marketing executive. In *Canadian Markets,* published by the *Financial Post,* the marketer will find a wide range of valuable data. Other good primarily U.S. summary data can be found in the annual survey of buying power published by *Sales and Marketing Management* magazine (which can be accessed at http://www.salesand marketing.com). For activities in a particular industry, trade associations are excellent resources. Advertising agencies continually collect information on the audiences reached by various media.

Several national firms offer information to business on a subscription basis. The largest of these, A.C. Nielsen Company, collects data that are reported weekly on product sales, retail prices, and promotional activities. The company also reports on consumer purchase behaviour, which is sourced from its 12 000 member Home Scan panel, an electronic consumer-based household panel. The Consumer Panel of Canada also gathers information on consumer purchases.

## ADVANTAGES AND LIMITATIONS OF SECONDARY DATA

Using secondary data offers two important advantages over that of primary data:

■ Assembling previously collected data is almost always less expensive than collecting primary data.
■ Less time is involved in locating and using secondary data. Table 7.3 shows the estimated time involved in completing a research study that requires primary data. The time involved will naturally vary considerably depending on such factors as the research subject and the scope of the study.

The researcher must be aware of two potential limitations to using secondary data: (1) the data may be obsolete, and (2) the classifications of the secondary data may not fit the information needs

**TABLE 7.3** Time Requirements for a Primary-Data Research Project

| STEP | ESTIMATED TIME REQUIRED FOR COMPLETION |
|---|---|
| Define problem | 1–3 days |
| Develop methodology | 1–3 days |
| Design questionnaire | 1–2 weeks |
| Pretest questionnaire and evaluate pretest results | 1–3 weeks |
| Conduct field interviews | 1–6 weeks |
| Code returned questionnaires | 1 week |
| Transfer data to computer | 1 week |
| Do data processing and statistical analysis | 7–10 days |
| Interpret output, write report, and present findings | 1–2 weeks |
|    Total elapsed time | 7–18 weeks |

of the study. Published information has an unfortunate habit of quickly going out of date. A marketing researcher analyzing the population of the Calgary metropolitan market in 2002, for example, may well discover that much of the 2001 census data are already obsolete due to an upturn or downturn in the economy or new developments in the oil and gas industry.

Data may also have been collected previously on such bases as county or city boundaries, when the marketing manager requires it to be broken down by city blocks or census tracts. In such cases, the marketing researcher may not be able to rearrange the secondary data in a usable form and must therefore collect primary data. Figure 7.2 provides an outline of how to get started when searching for published sources of secondary data.

Secondary information proved very valuable in the Infotech study. A wide range of information sources was found. For example, relevant articles were found in such magazines as *Maclean's*, *Popular Computing*, and *Businessweek*. An especially valuable publication was *Electronic Learning*, which had no fewer than eight articles relating to the topic.

In addition to such periodicals, the researchers found eleven different special reports on various aspects of the educational use of computers. Report titles included "School Uses of Computers" (from Johns Hopkins University, in the United States) and "Phase Two: A Periodical Reporting on Education Computing in Scotland."

Studying such secondary sources gave the researchers immense insight into the fundamental issues involved in using courseware in the educational system. But some important information was still needed before a decision could be made about proceeding with the courseware project. Thus, it was time to plan a primary-data collection process.

www.macleans.ca

## Design and Execute A Survey To Collect Primary Data

Often secondary data are incomplete or do not fully relate to the problem at hand, so the necessary information must be obtained through one of several primary research methods. Hopefully, the secondary data search will have narrowed the scope of the primary data that will have to be collected. If hypotheses have been stated, facts should be gathered in such a way as to allow direct testing of the hypotheses.

Collecting primary data requires a considerable amount of technical expertise. Companies have found that they get the best information when specially trained individuals handle the design and execution of the research. The marketing researcher has three alternative methods for collecting primary data: observation, survey, or controlled experiment. No one method is best in all circumstances.

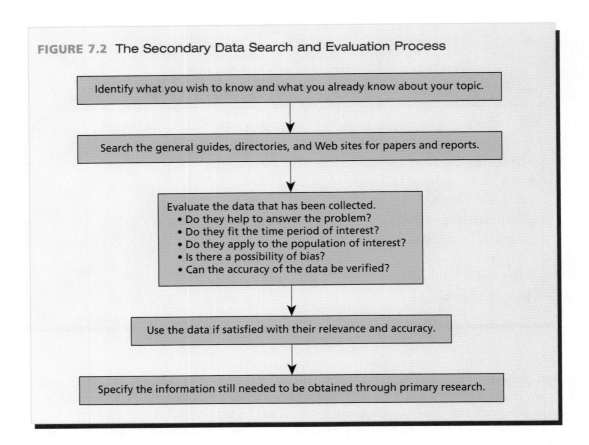

**FIGURE 7.2** The Secondary Data Search and Evaluation Process

Identify what you wish to know and what you already know about your topic.

Search the general guides, directories, and Web sites for papers and reports.

Evaluate the data that has been collected.
- Do they help to answer the problem?
- Do they fit the time period of interest?
- Do they apply to the population of interest?
- Is there a possibility of bias?
- Can the accuracy of the data be verified?

Use the data if satisfied with their relevance and accuracy.

Specify the information still needed to be obtained through primary research.

### THE OBSERVATION METHOD

Observational studies are conducted by actually viewing (either directly or through mechanical means such as hidden cameras) the overt actions of the respondent. Examples of this approach include conducting traffic counts at a potential location for a fast-food franchise, checking licence plates at a shopping centre to determine the area from which shoppers are attracted, or using supermarket scanners to record sales of certain products.

The observation method has both advantages and drawbacks. The advantages are that observation is often more accurate than questioning techniques like surveys and interviews, and that it may be the only way to get information about such things as actual shopping behaviour in a supermarket. Observation may also be the easiest way to get specific data. The drawbacks include observer subjectivity and errors in interpretation. For instance, researchers might incorrectly classify people's economic status because of the way they were dressed at the time of observation.

Sometimes firms use the observation method in evaluating advertisements. A specialist research service is hired to study patterns of viewer eye movements when looking at advertisements. This is done under laboratory conditions. The results from one such eye-tracking test led the advertiser to move the headline from the bottom of the ad to the top, since a majority of eye movements flowed to the top. Observation could also be used to determine the route shoppers take once inside a supermarket. From this information, positioning of items might be determined.

### THE SURVEY METHOD

The amount and type of information that can be obtained through merely observing overt consumer acts is limited. To obtain information on attitudes, motives, and opinions, the researcher must ask questions. The survey method is the most widely used approach to collecting primary data. There are three kinds of surveys: telephone interviews, self-completed surveys, and personal interviews.

*Telephone interviews* are inexpensive and fast ways to obtain limited quantities of relatively impersonal information. Many firms have leased toll-free wide area telephone services, which considerably reduce the cost of long-distance calls.

Telephone interviews account for the majority of all primary marketing research. They are limited to a small number of simple, clearly worded questions. Such interviews have two drawbacks: it is extremely difficult to obtain information about the personal characteristics of the respondent, and the survey may be prejudiced since two groups will be omitted—those households without telephones and those with unlisted numbers. One survey reported that alphabetical listings in telephone directories excluded one-quarter of large-city dwellers, and that they underrepresented service workers and separated and divorced persons. In addition, the mobility of the population creates problems in choosing names from telephone directories. As a result, a number of telephone interviewers have resorted to using digits selected at random and matched to telephone prefixes in the geographic area to be sampled. This technique is designed to correct the problem of sampling those with new telephone listings and those with unlisted numbers.

*Self-completed surveys* (often distributed by mail) allow the marketing researcher to conduct national studies at a reasonable cost. While personal interviews with a national sample may be prohibitively expensive, by using the mail the researcher can reach each potential respondent for the price of a postage stamp. Costs may be misleading, however, since *returned* questionnaires for such a study range between 10 and 80 percent, depending on the length of the questionnaire and respondent interest (a 20 percent return is not uncommon). When returns are low, the question arises as to the opinions of the majority (who did not respond). Some surveys use a coin or other incentive to gain the reader's attention, an approach that can increase returns but also increases costs. Unless additional information is obtained from nonrespondents, the results of the study are likely to be biased, since there may be important differences between the characteristics of these people and the characteristics of those who took the time to complete and return the questionnaire. For this reason, a follow-up questionnaire is sometimes mailed to nonrespondents, or telephone interviews may be used to gather additional information. These extra steps naturally add to the survey's cost. In spite of these difficulties, mail surveys are widely used.

Mail questionnaires must be carefully worded and pretested to eliminate any potential misunderstanding by respondents. But misunderstandings can occur with even the most clearly worded questions. When a truck operated by a government agency killed a cow, an official responded with an apology and a form to be filled out. It included a space for "disposition of the dead cow." The farmer responded "kind and gentle."

*Personal interviews* are typically the best means of obtaining more detailed information, since the interviewer has the opportunity to establish rapport with the respondent. The interviewer can also explain questions that might be confusing or vague to the respondent.

Personal interviews are slow and are the most expensive method of collecting data. However, their flexibility coupled with the detailed information that can be collected often offset these limitations. Marketing research firms sometimes rent locations in shopping centres, where they have greater access to potential buyers of the products in which they are interested. Downtown retail districts and airports are other on-site locations for marketing research.

The focus group interview is a special type of personal interview. *Focus group interviews* are widely used to gather preliminary research information. Eight to twelve people are brought together to discuss a subject of interest. Although the moderator typically explains the purpose of the meeting and suggests an opening discussion topic, he or she is interested in stimulating interaction among group members in order to develop the discussion of numerous points about the subject. Focus group sessions, which are often one to two hours long, are usually taped so that the moderator can devote full attention to the discussion. This process gives the researcher an idea of how consumers view a problem. Often it uncovers points of view that the researcher had not thought of. On the basis of these findings a broader study can be developed to verify the preliminary findings.

## THE CONTROLLED EXPERIMENT METHOD

The final and least-used method of collecting marketing information involves using *controlled experiments*. An experiment is a scientific investigation in which the researcher controls or manipulates a test group and observes this group as well as another group that did not receive the controls or manipulations. Such experiments can be conducted in the field or in a laboratory setting.

Although a number of marketing-related experiments have been conducted in the controlled environment of a laboratory, most have been conducted in the field. To date, the most common use of this method has been in test marketing.

Marketers face great risks in introducing new products. They often attempt to reduce this risk by **test marketing**: selecting areas considered reasonably typical of the total market, and introducing a new product to these areas with a total marketing campaign to determine consumer response before marketing the product nationally. Frequently used cities include Calgary, Lethbridge, and Winnipeg. Consumers in the test-market city view the product as they do any other new product, since it is available in retail outlets and is advertised in the local media. The test-market city becomes a small replica of the total market. The marketing manager can then compare actual sales with expected sales and project them on a nationwide basis. If the test results are favourable, the risks of

**test marketing**
Selecting areas considered reasonably typical of the total market, and introducing a new product to these areas with a total marketing campaign to determine consumer response before marketing the product nationally.

## THE PRACTISING MARKETER

### USING UNOBTRUSIVE MARKETING RESEARCH

Sometimes it is better to use unobtrusive methods of marketing research than to ask people direct questions about their attitudes or behaviour. "Garbology"—a technique whereby the researcher monitors consumption behaviour by rummaging through selected garbage—is a good example of such a method.

www.campbellsoup.ca

The *Saturday Evening Post* used this technique during the early 1900s to convince Campbell Soup that working-class, not upper-class, families were the appropriate target market for canned soup. Empty soup cans were widely found in trash in working-class neighbourhoods but not upper-class neighbourhoods. The success of this project resulted in Campbell becoming a regular advertiser in the *Saturday Evening Post*.

Restaurant managers have used garbology for years to monitor customer satisfaction. Patrons throw away what they don't want to eat or don't have room for. Thus, quality or quantity of food can be flagged by this method. See also http://bara.arizona.edu/gs.htm for a description of the University of Arizona garbage project.

**Can you think of other applications for garbology?**

The target market for Campbell's Soup changed after unobtrusive research (analysis of people's garbage).

a large-scale failure are reduced. Many products fail at the test-market stage; thus, consumers who live in these cities may purchase products that no one else will ever be able to buy.

The major problem with controlled experiments is the difficult task of controlling all the variables in a real-life situation. The laboratory scientist can rigidly control temperature and humidity, but how can the marketing manager determine the effect of varying the retail price through refundable coupons when the competition decides to retaliate against or deliberately confuse the experiment by issuing its own coupons?

In the future, experimentation will become more frequent as firms develop more sophisticated simulated competitive models that require computer analysis. Simulating market activities promises to be one of the great new developments in marketing.

In the Infotech market study, primary data were collected through four different research methods: (1) telephone surveys of departments of education across Canada and in selected American states, (2) personal and telephone interviews of principal Canadian textbook suppliers, (3) personal and telephone interviews of key hardware and software manufacturers and distributors, and (4) in-class surveys of teachers taking summer-school courses.

## The Data Collection Instrument

Most of the data collection methods depend on the use of a good questionnaire. Developing a good questionnaire requires considerable skill and attention. It should be done with reference to specified objectives concerning information that is needed to complete the study. With this list as a foundation, specific questions are written for the questionnaire. The questionnaire must then be pretested; a small sample of persons similar to those who will be surveyed are asked to complete it. Discussions with these sample respondents help uncover points that are unclear. The nature, style, and length of the questionnaire will vary depending on the type of data collection technique chosen. After pretesting and revising until the questionnaire works well, the researcher plans the necessary computer-coding set-up on the questionnaire to facilitate later data analysis.

The actual execution of the survey is beyond the scope of this book. Other important issues that need to be dealt with in planning the study are selecting, training, and controlling the field interviewers; editing, coding, tabulating, and interpreting the data; presenting the results; and following up on the survey. It is crucial that marketing researchers and research users cooperate at every stage in the research design. Too many studies go unused because marketing managers view the results as not meaningful to them.

For the Infotech study, a team of four researchers worked almost full-time for approximately three months to collect the secondary data, design and pretest questionnaires, and gather the primary data. The data were analyzed and presented in a 195-page report to the client.

The report highlighted the size and growth of the market. It also showed that despite the favourable market size, the idea as originally conceived would be extremely difficult to implement. As a result of the study, the sponsor was able to make an informed decision about whether or not to go ahead. The marketing research presented information that saved the sponsor a great deal of time and money.

## Sampling Techniques

Sampling is one of the most important aspects of marketing research. The total group that the researcher wants to study is called the **population** or **universe**. For a political campaign, the population would be all eligible voters. For a new cosmetic line, it might be all women in a certain age bracket. If this total group is contacted, the results are known as a **census**. Unless the group is small, the cost of such a survey will be overwhelming. Even the federal government attempts a full census only once every ten years.

Information, therefore, is rarely gathered from the total population during a survey. Instead, researchers select a representative group called a *sample*. Samples can be classified either as probability samples or as nonprobability samples. A **probability sample** is a sample in which every member of the population has a known chance of being selected, thus it is considered the ideal

**population or universe**
The total group that the researcher wants to study.

**census**
A collection of marketing data from all possible sources.

**probability sample**
A sample in which every member of the population has a known chance of being selected.

A concise questionnaire with an incentive to increase the number of responses.

**nonprobability sample**

A sample chosen in an arbitrary fashion so that each member of the population does not have a representative chance of being selected.

**convenience sample**

A nonprobability sample based on the selection of readily available respondents.

**judgement sample**

A nonprobability sample of people with a specific attribute.

**quota sample**

A nonprobability sample that is divided so that different segments or groups are represented in the total sample.

method. Because **nonprobability samples** are arbitrary, standard statistical tests cannot be applied to them. Marketing researchers like to base their studies on probability samples. However, for reasons of costs and ease of implementation other types of sampling methodologies are also used and are outlined below.

A **convenience sample** is a nonprobability sample based on the selection of readily available respondents. Broadcasting's "on-the-street" interviews are a good example. Marketing researchers sometimes use such samples in exploratory research, but not in definitive studies, because of the weakness of this method.

A nonprobability sample of people with a specific attribute is called a **judgement sample**. It is also known as a purposive sample. In this approach an experienced individual selects the sample based on his or her judgement about significant characteristics required of an individual to be included as a sample member. For example, test market cities are selected this way because they are viewed as representative of the greater population. Election-night predictions are usually based on polls of "swing voters" and are a type of judgement sample.

A **quota sample** is a nonprobability sample that is divided so that different segments or groups are represented in the total sample. An example would be a survey of imported-car owners that includes 33 Honda owners, 31 Toyota owners, 7 BMW owners, and so on.

A **cluster sample** is a probability sample that is generated by randomly choosing one or more areas or population clusters and then surveying all members in the chosen cluster(s). This approach can be helpful in a situation where it is difficult to obtain a complete list of all members of the population, but where there is good information on certain *areas* (such as census tracts).

The basic type of probability sample is the **simple random sample**, a sample in which every item in the relevant universe has an equal opportunity of being selected. Provincial lotteries are an example. Each number that appears on a ticket has an equal opportunity of being selected, and each ticket holder has an equal opportunity of winning. Using a computer to select 200 respondents randomly from a mailing list of 1000 would give every name on the list an equal opportunity of being selected.

A probability sample that takes every nth item on a list, after a random start, is called a **systematic sample**. Sampling from a telephone directory is a common example. This is a frequently used sampling procedure.

## Interpret and Present the Information

After going through the many steps to choose the best research method and the often complicated process of collecting data, the researcher faces the daunting task of making sense of the information. Key issues to be dealt with are:

- Who will handle the editing of the data?
- How will the data be coded?
- Who will supervise the coding?
- Will computer or hand tabulation be used?
- What tabulations are called for?
- What analysis techniques will be used?

The researcher is faced with a mass of numbers that must be compiled, organized, and interpreted. Computer programs are available to help with the task, but the responsibility of drawing conclusions and writing a report remains.

Once this process is complete, it is common procedure to present the analysis and conclusions to others in the marketing team and elsewhere in the organization. In the preparation of the report it is important to consider who will read the report, what is their technical level of sophistication, and what is their involvement with the project. Furthermore, in its preparation it must be decided whether managerial recommendations are called for. The marketing team will then combine the findings with other information to make strategic decisions and create marketing plans.

# MARKETING INFORMATION SYSTEMS

For all companies, some market data flow in on a regular basis from sales and other marketing activities. And companies that undertake marketing research gain other periodic bursts of facts from such studies.

The value of such material can vary significantly. Data and information are not necessarily synonymous terms. *Data* refer to statistics, opinions, facts, or predictions categorized on some basis for storage and retrieval. *Information* is data that is relevant to the marketing manager in making decisions. Often, the right information does not seem to be available when a marketing decision has to be made because the company simply does not have it, or because the information is not readily available in the firm's system.

The solution to the problem of obtaining relevant information appears simple—establish a systematic approach to information management by installing a planned marketing information system (MIS). Establishing an effective information system is, however, much easier said than done, as evidenced by the large number of firms that have attempted to develop an MIS and have succeeded only in increasing the amounts of irrelevant data available to them.

A **marketing information system** is a set of routine procedures to continuously collect, monitor, and present internal and external information on company performance and opportunities in the marketplace. Properly constructed, the MIS can serve as the nerve centre for the company, providing instantaneous information that is suitable for each level of management. It can act like a thermostat, monitoring the marketplace continuously so that management can adjust its actions as conditions change.

The analogy of an automatic heating system illustrates the role of marketing information in a firm's marketing system. Once the objective of a temperature setting (perhaps 20°C) has been established, information about the actual temperature in the house is collected and compared with the

**cluster sample**
A probability sample that is generated by randomly choosing one or more areas or population clusters and then surveying all members in the chosen cluster(s).

**simple random sample**
A probability sample in which every item in the relevant universe has an equal opportunity of being selected.

**systematic sample**
A probability sample that takes every nth item on a list, after a random start.

**marketing information system**
A set of routine procedures to continuously collect, monitor, and present internal and external information on company performance and opportunities in the marketplace.

## TOYOTA FACES BATTLE OVER CUSTOMER DATA

Toyota Canada Inc. dealers have warned that the automaker is heading toward a potential battle over ownership of customer data after it announced an exclusive agreement with information systems supplier Reynolds and Reynolds Canada Ltd.

The key issue, one Toyota dealer said, is "who truly owns those customers"—the sales outlet or the head office. Dealers also fear that Toyota may be setting up an Internet-based sales network that would sell directly to customers, then allocate those sales to various dealerships.

Under the deal, Reynolds and Reynolds will provide information systems to all Toyota dealers in Canada and create "a revolutionary retailing solution enabling Toyota Canada dealers to deliver superior value to Canadian car buyers," Pierre Blais, vice-president of Reynolds Canada Ltd., said.

The battle over customer information and who controls it is one of the key issues in the revolution sweeping the automotive retailing industry in North America, industry observers say. "Factories want to control the information, they want to control the customer data," said one industry insider. "The factory can't tell you who their customers are, so [information] systems, from a factory standpoint, are critical."

If the automakers don't control the information, they must rely on dealers to tell them who their customers are and, unless a dealer does so, the car companies can't maintain contact with their customers once they've bought a car, truck, or minivan.

**What are the implications and issues for consumers of trading personal information in data banks?**

www.toyota.ca

www.reyrey.com

Source: Adapted from Greg Keenan, "Toyota Faces Battle Over Customer Data," *The Globe and Mail*, December 3, 1998, p. B5. Reprinted with permission from *The Globe and Mail*.

---

objective, and a decision is made based on this comparison. If the temperature drops below an established figure, the decision is made to activate the furnace until the temperature reaches some established level. On the other hand, a high temperature may require a decision to turn off the furnace.

Deviation from the firm's goals of profitability, return on investment, or market share may necessitate changes in price structures, promotional expenditures, package design, or numerous marketing alternatives. The firm's MIS should be capable of revealing such deviations and possibly suggesting tactical changes that will result in attaining the established goals.

Some marketing executives feel that their company does not need a marketing information system, for various reasons. Two arguments are most often given: (1) the size of the company's operations does not warrant such a complete system, and (2) the information provided by an MIS is already being supplied by the marketing research department.

These contentions arise from a misconception regarding the services and functions performed by the marketing research department. Marketing research has already been described as typically focusing on a specific problem or project; the investigations involved have a definite beginning, middle, and end. Marketing information systems, on the other hand, are much wider in scope and involve continually collecting and analyzing marketing information. Figure 7.3 indicates the various information inputs—including marketing research studies—that serve as components of a firm's MIS.

By focusing daily on the marketplace, the MIS provides a continuous, systematic, and comprehensive study of areas that indicate deviations from established goals. The up-to-the-minute data allow problems to be corrected before they adversely affect company operations. Furthermore, such a system can be designed to collect information on the activities and effects of competitors. Competitor analysis is a very important component of a company's strategic planning process.

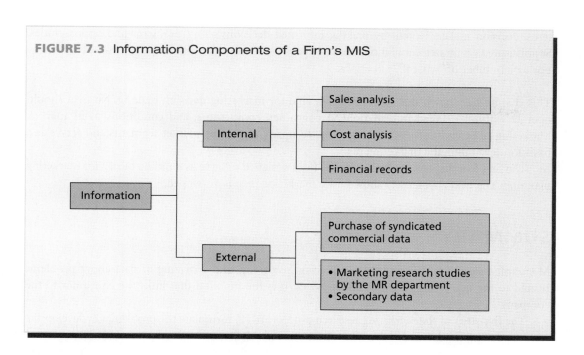

**FIGURE 7.3** Information Components of a Firm's MIS

- Information
  - Internal
    - Sales analysis
    - Cost analysis
    - Financial records
  - External
    - Purchase of syndicated commercial data
    - • Marketing research studies by the MR department
      • Secondary data

## Successful Marketing Information Systems

The Monsanto Company and General Mills Incorporated are examples of firms that have a successful MIS in operation.

Monsanto has designed one of the most advanced marketing information systems in operation. The system provides detailed sales analyses by product, sales, district, type of mill, and end use. Computer analyses are obtained from a continuing panel of households that represent a cross section of the national market. Information is collected on purchase patterns by socio-economic group and is then analyzed to determine current buying trends.

Monsanto also collects survey data to record the actions of competitors. In addition, the system generates short-, medium-, and long-range forecasts for the company and industry. Short-term forecasts are developed for each of about 400 individual products.

The General Mills computer supplies each zone, regional, and district manager with a daily report on the previous day's orders by brand and a comparison of current projections of monthly sales with the monthly total projected the week before. Each of approximately 1700 individual products is analyzed in terms of current profitability and projected annual profitability as compared with target projections made at the beginning of the year. The "problem" products that require management attention are then printed out on the daily reports. A similar report looks for problem areas in each region and breaks down the nature of the problem according to cause (i.e., profit margins, over- or underspending on advertising and sales promotion).[6]

As marketing research becomes increasingly scientific and is combined by a growing number of organizations into fully functional information sys-

www.monsanto.co.uk

www.generalmills.com

### THE ROOTS OF MARKETING

**AN INNOVATOR'S PERSPECTIVE ON INFORMATION SYSTEMS**

Robert J. Williams, creator of the first and still one of the most notable marketing information systems in 1961 at the Mead Johnson division of Edward Dalton Company, explains the difference between marketing research and marketing information systems this way:

> The difference between marketing research and marketing intelligence is like the difference between a flash bulb and a candle. Let's say you are dancing in the dark. Every 90 seconds you're allowed to set off a flash bulb. You can use those brief intervals of intense light to chart a course, but remember everybody is moving, too. Hopefully, they'll accommodate themselves roughly to your predictions. You may get bumped and you may stumble every so often, but you can go along.

> On the other hand, you can light a candle. It doesn't yield as much light, but it's a steady light. You are continually aware of the movements of the other bodies. You can adjust your own course to the courses of the others. The intelligence system is a kind of candle. It's no great flash on the immediate state of things, but it provides continuous light as situations shift and change.[5]

tems, decision makers benefit by making informed decisions about problems and opportunities. Sophisticated computer simulations make it possible to consider alternative courses of action by posing a number of "what if?" situations.

This chapter has shown that information is vital for marketing decision making. No firm should operate without detailed information on consumer, competitors, and conditions in its market. Marketing research information enables the company to identify market segments and serves as a basis for developing the marketing plan.

The first five chapters of this book have been designed to serve as building blocks for marketing planning. The next chapter will show how a marketing plan is developed.

## SUMMARY

Marketing research is the systematic gathering, recording, and analyzing of data about problems related to the marketing of goods and services. It is the function that links the consumer to the company.

The five steps of the marketing research process are (1) formulate the problem, (2) develop the research design, (3) determine the data collection method, (4) collect the data, and (5) interpret and present the information. The research design is a master plan or model for conducting the research.

Secondary data are previously published matter. They include any useful information published by sources such as Statistics Canada, information from the Web, and others. Secondary data can be very useful in that they provide a ready source of useful information at low or no cost. On the other hand, the value of the data may be limited because they might not directly relate to the problem, and the quality of the information may not be verifiable.

Primary data are data collected for the first time, by observation, survey, or controlled experiment. The three kinds of surveys are telephone interviews, self-completed surveys, and personal interviews.

Full- and partial-service research suppliers are often hired to handle various amounts of specific research needed by a firm. Another type of company, the syndicated service organization, collects and sells regularly collected information.

In drawing a sample of consumers to research, firms can choose between probability and non-probability samples. Probability samples represent all elements of the desired population because every member of the population has a known chance of being selected. A nonprobability sample is chosen in an arbitrary way that does not give everyone a chance of being selected.

A marketing information system (MIS) is a set of routine procedures to continuously collect, monitor, and present internal and external information on company performance, competitors' actions, and opportunities in the marketplace. Marketing information systems can provide better information for management decisions than periodic marketing research surveys.

## KEY TERMS

census, p. 157
cluster sample, p. 159
convenience sample, p. 158
exploratory research, p. 148
hypothesis, p. 148
judgement sample, p. 158
marketing information system, p. 159
marketing research, p. 144
nonprobability sample, p. 158

population or universe, p. 157
primary data, p. 150
probability sample, p. 157
quota sample, p. 158
research design, p. 150
secondary data, p. 151
simple random sample, p. 159
systematic sample, p. 159
test marketing, p. 156

# INTERACTIVE SUMMARY AND DISCUSSION QUESTIONS

1. Marketing research is the systematic gathering, recording, and analyzing of data about problems that relate to the marketing of goods and services. Does information collected in such a scientific manner reduce the scope of management decision making? Explain.

2. Full- and partial-service research suppliers handle various amounts of specific research needed by a firm. Syndicated service organizations collect and sell regularly collected information. Give examples of when each of these types of service would be used by a company.

3. The five steps of the marketing research process are (1) formulating the problem, (2) developing the research design, (3) determining the data collection method, (4) collecting the data, and (5) interpreting and presenting the information. A small firm recognizes that it has the ability to develop high-quality air-monitoring equipment. Illustrate how the marketing research process might be applied to help management decide whether or not to enter this market.

4. Explain how problem definition in marketing research can sometimes be confused with symptoms.

5. Research design is a master plan or model for conducting the investigation. Differentiate between research design and the steps of the marketing research process.

6. Secondary data are previously published matter. Give examples of sources of external secondary data.

7. Discuss the advantages and limitations of secondary data.

8. Primary data are data collected for the first time, by observation, survey, or controlled experiment. Give examples of each of these data collection methods.

9. The three kinds of surveys are telephone interviews, self-completed surveys, and personal interviews. Discuss the advantages and disadvantages of each.

10. Test marketing is one of the experimental designs used for collecting information. Why would a firm undertake test marketing? Why don't all firms do so?

11. In drawing a sample to research, firms can choose between probability and nonprobability samples. Why are nonprobability samples generally considered to be unreliable?

12. A marketing information system is a set of routine procedures to continuously collect, monitor, and present internal and external information on company performance and opportunities in the marketplace. Explain how a marketing information system could provide better information for management decisions than periodic marketing research surveys.

13. Assume that you are asked by your employer to research the market potential for a line of new miniature, but high-quality, speakers for computers. You are asked to start with an analysis of the British market. Go to the Web and write a report on the relevant information to be found there.

## WestJet

WestJet is Canada's leading no-frills discount airline. It focuses on price and customer service. The company has been profitable almost from the beginning, and despite Air Canada's introduction of discount services, WestJet has continued to grow profitably. Its marketing approach is low-key. Advertising is limited to price point newspaper ads plus a limited number of billboards and radio spots. The company also benefits from a great amount of free publicity from the news media.

As it expands into more and more markets in Central and Eastern Canada it would be useful to develop an understanding of customers in these markets as well as to determine the level of satisfaction of existing customers.

### You Be the Marketer

1. Suggest a secondary data research process, as well as possible secondary data that might be used.
2. Outline a proposal for primary research that would be useful to the company in accomplishing the objectives listed in the final paragraph above.

# LOCATING SECONDARY DATA*

As mentioned earlier in the chapter, secondary data can be an extremely important element in making business decisions. This appendix introduces you to the key sources of information. They will be helpful in working on your assignments for this course as well as others, and will serve as a valuable reference after graduation.

The publications and Internet sites listed and described in this appendix refer mainly to the Canadian market. Some international marketing sources are covered in the final sections.

These are by no means all the sources of secondary data available for Canada or for international markets. However, it is hoped that these sources will serve as a representative list and as a starting point in the search for secondary sources of marketing data.

Several practical comments are appropriate in regard to the Internet sites. Universal resource locators (URLs) can change or become obsolete due to many factors, such as a change of server or lack of maintenance. The most current URLs have been provided, but be prepared for a non-functioning address.

Also note that a print publication, such as a directory, may have a so-called Internet equivalent, but that in reality the Internet version, while providing a search capability for a directory, may not replicate the actual printed pages of the directory. This can reduce the usefulness of an electronic version of a printed publication.

---

* This appendix was developed by Dennis Felbel, Head, A.D. Cohen Management Library, University of Manitoba.

# CANADIAN GOVERNMENT PUBLICATIONS

The federal government generates a vast array of publications through its various departments and agencies. Two services are useful in keeping track of these publications. The *Weekly Checklist of Canadian Government Publications* put out by the Depository Services Program, Communications Canada lists the book and serial titles that have been released during the week by the Parliament of Canada, federal departments, and Statistics Canada. Depository institutions, those that have negotiated a depository status agreement with the federal government to receive the publications free, use the Checklist to select publications for their collections. Most major universities and provincial legislative libraries in Canada have full depository status. Check on the status of a library when using its federal government publications.

The second service is the Communications Canada, Depository Service Program (DSP) Internet site. The *Weekly Checklist* described above is also available electronically at this location. In addition, a full *Catalogue* is available for searching back issues of the *Checklist*. The records in the *Catalogue* go back to 1991. The titles can either be ordered or sought out in the libraries across Canada that collect government publications, particularly those with depository status. In many instances the *Catalogue* provides hot links to many of the publications that are available electronically on the Internet. Links are also provided to other federal government databases such as *Strategis*, Industry Canada's site described below, accessible through the Internet. The URL address for the DSP site is http://dsp-psd.pwgsc.gc.ca/.

## Industry Canada

www.strategis.ic.gc.ca

*Strategis*, Industry Canada's Internet site, is the federal government's major initiative in providing information on business, trade, and investment in Canada as well as on the international business environment. For information on major export opportunities, international intelligence, and key business contacts, one enters the site through the Trade and Investment, International Business Opportunities section. For domestic information one can consult a companies directory section, a business information by sector section, and a consumer information section amongst others. The *Strategis* site was launched in 1996 and now contains over 2 million electronic documents. The URL address is http://www.strategis.ic.gc.ca.

## Sector Competitiveness Frameworks Series

Industry Canada has published a series of sector analyses under the series name *Sector Competitiveness Frameworks*. There are some 25 industrial sectors covered, including the automotive industry, forest products, household furniture, and primary steel. Each focuses on the opportunities, both domestic and international, and challenges that face each sector. Each sector analysis specifically covers the highlights and key points of the industry, changing conditions and industry responses, and growth prospects. The series is available in both print and electronic format via Industry Canada's Internet site, *Strategis*, at http://www.strategis.ic.gc.ca/. Within *Strategis* select Business Information by Sector from the main menu. The Business Information by Sector section also includes other options for finding industry sector specific information.

## Statistics Canada

Statistics Canada publishes extensive statistical information gathered through various sources. In addition to standard print publications, data is disseminated on computer printouts, microform, and in electronic format. Maps and other geographic reference materials are also available for some types of data. With hundreds of titles available, it is not practical to describe all the publications and services. However, detailed information can be obtained in several ways. There is a Statistics Canada regional centre in each of the following locations:

- Halifax, Nova Scotia
- Montreal, Quebec
- Ottawa, Ontario
- Toronto, Ontario
- Winnipeg, Manitoba
- Regina, Saskatchewan
- Edmonton, Alberta
- Calgary, Alberta
- Vancouver, British Columbia

Each centre has a collection of current Statistics Canada publications and reference materials that can be consulted or purchased. Copying facilities for printed materials and microform are also available, as is access to CANSIM (Statistics Canada's computerized database).

www.statcan.ca

## Statistics Canada Catalogue

This catalogue is no longer published on a regular annual basis. The last edition was published in 1997 and contains only print products. Electronic data products and services are not listed in the catalogue, but rather are to be found in Statistic Canada's electronic Online Catalogue of Products and Services via their Web site. However, in addition to the print products, the catalogue still contains useful information in appendices that helps the first-time user of Statistics Canada products to understand their catalogue numbering system as well as to find and order their publications. Statistics Canada has also developed BiblioCat, an electronic library catalogue that provides information about current and historical paper and electronic publications, also available via their Web site. Items listed in it are not for sale but are listed for consultative purposes only.

Also remember that as a federal government agency Statistics Canada publications will be available at university and provincial legislative libraries across Canada that have a depository status agreement with the federal government.

## Statistic Canada's Web Site

The Statistics Canada site is available in both English and French. It is relatively easy to browse through the approximately half dozen major sections. Newly released data and announcements of new products and services are described in The Daily section. Under a Canadian Statistics section, free tabular data is available on all aspects of Canada's economy, land, people, and government. This free data is normally extracted from CANSIM, Statistics Canada's online statistical database. One also can access CANSIM and retrieve more detailed data at a nominal cost. The CANSIM time series database is also available to colleges and universities who have paid an annual fee via the Data Liberation Initiative. Free census data is available, as well as the option to purchase more detailed data series in the Census section. Community profile information on some 6000 communities in Canada is available in the Community Profile section. All of Statistics Canada's publications and services, print and electronic, are listed in the Online Catalogue of Products and Services. A particularly useful section is the links to other sites feature, whereby one can access other statistical Web sites, both provincial and international. The URL address is http://www.statcan.ca/.

## Canadian Economic Observer

Generally, the most readily available Statistics Canada publication is likely to be the *Canadian Economic Observer*. It was titled the *Canadian Statistical Review* up to 1988. It is published monthly and as of September 1993 has been split into two parts, a journal with feature articles and economic analysis, and a statistical summary. The journal part provides authoritative commentary on Canadian and international economic trends, analysis of current economic conditions including the composite leading indicator, and a monthly feature article. The statistical summary provides the complete range of hard data on critical economic indicators, prices, markets, trade, and demographics. Data on the provinces and the G7 international scene are also compiled. An annual *Historical Statistical Supplement* that compiles monthly data is also available individually or as part of the subscription to the *Canadian Economic Observer*.

# PROVINCIAL GOVERNMENT PUBLICATIONS

The provincial governments publish thousands of documents through their various departments and agencies. These publications cover a variety of topics, reflecting the nature of the department from which the document originated. They range across the entire information spectrum, from agriculture to urban affairs.

As available documents are too numerous to describe individually, one can only offer direction to the major sources that list and describe the documents published by the provincial governments. As an illustration, here is how one would find publications generated by the province of Manitoba. Documents published by other provincial jurisdictions can be identified and obtained in a similar fashion.

## The Province of Manitoba

Like a number of provinces, Manitoba makes its publications available through a department or agency of the government. It publishes a *Manitoba Government Publications Monthly Checklist* that lists the publications received during the month by the Legislative Library of Manitoba. The most recent issues of the *Monthly Checklist* are also available on-line under the Manitoba Legislative Library link of the province's Internet site indicated below. The publications are listed by their issuing department, and this means by department, their branches and subdivisions, as well as boards, committees, and other agencies or bodies of the government. The publications can be obtained from their issuing body or from Statutory Publications, a government department, as indicated in the *Monthly Checklist*.

Manitoba government publications are also available in eight major libraries in the province that operate under a provincial depository program. These depository libraries automatically receive current Manitoba government publications.

The province of Manitoba also has an agency known as the Manitoba Bureau of Statistics. Its main publication, the *Manitoba Statistical Review,* presents statistical information of a socio-economic nature for both the government and private sector. In general, the *Review* publishes statistics in the areas of population, the labour force, economics, and industrial sectoral analysis.

The Manitoba Government, like other provincial jurisdictions, also maintains a site on the Internet. The site provides access to the Statutory Publications department and the services offered at cost via the Internet. Links to other government sites are also provided. For research purposes specific links concerning Business and Economics, Trade and Investment, and the Manitoba Marketplace are noteworthy. The URL address is http://www.gov.mb.ca/index.shtml.

# CHAMBERS OF COMMERCE

Most major cities and towns have a Chamber of Commerce. A Chamber of Commerce is an association established to further the business interests of its community. The Chambers in most metropolitan cities publish information and maintain Web sites about their cities for promotional reasons. The types of information one can expect to find at most Chambers of Commerce include economic facts, employment figures, government descriptions, demographic data, and quality of life statistics.

As an illustration, the Winnipeg Chamber of Commerce maintains a Web site that provides a description of Chamber services, member listings, and resource links. The URL address is http://www.winnipeg-chamber.com/.

# OTHER BUSINESS/GOVERNMENT ORGANIZATIONS

Municipalities, cities, and towns, in their promotional efforts to stimulate business development, often create special agencies to act as a catalyst for economic development. As part of their efforts, such agencies create resource material that can be of great value to the researcher when gathering secondary material at the local level.

An example of such an agency is Economic Development Winnipeg (EDW). This agency is an initiative of the City of Winnipeg formed to act as a catalyst for business development. It does this by promoting success stories and business news, tracking Winnipeg events, and by marketing the city itself. It generates publications about the city that highlight and focus on the strengths of Winnipeg as a place to do business. One of its major print publications is entitled the *Winnipeg Community Profile.* It outlines Winnipeg's economic strengths, manufacturing diversity, transportation network, and workforce, along with other features of the city that make it an attractive location for business. In addition a Web site is maintained at www.winnipegedw.com.

Most of the information provided through EDW is available elsewhere, but when packaged as one entity as it is, the research process is made easier. Similar organizations to EDW exist in other jurisdictions across the country. The researcher seeking marketing data must be aware of their existence and potential usefulness.

# MARKET REPORTS, SURVEYS, DIRECTORIES, SPECIAL ISSUES, MAGAZINES, AND NEWSLETTERS

Many of the publications listed in the remainder of this appendix are available through university, public, and special business libraries. As many of them can be either fairly expensive or difficult to locate, consult with a librarian as to cost and possible locations where they may be held.

As to the Internet sites, free online searching is often available at university and public libraries, although printing costs may apply. Also remember that what one finds on an Internet site may not match in content and format the published print version.

Once again the annotated lists are not meant to be comprehensive, but rather a sampling of some of the more significant publications in each of the representative fields selected.

The publications are listed under major headings that describe the industry, trade, or sector to which they pertain. Remember that the headings are not clear-cut, there may be overlap and therefore a need to consult more than one heading.

Some "special issues" may appear in libraries under the title of the magazine with which they are associated. Furthermore, some of the "annual" publications may not always be published on a regular basis, and new special issues may appear with little or no prepublication announcement.

## Advertising

### Canadian Advertising Rates and Data

Published monthly. Known by its acronym *CARD*. Advertises itself as Canada's media information network. Provides addresses, advertising rates, circulation, mechanical requirements, and personnel and branch office information for radio and TV stations, newspapers, magazines, and Web and online advertising sites for all of Canada. (Rogers Media)

### Canadian Media Directors' Council Media Digest

Published annually as a supplement to *Marketing Magazine,* formerly called *Marketing.* Profiles the advertising and media industry in a statistical format. Provides net advertising revenues by medium as well as analysis of each medium, including the Internet, television, radio, newspapers, business publications, and consumer magazines. Also contains a useful media terminology dictionary. (Rogers Media)

### Ethnic Media and Markets

Published twice yearly by the Media Information Network/Rogers Media. Provides the same information as *Canadian Advertising Rates and Data (CARD),* see above, for the ethnic media. Coverage includes the print media, radio and television stations and programs, and ethnic media support services. (Rogers Media)

### National List of Advertisers

Published annually in December. Provides the addresses, telephone numbers, brand names, and personnel for over 5400 major advertisers in Canada. In a special section, the companies are arranged by their Standard Industrial Classification Code. Advertising agencies are also listed. (Rogers Media)

### Publication Profiles

An annual publication that is a supplement to the above described *Canadian Advertising Rates and Data (CARD).* Describes the editorial profile of all the major consumer, farm, and business publications published in Canada. An Internet version of this title, only accessible to CARD subscribers, but with a useful visitors area, is available at http://www.cardmedia.com/. (Rogers Media)

### The Rankings: Canada's Top Marketing Communications Service Companies

Published annually in a July issue of *Marketing Magazine.* Ranks companies by revenue for all forms of marketing communication services, not just traditional advertising. Along with the ranking, a description of the business breakdown, client listing, and address specifics are provided. (Rogers Media)

## Canadian Market, General

### Bank of Canada Review

www.bankofcanada.ca/en/index.htm

In summer 1999 the format of the *Review* was changed into two distinct publications, the *Bank of Canada Review,* published quarterly, and the *Bank of Canada Banking Financial Statistics,* published monthly. The former combines feature articles and economic commentary on monetary policy, while the latter uses extensive charts and tables on the major financial and economic statistical indicators collected by the bank. The Bank of Canada makes available most of the articles from the *Review,* other publications including its technical and working papers, and select financial statistics at its Web site at http://www.bankofcanada.ca/en/index.htm. (Bank of Canada)

### Canada Year Book

Published every two years. Records in narrative and statistical format the developments in Canada's economic, social, and political life. Useful for determining "where Canada is at" on general topics. (Statistics Canada)

## Canadian Economic Observer

Published monthly but now in two parts, a journal with feature articles and economic analysis, and a statistical summary. The data in both parts is retrieved from CANSIM, Statistics Canada's computerized data bank. An annual *Historical Statistical Supplement* that compiles monthly data is also available. All three combine to become the definitive source for Canadian statistical information. For a more complete description of the *Canadian Economic Observer*, see above under Statistics Canada. (Statistics Canada)

## Canadian Outlook: Economic Forecast

Published quarterly. Features forecasts on the major components of the Canadian economy, including consumer expenditures, housing, government, business, international trade, energy, employment, labour force, costs and prices, and the financial markets. Statistical tables covering the same range of topics follow. An *Executive Summary* of *Canadian Outlook* is also available on a quarterly basis. (Conference Board of Canada)

## Econoscope

Published monthly. Provides economic forecasts for the Canadian economy in both narrative and statistical formats. The forecasts and indicators are provided for both Canada and the U.S., which makes comparisons convenient. (Royal Bank)

## Editor and Publisher Market Guide

Published annually. A compilation of marketing data on all Canadian and U.S. markets where daily newspapers are published. The main sections survey each of the cities or communities supporting a daily. Other sections provide a nationwide summary of population, income, housing, and retail sales. Market ranking tables are shown for population, disposable income, income per household, and total retail sales. Retail sales are in turn broken down into nine categories. (Editor and Publisher)

## FP Markets, Canadian Demographics

Published annually. One of the most extensive sources for demographics on Canadian urban markets. Provides data and projections for population, households, retail sales, and personal income for markets nationwide. The markets are defined by the census divisions. Buying power indices are developed, allowing for market comparisons. Municipal and provincial profiles are also provided. (Financial Post)

## Market Research Handbook

Published annually. An authoritative source of socio-economic information on local and national markets in Canada. It is based on the latest census data available, as well as estimates of that data. It is very useful for locating target markets. The data is divided into a number of broad categories including population, employment and earnings, expenditures, industry statistics, and projections. (Statistics Canada)

## Provincial Outlook: Economic Forecast

Published quarterly. Similar in format to *Canadian Outlook*, but with individual sections for each of the Canadian provinces. Key economic indicators for each province follow the forecasts. An *Executive Summary* of *Provincial Outlook* is also available on a quarterly basis. (Conference Board of Canada)

### Survey of Buying Power and Media Markets

Published annually in September as a supplement to *Sales and Marketing Management*. Provides data from U.S. geographic markets and media markets in the form of market rankings, population, effective buying income, retail sales, buying power indices, merchandise line sales, and projections. It is known as the reference guide to American purchasing influence. (Bill Communications)

## Clothing

### Canadian Textile Journal Manual

Published annually. A comprehensive source of information that provides access to textiles, chemical specialties, yarn sources (importers and domestic producers), Canadian machinery agents, and textile mills. The largest section is a buyer's guide listing products and services, with the companies paying a fee for the listing. Other information sources cover business opportunities, associations, and conferences. (Textile Technology Centre)

### Style: Buyers' Guide

Published annually as a special issue of *Style*. A comprehensive guide to companies, services, agencies, designers, suppliers, associations, showrooms, and fashion schools in the Canadian clothing sectors. (Style Communications)

## Computers and Information Technology

### Computing Canada

Published weekly in newspaper format. Intended for professionals in information technology management. Provides news on current developments. Normally contains a special report featuring some aspect of the field. Articles providing industry statistics are common. Special issues published irregularly are devoted to major trends. (IT Business Group/Transcontinental Media)

### Information Week

Published weekly. Intended for business and technology managers. Two regularly released special issues are of note. The *Outlook* issue published in January forecasts developments for the near term looking at spending, networking, Web commerce, and other industry developments. In September, an *Information Week 500* highlights and ranks the top 500 information technology users. (CMP Media Inc.)

### National Post Magazine Branham 300

Published annually in March. The Branham 300 ranks Canada's leading software and information technology service companies. The information technology industry is also analyzed and major companies profiled. (National Post)

### PC Magazine's Top 100 Web Sites

www.pcmag.com

Published annually with the top sites broken down into categories. Although a number of the recommended sites are more appropriate for personal use, this listing will hit many aspects of one's information needs. Each site is described in brief. The categories covered include finance, news and entertainment, reference, business, and computing. A continually updated *Top 100* is available on the *PC Magazine* Internet site at www.pcmag.com. (Ziff Davis Inc.)

### PC World's Best Free Stuff Online

Published annually. As more and more Web sites begin charging for information content, this guide provides a guide to useful free sites. The sites range from financial information sites, to government sites, to Web and browser services. The online version is available through PC World's Internet site at www.pcworld.com. (PC World Communications)

## Electronics

### Electronic Bluebook

Published annually. Lists the names, products, and companies of the electrical equipment industry. (CLB Media Inc.)

### Electronic Products and Technology (EP&T): Electrosource Product Reference Guide and Telephone Directory

Intended audience is the buyers, technicians, and engineers in Canada's electronics industry. Lists companies, products and their suppliers, U.S. and foreign manufacturers, and manufacturers' representatives and distributors. An Internet version of the *Electrosource Directory*, searchable by company or product, is available at the Web site http://www.ept.ca/. (LPV Media Inc.)

## Financial and Insurance

### Benefits Canada: Benefits Consultants Directory

Published annually in August as a special issue of *Benefits Canada*. The *Directory* contains the services offered by benefit consultants, listed geographically by province. (Rogers Media)

### Benefits Canada: Group Insurance Directory

Published annually in May as a special section of *Benefits Canada*. The group insurance companies are arranged alphabetically, with address, contact, telephone number, and branch office information provided. Various rankings are also available in table format. (Rogers Media)

### Benefits Canada: Directory of Pension Fund Investment Services

Published annually in November as a special section of *Benefits Canada*. The *Directory* includes a sub-directory of pension money managers, a sub-directory of investment consultants, and a top 40 money managers listing. A snapshot of the pension fund investment management business is provided. (Rogers Media)

Back issues of *Benefits Canada* are also available at the magazine's Web site at http://www.benefitscanada.com/.

### Canadian Insurance: Annual Review of Statistics

Published annually in May as a special issue of *Canadian Insurance*. Reviews the Canadian insurance industry in a largely statistical format. The major portion of the publication is taken up by the company exhibits, which provide five years of underwriting experience for insurers in Canada. Five-year data are also provided for the various classes of insurance, such as liability, aircraft, accident and sickness, and marine insurance. Recent developments and trends in the industry are also highlighted in narrative form. (Stone and Cox Ltd. Publishers)

### Canadian Underwriter: Annual Statistical Issue

Published annually in May as a special issue of *Canadian Underwriter*. Provides insurance company financial results for the previous year. The summary tables are arranged by type of insurance and by company. The company tables also contain five-year underwriting results. A five-year record by class of insurance is included. Leading companies are also ranked by type of insurance and also by their rank within their provincial jurisdiction. (Southam Magazine Group)

## Foods and Restaurants

### Directory of Restaurant and Fast Food Chains in Canada

Published annually. Provides coverage for more than 600 companies, listing head and regional office information, personnel, financial and advertising data, and expansion plans. (Rogers Media)

### Food in Canada

Published nine times a year and serving the Canadian food and beverage processing industry. It publishes special reference issues such as *The Top Food and Beverage Processors in Canada,* an *Annual Economic Review and Forecast,* an *Industry Sources Directory,* and an annual *Buyers' Guide.* (Rogers Media)

### Food in Canada's Buyers' Guide Directory Online

The trade publication *Food in Canada* maintains an Internet site that is available free after a registration process. It is searchable by product, manufacturer, and distributor. The URL address is www.foodincanada.com.

www.foodincanada.com

## Forestry

### Canadian Pulp and Paper Association (CPPA) Homepage

The Library at the CPPA site provides access to the publications of this national association. Of particular note are the *Annual Review* and the *Trade Directory.* The former provides key statistics relating to the industry's economic and environmental performance. The latter lists products manufactured by member companies of the association. Links are supplied to member companies, government agencies, and other forestry organizations. The URL address is http://www.open.doors.cppa.ca/index.htm.

### Madison's Canadian Lumber Directory

Published annually. Provides products and services listings, addresses, phone and fax numbers, key contacts, and names for all sectors of the Canadian forest industry. Also provides statistics and five-year price graphs for the industry. (Madison's Canadian Lumber Reporter)

### Pulp and Paper Canada: Annual Directory

Published annually for professionals in the pulp and paper industry. Lists information on products, personnel, mills and their equipment, suppliers, and other sources required for purchasing. (Southam Magazine Group)

# Franchises

### Canadian Business Franchise Directory

Published annually. Contains over 1000 franchise listings in some 35 categories. In addition to a supporting services section, this publication contains articles on the basics of buying and running a franchise. (CGB Publishing)

### Directory of Franchising Organizations

This Directory is in its 38th edition. It is American in focus and lists 1300 franchise opportunities in 45 categories. (Pilot Books)

### Entrepreneur: Annual Franchise 500

Published annually for over 20 years. Ranks and rates U.S. and Canadian franchises based upon financial strength and stability, growth rate, and size amongst other criteria. An electronic version is available at http://franchise.entrepreneur.com. (Entrepreneur)

### Entrepreneur: Top 200 Global Franchises

Entrepreneur also makes available an electronic listing of international franchise opportunities that can be located at http://franchise.entrepreneur.com. (Entrepreneur)

## Industrial

### Heating-Plumbing-Air Conditioning: Buyer's Guide

Published annually in July/August as a special issue of *Heating-Plumbing-Air Conditioning*. A directory of manufacturers, wholesalers, distributors, and agents that supply products and services in the heating, plumbing, and air-conditioning industry. Lists of trade names and industry associations are included. (Rogers Media)

### PEM Sourcebook

Published in conjunction with *Plant Engineering and Maintenance*. A directory for plant engineers and industrial and purchasing managers. It provides address and name information for companies, organizations, and associations in the industry. An electronic version is available at www.industrialsourcebook.com. (CLB Media Inc.)

## Materials Handling

### MM&D's Handling Directory of Buying Sources

Published annually in June as the directory issue of *Materials Management and Distribution*. The companies are arranged in a classified equipment index and cover all aspects of the materials handling sector, from computers to conveyor belts. A free online, searchable version of the directory is available on the Internet at www.mmdonline.com. (Rogers Media)

## Metalworking

### Canadian Machinery and Metalworking: Census

Published annually as a special issue of *Canadian Machinery and Metalworking*. Focuses on computer numerically controlled (CNC) machine tools installed since the previous census, providing user name, location, and other specifics. Includes robotic installations. Market share information for the top vendors is also supplied. (Rogers Media)

### Canadian Machinery and Metalworking: Directory and Buying Guide

Published annually in December as a special issue of *Canadian Machinery and Metalworking*. Acts as a guide to worldwide sources of tooling, components, and supplies for the metalwork manufacturing industry. This is a significant directory, the 2002 edition numbers over 160 pages. (Rogers Media)

The *Census* and *Directory* are also available free after a registration process at the URL address www.canadianmetalworking.com.

## Office Equipment and Supplies

### Purchasing Profile and Salary Survey

Published annually as a special focus issue of *Purchasing 2b2* in conjunction with the Purchasing Management Association of Canada. Profiles the purchasing industry, looking at job titles, location within industry, education, salary levels, and trends. The *Survey* is also available free after a registration process at the Web site www.purchasingb2b.ca. (Rogers Media)

## Packaging

### Canadian Packaging: Buyers' Guide

Published annually in the summer as a special issue of *Canadian Packaging*. This is a significant publication providing access to companies involved in packaging materials and components, containers, machinery, and services in the packaging industry. Associations connected to the industry are also listed. The *Buyers' Guide* is also available free after a registration process at the Web site http://www.canadianpackaging.com/. (Rogers Media)

### Canadian Packaging: Machinery Specifications Manual

Published annually as the January issue of *Canadian Packaging*. Presents in table form performance and machinery specifications for manufacturers who supply packaging machinery to the Canadian market. (Rogers Media)

## Petroleum and Mining

### Canadian Mines Handbook

Published annually. Features listings of mining companies, mines, and advanced projects. Contains five years of stock exchange data, maps of major mining areas, and statistical data on the mining industry. (Southam Information Products)

### Canadian Mining Journal: Mining Sourcebook

Published annually as a special issue of *Canadian Mining Journal*. Provides technical operating and cost data for the mining and mineral-processing industry. Also, as a sourcebook, it details sources of supply for materials, equipment, and services. It includes a directory of mining managers and executives. (Southam Information Products)

### Canadian Oil Register

Published annually. Coverage of over 3500 companies in the oil and gas industry. Contains an 18 000-entry Who's Who of management and technical personnel, and sections on companies, products, and services. (Nickle's Energy Group)

### FP Survey of Mines and Energy Resources

Published annually. A comprehensive review of over 3000 publicly traded mining and energy resource companies in Canada. The financial statistical tables and ratios are useful for comparative investment analysis. Includes highlights of events that have affected the companies in the past year. (Financial Post)

### Mining Review: Directory and Buyers' Guide

Published annually as a special issue of *Mining Review*. Focus is on the Western Canadian mining industry and the equipment and services used in this geographic area. (Naylor Communications)

### Mining Review: Exploration and Development Review

Published annually as a special issue of *Mining Review*. Focuses on exploration and new developments in the Western Canadian mining industry over the past 12 months. (Naylor Communications)

## Printing, Publishing, and Graphic Arts

### Canadian Printer: Buyers' Guide and Directory

Published annually. Provides information on equipment, supplies, and suppliers, as well as statistical information on the printing industry. A searchable, online version of the *Buyers' Guide* is available free after a registration process on the Internet at www.canadianprinter.com. (Rogers Media)

### Estimators' and Buyers' Guide

An annual guide for the graphics industry published by the publisher of *Graphic Monthly*. Lists companies and graphic arts services of relevance to the graphics industry. (North Island Sound Ltd.)

## Product Design and Engineering

### Design Engineering: Fluid Power Buyers' Guide

Published annually as a special issue of *Design Engineering*. Lists information on suppliers, systems, and products in the engineering/fluid power sector. (Rogers Media)

### Design Engineering: Mechanical Power Transmission Buyers' Guide

Published annually as a special issue of *Design Engineering*. Lists information on products, suppliers, and manufacturers in the mechanical power transmission industry. (Rogers Media)

Both of these *Design Engineering Buyers' Guides* have an online equivalent searchable by product, manufacturer, and distributor. They are available free after a registration process. The Internet address is http://www.design-engineering.com/.

## Retailing

### Canadian Directory of Shopping Centres (3 Volumes)

Published annually. Provides information on over 2200 major shopping centres across the country. Lists include tenants and managers/owners contact information. Statistical data includes rent costs, traffic, sales, and market population. (Rogers Media)

www.cdngrocer.com

### Canadian Grocer

This trade journal monitors all the latest trends and news in food distribution and retailing. Special directory issues are published regularly, such as the *National Directory of Food Brokers and Brands* and the *Annual Survey of Chains and Groups*. The special directory issues are available free after a registration process on the Internet at www.cdngrocer.com. (Rogers Media)

### Directory of Retail Chains in Canada

Published annually. Provides information on over 2000 chains, including store location and size, head office particulars, and key contacts. Other details include projected openings and buyers' names. (Rogers Media)

### Monday Report on Retailers

Published weekly as a newsletter. Provides articles on the expansion plans of the major chain retailers in North America. Contains no advertising. (Rogers Media)

## Transportation

### Canadian Transportation Logistics: Buyers' Guide

Published annually as a special issue of *Canadian Transportation Logistics*. Arranged by transportation carrier: air, sea, motor, and rail. Other transport-related companies are listed under services such as customs brokers, logistic providers, and transportation intermediaries. (Southam Magazine Group)

### Purchasingb2b: Transportation Services Directory

Published annually. The *Directory* provides information on the major transportation carriers utilized by the purchasing sector. This includes air cargo, couriers, freight forwarders, and ports. The *Directory* is also available free after a registration process at the Web site www.benefitscanada.com. (Rogers Media)

## Regional and City Business Magazines

There are a number of regional and city business magazines published in Canada that devote themselves to a restricted geographic area. They often provide a wealth of information and analysis on the local scene that is available nowhere else. Some examples follow, with their respective publishers also indicated.

### BC Business Magazine

Features an annual Top 100 Companies issue and profiles Entrepreneurs of the Year in a special issue. (Canada Wide Magazines and Communications)

### Manitoba Business

Includes special issues focusing on the Top 100 Manitoba Companies and the 50 Fastest-Growing Manitoba Companies. (Manitoba Business Magazine Publishing Group)

### Northern Ontario Business

Reports on all aspects of business and industry that relate to Northern Ontario in a newspaper format. (Laurentian Publishing)

City business magazines like *Toronto Business Magazine* (Zanny Ltd.) and *Montreal Business Magazine* (Quebec Inc.) focus on the current business events of their respective cities. Other city magazines exist for urban areas across Canada generally, providing a combination of business and consumer information for that particular city.

# TRADE DIRECTORIES

### Canadian National Services Directory

Published annually. Contains listings of Canadian businesses in the services industry only. These businesses have to meet the criteria of having 20 or more employees, annual revenue of $1 million or more, and have a Standard Classification Code (SIC) in the service industry sector. Address and company specific information is provided. Also contains a business by SIC code and geographic index. (Dun & Bradstreet Canada)

### Canadian Trade Index

Published annually. A multi-volume directory that provides a classified list of some 27 000 Canadian products and an alphabetical list of some 32 000 Canadian companies. Also includes an exporters section, a catalogue section, and a section on ISO registered companies. (Nexport Media Inc.)

### FP Survey of Industrials

Published annually. Covers all publicly traded Canadian manufacturing and service companies. Provides a description of the companies' operations and highlights of events over the past year. Financial data and ratios are useful for investment purposes. The companies are also listed by Standard Industrial Classification (SIC) Code. (Financial Post)

### Fraser's Canadian Trade Directory

Published annually in four volumes. Provides a comprehensive listing of manufacturers by product classification, as well as an alphabetical listing. Trade names and their manufacturers and international firms who have agents or distributors in Canada also have their own specific listings. (Rogers Media)

### Moody's International Manual

Published annually, with a monthly updating service. One of the series of the Moody's manuals, this one provides coverage of major international corporations in over 110 countries, including Canada. Each entry contains a company history, business and product description, subsidiary and personnel listings, and financial statements. (Mergent)

### Scott's Industrial Directories

Published annually. The four major *Scott's Directories* are the Atlantic, Quebec, Ontario, and Western. They have identical formats, with four main sections. The first is a list of Canadian manufacturers in alphabetical order. The second is alphabetical by geographic location of the company, with addresses, products, and number of employees. The third section lists companies by their product, arranged by the North American Industry Classification System (NAICS). The fourth section contains indexes by company ISO registration number and by Internet address. (Southam Information Products)

# INTERNATIONAL MARKETING PUBLICATIONS

### European Marketing Data and Statistics

Published annually. This major reference work is a compendium of statistical information on the countries of Western and Eastern Europe that can be very useful for market planning. Some 25 principal subject areas are broken down into subcategories covering over 500 pages. Some representative subject areas are demographic trends/forecasts, economic indicators, labour force indicators, and advertising/media patterns. Within the subject of labour force indicators for example, there are 13 sub-categories ranging from employment level to average working week in manufacturing. The data compilation dates back to 1977 and allows for trend analysis and forecasting. The data itself is presented in spreadsheet format. The data for Eastern Europe is not quite as extensive and as complete as that for Western Europe, for obvious reasons. For example, countries that emerged from Czechoslovakia, Yugoslavia, and the USSR in the early 1990s are included as far as possible. Prior to that, the data is provided under the former country name. Brief geographic sketches and maps for each European country are included in a separate section. There is also a special chapter arranged by country that identifies the major information sources one can turn to for further research on the European market. (Euromonitor)

### International Marketing Data and Statistics

Published annually. A publication similar in format to the above-described *European Marketing Data and Statistics*, except that the 25 principal subjects deal with the Americas, Asia, Africa, and Oceania. The country coverage includes over 160 countries and is particularly useful for smaller countries for which it is difficult to find statistical information. Countries are grouped by major sub-region to make regional comparisons easier. Also includes a chapter dealing with other major information sources that can be consulted. (Euromonitor)

### Statistical Yearbook

Published annually. Provides information on some 200 countries and territories that are members of the United Nations. The data is presented mainly in table format. Some of the specific areas covered include education, science and technology, libraries, book publication, cultural information, and radio and television broadcasting. UNESCO maintains a Web site at http://www.unesco.org/ from which their documents can be identified, ordered, and downloaded in many cases. (UNESCO)

### World Economic Outlook

Published biannually. This survey of prospects and policies results from International Monetary Fund (IMF) staff drawing on information provided through member countries. The analysis is both current and detailed, with the late 2001 release dealing with the global economy after September 11. Implications from the terrorist attacks for the world economy, as well as the mature financial markets in the United States and Europe, are addressed. The narrative is supported in a comprehensive fashion by an extensive array of tables, boxes, and figures on all aspects of country, regional, and world statistics. The IMF maintains a Web site at http://www.imf.org/external/index.htm. A large number of IMF titles appear in full text, others have to be ordered. (International Monetary Fund)

### Yearbook of Labour Statistics

Published annually. Summarizes the principal labour statistics for some 190 countries, usually covering the most recent ten-year period. Data are drawn from national statistical services and are presented in nine chapters on such topics as wages, unemployment, and hours of work. A companion volume to the annual is the *Retrospective Edition on Labour Statistics, 1945–1989*. This volume pulls together data for the period and thus offers an opportunity to analyze participation rates of the population in the labour force over a 25-year period. The ILO Web site is located at http://www.ilo.org/. The majority of free data is in the ILO Library section of the site. (International Labour Organization)

# BIBLIOGRAPHIC DATABASES

### *ABI/INFORM*

This database is available in either CD-ROM or Internet versions. It contains thorough indexing and abstracting of articles from international business and management journals, including all the major marketing journals. The CD-ROM version known as *ABI Power Pages* carries more than 1000 journal titles, while the Internet version known as *Proquest Direct* carries more than 1700 journal titles. Over 400 of the journals in *ABI Power Pages* are available in full image, that is the full image of the entire article can be printed on request. For *Proquest Direct* over 1000 titles are available in either full image or full text, with the number continuing to grow. These articles can be viewed, printed, or e-mailed to a specific address. *ABI/INFORM* has search capabilities that make it easy to search for articles on a specific industry or company. The CD-ROM version is updated monthly, while the Internet version is updated on a continual basis. Coverage for indexing and abstracting dates back to 1981, and for full image access to 1987. *ABI/INFORM* is user friendly, with users requiring only a few minutes of instruction in order to feel comfortable with the system. It is available in many university and business libraries. (Proquest Information and Learning)

### *Canadian Business and Current Affairs (CBCA)*

This database provides indexing and abstracting to over 700 Canadian periodicals, including business, popular, trade, special interest, and academic publications, along with the major Canadian daily newspapers. Coverage goes back to 1982, with the full text of articles available from 1993 on for an increasing number of titles. Many of the special issues of periodicals described in the previous sections of this appendix are indexed in this database. Company, product, and industry information are readily searchable. CBCA is available in many public, university, and business libraries. It is relatively easy to use after a few minutes of instruction. (Micromedia Proquest)

Will Gap be successful in adapting to changing consumer behaviour?

# CONSUMER BEHAVIOUR

Imagine a world without the Gap. Imagine a landscape barren of thousands of big-windowed stores with navy awnings that call out: "All is safe. You're in a gentrified neighbourhood. Come inside and buy cotton twill."

Could it happen? As impossible as it might seem, yes. The Gap Inc., a retailer that transformed chinos and white T-shirts into a billion-dollar empire, is in distress. Since April 2000, sales for the San Francisco-based conglomerate, which also owns the Banana Republic and Old Navy chains, have been in steep decline.

The company's origins date back to 1969. At that time it was considered the place to buy counterculture items. By the '80s the Gap had expanded into a cult empire, making button-down shirts, chinos, and basic cotton T-shirts the boomer uniform.

Gap branding fed perfectly into the emergence of the ego-driven yuppie marketplace. Personality, rather than product was the focus. The Gap's trump card was that it transcended fashion. Nobody looked to the retailer for anything "directional," as the industry likes to put it. In other words, it didn't chase the latest trends. It didn't have to. The wearer brought style to the clothes, not the reverse. The firm expanded to GapKids in 1986 and then BabyGap was launched in 1990. It also developed the Old Navy chain. Some argue that ultimately Old Navy out-gapped Gap.

However, when the dot.com bubble burst, some of the Gap magic seemed to go too. The "dress-down revolution" suddenly looked empty—and old. The Gap brand was hit hard.

Critics have said that even the Gap's advertising, on which it spends lavishly, has lost its edge. A recent campaign, featuring images of low-profile, older celebrities such as the sculptor Robert Graham with his wife, actress Anjelica Huston, was thought to lack a clear message. New campaigns are being developed.

In the process, the company has succeeded in causing a "Gaplash" with twenty-something customers looking for individuality, not conformity. Gen Y doesn't identify with, or buy into, the Gap because the clothing is too homogeneous. Ad campaigns that show everyone dressed identically in Gap are the exact opposite of what that market wants.

The combination of changes in taste, managing change in a huge organization, and high-end competition such as Gucci and Prada, and lower-end competition from nimble operations such as Zara have resulted in a huge challenge for Gap. To try to satisfy emerging consumer needs without alienating current loyal customers is a major challenge.

Effective marketing depends on accurately assessing consumer behaviour. Gap has done this for many years. But as people's lifestyles change, the company is facing new challenges. A constant study of consumer behaviour is essential for the effective ongoing implementation of marketing plans.

Source: Excerpted from Anne Kingston, "Bridging the Gap," *National Post*, May 4, 2002, p. SP1. Reprinted with permission.

www.gap.com

# INTRODUCTION

This book has made a point of emphasizing the importance of understanding the consumer before developing a marketing plan. Consumer behaviour studies try to apply a microscope to the basic understanding of people and their purchase behaviour. This chapter and the next chapter provide an introduction to the extensive marketing literature concerning consumer behaviour.

**consumer behaviour**
The activities of individuals in obtaining, using, and disposing of goods and services, including the decision processes that precede and follow these actions.

**Consumer behaviour** consists of the activities of individuals in obtaining, using, and disposing of goods and services, including the decision processes that precede and follow these actions.[1] This definition includes both the ultimate consumer and the purchaser of products for business use. However, in the case of business consumers, a major difference is that additional influences from within the organization may be exerted on the purchasing agent. This will be discussed in more detail in the next chapter.

It is important to develop positive relationships with consumers. Therefore, the basic task of marketing is to understand the customer so sound marketing planning can occur. We can categorize people into various segments, but it is essential to go deeper than that. Marketing planners must consider *what* motivates potential consumers, and *why*. The study of consumer behaviour has become a well-established discipline within the field of marketing.

Much marketing research into consumer behaviour has been undertaken. In addition, the field of consumer behaviour borrows extensively from other areas, like psychology and sociology. The work of Kurt Lewin, for instance, provides an excellent classification of influences on buying behaviour. Lewin's proposition was that

$$B = f(P,E)$$

where behaviour ($B$) is a function ($f$) of the interactions of individual factors ($P$) and the pressures exerted on them by outside forces in the environment ($E$).[2]

This statement can be rewritten for consumer behaviour as follows:

$$B = f(E,I)$$

where consumer behaviour ($B$) is a function ($f$) of the interaction of environmental factors ($E$) such as culture and social influences, and individual factors and psychological processes ($I$) such as needs, motives, and attitudes. Understanding consumer behaviour, as Figure 8.1 illustrates, requires careful consideration of the many variables that comprise each of these two major categories.

# ENVIRONMENTAL FACTORS THAT AFFECT CONSUMER BEHAVIOUR

Countless facets of the environment affect behaviour. Two important groups of factors that can affect consumer behaviour are cultural and social influences. People are social animals. They often

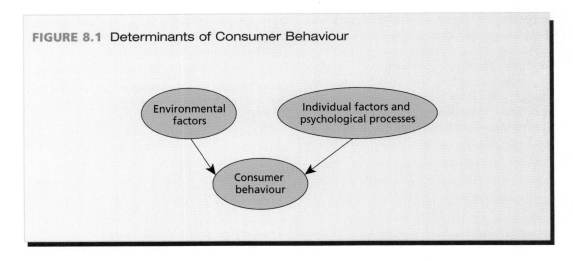

**FIGURE 8.1** Determinants of Consumer Behaviour

buy products and services because of a broad range of perceived influences of others, as well as the culture of which they are a part. The important social influences are group influences, reference groups, social class, and family influences. A general model of the environmental determinants of consumer behaviour is shown in Figure 8.2.

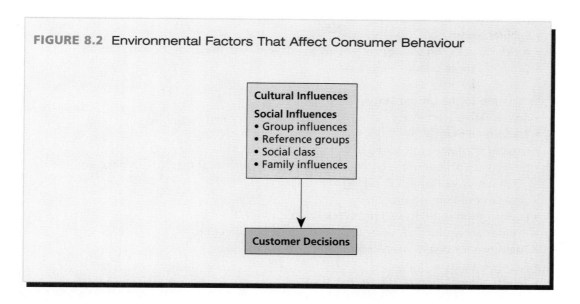

**FIGURE 8.2** Environmental Factors That Affect Consumer Behaviour

## Cultural Influences

Culture is the broadest environmental determinant of consumer behaviour. Sometimes it is a very elusive concept for marketers to handle. General Mills knew that few Japanese homes had ovens, so it designed a Betty Crocker cake mix that could be made in the electric rice-cookers widely used in that country. The product failed because of a cultural factor. Japanese homemakers regard the purity of their rice as very important, so they were afraid that a cake flavour might be left in their cookers.[3]

**Culture** can be defined as the complex of values, ideas, attitudes, institutions, and other meaningful symbols created by people that shape human behaviour, and the artifacts of that behaviour, transmitted from one generation to the next.[4] It is the way of life that is learned and handed down through generations that gives each society its own peculiar characteristics and values.

**culture**

The complex of values, ideas, attitudes, institutions, and other meaningful symbols created by people that shape human behaviour, and the artifacts of that behaviour, transmitted from one generation to the next.

### Core Values in the Canadian Culture

The list in Table 8.1 provides a useful summary of characteristics that are significant to the Canadian culture. There are trends and shifts in cultural values, yet traditionally these changes have been gradual. Nevertheless, marketers must constantly assess cultural norms. One strong cultural thread is an awareness of the distinctiveness of the Canadian "identity," despite the difficulty of being able to easily define it. Thus a number of television programs and commercials created in other countries, including the United States, often do not quite fit in the Canadian context.

### Cultural Influences: An International Perspective

An awareness of cultural differences is particularly important for international marketers. Different attitudes, mores, and folkways all affect marketing strategy. Examples of cultural influences on marketing strategy are abundant in the international environment. Look at the marketing implications of the following situations:

■ In Malaysia and Indonesia, the left hand is considered unclean. Therefore, it is insulting to hand an object to someone using the left hand.

> **TABLE 8.1** Summary of Significant Canadian Characteristics
>
> **As a Function of Being a Part of the North American Reality**
> - Modern orientation
> - Openness to new ideas
> - Egalitarianism
> - A rich, developing society with many needs and high materialistic expectations
> - Growing, more diffuse middle class
>
> **In Relation to the United States**
> - Conservative tendencies
> - Traditional bias
> - Greater confidence in bureaucratic institutions
> - Collectivity orientation—reliance on institutions such as state, big business, and the church vs. personal risk taking
> - Less achievement-oriented
> - Lower optimism—less willing to take risks
> - Greater acceptance of hierarchical order and stratification
> - Tolerance for diversity—acceptance of cultural mosaic
> - Family stability
> - Selective emulation of the United States—resistance to some American characteristics and dominance, yet willingness to emulate
> - Elitist and ascriptive tendencies

■ In Japan, as well as some other Asian countries, it is much easier to get things done, or to get to see a prospective client, if you have been recommended or introduced by a mutual acquaintance.

■ In Ethiopia, the time required to make a decision is directly proportional to its importance. This is so much the case that lower-level bureaucrats there attempt to elevate the prestige of their work by taking a long time to make decisions. Unaware North Americans therefore may innocently downgrade their work in the local people's eyes by trying to speed things up.

Often a marketing program that has been successful in Canada cannot be applied directly in international markets because of cultural differences. Real differences exist among different countries, and the differences must be known and evaluated by the international firm. Purdy's Chocolates not only discovered that Taiwanese consumers did not like some of their products and packaging, but also that channels of distribution were not what they expected. When Helene Curtis introduced its Every Night shampoo line in Sweden, it renamed the product Every Day, since Swedes usually wash their hair in the morning.

World marketers must become familiar with many aspects of the local population—including their cultural heritage. The local market segments in each country must be thoroughly analyzed prior to developing a marketing plan, just as they are at home. The topic of cultural influences in international marketing is explored more fully in Chapter 19.

www.helenecurtis.com

### Subcultures

**microculture**

A subgroup with its own distinguishing modes of behaviour.

Within each culture are numerous **microcultures**—subgroups with their own distinguishing modes of behaviour. Any culture as heterogeneous as that existing in Canada is composed of significant microcultures based on such factors as race, nationality, age, rural–urban location, religion, and geographic distribution. The size of such microculture groups can be significant. For example, the Italian population in the Toronto area is about 500 000—larger than the entire population of most Canadian cities.

## RETAIL OXYMORON: LOYAL SHOPPER

Erica George spends about $75 a month at her local Shoppers Drug Mart on toiletries and cosmetics, an increase of 25 percent since she signed up for an Optimum loyalty card a year ago. An admitted loyalty junkie, Ms. George, 33, carries nine such cards in her wallet but says she likes Optimum best because she can redeem her points for discounts on goods right at the checkout counter.

"I hate having all of these cards," she says, gesturing at her blue Air Miles card, a car-wash card, and a Coltee card. It's a sentiment echoed all too frequently among consumers, and no wonder. Retail loyalty programs have risen about 60 percent since the mid-1990s. A Kubas Consultants survey last year of Canada's biggest markets indicated that 73 percent of consumers participated in one or more loyalty programs.

But despite this, few actually encourage customers to be loyal, experts say, because they require too much effort to redeem the rewards—usually discounts, free merchandise, or services. "We've hit the peak with these programs and I think most of them are just going to die off," says retail consultant Joan Pajunen, president of TrendSpeak International and author of *The Butterfly Customer: Capturing the Loyalty of Today's Elusive Consumer.*

Most egregious, in her view, are reward programs that charge a fee to join or require customers to redeem their points through a catalogue or coupons offering merchandise or services.

In fact, says Ms. Pajunen, most loyalty programs aren't about encouraging loyalty but about mining consumers for information about purchases and preferences. Because customers provide their names, addresses, birth date, and telephone number when they apply for membership, each swipe of a magnetically encoded plastic card records valuable information about their preferences and preferences of people like them. The data might show, for example, that women over 35 prefer a certain brand or price range of face cream in a particular region of Canada.

Programs that don't yield that type of information to retailers are regarded as outmoded and costly, says Steve Boase, a retail consultant at J.C. Williams Group: "Loyalty programs are expensive to run, but the costs to retailers are presumably offset by the quality of the feedback they are getting." Music retailer HMV dropped its "buy 10 CDs, get one free" loyalty program, which did not collect information, earlier this year.

Canadian Tire operates the country's oldest loyalty program, doling out $100 million in Canadian Tire money each year. But it too has tried to modernize (and collect sales data) with a house credit card that offers discounts for accumulated points.

**Do you agree with the practices discussed, and the conclusions drawn in this article?**

Source: Excerpted from Hollie Shaw, "Retail Oxymoron: Loyal Shopper," *National Post*, April 13, 2002, p. FP1. Reprinted with permission.

Many people on the West Coast display a lifestyle that emphasizes casual dress, outdoor entertaining, and water recreation. Mormons refrain from purchasing tobacco and liquor; orthodox Jews purchase kosher or other traditional foods; Chinese people may exhibit more interest in products and symbols that reflect their Chinese heritage.

### THE FRENCH-CANADIAN MARKET

Although Canada has many microcultures, the two founding cultures—English and French—are the most influential, through sheer force of numbers. The francophone population is a significant market in Canada. Twenty-two percent of the Canadian population identify French as their mother tongue.[5] While most of this population resides in Quebec, there are significant French-speaking segments in other provinces. Proportionately, the largest is in New Brunswick, where 32.9 percent of the population (or 239 700 people) have French as their mother tongue. Numerically, Ontario has the largest group outside Quebec, with 479 300.

The Quebec market is large enough and different enough to create an entire advertising industry of its own. Quebec's share of Canadian GDP is 21.7 percent.[6] It is the second-largest market in Canada.

While there is no doubt that the Quebec market is substantially different from the rest of Canada, it is difficult to define those differences precisely. Considerable research over the years has suggested many characteristics specific to the area—French-Canadians, for example, are said to be fonder of sweets than other Canadians. However, other data can usually be found to contest any such find, or at least to show that it is no longer true.

Such statements reflect measurement of traits in the Quebec culture at only one particular period. These measurements may be legitimate and necessary for a firm that wishes to market a product in that segment at a particular point in time. However, similar differences can probably be detected between consumers in Nova Scotia and consumers in British Columbia, if you look for them.

Attention should not be concentrated on *specific* differences between the Quebec market and the rest of Canada, but rather on the fact that there is a basic cultural difference between the two markets. "Culture is a way of being, thinking, and feeling. It is a driving force animating a significant group of individuals united by a common tongue, and sharing the same customs, habits and experiences."[7] Because of this cultural difference, some marketing programs may be distinctly different in Quebec than in the rest of Canada. In the French-Canadian market, it is not the products that are different, but the state of mind. For example, Renault achieved a Quebec market penetration ten times greater than in the rest of Canada. Since the product and price were the same, the difference must have been in the marketing program attuned to the Quebec market.

As cultures in Canada are affected by similar political and technological influences, the differences in values and consumption patterns also narrow. Nevertheless, it appears that for some francophones some frames of reference and significant cues will continue to be different, requiring the marketer to be astute in dealing with these market segments.

The key to success in this important Canadian market is having marketing specialists who understand people and how to deal in that specific market. Sophisticated marketers now realize this. That is why there are so many Quebec advertising agencies producing unique advertising programs for the francophone market.

## THE CANADIAN MARKETPLACE

### IS THERE A DIFFERENCE? FRANCOPHONE QUEBECKERS VS. ENGLISH CANADIANS

- Percentage of francophone Quebeckers who prefer people who choose happiness over duty: 51. Of English Canadians: 25.

- Percentage of francophone Quebeckers who think buying something new is one of life's great pleasures: 71. Of English Canadians: 51.

- Percentage of Quebec couples living common-law in 1996: 25. Of couples elsewhere in Canada: 14. Of Quebec couples under 30: 64. Of under-30 couples in the rest of Canada: 42.

- Number of Quebec-made television shows among the ten most highly rated programs in the province during the 1995–96 season: 10. Of Canadian-made shows in the top ten in English Canada: 3.

- Percentage of francophone women who say that dressing elegantly is an important facet of their lives: 45. Of anglophone women: 29.

- Percentage of Quebeckers who conduct their ordinary banking transactions through a credit union or caisse populaire: 60. Of English Canadians: 3.

- Percentage of francophone men who said they purchased more than three pairs of shoes in the preceding 12 months: 23. Of anglophone men: 8.

www.nielsenmedia.com

- Percentage of francophone Quebeckers who say they've purchased no-name grocery products: 42. Of English Canadians: 70.

- Percentage of francophone Quebeckers who read the comics section of their newspaper: 17. Of English Canadians: 38.

- Percentage of Quebeckers who acknowledge having had an affair: 16. Of Ontarians: 9.

**How might a marketer make use of this information?**

Source: Excerpted from Leger & Leger, Decima Research, Statistics Canada, Nielsen Media Research, and Print Measurement Bureau, in *The Globe and Mail* (July 19, 1997), p. D1.

# Social Influences

The earliest awareness of children confirms that they are members of a very important group—the family—from which they seek total satisfaction of their physiological and social needs. As they grow older, they join other groups—neighbourhood play groups, school groups, Cub Scouts, Brownies, minor league hockey teams—as well as groups of friends. From these groups they acquire both status and role. **Status** refers to relative position in a group. **Role** refers to the rights and duties expected of an individual in a group by other members of the group. Some of these are formal groups (for example, Cub Scouts) and others are informal (friendship groups). But both types supply their members with status and roles and, in doing so, influence the activities, including the consumer behaviour, of each member.

## Group Influence Affects Conformity

Although most people view themselves as individuals, groups are often highly influential in purchase decisions. In situations where individuals feel that a particular group or groups are important, they tend to adhere in varying degrees to the general expectations of that group. Consider the pressure faced by young teens to conform to clothing styles.

The surprising impact that groups and group norms can exhibit on individual behaviour has been called the **Asch phenomenon**. The phenomenon was first documented in a classic study by psychologist S.E. Asch:

> Eight subjects are brought into a room and asked to determine which of a set of three unequal lines is closest to the length of a fourth line shown some distance from the other three. The subjects are to announce their judgements publicly. Seven of the subjects are working for the experimenter, and they announce incorrect matches. The order of announcement is arranged such that the naive subject responds last. In a control situation, 37 naive subjects performed the task 18 times each without any information about others' choices. Two of the 37 subjects made a total of 3 mistakes. However, when another group of 50 naive subjects responded *after* hearing the unanimous but *incorrect* judgement of the other group members, 37 made a total of 194 errors, all of which were in agreement with the mistake made by the group.[8]

This widely replicated study illustrates the influence of groups on individual choice making. Marketing applications range from the choice of car models and residential locations to the decision to purchase at least one item at a Tupperware party.

**status**
Relative position in a group.

**role**
The rights and duties expected of an individual in a group by other members of the group.

**Asch phenomenon**
The impact that groups and group norms can exhibit on individual behaviour.

UNITED COLORS OF BENETTON.

Group influence is used here to suggest that, because others have been satisfied, you will be too.

## Reference Groups

Groups that exert such influence on individuals are categorized as **reference groups**, or groups whose value structures and standards influence a person's behaviour. Consumers usually try to keep their purchase behaviour in line with what they perceive to be the values of their reference group.

The status of the individual within the reference group produces three subcategories: **membership groups**, in which the person actually belongs (as is the case with, say, a country club); **aspirational groups**, a situation where a person wishes to associate with a group; and **disassociative groups**, ones with which an individual does not want to be identified. For example, teenagers are unlikely to enjoy the middle-of-the-road music played on radio stations that cater to their parents' generation.

It is obviously not essential that the individual be a member in order for the group to serve as a point of reference. This partly explains the use of famous athletes and celebrities in advertisements. Even though few possess the skills necessary to pilot a racing car, all racing fans can identify with the Mosport winner by injecting their engines with STP.

The extent of reference-group influence varies widely among purchases. For reference-group influence to be great, two factors must be present:

- The item purchased must be one that can be seen and identified by others.
- The item purchased must also be conspicuous in the sense that it stands out, is unusual, and is a brand or product that not everyone owns.

Figure 8.3 shows the influence of reference groups on both the basic decision to purchase a product and the decision to purchase a particular brand. The figure shows that reference groups had a significant impact on both the decision to purchase a car *and* the type of brand that was actually selected. By contrast, reference groups had little impact on the decision to purchase canned peaches or the brand that was chosen.

## Social Classes

Consumer behaviour is affected by **social class**, the relatively permanent divisions in a society into which individuals or families are categorized based on prestige and community status. A six-class

**FIGURE 8.3** Group Influence as a Function of Product Type and Consumption Situation

| Product or Brand | Publicly Consumed | |
|---|---|---|
| | Weak reference group influence (–) | Strong reference group influence (+) |
| Strong reference group influence (+) | Public necessities<br>Influence: Weak product and strong brand<br>Examples: Wristwatch, automobile, man's suit | Public luxuries<br>Influence: Strong product and brand<br>Examples: Golf clubs, snow skis, sailboat |
| Weak reference group influence (–) | Private necessities<br>Influence: Weak product and brand<br>Examples: Mattress, floor lamp, refrigerator | Private luxuries<br>Influence: Strong product and weak brand<br>Examples: TV game, trash compactor, icemaker |

NECESSITY             LUXURY

Source: William O. Bearden and Michaeli Etzei, "Reference Group Influence on Product and Brand Purchase Decisions," *Journal of Consumer Research* 9 (September 1982), p. 185, published by the University of Chicago Press. Reprinted with permission.

system within the social structure has been identified. Families have been grouped into two categories each of lower, middle, and upper classes on the basis of occupation, source of income (not amount), education, family background, and dwelling area. Research has shown that activities, interests, opinions, and buying behaviour are significantly affected by social class.

Income is not the main determinant of social-class behaviour, and the view that "a rich person is just a poor person with more money" is incorrect. Pipe-fitters paid at union scale will earn more money than many university professors, but their purchase behaviour may be quite different. For example, a professor may be more interested in expenditures related to the arts and similar entertainment, whereas a pipe-fitter may have quite different tastes and interests in satisfying aesthetic and entertainment needs.

Marketers have found that it is more meaningful to think about such differences in terms of variations in *lifestyle*. Market segmentation by lifestyle is described in the next section.

## Relating Social-Class Hierarchy and Lifestyles

Analysis of people's lifestyles can be very revealing. It can indicate where they live, how they live, where they travel, what motivates them. More important, it can reveal the kinds of things they purchase, because it is lifestyle, not just income, that determines what a person buys.

Without knowledge of a person's lifestyle it is difficult to intelligently target a product or service. That knowledge provides the means to accurately profile the consumer base. You will know where to market a new product, where to best locate a new store, where to promote with direct mail, where to spend the advertising budget wisely. In fact, lifestyle analysis can provide the answers to most important marketing questions.

To meet marketers' needs for better information, Compusearch has developed a system that groups all the neighbourhoods in Canada into unique clusters. Its **PSYTE** system identifies 60 different lifestyles (PSYTE cluster profiles) with specific locations across Canada.

Table 8.2 summarizes the PSYTE cluster profiles. Fifteen different major groups are classified as urban, suburban, town, and rural. As an example, the urban subgroup Urban Young Singles (U4) is highlighted. This subgroup is further subdivided into six smaller clusters, including University Enclaves. A brief description of this cluster is shown; Compusearch actually provides a more extensive description. Compusearch calls PSYTE a geodemographic neighbourhood classification system.

According to Compusearch's Web site, the basic tenet of geodemographic neighbourhood classification systems is that people with similar cultural backgrounds, means, and perspectives naturally gravitate toward one another, or form relatively homogeneous communities. Once settled in, people emulate their neighbours; adopt similar social values, tastes, and expectations; and, most important of all, share similar patterns of consumer behaviour toward products, services, media, and promotions. This behaviour is the basis for developing classification systems such as LIFESTYLES, PRIZM, CLUSTER PLUS, and Compusearch's PSYTE system.

Such cluster systems have already proven themselves where it counts—in the marketplace. At a conservative estimate, more than 15 000 companies in Canada and the United States alone used clusters as part of their marketing information mix in 1998.[9]

The major contributions of PSYTE's geodemographic clustering to modern marketing are as follows:

- *Discriminating power.* It is superior to most single-factor demographic measures such as age, gender, income, and so on.
- *Medium of integration.* You can build a consumer target market by profiling your own customer files, or you can use a profile of your particular product or service, and then compare or correlate that profile with more than 50 databases that have been coded with PSYTE. This can help you decide which cluster targets you want. You can then rank TV programs, select names from a mailing list, rank telephone exchanges and postal walks, and target retail distribution, all using the same target definition.
- *Accountability.* The results of cluster targeting can be easily measured. To see if cluster targeting works, companies simply have to track their sales, shipments, subscriptions, or whatever indi-

**PSYTE**
A geodemographic classification system that identifies lifestyle cluster profiles across Canada.

**TABLE 8.2** PSYTE Cluster Profile, Estimated 1999 Canadian Households

| PSYTE MAJOR GROUPS | NO. OF CLUSTERS | PERCENTAGE OF ALL HOUSEHOLDS |
|---|---|---|
| **Urban** | | |
| Urban Elite (U1) | 3 | 2.71 |
| Urban Ethnic (U2) | 3 | 4.05 |
| Urban Older Singles and Couples (U3) | 2 | 5.01 |
| | | |
| **Urban Young Singles (U4)** | **6** | **11.05** |
| Urban Quebec Grey Collar (U5) | 5 | 8.18 |
| Urban Downscale (U6) | 4 | 6.07 |
| | | |
| **Suburban** | | |
| Suburban Affluent (S1) | 4 | 6.63 |
| Suburban Upscale Families (S2) | 4 | 6.67 |
| Suburban Older Singles and Couples (S3) | 3 | 4.09 |
| Suburban Younger Families (S4) | 2 | 5.64 |
| Suburban Quebec (S5) | 4 | 9.39 |
| | | |
| **Town** | | |
| Town Upscale (T1) | 3 | 7.53 |
| Town Grey Collar (T2) | 5 | 8.68 |
| | | |
| **Rural** | | |
| Rural Comfortable Families (R1) | 6 | 6.10 |
| Rural Downscale (R2) | 6 | 7.95 |
| **Total** | **60** | **100.00** |

| URBAN YOUNG SINGLES (U4) | CANADA HOUSEHOLDS (#) | CANADA HOUSEHOLDS (%) |
|---|---|---|
| 20 Young Urban Professionals | 235 324 | 1.91 |
| 29 Young Urban Mix | 258 772 | 2.10 |
| 36 Young Urban Intelligentsia | 193 761 | 1.57 |
| **40 University Enclaves** | **250 766** | **2.04** |
| 51 Young City Singles | 275 822 | 2.24 |
| 56 Urban Bohemia | 145 335 | 1.18 |
| **Total Urban Young Singles** | **1 359 780** | **11.05** |

**Cluster 40 (Group U4)**: University Enclaves (1.84% of Canadian households). Neighbourhood concentrations of urban university students, artists, musicians, etc. Most residents rent high-rise or low-rise apartments or older, subdivided houses. Education levels are very high. Occupations are white and grey collar. There are some immigrants, including recent immigrants, in these areas.

Source: MapInfo Canada, Inc. Copyright © 2002 by MapInfo Canada Inc. PSYTE is a trademark of MapInfo. Reprinted with permission.

cator by postal code, summarize them up to each of the 60 clusters, and see if sales have, in fact, increased in the targeted clusters.

- *Longitudinal time series.* PSYTE delivers the ability to track market share for groups of products or individual products on a cluster-by-cluster basis, both at the national and the individual market level, month over month, year over year.

- *Addressable, mapable targets.* Using a desktop mapping system, companies can illustrate targets at any level, right down to individual postal walks, proprietary distribution/sales zones, grocery store trade areas, or whatever.[10]

More detail on the PSYTE system can be found at http://www.dynamo.mapinfo.com/miproducts/overview.cfm?productid=787.

## Opinion Leaders

Each group usually contains a few members who can be considered **opinion leaders** or trendsetters. These individuals are more likely to purchase new products early and to serve as information sources for others in a given group. Their opinions are respected, and they are often sought out for advice.

Generalized opinion leaders are rare. Individuals tend to be opinion leaders in specific areas. Their considerable knowledge about and interest in a particular product or service motivates them to seek out further information from mass media, manufacturers, and other sources, and, in turn, they transmit this information to their associates through interpersonal communication. Opinion leaders are found within all segments of the population.

Opinion leaders play a crucial role in interpersonal communication. The fact that they distribute information and advice to others indicates their potential importance to marketing strategy. Opinion leaders can be particularly useful in launching new products.

General Motors once provided a popular small car to college marketing classes as a basis for a course project. Rock stations have painted teenagers' cars for them; of course, the paint job included the stations' call letters and slogans. Politicians sometimes hold issues forums for community leaders. All these efforts are directed at the opinion leaders in a particular marketplace. These people play an important role in how successfully a new or established product, idea, or political candidacy is communicated to consumers.

## Family Influences

The family is an important interpersonal determinant of consumer behaviour. The close, continuing interactions among family members are the strongest group influences for the individual consumer.

Most people in our society are members of two families during their lifetime: the family into which they are born, and the family they eventually form as they marry and have children. With divorce an increasingly common phenomenon, many people become involved with three or more families.

**opinion leaders**
Trendsetters—individuals who are more likely to purchase new products early and to serve as information sources for others in a given group.

This TV ad shows a man tired from work, asking himself why he does it. Then he looks down and sees his son and remembers why he works so hard — so he can buy a SEA-DOO® for his family.

Showing how a family enjoys using a product can be a powerful buying influence.

The establishment of a new household upon marriage produces marketing opportunities. A new household means a new home and accompanying furniture. The need for refrigerators, vacuum cleaners, and an original oil painting for the living room depends not on the number of people in each household but on the number of *households* themselves.

As children are added to the household, sizes of some products purchased naturally increase. Two litres of milk will be purchased instead of one. Some larger families will purchase larger vehicles. Many other child-related purchases will be made over the period of time the youngsters remain in the home. Marketers find many opportunities in this market segment. For example, Chrysler achieved great success with its minivan, the Magic Wagon, a vehicle with ample capacity for families that nevertheless handled as easily as a car.

Another market evolves as parents are left alone when the children move away from home. These parents find themselves with a four-bedroom "empty nest" and a sizable lawn to maintain each week. Lacking assistance from their children and no longer needing the extra space, they become customers for townhouses, condominiums, and high-rise luxury apartments in the larger cities. This market segment also eventually purchases bifocals, and is a good target for organized tour packages.

### Identifying Target Markets by Lifestage

A related approach to understanding consumer behaviour is to identify lifestages—stages in the life of consumers rather than stages within the family. Using this method, one could, for example, categorize young singles who are quite independent but live with their parents without trying to fit them into a category within a family.

The lifestages are At Home Singles, Starting Out Singles, Young Couples, Young Parents, Single Parents, Mature Singles, Empty Nesters, and Left Alone Singles.

The marketer can determine the type of products each group is buying and how much they are spending on them. It is easy to see that a Starting Out Single's purchases will be quite different from those of a Mature Single. Following this line of analysis, marketers can identify the logical customer for their product and develop a marketing program to appeal to the needs of that customer group.[11]

### Marital Roles in Purchase Decisions

Although an infinite variety of roles are played in household decision making, four role categories are often used: (1) *autonomic*—situations in which an equal number of decisions is made by each

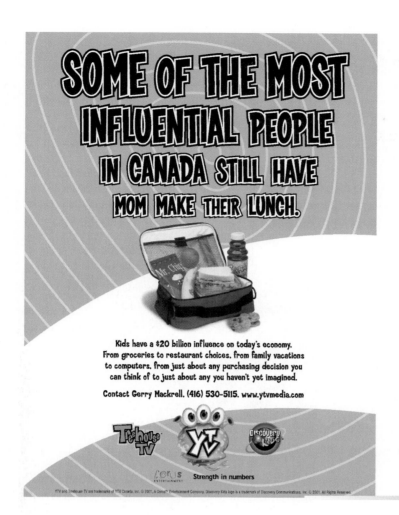

partner, but each decision is made individually by one partner or the other; (2) *husband-dominant;* (3) *wife-dominant;* and (4) *joint*—situations in which decisions are made jointly by male and female.[12] Figure 8.4 shows the roles commonly played by household members in purchasing a number of products.

### Changing Family Roles

Two forces have changed the female's role as sole purchasing agent for most household items. First, a shorter workweek provides each wage-earning household member with more time for shopping. Second, a large number of women are now in the workforce. In 1950, only about a quarter of married women were also employed outside the home; by 1981, that figure had doubled. Currently, over half of all married women with school-age children hold jobs outside the home. Women's share of employment is now 48 percent. Between 1989 and 1996, women filled two-thirds of the new managerial and professional jobs. Studies of family decision making have shown that wives who work outside the home tend to exert more influence than wives who work in the home only. Households with two wage earners also exhibit a large number of joint decisions and an increase in night and weekend shopping.

These changing roles of household members have led many marketers to adjust their marketing programs. Men's clothing stores, such as Stollery's in Toronto, now offer suits and accessories for the career woman. Although demand for men's suits has been sluggish in recent years, sales of women's suits increased 70 percent. Meanwhile, a survey of 1000 married men revealed that 77 percent participate in grocery shopping and 70 percent cook. A Del Monte promotional campaign recognized these changes and de-emphasized women as the sole meal preparers. Its theme, "Good things happen when you bring Del Monte home," applies to both male and female food shoppers.

## FIGURE 8.4 Relative Influence of Husbands and Wives in Decision Making

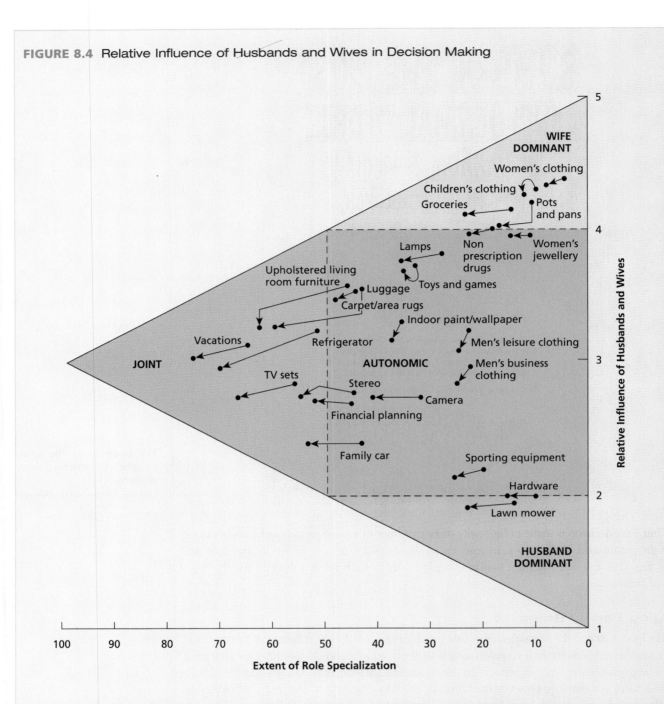

Source: From *Consumer Behavior*, 7th edition by James F. Engel, Roger Blackwell, and Paul Miniard, page 176. Copyright © 1993. Reprinted with permission of South-Western, a division of Thomson Learning: www.thomsonrights.com. Fax 800-730-2215.

## Children's Roles in Household Purchasing

The role of the children evolves as they grow older. Their early influence is generally centred on toys to be recommended to Santa Claus and the choice of brands of cereals. Younger children are important to marketers of fast-food restaurants. Even though the parents may decide when to eat out, the children often select the restaurant. As they gain maturity, they increasingly influence other purchases.

Young teenage boys spend most of their money on food, snacks, movies, and entertainment. Girls in this same age group buy clothing, food, snacks, movies, entertainment, cosmetics, and fragrances. Older boys spend most of their money on entertainment, dating, movies, cars and gasoline,

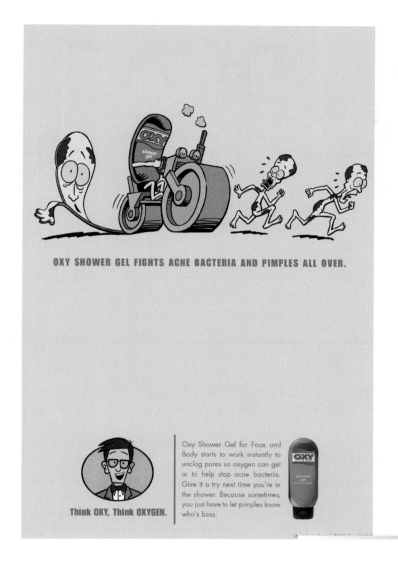

OXY SHOWER GEL FIGHTS ACNE BACTERIA AND PIMPLES ALL OVER.

Oxy Shower Gel for Face and Body starts to work instantly to unclog pores so oxygen can get in to help stop acne bacteria. Give it a try next time you're in the shower. Because sometimes, you just have to let pimples know who's boss.

Think OXY, Think OXYGEN.

**An appeal directly targeted to a teenaged audience.**

clothing, food, and snacks; while girls of the same age buy clothing, cosmetics, fragrances, cars and gasoline, movies, and entertainment.

# INDIVIDUAL FACTORS AND PSYCHOLOGICAL PROCESSES

In addition to environmental influences on behaviour, many individual factors are involved. These include needs and motives, perceptions, attitudes, and learning. Furthermore, the psychological processes that occur in the development of these factors have a significant bearing on buyer behaviour. After discussing these elements, a model of the consumer decision process will be presented. A general model of the factors that influence consumer behaviour is shown in Figure 8.5.

## Needs and Motives

The starting point in the purchase decision process is the recognition of a felt need. A **need** is the perceived difference between the current state and a desired state. The consumer is typically confronted with numerous unsatisfied needs. Note that a need must be sufficiently aroused before it may serve as a motive.

**need**

The perceived difference between the current state and a desired state.

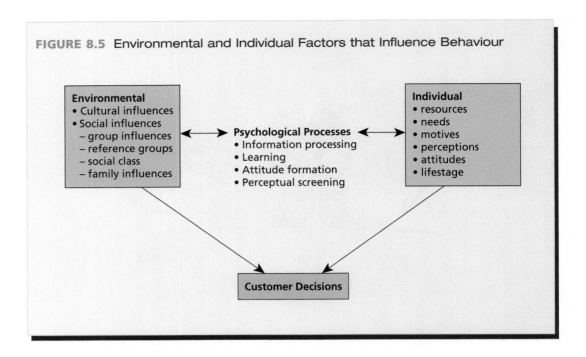

**FIGURE 8.5** Environmental and Individual Factors that Influence Behaviour

**Environmental**
• Cultural influences
• Social influences
  – group influences
  – reference groups
  – social class
  – family influences

**Psychological Processes**
• Information processing
• Learning
• Attitude formation
• Perceptual screening

**Individual**
• resources
• needs
• motives
• perceptions
• attitudes
• lifestage

**Customer Decisions**

**motive**

An inner state that directs us toward the goal of satisfying a felt need.

**Motives** are inner states that direct us toward the goal of satisfying a felt need. The individual is *moved* (the root word of motive) to take action to reduce a state of tension and to return to a state of equilibrium.

### Hierarchy of Needs

Although psychologists disagree on specific classifications of needs, a useful theory that may apply to consumers in general was developed by A.H. Maslow.[13] He proposed a classification of needs (sometimes referred to as a hierarchy), as shown in Figure 8.6. It is important to recognize that Maslow's hierarchy *may not apply to every individual,* but seems to be true of groups in general. His theory is based on two important assumptions:

1. People are wanting animals whose needs depend on what they already possess. A satisfied need is not a motivator; only those needs that have not been satisfied can influence behaviour.
2. Once one need has been largely satisfied, another emerges and demands satisfaction.

**PHYSIOLOGICAL NEEDS**

The primary needs for food, shelter, and clothing normally must be satisfied before the higher-order needs are considered. A hungry person is possessed by the need to obtain food, while other needs are ignored. Once the physiological needs are at least partly satisfied, other needs come into the picture.

**SAFETY NEEDS**

Safety needs include protection from physical harm, the need for security, and avoidance of the unexpected. Fulfillment of these needs may take the form of a decision to stop smoking, life insurance, the purchase of radial tires, or membership in the local health club. Antismoking advertisements target this need.

**SOCIAL NEEDS**

Satisfaction of physiological and safety needs may be followed by the desire to be accepted by members of the family and other individuals and groups—that is, the social needs. Individuals may be motivated to join various groups and to conform to their standards of dress, purchases, and behaviour, and may become interested in obtaining status as a means of fulfilling these social needs. Social

FIGURE 8.6 Need Classification Structure

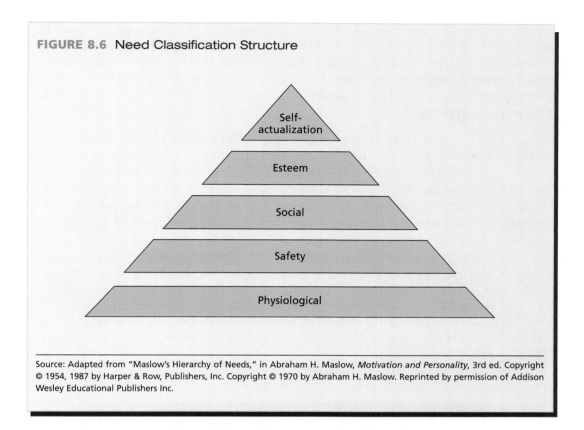

Source: Adapted from "Maslow's Hierarchy of Needs," in Abraham H. Maslow, *Motivation and Personality*, 3rd ed. Copyright © 1954, 1987 by Harper & Row, Publishers, Inc. Copyright © 1970 by Abraham H. Maslow. Reprinted by permission of Addison Wesley Educational Publishers Inc.

needs seem to be becoming a more important cultural value. Many "lifestyle" advertisements, such as those often used by Coca-Cola and Pepsi, appeal to social needs.

## ESTEEM NEEDS

These higher-order needs are prevalent in all societies. In developed countries with high per capita income, most families have been able to satisfy the basic needs. Therefore, Maslow predicts that such consumers will concentrate more on the desire for status, esteem, and self-actualization. These needs are more difficult to satisfy. At the esteem level is the need to feel a sense of accomplishment, achievement, and respect from others. The competitive need to excel—to better the performance of others and "stand out" from the crowd—is an almost universal human trait.

Esteem needs are closely related to social needs. At this level, however, the individual desires not just acceptance but also recognition and respect in some way. Membership in prestigious organizations or purchase of a specialty car are ways of fulfilling such needs.

## SELF-ACTUALIZATION NEEDS

Self-actualization needs are the desire for fulfillment, for realizing one's own potential, for using one's talents and capabilities totally. Maslow defines self-actualization this way: "The healthy man [sic] is primarily motivated by his needs to develop and actualize his fullest potentialities and capacities. What man can be, he must be."[14] The author Robert Louis Stevenson was describing self-actualization when he wrote, "To be what we are, and to become what we are capable of becoming, is the only end in life."

As already noted, Maslow argues that a satisfied need is no longer a motivator. Once the physiological needs are satiated, the individual moves on to the higher-order needs. Consumers are periodically motivated by the need to relieve thirst or hunger, but their interests are most often directed toward the satisfaction of safety, social, and other needs.

Caution must be used in applying Maslow's theory. Empirical research shows little support for a universal hierarchical ordering of needs in *specific individuals*.[15] It would therefore be unsafe to use the theory to explain a particular purchase. The needs hierarchy and motive strength concept may be useful in considering the behaviour of consumers *in general,* however. It has been verified that in consumer buying, previously ignored desires often surface only after a purchase has satisfied a predominant (and *perhaps* lower-order) motive.[16]

## Perceptions

In some Asian countries, a prized product is ginseng root. This is used as a key ingredient in certain drinks and medications. The product is not cheap, but demand is huge, because many Asians perceive that ginseng has positive medicinal benefits for a number of conditions. In the West, however, the vast majority see no value in ginseng and are not at all interested in buying or using it.

Individual behaviour resulting from motivation is affected by how we perceive stimuli. **Perception** is the meaning that each person attributes to incoming stimuli received through the five senses.

Psychologists once assumed that perception was an objective phenomenon—that is, that the individual perceived what was there to be perceived. It is now recognized that what we perceive is as much a result of what we *want* to perceive as of what is actually there. This does not mean that people view dogs as pigeons. We can distinguish shopping centres from churches, and a retail store stocked with well-known brand names and staffed with helpful, knowledgeable sales personnel is perceived differently from a largely self-serve discount store. Zellers and Birks are both important retailers, but they carry quite different images.

**perception**

The meaning that each person attributes to incoming stimuli received through the five senses.

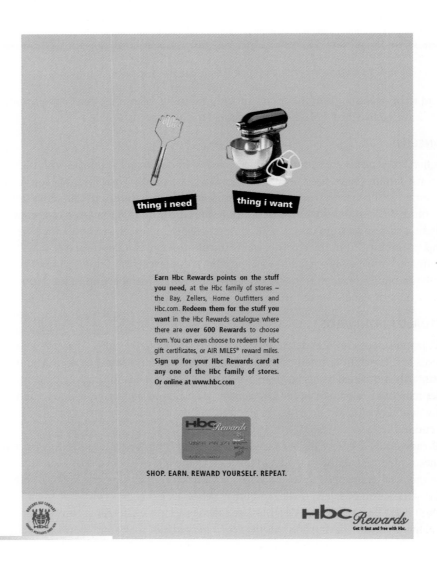

**We always have more wants to satisfy.**

Our perception of an object or event is the result of the interaction of two types of factors:

- Stimulus factors, which are characteristics of the physical object, such as size, colour, weight, or shape. For example, a beautifully decorated and appointed lawyer's office results in a different perception of the lawyer than a plain, "storefront" operation.
- Individual factors, which are characteristics of the perceiver. These factors include not only sensory processes but also past experiences with similar items and basic motivations and expectations. The fancy law office will be reassuring to some and threatening to others.

## Perceptual Screens

We are continually bombarded with myriad stimuli, but ignore most of them. In order to have time to function, each of us must respond selectively to stimuli. What stimuli we respond to, then, is the problem of all marketers. How can they gain the attention of individuals so that they will read the advertisement, listen to the sales representative, react to a point-of-purchase display?

Even though studies have shown that the average consumer is exposed to more than 1000 ads daily, most of them never break through our **perceptual screen**, the filter through which messages must pass. Sometimes breakthroughs may be accomplished in the print media through larger ads, since doubling the size of an ad increases its attention value by approximately 50 percent. Black-and-white TV ads that selectively use one colour, in contrast with the usual colour ads, are another device to break the reader's perceptual screen. Another method of using contrast in print advertising is to include a large amount of white space to draw attention to the ad, or to use white type on a black background. In general, the marketer seeks to make the message stand out, to make it sufficiently different from other messages that it gains the attention of the prospective customer. Piercing the perceptual screen is a difficult task.

With such selectivity at work, it is easy to see the importance of the marketer's efforts to develop brand loyalty to a product. Satisfied customers are less likely to seek or pay attention to information about competing products. They simply tune out information that is not in accord with their existing beliefs and expectations.

**perceptual screen**
The filter through which messages must pass.

**Creative new uses of standard images may break through perceptual screens.**

### Can Subliminal Messages Sneak Through the Perceptual Screen?

Is it possible to communicate with people without their being aware of the communication? In other words, does **subliminal perception**—a subconscious level of awareness—really exist? In 1957, the phrases "Eat popcorn" and "Drink Coca-Cola" were flashed on the screen of a New Jersey movie theatre every 5 seconds for 1/300th of a second. Researchers then reported that these messages, although too short to be recognizable at the conscious level, resulted in a 58 percent increase in popcorn sales and an 18 percent increase in Coca-Cola sales. After the publication of these findings, advertising agencies and consumer protection groups became intensely interested in subliminal perception.[17] Subsequent attempts to duplicate the test findings have, however, invariably been unsuccessful.

If used, subliminal advertising would be aimed at the subconscious level of awareness to avoid the perceptual screens of viewers. The goal of the original research was to induce consumers to purchase products without being aware of the source of the motivation. Although subliminal advertising has been universally condemned (and declared illegal in Canada and California), experts believe that it is in fact unlikely that such advertising can induce purchases anyway. There are several reasons for this: (1) strong stimulus factors are typically required even to gain attention, as discussed earlier; (2) only a very short message can be transmitted subliminally; (3) individuals vary greatly in their thresholds of consciousness[18] (a message transmitted at the threshold of consciousness for one person will not be perceived at all by some people and will be all too apparent to others; when exposed subliminally, the message "Drink Coca-Cola" might go unseen by some viewers, while others read it as "Drink Pepsi-Cola," "Drink Cocoa," or even "Drive Slowly");[19] and (4) perceptual defences also work at the subconscious level.

Contrary to earlier fears, research has shown that subliminal messages cannot force the receiver to purchase goods that she or he would not consciously want.[20]

## Attitudes

Perception of incoming stimuli is greatly affected by attitudes regarding these stimuli. In fact, decisions to purchase products are based on currently held attitudes about the product, the store, or the salesperson.

**Attitudes** may be defined as a person's enduring favourable or unfavourable evaluations of some object or idea. Attitudes are formed over a period of time through individual experiences and group contacts, and are highly resistant to change.

### Components of an Attitude

Attitudes consist of three related components: cognitive, affective, and conative. The **cognitive component** is the knowledge and beliefs one has about an object or concept. The **affective component** is one's feelings or emotional reactions. The **conative component** is the way one tends to act or behave. In considering the decision to shop at a warehouse-type food store, a person obtains information from advertising, trial visits, and input from family, friends, and associates (cognitive). A consumer also

---

## THE PRACTISING MARKETER

### WHAT IT TAKES TO BREAK THROUGH THE PERCEPTUAL SCREEN

Many businesses fail to understand what it takes to get attention. They often fail to consider how great a change in stimulus is necessary to make a difference to customers. The relationship between the actual stimulus (such as price, size, loudness, or texture) and the corresponding sensation produced in the individual must be evaluated. This can be expressed as a mathematical equation:

$$\frac{\Delta I}{I} = k$$

where $\Delta I$ = the smallest increase in stimulus that will be noticeably different from the previous intensity

$I$ = the intensity of the stimulus at the point where the increase takes place

$k$ = a constant (that varies from one sense to the next)

In other words, the higher the initial intensity of a stimulus, the greater the amount of the change in intensity that is necessary in order for a difference to be noticed.

This relationship, known as **Weber's Law**, has some obvious implications in marketing. A price increase of $300 for a Chrysler Neon is readily apparent for prospective buyers; the same $300 increase on a $70 000 Lexus seems insignificant. A large package requires a much greater increase in size to be noticeable than a smaller-sized package requires. People perceive by *exception*, and the change in a stimulus must be sufficiently great to gain the individual's attention.[21]

**How can this finding be applied to advertising?**

receives inputs from others about their acceptance of shopping at this new type of store, as well as impressions about the type of people who shop there (affective). The shopper may ultimately decide to make some purchases of canned goods, cereal, and bakery products there, but continue to rely on a regular supermarket for major food purchases (conative).

As Figure 8.7 illustrates, the three components exist in a relatively stable and balanced relationship to one another and combine to form an overall attitude about an object or idea.

## Producing Attitude Change

Given that a favourable consumer attitude is a prerequisite to market success, how can a firm lead prospective buyers to adopt a more favourable attitude toward its products? The marketer has two choices: either attempt to change attitudes to bring them into accord with the product, or determine consumer attitudes and then change the product to match them. The latter is the easiest choice.

If consumers view the product unfavourably, the firm may choose to redesign the product to better conform with their desires. To accommodate the consumer, the firm may make styling changes, variations in ingredients, changes in package size, and changes in retail stores handling the product. The other course of action—changing consumer attitudes toward the product without changing the product—is much more difficult.

## Affecting Attitude by Modifying One Attitudinal Component

Attitude change may occur when inconsistencies are introduced among the three attitudinal components. If one component can be influenced, the other two may be brought into congruence with the changed component, and the attitude will be modified.

### COGNITIVE COMPONENT

One way to create an inconsistency in the cognitive component involves providing new information. In the early 1990s, General Motors mounted a huge advertising program showing that its cars were more fuel-efficient and reliable than Japanese-produced cars. This information was expected to counteract "common knowledge" that Japanese-produced cars were superior on these characteristics. In another instance, beef producers first modified their product, then undertook comparative advertising to show the low amount of fat now contained in beef.

### AFFECTIVE COMPONENT

The affective component of attitude may be altered by relating the use of the product to desirable consequences for the user. This is a common appeal for health and beauty-aid products. Advertisements for a new perfume or cologne may imply that it will make one more attractive to the opposite sex.

**attitudes**
A person's enduring favourable or unfavourable evaluations of some object or idea.

**cognitive component**
The knowledge and beliefs one has about an object or concept.

**affective component**
One's feelings or emotional reactions.

**conative component**
The way one tends to act or behave.

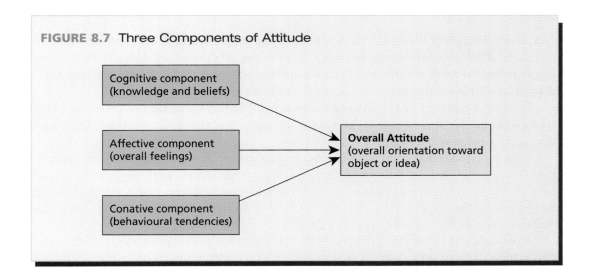

**FIGURE 8.7** Three Components of Attitude

Cognitive component
(knowledge and beliefs)

Affective component
(overall feelings)

Conative component
(behavioural tendencies)

**Overall Attitude**
(overall orientation toward object or idea)

Consumer Behaviour    Chapter 8

got milk?

Try this at home.*

*We mean the drinking milk part.
Lowfat milk helps prevent osteoporosis
and keeps your bones supple.

**Using a health appeal to influence the affective attitude component concerning milk.**

## CONATIVE COMPONENT

The third alternative in attempting to change attitudes is to focus on the conative component by inducing someone to engage in behaviour that is contradictory to the person's currently held attitudes. Attitude-discrepant behaviour of this type may occur if the consumer is given a free sample of a product. Such trials may lead to attitude change.

## Learning

Consumers *learn* about the values and uses of products. Since marketing is as concerned with the process by which consumer decisions change over time as with describing those decisions at one point in time, the study of how learning takes place is important. A useful definition of **learning** is changes in knowledge, attitudes, and behaviour, as a result of experience.[22]

The learning process includes several components. The first component, **drive**, refers to any strong stimulus that impels action. Examples of drives include fear, pride, the desire for money, thirst, pain avoidance, and rivalry.

**Cues,** the second component of the learning process, are any objects existing in the environment that determine the nature of the response to a drive. Cues might include a newspaper advertisement for a new French restaurant, an in-store display, or a Petro-Canada sign on a major highway. For the hungry person, the shopper seeking a particular item, or the motorist needing gasoline, these cues may result in a specific response to satisfy a drive.

A **response** is the individual's reaction to the cues and drives, such as purchasing a bottle of Pert Plus shampoo, dining at Earl's, or deciding to enrol at a particular university or community college.

**learning**
Changes in knowledge, attitudes, and behaviour, as a result of experience.

**drive**
Any strong stimulus that impels action.

**cue**
Any object existing in the environment that determines the nature of the response to a drive.

**response**
The individual's reaction to the cues and drives.

**Reinforcement** is the reduction in drive that results from a proper response. The more rewarding the response, the stronger the bond between the drive and the purchase of that particular item becomes. Should Pert Plus result in shiny, manageable hair through repeated use, the likelihood of its being purchased in the future increases.

**reinforcement**
The reduction in drive that results from a proper response.

## Applying Learning Theory to Marketing Decisions

Learning theory has some important implications for marketing strategists.[23] A desired outcome such as repeat purchase behaviour may have to be developed gradually. **Shaping** is the process of applying a series of rewards and reinforcement so that more complex behaviour (such as the development of a brand preference) can evolve over time. Both promotional strategy and the product itself play a role in the shaping process.

**shaping**
The process of applying a series of rewards and reinforcement so that more complex behaviour can evolve over time.

## THE INFORMED CONSUMER

### ARE EXTENDED WARRANTIES WORTH IT?

These days, you can hardly buy anything with a bit of electronic gadgetry in it without the salesperson offering to sweeten the deal with an extended warranty. It is not free, of course, but paying out a little more seems a small price for peace of mind—or is it?

"Extended warranties are just about the most expensive form of insurance that you can buy," says Paul Reynolds, an Ottawa native who is products editor with *Consumer Reports* in Yonkers, N.Y. "You can be almost assured that a retailer is going to make more on selling you the extended warranty than they are making on selling you the item itself, particularly with lower-priced items—smaller-sized TV sets, VCRs, DVD players," he says. "They are making a pretty small margin on those items, and that is where some retailers are aggressive in trying to sell you an extended warranty."

In the fall of 2001, the magazine concluded that extended warranties are generally not a wise investment. *Consumer Reports* found that the average cost of repairing a wide range of household appliances and electronics was typically comparable with the warranty cost.

With some, the repair costs more. However, consumers are only saving money if it needs repair—and that, it turns out, is unlikely. Most often, *Consumer Reports* found, the goods did not require any fixing within three years. The most likely in need of fixing were lawn tractors—nearly three in ten needed repair—while almost four in ten desktop computers needed something repaired.

Meanwhile, popular items such as televisions, microwaves, and VCRs all had a less than one in ten chance of needing any repair within the warranty period.

In other words, the odds are people are buying a warranty they will never need. "There is a slight chance with some of these items that you can end up with a repair that might be higher than the warranty cost. And if that possibility keeps you awake at night, you might consider buying an extended warranty," Mr. Reynolds says. "But we think that they are really, overall, a poor buy."

Furthermore, credit card companies often extend a product warranty against both defect and accident if you pay for the goods with their gold or platinum cards. Sometimes, too, the protection for items such as laptops can be added to a home insurance policy for a lower cost than the extended warranty, so it is a good idea to check with your insurer.

On the other hand, convenience and peace of mind is a consideration. If consumers are buying something for their own business and having it out of commission will be costly, a hassle-free service or over-the-counter exchange warranty may well be worth the extra price. One of the largest companies in the business estimates that as many as one in four consumers pay out for extended warranties for products worth more than $250. Of those who do have coverage, VAC Service Ltd. of Middletown, N.Y., estimates that only 15–20 percent ever take advantage of it. "It's like life insurance," says Charles Romano, the company's senior vice-president of sales and marketing. "You don't buy it to cash in on it. You buy it as peace of mind." Buying peace of mind for consumer goods has turned out to be a big industry.

Michael Bailey, Canadian president for Texas-based Warrantech Corp., advises consumers who do choose extended warranties to make sure those warranties are insured, noting that guarantees are no good if they are backed by retail chains that go out of business. He cites stores such as Multitech Warehouse Direct stores as examples: Anyone who bought a warranty from them was out of luck because they are no longer in business. "There is a long list of retailers that have gone down. There are a lot of majors who do not insure their program," says Mr. Bailey.

**What will you do the next time an extended warranty is suggested to you?**

Source: Excerpted from David Stonehouse, "Are Extended Warranties Worth It?" *Financial Post*, March 18, 2002, p. IT2. Reprinted with permission of the author.

Figure 8.8 shows the application of learning theory and shaping procedures to a typical marketing scenario, in which marketers attempt to motivate consumers to become regular buyers of a certain product. An initial product trial is induced by a free sample package that includes a coupon offering a substantial discount on a subsequent purchase. This illustrates the use of a cue as a shaping procedure. The purchase response is reinforced by satisfactory product performance and a coupon for the next purchase.

The second stage is to entice the consumer to buy the product with little financial risk. The large discount coupon enclosed with the free sample prompts such an action. The package that is purchased has a smaller discount enclosed. Again, the reinforcement is satisfactory product performance and the second coupon.

The third step would be to motivate the person to buy the item again at a moderate cost. The discount coupon accomplishes this objective, but this time there is no additional coupon in the package. The only reinforcement is satisfactory product performance.

The final test comes when the consumer is asked to buy the product at its true price, without a discount coupon. Satisfaction with product performance is the only continuing reinforcement. Thus, repeat purchase behaviour has literally been shaped.

Kellogg has used learning theory and shaping when introducing some of its cereals. Coupons worth 40 cents off have been distributed to elicit trial purchases by consumers. Inside boxes of the new cereal were additional cents-off coupons of lesser value. Kellogg has clearly tried to shape future purchase behaviour by effectively applying a learning theory within a marketing strategy context.

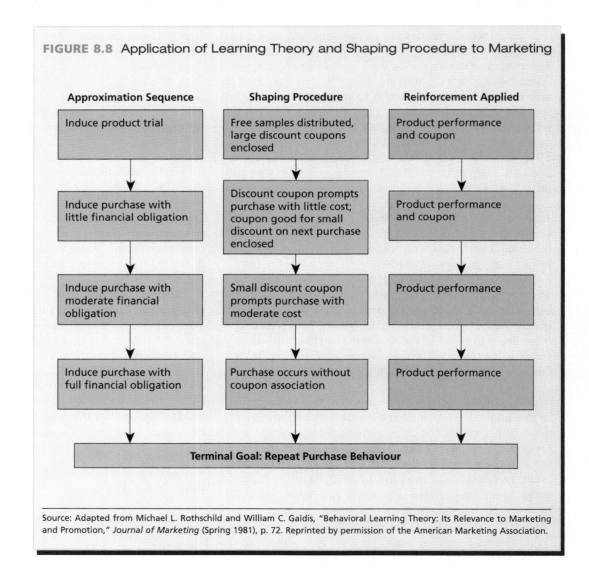

**FIGURE 8.8** Application of Learning Theory and Shaping Procedure to Marketing

Source: Adapted from Michael L. Rothschild and William C. Gaidis, "Behavioral Learning Theory: Its Relevance to Marketing and Promotion," *Journal of Marketing* (Spring 1981), p. 72. Reprinted by permission of the American Marketing Association.

# THE CONSUMER DECISION PROCESS

This chapter has shown that consumer behaviour is the result of two main categories of influences: environmental and individual. The purchase of all goods and services will be affected by some or all of the many variables discussed.

In the light of all this information, researchers have spent considerable effort trying to identify the process that a consumer goes through in making a purchase decision. One commonly accepted hypothesis suggests that the consumer decision process consists of six stages: (1) problem recognition, (2) information search, (3) alternative evaluation, (4) purchase decision, (5) purchase act, and (6) postpurchase evaluation. Figure 8.9 is a model of this process. Each step of the model is covered in the discussion that follows.

## Problem Recognition

This first stage in the decision process occurs when the consumer becomes aware of a discrepancy of sufficient magnitude between the existing state of affairs and a desired state of affairs. Once the problem has been recognized, it must be defined so that the consumer may seek out methods to solve it. Having recognized the problem, the individual is motivated to achieve the desired state.

What sort of problems might a person recognize? Perhaps the most common is a routine depletion of the stock of products. A large number of consumer purchases involve replenishing items ranging from gasoline to groceries. In other instances, the consumer may possess an inadequate assortment of products. The individual whose hobby is gardening may make regular purchases of different kinds of fertilizers, seeds, or gardening tools as the size of the garden grows.

A consumer may also be dissatisfied with a present brand or product type. This situation is common in the purchase of a new car, new furniture, or a new fall wardrobe. In many instances, boredom with current products and a desire for novelty may be the underlying rationale for the decision process that leads to new-product purchases.

Another important factor is changed financial status. Added financial resources from such sources as a salary increase, a second job, or an inheritance may permit the consumer to recognize desires and make purchases that previously had been postponed due to their cost.[24]

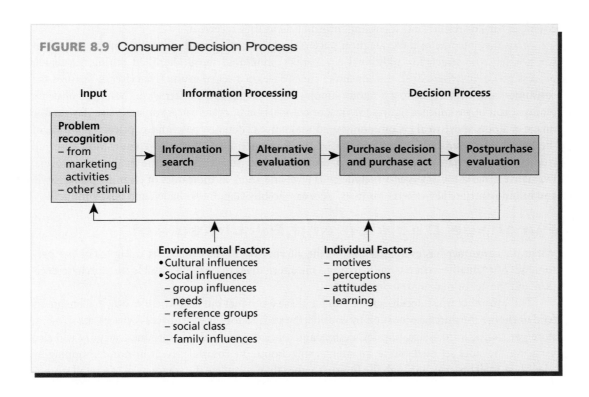

FIGURE 8.9 Consumer Decision Process

# Information Search

Information search, the second stage in the decision process, involves gathering information related to attaining a desired state of affairs. This stage also involves identifying alternative means of solving the problem.

An *internal search* is a mental review of the information that a person already knows that is relevant to the problem. This includes actual experiences and observations, plus remembered reading or conversations, and exposure to various persuasive marketing efforts.

An *external search* is the gathering of information from outside sources. These may include family members, friends and associates, store displays, sales representatives, brochures, and such product-testing publications as *Consumer Reports,* as well as contacts with competing suppliers.

In many instances, the consumer does not go beyond an internal search but merely relies on stored information in making a purchase decision. Achieving a favourable experience flying with Air Canada may sufficiently motivate a consumer to purchase another ticket from Air Canada rather than consider possible alternatives. Furthermore, the Aeroplan frequent flyer program reinforces past purchases. Since an external search involves both time and effort, the consumer will rely on it only in instances in which, for some reason, the information remembered is inadequate.

The search process will identify alternative brands for consideration and possible purchase. The number of brands that a consumer actually considers in making a purchase decision is known as the **evoked set**. In some instances, the consumer will already be aware of the brands worthy of further consideration; in others, the external search process will permit the consumer to identify those brands. Not all brands will be included in the evoked set. The consumer may remain unaware of certain brands, and others will be rejected as too costly or as having been tried previously and considered unsatisfactory. In other instances, unfavourable word-of-mouth communication or negative reactions to advertising or other marketing efforts will lead to the elimination of some brands from the evoked set. While the number of brands in the evoked set will vary by product categories, research indicates that the number is likely to be as few as four or five brands.[25]

## Alternative Evaluation

The third step in the consumer decision process involves evaluating the alternatives identified during the search process. Actually, it is difficult to completely separate the second and third steps, since some evaluation takes place simultaneously with the search process as consumers accept, discount, distort, or reject some incoming information as they receive it.

Since the outcome of the evaluation stage is the choice of a brand or product in the evoked set (or, possibly, the search for additional alternatives, should all those identified during the search process prove unsatisfactory), the consumer must develop a set of **evaluative criteria**, features the consumer considers in making a choice among alternatives. These criteria can be either *objective* (comparison of gas mileage figures for cars, or comparison of retail prices) or *subjective* (favourable image of Roots sportswear). Commonly used evaluative criteria include image, price, reputation of the brand, perceived quality, packaging, size, performance, durability, and colour. Most research studies indicate that consumers seldom use more than six criteria in the evaluation process. Evaluative criteria for detergents include suds level and smell as indicators of cleaning power. Style and brand name are key criteria for many people who buy Gap, Eddie Bauer, and Nike products.

## Purchase Decision and Purchase Act

When the consumer has evaluated each of the alternatives in the evoked set using his or her personal set of evaluative criteria, and narrowed the alternatives to one, the result is the purchase decision and the act of making the purchase.

The consumer must decide not only to purchase a product but also where to buy it. Consumers tend to choose the purchase location by considering such factors as ease of access, prices, assortment, store personnel, store image, physical design, and services provided. The product category will also influence the store selected. Some consumers will choose the convenience of in-home shopping by telephone, mail order, or through the Internet rather than complete the transaction in a retail store.[26]

**evoked set**
The number of brands that a consumer actually considers in making a purchase decision.

**evaluative criteria**
Features the consumer considers in making a choice among alternatives.

Jamie Sale and David Pelletier 2002 Gold Medalists.

## Postpurchase Evaluation

You may have narrowed the choice down to a jacket by Tommy Hilfiger or Eddie Bauer—a discrepancy in your beliefs about which would be best. But after some debate you choose Eddie Bauer. The purchase act results in the removal of the discrepancy between the existing state ("My jacket needs replacing") and the desired state ("I want a stylish jacket so I will look good"). Logically, it should result in satisfaction to the buyer. However, even in many purchase decisions where the buyer is ultimately satisfied, it is common for that person to experience some initial postpurchase anxieties. She or he often wonders if the right decision has been made ("Maybe that Hilfiger jacket would have been better"). This postpurchase doubt is known as cognitive dissonance.

**Cognitive dissonance** is the postpurchase anxiety that occurs when there is a discrepancy between a person's knowledge and beliefs (cognitions) about certain attributes of the final products under consideration. This occurs because several of the final product-choice candidates have desirable characteristics, making the final decision difficult. Consumers may, for example, experience dissonance after choosing a particular car over several alternative models, when one or more of the rejected models have some desired features that the purchased car lacks.

Dissonance is likely to increase (1) as the dollar value of the purchase increases, (2) when the rejected alternatives have desirable features that are not present in the chosen alternative, and (3) when the decision is a major one. The consumer may attempt to reduce dissonance in a variety of ways. He or she may seek out advertisements and other information supporting the chosen alternative, or seek reassurance from acquaintances who are satisfied purchasers of the product. At the same

**cognitive dissonance**
The postpurchase anxiety that occurs when there is a discrepancy between a person's knowledge and beliefs (cognitions).

time, the individual will avoid information that favours unchosen alternatives. The Toyota purchaser is more likely to read Toyota ads and to avoid Honda and Ford ads. The cigarette smoker may ignore magazine articles that report links between smoking and cancer.

Marketers should try to reduce cognitive dissonance by providing informational support for the chosen alternative. Car dealers recognize "buyer's remorse" and often follow up purchases with a warm letter from the president of the dealership, offering personal handling of any customer problems and including a description of the quality of the product and the availability of convenient, top-quality service.

The consumer may ultimately deal with cognitive dissonance by concentrating on positive aspects of the purchase, changing opinions or deciding that one of the rejected alternatives would have been the best choice, and forming the intention of purchasing it in the future.

Should the purchase prove unsatisfactory, the consumer will revise her or his purchase strategy to obtain need satisfaction. Feedback from the results of the decision process, whether satisfactory or not, will be called upon in the search and evaluation stages of similar buying situations.

## Classifying Consumer Problem-Solving Processes

The consumer decision process depends on the type of problem-solving effort required. Problem-solving behaviour has been divided into three categories: routinized response, limited problem solving, and extended problem solving.[27]

### Routinized Response

Many purchases are made as a routine response to a need. The selection is a preferred brand or is made from a limited group of acceptable brands. The consumer has set the evaluative criteria and identified the available options. Routine purchases of a particular newspaper or regular brands of soft drinks or hand soap are examples.

### Limited Problem Solving (LPS)

Consider the situation in which the consumer has set evaluative criteria but encounters a new, unknown brand. The introduction of a new fragrance line might create a situation that calls for limited problem solving. The consumer knows the evaluative criteria but has not assessed the new brand on the basis of these criteria. A certain amount of time and external search will be required. Limited problem solving is affected by the multitude of evaluative criteria and brands, the extent of external search, and the process by which preferences are determined. Some products—those with little significance, either materially or emotionally—a consumer may purchase first and evaluate later (while using them). These are known as **low-involvement products**.

### Extended Problem Solving (EPS)

Extended problem solving occurs with important purchase decisions when evaluative criteria have not been established for a product category or when the individual wishes to review such criteria. Today, many individuals are in the process of purchasing a scanner for their personal computer. Since many have never owned one before, they generally engage in an extensive search process. The main aspect of this process is determining appropriate evaluative criteria that are relevant to the needs of the decision maker. How much precision is required? Is the scanner to be used for images or optical character recognition (OCR)? What will be the machine's main uses? What special features are required? As the criteria are being set, an evoked set of brands is also established. Most extended problem-solving efforts are lengthy and involve considerable external search. A considerable amount of this research can be done on the Internet. Products for which the purchaser is highly involved in making the purchase decision are known as **high-involvement products**.

**low-involvement products**
Products with little significance, either materially or emotionally, that a consumer may purchase first and evaluate later (while using them).

**high-involvement products**
Products for which the purchaser is highly involved in making the purchase decision.

You woke up in a new place today.     THE TORONTO STAR   It's where you live.

**Attracting attention to a low-involvement product.**

## SUMMARY

Consumer behaviour consists of the activities of individuals in obtaining, using, and disposing of goods and services, including the decision processes that precede and follow these actions. Buyer behaviour is a function of the interactions of environmental, individual, and psychological processes, and can be summarized by the formula $B=f(E,I)$.

Environmental factors can be subdivided into cultural influences and social influences. Key social influences are group influence, reference groups, social class, and family influences.

The impact that groups and group norms can exhibit on individual behaviour has been called the Asch phenomenon. Its effect can be seen in the influence of membership, aspirational, and disassociative reference groups. Opinion leaders are individuals who are more likely to purchase new products early and to serve as information sources for others in the group. Therefore, they are important for the marketer when introducing new products.

Marital roles vary in purchase decisions. These roles have been categorized as autonomic, husband-dominant, wife-dominant, and joint.

Individual factors also significantly affect consumer behaviour. These include needs, motives, perceptions, attitudes, and learning. A need is the perceived difference between the current state and a desired state. Abraham Maslow established a need classification system with the following categories: physiological needs, safety needs, social needs, esteem needs, and self-actualization needs.

Motives are inner states that direct us toward the goal of satisfying a felt need.

Perception is the meaning that each person attributes to incoming stimuli received through the five senses. There are so many stimuli that individuals establish a perceptual screen to filter out undesired stimuli.

Attitudes are comprised of three related components: cognitive, affective, and conative. Marketers sometimes try to affect one or more of these components in order to change attitudes and therefore consumer behaviour.

The consumer decision process can be divided into the following steps: problem recognition, information search, alternative evaluation, purchase decision, and postpurchase evaluation. The outcome of this process is affected by environmental influences and individual factors.

Cognitive dissonance is the postpurchase anxiety that occurs after a purchase when there is a discrepancy between a person's knowledge and beliefs (cognitions) about certain attributes of the final products under consideration.

The consumer problem-solving process depends on the type of problem-solving effort that is required: routinized response, limited problem solving, or extensive problem solving. The products that are considered in the purchasing process can be grouped into low-involvement and high-involvement categories.

## KEY TERMS

affective component, p. 203
Asch phenomenon, p. 189
aspirational group, p. 190
attitudes, p. 203
cognitive component, p. 203
cognitive dissonance, p. 209
conative component, p. 203
consumer behaviour, p. 184
cue, p. 204
culture, p. 185
disassociative group, p. 190
drive, p. 204
evaluative criteria, p. 208
evoked set, p. 208
high-involvement products, p. 210
learning, p. 204
low-involvement products, p. 210

membership group, p. 190
microculture, p. 186
motive, p. 198
need, p. 197
opinion leaders, p. 193
perception, p. 200
perceptual screen, p. 201
PSYTE, p. 191
reference group, p. 190
reinforcement, p. 205
response, p. 204
role, p. 189
shaping, p. 205
social class, p. 190
status, p. 189
subliminal perception, p. 202
Weber's Law, p. 202

## INTERACTIVE SUMMARY AND DISCUSSION QUESTIONS

**1.** The work of Kurt Lewin provides a proposition of influences on buying behaviour: $B = f(P,E)$. Explain this equation, and apply it to the purchase of a service.

**2.** A major category of determinants of consumer behaviour is interpersonal determinants: cultural influences, social influences, and family influences. Based on Figure 8.3, for which of the following products is a reference-group influence likely to be strong?
a. Rolex watch
b. skis
c. shaving foam
d. mountain bike
e. deodorant
f. portable radio
g. personal computer
h. contact lenses

**3.** Compare and contrast influences on product use that you are aware of between two cultural groups. Outline the implications for marketing the product(s) specified.

4. The impact that groups and group norms can exhibit on individual behaviour has been called the Asch phenomenon. Its effect can be seen in the influence of membership, aspirational, and disassociative reference groups. Give an example of each type of group, and how such influence might influence product usage.

5. Opinion leaders are individuals who are more likely to purchase new products early and to serve as information sources for others in the group. Give an example of how a salesperson might make use of the phenomenon of opinion leadership in promoting her or his product.

6. Marital roles vary in purchase decisions. They have been categorized as autonomic, husband-dominant, wife-dominant, and joint. List a number of products whose purchase would be influenced more by a female. Explain how this knowledge could be used in developing an advertising program for a product in this category.

7. Consumer behaviour is also affected by personal determinants, which include needs, motives, perceptions, attitudes, and learning. A need is the perceived difference between the current state and a desired state. Maslow established a need classification system with the following categories: physiological needs, safety needs, social needs, esteem needs, and self-actualization needs. Which needs are being referred to in the following slogans?
   a. No caffeine. Never had it. Never will. (7-Up)
   b. Swedish engineering. Depend on it. (SAAB)
   c. Conformity breeds mediocrity. (Levi Strauss)
   d. Best bed a body can buy. (Simmons)
   e. Don't leave home without it. (American Express)

8. Motives are inner states that direct us toward the goal of satisfying a felt need. Explain this statement using one of Maslow's need categories.

9. Perception is the meaning that each person attributes to incoming stimuli received through the five senses. There are so many stimuli that individuals establish a perceptual screen to filter out undesired stimuli. Name some methods that a marketer might use to break through such a screen. Consider selective perception and Weber's Law in your answer.

10. Attitudes consist of three related components: cognitive, affective, and conative.
    a. Explain each component.
    b. How do attitudes influence consumer behaviour?
    c. How can negative attitudes be changed?

11. The consumer decision process is outlined in Figure 8.9. Relate a recent purchase you made to this consumer decision process model.

12. Cognitive dissonance is the postpurchase anxiety that occurs after a purchase when there is a discrepancy between a person's knowledge and beliefs (cognitions) about certain attributes of the final products under consideration. Describe a purchase situation in which you or someone you know experienced cognitive dissonance. Explain how the company that produced the good or service helped or could have helped to reduce that dissonance.

13. Low-involvement products are those with little significance that a consumer might purchase first and evaluate later. High-involvement products are those for which the consumer is highly involved in making the purchase decision. Explain the type of distribution and advertising messages that would be appropriate for each category.

14. Discuss how access to the Internet might affect the consumer decision process, as outlined in Figure 8.9. Explain both the positive and possible negative aspects.

# Case

## BeautySong Cosmetics

Ms. Angela Rubick is marketing manager of BeautySong Cosmetics, a large cosmetic manufacturing company. She has just read the article produced below.

### You Be the Marketer

1. What should she do about this new information?
2. What are the pros and cons of her firm trying to enter this market segment?

### Teen Boys Taking up Tweezers, Tints, and Hair Gel

Far from being the shaggy bed-heads who once sneered at even basic hygiene habits, more of today's teenage boys are becoming grooming gurus, spending nearly as much time in front of the mirror as their sisters.

Stylists at cosmetic counters and beauty salons across the country say young men are asking about concealers, moisturizer, and how to accentuate their eyes. "You're seeing things like lash tinting and tweezing," says Michael Levine, owner of Statik salon on south Granville.

"Every guy's got sculptured eyebrows now—the young ones. It's incredible." Where the imperative to look good once rarely extended beyond brand-name clothes and sneakers, it now includes gym memberships, hair dye, and depilatories for the more style-conscious. "It's starting at, like, 16," says Levine. "It's this whole new kind of genre of guys that are extremely well dressed—they look incredible."

Looking good is always important, says teen Jeremy Yeckler, who spends up to 45 minutes getting ready for a special night out and never leaves the house without a necklace or two. The 17-year-old admits his style regimen at one time included hairspray and gel but now focuses more on clothes.

"I organize it so I don't wear something twice the same week," says Yeckler, who visits the mall once a week to check out the latest fashions. "I like to see what everyone has and get it when it goes on sale right away."

Tom Rennie, 13, says it was his 17-year-old sister who taught him to use hair gel and advises him on what looks good. Older brother Alex, who considers himself low maintenance, says it's because the pressure to fit in is heavy once kids enter high school. "He showers a lot more than necessary," notes Alex, 15. "At his age, I wanted to impress my friends a lot more, too."

Trend experts say boys and girls are flirting with interests and hobbies previously considered to be the exclusive domain of each other.

Stereotypes about what teens consider attractive are dissolving, says the director of youth-culture research at a Toronto

publisher. "There's a blending of the gender differences—boys being more worried about their appearances and girls being less so," says Michele Erskine of Youth Culture Inc., which publishes teen magazines *Verve* and *Fuel*.

"They're not afraid to say they wear hair gel or that looking good is important to them." Girls, meanwhile, can flaunt their athleticism without fear of seeming butch, she says. Erskine credits heavily coiffed boy bands such as 'N Sync, the Backstreet Boys, and B2K. And hip-hoppers laden with heavy gold chains, chunky rings, and garish pendants make wearing jewellery cool.

"The media can be very powerful," says Erskine, who sees boys as young as eight showing up at focus groups with tinted hair. "Suddenly popular music became a forum for cultivated bands of really good-looking guys who clearly had been groomed for the spotlight."

These preening princes know their way around a tweezer and it's spelling big business for the beauty industry. Ron Wood, editor of *Cosmetics* magazine which tracks industry trends, says beauty products are now specifically targeting young men in a way never seen before.

Most push hair care products, such as temporary hair dyes and styling gel. But they're starting to branch into skin care, too, with Holt Renfrew now featuring a wall of skin-care products for men.

"This is the growing market," says Wood, pointing to consumer sales reports from last year. When it comes to hair colour, men bought 13 percent more dye at drugstores than they did the previous year and 18 percent more at grocery stores. That's opposed to women who only bought one percent more at drugstores and 16 percent more at groceries.

"When you see something like 16-, 18-percent growth, you know that's something significant," says Wood, who credits the leap to younger men who are more likely to experiment. Annual surveys by Youth Culture suggest similar trends.

Erskine says boys are generally more label conscious than girls when it comes to clothes. "It's more an emblem or a badge—it shows they're part of the group," says Erskine, whose company surveys 1800 Canadian youth aged 12 to 24 every fall. "With girls, it's all about style and keeping up with what's current, whether the peasant look is in and that sort of thing." Kids on average have $107 a week in their pocket, making the teen population worth about $19 billion, according to Youth Culture studies. And that doesn't include the billions more teens get their parents to spend on them.

For salons such as Statik, that is good news. "We're literally seeing the guys within four weeks," says Levine. "Before, it was almost non-existent unless mother dragged them in. Whether it's a good thing or a bad thing, it's great for our business."

Source: "Teen Boys Taking up Tweezers, Tints and Hair Gel," *The Province*, May 24, 2001, p. A28. Reprinted with the permission of The Canadian Press.

INTRINSYC

Intrinsyc provides unique software and hardware solutions that enable companies to cost-effectively create, network and manage a wide range of consumer and industrial devices.

Accelerate your Vision

Intrinsyc is one of a vast number of firms whose market is other businesses, not consumers.

## Chapter 9

# BUSINESS-TO-BUSINESS MARKETING

## CHAPTER OBJECTIVES

After reading and studying this chapter, you should be able to

1. Provide an overview of the buying process between business buyers and sellers.
2. Differentiate among the three types of business markets.
3. Identify the three distinctive features of business markets.
4. Explain the characteristics of business market demand.
5. Identify the basic categories of business products.
6. Describe the nature and importance of government markets.

**W**arp speed, quantum mechanics, and hyperspace are just a few terms in the time-travel lexicon. Intrinsyc Software of Vancouver is adding "pop machine" to the list.

No, buying a Coke won't fling you forward in time. But the pop machine is one place you can find Intrinsyc's embedded-systems technology—and catch a glimpse of a future full of "smart devices" that talk to one another in real time, all the time.

Embedded systems are small, specialized computers that help everyday devices—from clock radios to cars—do their thing even better. Intrinsyc builds embedded devices and the software that lets them communicate over the Internet. "You can put these intelligent devices in anything," raves president and CEO Neil McDonnell. Here's how it works in a pop machine. An embedded computer displays price on an LCD screen and tracks every soda sale; when stock runs low, it e-mails an order for more. The vendor can also check inventory over the Web or pump up prices, say, during hot weather or a nearby sporting event.

It might not sound like rocket science, but large manufacturers—including Ford, Siemens, and General Electric—count on Intrinsyc to build embedded devices into anything from handheld computers to industrial air-conditioning systems. "They want to specialize in developing their business application," says McDonnell, "not in developing the devices and infrastructure to make it work."

By riding the embedded-systems wave, Intrinsyc has grown its sales by 13 166 percent since 1996. Future success could hinge on its versatility. Unlike most of its rivals, Intrinsyc sells a total package of hardware, software, and engineering services. And while other firms are wed to a single operating system, Intrinsyc's software can link, say, a salesperson's Windows-based PDA to the Linux-based computers at head office. Analyst Glen Tracey of Vancouver's Pacific International Securities Inc. says such flexibility will help Intrinsyc do battle in an industry expected to be worth $27 billion by 2004. But with sales of just $10.9 million, says Tracey, Intrinsyc is below the radar of many potential clients. (Industry "giant" BSquare Corp. had 2001 sales of US$62 million): "They have to get the message out about the value that they add, and that can only come through size."

McDonnell, a seasoned tech exec who joined Intrinsyc from lending-software developer Plexus Systems Design in 2000, is responding to this need. Intrinsyc recently announced an agreement to acquire NMI Electronics, a U.K. developer of wireless technology for the Windows CE platform. The deal could help Intrinsyc access Europe and tap growing demand for embedded systems for PDAs. Intrinsyc is also pumping more money into sales and R&D. "We're confident we can do between $16 million and $18 million this year," he says. "We've got a bunch of really smart people here that don't let the customer down."

Source: Adapted from "Ghost in the Machine" by Susanne Baillie, from http://www.profitguide.com/profit100/2002/features.asp?ID=947 June 2, 2002. Reprinted with permission from *Profit: The Magazine for Canadian Entrepreneurs.*

# INTRODUCTION

Intrinsyc does not operate in the consumer market. It is one of a vast number of firms whose market is other businesses. Electronic components companies do not sell to the final customer, but to car and appliance manufacturers and countless other firms. In turn, many of these same companies produce and sell products to electronic components companies. The huge variety of products and services needed by companies to produce countless products constitutes the business market.

Business-to-business (B2B) marketing is quite different from the marketing practised by consumer-product companies such as Chanel or Procter & Gamble. Many companies that have consumers that might cross over into the business market, and vice versa, have found that marketing practices that are successful in one market will not necessarily be successful in another.

The consumer market consists of individuals who purchase goods and services for *personal* use. The **business-to-business market** consists of firms that produce or acquire goods and services to be used, directly or indirectly, in the production of other goods and services or to be resold. The business-to-business market is also sometimes called the *industrial market*.

Important differences from the consumer market exist in the motivations and buying process followed by business buyers. As a result, marketing planning and the resulting marketing mix for the business-to-business market often are considerably different from those of consumer marketing.

www.chanel.com

**business-to-business market**

Firms that produce or acquire goods and services to be used, directly or indirectly, in the production of other goods and services or to be resold.

A communication designed to meet the specialized needs of a business customer.

# DISTINCTIVE FEATURES OF THE BUSINESS MARKET

The business market has three distinctive features: geographic market concentration, a relatively small number of buyers, and a complex purchase decision process.

## Geographic Market Concentration

The market for business goods in Canada is much more concentrated geographically than that for consumer goods. The largest markets are in Ontario and Quebec. However, business markets for specific items often do not follow the general pattern. As an example, the market for marine engines and fishing gear is concentrated on the Atlantic and Pacific coasts, while that for oil-drilling equipment centres on Alberta, British Columbia, and, to a lesser extent, Saskatchewan. The latter market has now expanded into Newfoundland.

## Small Number of Buyers

The business market is concentrated not only on a geographical basis, but also by a limited number of buyers. Although there are approximately 36 000 manufacturing firms in Canada, a small proportion of firms—those with 500 or more employees—are typically responsible for approximately half the total value added by manufacturing.

The concentration of the business market greatly influences the strategy used in serving this market. The business marketer can usually make more profitable use of a sales force to provide regular personal contacts with a small, geographically concentrated market than consumer goods companies can provide with ultimate consumers. Wholesalers are less frequently used, and the marketing channel for business goods is typically much shorter than that for consumer goods. Advertising plays a much smaller role in this market, as funds may be more effectively spent on the sales force and other means of promotion than with consumer goods.

## Complex Purchase Decision Process

Another distinctive feature of the business-to-business market is the purchase decision process. Compared with the consumer decision process, the business decision process is generally more complex. The magnitude of the decision is greater, more people are involved, and organizations set up more formal procedures that have to be met. This topic will be discussed later in the chapter in more detail.

# TYPES OF BUSINESS MARKETS

In assessing the buyer behaviour of businesses, it is helpful to think about it in terms of the types of business markets. The business-to-business market can be divided into three categories: producers, trade industries (wholesalers and retailers), and governments.

**Producers** are those who transform goods and services through production into other goods and services. Producers include manufacturing firms, farms and other resource industries, construction contractors, and providers of services (such as transportation companies, public utilities, and banks). In the production process, some products aid in producing another product or service (for example, an airplane provides transportation), others are physically used up in the production of a product (wheat becomes part of cereal), and still others are routinely used in the day-to-day operations of a firm (light bulbs and cleaning materials are maintenance items).

**Trade industries** are organizations, such as retailers and wholesalers, that purchase for resale to others. In most instances, resale products (for example, clothing, appliances, sports equipment, and car parts) are finished goods that are marketed to customers. In other instances, some processing or

**producers**
Those who transform goods and services through production into other goods and services.

**trade industries**
Organizations, such as retailers and wholesalers, that purchase for resale to others.

repackaging may take place. Retail meat markets may make bulk purchases of sides of beef and convert them into individual cuts for their customers. Lumber dealers and carpet retailers may purchase in bulk, then provide quantities and sizes to meet customers' specifications. In addition to resale products, trade industries also buy cash registers, computers, display equipment, and other products required to operate their business. These products (as well as maintenance items and the purchase of such specialized services as marketing research studies, accounting services, and consulting) all represent industrial purchases. Retailing and wholesaling activities are discussed in separate chapters later in the text.

Governments at the federal, provincial, and local level represent the final category of business purchasers. This important component of the business market purchases a wide variety of products, ranging from highways to education to fighter aircraft. The primary motivation of government purchasing is to provide some form of public benefits, such as transportation infrastructure, education, or health services. Buying behaviour in government markets is discussed separately in this chapter because of its immense size and importance.

## SCOPE OF THE BUSINESS MARKET

The business market is enormous. As Table 9.1 shows, in the manufacturing sector alone there are over 36 000 establishments, and they employ more than 1.7 million people. The significance of this market is dramatized in the amount of materials and supplies used in their operations—almost $233 billion worth! In total, the industrial market accounts for some 50 percent of purchases of manufactured goods in Canada.

**value added**

The increase in value of input material when transformed into semifinished or finished goods.

One measure of industrial output is the **value added** by manufacturing: the increase in value of input material when transformed into semifinished or finshed goods. For example, value is added to a tonne of iron ore when it is made into steel plate, and more value is added when the plate is stamped into refrigerator bodies. As shown in Table 9.1, the value added by manufacturing in Canada totalled approximately $164.9 billion in 1996.

# THE PRACTISING MARKETER

## CRM IN B2B—A BETTER WORLD

Bo Manning can dream of a world where the substance of every meeting, phone call, e-mail, and Web chat with every customer is recorded, organized, and delivered to your fingertips on demand. Better yet, it's merged with your customer's purchase history, how they like to pay and whether they subscribe to your e-mail newsletter. Suddenly, you can assemble all that disparate information to serve today's most demanding clients better.

Cool, huh? Manning's Pivotal Corp. is delivering the dream. By producing top-notch customer-relationship management software for a mid-market niche, Pivotal has built a US$95-million dollar business with five-year growth of 23 782 percent, good for second spot (for the second year in a row) among Canada's Fastest-Growing Companies.

Founders Norm Francis and Keith Wales—the same duo who created ACCPAC accounting software—established Pivotal in 1994 to help firms handle the growing proliferation of customer-contact channels, including e-mail and the Web. They concentrated on producing sophisticated yet flexible software that appeals to mid-sized firms, which were largely ignored by other CRM players. And they spent heavily on R&D, marketing, and strategic acquisitions in an effort to build barriers against would-be rivals.

Manning counts some 45 000 potential clients in the CRM mid-market. However, some analysts wonder if—or when—Microsoft will take over the category with a mid-level CRM product of its own. (It's scheduled to release a small-business package before year's end.) This is a worry but Manning is too happy with Pivotal's current prospects to buy into any doom and gloom. "We're pretty excited about where we stand," he says. "We're back to winning, and it feels pretty good."

**What do you think about the company's objectives outlined in the first paragraph?**

Source: Adapted from "CRM in B2B – A Better World" by Camilla Cornell, from http://www.profitguide.com/profit100/2002/features.asp?ID=952 downloaded June 2, 2002. Reprinted with permission from *Profit: The Magazine for Canadian Entrepreneus.*

**TABLE 9.1** Summary of Manufacturers by Province, 1996

| PROVINCE | NUMBER OF ESTABLISHMENTS | TOTAL EMPLOYEES | MATERIALS AND SUPPLIES USED ($ MILLIONS) | TOTAL VALUE ADDED ($ MILLIONS) |
|---|---|---|---|---|
| All Canada[a] | 36 239 | 1 703 734 | 232 872.8 | 164 940.1 |
| Newfoundland | 323 | 10 335 | 734.5 | 793.0 |
| Prince Edward Island | 143 | 4 177 | 419.7 | 254.6 |
| Nova Scotia | 748 | 34 402 | 3 788.4 | 2 293.5 |
| New Brunswick | 705 | 32 069 | 5 235.2 | 2 780.4 |
| Quebec | 10 603 | 484 068 | 52 261.2 | 42 541.8 |
| Ontario | 14 471 | 813 504 | 124 541.2 | 84 495.5 |
| Manitoba | 1 143 | 53 114 | 4 784.7 | 3 949.9 |
| Saskatchewan | 800 | 22 298 | 3 155.6 | 1 958.3 |
| Alberta | 2 884 | 100 746 | 18 154.6 | 12 334.4 |
| British Columbia | 4 378 | 148 528 | 19 773.0 | 13 517.4 |
| NWT and Yukon | 41 | 493 | 24.8 | 21.4 |

[a] There may be a discrepancy between figures for Canada and the total of all provinces due to varying sources of information.

Source: Adapted from the Statistics Canada publication *Market Research Handbook, 1999*, Catalogue No. 63-224-XPB, 1999, p. 180. Reprinted with permission of the Minister of Industry Canada.

# MARKET DEMAND

Demand for goods and services is affected by many factors. Beyond the strength or weakness of the general economic environment, four primary characteristics distinguish business requirements: derived demand, joint demand, inventory adjustments, and demand variability.

## Derived Demand

The demand for products used by business is typically **derived demand**—demand derived from (or linked to) demand for a consumer good. The demand for cash registers (an industrial good) is partly derived from demand at the retail level (consumer products). Lower retail sales may ultimately result in lower demand for cash registers.

The "downsizing" of automobile engines by auto manufacturers in an attempt to develop smaller, fuel-efficient cars adversely affects spark-plug manufacturers like Champion. Since four-cylinder engines use half as many plugs as V-8s, Champion's total sales may decline drastically unless total car sales increase dramatically, or unless Champion can increase its share of the total market. On the other hand, booming personal computer sales, along with advances in computing power, have boosted shipments of CD-ROM disk drives.

## Joint Demand

The demand for some industrial products is related to the demand for other industrial goods. There is a **joint demand** for paper and printing ink in the manufacture of newspapers, for example. If the paper supply is reduced, there will be an accompanying reduction in the demand for printing ink.

## Inventory Adjustments

Changes in the amounts of materials a manufacturer keeps on hand can have an impact on demand. Suppose a two-month supply of raw materials is considered the optimal inventory in some manufacturing industries. But suppose economic conditions or other factors dictate that this level be increased to a 90-day supply. The raw materials supplier would then be bombarded with a tremendous increase in new orders. Thus, **inventory adjustments** can be a major determinant of demand for products used by business.

## Demand Variability

Derived demand in the business market is related to and often creates immense variability in the amount of products required. Assume the demand for industrial product A is derived from the demand for consumer product B—an item whose sales volume has been growing at an annual rate of 10 percent. Now suppose that the demand for product B slowed to a 5 percent annual increase. Management might decide to delay further purchases of product A, using existing inventory until the market conditions were clarified. Therefore, product A's **demand variability** becomes significantly affected by even modest shifts in the demand for product B. The disproportionate impact that changes in consumer demand have on business market demand is called the **accelerator principle**.

An example of shifting demand is in the market for coal. Several countries, including Canada, the United States, South Africa, and Australia, have the potential to produce and sell great quantities of coal, but the market is extremely volatile. Demand has been declining for some time, which has led to significant price falls. One of the reasons for the decline in demand has been technological change. Demand for steel has levelled off, and electric-arc furnaces are being used to make steel from scrap. Also, pulverized coal injection, which allows steelmakers to replace half their coking coal with cheaper steam coal, is eroding the value of sales in the market that remains. Another effect on demand is the availability of substitutes such as gas and oil. As gas supplies have increased, its clean-burning properties have made it the fuel of choice in some applications.

Is there any hope for coal? Over the next few years, new materials and technologies for generating electricity from coal are expected to become available. This will increase the percentage of energy in coal that can be converted into electricity. In addition, rapidly developing nations such as China are expected to buy more coal. Demand will fluctuate, but the prospects are not all bad.

# BASIC CATEGORIES OF BUSINESS PRODUCTS

There are two general categories of business products: capital items and expense items. **Capital items** are long-lived business assets that must be depreciated over time. **Depreciation** is the accounting concept of charging a portion of the cost of a capital item as a deduction against the company's annual revenue for purposes of determining its net income. Examples of capital items include major installations like new plants and office buildings as well as equipment.

**Expense items**, by contrast, are products and services that are used within a short period of time. For the most part, they are charged against income in the year of purchase. Examples of expense items include the supplies that are used in operating the business, ranging from raw materials and fabricated parts to paper clips and machine lubricants.

Chapter 10 presents a comprehensive classification of business products. This initial breakdown into capital and expense items is useful, because buying behaviour varies significantly depending on how a purchase is treated from an accounting viewpoint. Expense items may be bought routinely and with minimal delay, while capital items involve major fund commitments and are thus subject to considerable review by the purchaser's personnel.

**capital items**
Long-lived business assets that must be depreciated over time.

**depreciation**
The accounting concept of charging a portion of the cost of a capital item as a deduction against the company's annual revenue for purposes of determining its net income.

**expense items**
Products and services that are used within a short period of time.

Rational or economic appeals are commonly used in advertising to business customers.

# THE NATURE OF BUSINESS PURCHASES

The purchasing process for business tends to be more complex than the consumer decision process described in Chapter 8. There are several reasons for this increased complexity:

1. Many people may exert influence in business purchases, and considerable time may be spent obtaining the input and approval of various organizational members.
2. Organizational purchasing may be handled by committees with greater time requirements for majority or unanimous approval.
3. Many organizations attempt to use several sources of supply as a type of insurance against shortages.

Most firms have attempted to systematize their purchases by employing a professional buyer, or purchasing manager, who is responsible for handling most of the organization's purchases and for securing needed products at the best possible price. Unlike the ultimate consumer (who makes periodic purchase decisions), a firm's purchasing department devotes all of its time and effort to determining needs, locating and evaluating alternative sources of supply, and making purchase decisions.

## The Complexity of Business Purchases

Where major purchases are involved, negotiations may take several weeks or months, and the buying decisions may rest with a number of people in the organization. The choice of a supplier for industrial drill presses, for example, may be made jointly by the purchasing manager and the company's production, engineering, and maintenance departments. Each of these principals has a different point of view, and these must all be reconciled in making a purchase decision. As a result, representatives of the selling firm must be well versed in all aspects of the product or service and be capable of interacting with the managers of the various departments involved. In the industrial instruments industry, for instance, it takes an average of 4.6 face-to-face presentations to make a sale.[1] The average cost of closing the sale—including salesperson compensation and travel and entertainment expenses—is $1197.80.[2] Table 9.2 shows the sales force total cost as a percentage of sales, the average number of sales calls required to complete a sale in several industries, and the average number of calls made per day.

Many industrial goods are purchased over long periods of time on a contractual basis. A manufacturing operation requires a continual supply of materials, and a one- or two-year contract with a supplier ensures a steady supply of raw materials as they are needed. Other products, such as conveyors, typewriters, and forklifts, generally last several years before they need to be replaced.

Purchase decisions are frequently made on the basis of service, certainty of supply, and efficiency of the products. These factors may be even more important than the prices quoted for the products. Car manufacturers purchase steel, glass windows, spark plugs, and batteries as ingredients for their output. Since demand for these parts is derived entirely from the demand for cars, price changes do not substantially affect their sale. Price increases for paint will have little effect on car sales at General Motors, since paint represents a minute portion of the total costs of the car.

## Purchasing a Capital Item

A utility company that was considering buying a reinforced Fiberglas utility pole faced a complicated decision process. The sales representative dealt with the members of several departments of the utility company and went through months of negotiations before a purchase was made. The new pole had several advantages over the traditional wood post: it was lightweight, had noncorrosive properties, never needed painting, and met all strength requirements. Its major disadvantage, other than its unfamiliarity to the purchaser, was its high initial purchase price compared with the alternatives. The decision process began when the manager of the utility consulted the engineering head, who in turn brought in the purchasing manager. Purchasing then prepared a list of alternative suppliers and materials, which was approved by engineering. The purchasing manager then discussed the organization's needs in detail with the sales representatives of three suppliers. The

**TABLE 9.2** Sales Call Statistics

| INDUSTRY GROUP | AVERAGE SALES FORCE TOTAL COST AS A PERCENTAGE OF SALES | AVERAGE NUMBER OF CALLS TO CLOSE SALE | AVERAGE NUMBER OF CALLS PER DAY |
|---|---|---|---|
| Banking | 0.9 | 3.5 | 2.5 |
| Business services | 10.5 | 4.2 | 2.2 |
| Chemicals | 3.4 | 5.4 | 3.2 |
| Communications | 9.9 | 4.0 | 3.1 |
| Construction | 7.1 | 6.2 | 2.2 |
| Educational services | 12.7 | 5.0 | 1.8 |
| Electronics | 12.6 | 5.0 | 2.5 |
| Electronic components | 4.9 | 5.0 | 2.6 |
| Fabricated metals | 7.2 | 3.7 | 2.5 |
| Food products | 2.7 | 2.3 | 2.3 |
| Health services | 13.4 | 4.0 | 3.5 |
| Hotels and other lodging places | 1.9 | 3.8 | 2.8 |
| Instruments | 14.8 | 4.6 | 2.8 |
| Machinery | 11.3 | 2.8 | 3.1 |
| Manufacturing | 6.6 | 4.0 | 2.6 |
| Office equipment | 2.4 | 3.5 | 2.9 |
| Paper and allied products | 8.2 | 3.8 | 2.7 |
| Pharmaceuticals | 5.6 | 0.0 | 4.0 |
| Printing and publishing | 22.2 | 4.2 | 4.0 |
| Real estate | 2.8 | 4.9 | 2.5 |
| Retail | 15.3 | 3.8 | 2.7 |
| Rubber/plastics | 3.6 | 3.5 | 4.2 |
| Transportation equipment | 6.2 | 3.8 | 3.5 |
| Wholesale (consumer goods) | 11.2 | 2.6 | 3.9 |
| Average | 10.0 | 3.8 | 3.0 |

Source: Dartnell Corporation, "Dartnell's 30th Sales Force Compensation Survey" (Palm Beach Gardens, FL: The Dartnell Corporation, 1999), Figures 70 and 104. © 1999, Dartnell Corporation.

salespeople met with the managers of the stores department, the marketing department, and the engineering department. After a series of meetings with the salespeople and numerous discussions among the utility's department heads, the utility company decided to submit the new Fiberglas pole to a test conducted by the engineering department. The results of the test were reported to the various department heads, and bids were then requested from suppliers A, B, and C. These bids were reviewed by the department heads, who ultimately decided to select the Fiberglas pole offered by supplier B. This complex decision process is diagrammed in Figure 9.1.[3]

# CLASSIFYING BUSINESS PURCHASING SITUATIONS

Business buying behaviour is affected by the degree of effort and involvement by different levels within the organization. There are three generally recognized industrial purchasing situations: straight rebuy, modified rebuy, and new task buying.

# FIGURE 9.1 The Decision to Purchase a New Type of Utility Pole

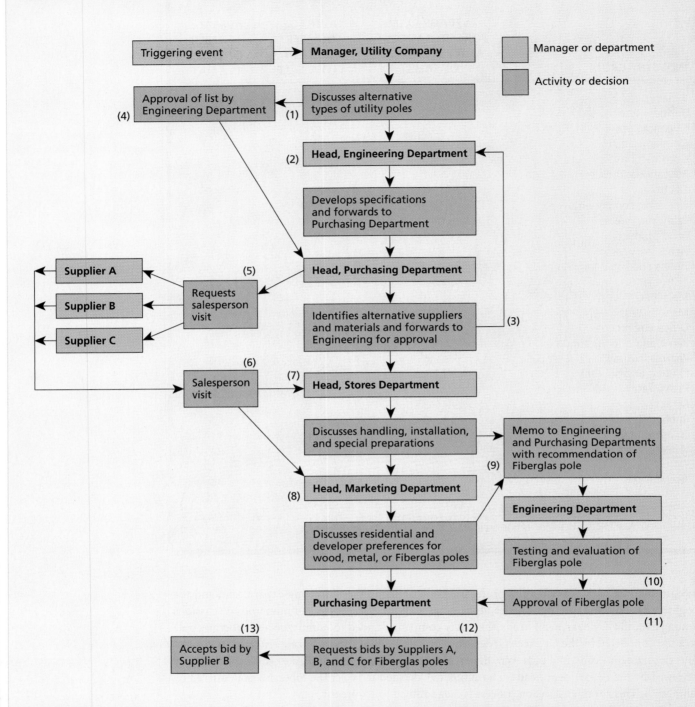

Source: Adapted from Arch G. Woodside, "Marketing Anatomy of Buying Process Can Help Improve Industrial Strategy," *Marketing News* (May 1, 1981), Section 2, p. 11. Reprinted with permission by the American Marketing Association.

## Straight Rebuy

A **straight rebuy** is a recurring purchase decision involving an item that has performed satisfactorily and is therefore purchased again by a customer. This industrial buying situation occurs when a purchaser is pleased with the good or service and the terms of sale are acceptable. Seeing little reason to assess other options, the purchaser follows some routine buying format.

Low-cost items like paper clips and pencils are typically rebought. If the purchaser is pleased with the products, their prices, and their terms, future purchases will probably be treated as a straight rebuy from the current vendor. Even expensive items specially designed for a customer's needs can be treated as a straight rebuy in some cases. For example, a manufacturer might be virtually committed to buying additional lathes from a certain company because it purchased them before and wants to keep a standardized production process.

Marketers facing straight rebuy situations should concentrate on maintaining good relations with the buyer through prompt attention and adequate service. Competitors are faced with the difficult task of presenting a unique sales proposal that will break this chain of repurchases.

**straight rebuy**
A recurring purchase decision involving an item that has performed satisfactorily and is therefore purchased again by a customer.

## Modified Rebuy

A **modified rebuy** is a situation in which purchasers are willing to reevaluate their available options. The decision makers feel that it is to their advantage to look at alternative product offerings using established purchasing guidelines. A modified rebuy situation may occur if a marketer allows a straight rebuy situation to deteriorate because of poor service or delivery or if quality, cost, and service differences are perceived by the customer.

Business-to-business marketers want to move purchasers into a straight rebuy position by responding to all their product and service needs. Competitors, on the other hand, try to move buyers into a modified rebuy situation by correctly assessing the factors that would make buyers reconsider their decisions.

**modified rebuy**
A situation in which purchasers are willing to reevaluate their available options.

## New Task Buying

**New task buying** refers to first-time or unique purchase situations that require considerable effort on the part of the decision makers. Once a need has been identified, evaluative criteria can be established and an extensive search for a product launched. Alternative product and service offerings and vendors are considered. A new task-buying situation may arise when a firm enters a new field and has to seek out suppliers of component parts that have not previously been purchased.

Business-to-business marketers should work closely with the purchaser in the case of new task buying situations. This will allow them to study the factors the purchaser considers important and to design their marketing proposal to match the needs of the purchaser.

**new task buying**
First-time or unique purchase situations that require considerable effort on the part of the decision makers.

# THE BUYING CENTRE

The **buying centre** concept is an important key to understanding industrial purchase behaviour. It denotes the fact that important purchases are normally decided with the input of several different individuals, each person often playing a unique role. The buying centre simply refers to the key individuals who participate in a buying decision. It is not one central location where buying decisions are made. For example, a buying centre may include the architect who designs a new research laboratory, the scientist who will use the facility, the purchasing manager who screens contractor proposals, the chief executive officer who makes the final decision, and the vice president of research who signs the formal contracts for the project.

Buying centres are not normally part of a firm's formal organizational structure. They are informal groups whose composition will vary from one purchase situation to another and from one firm to the next. Buying centres typically include anywhere from four to twenty participants, and tend to evolve as the purchasing process moves through its various stages.

**buying centre**
The key individuals who participate in a buying decision.

### BUSINESS-TO-BUSINESS MARKETING IN A GLOBAL SETTING

If you've ever shopped at a Club Monaco or Suzy Shier store in Canada, or a Tommy Hilfiger, Warner Brothers, or Armani store in the United States, you've seen STS Systems Inc. of Pointe-Claire, Quebec, in action.

You probably didn't notice it, though. STS is the company that provided the information technology that runs those chain stores—the point-of-sale terminals, software, and back-end computers. Doing it and doing it well will see the company posting revenue of $110 million this year, up from $95 million last year—90 percent of it in the United States. With 650 staff and offices in Montreal, New Jersey, Indiana, New York, and Georgia, it's also expanding into Europe through a new office in Britain. "Long term, we want to be a global player," says Howard Stotland, president. "Our new U.K. office is a step in that direction."

While, in the past, STS focused on providing total solutions—its own software plus hardware from business partners General Data and IBM—the company is now also marketing its own packaged best-of-breed products. One such product is AuditWorks—software, Mr. Stotland says,

that can manage a retailer's entire audit process. "We're finding best-of-breed packages to be excellent door-openers for our other services," he explains. "Chances are, if they buy one of our solutions, they'll also come to us for other projects."

www.stssystems.com

Behind the company's success is a team of highly motivated, creative people. "We focus on our staff," Mr. Stotland says. "That's what has and will drive this company in the long run.... [We have] a team ... that's always under budget and exceeds expectations."

This is another of the *Financial Post*'s 50 best-managed private companies in Canada.

**How are the marketing efforts of the company enhanced by having offices in the various world locations?**

Source: Adapted from Deborah Stokes, "Going Global, after a Fashion," *National Post* (December 28, 1998), p. C17. Reprinted with permission.

Buying centre participants play the roles of users, gatekeepers, influencers, deciders, and buyers in the purchasing decision process. Each of these roles is described in Table 9.3.

A critical task for the business-to-business marketer is to determine the specific role and the relative buying influence of each buying centre participant. Sales presentations and information can then be tailored to the role that the individual plays at each step in the purchase process. Marketers have also found that while their initial, and in many cases most extensive, contacts are with the purchasing department, the buying centre participants with the greatest influence are often elsewhere in the company.

# THE PROCESS OF BUYING BUSINESS GOODS AND SERVICES

The exact procedures that are used in buying business goods and services vary according to the buying situation confronted—straight rebuy, modified rebuy, or new task buying. However, most business purchases follow the same general process. A model of the business buying process is presented in Figure 9.2. The specific steps of this process are outlined below. Some steps may be omitted for a modified or straight rebuy.

### Need Recognition

A triggering event, such as an equipment failure, stimulates recognition of a perceived need for a business purchase.

**TABLE 9.3** Roles of Buying Group Members

| ROLE | EXPLANATION |
| --- | --- |
| Users | Individuals who will actually be using the product. They normally have an important role in influencing the purchase decision. |
| Gatekeepers | Those who control the information about the product. For example, the purchasing agent will likely have catalogues, brochures, and advertisements that may or may not be passed on to the buying group. This individual may control which salespeople get to meet the buying group members. |
| Influencers | Those who affect the purchasing decision by setting buying specifications, or by providing information (e.g., engineers) or influence (e.g., senior or knowledgeable users). |
| Deciders | Those who make the purchase decision. The range of possible deciders is wide. They could be users, engineers, purchasing managers, or senior managers. It is important for the marketer to try to determine who the deciders are. |
| Buyers | Those who have formal authority for making the actual purchase after the decision has been made. Often this is the purchasing manager. |

**FIGURE 9.2** A Model of the Business Buying Process

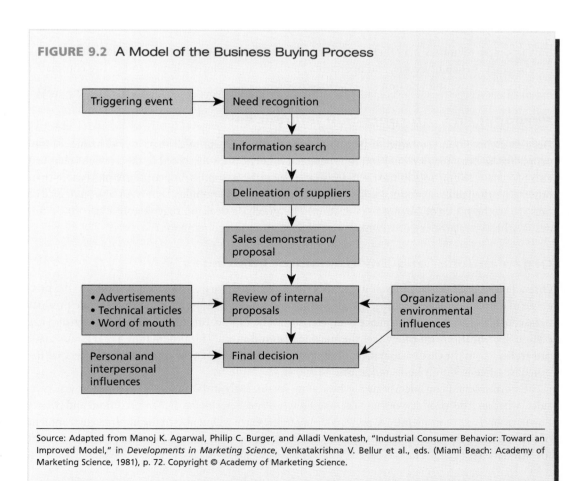

Source: Adapted from Manoj K. Agarwal, Philip C. Burger, and Alladi Venkatesh, "Industrial Consumer Behavior: Toward an Improved Model," in *Developments in Marketing Science*, Venkatakrishna V. Bellur et al., eds. (Miami Beach: Academy of Marketing Science, 1981), p. 72. Copyright © Academy of Marketing Science.

## Information Search

Buying centre members begin to collect information on potential suppliers from sales personnel, advertisements, word of mouth, pamphlets, and other sources. The net result is to delineate the technical nature of the purchase and the available alternatives.

## Delineation of Suppliers

Given the specifications established in the previous step, potential suppliers are determined. Budget considerations may also be a factor in this step.

## Sales Demonstration/Proposal

Vendors' representatives are invited to provide proposals and demonstrations and sales proposals. This is known as **RFP (request for proposal)** or **RFQ (request for quotation)**. These proposals typically include technical and economic options as well as prices.

## Advertisements

Advertisements have the effect of informing and persuading. Often, industrial advertising will invite a reader response requesting further information to be supplied.

## Technical Articles

The buying group examines technical articles for an in-depth analysis of the product, its features, and its performance.

## Word of Mouth

Buying centre members may then contact current users of the product for their evaluation of its performance. Reliability, costs, and operational abilities are explored. Some vendors are eliminated because of negative information.

## Personal and Interpersonal Influences

Despite the fact that the business buying process is generally more deliberate and involves more people in the decision, personal and interpersonal influences (as discussed in the previous chapter) also play a significant role in the final decision. For example, some salespeople are *liked* more than others. In other cases, a product will be purchased because it is popular, trendy, or gives a degree of prestige to the buyer or buying organization. The purchase decision may favour a known brand, despite the better promise of an unknown product, as a risk-reducing measure.

## Organizational and Environmental Influences

Often a number of organizational influences affect the purchase decision. For example, in the purchase of a metal milling machine, the marketing and product design group may want the product to be capable of certain performance characteristics. The engineering and manufacturing group has certain specifications that they feel the machine should meet. The production workers also have preferences as to the ease of operation of the machine, and the financial officer wants to see that the purchase price is within budgeted limits.

Environmental considerations are becoming increasingly important. The company must consider whether the product being purchased fits within set standards for pollution and waste. Furthermore, such considerations apply not only to the external but also to the internal environment of the organization. For example, with some photocopiers, proper ventilation has become important for worker safety.

## Review of Internal Proposals

In some business purchase decisions, more than one group within the organization may have an interest in the purchase. For example, accounting, production scheduling, and research and forecasting departments would be interested in the purchase of a new computer system. After all of the information on various systems has been gathered, such interest groups should each be asked to recommend a system. These proposals would be taken into consideration in the process of coming to a final decision.

## Final Decision

Eventually a purchase decision is made. In many cases, this extensive process leads to a consensus decision, but some buying centre members have more influence than others in this final decision stage.

## Reciprocity

A somewhat controversial practice in a number of business purchasing situations is **reciprocity**, extending purchasing preference to suppliers who are also customers. For example, an office equipment manufacturer may favour a particular supplier of component parts if the supplier has recently made a major purchase of the manufacturer's office equipment. Reciprocal arrangements have traditionally been used in industries with homogeneous products with similar prices, such as the chemical, paint, petroleum, rubber, and steel industries.

Two other forms of reciprocity are sometimes used. *Reverse reciprocity* is the practice of supplying parts and raw materials that are in short supply to firms that can provide other needed supplies in return. In times of shortages, reverse reciprocity occasionally emerges as firms attempt to obtain raw materials and parts to continue operations. A more recent reciprocity spinoff is the *voluntary price roll-back,* in which purchasers request vendors to agree to temporary price cuts or freezes. While no threats are made, it is difficult for a supplier to refuse a request from a major purchaser. This sometimes forces the vendor to ask for concessions from its own workforce and suppliers. The various forms of reciprocity are evidence of the close links that exist among the different elements of the industrial marketplace.

> **reciprocity**
> Extending purchasing preference to suppliers who are also customers.

# NORTH AMERICAN INDUSTRIAL CLASSIFICATIONS

The marketer who focuses on the business market is aided by a wealth of information collected by the federal government, including data on the number of firms, their sales volumes, and the number of employees by category for firms in each industry. The data are broken down using a system known as the **North American Industrial Classification System (NAICS)** (formerly SIC) codes. The NAICS codes begin with 20 divisions; under each division is a list of major groups into which all types of businesses are divided. Table 9.4 lists the main divisions and groups.

These broad groups are further divided into classes. For example, Division 31–33 (Manufacturing) and Division 52 (Finance and Insurance) are divided as shown in Table 9.5. Statistics Canada collects statistics for each of the classes. The NAICS code system can thus help greatly in analyzing the business market.

Beyond the NAICS data, trade associations and business publications provide additional information on the industrial market. Many such publications are listed in the Appendix which follows Chapter 7. Such secondary sources often serve as useful starting points for analyzing industrial markets.

Differences in business purchasing behaviour are discussed in the sections that follow.

> **North American Industrial Classification System (NAICS)**
> A coding system used to categorize different types of businesses and products (formerly the Standard Industrial Classification, or SIC).

**TABLE 9.4** North American Industrial Classifications

| DIVISION | INDUSTRY | GROUPS | NUMBER OF GROUPS |
|---|---|---|---|
| 11 | Agriculture, forestry, fishing and hunting | 111–115 | 5 |
| 21 | Mining and oil and gas extraction | 211–213 | 3 |
| 22 | Utilities | 221 | 1 |
| 23 | Construction | 231–232 | 2 |
| 31–33 | Manufacturing | 311–339 | 20 |
| 41 | Wholesale trade | 411–419 | 8 |
| 44–45 | Retail trade | 441–454 | 12 |
| 48–49 | Transportation and warehousing | 481–493 | 11 |
| 51 | Information and cultural industries | 511–514 | 4 |
| 52 | Finance and insurance | 521–526 | 5 |
| 53 | Real estate and rental and leasing | 531–533 | 3 |
| 54 | Professional, scientific, and technical services | 541 | 1 |
| 55 | Management of companies and enterprises | 551 | 1 |
| 56 | Administrative and support, waste management, and remediation services | 561–562 | 2 |
| 61 | Educational services | 611 | 1 |
| 62 | Health care and social assistance | 621–624 | 4 |
| 71 | Arts, entertainment, and recreation | 711–713 | 3 |
| 72 | Accommodation and food services | 721–722 | 2 |
| 81 | Other services (except public administration) | 811–814 | 4 |
| 91 | Public administration | 911–919 | 5 |

Source: Adapted from the Statistics Canada publication, *North American Industry Classification System — NAICS Canada*, Catalogue No. 12-501, 1997, pp. 17–69. Reprinted with permission of the Minister of Industry Canada.

# GOVERNMENT MARKETS

The various levels of government make up a sizable segment of the market for industrial products. There are many similarities between the government market and business markets, for they seek to purchase many similar goods and services. However, the numerous regulations that affect government purchases create differences in the way items are procured.

## The Basics of Selling to Government

The Government of Canada buys approximately $14 billion worth of goods and services every year from thousands of suppliers. There are over 100 departments, agencies, Crown Corporations, and Special Operating Agencies. Public Works and Government Services Canada (PWGSC) is the government's largest purchasing organization, averaging 50 000 contracts totalling $8 billion annually. While PWGSC buys goods for most departments of the federal government, the departments buy most services themselves.[4] Provincial governments and governments of other countries are also major buyers. Selling to them requires similar approaches as to the Canadian government, which is used here as an example.

There are several ways of doing business with the Canadian government.

1. By selling directly to government departments and agencies via cash, acquisition card (credit card), local purchase order, or contract.

**TABLE 9.5** NAICS Examples

### DIVISION 31–33—MANUFACTURING

| | |
|---|---|
| Group | 311 Food manufacturing |
| Class | 3111 Animal food manufacturing<br>31111 Animal food manufacturing<br>311111 Dog and cat food manufacturing<br>311119 Other animal food manufacturing |
| Class | 3112 Grain and oilseed milling<br>31121 Flour milling and malt manufacturing<br>311211 Flour milling<br>311214 Rice milling and malt manufacturing |

### DIVISION 52—FINANCE AND INSURANCE

| | |
|---|---|
| Group | 521 Monetary authorities—Central Bank |
| Class | 5211 Monetary authorities—Central Bank<br>52111 Monetary authorities—Central Bank |
| Group | 522 Credit intermediation and related activities |
| Class | 5221 Depository credit information<br>52211 Banking<br>522111 Personal and commercial banking industry<br>522112 Corporate and institutional banking |

Source: Adapted from the Statistics Canada publication, *North American Industry Classification System — NAICS Canada*, Catalogue No. 12-501, 1997. Reprinted with permission of the Minister of Industry Canada.

■ Goods: Departments have authority to buy up to $5000 directly from suppliers. Over $5000 they must go to PWGSC.
■ Services: Departments can buy services directly (with a few exceptions).
2. By accessing MERX™, the electronic tendering service.
3. By registering online as a supplier for goods and services.

The overall procurement and contracting policies of the Government of Canada are established by the Treasury Board. The objective of government contracting is to acquire goods and services, and to carry out construction, in a manner that enhances access, competition, and fairness and results in best value to the Canadian government.

Government policy requires that contracting be conducted in a manner that will:

■ stand the test of public scrutiny, increase access, encourage competition, and reflect fairness;
■ comply with Canada's trade obligations.

## What the Government Buys

The Government of Canada buys just about every kind of product and service, from aircraft to paper clips, from training services to scientific research. Public Works and Government Services Canada (PWGSC) is a common service agency responsible for a significant portion of these government requirements.

For most goods and services below $25 000, PWGSC seeks competitive bids from companies registered on PWGSC source lists. For goods and services above this threshold PWGSC advertises requirements through an electronic tendering service known as MERX™.

Many of the requirements the department buys below $25 000 are handled by its regional offices, through an Automated Vendor Rotation System designed to ensure that suppliers have an equal chance to compete for government business.

### MERX™—The Electronic Tendering Service

www.merx.bmo.com/
Services/AboutMERX/
English/MK_SiteMap.asp

MERX™ is an online service that advertises government contracting opportunities to potential bidders. It is owned and operated by the Bank of Montreal, which provides the service to the federal government under contract. More and more of the Government of Canada's requirements are advertised on MERX™—about $5 billion annually.

The buying process starts when a government department or agency sends a requisition to PWGSC. Depending on the requirements, the requisition may be handled by a procurement officer at headquarters or in a regional office. For some requirements valued at less than $25 000, source lists of known suppliers may be used. Normally the previous supplier will be among those invited to bid. PWGSC uses source lists for regional opportunities valued at less than $25 000; and for certain contracts that require pre-qualified bidders.

### How Bids Are Solicited

Depending on the dollar value and the particular requirements of the proposed contract, the procurement officer and the client may choose one of the following bid solicitation methods:
- Telephone Buy (T-buy)
- Request for Quotation (RFQ)
- Invitation to Tender (ITT)
- Request for Proposal (RFP)
- Request for Standing Offer (RFSO).

### How Bids Are Evaluated

The bids received are evaluated using criteria specified in the bid document. As a rule, the bidder who fulfils all the terms and conditions of the requirement, and offers the lowest price, is generally selected. If only one bidder is responsive, PWGSC may negotiate contract terms and prices with that individual or company.

## Selling to Government Markets

Sometimes it is difficult for government to obtain bidders, even for relatively large contracts. Despite its immense size, the government market is often viewed as too complex and unprofitable by many suppliers. Excessive paperwork, bureaucracy, emphasis on low bid prices, decision-making delays, frequent shifts in procurement personnel, and excessive policy changes discourage some suppliers from attempting to service government supply needs.

On the other hand, marketers generally credit the government with being a relatively stable market. Once an item is purchased from a firm by the government, the probability of more sales is good. Other marketers cite such advantages as the instant credibility established by sales to the federal or a provincial government, timely payment, acceptance of new ideas, and reduced competition.

Only a few firms maintain a separate government sales manager or sales force. But many have experienced success with specialized government marketing efforts. It is expected that a growing number of large companies will organize to deal with government purchasers. This is especially true since the North American Free Trade Agreement opened the possibility of selling to U.S. and Mexican governments.

# B2B E-COMMERCE

In order to implement the various facets of business-to-business marketing in an optimal manner, organizations must utilize the power of Internet interconnectivity. Software producer, Oracle, puts it dramatically : "Your competition is on-line. Companies you've never heard of are stealing your customers. 'Business-as-usual' is not an option. Ignoring the Internet means 'no business at all.'"[5] Some may claim this is overstatement; however, small and large companies are proving there are major benefits to connecting all their suppliers and customers into one **electronic exchange network**.

RBC Financial Group has made a powerful statement about **e-commerce**. They have publicly announced on their Web site, with special attention given to their suppliers, their intentions to move as fully into e-commerce as is possible. They ask all who wish to do business with them, "Does your business have the eProcurement advantage?" RBC then makes the following points:[6]

- 93% of businesses surveyed recently had revenue growth after joining Internet business-to-business (B2B) marketplaces, with 11% reporting gains of 21% or more, and 65% experiencing cost reductions.

- By 2002, says Forrester Research, 72% of companies polled expect 20%–50% of their sales will take place over the Internet.

- By 2004, according to AMR Research, B2B marketplaces will involve global transactions worth US$5.7 trillion.

Today, the companies of RBC Financial Group are rapidly implementing an electronic or eProcurement system that will greatly increase supply chain efficiencies, reduce costs, centralize supplier information, speed payment of invoices, and open up many new opportunities for both suppliers and RBC Financial Group alike.

**electronic exchange network**
A single point of access to suppliers and customers through the Internet.

**e-commerce**
Commerce conducted via the Internet.

RBC Financial Group announced on their Web site their intentions to move as fully into e-commerce as is possible.

As we move forward, eProcurement capability will be very important for doing business with RBC Financial Group. If you offer high-quality goods and services with top-notch customer service and have or will soon have eProcurement capability, you could be one of the many small, medium, and large businesses supplying RBC Financial Group.

The companies of RBC Financial Group want to efficiently and cost-effectively buy goods and services, from office equipment to flowers.

We're also introducing existing and prospective vendors to our eProcurement system, which uses inexpensive Internet-based technology to purchase goods and services, track vendors and their offerings, and electronically make payments.

This will be an exciting time for our vendors, with many new opportunities to do business not only with RBC Financial Group but also the dozens of other major organizations in Canada and abroad moving to similar electronic purchasing systems.

You Could Be A RBC Financial Group Supplier, But You Need To Know This… Electronic procurement is the future at Royal Bank. We have already begun implementing our eProcurement system and it's important for potential and existing suppliers to understand how eProcurement will affect supplier relationships.

RBC's strong message, " We want to do business with technologically advanced, innovative companies" is just one example of the significant changes occurring in business-to-business relationships. E-commerce has had a much greater impact in the realm of B2B than business to consumer.

The Internet has made possible tremendous changes in the way business is done. It improves the flow, accuracy, and timeliness of information. Thus Internet-enabled systems provide greater transparency and efficiency at all points along the supply chain. It speeds up search and transaction costs, and improves the transporting and inventorying of products.

The Web enables documents, sound, video, images, and other information forms to be instantly viewed and inexpensively accessed from anywhere in the world. The number of Web sites has grown from 10 000 in January 1995 to over 29 million today. There are currently more than 2.7 billion pages on the Web, and the number is rising by 5 million every day. **B2B e-commerce** includes the creation of Internet-enabled marketplaces for trading goods and services online and business process improvements for transferring information and transactions from the physical world to secure business intranets.[7]

**B2B e-commerce**
Doing business online through Internet-enabled marketplaces.

The part of B2B e-commerce expected to grow the fastest is electronic exchanges, also known as electronic marketplaces. These use vast amounts of information and bring together multiple sellers and buyers online. To understand electronic exchanges, it is useful to remember how businesses buy, and what they buy. Businesses buy a diverse set of products and services ranging from paper clips to computer systems, and steel to machinery. This complex set of buying needs, and supply systems, are the focus of B2B electronic exchanges.

The Internet, and associated software systems, enable buyers and sellers to connect more efficiently than ever before. E-marketplaces provide participants with greater knowledge of prices, availability, supplier capacities and abilities, and alternative products. It is less expensive to search for products and compare prices through e-marketplaces than to hunt through catalogues and make phone calls. British Telecom estimates that moving procurement functions to the Internet has reduced costs from $113 to $8 per transaction.[8] MasterCard® estimates that the internal cost of processing its purchase orders has fallen from $125 to $40, with the time cut from four days to 1.25 days.[9]

### INTERNET-ENABLED SYSTEMS

Some Internet exchange systems have been established and run by individual companies. Others have been sponsored by an industry to serve the needs of various members in that industry. Both private networks and industry-established online exchanges can help participants better manage production schedules and inventory levels. Dell Computer Corp. has turned traditional manufac-

Use .NET™ connected software to work closer with your suppliers. Your product, no matter how good it is, isn't going to make you money unless you can get it off your plant floor and onto the road – fast. How you do it? Easy. With .NET connected software from Microsoft. Quickly link all of your suppliers' systems together – on a large scale. Suddenly, all your suppliers will work together seamlessly. Allowing you to instantly gather quotes, make purchases, check orders and easily manage hectic delivery schedules. You'll know your suppliers better than the back of your hand. And they'll know you better than you know yourself. That's one degree of separation. That's business with .NET. For more information, visit microsoft.ca/business. Software for the Agile Business.

Dollar Rent A Car wanted to let potential partners directly access its mainframe-based reservation system via the Internet. Using .NET connected software from Microsoft, they built an interface application that has already produced thousands of new reservations and millions of dollars in additional revenue.

*Microsoft®*

By using the Internet to enable software applications to work together, Microsoft® .NET™ allows all of a company's suppliers' systems to work together to better manage purchasing functions.

turing on its head by saying it will not build anything until it receives an order. Almost 50 percent of Dell's revenues come through its Web site, which generates roughly $40 million in sales each day. With perfect information about what customers want, Dell operates with five days' inventory, down from 31 days in 1996, before the company implemented its Internet-based build-to-order system. The moral of this story is that accurate information provided in real time through Internet-enabled systems leads to greater production efficiencies.[10]

## E-Commerce Applications

E-commerce is a term that encompasses several different interconnected relationships and applications. Essentially, e-commerce applications bring people (users) using computer systems (tools) that manipulate data, information, knowledge, and wisdom (content) in order to accomplish a set of purposes (tasks).

The most typical types of e-commerce include:

- e-business/retailing (electronic storefronts)
- e-brokerages
- Information utilities
- Customized marketing
- Custom manufacturing
- Online procurement

- Supplier-customer system integration (electronic exchanges/e-hubs)
- Logistical management of commodity suppliers
- Support for non-profit organizations

There is a considerable overlap between these types of e-commerce applications. With respect to B2B, electronic exchanges have shown a great deal of potential.

B2B exchanges are virtual trading posts. On a particular site, buyers and sellers come together to offer products for sale, or to specify items that are needed.

A B2B **electronic exchange** is an organized group of buyers and sellers from a specific industry linked together electronically. Electronic exchanges benefit buyers and sellers through the close linkage that they achieve. For example, a business purchaser might post a request for quotations for 10 000 automotive CD players. An attachment would include drawings and precise specifications. The posting would be placed through an Internet exchange network operated by the company (if the business is large enough) or by other providers. On the closing date, the purchaser would review the quotations that had been received from around the world, and would then issue the purchase order electronically. All other parts of the transaction, except physical delivery and handling, would be handled electronically, including the relaying of information to relevant units of the organization. The CD players would arrive on the production line in the right quantities and at the specified delivery times.

An example of an electronic exchange network is VerticalNet, Inc., a leading creator and operator of numerous vertical trade communities on the Internet, including advanced technologies, communications, food and packaging, healthcare, and other service industries. A **vertical Web community** acts as a comprehensive source of information and dialogue for a particular vertical market.

Companies can take advantage of the interactive features and global reach of the Internet to facilitate business-to-business trading. Buyers and sellers from around the world with similar professional interests are brought together in ways that were never possible before the Internet. The VerticalNet Web site features highly focused target markets that draw business Web users to visit the site to obtain information, or to search for products and services to buy and sell. Another site that facilitates business-to-business trade is PurchasePro.com.

It is possible to define online exchanges in two ways: 1) by the primary means of transaction that they offer, or 2) by the market that they serve. e-STEEL can be defined as industry-specific. A different type of exchange, exemplified by Freemarkets is a horizontal player serving the auction needs of multiple industries. But as the industry matures and the online marketplaces grow correspondingly more complex, alternate definitions need to emerge.

Some online marketplaces will begin serving both horizontal and vertical markets. Covisint is a remarkable exchange in that it is an auto industry exchange backed by three major companies, GM, Ford, and DaimlerChrysler. It will eventually facilitate the purchase of not only auto parts, but non-production goods such as office supplies and maintenance equipment. Others will begin offering more than one transaction mechanism as well.

Covisint and similar ventures have already had significant impact on the way Web marketplaces are visualized and executed. And these new models require new classifications.

## Three Types of Online Exchanges

In Table 9.6, eMarketer has defined exchanges by their ownership, distinguishing between those that are run by third parties, industry consortia, or private companies.

E-commerce works. Nygard International's Winnipeg production site formerly took five weeks to turn orders around. Today, with electronic ordering that time is cut to a maximum of 72 hours. When a retail customer places an order electronically, a process is triggered that first places automatic orders with fabric and component suppliers linked to the system enabling manufacturing to be scheduled and started quickly. Another firm found that by utilizing a similar system, a purchasing assignment that once took six or seven hours to complete now takes about 45 minutes to an hour.[11]

B2B e-commerce has come a long way. However, it is still in its early stages, and thus it is still subject to a great deal of development. It is clear that there is an increasing trend to use the Internet

**electronic exchange**
An organized group of buyers and sellers from a specific industry linked together electronically.

**vertical Web community**
A site that acts as a comprehensive source of information and dialogue for a particular vertical market.

www.verticalnet.com

www.corp.purchasepro.com

# INTERNET IMPACT

## MOTOROLA'S EXPERIENCE

The enterprise tackles e-procurement, e-sourcing, supplier relationships, and spending visibility; the bottom line is still savings.

Communications and electronics specialist Motorola is no stranger to e-business, having been involved in electronic data interchange (EDI) for years. However, in the mid-'90s, Motorola became interested in the potential of Internet-based technologies and applications to transform the business. Since then, Motorola has moved aggressively to take advantage of the newer strains of e-business.

In a recent conversation, Robert Harlan, director of Motorola's Internet negotiation program (covering all e-sourcing, e-RFQ, and reverse auction initiatives), said, "In May of last year, we [contracted] eBreviate to run e-auctions for us. They did 60 auctions, and we spent $800 million online." For an investment of $1 million, Motorola won nearly $50 million in savings. Understandably pleased with the results, the company became more ambitious, and laid plans to develop an enterprise-wide e-sourcing system. Among the needs: better scalability and data capture. "We were saving money, but we weren't encompassing the full breadth of e-sourcing," he says. "For example, we weren't connecting RFQs with the ability to go to online auctions, and we didn't have flexibility around Internet negotiations [with suppliers]."

This year, Motorola expects to channel $2 billion in auction spending through services provided by the Emptoris ePASS auction platform, and an additional $2–4 billion through Emptoris' eRFQ functionality.

Motorola's grand vision is to get both direct and indirect spending into the Emptoris system. "I see us achieving that within the next year or two," Harlan predicts. He also reveals that Motorola expects to shave a significant percentage of its historic costs of spending by using Emptoris. "Historically, we've seen over eight percent incremental reductions above and beyond our expectations," Harlan says. "We thought we'd get 20 percent, we got 28." But, significant though these savings may be, Harlan is just as excited about the long-term value of the Emptoris solution in its role as a data capture tool.

Traditionally, he says, "It's difficult for us to find out what we sourced from a particular supplier. It's time-intensive to answer that, and there's an exposure for us there." With Emptoris, the situation changes, as spending information is captured—and the resulting visibility improves Motorola processes. "I spent half of today with the commodities manager, trying to locate demand data for PCBs. But his job is not to chase data; his job is to think high-level strategy. Saving his time can save the company a lot of money every day." There are 600 Motorola employees who deal with sourcing, and Harlan thinks that Emptoris' data capture/spending analysis function will have a similar impact across the constituency.

**Explain how Motorola will benefit by initiating this system.**

Source: Demir Barlas, Line56 http://www.line56.com/articles/default.asp?ArticleID=3686, June 6, 2002.

---

**TABLE 9.6** The Three Primary Business Models for Online Exchanges

| | Description | Example |
|---|---|---|
| 1. Third-Party Exchange | Exchange is owned and operated by a third-party that is not considered to be a trading partner, often a B2B startup. | Ventro (formerly Chemdex) |
| 2. Consortia-Led Exchange | Exchange ownership is shared between industry-leaders and a technology partner. | GM/DaimlerChrysler/ Ford exchange, Covisint |
| 3. Private/Proprietary Exchange | Exchange is owned and operated by a single large firm. | Wal-Mart's RetailLink |

Source: Steve Butler, "The Three Primary Business Models for Online Exchanges," *eMarketer*, www.emarketer.com, June 19, 2000. Reprinted by permission.

to improve supply chain efficiency and thereby reduce production costs. Furthermore, it should be noted that B2B e-commerce goes beyond online buying and selling via the Internet, and includes the entire spectrum of business automation. The potential for generating efficiencies through Supply Chain Management (SCM) is a crucial element of exchange-based trade.

Perhaps the most important point to remember about online business is that the adoption of e-commerce technology is more evolutionary than revolutionary. Commerce conducted via the Internet is not about to change the fundamental way that business is conducted. E-commerce is being adapted to established business processes; the firms that will succeed in the New Economy are those that most effectively use the new technologies.

## SUMMARY

The business-to-business market consists of firms that produce or acquire goods and services to be used, directly or indirectly, in the production of other goods and services or to be resold. Important differences from the consumer market exist with business buyers.

Categorizing business buyers is important for assessing buyer behaviour. The three categories are producers, trade industries, and governments. The business market also has three distinctive features: geographic market concentration, a relatively small number of buyers, and a complex purchase decision process.

Business market demand is distinguished by four characteristics: derived demand, joint demand, inventory adjustments, and demand variability.

The business purchase is generally more complex than a typical consumer purchase. The purchase often involves a group of individuals (the buying centre) with different interests and skills in assessing the value of the purchase. There are three generally recognized purchasing situations: straight rebuy, modified rebuy, and new task buying. The straight rebuy is the simplest business buying situation.

The business buying process generally involves the following phases: (1) need recognition, (2) information search, (3) delineation of suppliers, (4) sales demonstration/proposal, (5) review of internal proposals, and (6) final decision.

Governments are often very large buyers. Their purchases are normally made on the basis of bids, which are based on specifications.

B2B e-commerce is a major part of business marketing. It has many components including electronic online exchanges, e-procurement, e-sourcing, and it affects supplier relationships in a major way. Its implementation saves time and reduces costs significantly.

## KEY TERMS

accelerator principle, p. 222

B2B e-commerce, p. 236

business-to-business market, p. 218

buying centre, p. 227

capital items, p. 223

demand variability, p. 222

depreciation, p. 223

derived demand, p. 222

e-commerce, p. 235

electronic exchange network, p. 235

electronic exchange, p. 238

expense items, p. 223

inventory adjustments, p. 222

joint demand, p. 222

modified rebuy, p. 227

new task buying, p. 227

North American Industrial Classification System (NAICS), p. 231

producers, p. 219

reciprocity, p. 231

RFP (request for proposal) or RFQ (request for quotation), p. 230

straight rebuy, p. 227

trade industries, p. 219

value added, p. 220

vertical Web community, p. 238

# INTERACTIVE SUMMARY AND DISCUSSION QUESTIONS

1. Categorizing business buyers is important for assessing buying behaviour. The three categories are producers, trade industries, and government. Why is this categorization useful?
2. The business market accounts for approximately 50 percent of purchases of manufactured goods. What significance does this have for jobs for business graduates?
3. The business market has three distinctive features: geographic market concentration, a relatively small number of buyers, and a complex purchase decision process. Give an example and discuss some of the implications for a marketing program targeted at that market.
4. Business market demand is distinguished by four characteristics: derived demand, joint demand, inventory adjustments, and demand variability. Explain and give examples of each.
5. The two general categories of industrial products are capital items and expense items. Distinguish between the two.
6. Illustrate how a marketing planner can use the North American Industrial Classification System (NAICS).
7. A business purchase is generally characterized by being systematic and complex. Explain and illustrate with an example.
8. There are three generally recognized business purchasing situations: straight rebuy, modified rebuy, and new task buying. Describe each type, and discuss the marketing task in each.
9. Figure 9.2 shows a model of the business buying process. Compare and contrast salesperson influence, advertising influence, and word-of-mouth influence. In which type of buying situations might each be more influential?
10. Prepare a report on a recent purchase by a local organizational buyer. What can be learned from this exercise?
11. The Canadian International Development Agency (CIDA) is a government agency that supports development in less developed countries. Go to the CIDA Web site and prepare a brief report on the business opportunities that exist through its work.

www.acdi-cida.gc.ca

# Case

## Step Aside, Spider-Man!

When it comes to averting computer-network disasters, Captain Nuvo will take the call. The mention of "network-management solutions" is enough to send most businesspeople screaming for the door. That's why Nuvo Network Management created Captain Nuvo, the comic-book superhero who pervades the firm's marketing materials.

The buff, blonde Captain sports a blue-and-gold bodysuit and a Lone Ranger mask. His territory: Netropolis. His arch-nemesis: Crash, whose "evil powers are having horrific effects on global industries." (To see the good Captain in action, download Nuvo's 2001 annual report at www.nuvo.com.)

"Selling complex services is all about simplification," explains CEO Kevin Vachon. "We simplified our value proposition through a superhero vs. villain approach." Vachon says spawning Captain Nuvo—who debuted 18 months ago—helped Nuvo achieve its 2001 sales of $12 million.

### You Be the Marketer

1. Sales are a result of many things, including good products. What do you think about the idea of having a Captain Nuvo as a major part of promoting and explaining a product in the business-to-business product?
2. Would this be a more acceptable approach in the business-to-consumer market?

Source: Adapted from "Step Aside, Spider-Man!" from http://www.profitguide.com/profit100/2002/features.asp?ID=947 June 2, 2002. Reprinted with permission from *Profit: The Magazine for Canadian Entrepreneurs.*

Ford demonstrates the value of a powerful brand by reintroducing the Marauder.

## Chapter 10

# MARKETING THE TOTAL PRODUCT: BRAND, IMAGE, WARRANTY, AND PACKAGING

## CHAPTER OBJECTIVES

After reading and studying this chapter, you should be able to

1. Explain the concept of a total product and of product management.
2. Discuss the role of brands, brand names, and trademarks.
3. Elaborate on basic approaches to brand management.
4. Understand brand equity and what contributes to it.
5. Explain the importance, role, and functions of packaging.
6. Identify the classifications for consumer products and briefly describe each category.
7. Classify the types of industrial products.

The announcement by Ford that they're reintroducing the Mercury Marauder brand indicates that a trend toward "revivals" might be under way.

Ford isn't the only automaker to look back in time for inspiration recently, and analysts predict that we'll see a few more hallowed nameplates making a second debut over the next year or two.

Ford's St. Thomas Assembly Plant in Ontario is producing a modern version of the "muscle car" icon. The original Marauder was launched back in 1963 and was still benefiting from engine power hikes as late as 1969, before fading from the scene.

Ford will build just 18 000 of the new Marauders and they'll be powered by a 302 horsepower V8 in the best muscle-car tradition. Other features include performance suspension, full instrumentation, high performance tires, leather trim, and any colour you want as long as it's gloss black.

Of course, Ford is no newcomer to the business of reviving and updating old nameplates. Most recently, the 2002 Thunderbird has proved itself a tremendously popular modern interpretation of the '50s sports car legend. The only problem with this model is that if you want one, you'll have to join a long waiting list.

Ford is not the only automaker to look back to a distinguished past for new model inspiration. Chrysler's 300M is a modem interpretation of this automaker's "letter series" cars of the l950s and 1960s. With its 250 horsepower V6, semi-manual AutoStick transmission and agile handling, the 300M is a worthy successor to those legends.

Over at General Motors, the Impala name was revived for a low-run specialty model—the SS—and then used for what is now a very popular large sedan. The latest auto manufacturer to revive an old nameplate is no less than Mercedes-Benz, which announced its spin-off Maybach brand earlier this year.

Back in the 1930s, Maybach was one of the world's most distinguished luxury marques, but like so many of its contemporaries, it disappeared from the scene.

**Ford, and the other automakers, are continually monitoring their product line looking for ways to increase the attractiveness of the product, and hence its value to their customers. Ford realizes that there is a great deal more to their cars than simply the metal and other components from which they're made. Given that the new model being introduced is based on the Crown Victoria platform, they could have retained the Crown Victoria nameplate—but somehow the overall impact would have been very different. Ford executives know that as well as the Marauder brand, customers will consider the warranty of the car and the overall image that a muscle car projects. (In smaller products, customers would also be looking at the package and label.) All in all, marketers have to manage the total product, and that's the focus of this chapter.**

**Marketing managers not only face many decisions about designing and positioning new products, but also about managing existing ones. Over the life of each product, they have to determine whether prices should be lowered or raised, whether money should be spent on redeveloping older products, and how such products should be promoted and distributed. Finding and introducing new products and managing older ones are major aspects of marketing management.**

Source: Excerpted from Tony Whitney, "Marauder Makes Comeback," *The Star Phoenix*, June 7, 2002. Reprinted with permission of the author.

www.ford.ca

www.mercedes.ca

www.gmcanada.com

# INTRODUCTION

This is the first of three chapters dealing with the "product" component of the marketing mix. Here the basic concepts and definitions of this marketing element are laid out.

Marketing planning efforts begin with the choice of products to offer the target market. Pricing, marketing channels, and marketing communication (the other variables of the marketing mix) are all based on the nature of the product.

Everyone knows what a product is—or do they? We must first make sure we understand what a product really is.

## Product: A Definition

A narrow definition of the word *product* might focus on the physical or functional characteristics of a good that is offered to consumers. For example, a Sony videocassette recorder is a rectangular container of metal and plastic wires connecting it to a television set, accompanied by a series of special tapes for recording and viewing. This is the core product. But purchasers have a much broader view of the VCR. They have bought the convenience of viewing television programs at their leisure; the warranty and service that Sony, the manufacturer, provides; the prestige of owning this fine product; and the ability to rent or purchase recently released movies for home viewing. Thus, the brand image, warranty, and service are also all parts of the product as seen by the consumer.

Marketing decision makers must have this broader concept in mind and realize that people purchase more than just the physical features of products. *They are buying want satisfaction.* Most drivers know very little about the gasoline they regularly purchase. If they bother to analyze it, they discover that it is almost colourless and emits a peculiar odour. However, most drivers do not think of gasoline as a product at all—to them, gasoline is a tax. It is a payment that they must make periodically for the privilege of driving their cars on the streets and highways, and the friendly service-station attendant is a tax collector. Petroleum retailers should be aware of this image in the minds of many customers before spending huge sums to promote dozens of secret ingredients designed to please the motorist.

The shopper's conception of a product may be altered by such features as packaging, labelling, or the retail outlets in which the product may be purchased. An image of high quality has been created for Maytag appliances, whose television commercials describe the Maytag repairer as "the loneliest person in town." More than 30 years ago, the firm's president set a standard of "10 years of trouble-free operation" for washing machines. The company's success in achieving a reputation for high quality is evident in Maytag's continued sales growth record, even though the washer's retail price is higher than the nearest competitor's.

Some products have no physical ingredients. A haircut and blow-dry at the local hairstylist produces only well-groomed hair. A tax counsellor produces only advice. Thus, a broader view of product must also include services.

A **total product**, then, may be defined as a total bundle of physical, service, and symbolic characteristics designed to produce customer want satisfaction. Figure 10.1 reflects this broader definition—known as the total product concept—by identifying the various components of the total product.

### The Warranty

An important feature of many products is a product **warranty**. The warranty is a guarantee to the buyer that the supplier will replace a defective product (or part of a product) or refund its purchase price during a specified period of time. Such warranties serve to increase consumer purchase confidence and can prove to be an important means of stimulating demand. Sangoma, an electronics components manufacturer, warranties its products for up to 36 months. Many retailers have a broad, unwritten, but frequently honoured warranty of satisfaction or your money back.

---

**total product**

A total bundle of physical, service, and symbolic characteristics designed to produce customer want satisfaction.

**warranty**

A guarantee to the buyer that the supplier will replace a defective product (or part of a product) or refund its purchase price during a specified period of time.

## UNDERSTANDING WARRANTIES

Laws governing warranties are a provincial matter, so there are some differences from province to province. Nonetheless, the provincial legislation is broadly similar. Many consumers are not aware that regardless of written warranties, or the lack of written warranties, they have certain rights assured by legislation.

A new product must be free from encumbrances; that is, the seller must have clear title, or be able to bestow clear title, and must have the right to sell the product in the first place. Descriptions of the product on the package must be accurate. The product must be of acceptable quality unless defects are specifically drawn to the consumer's attention or an inspection of the goods might reasonably be expected to reveal imperfections (e.g., cosmetic imperfections in a paint job). The product must be fit for its purpose. If the purchase is made based on a sample, the purchased goods must match the sample and be of acceptable quality. The product must be of reasonable durability—reasonable will, of course, vary from one product to another. Finally, spare parts and repair facilities must be available, although not necessarily in the immediate vicinity.

On the other hand, many written warranties provide less protection than one might think. Many have an abuse clause by which the warranty will be void if, in the seller's opinion, the problems with the product are caused by abuse. Most manufacturers have that clause to protect themselves from flagrant consumer abuse. A few, however, define abuse as anything that might damage the product, in which case a consumer can literally hear, for example, a golf club manufacturer say, "You must have abused the club, because our clubs don't break in normal play."

Many written warranties have explicit service schedules. Failure to follow the schedule will void the warranty.

Another interesting phrase used in some warranties is "Guaranteed for life." The warranty should specify whether that means the life of the consumer or the life of the product. Obviously, a warranty for the life of the product is not terribly meaningful.

For more information about warranties and consumer rights, visit Industry Canada's Web page on consumer information. The site also has links to provincial pages.

**Can you think of an example of a questionable warranty for a product you've recently bought? How could the warranty have been improved to make it more meaningful?**

www.industrycanada.ca

www.strategis.ic.gc.ca/
sc_consu/engdoc/
homepage.html

Source: Based on information from Sandra Hornung, *Consumer Power: A Guide to the Basics of Consumer Law in Saskatchewan* (Saskatoon: Public Legal Education Association of Saskatchewan, 1997), pp. 13–22.

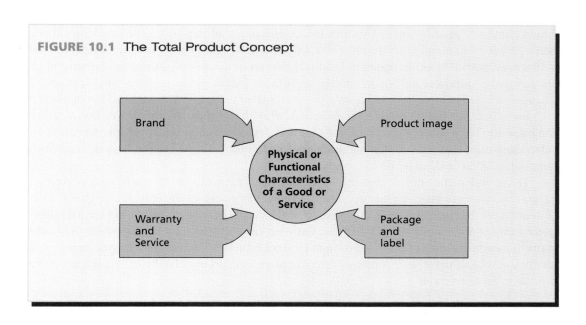

FIGURE 10.1 The Total Product Concept

Brand

Product image

Physical or Functional Characteristics of a Good or Service

Warranty and Service

Package and label

# BRAND MANAGEMENT

Manufacturers identify their products through the use of brand names, symbols, and distinctive packaging. So do large retailers such as Canadian Tire, with its line of Mastercraft products, and The Bay, with its Beaumark brand. Almost every product that is distinguishable from another contains a means of identification for the buyer. Even a five-year-old can distinguish a Chiquita banana from other ones. And the California Fruit Growers Exchange brands its oranges with the name Sunkist. The purchasing manager for a construction firm can turn over an ordinary sheet of roofing and find the name and symbol for Domtar. Choosing the means of identification for the firm's output often represents a major decision area for the marketing manager.

## Brands, Brand Names, and Trademarks

**brand**

A name, term, sign, symbol, or design (or some combination of these) used to identify the products of one firm and to differentiate them from competitive offerings.

**brand name**

Words, letters, or symbols that make up a name used to identify and distinguish the firm's offerings from those of its competitors.

**trademark**

A brand that has been given legal protection and has been granted solely to its owner.

A brand is more, though, than simply a means of identifying the product. A **brand** is a name, term, sign, symbol, or design (or some combination of these) used to identify the products of one firm and to differentiate them from competitive offerings. A **brand name** is that part of the brand consisting of words, letters, or symbols that make up a name used to identify and distinguish the firm's offerings from those of its competitors.[1] The brand name is, therefore, that part of the brand that can be spoken. A **trademark** is a brand that has been given legal protection and has been granted solely to its owner. Thus, the term "trademark" includes not only pictorial design but also the brand name. Many thousands of trademarks are currently registered in Canada. Today, virtually all trademarks are developed with careful consideration of the visual and emotional impact of the name. Some other common trademarks have emerged through various iterations over the years. The Procter & Gamble "moon and stars" trademark is one example.

For the consumer, brands facilitate repeat purchases of products that have been found satisfactory. The brand assures a uniform quality and identifies the firm producing the product. The purchaser associates the satisfaction derived from a carbonated soft drink with the brand name Pepsi-Cola.

## What Constitutes a Good Brand Name?

Good brand names are easy to pronounce, recognize, and remember. Short names like Vim, Gleem, Dash, and Kodak meet these requirements. Multinational marketing firms face a particularly acute problem in selecting brand names: a brand name that works terrifically well in one country may prove disastrous in another due to language problems.

For 21 years, Nissan Motor Corporation marketers struggled with an easily mispronounced brand name—"Datsun"—for its cars and trucks. Nissan found that in English-speaking nations some people pronounced the *a* like the *a* in *hat*, while others pronounced it like the *o* in *got*, and the difference hindered brand recognition. Finally, Nissan marketers decided to change the name of all its automobile products to "Nissan" beginning with its Stanza model in 1982. Total cost of the change—effected in more than 135 countries—is estimated to have been as high as $150 million.[2]

Every language has "O" and "K" sounds, and "okay" has become an international word. Every language also has a short "a," so that Coca-Cola and Texaco are good in any tongue. An American advertising campaign for E-Z washing machines failed in the United Kingdom because the British pronounce "Z" as "zed," as we do in Canada.

The brand name should give the buyer the right connotation. Mercury Marine presents favourable images of boating pleasures. The Craftsman name used on the Sears line of quality tools also produces the correct image. Accutron suggests the quality of the high-priced and accurate timepiece made by the Bulova Watch Company. But what can the marketing manager do if the brand name is based on a strange-sounding company name? Sometimes the decision may be to poke fun at this improbable name, as in a promotional campaign built around the theme "With a name like Koogle, it has to be good!"

www.pg.com/rumor/
index.html

# The Brand Name Should Be Legally Protectable

S.C. Johnson and Son, makers of OFF, lost a court case against Bug Off since it was held that OFF was an improper trademark because it was not unusual enough to distinguish it from other, similar products.

When all offerings in a class of products become generally known by the brand name of the first or leading brand in that product class, the brand name may be ruled a descriptive or **generic name**, after which the original owner loses all right to the exclusive use of it. Generic names like nylon, zipper, kerosene, linoleum, escalator, and shredded wheat were once brand names.

Bayer's Aspirin is the only ASA tablet permitted to carry that protected trademark in Canada. All other acetylsalicylic acid tablets are called ASA. In the United States, because Bayer did not protect its trade name, the generic name "aspirin" is given to all acetylsalicylic acid tablets. Most drug purchasers there would not know what an ASA tablet is.

There is a difference between brand names that are legally generic and those that could be perceived to be generic in the eyes of many consumers. Jell-O is a brand name owned exclusively by General Foods. But to most grocery purchasers the name Jell-O is the descriptive generic name for gelatin dessert. Legal brand names—such as Formica, Xerox, Frigidaire, Kodak, Frisbee, Styrofoam, Kleenex, Scotch Tape, Fiberglas, Band-Aid, and Jeep—are often used by consumers in a descriptive manner. Xerox is such a well-known brand name that it is frequently used as a verb. British and Australian consumers often use the brand name Hoover as a verb for vacuuming.

To prevent their brand names from being ruled descriptive and available for general use, companies must take deliberate steps to inform the public of their exclusive ownership of brand names. They may resort to legal action in cases of infringement. The Eastman Kodak Company developed a series of advertisements around the theme "If it isn't an Eastman, it isn't a Kodak." The Coca-Cola Company and many other companies use the ® symbol for registration immediately after their brand names. Coca-Cola sends letters to newspapers and novelists and other writers who use the name Coke® with a lowercase first letter, informing them that the trademark is owned by Coca-Cola. Walt Disney Co. actively protects its brand names and is prepared to sue if necessary. West Edmonton Mall learned this the hard way when it lost a ten-year court battle with Disney over its indoor amusement park named Fantasyland. It lost an estimated $5 million in replacing all the Fantasyland signs and paraphernalia associated with the name. Thus, companies may face the ironic dilemma of attempting to retain the exclusive rights to a brand name that, chiefly due to the success of their own marketing efforts, could become generic to a large market segment if they do not take appropriate steps to protect their trademarks.

Since any dictionary word may eventually be ruled to be a generic name, some companies create new words to use for brand names. Such brand names as Keds, Rinso, and Kodak have obviously been created by their owners.

For the marketing manager, the brand serves as the cornerstone around which the product's image is developed. Once consumers have been made aware of a particular brand, its appearance becomes further advertising for the firm. The Shell Oil Company symbol is instant advertising to motorists who view it while driving. Well-known brands also allow the firm to escape some of the rigours of price competition. Although any chemist will confirm that all ASA tablets contain the same amount of the chemical acetylsalicylic acid, Bayer has developed so strong a reputation that it can successfully market its Aspirin at a higher price than competitive products. Similarly, McDonald's "golden arches" attract customers to its outlets.

The "attractiveness" of Bayer, McDonald's, and hundreds of other respected brands is called **brand equity**. Brand equity really represents the value customers (and the stock markets) place on the sum of the history the customer has had with a brand. If a brand has consistently been associated with high quality and resulted in high customer satisfaction, the equity of that brand will be high. Sony is a valuable brand, with high brand equity, because the company has delivered high-quality electronic products for decades. On the other hand, the Russian car manufacturer Lada has

**generic name**
A brand name over which the original owner has lost exclusive claim because all offerings in the associated class of products have become generally known by the brand name (usually that of first or leading brand in that product class).

**brand equity**
Represents the value customers (and the stock markets) place on the sum of the history the customer has had with a brand.

### ESTABLISHING THE COCA-COLA BRAND

"Coca-Cola" and "Coke" are two famous trademarks that identify one of the world's most widely recognized brands. This high recognition has not been accidental, but rather reflects years of effort and advertising investment by The Coca-Cola Company.

Here is an early advertisement that very explicitly distinguishes Coca-Cola from other colas and also reserves the abbreviation "Coke" as exclusively referring to Coca-Cola.

The company continues to protect its trademarks with great persistence and consistency.

www.coca-cola.com

struggled for years to overcome an initial public perception of poor quality. Lada is not considered a particularly valuable brand in North America.

We shall see that many brand-related decisions—from initially choosing a name, to protecting the name in court if necessary, to brand extension strategies—are driven by a company's desire to create, preserve, and exploit brand equity.

Brand equity has four components (Figure 10.2)[3] *Brand awareness* is a measure of how well and widely a brand is known. *Perceived quality* reflects customers' assessments of the quality of the product that carries a particular brand. *Brand associations* are the connections customers make between the brand and other aspects of their experience and understanding. For example, Nike tends to be associated with high performance as well as individualism. Brand loyalty is the single most important aspect of brand equity. *Brand loyalty* reflects the level of commitment a customer has to a particular brand. This aspect of brand equity is so important that we need to discuss it in more detail.

## Brand Loyalty Categories

Brands vary widely in consumer familiarity and acceptance. While a shopper may insist on Robin Hood flour for use in the family bread maker, that same shopper may not be able to recall the name of even one brand of powdered milk to be used in the same bread maker.

Brand loyalty may be measured in three stages: brand familiarity, brand preference, and brand insistence.

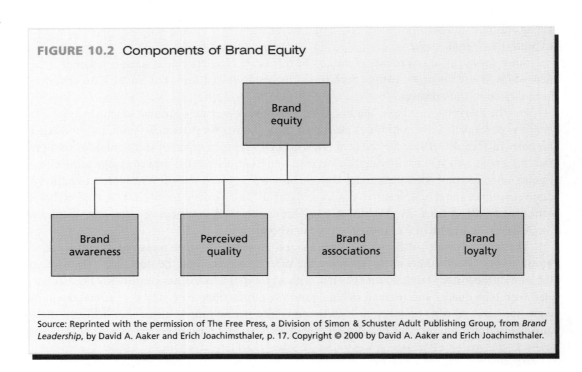

FIGURE 10.2 Components of Brand Equity

Source: Reprinted with the permission of The Free Press, a Division of Simon & Schuster Adult Publishing Group, from *Brand Leadership*, by David A. Aaker and Erich Joachimsthaler, p. 17. Copyright © 2000 by David A. Aaker and Erich Joachimsthaler.

**Brand familiarity** is a company's first objective for newly introduced products—to make them familiar to consumers. Often the company achieves this goal through advertising. Sometimes it uses free samples or coupons offering discounts for purchases. Several new brands of toothpaste have been introduced on college campuses through free samples contained in Campus Pacs. Once the consumer has used the product, it moves from the "unknown" to the "known" category, and provided the consumer was satisfied with the trial sample, he or she is more likely to repurchase it.

**Brand preference** is the second stage of brand loyalty. Because of previous experience with the product, consumers will choose it rather than one of its competitors—if it is available. Even if university students prefer Coca-Cola as a means of quenching their thirst, almost all of them will quickly switch to Pepsi-Cola or 7-Up when they discover that the vending machine has no Coca-Cola and the nearest supply is two buildings away. Companies with products at the brand preference stage are in a favourable position with respect to competing in their industries.

The ultimate stage in brand loyalty is **brand insistence**, which occurs when consumers will accept no alternatives and will search extensively for the product. Such a product has achieved a monopoly position with this group of consumers. Even though brand insistence may be the goal of many firms, it is seldom achieved. Only the most exclusive specialty goods attain this position with a large segment of the total market.

## The Importance of Brand Loyalty

A study of twelve patented drugs (including well-known drugs like Librium and Darvon) illustrates the importance of brand loyalty. The research indicated that patent expiration had a minimal effect on the drugs' market shares or price levels, a resiliency credited to the brand loyalty for the pioneer product in the field.[4] Another measure of the importance of brand loyalty is found in the Brand Utility Yardstick used by the J. Walter Thompson advertising agency. These ratings measure the percentage of buyers who remain brand-loyal even if a 50 percent cost savings is available from generic products. Beer consumers were very loyal, with 48 percent refusing to switch. Sinus-remedy buyers were also brand-loyal, with a 44 percent rating. By contrast, only 13 percent of the aluminum-foil buyers would not switch to the generic product.[5]

## Building Strong Brands

Professor David Aaker is one of the leading researchers and writers in the field of brand management. He argues that four factors contribute to strong brands (see Figure 10.3).

1. The organization's structure and processes must be supportive of the brand: it must be clear who is responsible for the brand and management must have adequate systems and processes in place to actually track brand performance.
2. There must be intentional brand building programs in the form of integrated communication plans.
3. The brand's identity and position—what it stands for and symbolizes in the marketplace—must be clearly understood.
4. The brand's architecture must be consistent with the overall brand strategy.

Let's look at the issue of brand architecture in more detail.

**Brand architecture** refers to the relationships that a company's brands have with each other—the structure of the company's brands. The most common way to classify brands is as either family brands or individual brands.[6] A **family brand** is one brand name used for several related products. E.D. Smith markets dozens of food products under the E.D. Smith brand. Black & Decker has a complete line of power tools under the Black & Decker name. Johnson & Johnson offers parents a line of baby powder, lotions, plastic pants, and baby shampoo under one name.

On the other hand, such manufacturers as Procter & Gamble market hundreds of products with **individual brands** (for example, Tide, Cheer, Crest, Gleem, Oxydol, and Dash). Each such item is known by its own brand name rather than by the name of the company producing it or an umbrella name covering similar items. Individual brands are more expensive to market, since a new promo-

**brand familiarity**
The first stage of brand loyalty, when a firm has developed enough publicity for a brand that its name is familiar to consumers.

**brand preference**
The second stage of brand loyalty, when, based on previous experience, consumers will choose a product rather than one of its competitors—if it is available.

**brand insistence**
The ultimate stage of brand loyalty, when consumers will accept no alternatives and will search extensively for the product.

**brand architecture**
The relationship between a company's products, brands, and sub-brands.

**family brand**
Brand name used for several related products.

**individual brand**
Brand that is known by its own brand name rather than by the name of the company producing it or an umbrella name covering similar items.

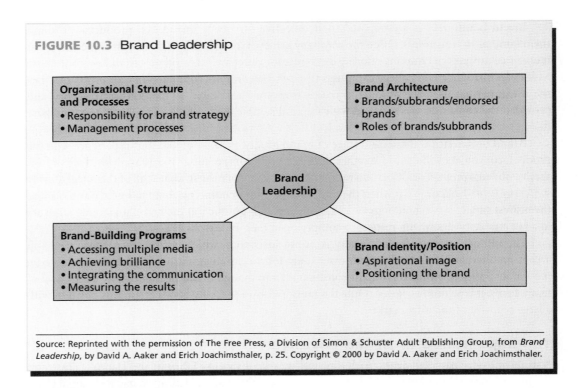

**FIGURE 10.3** Brand Leadership

**Organizational Structure and Processes**
• Responsibility for brand strategy
• Management processes

**Brand Architecture**
• Brands/subbrands/endorsed brands
• Roles of brands/subbrands

**Brand Leadership**

**Brand-Building Programs**
• Accessing multiple media
• Achieving brilliance
• Integrating the communication
• Measuring the results

**Brand Identity/Position**
• Aspirational image
• Positioning the brand

Source: Reprinted with the permission of The Free Press, a Division of Simon & Schuster Adult Publishing Group, from *Brand Leadership*, by David A. Aaker and Erich Joachimsthaler, p. 25. Copyright © 2000 by David A. Aaker and Erich Joachimsthaler.

# THE PRACTISING MARKETER

## ADJUSTING ORGANIZATIONAL STRUCTURE TO BUILD BRANDS

The Chrysler Group of DaimlerChrysler AG is forming new marketing teams designed to strengthen the division's brands.

www.daimlerchrysler.ca

Dieter Zetsche, Chrysler Group president and chief executive officer, said the initiative consolidates marketing and product-planning structures into "vehicle brand teams."

"These teams have one goal—to strengthen our brands," Zetsche said.

"Therefore, we're organizing marketing into three teams—Chrysler, Jeep, and Dodge—with executives in charge of each who will be held accountable for the overall success of all vehicles, marketing programs, and the dealer experience for their respective brands."

Jim Schroer, Chrysler's executive vice-president for global sales and marketing, said the idea is to make the division's brands as desirable and as strong as Mercedes-Benz.

Schroer said the newly appointed marketing vice-presidents will have direct control over the budgets for their brands.

Each marketing VP will have a communication and advertising-agency team assigned to the brand, a dealer marketing programs department, and a newly assigned marketing and product planning director, Schroer said.

Source: Anonymous, "Chrysler Forms 'Teams' to Boost Brands' Strength," Associated Press, June 21, 2002. http://www.autonet.ca/AutonetStories/stories.cfm?storyID=5910. Reprinted with permission of The Associated Press.

tional program must be developed to introduce each new product to its target market.

Using family brands allows promotional outlays to benefit all products in the line. The effect of the promotion is spread over each of the products. A new addition to the products marketed by the H.J. Heinz Company gains immediate recognition due to the well-known family brand. Family brands also facilitate the task of introducing the product—for both the customer and the retailer. Since supermarkets carry an average of nearly 10 000 items in stock, they are reluctant to add new products unless they are convinced of potential demand. A marketer of a new brand of turtle soup would have to promise the supermarket-chain buyer huge advertising outlays for promotion and evidence of consumer buying intent before getting the product into the stores. The Campbell Soup Company, with approximately 85 percent of the market, would merely add the new flavour to its existing line and could secure store placements much more easily than could a company using individual brand names.

Family brands should be used only when the associated products are of similar quality, or the firm risks the danger of harming its product image. Using the Mercedes brand name on a new, less expensive car model might severely tarnish the image of the other models in the Mercedes product line. Even the most affordable Mercedes starts at a retail price of almost $40 000. With the merger of Chrysler and Daimler-Benz, it is very unlikely that a Mercedes priced below the C-class will appear. Less expensive models will wear a Chrysler brand.

Individual brand names should be used for dissimilar products. Campbell Soup once marketed a line of dry soups under the brand name Red Kettle. Large marketers of grocery products (such as Procter & Gamble, General Foods, and Lever Brothers) employ individual brands to appeal to unique market segments. Unique brands also allow the firm to stimulate competition within the organization and to increase total company sales. Product managers are also more free to try different merchandising techniques with individual brands. Consumers who do not prefer Tide may choose Dash or Oxydol rather than purchase a competitor's brand.

Some brands are so popular that they are carried over to unrelated products because of their marketing advantages. The decision to use a popular brand name for a new product entry in an unrelated product category is known as **brand extension**. This should not be confused with line extension (discussed in Chapter 11), which refers to adding new sizes, styles, or related products. Brand extension, by contrast, refers only to carrying over the brand name.

Examples of brand extension are abundant in contemporary marketing. Pears soap has been extended to the Pears shampoo line. Bic applied the brand name developed for its pens to disposable razors. Similarly, General Foods is extending its Jell-O brand: in some markets the company now has Jell-O Pudding Pops, Jell-O Slice Creme, and Jell-O Gelatin Pops.

In other situations a company will choose a new brand name for related products. One reason for this approach is to protect the image of the established brand in case the new introduction fails. In other instances the company may wish to protect the established brand from attack (usually price-based) by competitors. Brands that are intended to protect an established brand from attack are called *flanker brands*. Loblaws' No Name brand is a flanker brand for its President's Choice brand. No Name offers a low-price alternative to President's Choice but assures that the consumer is still buying a Loblaws brand.

www.heinz.com

www.campbellsoup.ca

www.mercedes-benz.ca

daimlerchrysler.ca

**brand extension**
The decision to use a popular brand name for a new product entry in an unrelated product category.

**Procter & Gamble employs individual brands to appeal to unique market segments.**

Life ahead of you.
A legacy behind you.

SWISS ARMY

Swiss Army has successfully extended its brand to several new product categories.

## National Brands or Private Brands?

**national brand (manufacturer's brand)**
A brand promoted and distributed by a manufacturer.

**private brand**
A brand promoted and distributed by a wholesaler or retailer.

www.canadiantire.ca

www.safeway.com

Most of the brands mentioned in this chapter have been **national brands**, also commonly called **manufacturer's brands**. But, to an increasing extent, large wholesalers and retailers operating over a regional or national market are placing their own brands on the products that they market. These brands offered by wholesalers and retailers are usually called **private brands**. Loblaws' popular President's Choice line is one example. Canadian Tire carries its own brands, such as Mastercraft, MotoMaster, Supercycle, and Playmaker. Safeway store shelves are filled with such company brands as Edwards, Town House, Empress, and Taste Tells. Safeway brands represent a large percentage of all products in an average Safeway supermarket.

For a large retailer such as Loblaws, Canadian Tire, or Safeway, private brands allow the firm to establish an image and to attain greater control over the products that it handles. Quality levels, prices, and availability of the products become the responsibility of the retailer or wholesaler who develops a line of private brands.

Even though the manufacturers' brands are largely presold through national promotional efforts, the wholesaler and retailer may easily lose customers, since the same products may be available in competing stores. But only Canadian Tire handles the Mastercraft line of power tools. By eliminating the promotional costs of the manufacturers' brands, the dealer may be able to offer a private brand at a lower price than the competing national brands—or make higher margins. Both consumers and the company benefit. As private brands achieve increasing brand loyalty they may even enable a retailer to avoid some price competition, since the brand can be sold only by the brand owner.

### Battle of the Brands

Competition among manufacturers' brands and the private brands offered by wholesalers and large retailers has been called the "battle of the brands." Although the battle appears to be intensifying, the marketing impact varies widely among industries. One survey showed that private brands represented 36 percent of the market in replacement tires but only 7 percent in portable appliances. A full 52 percent of shoe sales involve private brands. For example, Sears and Bata stores distribute their own private brands. Department stores capture about 53 percent of heavy-appliance sales, most of which are private brands.[7]

Retailers with their own brands become customers of the manufacturer, who place the chains' private brands on the products that the firm produces. Such leading corporations as Westinghouse, Armstrong Rubber, and Heinz obtain an increasingly larger percentage of total sales through private labels.

Manufacturers often debate whether they should serve the private brand market. On the one hand, potential orders are large, so marketing efforts can be reduced. On the other hand, the manufacturer can become dependent on one or two retailers rather than remaining independent by serving a broad range of customers.

## Generic Products

Food and household staples characterized by plain labels, little or no advertising, and no brand names are called **generic products**. Generic products were first sold in Europe, where their prices were as much as 30 percent below brand-name products. By 1979, they had captured 40 percent of total volume in European supermarkets.

This new version of private brands has received significant acceptance in Canada. Surveys indicate that both professional, college-educated consumers and lower-income, blue-collar consumers are heavy purchasers of generics. Most shoppers have experimented with generic products and formed opinions about those that are acceptable to them.

**generic products**
Food and household staples characterized by plain labels, little or no advertising, and no brand names.

## THE CANADIAN MARKETPLACE

### HUDSON'S BAY TO SELL FEDERATED PRIVATE LABELS

Hudson's Bay Co. has struck a three-year deal with Federated Department Stores Inc. enabling the Canadian department store retailer to sell the U.S. giant's popular private label brands exclusively.

At the Hudson's Bay general meeting yesterday the company's executives would not speculate on whether the deal will forge further business ties with the parent company of Macy's and Bloomingdale's, but the news made retail industry watchers' tongues wag.

"There's really a globalization going on at department stores," said George Heller, chief executive of Hudson's Bay.

He said the company has a strong relationship with Federated and is also talking with European chains with a view to introduce fresh merchandise into a prosaic Canadian department store scene. Mr. Heller said Canadians are bored with the merchandise offerings in this country. Susan Bertelsen, senior vice-president of Federated Merchandising Group, said the 460-store corporation is working to leverage its assets around the world.

"Right now this is a private brand alliance ... and that's where I see this relationship beginning," she said.

Federated's merchandising unit will design and manufacture eight lines that will be sold at The Bay, starting this fall with I.N.C. International Concepts, Federated fastest-growing fashion line, Style & Co., a sportswear label, and Tools of the Trade, a housewares brand. The three lines produce 16 percent of overall sales at Federated.

The agreement signals Hudson's Bay's growing reliance on private label merchandise to fatten its sales margins and encourage customer loyalty. Private label sales account for 26 percent of chain-wide sales since the program was revitalized three years ago.

Hudson's Bay is hoping the strategy implemented to great success by Loblaw Cos., producer of the President's Choice line, will fend off stiff competition in the difficult apparel business from specialty retailers and mass merchants such as Wal-Mart.

**What brands does The Bay itself own that you're familiar with? Why would The Bay distribute another department store's private label goods rather than develop their own brands?**

www.hbc.com/bay

www.fds.com/cpsc

Source: Hollie Shaw, "Hudson's Bay to Sell Federated Private Labels," *Financial Post*, May 23, 2002, FP8. Reprinted with permission.

In the retail food industry there are thus three types of brands. Manufacturers promote their own national brands. Retailers promote, to a limited degree, private brands (for example, Canadian Tire and President's Choice), and generic brands are available at the low end for those who are prepared to accept a wider variation in quality and little information about the product. (Loblaws has muddied the waters somewhat with its No Name brand mentioned earlier. No Name is not a true generic product, but is rather Loblaws' price-fighting brand that it has named, a little perversely, No Name.)

### Product Image

Another aspect of the total product is product image. Product image and brand image are related but distinct concepts with product image being the more general term. Product image refers to the perceptions and reactions customers have to a type of product, say DVD players. Brand image refers to perceptions and reactions customers have to a particular brand of that product, say Sony versus Magnavox.

# PACKAGING AND LABELLING

Although packaging can be put to multiple purposes within the marketing mix, including marketing communication, at root, the package is a vital part of the total product. Indeed, in an overcrowded supermarket, packaging very often *is* the significant difference between one product and another. In the spring of 2000, for example, Procter & Gamble revamped its Cover Girl line of cosmetics. Carefully redesigned packaging was an important complement to Cover Girl's modified product line and more convenient in-store displays.

Packaging represents a vital component of the total product concept. Its importance can be inferred from the size of the packaging industry. Approximately $9.1 billion is spent annually on packaging in Canada.[8] Packaging costs in the food industry as a percentage of net processed food sales range from 4 to 59 percent, averaging about 22 percent. In cases where packaging costs seem to be disproportionately high, costs of ingredients (e.g., salt) have been found to be very low.

The package has several objectives, which can be grouped into three general categories: (1) protection against damage, spoilage, and pilferage; (2) assistance in marketing the product; and (3) cost-effectiveness.

## Protection against Damage, Spoilage, and Pilferage

The original purpose of packaging was to offer physical protection. The typical product is handled several times between manufacture and consumer purchase, and its package must protect the contents against damage. Perishable products must also be protected against spoilage in transit, in storage, or while awaiting selection by the consumer.

Another important role of many packages is preventing pilferage, which at the retail level is very costly (even "sampling" from bulk food displays has become a major cost concern for retailers). Many products are packaged with oversized cardboard backings too large to fit into a shoplifter's pocket or purse. Large plastic boxes are used for a similar reason on such products as cassette tapes.

## Assistance in Marketing the Product

Package designers frequently use marketing research in testing alternative designs. Increasingly, scientific approaches are used in designing a package that is attractive, safe, and aesthetically appealing. Kellogg, for instance, has been known to test the package for a new product as well as the product itself.[9]

In a grocery store that contains as many as 15 000 different items, a product must capture the shopper's attention. Walter Margulies, chairman of Lippincott & Margulies advertising agency, sum-

Tetra Pak developed packaging that dramatically extended the shelf life of perishable foods such as apple juice. As well, its cube shape makes more efficient use of shelf and storage space.

marizes the importance of first impressions in the retail store: "Consumers are more intelligent [these days], but they don't read as much. They relate to pictures." Margulies also cites another factor: one of every six shoppers who needs eyeglasses does not wear them while shopping. Consequently, many marketers offering product lines are adopting similar package designs throughout the line in order to create more visual impact in the store. The adoption of common package designs by such product lines as Weight Watchers foods and Planter's nuts represents attempts to dominate larger sections of retail stores the way Campbell does.[10]

Packages can also offer the consumer convenience. Pump-type dispensers facilitate the use of products ranging from mustard to insect repellent. Pop-top cans provide added convenience for soft drinks and for other food products. The six-pack carton, first introduced by Coca-Cola in the 1930s, can be carried with minimal effort by the food shopper.

A growing number of firms provide increasing consumer utility with packages that are designed for reuse. Peanut butter jars and jelly jars have long been used as drinking glasses. Bubble bath can be purchased in plastic bottles shaped like animals that are suitable for bathtub play. Packaging is a major component in Avon's overall marketing strategy. The firm's decorative reusable bottles have even become collectibles.

## Cost-Effectiveness

Although packaging must perform a number of functions for the producer, marketer, and consumer, it must accomplish them at a reasonable cost. Packaging currently represents the single largest item in the cost of producing numerous products. For example, it accounts for 70 percent of the total cost of the single-serving packets of sugar found in restaurants. However, restaurants continue to use the packets because of the saving in wastage and in washing and refilling sugar containers.

Environmentally safer packaging has become a concern in recent years, as evidenced by this example:

> Procter & Gamble has introduced a new, less expensive, more environmentally compatible package for eight of its liquid products. The company estimates that 15 to 25 percent of consumers who use those products will choose to buy them in the new format. That would mean five million fewer plastic bottles—about 700 fewer dump trucks—going to Canadian dumps annually.[11]

An excellent illustration of how packaging can be cost-effective is provided by the large Swedish firm Tetra-Pak, which pioneered aseptic packaging for products like milk and juice. Aseptic packaging wraps a laminated paper around a sterilized product and seals it off. The big advantage of this packaging technology is that products so treated can be kept unrefrigerated for months. Aseptically packaged sterilized milk, for instance, will keep its nutritional qualities and flavour for six months. With 60 percent of a supermarket's energy bill going for refrigeration, aseptic packaging is certainly cost-effective. The paper packaging is also cheaper and lighter than the cans and bottles used for unrefrigerated fruit juices. Handling costs can also be reduced in many cases.[12] These containers have recently been criticized because of ecological concerns over recycling. Tetra-Pak has responded aggressively, showing that its containers can be recycled into such items as picnic furniture.

## Labelling

**label**

The part of a package that contains (1) the brand name or symbol, (2) the name and address of the manufacturer or distributor, (3) information about product composition and size, and (4) information about recommended uses of the product.

Sometimes the label is a separate item applied to the package, but most of today's plastic packages contain the label as an integral part of the package. Labels perform both a promotional and an informational function. A **label** in most instances contains (1) the brand name or symbol, (2) the name and address of the manufacturer or distributor, (3) information about product composition and size, and (4) information about recommended uses of the product.

Government-set and voluntary packaging and label standards have been developed in most industries. The law requires a listing of food ingredients, in descending order of the amounts used, and the labels of such companies as the Del Monte Corporation now show specific food values and include a calorie count and a list of vitamins and minerals. In other industries (such as drugs, fur, and clothing), federal legislation requires various information to be provided and prevents false branding. The marketing manager in such industries must be fully acquainted with these laws and must design the package and label in compliance with these requirements.

The informational aspect of a label is particularly noteworthy. People who condemn all types of elaborate or fancy packaging fail to realize that the information on the label and the nature of the container enhance the product itself. In some cases, the dispenser is almost as important as the contents and is really an integral part of the total "product." Furthermore, with the advent of self-service nearly everywhere, the information on the label takes the place of a salesperson. Self-service improves marketing efficiency and lowers costs.

## Universal Product Code (UPC)

**Universal Product Code**

A code readable by optical scanners that can print the name of the item and the price on the cash register receipt.

The Universal Product Code (UPC) designation is another very important part of a label or package. Most grocery items display the bar code UPC on the label or package. The **Universal Product Code**, which was introduced to cut expenses in the supermarket industry, is a code readable by optical scanners that can print the name of the item and the price on the cash register receipt.

The advantages of optical scanning include
- labour savings (because products are no longer individually priced)
- faster customer check-out
- better inventory control, since the scanner can be tied to inventory records
- easier marketing research for the industries involved with it
- fewer errors in entering purchases at the check-out counter

### BOTTLED WATER—WHAT'S IN A LABEL?

Sales of bottled water are booming around the globe. According to the World Wildlife Fund, it's the fastest-growing beverage sector in the world, worth about $33 billion (Canadian).

It's so big, both Coke and Pepsi have waded into the market with their own brands.

So far, there are no scientific studies that indicate bottled water is healthier for you than tap water. Bottled water, however, does not contain chlorine or fluoride.

What makes one brand different than the other? You may notice a number of terms listed on the label.

Here's a quick reference guide to what it all means.

**Mineral and Spring Water**—must come from an underground source (not a public water supply) and can't be changed in any way by chemicals. Mineral water has a higher amount of dissolved mineral salts.

**Bottled Water**—water from any source that can be distilled or carbonated or treated in any other way.

The water in brand "Dasani" (owned by Coca-Cola) comes from municipal supplies in Brampton, Ontario, and Calgary, Alberta, and is then filtered and remineralized.

www.dasani.com

**Artesian Water/Artesian Well Water**—bottled water from a well that taps a confined aquifer (a water-bearing underground layer of rock or sand) in which the water level stands at some height above the top of the aquifer.

**Sparkling Water**—water that has been carbonated. Soda water, seltzer water, and tonic water are not considered bottled waters.

**Glacial Water**—water from a source directly from a glacier.

**Natural Water**—water (such as spring, mineral, artesian, or well water) obtained from an approved underground source and not from a municipal or public water supply system. This water has undergone no treatment other than physical filtration and iron removal.

**Purified Water**—water produced by distillation, de-ionization or reverse osmosis, which contains not more than 10 mg/L of total dissolved solids.

**What's in the Water?**
*Mineral Water:*
• **Naturally-carbonated natural mineral water** is water which—after treatment, replacement of gas, and packaging—has the same content of gas from the source.
• **Non-carbonated natural mineral water** is water which, after treatment and packaging, prevents hydrogen carbonate salts from dissolving.
• **De-carbonated natural mineral water** is water which,

## 11,820 perfect little drops in each bottle. (Feel free to check.)

**DASANI**

FILTERED 5x
FOR PERFECTION™

*"Dasani" bottled water has become a dominant brand in the bottled water market.*

after treatment, does not have the same carbon dioxide content as when it first came out of the ground.
• **Carbonated natural mineral water** is water which, after treatment and packaging, has been made bubbly by adding carbon dioxide.
• **Demineralized**—the dissolved solids (minerals) have been removed.
• **Re-mineralized**—after filtration that removes all the solids, some are put back in.
• **Ozonized**—ozone is added to kill bacteria.
• **Super-oxygenated**—oxygen is added, most of which escapes when you twist the cap.

Source: Adapted from "Bottled Water — What's in a Label." Copyright © Canadian Broadcasting Corporation. http://www.cbc.ca/consumers/consumertips/ tips_bottled water.html

# OTHER ISSUES IN PRODUCT MANAGEMENT

## Consumer and Business-to-Business Products

How a firm markets its products depends largely on the product itself. For example, a perfume manufacturer stresses subtle promotions in prestige media such as *Chatelaine* and *Vogue* magazines, and markets the firm's products through exclusive department stores and specialty shops. Cadbury Schweppes Powell Ltd. markets its candy products through candy wholesalers to thousands of supermarkets, variety stores, discount houses, and vending machines. Its marketing objective is to saturate the market and make buying its candy as convenient as possible for potential buyers. A firm that manufactures and markets forklifts may use sales representatives to call on purchasing managers, and ship its product either direction from the factory or from regional warehouses.

Marketing strategy differs for consumer products and business-to-business products. As defined earlier, consumer products are those destined for use by the ultimate consumer, and business-to-business products are those used directly or indirectly in producing other goods for resale. These two major categories can be broken down further.

## Characteristics of Consumer Products

The consumer assesses satisfaction by calculating benefits expected minus costs incurred. Costs involve *effort* and *risk*.[13] Effort is the amount of money, time, and energy the buyer is willing to expend to acquire a given product. In addition, there are risks that the product will not deliver the benefits sought. There are five types of such possible risk: financial, psychological, physical, functional, and social.

IT COULD BE THE BIGGEST
NEW PRODUCT IDEA
YOUR COMPANY HAS THIS YEAR

The Sweetened Dried Cranberry: small fruit – big idea. Great new products need great new ingredients – healthy, natural, tasty and nutritious and that special something which keeps consumers coming back for more.

Not only do consumers love sweetened dried cranberries (SDCs), so do food manufacturers! Superb processing tolerance, low water activity, long shelf-life and extraordinary versatility across the bakery, confectionery, cereals and snacks industries make the SDC a real value added ingredient.

Be inspired! Add the sensational SDC with its beautiful red colour and tangy, sweet taste and texture to your recipes and see the results.

STILL STUCK FOR IDEAS? ONE SMALL CALL COULD MAKE A BIG DIFFERENCE.
For your local distributor, please contact: Tel: +44 (0)161 236 6771 Fax: +44 (0)161 236 9730

Ocean Spray's new product Craisins™, Sweetened Dried Cranberries, is sold as both a consumer and a business good.

# Classifying Consumer and Business-to-Business Products

A product is classified as a consumer or business-to-business product based on its end user rather than on intrinsic attributes. Sometimes the same product is sold both to consumers as a consumer product and to other producers as a business-to-business product.

The Ocean Spray ad (opposite) is directed towards business customers. What are some examples of Ocean Spray's consumer products? Can you think of other products that have both consumer and business-to-business applications?

There are four categories of products: convenience, preference, shopping, and specialty. Each category can be defined according to the buyer's evaluation of the effort and risk required to obtain the product. Figure 10.4 illustrates the classification system. Two points shown in the figure should be especially noted. First, increasing risk and effort permits the marketer to broaden the scope of marketing strategy (shown by the widening arrow). That is, a wider variety of marketing mix combinations can be used to gain a differential advantage for shopping and specialty products than can be used for convenience and preference products. Second, the concept of high and low product involvement is incorporated into this classification. The blue area represents low involvement.

www.oceanspray.ca

## Convenience Products

As shown in Figure 10.4, **convenience products** are defined as lowest in terms of both effort and risk. That is, consumers will not spend much money or time in purchasing these products, nor do

**convenience products**
Products that are lowest in terms of both effort and risk.

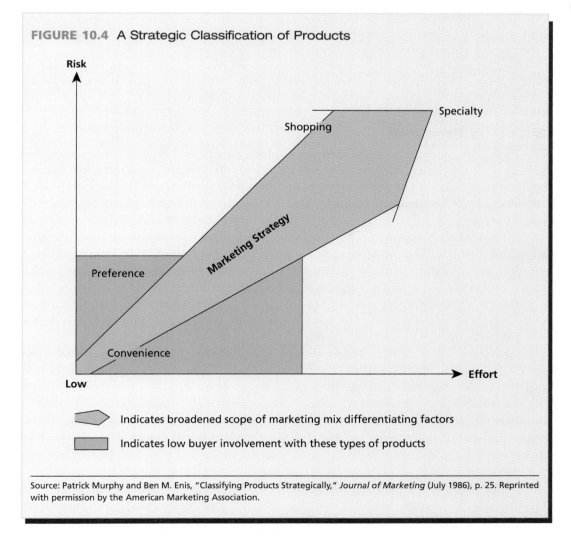

**FIGURE 10.4** A Strategic Classification of Products

Indicates broadened scope of marketing mix differentiating factors

Indicates low buyer involvement with these types of products

Source: Patrick Murphy and Ben M. Enis, "Classifying Products Strategically," *Journal of Marketing* (July 1986), p. 25. Reprinted with permission by the American Marketing Association.

they perceive significant levels of risk in making a selection. These are the products consumers want to purchase frequently, immediately, and with a minimum of effort; common illustrations are commodities and impulse products.

Examples of consumer goods that fall into the convenience category include fresh produce and grocery staples, umbrellas, gum, and batteries. Convenience services include taxis and mass transit.

### Preference Products

The second category shown in Figure 10.4 is termed **preference products**. Such products are slightly higher on the effort dimension and much higher on risk than convenience products. In fact, the distinction between convenience and preference products is primarily one of buyer-perceived risk. Often the consumer perceives a higher level of risk chiefly due to the marketer's efforts, particularly in branding and advertising. Some companies, for example, have successfully convinced consumers that their brand of a low-priced product conveys greater benefits than competing ones—as, for example, with Bayer aspirin.

The most prominent examples of preference products are in the consumer packaged goods industry (for example, toothpaste and soft drinks). Consumers may "prefer" the taste and image of Diet Coke, based on advertising appeals or brand preference. However, they are likely to substitute Diet Pepsi or perhaps a low-calorie brand of iced tea if the monetary or time effort involved in acquiring the preferred product is too large.

Since the consumer is unwilling to expend much effort in purchasing convenience or preference goods, the manufacturer must strive to make obtaining them as convenient as possible. Newspapers, soft drinks, and candy are sold in almost every supermarket, variety store, service station, and restaurant. Where retail outlets are physically separated from a large number of consumers, the manufacturers may use vending machines for their customers' convenience. They must protect fragile brand loyalty by ensuring that their product is easily available.

Retailers usually carry several competing brands of preference products and are unlikely to promote any particular brand. The promotional burden therefore falls on the manufacturer. Firms must advertise extensively to develop consumer acceptance of their products.

### Shopping Products

In contrast with convenience goods, **shopping products** are usually purchased only after the consumer has compared competing products on such bases as price, quality, style, and colour in competing stores. Consumers are willing to forgo consumption for a period in order to evaluate product offerings because they anticipate gaining monetary savings or greater satisfaction of needs by evaluating alternatives.

The purchaser of shopping products lacks complete information prior to the actual purchase and gathers additional information during the shopping trip. A woman who is intent on adding a new dress to her wardrobe may visit many stores, try on perhaps 30 dresses, and spend days making the final decision. She may follow a regular route from store to store in surveying competing offerings and will ultimately select the dress that most appeals to her. New stores that carry assortments of shopping products must ensure that they are located near other shopping-product stores so that they will be included in shopping expeditions.

Shopping products are typically more expensive than convenience or preference products and are most often purchased by women. In addition to women's apparel, shopping products include such items as jewellery, furniture, appliances, shoes, and used cars.

Some shopping products, such as children's shoes, may be classified as *homogeneous*—that is, the consumer views them as essentially the same—while others, such as furniture and clothing, are *heterogeneous*—essentially different. Price is a more important factor in the purchase of homogeneous shopping products, while quality and styling are more important in the purchase of heterogeneous products.

Brands are often less important for shopping than for convenience products. Although some furniture brands may come to mind, they are typically less important than the physical attributes of the product, its price, styling, and even the retail store that handles the brand. And although apparel companies have spent large amounts of money in promoting their brands, the dress buyer knows that the brand is (usually) inside the dress, and is generally more impressed with how the dress looks on her and with its fit than with the hidden label.

Manufacturers of shopping products use fewer retail stores than is common for convenience or preference products, since purchasers can be expected to expend some effort in finding what they want to buy and retailers will expend more effort in selling an exclusively distributed product. Thinness of the market may also affect the number of outlets. Retailers often purchase directly from the manufacturer or its representative rather than going through the wholesalers. Fashion merchandise buyers for department stores and specialty shops make regular visits to Toronto, Montreal, New York, and Winnipeg on buying trips. Manufacturers often visit regional centres such as Vancouver, Edmonton, or Moncton to meet retailers there. Buyers for furniture retailers often go directly to the factories of furniture manufacturers or visit major furniture trade shows.

## Specialty Products

As the arrowhead in Figure 10.4 shows, marketing managers may attempt to move their shopping products into the specialty category. This means that consumers will no longer "shop" for alternatives but will accept only one brand. The major distinction between shopping products and specialty products revolves around effort rather than risk. The specialty-products purchaser is well aware of what he or she wants and is willing to make a special effort to obtain it. The nearest Leica camera dealer may be 20 km away, but the camera enthusiast will go to that store to obtain what he or she may consider to be the ultimate in cameras. The Campbell River, B.C., collector who longs for a $2500 *objet d'art* of Steuben glassware is willing to journey to Vancouver to find the nearest Steuben dealer.

**Specialty products** are the highest in both effort and risk, due to some unique characteristics that cause the buyer to prize that particular brand. The buyer possesses relatively complete information about the product prior to the shopping trip and is unwilling to accept substitutes.

Specialty products are typically high-priced and are frequently branded. Since consumers are willing to exert a considerable effort in obtaining such goods, fewer retail outlets are needed. Mercury outboard motors and Porsche sports cars may be handled by only one or two retailers for each 100 000 population.

**specialty products**
Products that are highest in both effort and risk, due to some unique characteristics that cause the buyer to prize that particular brand.

## Unsought Products

Some products are not sought by consumers. They are products that people know about but normally do not think of buying. Products that are usually thought of in this category are funerals and life insurance. University textbooks are another example of unsought products.

## Applying the Consumer Goods Classification System

The four-way classification system described above gives the marketing manager additional information to use in developing a marketing strategy. For example, if a new food product sells well in a test market as a preference good, this provides insights about marketing needs in branding, promotion, pricing, and distribution methods. The impact of the product classifications on their associated consumer factors and to marketing mix variables is shown in Table 10.1.

But the classification system also poses problems of which the marketing manager must be aware. One pitfall is that it suggests a neat, four-way series of demarcations into which all products can easily be fitted. Some products do fit neatly into one of the classifications, but others fall into grey areas between categories.

How, for instance, should a new car be classified? It is expensive, is branded, and is handled by a few exclusive dealers in each city. But before it is classified as a specialty good, other characteristics must be considered. Most new-car buyers shop extensively among competing models and dealers before deciding on the best deal. A more effective method of using the classification system, therefore, is to consider it a continuum representing degrees of effort expended by the consumer. The new-car purchase can then be located between the categories of shopping and specialty products, but nearer the specialty-products end of the continuum.

A second problem with the classification system is that consumers differ in their buying patterns. One person will make an unplanned purchase of a new Toyota Corolla, while others will shop extensively before purchasing a car. One buyer's impulse purchase does not make the Corolla a convenience product. Products are classified by the purchase patterns of the *majority* of buyers.

www.toyota.ca

**TABLE 10.1** Managerial Implications of Classifying Products Strategically

| MANAGERIAL FOCUS | PRODUCT CATEGORY | | | |
| --- | --- | --- | --- | --- |
| | Convenience | Preference | Shopping | Specialty |
| Buyer's perception of price | Low effort, low risk | Low effort, medium risk | High effort, medium risk | High effort, high risk |
| Buyer behaviour | Impulse or habit (auto reorder) | Routine (straight rebuy) | Limited (modified rebuy) | Extensive (new task) |
| Marketer's objective | Move to preference or shopping category, or dominate via low cost | Brand loyalty | Source or store loyalty | Absolute (source *and* brand) loyalty |
| Marketer's basic strategy | High volume, cost minimized, or move product | High volume, brand identity, differentiation | High volume or high margin, segmentation | High margin, limited volume, market "niche" |
| Product strategy | Standard grades and quantities, quality control, innovations copied quickly | Standard grades and quantities, quality control, some R & D | Standard base, many options, much R & D, warranties | Custom design, much R & D, warranties, personalized service |
| Price strategy | Market | Market | Bundled or negotiated | Negotiated |
| Monetary, nonmonetary | Minimize time and risk | Minimize time, warrant risk | Accommodate time, warrant risk | Pamper for time and risk |
| Place strategy | Saturation distribution | Intensive distribution | Selective distribution | Exclusive distribution |
| Promotion | Point-of-purchase, some sales promotion | Mass advertising, sales promotion, some personal selling | Personal selling, some advertising | Publicity, personal selling, testimony |

Source: Patrick Murphy and Ben M. Enis, "Classifying Products Strategically," *Journal of Marketing* (July 1986), p. 35. Reprinted with permission by the American Marketing Association.

# Classifying Business-to-Business Products

The foregoing classification system can also be used for business-to-business products. But a more common system categorizes business-to-business products into five categories: installations, accessory equipment, component parts and materials, raw materials, and business-to-business supplies. Business-to-business buyers are professional customers; their job is to make effective purchase decisions. Although details may vary, the purchase decision process involved in buying supplies of flour for General Mills, for example, is much the same as that used in buying the same commodity for Robin Hood. Thus this classification system for business-to-business goods is based on product uses rather than on consumer buying patterns.

ON-RAMPS ARE FOREPLAY.

MINI.CA

New cars, such as this MINI, are categorized somewhere between shopping and specialty products.

## Installations

**Installations** are major capital assets (like factories and heavy machinery) that are used to produce products and services. Installations are the specialty products of the business-to-business market. New aircraft for Air Canada, locomotives for Canadian National, or a new pulp mill for MacMillan Bloedel are examples of installations.

Since installations are relatively long-lived and involve large sums of money, their purchase represents a major decision for an organization. Sales negotiations often extend over a period of several months and involve the participation of numerous decision makers. In many cases, the selling company must provide technical expertise. When custom-made equipment is involved, representatives of the selling firm work closely with the buyer's engineers and production personnel to design the most feasible product.

Price is almost never the deciding factor in the purchase of installations. The purchasing firm is interested in the product's efficiency and performance over its useful life. The firm also wants a minimum of breakdowns. "Downtime" is expensive because employees are non-productive (but must still be paid) while the machinery is being repaired.

Since most of the factories of firms that purchase installations are geographically concentrated, the selling firm places its promotional emphasis on well-trained salespeople, who often have a technical background. Most installations are marketed directly on a manufacturer-to-user basis. Even though a sale may be a one-time transaction, contracts often call for regular product servicing. In the

**installations**

Major capital assets that are used to produce products and services.

www.aircanada.ca

www.cn.ca

www.mbltd.com

case of extremely expensive installations, such as computers and electronic equipment, some firms lease the installations rather than sell them outright and assign personnel directly to the lessee to operate or to maintain the equipment.

## Accessory Equipment

Fewer decision makers are usually involved in purchasing **accessory equipment**—second-level capital items that are used in the production of products and services but are usually less expensive and shorter-lived than installations. Although quality and service remain important criteria in purchasing accessory equipment, the firm is likely to be much more price-conscious. Accessory equipment includes such products as desktop calculators, hand tools, portable drills, small lathes, and office equipment. Although these goods are considered capital items and are depreciated over several years, their useful life is generally much shorter than that of an installation.

Because of the need for continuous representation and the more widespread geographic dispersion of accessory equipment purchasers, a wholesaler, often called an **industrial distributor**, may be used to contact potential customers in each geographic area. Technical assistance is usually not necessary, and the manufacturer of accessory equipment can often use such wholesalers quite effectively in marketing the firm's products. Advertising is more important for accessory manufacturers than it is for installation procedures.

## Component Parts and Materials

While installations and accessory equipment are used in producing the final product, **component parts and materials** are the finished business-to-business goods that actually become part of the final product. Champion spark plugs make a new Chevrolet complete, nuts and bolts are part of a Rocky Mountain bike, tires are included with a Dodge pickup truck. Some materials, such as flour, undergo further processing before producing a finished product.

Purchasers of component parts and materials need a regular, continuous supply of uniform-quality goods. These goods are generally purchased on contract for a period of one year or more. Direct sale is common, and satisfied customers often become permanent buyers. Wholesalers are sometimes used for fill-in purchases and in handling sales to smaller purchasers.

## Raw Materials

Farm products (such as cattle, wool, eggs, milk, pigs, and canola) and natural products (such as coal, copper, iron ore, and lumber) constitute **raw materials**. They are similar to component parts and materials in that they become part of the final products.

Since most raw materials are graded, the purchaser is assured of standardized products with uniform quality. As with component parts and materials, direct sale of raw materials is common, and sales are typically made on a contractual basis. Wholesalers are increasingly involved in purchasing raw materials from foreign suppliers.

Price is seldom a controllable factor in purchasing raw materials, since it is often quoted at a central market and is virtually identical among competing sellers. Purchasers buy raw materials from the firms they consider most able to deliver in the quantity and the quality required.

## Supplies

If installations represent the specialty products of the business-to-business market, then operating supplies are the convenience products. **Supplies** are regular expense items necessary in the daily operation of a firm, but not part of its final product.

Supplies are sometimes called **MRO items**, because they can be divided into three categories: (1) maintenance items, such as brooms, floor-cleaning compounds, and light bulbs; (2) repair items, such as nuts and bolts used in repairing equipment; and (3) operating supplies, such as heating fuel, lubricating oil, and office stationery.

The regular purchase of operating supplies is a routine aspect of the purchasing manager's job. Wholesalers are very often used in selling supplies due to the items' low unit prices, small sales, and large number of potential buyers. Since supplies are relatively standardized, price competition is frequently heavy. However, purchasing managers spend little time in making purchase decisions about such products. They frequently place telephone orders or mail orders, or make regular purchases from the sales representative of the local office-supply wholesaler.

Managers must understand the total product if they are going to successfully market their company's product offerings. It is also important to understand how a particular product fits into a company's complete product portfolio and how the marketing requirements for products change over time. Chapter 11 picks up these issues.

## SUMMARY

A product is a total bundle of physical, service, and symbolic characteristics designed to produce consumer want satisfaction. The total product concept includes the brand, image, warranty, and packaging.

A brand is a name, term, sign, symbol, or design (or some combination of these) used to identify and differentiate the products of a firm. Brand equity results from brand awareness, perceived quality, brand associations and brand loyalty. Three brand-loyalty categories are brand familiarity, brand preference, and brand insistence. Building strong brands depends on a supportive organizational structure, intentional brand building programs, the brand's identity and position, and brand architecture. There are four basic types of brands: family brands, individual brands, national brands, and private brands.

Packaging has the following main objectives: protection against damage, spoilage, and pilferage; assistance in marketing the product; and cost-effectiveness.

Consumer products can be categorized as convenience products, preference products, shopping products, and specialty products. Business-to-business products are categorized as installations, accessory equipment, component parts and materials, raw materials, and supplies.

## KEY TERMS

accessory equipment, p. 266
brand, p. 248
brand architecture, p. 251
brand equity, p. 249
brand extension, p. 253
brand familiarity, p. 251
brand insistence, p. 251
brand name, p. 248
brand preference, p. 251
component parts and materials, p. 266
convenience products, p. 261
family brand, p. 251
generic name, p. 249
generic products, p. 255
individual brand, p. 251

industrial distributor, p. 266
installations, p. 265
label, p. 258
MRO items, p. 266
national brand (manufacturer's brand), p. 254
preference products, p. 262
private brand, p. 254
raw materials, p. 266
shopping products, p. 262
specialty products, p. 263
supplies, p. 266
total product, p. 246
trademark, p. 248
Universal Product Code, p. 258
warranty, p. 246

# INTERACTIVE SUMMARY AND DISCUSSION QUESTIONS

**1.** A product is a total bundle of physical, service, and symbolic characteristics designed to produce customer want satisfaction. Explain how this definition applies to
a. a lawyer's service in drafting a will
b. a pail of chemical fertilizer used by a farmer
c. Alfred Sung perfume

**2.** A brand is a name, term, sign, symbol, or design (or some combination of these) used to identify and differentiate the products of a firm. What constitutes a good brand name?

**3.** Three brand-loyalty categories are brand recognition, brand preference, and brand insistence. Explain and discuss the importance of these categories to the marketer.

**4.** Companies choose different types of branding strategy: family brands, individual brands, national brands, and private brands. Explain and discuss each.

**5.** Packaging has the following main objectives: protection against damage, spoilage, and pilferage; assistance in marketing the product; and cost-effectiveness. Find examples of products that fulfill all of these objectives.

**6.** Consumer products can be categorized as convenience products, preference products, shopping products, and specialty products. Describe how the marketing mix varies for products in each category.

**7.** Business-to-business products are categorized as installations, accessory equipment, component parts and materials, raw materials, and supplies. Explain how the marketing mix varies for products in each category.

**8.** Compare the Cadbury Web site to the Ford Canada Web site. What types of products are these? How has product type affected the way the products are promoted? How are the Web sites different? Can you attribute any of these differences to differences in product type?

www.cadbury.co.uk

www.ford.ca

## When Is a Fruit Dot Not a Froot Loop? The Federal Court Rules

A prolonged trademark battle between two cereal giants has ended in victory for Weetabix's Fruit Dots over Kellogg's Froot Loops.

For nearly 10 years, Kellogg Canada Inc. has blocked Weetabix of Canada Ltd. from selling Fruit Dots in Canada.

Kellogg argued that the name Fruit Dots, which are small coloured balls of cereal, was too similar to Froot Loops and would cause confusion among consumers. Trademark officials agreed and prohibited Weetabix from using the brand name in Canada.

But in a recent decision, the Federal Court of Canada overruled those officials and said the brands are not alike. The court ruled that the words in both names are not confusing to consumers.

Chantal Bertosa, an Ottawa lawyer who represented Weetabix, said the ruling will allow the British company to market Fruit Dots in Canada. Currently, the cereal is made in Cobourg, Ontario and sold wholesale to retailers in the United States and Canada who package it under their own names. Weetabix has had a trademark for Fruit Dots in the United States since 1988 and the ruling means the company can now sell a retail brand of Fruit Dots in Canada.

Ms. Bertosa said it was not easy taking on one of the world's most recognized brands.

"Froot Loops is known by everybody in the trade," she said. "However, it still remains that you use the word 'Froot' to describe the flavouring of the cereal and 'Loop' describes the shape of the cereal so why should you be entitled to monopolize this idea over other traders?"

Tony Bortolin, a Toronto lawyer who represented Kellogg, said the Toronto-based company is considering an appeal. He added that the ruling only deals with the words and Kellogg will be watching closely to see what kind of packaging Weetabix uses.

"They may still have legal problems depending on how they design the package. If they have the same character, same colours and all that, there's other legal issues. This decision focuses only on the name and how it is spelled."

The battle began on Feb. 23, 1993, when Kellogg Canada opposed a trademark registration by Weetabix for Fruit Dots.

Kellogg's parent, Kellogg Co. of Battle Creek, Michigan, is one of the world's largest cereal makers with $9 billion (U.S.) in annual sales. Froot Loops have been around since 1964 and the cereal is among Kellogg's oldest and best-selling brands. According to documents filed in court, Kellogg sold more than $30 million (Canadian) worth of Froot Loops in Canada annually in the 1990s.

Weetabix is the largest cereal company in Britain and has about $815 million in annual sales.

The trademark office rejected the Weetabix application and the two companies spent years in court and trying to negotiate a settlement.

The Federal Court ruled that there are already several trademarks with variations on the word "fruit," including Fruit Rings, Fruit Whirls, Fruitful Bran, and Tootie Fruities.

"Therefore, it would seem that the trademark Fruit Dots is no different from some of the aforementioned trademarks," the court said.

It also ruled that "the word 'Fruit' (or its phonetic equivalent 'Froot') is merely descriptive of the flavouring of the product. The words 'Dots' and 'Loops' allude to the shape of the product and again do not enhance any inherent distinctiveness of the trademarks as the words are merely descriptive."

Ms. Bertosa said the case dragged on longer than most trademark cases.

"Generally speaking, it takes only a few years," she said. "But if the mark is important then you will do whatever you have to do."

### You Be the Marketer

1. Why would Weetabix pursue this case for so long—and why would Kellogg's defend Froot Loops so tenaciously?
2. Aside from legal action, what options does Kellogg's have available?

---

Source: Paul Waldie, "When Is a Fruit Dot Not a Froot Loop?" *The Globe and Mail*, p. B1, Friday, July 5, 2002. Reprinted with permission from *The Globe and Mail*.

New product development is a key aspect of a company's product management strategy.

# PRODUCT STRATEGY

**CHAPTER OBJECTIVES**

After reading and studying this chapter, you should be able to

1. Explain the concept of the product mix, and indicate various mix decisions that can be made.
2. Describe the importance of developing a line of related products.
3. Explain the concept of the product life cycle, as well as its uses and limitations.
4. Relate product strategy to the other variables of the marketing mix.
5. Identify the determinants of the speed of the adoption process.
6. Explain the methods of accelerating the speed of adoption.
7. Outline new-product strategies and the determinants of their success.
8. Describe various organizational arrangements for new-product development.
9. Examine the stages in the product development process.

Imagine being able to take 200 compact discs with you wherever you go.

That's exactly what Sandra Wear, a co-founder at docSpace Company Inc., the Canadian software company that was sold for around $500 million, does every day when she takes her Creative Labs Nomad Jukebox out while jogging.

Ms. Wear currently works as the chief executive of strategic consulting company Tykra Inc., a Vancouver business that helps early stage companies reach profitability more quickly.

Ms. Wear takes her Nomad, which she discovered through an advertisement in *Red Herring*, with her during her extensive travels. While it looks like a CD walkman, the Nomad plays MP3 music files that can be stored on its 6-GB hard drive. The large storage capacity means that the unit will hold more than 100 hours worth of CD-quality music.

The portability of the unit is what appeals to Ms. Wear.

"My Nomad weighs less that what a CD Walkman does but with the ability to search, sort and best of all listen to play lists for whatever mood I'm in, whether that is a cathartic run, intense work-out, or melodic scenic drive."

Ms. Wear admits she should upgrade her Nomad, which is two years old. One of Creative Labs' most successful products, the Nomad Jukebox 3 comes with a 20-GB or 40-GB hard drive and up to 22 hours of battery life. The average cost in Canada is about $699.

Despite its age, Ms. Wear says her Nomad's features, like allowing users to create MP3 playlists, makes it invaluable.

"I love the colour, size and versatility of creating play lists," she says. "This thing was way ahead of its time."

---

Source: Robert Thompson, "MP3 Nomad Lets You Take 200 CDs Wherever You Go 'Way Ahead of Its Time,'" *Financial Post*, August 2, 2002. http://www.nationalpost.com/financialpost/story.html?id= {68047716-B244-46AC-8F32-574FABA60D97}. Reprinted with permission.

www.americas.creative.com

# INTRODUCTION

Setting product strategy is a dynamic, ever-changing challenge. The marketer must get the most value from existing products throughout their life—all the while looking for exciting new ways to anticipate and meet customer needs. Product strategy requires continual diligence in assessing the changing needs of the market. Normally it is important to have products that provide a range of opportunities for the company. This range of products is described as a product mix. A **product mix** is the assortment of product lines and individual offerings available from a company. Its two components are the **product line**, a series of related products, and the **individual offerings**, or single products within those lines. The product mix should contain products at various stages of their life cycle.

Product mixes are typically measured by width and depth of assortment. Width of assortment refers to the number of different product lines that the firm offers, while depth of assortment refers to the extension or variety within a particular product line. Maple Leaf Foods International offers an assortment of consumer product lines—meats, and several unrelated grocery items such as peanut butter (see Table 11.1). These product lines would be considered the width of the Maple Leaf product mix. The depth is determined by the number of individual offerings within each product line. For example, the company's meat line consists of fresh meats, smoked meats, and processed meats, while the grocery line is represented by peanut butter and several types of canned vegetables. The company also sells a nonedible line of by-products.

# THE EXISTING PRODUCT MIX

The starting point in any product-planning effort is to assess the firm's current product mix. What product line does it now offer? How deep are the offerings within each of the product lines? The marketer normally looks for gaps in the assortment that can be filled by new products or by modified versions of existing products. Expansion or redevelopment of existing product lines is usually the easiest approach for a firm to take, since the market requirements for these lines are generally well known.

## Cannibalization

The firm wants to avoid a costly new-product introduction that will adversely affect sales of one of its existing products. A product that takes sales from another offering in a product line is said to be **cannibalizing** the line. Marketing research should ensure that cannibalization effects are minimized or at least anticipated. When Clearly Canadian, the beverage company, introduced new flavours, its marketers were resigned to the fact that sales of their existing brand would be negatively affected.

**TABLE 11.1** The Maple Leaf Foods International Mix

| | WIDTH OF ASSORTMENT | | |
|---|---|---|---|
| | **Meats** | **Groceries** | **Nonedible** |
| **DEPTH OF ASSORTMENT** | Fresh and frozen meats | Peanut butter | By-products |
| | Bacon | Canned vegetables and fruit | Hides |
| | Sausages | | |
| | Wieners | Vegetable oils | |
| | Luncheon meats | Lard | |
| | Canned meat | Shortening | |
| | Poultry | French fries | |
| | | Maple syrup | |
| | | Jams | |

## Line Extension

An important rationale for assessing the current product mix is to determine whether line extension is feasible. A **line extension** refers to the development of individual offerings that appeal to different market segments but are closely related to the existing product line. If cannibalization can be minimized, line extension provides a relatively cheap way of increasing sales revenues at minimal risk. Oh Henry chocolate bars can be purchased in an ice-cream bar format, in addition to their traditional form. This illustrates the line extension of an existing product.

Once the existing product mix has been assessed and the appropriate line extensions considered, marketing decision makers must turn their attention to product-line planning and new-product development.

**line extension**

The development of individual offerings that appeal to different market segments but are closely related to the existing product line.

# THE IMPORTANCE OF PRODUCT LINES

Firms that market only one product are rare today. Most offer their customers a product line—a series of related products. Bombardier, for example, was formed in 1942 and specialized in manufacturing enclosed multipassenger snowmobiles for military use. In 1959 it introduced the SKI-DOO® snowmobile. SKI-DOO® was Bombardier's primary product until the early 1970s. In 1974 the company won a contract to build rolling stock for the Montreal subway. Since that time it has diversified well beyond its original product base. In addition to the SKI-DOO® and a personal watercraft branded as SEA-DOO®, Bombardier manufactures subway and railway stock, corporate

Procter & Gamble Inc. expands the product line by creating modified versions of its Pampers® Wipes.

and regional commercial jets, short-range surface-to-air defence systems, and the electric Neighbourhood Vehicle, or NV, designed to carry people around a golf course, neighbourhood, or other short route. The company also offers various industrial and financial services.[1]

Bombardier's addition of products and product lines has been extremely successful, but the strategy is hardly unique. Several factors account for the inclination of firms to develop complete product lines rather than relying on just one product.

www.bombardier.com

## Desire to Grow

A company places definite limitations on its growth potential when it concentrates on a single product. Lever Brothers once introduced 21 new products in a single 12-month period in its search for market growth and increased profits. A study by a group of management consultants revealed that firms expect newly developed products to account for 37 percent of their sales and 51 percent of their profits over the five years following the products' introduction.[2]

Firms often introduce new products to offset seasonal variations in the sales of their current products. Since the majority of soup purchases are made during the winter months, Campbell Soup Company has attempted to tap the warm-weather soup market. A line of fruit soups to be served chilled was test-marketed, but results showed that consumers were not yet ready for fruit soups. The firm continued to search for warm-weather soups, however, and in some markets it has added gazpacho (and other varieties meant to be served chilled) to its product line.

## Making Optimal Use of Company Resources

By spreading the costs of operations over a series of products, a company may find it possible to reduce the average costs of all products. Texize Chemical Company started with a single household cleaner and learned painful lessons about marketing costs when a firm has only one major product. Management rapidly added the products K2r and Fantastik to the line. The company's sales representatives can now call on intermediaries with a series of products at little more than the cost of marketing a single product. In addition, Texize's advertising produces benefits for all products in the line. Similarly, production facilities can be used economically in producing related products. For example, car companies regularly produce a range of products, from convertibles to vans to sports cars, from a basic car design. Finally, the expertise of all the firm's personnel can be applied more widely to a line of products than to a single one.

## Increasing Company Importance in the Market

www.maytag.com

www.gillette.com

Consumers and marketing intermediaries often expect a firm that manufactures and markets small appliances to also offer related products under its brand name. The Maytag Company offers not only washing machines but also dryers, since consumers often demand matching appliances. Gillette markets not only razors and blades but also a full range of grooming aids, including Foamy shaving cream, Right Guard deodorant, Gillette Dry Look hair spray, and Super Max hair dryers.

The company with a line of products is often more important to both the consumer and the retailer than is the company with only one product. Shoppers who purchase a tent often buy related items, such as tent heaters, sleeping bags, air mattresses, camp stoves, and special cookware. Recognizing this tendency, the Coleman Company now includes in its product line dozens of items associated with camping. The firm would be little known if its only product was lanterns. Similarly, new cameras from Eastman Kodak help the firm sell more film—a product that carries a significant profit margin.

## Exploiting the Product Life Cycle

As its output enters the maturity and decline stages of the life cycle of a product category, the firm must add new products if it is to prosper. The regular addition of new products to the firm's line helps ensure that it will not become a victim of product obsolescence. The car industry continually adds new products, deletes those that are not doing well, and upgrades popular models.

# THE PRODUCT LIFE CYCLE

Product *types,* like individuals, pass through a series of stages. The life cycle for humans is quite specific: infancy to childhood to adulthood to retirement to death. Product types also progress through stages, although a product's progress through the stages is sometimes not very clear-cut. This progression of introduction, growth, maturity, and decline is known as the **product life cycle**. An idealized model of the cycle is depicted in Figure 11.1, with examples of products currently at each stage of development.[3] The length of time in each stage varies widely, as represented by the broken line on the bottom axis. The model is representative of many, but not all, situations. For example, there is little evidence that refrigerators enter a decline or death stage.

At each stage of the life cycle, the emphasis and focus of the marketing program should change to fit the requirements at that phase. For example, at the introductory stage, communication efforts should emphasize information. At the growth stage, with competitors entering the market, communication should emphasize comparative features and advantages. Taking into consideration this need to change the marketing mix emphasis, particularly in the introduction and growth stages, can be useful in guiding marketing planning.

**product life cycle**
A product's progress through introduction, growth, maturity, and decline stages.

## Stages of the Cycle

### Introductory Stage

The firm's objective in the early stages of the product life cycle is to stimulate demand for the new market entry. Since the product is not known to the public, promotional campaigns stress information about its features. Promotion may also be directed toward channels of distribution to induce them to carry the product. In this initial phase, the public is being acquainted with the merits of the new product, and acceptance is being gained.

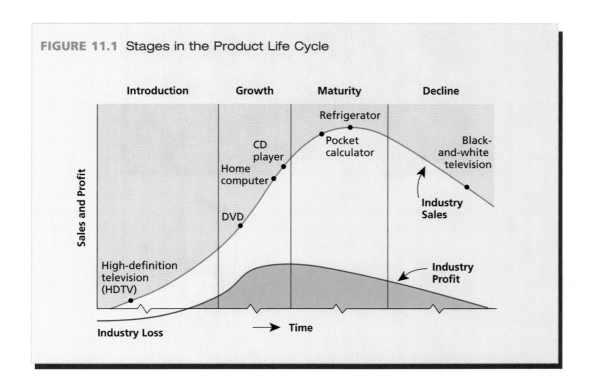

**FIGURE 11.1** Stages in the Product Life Cycle

As Figure 11.1 indicates, losses are common during the introductory stage due to heavy promotion as well as extensive research and development expenditures. But the groundwork is being laid for future profits. Firms expect to recover their costs and to begin earning profits when the product moves into the second phase of the cycle—the growth stage.

The costs of development and promotion at this stage are very high. New small business innovators often badly underestimate the costs of even a simple product launch. Big electronics companies such as Philips have spent more than $200 million in this stage of the product life cycle.

### Growth Stage

Sales volume rises rapidly during the growth stage as new adopters make initial purchases and as repurchases are made by the early users of the product. Word of mouth and mass advertising induce hesitant buyers to make trial purchases. Home computers are now in this phase of the cycle.

As the firm begins to realize substantial profits from its investment during the growth stage, it attracts competitors. Success breeds imitation, and firms rush into the market with competitive products in search of profit during the growth stage. As soon as the dramatic market acceptance of mountain bikes was realized, for instance, many manufacturers jumped into the market with their versions of the product.

### Maturity Stage

Industry sales continue to grow during the early portion of the maturity stage, but eventually reach a plateau as the backlog of potential customers is exhausted. By this time a large number of competitors have entered the market, and profits decline as competition intensifies.

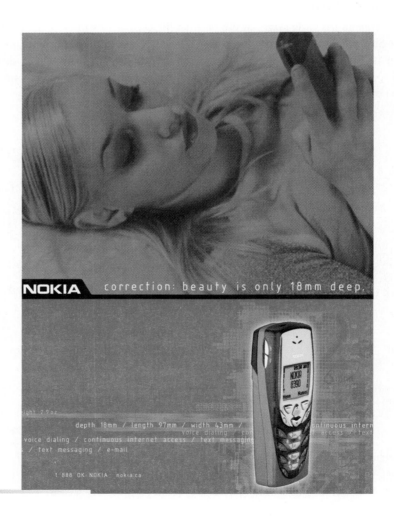

**Cell phones are in the late growth or early maturity stage of the product life cycle. How does Nokia's ad match the recommended strategies for this product life cycle stage?**

In the maturity stage, differences among competing products have diminished as competitors have discovered the product and promotional characteristics most desired by the market. Heavy promotional outlays emphasize subtle differences among competing products, and brand competition intensifies.

Available products now exceed demand. Companies attempting to increase sales and market share must do so at the expense of competitors. As competition intensifies, the tendency grows among competitors to cut prices in a bid to attract new buyers. Even though a price reduction may be the easiest method of inducing additional purchases, it is also one of the simplest moves for competitors to duplicate. Reduced prices will result in decreased revenues for all firms in the industry unless the price cuts produce enough increased purchases to offset the loss in revenue on each product sold.

### Decline Stage

In the final stage of the product's life, new innovations or shifting consumer preferences bring about an absolute decline in total industry sales. The safety razor and electric shavers replace the straight razor, a new PlayStation game replaces an earlier version as the latest fad, and the slower personal computer is replaced by a faster, more powerful model. As Figure 11.2 indicates, the decline stage of the old product is often also the growth stage for the new market entry.

Industry profits decline and in some cases actually become negative as sales fall, and firms cut prices in a bid for the dwindling market. Manufacturers gradually begin to leave the industry in search of more profitable products.

# DEPARTURES FROM THE TRADITIONAL PRODUCT LIFE-CYCLE MODEL

The preceding discussion has examined what is considered the traditional product life cycle, with its four clearly delineated stages. Some marketing theorists divide the life cycle into additional stages, but these four, identified in Figure 11.1, are generally accepted within the marketing discipline.

Yet despite the vast body of material written on the subject, considerable controversy surrounds the format and usefulness of product life-cycle theory. On the one hand, the concept has an enduring

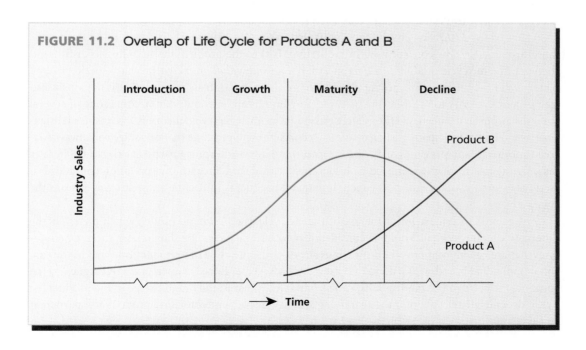

**FIGURE 11.2** Overlap of Life Cycle for Products A and B

## MOVE OVER POKÉMON!

Eric Rodriguez can't stop buying the trading cards.

So far, the 14-year-old Vancouver boy has spent $600 on the game he says is even better than Pokémon.

"It's hot," Rodriguez said yesterday with a smile. "Everyone's playing it."

The slick new item he's talking about is Yu-Gi-Oh!, a trading-card game that originated in Japan and is licensed to 4Kids Entertainment, the same company that holds the licensing rights to Pokémon.

And the Yu-Gi-Oh! craze seems to be catching on so wildly that after only about six weeks of sales, the decks may be stacked against any competition.

"We were sold out in two days," said Sam Kassam, manager of the Gem Mint Collectables store in Vancouver. "We've seen kids cry because we're sold out."

The game is based on a popular Japanese comic book and TV series that follows the adventures of Yugi and his best buddies, Joey, Tristan, and Tea. Kids pair up different mystical creatures in magical duels.

Yu-Gi-Oh! made its debut in Japan nearly three years ago. *KidScreen* magazine reported that at a swap meet and card tournament a few months later, 55 000 children and parents showed up for the event held in the Tokyo Dome baseball stadium.

When about 10 000 people were denied entry, the crowd became so unruly organizers had to call in riot police.

And distributors of the game say North America is catching the same fever. Mary Mancera, spokeswoman for The Upper Deck Company—a California-based firm that manufactures and distributes the game in North America—said demand is so high they can barely keep the stuff in stock.

www.yugioh-card.com

"We printed the product based on orders that we had gotten initially and sold out of it immediately," Mancera said.

"We had to go back and print a second time for the orders that continued to come in, and sold out of that immediately. This last reprint sold out in about 15 minutes."

"Usually on our products we only do one print and demand for other products hasn't even been in the same league."

None of this matters to Rodriguez and other kids who file into the Vancouver store after school to buy Yu-Gi-Oh! cards.

"I just like to play," he said with a shrug.

**In what stage of its life cycle is Yu-Gi-Oh!? Do you think it will have a normal product life cycle?**

Source: Excerpted from Salma Nurmohamed, "Move Over Pokémon, Yu-Gi-Oh! Is the Hot New Game in Town," *The Province*, May 24, 2002, p. A8. Reprinted with permission Pacific Newspaper Group.

---

appeal because of the intuitive logic of the birth-to-decline biological analogy.[4] As such, it has considerable descriptive value when used as a systematic framework for explaining market dynamics.

However, the simplicity of the concept has led to simplistic uses and expectations for the model, and this has called the concept itself into question. Part of the problem lies in failing to distinguish between the life cycle of a *product type* and that of an *individual brand* within that generic product category. Life-cycle theory is most applicable to product types. A truly new product is obviously also the generic category for a while, but as competing brands are introduced, it becomes one of several brands within that category. The greatest misuse of product life-cycle theory is to consider it a *predictive* model for anticipating when changes will occur and to presume that one stage will always succeed another. Managers can make grave errors if they naively interpret a particular rise or fall in sales as a sign that a product has moved from one stage to another. Such an interpretation could lead to serious errors in strategy, such as concluding that a product is in decline and removing it from the market.

A second criticism involves the use of the life cycle as a *normative* model, which *prescribes* the alternative strategies that should be considered at each stage. As will be shown later, there are strategies that are generally appropriate at various stages of the life cycle of a product *category*. In the case of an individual brand *within* a product category, however, as Enis, LaGrace, and Prell argue, "[T]he product life cycle [of a brand] is a *dependent* variable.... That is, the brand's stage in the product life cycle depends primarily upon the marketing strategy implemented for that product at a particular time."[5]

A more realistic view is that life-cycle analysis serves several different roles in the formulation of strategy. In the case of both generic product type and individual brand, the life cycle serves as an *enabling condition* in the sense that the underlying forces that inhibit or facilitate growth create opportunities and threats with strategic implications. The stage of the life cycle also acts as a *moderating variable* through its influence on the value of market-share position and the profitability consequences of strategic decisions. In the case of an individual brand, a stage in the life cycle is partly a *consequence* of managerial decisions. Its position is not necessarily a *fait accompli,* which can only be reacted to, but instead is only one of several scenarios that are conditional on the life cycle of the product category, on competitive actions, and on managerial decisions.

## Other Life-Cycle Issues

Three other issues that modify the original life-cycle concept are (1) the length of each product life-cycle stage, (2) the existence of product life-cycle variants, and (3) the current role of product and service fashions and fads.

### Length of Cycle Stages

Professor John O. King has argued that product life-cycle models should reflect the reality that goods and services move through the cycle at varying speeds. He suggests that the model should be drawn to show a broken horizontal axis to reflect the fact that the stages may be of varying lengths, as we did in Figures 11.1 and 11.2. Research now suggests that product life cycles may be getting shorter, especially in the introductory and growth stages.[6] While definitive conclusions are not yet available, most marketers do accept the fact that product life cycles and their stages show considerable variation in length.

### Alternative Product Life Cycles

Thus far, an idealized product life-cycle model has been presented. Because of the realities of the marketplace, the actual resulting life cycle can take on several other shapes. Some common variants of the traditional model are shown in Figure 11.3.

As shown in Figure 11.3, some products simply do not make it. These can be labelled the "instant busts"—failures that simply do not go through the four steps of the traditional model. Still other products are introduced, but information derived from test-market situations indicates that changes will be necessary if the product launch is to be successful (test markets are described later in this chapter). The products then have to be modified in some way—such as in design, packaging, or promotional strategy—before they are reintroduced. This type of start-up, start-again launch is labelled the "aborted introduction" in Figure 11.3.

Still other products become market specialty items (discussed in Chapter 10) and provide long and stable maturity stages. A common variant is the "pyramid cycle," where the product is adapted through new technology or a revised marketing strategy. The pyramid cycle (also discussed later in this chapter under "Extending the Product Life Cycle") is characterized by a series of regrowth periods.

### Fashions and Fads

Fashions and fads are also important to marketers. **Fashions** are currently popular products that tend to follow recurring life cycles.[7] The miniskirt was reintroduced in 1982 after being out of fashion for over a decade. In 1990 it appeared again. Wide-leg pants reappeared after having been the dominant style in the 1970s.

In contrast, **fads** are fashions with abbreviated life cycles. Consider the case of popular music for teenagers. Disco gave way to punk and new wave, which was replaced by the "new music," a take-off on rock and roll. Rap music is another example of the many music fads that come and go. Most fads experience short-lived popularity and then fade quickly. However, some maintain a residual market among certain market segments. Both of these fad cycles are shown in Figure 11.4.

**fashions**
Currently popular products that tend to follow recurring life cycles.

**fads**
Fashions with abbreviated life cycles.

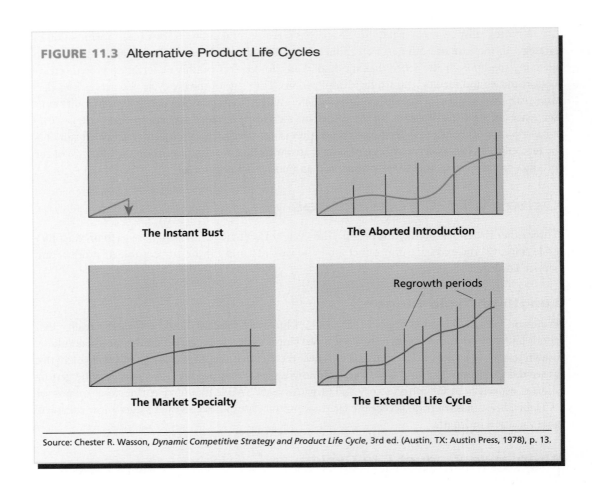

**FIGURE 11.3** Alternative Product Life Cycles

The Instant Bust

The Aborted Introduction

The Market Specialty

Regrowth periods

The Extended Life Cycle

Source: Chester R. Wasson, *Dynamic Competitive Strategy and Product Life Cycle*, 3rd ed. (Austin, TX: Austin Press, 1978), p. 13.

# PRODUCT LIFE-CYCLE CONSIDERATIONS IN MARKETING STRATEGY

Marketing strategy related to the product life cycle is most useful when it is carried out on an individual *brand* basis rather than a generic product category basis.[8] There are too many uncontrollable variables at the generic level.

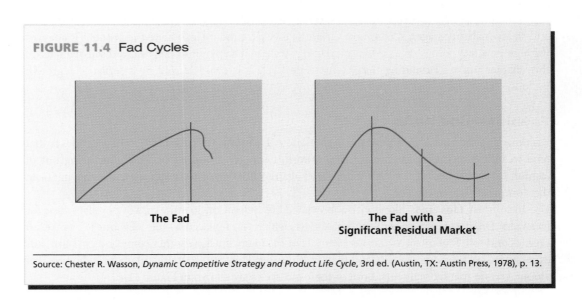

**FIGURE 11.4** Fad Cycles

The Fad

The Fad with a
Significant Residual Market

Source: Chester R. Wasson, *Dynamic Competitive Strategy and Product Life Cycle*, 3rd ed. (Austin, TX: Austin Press, 1978), p. 13.

The product life cycle—with all its variants—is a useful tool in marketing strategy decision making. The knowledge that profits assume a predictable pattern through the stages and that promotional emphasis must shift from product information in the early stages to brand promotion in the later ones allows the marketing decision maker to take advantage of conditions that often exist in each stage of the product life cycle through appropriate marketing efforts.

A firm's marketing efforts should emphasize stimulating demand at the introductory stage. The emphasis shifts to cultivating selective demand in the growth period. Market segmentation should be used extensively in the maturity period. During the decline, the emphasis again shifts to increasing primary demand. Table 11.2 suggests possibilities for appropriate pricing, distribution, product development, and service and warranty strategies for each life-cycle stage. The reader is again cautioned that the life cycle does not determine the strategy.

## Extending the Product Life Cycle

The life cycle of a *brand* can often be affected by managerial strategy. One example is the practice of extending the cycle as long as possible. Marketing managers can accomplish this objective if they take action early in the maturity stage. Product life cycles can sometimes be extended indefinitely by actions designed to accomplish one or more of the following:

1. Increase the frequency of use by present customers.
2. Add new users.
3. Find new uses for the product.
4. Change product quality or packaging.

Examples of such actions follow.

### Increase the Frequency of Use

Noxzema was originally intended as an occasional-use skin medicine, but it was repositioned as a routine-use beauty-care item. This substantially increased the rate of use—and the amount purchased.

### Add New Users

Cadillac introduced its CTS, a more sporty model, to attract non-Cadillac buyers who usually purchased cars like BMWs. Crest and Colgate have introduced a number of variations ranging from sweeter-tasting gels to appeal to younger consumers to antibacterial formulations aimed at freshening breath and producing healthier gums. Each formulation further extends the life cycles of these well-known brands. Finding new users is often difficult, however. Gerber, for example, failed in attempts to sell its products to the 15-to-22 age group as desserts and snacks. Many still regarded Gerber products as baby food.[9]

### Find New Uses

Q-tips cotton swabs were originally sold as a baby-care item, but Cheseborough-Pond's Inc.'s marketers found a new use for them as makeup applicators. Baking soda was used primarily in cooking until its product life cycle was extended by finding new uses for it as a denture cleaner, swimming-pool pH adjuster, cleaning agent, flame extinguisher, first-aid remedy, and refrigerator freshener.

### Change the Product Quality or Packaging

One of the best examples of a product that has been managed well and has avoided the decline stage is Tide. This synthetic detergent, introduced in 1947, dominates the laundry detergent market. But more than 50 modifications of packaging, cleaning performance, sudsing characteristics, aesthetics, and physical properties have been made during its lifetime.

**TABLE 11.2** Organizational Conditions, Environmental Conditions, and Marketing Efforts at Each Stage of the Product Life Cycle

| INTRODUCTION | GROWTH | MATURITY | | DECLINE |
| | | Early Maturity | Late Maturity | |
| --- | --- | --- | --- | --- |
| **Organizational Conditions** | | | | |
| High costs | Smoothing production | Efficient scale of operation | Low profits | |
| Inefficient production levels | Lowering costs | Product modification work | Standardized production | |
| Cash demands | Operation efficiencies Product improvement work | Decreasing profits | | |
| **Environmental Conditions** | | | | |
| Few or no competitors | Expanding markets | Slowing growth Strong competition | Faltering demand Fierce competition | Permanently declining demand |
| Limited product awareness and knowledge | Expanded distribution | Expanded market | Shrinking number of competitors | Reduction of competitors |
| Limited demand | Competition strengthens Prices soften a bit | Heightened competition | Established distribution patterns | Limited product offerings Price stabilization |
| **Marketing Efforts** | | | | |
| Stimulate demand | Cultivate selective demand | Emphasize market segmentation | Ultimate in market segmentation | Increase primary demand |
| Establish high price | Product improvement | Improve service and warranty | Competitive pricing | Profit opportunity pricing |
| Offer limited product variety | Strengthen distribution | Reduce prices | Retain distribution | Prune and strengthen distribution |
| Increase distribution | Price flexibility | | | |

Source: Adapted from Burton H. Marcus and Edward M. Tauber, *Marketing Analysis and Decision Making* (Boston: Little, Brown, 1979), pp. 115–16. Copyright © 1979 by Burton H. Marcus and Edward M. Tauber. Reprinted with permission.

# NEW-PRODUCT PLANNING

The product development effort requires considerable advance planning. New products are the lifeblood of many business firms, and a steady flow of new entries must be available if such firms are to survive. Some new products represent major technological breakthroughs. For instance, biotechnology, which permits the transfer of genes from any living organism to another, has the potential to spur the invention of many new pharmaceutical products. Other new products are simple product-line extensions—that is, the "new" product is new only to the company or to the customer. One survey found that for products introduced in one five-year period, about 85 percent were line extensions, and only 15 percent were truly new products.[10]

## The Product Decay Curve

New-product development is risky and expensive. In 1989, despite the continuing potential of biotechnology, only 1 of 400 North American start-ups, Geneutech, had made a sustained profit.[11] A Conference Board study of 148 medium and large North American manufacturing companies revealed that one out of three new industrial and consumer products introduced within the previous five years had failed. The leading cause of new-product failure was insufficient or poor marketing research.[12]

Dozens of new-product ideas are required to produce even one successful product. Figure 11.5

### THE CANADIAN MARKETPLACE

**CANADIANS LOVE THEIR KRAFT DINNER**

Canadians eat about 246 000 boxes of Kraft Dinner every day. That's roughly three times, per capita, what Americans eat. Moreover, nine of ten households here have purchased it at one time or another. Canadians even invented the name Kraft Dinner, which was originally a nickname. (Outside Canada, it's called Kraft Macaroni and Cheese.)

West Gidluck, a farmer in Saskatchewan, is the champion of Kraft Dinner consumption. He goes through about 800 boxes a year, and recently won a Kraft Canada contest aimed at finding the most ardent Kraft Dinner fans in Canada.

**With a household penetration rate of 90 percent, what steps can Kraft take to continue expanding sales of Kraft Dinner? Have you noticed Kraft making any changes in its marketing approaches in the last year or two?**

www.kraftfoods.com/index.cgi

Source: Adapted from John Heinzl, "Kraft Dinner Serves Up a New Look," *The Globe and Mail* (January 13, 1999), p. B29. Reprinted with permission from *The Globe and Mail*.

depicts the product decay curve from a 1968 survey of 51 companies. Of every 58 ideas produced in these firms, only 12 passed the preliminary screening test designed to determine whether they were compatible with company resources and objectives. Of these 12, only 7 showed sufficient profit potential in the business analysis phase. Three survived the development phase, two made it through

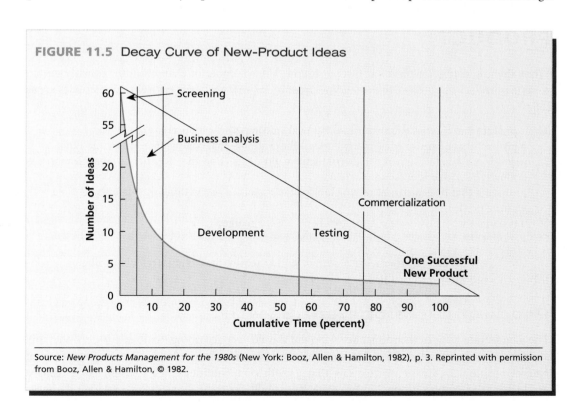

**FIGURE 11.5** Decay Curve of New-Product Ideas

Source: *New Products Management for the 1980s* (New York: Booz, Allen & Hamilton, 1982), p. 3. Reprinted with permission from Booz, Allen & Hamilton, © 1982.

the test-marketing stage, and only one, on the average, was commercially successful. Thus, less than 2 percent of new ideas resulted in a successful product.

A 1981 follow-up study reported that while the success rate had not improved, new-product development was becoming more cost-effective. According to the new data, some 54 percent of total new-product expenditures were made on products that became successes, compared with 30 percent in 1968. Capital investment in new products had fallen from 46 percent to 26 percent of total new-product spending.[13] These figures suggest that new-product development has become more efficient.

## Determinants of Success for New Products

What determines the success or failure of a new product? A research effort known as Project New Product suggests the following nine categories as determinants of new-product outcomes:

1. product superiority/quality
2. economic advantage to the user
3. overall company/project fit
4. technological compatibility
5. familiarity to the company
6. market need, growth, and size
7. competitive situation
8. defined opportunity (whether the product has a well-understood category and market, as opposed to truly revolutionary innovations that must define new categories and markets)
9. project definition[14]

These hypothetical variables allowed Robert Cooper of McMaster University to classify types of new products. Cooper contends that the most important key to new-product success lies in the product strategy itself. In his research, he found that in the cases he studied, the best 20 percent of the products had an astounding success rate of 82 percent. In contrast, 20 percent at the other end of the scale (the "me-too" products) suffered a *failure* rate of 78 percent.[15]

# CHARACTERISTICS OF THE SUPERIOR PRODUCT

What, then, *is* a superior product? Cooper found that a number of characteristics constituted the superior-product dimension. In descending order of importance, these critical characteristics are as follows:

1. a product that meets customers' needs better than competing products
2. a product that offers features or attributes to the customer that competing products do not
3. a product of higher quality than competitive products (one that has tighter specifications, is stronger, lasts longer, or is more reliable)
4. a product that does a special task or job for the customer—something that cannot be done with existing products
5. a product that is highly innovative, totally new to the market
6. a product that permits the customer to reduce costs[16]

Products with these characteristics, supported by creative marketing strategies, will greatly contribute to a profitable product line.

## Product Development Strategies

The firm's strategy for new-product development should vary according to the existing product mix and the determinants cited above. Marketing decision makers also need to look at the firm's current market position. In Chapter 5, we saw that growth opportunities can be summarized using a product/market matrix. Product improvement possibilities can be discussed in a very similar way.

Table 11.3 provides a means of looking at overall product development strategy. Four forms of product development are suggested: product improvement, market development, product development, and product diversification.

A **product improvement strategy** refers to a modification in existing products. Tide is an example of a product that has undergone constant product improvement over the years. Because of such improvements, it continues to be a leading product. Another example is the "Quality Is Job One" program established by Ford. And this was more than just a slogan: Ford's products are now more competitive with Japanese cars.

**product improvement strategy**
A modification in existing products.

**TABLE 11.3** Forms of Product Development

|  | OLD PRODUCT | NEW PRODUCT |
| --- | --- | --- |
| **OLD MARKET** | Product improvement | Product development |
| **NEW MARKET** | Market development | Product diversification |

Source: Charles E. Meisch, "Marketers, Engineers Should Work Together in 'New Product' Development Departments," *Marketing News* (November 13, 1981), p. 10. Used by permission of the American Marketing Association. Earlier discussion of these strategies is credited to H. Igor Ansoff, "Strategies for Diversification," *Harvard Business Review* (September–October 1957), pp. 113–24; see also Philip Kotler, *Principles of Marketing*, 2nd ed. (Englewood Cliffs, NJ: Prentice Hall, 1983), pp. 34, 52. Reprinted with permission by the American Marketing Association.

A **market development strategy** concentrates on finding new markets for existing products. Market segmentation (discussed in Chapters 3 and 4) is a useful tool in such an effort. Penetrating the home market with the fax machine—a product already established in the office—illustrates such a strategy. Cellular phone companies have consistently practised market development. Originally

**market development strategy**
Finding new markets for existing products.

A teeth whitening system you've never seen before.

New Crest Whitestrips. Thin, flexible strips coated with the same enamel-safe ingredient that dentists use. They get at stains below the enamel surface to whiten teeth 10 times better than a leading whitening toothpaste in just two weeks.* Guaranteed.

Start
Peel
Apply
Reveal*

*Crest* *Whitestrips* Reveal Your Whiter Smile.

**Procter and Gamble's new Crest Whitestrips is an example of product development. It extends the Crest brand to a new product that is intended to appeal to current customers—either of Crest toothpaste or of competing oral health products.**

**product development strategy**

Introducing new products into identifiable or established markets.

**product diversification strategy**

The development of new products for new markets.

attractive primarily to businesspeople who were frequently away from conventional phones, cell phones are now purchased by consumers for convenience or occasional emergency use.

A **product development strategy** refers to introducing new products into identifiable or established markets. Chrysler's Magic Wagon, for example, was a tremendous success because it provided consumers with a spacious vehicle that was as easy to drive, and as comfortable, as a car. This is a major strategy of the computer industry. A continuous flow of products makes the computer you just bought somewhat obsolete within a few months of purchase.

Sometimes the new product is the firm's first entry in a particular market. In other cases, firms choose to introduce new products into markets in which they have already established positions, in an attempt to increase overall market share.

A **product diversification strategy** refers to the development of new products for new markets. The introduction of the CD-ROM is an example. In some cases, the new target markets complement existing markets; in others, they do not. For example, a computer company might develop a range of products for the home security market.

Each of these strategies has advantages and disadvantages and must carefully be considered in the light of consumer needs and behaviour, competitors' strengths, and the strengths and abilities of the company. New products should be consistent with the firm's overall strategic orientation. Bombardier's recent introduction of a four-wheel all-terrain vehicle (ATV) nicely complements its SKI-DOO® snowmobile and SEA-DOO® watercraft product in its Recreational division. It would have made far less sense for Bombardier to have introduced a touring class two-wheel motorcycle. In general, a new product should fit well with the orientation, skills, and resources of the firm.

**Expanding its line of recreational vehicles, Bombardier recently introduced a four-wheel all-terrain vehicle (ATV).**

# THE ORGANIZATIONAL STRUCTURE FOR NEW-PRODUCT DEVELOPMENT

As the above section indicates, new-product planning is a complex area. The critical nature of product-planning decisions requires an effective organizational structure to make them. A prerequisite for efficient product innovation is an organizational structure designed to stimulate and coordinate new-product development. New-product development is a specialized task that requires the expertise of many departments. A company that delegates new-product development responsibility to the engineering department often discovers that engineers sometimes design products that are good from a structural standpoint but poor in terms of consumer needs. Many successful medium and large companies assign new-product development to one or more of the following: (1) new-product committees, (2) new-product departments, (3) product managers, or (4) venture teams.

## New-Product Committees

The most common organizational arrangement for new-product development is the *new-product committee*. Such a committee typically comprises representatives of top management in such areas as marketing, finance, manufacturing, engineering, research, and accounting. Committee members are less concerned with conceiving and developing new-product ideas than with reviewing and approving new-product plans.

Since key executives in the functional areas are committee members, their support for a new-product plan is likely to result in its approval for further development. However, new-product committees tend to be slow, are generally conservative, and sometimes compromise in order to expedite decisions so that members can get back to their regular company responsibilities.

## New-Product Departments

To overcome the limitations of the new-product committee, a number of firms have established a separate, formally organized department responsible for all phases of a product's development within the firm, including making screening decisions, developing product specifications, and coordinating product testing. The head of the department is given substantial authority and usually reports to the president or to the top marketing officer.

## Product Managers

**Product managers** (also called **brand managers**) are individuals assigned one product or product line and given responsibility for determining its objectives and marketing strategies. Procter & Gamble assigned the first product manager back in 1927 when it made one person responsible for Camay soap.[17] The role of product manager is now widely accepted by marketers. Johnson & Johnson, Maple Leaf Foods, and General Mills are examples of firms that employ product managers.

Product managers are deeply involved in setting prices, developing advertising and sales promotion programs, and working to provide assistance to sales representatives in the field. Although product managers have no line authority over the field sales force, they share the objective of increasing sales for the brand, and they try to help salespeople accomplish this task. In multiproduct companies, product managers are key people in the marketing department. They provide individual attention to each product, while the firm as a whole has a single sales force, a marketing research department, and an advertising department that all product managers can use.

In addition to performing product analysis and planning, the product manager must use interpersonal skills and sales skills to gain the cooperation of people over whom he or she has no authority. This occurs with levels above the manager, as well as with those in sales and advertising.

Besides having primary responsibility for marketing a particular product or product line, the product manager often is also responsible for new-product development, creating new-product ideas, and making recommendations for improving existing products. These suggestions become the basis for proposals submitted to top management.

**product managers (brand managers)**
Individuals assigned one product or product line and given responsibility for determining its objectives and marketing strategies.

The product manager system is open to one of the same criticisms as the new-product committee: new-product development may get secondary treatment because of the manager's time commitments for existing products. Although a number of extremely successful new products have resulted from ideas submitted by product managers, it cannot be assumed that the skills required for marketing an existing product line are the same as those required for successfully developing new products.[18]

## Venture Teams

Many companies have found that new venture teams have provided a good method of bringing new products to the market.

**venture-team concept**

An organizational strategy for developing new products through combining the management resources of marketing, technology, capital, and management expertise in a team.

The **venture-team concept** develops new products through combining the management resources of marketing, technology, capital, and management expertise in a team. Like new-product committees, venture teams are composed of specialists from different functions in the organization: engineering representatives for expertise in product design and the development of prototypes; marketing staff members for development of product-concept tests, test marketing, sales forecasts, pricing, and promotion; and financial accounting representatives for detailed cost analyses and decisions concerning the concept's probable return on investment.

Unlike new-product committees, venture teams do not disband after every product developed. Members are assigned to the project as a major responsibility, and the team possesses the necessary authority to both plan and carry out a course of action.

As a means of stimulating product innovation, the team is typically separated from the permanent organization and is also linked directly with top management. One company moved its three-member venture team from its divisional headquarters to the corporate head office. Since the venture-team manager reports to the division head or to the chief administrative officer, communications problems are minimized and high-level support is assured.

The venture team usually begins as a loosely organized group of members with a common interest in a new-product idea. Team members are frequently given released time during the workday to devote to the venture. If viable product proposals are developed, the venture team is formally organized as a task force within a venture department or as a task force reporting to a vice president or to the chief executive officer. When the commercial potential of new products has been demonstrated, the products may be assigned to an existing division, may become a division within the company, or may serve as the nucleus of a new company. The flexibility and authority of the venture team allows the large firm to operate with the manoeuvrability of smaller companies.

# STAGES IN THE NEW-PRODUCT DEVELOPMENT PROCESS

New-product development strategy should be built on the existing business strategy of the company. Companies that have successfully launched new products are more likely to have had a formal new-product process in place for some time. They are also more likely to have a strategic plan and to be committed to growth through internally developed new products.[19]

Once the firm is organized for new-product development, it can establish procedures for evaluating new-product ideas. The product development process may be thought of as involving seven stages: (1) development of overall new-product strategy, (2) new-product idea generation, (3) screening, (4) business analysis, (5) final product development, (6) test marketing, and (7) commercialization. At each stage, management faces the decision to abandon the project, continue to the next stage, or seek additional information before proceeding further. The process is illustrated in Figure 11.6.

## New-Product Strategy

New-product strategy links corporate objectives to the new-product effort, provides direction for the new-product process, and identifies the strategic roles in the product line that the new products

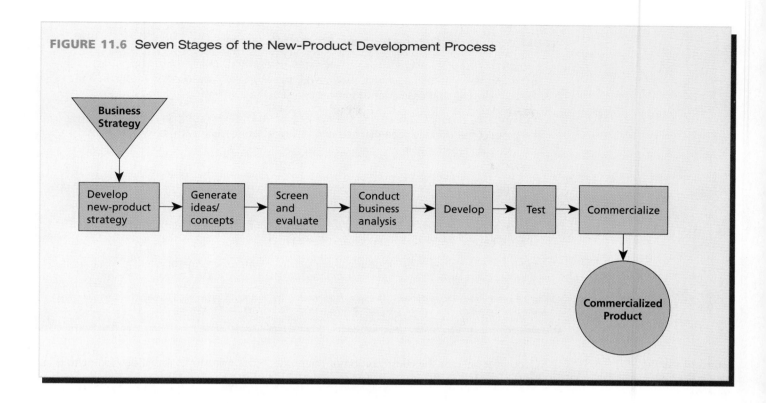

**FIGURE 11.6** Seven Stages of the New-Product Development Process

should play. It also helps set the formal financial criteria to be used in measuring new-product performance and in screening and evaluating new-product ideas.[20]

## Idea Generation

New-product development begins with an idea. Ideas emanate from many sources: the sales force, marketing employees, research and development (R & D) specialists, competitive products, retailers, inventors outside the company, and customers who write letters asking, "Why don't you ...?" It is extremely important for the firm to develop a system of stimulating new ideas and rewarding people who develop them.

## Screening

This crucial stage involves separating ideas with potential from those incapable of meeting company objectives. Some organizations use checklists to determine whether product ideas should be eliminated or subjected to further consideration. These checklists typically include such factors as product uniqueness, availability of raw materials, and compatibility of the proposed product with current product offerings, existing facilities, and capabilities. In other instances, the screening stage consists of open discussions of new-product ideas among representatives of different functional areas in the organization. This is an important point in the product development process, since any product ideas that go beyond this point will cost the firm considerable time and money. Table 11.4 lists some issues that should be considered in the screening process.

## Business Analysis

Product ideas that survive the initial screening are then subjected to a thorough business analysis. This involves assessing the potential market, its growth rate, and the likely competitive strength of the new product. Decisions must be made about the compatibility of the proposed product with such company resources as financial support for necessary promotion, production capabilities, and distribution facilities.

> **TABLE 11.4 Basic Criteria for New-Product Screening**
>
> 1. *Company's resources and abilities.* Financial resources, R & D skills, engineering skills, marketing research, management, production, sales force and distribution resources and skills, advertising and promotion resources and skills.
>
> 2. *Nature of the product.* Newness to the market, newness to the company, how completely the product has actually been planned and technical issues dealt with, fit with current product line, superiority in meeting customer needs, quality relative to current competitive products.
>
> 3. *Potential customers for the product.* Similarity to current customers, level of felt need for the product.
>
> 4. *Nature of competition.* Similarity to current competition, intensity of competition, presence of price bases competition, number and size of competitors.
>
> 5. *Nature of the market.* Size or potential, growth rate, rate of change of needs of customers.
>
> Source: Adapted from Robert Cooper, "The New Prod System: The Industry Experience," *Journal of Product Innovation Management* (June 1992), pp. 125–26. Copyright © 1992, with permission from Elsevier Science.

**concept testing**

A marketing research project that attempts to measure consumer attitudes and perceptions relevant to a new-product idea.

Concept testing, or the consideration of the product idea prior to its actual development, is an important aspect of the business analysis stage. **Concept testing** is a marketing research project that attempts to measure consumer attitudes and perceptions relevant to a new-product idea. Focus groups (see Chapter 7) and in-store polling can be effective methods of assessing a new-product concept.

## Product Development

Those product ideas with profit potential are then converted into a physical product. The conversion process becomes the joint responsibility of development engineering, which is responsible for developing the original concept into a product, and the marketing department, which provides feedback on consumer reactions to alternative product designs, packages, features, colours, and other physical appeals. Numerous changes may be necessary before the original mock-up is converted into the final product.

Even after basic production processes have been solved, there is often a considerable amount of testing with potential consumers. Such testing is done in many ways. Sometimes employees are given the product and asked to report on performance on a regular, structured basis. As a textbook such as this one is written, it is subject to review by faculty members across the country. In other cases, limited market tests are undertaken under carefully monitored conditions, as discussed in Chapter 7. The series of revisions, tests, and refinements should result in the ultimate introduction of a product with a greater likelihood of success.

Despite such careful testing, further problems are often uncovered in daily use. For example, the first release of computer software often has some "bugs" that have to be corrected. And the first printing of this book might have some typographical or other errors that will be corrected with the next printing a few months later. Cars are sometimes recalled to dealers to replace a part that does not work as expected.

## Test Marketing

To determine consumer reactions to their products *and* to the proposed marketing plan under normal shopping conditions, a number of firms test-market their new offerings. Up to this point, consumer information has been obtained by giving free products to consumers, who then gave their reactions. Other information may have been gathered by asking shoppers to evaluate competitive products, but test marketing is the first point at which the product must perform in a "real-life" environment.

**Test marketing** involves selecting usually one to three cities or television-coverage areas considered reasonably typical of the total market, and introducing a new product to these areas with a total marketing campaign. A carefully designed and controlled test allows management to develop estimates of the effectiveness of marketing mix decisions and projections of sales following full-scale introduction.

Some firms omit the test-marketing stage and move directly from product development to full-scale production. They cite three problems with test marketing:

1. Test marketing is expensive. As one marketing executive pointed out,

   It's very difficult to run a little [test market] for six months or a year in three or four markets across the [country] and then project what your sales volume is going to be two or three years in the future, mainly because you're testing in such small localities, generally to keep your costs down.

   You simply can't afford to test your products in markets like [Toronto or Montreal]. So you run your test in [smaller cities]. And your test costs are over $1 million even in places like that.[21]

2. Competitors who learn about the test market may disrupt the findings by reducing the price of their products in the test area, distributing cents-off coupons, installing attractive in-store displays, or giving additional discounts to retailers to induce them to display more of their products.

   Test-marketing a new product also communicates company plans to competitors before the product's introduction. The Kellogg Company discovered a new product with suspected sales potential by learning of the test marketing of a new fruit-filled tart designed to be heated in the toaster and served hot for breakfast. Kellogg rushed a similar product into full-scale production and became the first national marketer of the product they named Pop Tarts.

3. Long-lived durable goods (such as dishwashers, hair dryers, and VCRs) are seldom test-marketed due to the major financial investment required for the development, the need to develop a network of dealers to distribute the products, and the parts and servicing required. A company such as Whirlpool invests from $1 million to $33 million in the development of a new refrigerator. To develop each silicon chip in an Apple microcomputer costs approximately $1 million and takes from one to fifteen months. Producing a prototype for a test market is simply too expensive, so the "go/no-go" decision for the new durable product is typically made without the benefit of test-market results.[22]

www.kelloggs.com

www.poptarts.com

A decision to skip the test-marketing stage should be based on there being a very high likelihood of the product's success. The cost of developing a new detergent from idea generation to national marketing has been estimated at $10 million. Even though a firm will experience losses on any product that passes the initial screening process but is not introduced, it will still be much better off if it stops as soon as it discovers that the product cannot succeed. Otherwise, it may be faced with a failure like Corfam, an artificial leather that DuPont introduced; the company suffered losses of more than $100 million over the lengthy period it tried to make Corfam a success.

## Commercialization

The few product ideas that have survived all the steps in the development process are now ready for full-scale marketing. Marketing programs must be established, outlays for production facilities may be necessary, and the sales force, intermediaries, and potential customers must become acquainted with the new product.

New-product development should follow the step-by-step approach outlined in Figure 11.6. Systematic planning and control of all phases of development and introduction can be accomplished through the use of such scheduling methods as the Program Evaluation and Review Technique (PERT) and the Critical Path Method (CPM). These techniques map out the sequence in which each step must be taken and show the time allotments for each activity. Detailed PERT and CPM flow charts not only assist in coordinating all activities in the development and introduction of new products, but can also highlight the sequence of events that will be the most critical in scheduling.

## SOME IDEAS TAKE A LITTLE LONGER

What's a good idea worth? On its own, not much.
It might have been the worst product launch of the century. Or several centuries.

The inventor's name was Merlin but he quickly proved himself to be something less than a magician at marketing.

Joseph Merlin is recorded in history books as the first person to wear roller skates. The Belgian inventor introduced them to the world at a party in London in 1760.

He lost control and skated into an expensive mirror, smashing it to pieces and quite probably shattering the market for his product at the same time.

In Waterloo, Ontario, Gary Svoboda laughs. He's the vice-president of the Canadian Innovation Centre, a non-profit organization dedicated to helping inventors.

"Most of our inventor clients are going to crash into the mirror," he says. "We have an invention assessment service. Sometimes I think what we really need is an inventor assessment service."

His point: it's not enough to have a great idea. Once you emerge from your basement workshop with your perfect invention, you have to reinvent yourself—as a businessperson with marketing skills.

"The patent office is full of good ideas going nowhere," says Svoboda. "The inventor is more important than the invention."

Want proof?

The most successful product ever to pass through the CIC is probably the Abdominizer. A simple home exercise device that sold—and made—millions.

"It's probably not the best idea of the month, let alone the best idea of the last 20 years that came through our service," says Svoboda. "The Abdominizer is simply a seat which you sit on and you do sit ups. It's not rocket science."

So why did people buy eight million units of this product? The inventor was a shrewd businessperson with good timing. Back in the '80s, interest in fitness equipment was exploding when the Abdominizer was launched into living rooms via infomercials.

"It was an OK idea, well marketed," says Svoboda.

So what about that roller skating idea?

After Mr. Merlin smashed his chances, other inventors worked on ways to put people on wheels. Finally, in 1863, an inventor developed skates that made turning simple—and the sport took off.

"A lot of ideas are waiting for technology to catch up," says Svoboda. "Something too far ahead of its time isn't going to be successful."

That isn't the whole story, though. Check out this ad for in-line roller skates—from 1947.

The technology seems to be in place. The manufacturer had solved Mr. Merlin's big problem.

"Note the exclusive brake," the copy trumpets. "To stop quick SIMPLY RAISE THE TOE. The 'JET' Skate is the ONLY SKATE WITH THIS FEATURE."

The patent was in place, and judging by the generous use of capitals, the marketing department was motivated. So why didn't in-line skating take off back in 1947? Why didn't everyone in North America scramble to "Be first in your locality"?

We were unable to find Afco Products. Several companies with similar names had no knowledge of an early foray into in-line skates.

Gary Svoboda, however, is willing to speculate. "Timing counts," he says. "The marketplace has to be ready for the idea. And maybe the postwar society just wasn't interested."

In-line skates, by the way, were first patented back in 1819. So the concept sat on the shelf for a very long time before the explosion of interest that started in the 1980s.

That's when consumers were offered in-line skates with better boots and high-tech wheels. It didn't hurt that smooth roads were everywhere. But you still have to wonder why a really good idea like in-line skates didn't move for so long.

What about the notion that all you have to do is build the better mousetrap?

Gary Svoboda laughs again.

"The world is not going to beat a path to your door," he says. "It's not about the power of an idea. It's about communicating that idea and convincing the market."

**Why are some good ideas not successful? What reasons, other that those suggested in the article, may explain the failure of the in-line skate in 1947?**

Source: Havard Gould, *Venture* reporter, http://cbc.ca/business/indepth/inventors.html

www.innovationcentre.ca

# CONSUMER ADOPTION PROCESS

Once a new product is launched, consumers begin a process of evaluating it. This evaluation is known as the **adoption process**—the process whereby potential consumers go through a series of stages from learning of the new product to trying it and deciding to purchase it regularly or to reject it. The process has some similarities to the consumer decision process discussed in Chapter 8. The stages in the consumer adoption process can be classified as follows:

1. *Awareness.* Individuals first learn of the new product but lack information about it.
2. *Interest.* They begin to seek out information about it.
3. *Evaluation.* They consider whether the product is beneficial.
4. *Trial.* They make a trial purchase, test it, or mentally visualize its use to determine its usefulness.
5. *Adoption/Rejection.* If the trial purchase is satisfactory, they decide to make regular use of the product.[23] Of course, rejection may take place at any stage of the process.

Marketing managers need to understand the adoption process so that they can move potential consumers to the adoption stage. Once the manager is aware of a large number of consumers at the interest stage, steps can be taken to stimulate sales. For example, when consumer interest in buying a combined shampoo/conditioner began to grow, Procter & Gamble introduced Pert Plus with samples sent to homes in addition to its regular advertising campaign. Sampling, if it is successful, is a technique that reduces the risk of evaluation and trial, moving the consumer quickly to the adoption stage.

**adoption process**
A series of stages consumers go through, from learning of a new product to trying it and deciding to purchase it regularly or to reject it.

## Adopter Categories

Some people will purchase a new product almost as soon as it is placed on the market. Others wait for additional information and rely on the experiences of the first purchasers before making trial purchases. **Consumer innovators** are the first purchasers at the beginning of a product's life cycle. They are found to be the first in the community to buy high-definition television (HDTV), for example.

A number of investigations analyzing the adoption of new products have resulted in the identification of five categories of purchasers based on relative time of adoption: innovators, early adopters, early majority, later majority, and laggards. These categories are shown in Figure 11.7, as well as the proportion of the population in each category.

The **diffusion process** refers to the filtering and acceptance of new products and services by the members of a community or social system. Figure 11.7 shows this process as following a normal distribution. A few people adopt at first, and then the number of adopters increases rapidly as the value

**consumer innovators**
The first purchasers—those who buy a product at the beginning of its life cycle.

**diffusion process**
The filtering and acceptance of new products and services by the members of a community or social system.

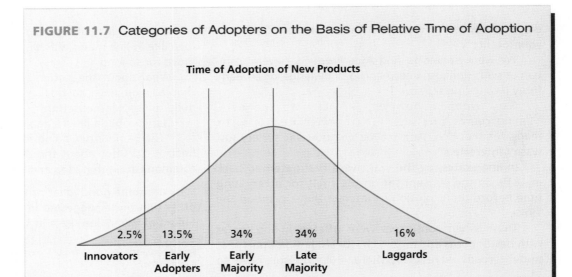

**FIGURE 11.7** Categories of Adopters on the Basis of Relative Time of Adoption

Source: Everett M. Rogers, *Diffusion of Innovations*, 4th ed. (New York: The Free Press, 1995). Copyright © 1995 by Everett M. Rogers. Copyright © 1962, 1971, 1983 by The Free Press. Reprinted with the permission of The Free Press, a Division of Simon & Schuster.

of the innovation becomes apparent. The rate finally diminishes as fewer potential consumers remain in the nonadopter category.

Since the categories are based on the normal distribution, standard deviations are used to partition each category. Innovators are defined as the first 2.5 percent of those individuals who adopt the new product; laggards are the final 16 percent to adopt. Excluded from the figure are the non-adopters—people who never adopt the new product.

## Identifying the First Adopters

Locating first buyers of new products represents a challenge for the marketing manager. If the right people can be reached early in the product's development or introduction, they may serve as a test market, evaluating the product and possibly making suggestions for modifications. Since early purchasers are frequently opinion leaders from whom others seek advice, their attitudes toward new products are communicated in their neighbourhoods, clubs, and organizations. Acceptance or rejection of the innovation by these purchasers may serve as a kind of signal for the marketing manager that indicates the probable success or failure of the new product.[24]

Unfortunately, people who are first adopters of one new product may not necessarily be first adopters for other products or services. A large number of studies have, however, established some general characteristics possessed by most first adopters.

In general, first adopters tend to be younger, have a high social status, be better educated, and enjoy a higher income. They are more mobile than later adopters, and change both their jobs and their home addresses more often. They are more likely to rely on impersonal information sources than are later adopters, who depend more on promotional information from the company and word-of-mouth communication.[25]

## What Determines the Rate of Adoption?

The electronic calculator replaced the slide rule as the engineering student's friend as soon as prices came within range of the student budget. On the other hand, it took thirteen years to convince most corn farmers to use hybrid seed corn—an innovation capable of doubling corn yields—even though some progressive farmers adopted it at once. The adoption rate is influenced by five characteristics of the innovation.[26]

- *Relative advantage.* The degree to which the innovation appears superior to previous ideas. The greater the relative advantage—whether manifested in lower price, physical improvements, or ease of use—the faster the adoption rate.
- *Compatibility.* The degree to which the innovation is compatible with existing facilities or consistent with the values and experiences of potential adopters. The business student who purchases a personal computer will likely buy one that is compatible with those at the school he or she attends or with those of his or her friends.
- *Complexity.* The more difficult it is to understand or use the new product, the longer it will take to be generally accepted in most cases.
- *Divisibility.* The degree to which the innovation may be used on a limited basis. First adopters face two types of risk—financial losses and the risk of ridicule by others—if the new product proves unsatisfactory. The option of sampling the innovation on a limited basis allows these risks to be reduced and, in general, should accelerate the rate of adoption.
- *Communicability.* The degree to which the results of the product may be observable by or communicated to others. If the superiority of the innovation can be displayed in a tangible form, this will increase the adoption rate.

These five characteristics can be used, to some extent, by the marketing manager in accelerating the rate of adoption. First, will consumers perceive the product as complex, or will its use necessitate a significant change in typical behavioural patterns? Product complexity must be overcome with promotional messages of an informational nature. Products should be designed to emphasize their relative advantages and, whenever possible, be divisible for sample purchases. If divisibility is physically impossible, in-home demonstrations or trial placements in the home may be used. Positive attempts must also be made to ensure compatibility of the innovation with the adopters' value systems.

These actions are based on extensive research studies of innovators in agriculture, medicine, and consumer goods. They should pay off in increased sales by accelerating the rate of adoption in each of the adopter categories.

# PRODUCT DELETION DECISIONS

While many firms devote a great deal of time and resources to developing new products, the thought of eliminating old products from the firm's line is painful for many executives. Often sentimental attachments to marginal products prevent objective decisions to drop products with declining sales. Management finds it difficult to say good-bye to an old friend.

If waste is to be avoided, product lines must be pruned, and old unprofitable products must eventually be eliminated from the firm's line. This decision is typically faced in the late-maturity and early-decline stages of the product life cycle. Periodic reviews of all products should be conducted in order to prune weak products or to justify their retention.

In some instances, a firm will continue to carry an unprofitable product so as to provide a complete line of goods for its customers. Even though most supermarkets may not make much money on low-unit-value items such as salt, they continue to carry these items to meet shopper demands.

Other cases arise in which profitable products are dropped because of failure to fit into the firm's existing product line. IBM found that its marketing system, including the training of representatives, was so focused on computers that it was difficult to do an adequate job in marketing printers. Therefore, it removed printers from the main product line and turned them over to a subsidiary company, Lexmark.

# PRODUCT SAFETY

If the product is to fulfill its mission of satisfying consumer needs, it must above all be safe. Manufacturers must design their products in such a way as to protect not only children but all consumers who use them. Packaging can play an important role in product safety. The law requires that bottle tops on dangerous products such as pharmaceuticals be child-proof (some are virtually parent-proof). This safety feature has reduced by two-thirds the number of children under five years of age who swallow dangerous doses of ASA. Prominent safety warnings on the labels of such potentially hazardous products as cleaning fluids and drain cleaners inform users about the dangers of these products and urge purchasers to store them out of the reach of children. Changes in product design have reduced the dangers involved in the use of such products as lawn mowers, hedge trimmers, and toys.

The need for fire-retardant fabrics for children's sleepwear was recognized long before federal regulations were established. While fire-retardant fabrics were available, the problems lay in how to produce them to meet consumer requirements for softness, colour, texture, durability, and reasonable cost. Today, government flame-retardancy standards are strictly enforced.

Federal and provincial legislation has long played a major role in promoting product safety. The **Hazardous Products Act**, passed in 1969, was a major piece of legislation that consolidated previous legislation and set significant new standards for product safety. The Act defines a hazardous product as any product that is included in a list (called a schedule) compiled by Consumer and Corporate Affairs Canada or Health and Welfare Canada. Any consumer product considered to be a hazard to public health or safety may be listed in the schedule. Table 11.5 lists some of the main items and outlines the regulations that affect them.

The Act itself comprises just fifteen clauses. Those relating to criminal penalties and seizure put sharp teeth in the law. Inspectors designated under the Act have powers of search and seizure. Hazardous products inspectors may enter, at any reasonable time, any place where they reasonably believe a hazardous product is manufactured, prepared, packaged, sold, or stored for sale. They may examine the product, take samples, and examine any records believed to contain information relevant to enforcing the Act. Products that an inspector has reasonable grounds to believe are in contravention of the Act may be seized.

These regulatory activities have prompted companies to voluntarily improve safety standards for their products. For many companies, safety has become a very important ingredient in the broader definition of product.

The management of products is a many-faceted affair. It can involve the way that the organization is structured, both in developing new products and in managing them. Product management

**Hazardous Products Act**
A major piece of legislation that consolidated previous legislation and set significant new standards for product safety; defines a hazardous product as any product that is included in a list (called a schedule) compiled by Consumer and Corporate Affairs Canada or Health and Welfare Canada.

---

### Table 11.5 Some Hazardous Products Act Regulations

- Bedding may not be highly flammable.
- Children's sleepwear, dressing gowns, and robes must meet flammability standards.
- Children's toys or equipment may not contain toxic substances (such as lead pigments) beyond a prescribed limit.
- Certain household chemical products must be labelled with appropriate symbols to alert consumers to their hazards.
- Hockey helmets must meet safety standards to protect young hockey players.
- Pencils and artists' brushes are regulated to limit lead in their decorative coating.
- Matches must meet safety standards for strength and packaging.
- Safety glass is mandatory in domestic doors and shower enclosures.
- Liquid drain cleaners and furniture polishes containing petroleum-based solvents must be sold in child-proof packaging.
- Toys and children's playthings must comply with safety standards.
- Crib regulations provide for increased child safety.

also includes an analysis of the product mix, as well as the appropriate branding and packaging of each product. And, as always, such decisions must be made in the light of the marketing strategy, and in harmony with the rest of the elements of the marketing mix.

## SUMMARY

A product mix is the assortment of product lines and individual offerings available from a company. Product mixes are typically measured by width and depth of assortment.

A line extension is the development of individual offerings that appeal to different market segments but are closely related to the existing product line.

Over time, products are characterized by a product life cycle. The stages of this life cycle are introduction, growth, maturity, and decline. The most appropriate marketing strategy changes for different stages of the life cycle. Fads have short life cycles, while other products can have very long life cycles. Marketing activity can extend the product life cycle by increasing the frequency of use of a product, or by changing product quality or packaging. The product life cycle concept applies best to product groups rather than to individual brands.

In product development, many initial ideas fall by the wayside. This is known as the product decay curve.

Contributors to the success of new products include overall superiority, advantages to the user, fit and compatibility of the product with the company, market need, competitive situation, and how well the opportunity and project have been defined.

There are four product development strategies: product improvement, market development, product development, and product diversification.

Organizational structures used to make product-planning decisions are new-product committees, new-product departments, product managers, and venture teams. Product managers are individuals assigned one product or product line who are responsible for determining its objectives and marketing strategies.

The stages of the new-product development process are (1) develop new-product strategy, (2) generate ideas and concepts, (3) screen and evaluate, (4) conduct business analysis, (5) develop the product, (6) test the product, and (7) commercialize it.

Consumers go through a process from learning about a product to deciding whether to purchase it or not. This adoption process proceeds in stages consisting of awareness, interest, evaluation, trial, and adoption/rejection. Different people will adopt a particular innovation at different times. Adopters are classified as innovators, early adopters, early majority, late majority, and laggards. Rate of adoption is influenced by the five characteristics of innovation: relative advantage, compatibility, complexity, divisibility, and communicability.

In parallel with product introduction decisions, there will normally be product deletion decisions.

## KEY TERMS

adoption process, p. 293
cannibalizing, p. 272
concept testing, p. 290
consumer innovators, p. 293
diffusion process, p. 293
fads, p. 279
fashions, p. 279
Hazardous Products Act, p. 296
individual offering, p. 272
line extension, p. 273

market development strategy, p. 285
product development strategy, p. 286
product diversification strategy, p. 286
product improvement strategy, p. 285
product life cycle, p. 275
product line, p. 272
product managers (brand managers), p. 287
product mix, p. 272
test marketing, p. 291
venture-team concept, p. 288

# INTERACTIVE SUMMARY AND DISCUSSION QUESTIONS

1. A product mix is the assortment of product lines and individual offerings available from a company. Product mixes are typically measured by width and depth of assortment.
   a. Describe the product mix by depth and width for a company that has ten or more products.
   b. Indicate where each product type is in the life cycle for that product category.
2. A line extension is the development of individual offerings that appeal to different market segments but are closely related to the existing product line. Explain this using the photocopier market as an example.
3. The product life-cycle stages are introduction, growth, maturity, and decline. Draw the typical life-cycle model, and then the way the model would appear for a fad, a fashion item, and an aborted (re)introduction.
4. At different stages in the product life cycle, the emphasis differs for the elements of the marketing mix. Discuss, and give examples.
5. Fashions are currently popular products that tend to follow recurring life cycles. For some marketers, it would be desirable to speed up the cycle so there would be a revived demand for the new fashion. Is this possible? Why or why not?
6. The life-cycle concept is most applicable to a product category, not to individual brands. Discuss, using examples.
7. The product life cycle may be extended by increasing the frequency of use by present customers, adding new users, finding new uses for the product, or changing product quality or packaging. Discuss the pros and cons of such efforts in comparison with introducing a completely new product.
8. Consumers go through a process from first learning about a product to deciding whether to purchase it or not. This adoption process has the following stages: awareness, interest, evaluation, trial, and adoption/rejection. Discuss how a marketer can use this information.
9. The rate of adoption is influenced by the five characteristics of the innovation: relative advantage, compatibility, complexity, divisibility, and communicability. Using these characteristics, give an example of a product that would be adopted relatively quickly, and one that would be adopted more slowly.
10. In product development, many initial ideas fall by the wayside. This is known as the product decay curve. Draw a typical decay curve of new-product ideas, indicating the related phases: screening, business analysis, development, testing, and commercialization.
11. Assume you work for the product manager of a company in the consumer electronics business. You have been asked to write your manager a memo on determinants of success for new products. Base your memo on the chapter material.
12. There are four product development strategies: product improvement, market development, product development, and product diversification. In what instances would each strategy be appropriate?
13. Organizational structures used to make product-planning decisions are new-product committees, new-product departments, product managers, and venture teams. Explain and discuss the advantages of each.
14. Product managers are individuals assigned one product or product line and given responsibility for determining its objectives and marketing strategies. Do you think they would do as good a job at suggesting and initiating new products as they do at managing existing products? Why or why not?
15. The stages of the new-product development process are outlined in Figure 11.6. With two or three classmates, develop a product strategy for a product category of your choice. Then brainstorm an extensive list of product ideas. Following this, look more closely at the list and pick out those that seem to have the most potential. Finally, suggest some ways of performing a business analysis for the most promising candidates.
16. In parallel with product introduction decisions, there will normally be product deletion decisions. Give some examples of products that have been (or should be) deleted.
17. Allproducts.com is a directory of over 60 000 products. Go to their home page and click on the New Products category. Choose two products that look interesting to you. Evaluate them using the criteria listed on page 284. Do you think the products will be successful? Explain.

www.allproducts.com

## A Smarter Slice of Toast

I will never eat again. It is the day after Thanksgiving and I am seriously regretting every bite I took in the past 24 hours. Unfortunately, instead of a turkey dinner to gorge on, my holiday feast consisted solely of toast—white toast with butter, toasted English muffins with jam, toasted pumpernickel bagels with cream cheese and lox. But I know all too deep in my gut that what really put me over the edge was the toasted Pop-Tarts I had for breakfast this morning.

It all started when I saw a new toaster from Oster that offered 63 different settings. Called the Perfectionist, this $60 microprocessor-controlled box has separate calibrations for bagels, English muffins, and regular bread. It reheats and defrosts. And it charts its progress on a blinking, beeping, digital pie chart you can watch while you wipe the sleep from your eyes.

Surely this must be a joke, I thought. People have been toasting bread for centuries, and they've never needed a computer to get the job done. Like answering machines, microwaves, and VCRs before it, even the humble toaster seemed to have become too smart for its own good. To find out for sure, I put to the test four of the fanciest models I could find.

I soon learned that Oster's Perfectionist isn't the only toaster that asks humans to make far too many decisions before their first cup of coffee. Krups' ToastControl Digital, which sells for $70, packs in even more options, including two for saving your favourite settings, like the bookmarks on your Web browser. Two glass-sealed quartz rods replace the usual wire heating elements inside and are supposed to toast your bread faster without drying it out. A built-in digital timer tells you precisely how many seconds are left to go.

Too bad the resulting toast proved to be merely ordinary. While bagels came out nicely and white bread toasted almost evenly, both took longer to brown in the Krups than in the three other models I tried. And for some reason, frozen English muffins came out slightly soggy, even on the defrost setting.

www.oster.com

The Perfectionist also proved less than perfect. One side of my toast tended to come out darker than the other—fine for bagels, but not for bread. And while I had 63 options for browning, the short, 50-cm cord gave me too few options for where to put the thing.

That left me with two popular older models: KitchenAid's $100 Ultra Power Plus, which comes in fun colors like green, blue, and red, and Cuisinart's Custom Control Total Touch, which typically sells for $70. The KitchenAid was cute and compact, but I finally settled on the slightly bulkier Cuisinart because it consistently turned out the most evenly browned bread, bagels, Pop-Tarts, and muffins with the least amount of thought or effort on my part. Now that's what I call a smart toaster—not that I'll ever get near a piece of toast again.

### You Be the Marketer

1. Why would toaster manufacturers take a relatively simple product, like a toaster, and increase its complexity to the levels described by the reviewer?

2. What are they trying to accomplish? What other strategies could they use?

Source: Anita Hamilton, "A Smarter Slice of Toast," *Time*, December 3, 2001, p. 57. Copyright © 2001 TIME Inc. Reprinted by permission.

The Four Seasons Hotel carefully manages all aspects of their service provision so that their customers' experience consistently matches or exceeds their expectations.

## Chapter 12

# SERVICES

**CHAPTER OBJECTIVES**

After reading and studying this chapter, you should be able to

1. Elaborate on the discussion of products by exploring the "service product."
2. Discuss the similarities and differences between goods and services.
3. Explain the four main characteristics of services.
4. Outline the major issues that must be addressed by marketers for each of the characteristics.
5. Describe the main methods marketers use to address these issues.

Susan Helstab says foreign contacts often do a double take when she tells them Four Seasons is a Canadian company. They think British-owned perhaps, maybe American.

When she reassures them that she isn't joking, they then conclude that the luxury hotel chain's birthplace must be the secret to its success. "They think it is in our inherent nature as Canadians to offer a high level of personal service because we are kind and sensitive," says Helstab, Four Seasons' senior vice-president of corporate marketing.

It's hardly surprising that the foreigners question the company's origin, given Canada isn't noted as a hotbed of companies that are global leaders in luxury service. But make no mistake, Toronto-based Four Seasons Hotels and Resorts has emerged—under the Four Seasons and Regent brands—as the world's largest provider of upscale lodging for the rich and famous. Now its challenge is to maintain this status in a tough travel market, while expanding into more residential-style resorts.

"We're very discreet," explains Helstab, talking about the company's success. "There's an intimacy and residential feeling to our hotels, so someone who is, say, in the film industry and recognizable appreciates that discretion."

For evidence of that discretion, look no further than the Four Seasons Hotel Toronto, which each year plays host to celebrities in town for the International Film Festival. Most recently, überfamous Tom Cruise stayed there while promoting his new film *Vanilla Sky.* U.K. journalist Lynn Middlehurst, publisher of *The Gallivanter's Guide*—a newsletter for high-end travellers—said in a recent editorial that celebrities like it when Four Seasons treats them as ordinary people, and ordinary people like it when Four Seasons treats them as celebrities.

The key to this kind of service is great staff and, surprisingly, Helstab says the chain doesn't mind hiring employees with no prior hotel experience. "We want to hire people who feel serving another human being is their calling," she says. "No isn't part of their vocabulary."

The chain's highly personalized service originated with Four Seasons' legendary founder Isadore Sharp. His goal was to create a group of medium-size hotels with exceptional quality, and he's succeeded.

"Four Seasons is not a substitute for a Marriott or Hilton. Four Seasons is a destination itself," says Jacques Kavafian, analyst at Toronto-based Yorkton Securities. "They've been able to build a brand that truly means luxury, by offering consistently exclusive services. A Four Seasons in Tokyo, Milan and Paris all have personalized service. They even have good service in New York."

That consistency has enabled Four Seasons to become the world's largest luxury hotel brand. Back in 1990, it managed just 22 hotels in three countries: Canada, the U.S., and the U.K. Today it operates 51 properties in 22 countries, ranging from the chain's largest hotel, with 539 rooms— the Formosa Regent Taipei in Taiwan—to the smallest, with just 54 rooms—Indonesia's Four Seasons Resort Bali at Sayan. Its high-priced real estate includes luxury hotels on 57th Street in New York and on the Champs Élysées in Paris. This year, the chain is undergoing its largest expansion effort with more than 20 properties under construction.

And Four Seasons gets it right. In 2001, the luxury hotel chain nabbed 17 of the 59 AAA Five Diamond Lodging Awards—the highest measurement bestowed in the accommodation industry—winning more awards than any other hotel operator.

Source: Excerpted from Chris Daniels, "A Room for All Seasons," *Marketing*, February 4, 2002, pp. 6, 7.

www.fourseasons.com

# INTRODUCTION

A service is a type of product. For the most part, discussions about the marketing of goods apply to services as well. But services have a number of important special characteristics that differentiate them from goods. One of the most important differences, as the opening vignette implies, is that service marketers are really selling *experiences*—and people bring very definite expectations with them when they are buying an experience.

General marketing notions, approaches, and theories apply to both goods and services. However, some techniques and ideas are relatively exclusive to services marketing; others, to goods marketing. And within either type of marketing, distinctions may also be made among various industries or marketing situations.

The service sector today is so large that a good understanding of it is necessary. In Canada, services account for 74 percent of employment and 67 percent of Gross Domestic Product (GDP).[1] The World Trade Organization (WTO) estimates that in 2001 total international trade in commercial services was $1.44 trillion (U.S.).[2]

# SERVICES VERSUS GOODS

**service**
A product without physical characteristics—a bundle of performance and symbolic attributes designed to produce consumer want satisfaction.

**tangible attributes**
Those attributes that can be experienced by the physical senses, such as sight, touch, and smell.

**intangible attributes**
Those attributes that cannot be experienced by the physical senses.

A **service** is a product without physical characteristics—a bundle of performance and symbolic attributes designed to produce consumer want satisfaction. Leonard Berry states that "the pivotal difference between goods businesses and services businesses is that goods businesses sell *things* and service businesses sell *performances.*"[3] In other words, goods are produced, whereas services are performed.

Despite the relatively clear-cut definition of a service, many products have *both* **tangible** and **intangible attributes.** For example, a pail of fertilizer sold by a farm-supply dealer to a farmer seems like a pure good. However, if that dealer also provides expertise—for example, counselling about fertilizer application—a service is added. Consequently, it is more accurate to consider products as falling on a spectrum between "tangible elements dominant" and "intangible elements dominant" (see Figure 12.1).

## Buying Promises

Potential customers often have difficulties conceptualizing the service product, because it has no physical properties. Basically, they are buying promises. No product trial or return is possible. Three

**FIGURE 12.1** The Tangibility Spectrum

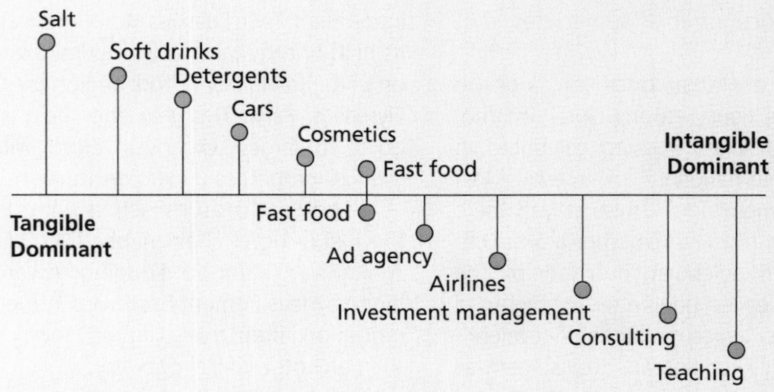
Salt
Soft drinks
Detergents
Cars
Cosmetics
Fast food
Intangible Dominant
Tangible Dominant
Fast food
Ad agency
Airlines
Investment management
Consulting
Teaching

Source: G. Lynn Shostack, "Breaking Free from Product Marketing," *Journal of Marketing* 41 (April 1977), p. 77. Reprinted with permission by the American Marketing Association.

Services, such as insurance services, account for a large proportion of Canada's economic activity.

types of product properties are attached to every good or service: **search qualities**, **experience qualities**, and **credence qualities**.[4] Products that can be physically examined and compared are high in search qualities. Household furniture is high in search qualities. Others are primarily assessed on the basis of the experience of using them. They include a large proportion of both tangible and intangible attributes. A meal at a fine restaurant or a musical performance are both high in experience qualities. Products with credence qualities are those for which, even after purchasing, the buyer must simply trust that the supplier has performed the correct service. Car repairs, medical procedures, and most professional services are high in credence qualities. Figure 12.2 shows this range of product properties. In intangibles, credence (buying a promise) and experience qualities dominate, while search qualities are central for tangible products.

## CHARACTERISTICS OF SERVICES

Four unique characteristics of services distinguish them from goods: intangibility, inseparability of production and consumption, heterogenetiy, and perishability.

### Intangibility

Unlike goods, which can be displayed before the sale, services cannot be seen, smelled, or touched. The student who goes to a counsellor for assistance in deciding what kind of a career to choose cannot foretell the result of that counselling service. Intangibility means that services have no physical substance. J. Bateson believes that besides being physically intangible, services can also be mentally intangible, because it is sometimes hard for the human mind to grasp them.[5]

**search qualities**
Physical qualities that enable products to be examined and compared. This eases the task of choosing among them.

**experience qualities**
Characteristics of products that can be assessed mainly through using them.

**credence qualities**
Qualities for which, even after purchasing, the buyer must simply trust that the supplier has performed the correct service.

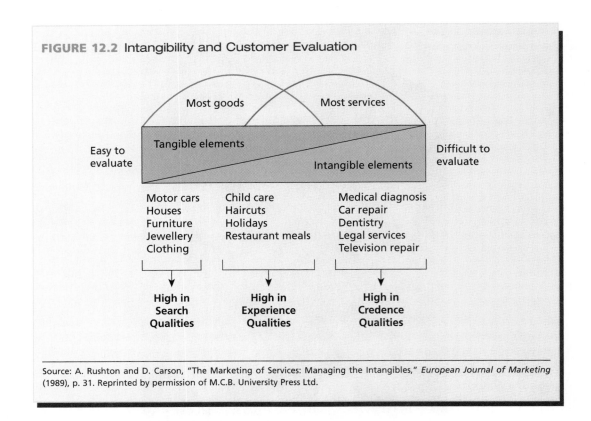

**FIGURE 12.2** Intangibility and Customer Evaluation

Most goods

Most services

Easy to evaluate

Tangible elements

Intangible elements

Difficult to evaluate

| Motor cars | Child care | Medical diagnosis |
| Houses | Haircuts | Car repair |
| Furniture | Holidays | Dentistry |
| Jewellery | Restaurant meals | Legal services |
| Clothing | | Television repair |

**High in Search Qualities**

**High in Experience Qualities**

**High in Credence Qualities**

Source: A. Rushton and D. Carson, "The Marketing of Services: Managing the Intangibles," *European Journal of Marketing* (1989), p. 31. Reprinted by permission of M.C.B. University Press Ltd.

The intangibility of services creates a number of marketing problems:

- *Services cannot be stored.* An Air Canada plane provides a transportation service for 90 people to fly from Montreal to Vancouver. Revenue from empty seats is lost forever.
- *Services cannot be protected through patents.* Patents apply to physical objects. Thus, because they are intangible, services are ineligible for patents. This can create a real problem for a services marketer, since the service can easily be copied.
- *It is hard to readily display or communicate services.* It is easy to show a good, allowing potential customers to hold, handle, or try it out before purchase. That way, they can get a good idea of whether or not the good will satisfy their needs. In the case of a service, a purchaser must purchase in order to experience it.

Playland is really selling an experience to its customers.

- *Prices are difficult to set.* At the best of times, pricing is complex. In the case of a good, each of its components can be costed out, which helps in determining what it is worth. Costing out, say, an accountant's services proves to be much more complex.

A second complicating factor is that a very high proportion of the cost of some services is fixed. The cost of performing one additional service can be virtually zero. The seat on the Air Canada flight mentioned earlier is a good example. If there is an empty seat on the flight just before takeoff, it costs the airline practically nothing to accept an additional passenger. That's one reason stand-by tickets—when the passenger flies only if there is an available seat—can be so much cheaper than the regular fare.

The difficulty facing the marketer is to find a price that is low enough to encourage near-maximum usage but high enough to cover all costs over time. Airlines use differential pricing—charging different types of customers different amounts—to try to accomplish this end.

### Marketing Strategies to Solve the Problems of Intangibility

Some of the problems facing service providers cannot be avoided. But certain marketing strategies can help resolve others, particularly the problem of marketing communication. Because services are so intangible, many marketers *stress tangible cues* in advertising and selling. For example, advertisements for long-distance phone calling dramatize the pleasure on the face of a loved one receiving a call. Marketing messages should also *use personal sources more than nonpersonal sources.* Thus a recommendation for life insurance would likely be more persuasive if it came from John Hanchuck, rather than the more impersonal Life Insurance Council. The personal source adds tangibility to the service.

Service marketers also have found that it is helpful to *stimulate word-of-mouth communications.* If a purchaser can be induced—through the superior service received or by other incentives—to speak to friends and acquaintances positively about a service, that service will tend to be purchased by those people. *Engaging in postpurchase communications* is a related useful strategy. For example, a provider of financial counselling services might write a letter to a new client assuring the client of the wise choices she or he made.

Services marketers also try to *create a strong image* of their organization. This is a very important approach affecting the choice of a service. Since potential purchasers cannot physically evaluate the product that is offered, they may be reassured that they are purchasing a service from a well-known organization.

Finally, with respect to the difficulty of setting prices, it has been found useful to *develop a strong cost accounting system.* Such a system enables an accurate and realistic analysis of various costs involved in the operation. This information provides a strong foundation for setting the ultimate price of the service.

## Inseparability of Production and Consumption

Goods are first produced, then sold, and then consumed, but services are first sold, then produced and consumed simultaneously.[6] For services then, production and consumption are said to be inseparable. The customer therefore has an active role during production of the service. For instance, professional legal counselling is consumed at the same time as the service of providing legal advice is performed. The client raises questions, seeks opinions, and responds with the details required by the lawyer.

The **inseparability** of production and consumption also results in marketing problems:

**inseparability**
A characteristic of services in which the product is produced and consumed simultaneously.

- *Consumers are involved in production.* Performance depends on the quality of input from the customer, as well as on the relationship between the customer and the provider.

- *Other consumers are involved in production.* Many services are offered in a setting with other people present. For example, the service provided by a restaurant server is performed not just for one customer, but for many simultaneously. This fact can have a number of positive and negative influences on the service actually experienced by an individual buyer. For instance, the presence of others can distract a server, or create so much pressure that service is negatively affected.

■ *Centralized mass production of services is difficult.* Services are normally provided where the people are. Whereas Honda might have one or two factories to serve the entire country, Royal Bank must have many "little factories" (branches) in each city. Cost efficiencies and standardization are therefore difficult to achieve because there are so many producers (people) involved.

## Marketing Strategies to Solve the Problems of Inseparability

With services, since production and consumption occur simultaneously and in the same place, production personnel have a tremendous impact on consumers' perceptions of product acceptability. It is therefore essential to *emphasize the selection and training of public-contact personnel.* Personnel not only have to perform the service well, but must be able to interact positively with the customer. The famous Avis "We Try Harder" program was based on this principle.

*Multisite locations* may help offset the fact that services cannot be "sent" from a warehouse to a retail outlet. Banking, travel counselling, and other such services must be produced and consumed where consumers shop. Developing, managing, and maintaining so many locations is a major task for the marketer. This is one of the reasons why employment in the service sector is so high.

*Managing customer flows* also helps to make the "inseparability" condition positive for both buyer and seller. Customer flows can be facilitated by guiding, directing, and expediting their movements and interactions in the service situation. For example, banks channel the flow of customers to tellers through specially laid-out queues. Restaurants provide chairs for customers, or seat them in lounges, while they wait for a table to become available.

A musical performance is inseparable: it is produced and consumed simultaneously. Web sites, such as CBC's ArtsCanada site, attempt to overcome inseparabiliity by providing artistic entertainment, and other arts-related services, on demand.

Increasingly, the Internet is being used to bring service providers and customers together. For example, the Bank of Montreal has created Mbanx, a bank that exists only on-line.

www.mbanx.com

## Heterogeneity

Services are highly variable. Heterogeneity means that each service performance is different than other service performances. Because they are performed by a provider who is a fallible human being, services are difficult to standardize. Service providers can vary in skill and training, and individual performance can vary from day to day. Furthermore, performance varies from individual to individual. A customer may pay the same price for a haircut at the same shop on subsequent dates from two different people—or even the same person—and experience far different outcomes.

The main marketing problem arising from heterogeneity is that standardization and quality control are difficult to achieve. Services marketers try to overcome this problem by industrializing the service or customizing it. To industrialize a service, Theodore Levitt has suggested substituting organized, preplanned systems for individual service operations. For example, a travel agency could offer prepackaged vacation tours to remove the need for the selling, tailoring, and haggling involved in customization.[7] Customization—the opposite of industrialization—is another possible solution. If each service is produced for an individual customer, the problem of standardization disappears.

## Perishability

Because services are produced and consumed similtaneously, they cannot be stored. Because they cannot be stored, services are said to be perishable. No service can be produced before required and then stocked up to meet future demand. Whatever is not used when available is wasted. Unoccupied motel rooms and airline seats and unused telephone line capacity cannot be reclaimed. Because of this, service businesses frequently find it difficult to balance supply and demand. The fact that services cannot be inventoried is a major problem for service providers.

The problem of perishability can be solved to some degree by using strategies to cope with fluctuating demand. Restaurants, airlines, and other service businesses often give special discounts to those who use the service in periods of low demand. This shifts some demand from high to low periods. A second approach to the perishability problem is to make simultaneous adjustments in demand and capacity to achieve a closer match between the two. Capacity can often be increased by adding staff or equipment at peak times. This approach may be used simultaneously with the previous solution.

Table 12.1 summarizes the discussion of features that are unique to services, the resulting marketing problems, and suggested marketing solutions. Ziethaml et al. (from whose important study Table 12.1 is adapted) found that service firms did not view most of the problems as especially serious. The authors speculated that this viewpoint may be founded on the providers' being used to facing these problems, or the problems may not in fact be as significant as they first seem.

# OTHER STRATEGIES IN SERVICES MARKETING

## Internal Marketing

Traditionally, the marketing mix is thought to be oriented toward the external market. While services do face a competitive external environment, they must also be responsive to an internal market—those who provide the service. Since service producers interact so directly with consumers, the way they feel about their task within the marketing strategy is extremely important. In fact, their feelings directly influence the quality of the service they perform. Leonard Berry has suggested that "internal marketing means applying the philosophy and practices of marketing to the

**TABLE 12.1** Unique Service Features and Resulting Marketing Problems and Solutions

| UNIQUE SERVICE FEATURES | RESULTING MARKETING PROBLEMS | MARKETING STRATEGIES TO SOLVE PROBLEMS |
|---|---|---|
| Intangibility | • Service cannot be stored.<br>• Cannot protect services through patents.<br>• Cannot readily display or communicate services.<br>• Prices are difficult to set. | • Stress tangible cues.<br>• Use personal sources more than nonpersonal sources.<br>• Simulate or stimulate word-of-mouth communications.<br>• Create strong organizational image.<br>• Use cost accounting to help set prices.<br>• Engage in postpurchase communications. |
| Inseparability | • Consumer involved in production.<br>• Other consumers involved in production.<br>• Centralized mass production of services difficult. | • Emphasize selection and training of public-contact personnel.<br>• Manage consumers.<br>• Use multisite locations. |
| Heterogeneity | • Standardization and quality control difficult to achieve. | • Industrialize service.<br>• Customize service. |
| Perishability | • Services cannot be inventoried. | • Use strategies to cope with fluctuating demand.<br>• Make simultaneous adjustments in demand and capacity to achieve a closer match between the two. |

Source: Adapted from Valarie A. Zeithaml, A. Parasuraman, and Leonard L. Berry, "Problems and Strategies in Services Marketing," *Journal of Marketing* (Spring 1985), p. 35. Reprinted with permission by the American Marketing Association.

people that serve the external customers so that (1) the best possible people can be employed and retained, and (2) they will do the best possible work."[8]

**internal marketing**

A marketing effort aimed at those who provide the service so that they will feel better about their task and therefore produce a better product.

The objective of the **internal marketing** function is to develop motivated, customer-conscious, market-oriented, and sales-minded employees. The successful service company must first sell the job to its employees before it can sell its services to customers.[9]

The practice of internal marketing has direct human resource management implications. According to Christian Grönroos, a leading European researcher in services marketing, there are three direct consequences of practicing internal marketing:

> employees are a first market, an internal market, for the firm's offerings as well as for its external marketing programs; an active, coordinated and goal-oriented approach to all employee-oriented efforts which combines these internal efforts and processes with the external efficiency of the firm (that is, interactive marketing performance in customer relationships); and an emphasis on the need to view people, functions and departments internal to the firm as internal customers, to whom internal services have to be provided in the same customer-oriented manner as to external customers.[10]

The interaction between the employee, or service provider, and the customer is critical to the success of the service and the satisfaction of the customer. **Interactive marketing** describes this interrelationship between the employee and the customer.

**interactive marketing**
Term used to describe the interrelationship between the employee and the customer.

In total, then, there are actually three aspects of marketing that must take place in order for a service firm to be successful: external marketing, which takes place between the firm and the customer; internal marketing, which takes place between the firm and its employees; and interactive marketing, which takes place between the employees and the customer. External marketing is really making a commitment to customers that certain things will happen in their service encounter. Internal marketing allows that commitment to be carried out. Finally, interactive marketing actually delivers the promise.[11] Figure 12.3, the services marketing triangle, shows that these three tasks are mutually supporting.

## Managing Evidence

As discussed earlier, prospective customers like to associate tangibles with a service for cues as to its quality. Marketers, therefore, must try to manage tangibles to convince customers about the service.

Goods marketing tends to give prime emphasis to creating abstract associations with the product. Services marketers, on the other hand, should focus on enhancing and differentiating the "realities" by manipulating tangible cues. Managing evidence comes first for service marketers.[12] There are several ways that the evidence can be managed.

### The Environment

Services are totally integrated with their environment. The physical setting—where the service is performed—has a great influence on the customer's perception. The physical milieu should be intentionally created so as to provide the appropriate situation-specific atmosphere to impress the customer. For example, even though two lawyers may provide identical services, customers still differentiate between the two by the environmental differences. If one lawyer decorates her office with leather and subdued lighting and the other has a plain painted office with steel-and-formica furniture, customers will judge them accordingly.

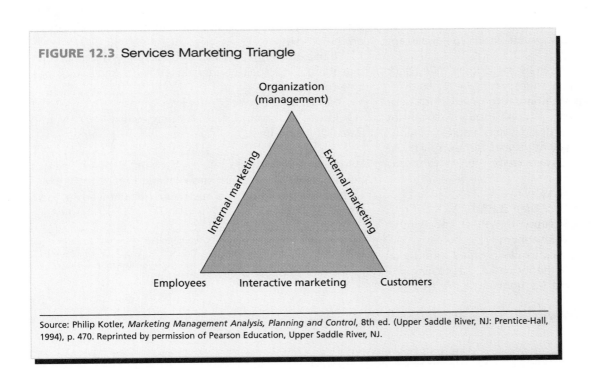

**FIGURE 12.3** Services Marketing Triangle

Source: Philip Kotler, *Marketing Management Analysis, Planning and Control*, 8th ed. (Upper Saddle River, NJ: Prentice-Hall, 1994), p. 470. Reprinted by permission of Pearson Education, Upper Saddle River, NJ.

## RETAILERS ARE STILL WORKING ON SERVICE

The offending screen door lay on the counter, its cardboard sleeve torn in several places—evidence of inexpert repacking at the hands of a customer.

A tribunal of sales clerks stood together, peering down but not touching the door, like judges from the bench assessing an unpleasant exhibit at a criminal trial.

"Did you measure the opening?" one asked, frowning.

The frustrated do-it-yourselfer, who had measured the opening not twice but thrice, considered a sarcastic reply, since custom ordered doors could not be purchased without measurements.

"Yes," he said. "I measured."

Then he pulled a crumpled order form out of his pocket, smoothing it, the paper still damp from the sweaty struggle with the door.

"I ordered a door 28½ inches wide," he said.

He paused, as a confident defence attorney might, still holding the paper.

"This door is 29 inches," he said.

One of the clerks shook her head slowly.

"Twenty eight and a half inches," she said deliberately.

She too, paused.

"Sorry, sir," she said in a voice that conveyed neither sorrow nor respect. "Custom doors only come in standard sizes."

The colliding concepts did not prevent her from completing her judgment.

"You can have a door that's 28 or 29. Not 28½," she said, closing the case.

On appeal, head office would later apologize and even install a new door.

It was, after all, a mistake by the original sales clerk, who didn't know how the product was made. Or sold.

The store had accepted an order for a 28½ inch door. And accepted payment too. No one thought to call the customer to say he had ordered something he couldn't have. Something close was sent instead. But even with the traditional tools of the do-it-yourselfer—brute force and cursing—it wouldn't fit.

What's the point of the story?

Retailers have a problem. Their staff.

"For the first time in history, the buyer knows more than the seller," says Elliott Ettenberg.

He's the marketing executive we profiled recently on *Venture*. He has a gloomy theory about the coming collapse of consumer demand (as boomers age). He's also appalled by the way many retailers deal with their customers.

As in, badly.

"What have we done? We've hired a bunch of young kids who churn out (quit) at 60 per cent a year, who are part time because we don't want to put full time people in there," Ettenberg tells an audience of high-end retailers in New York.

Ettenberg, a Canadian who lives in Quebec and Florida while maintaining an office in New York, surveys the retail landscape of North America and is not impressed. He argues retailers will have to change the way they deal with customers in the future.

"There's no passion for it," he laments. "And in the next economy, you will have to delight your customers."

In his book, *The Next Economy*, Ettenberg argues that most aging baby boomers will start putting away their wallets in a few years.

"How many more houses do you want to own? How much more clothing do you want to own as your life actually simplifies?" he asks.

Ettenberg believes that boomers will have almost everything they need. So retailers will need highly trained, highly motivated salespeople to coax aging boomers to buy luxuries they might want.

But will big retailers, like the big box hardware chain with the custom door problem, be willing to spend on staff and training, reinventing their standards of customer service?

"It will be a major survival issue for big companies in the near future," writes Ettenberg in his book. "My bet is on the little guy."

That's not a final verdict. But Ettenberg is sure about one thing. Underpaid, undertrained sales staff won't be able to deliver.

"It just doesn't work," says Ettenberg.

Just as a custom door that's only available in a standard size won't fit.

**What steps would you take to prevent a recurrence of his problem? How might internal marketing have prevented the situation the customer experienced in this story?**

Source: Adapted from Havard Gould, "Coming Soon to a Store Near You (If We're Lucky): A Retail Experience That Will Delight" broadcast on *Venture*, CBC Television. Copyright © Canadian Broadcasting Corporation. http://www.cbc.ca/business/indepth/ettenberg_gould.html

## Appearance of Service Providers

The appearance of service providers also affects customers' perception of the product. Salespeople in an optical shop who wear white lab coats look more "professional" than those with ordinary attire.

## Service Pricing

Research confirms that there is a high tendency for customers to perceive a direct relationship between price and quality of service.[13] Price is seen as an index of quality. Professional practitioners may charge an unusually high price for their services in order to assure clients. Setting the right price can be critical in differentiating one service from the crowd.

# Quality in Services Marketing

Quality in services marketing is generally defined as the degree that customers' experiences match or exceed their expectations. If there is a match, the service is of high quality. If there is a gap between customers' expectations and their experiences, the service is of low quality.[14] One of the primary reasons for the success of McDonald's over the years has been its ability to clearly set, and then meet, customer expectations. If you go to a McDonald's you expect a clean facility, quick service, consistent food served at the appropriate temperature, and a relatively low price. The majority of the time, that's exactly what you get.

An experience-based definition implies that quality is somewhat specific to an institution, or at least a type of institution. For example, from a marketing point of view, the McDonald's that meets your expectations is of higher quality than the upscale restaurant that fails to meet your expectations.

Figure 12.4 illustrates how gaps between customer expectations and experiences can occur. Initial expectations of the customer are a result of word-of-mouth communications, personal needs, and past experience. The gap between customer expectations and perceived service (Gap 5) actually results from four other gaps. Gap 1 is the difference between what customers want from a service and what management *thinks* they want. Reducing Gap 1 involves increasing formal and informal market research.

Gap 2 is the difference between management's understanding of customer expectations and how the service is actually designed. Management may be aware of customer expectations or desires but be unable or unwilling to meet those desires. Many passengers who fly economy class would like, and first-time flyers may innocently expect, more spacious seating. To meet that expectation, though, would reduce the capacity of the airplane and consequently be prohibitively expensive.

Gap 3 is the difference between how management designed the service and how it is actually delivered. Service delivery personnel may not agree with management specifications, may not understand them, or may be unable to fully implement them. The Practising Marketer box, "Retailers Are Still Working on Service," is really describing a Gap 3 problem. No retail owner or manager intends that customers encounter the type of frustration described in the box. But it seems to happen anyway.

Gap 4 is the difference between the service and what management has communicated about the service through advertising and other promotions. Overpromising is a particular problem for service industries. A video store that promises to have current titles always in stock and then doesn't creates greater dissatisfaction than if the promise had not been made at all.

The final gap, Gap 5, is the net effect of the other four gaps. If they are small, customers' perceptions should be close to their expectations. If the other gaps are large, customers' perceptions will not match their expectations and they will judge the service provider to have low quality. Figure 12.5 summarizes the five gaps.

w(W)w

www.mcdonalds.com/
countries/canada/index.html

## FIGURE 12.4 A Model of Service Quality

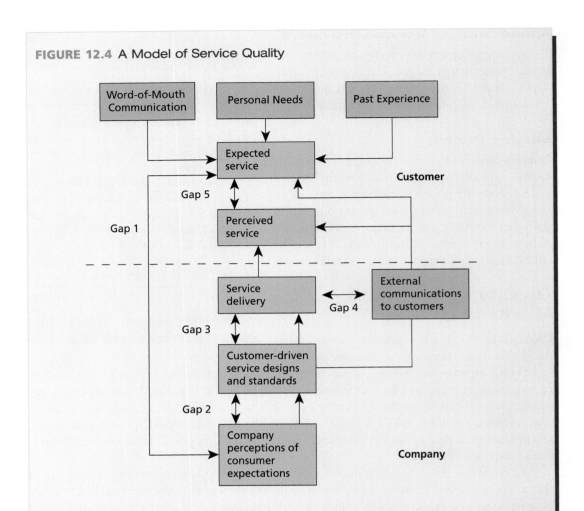

Source: A. Parasuraman, Valarie Zeithaml, and Leonard Berry, "A Conceptual Model of Service Quality and Its Implications for Future Research," *Journal of Marketing* 49 (Fall 1985), p. 44. Reprinted with permission by the American Marketing Association.

## FIGURE 12.5 Summary of the Five Gaps

| Gap | Cause |
|---|---|
| 1 | Not knowing what the customer expects |
| 2 | Not developing the right service design |
| 3 | Not delivering to service standards |
| 4 | Not matching performance to promises |
| 5 | Not matching experience with expectations |

# Organizational Responsibility for Marketing

In many service firms, the organizational responsibility for marketing may be considerably different than in manufacturing companies. In any company there may be confusion about what marketing is. It is frequently considered to be what the marketing department does. Marketing is, however, often carried out by others in the company to some degree. This confusion may be much more acute for service firms than for manufacturing firms, and may in fact constitute an organizational dilemma. In many professional service organizations, the marketing department's role may be lim-

---

## THE INFORMED CONSUMER

### THE CASE FOR COMPLAINING IN A RESTAURANT

Many friends, colleagues and acquaintances who are assertive, articulate and outspoken turn into wimps when we dine out. When the chicken is dry or the service is inadequate, they can't seem to muster the courage to complain. I don't understand why they find this so difficult.

All the professionals I've spoken with in the restaurant industry swear they want to know the truth when they wander over to ask, "How is everything this evening?" But they know people lie to them—and they told me how they spot the liars. They say they'd prefer to be given a chance to fix a problem than to see a customer leave the restaurant unhappy. Unfortunately, they're seldom given that chance.

Some people have told me they say everything is okay when it's not because they don't believe the waiter really wants to know when something goes wrong. I don't think that's a reason to clam up. If you're paying a lot of money for dinner, you have every right to expect a good experience and you certainly shouldn't return to a restaurant that doesn't handle your complaint properly. My own experience is that the vast majority of foodservice professionals do care what you think.

So why are people afraid to complain? Sometimes they're intimidated—by the menu, by the posh surroundings or by the uniformed servers—and sometimes they're afraid of a confrontation. Will the chef be insulted if the plate goes back to the kitchen? However, when I've questioned people more closely, what inevitably comes out is that they're afraid of being branded as a "troublemaker" or a "complainer." Some people see that as a negative thing, but the irony is that a good restaurateur loves complainers.

I prefer to think of a complaint as a gift to the restaurant, and the professionals I spoke with agree. What's critical is that you do it in the right way. There's no need to raise your voice or to be angry. Be polite, stay calm and explain the problem as clearly as you can. If you're unhappy with the food, speak up right away. It's bad form to say you didn't enjoy your meal after you've licked your plate clean.

You may not want to spoil the mood of the evening.

In that case, excuse yourself from the table and discreetly seek out the waiter or maitre d'. And if it's a very special occasion or a business meeting, you may not want to focus any attention on your unhappiness with the meal.

Try this: as you're leaving the restaurant, inform the maitre d' that you'll be calling the next day because you were unhappy about something. Before you phone, think about what kind of recourse you want. For example, would you like to give the restaurant a second chance or do you want some money back because you were overcharged?

I don't believe in leaving a small tip for bad service. That only sends a message that you're a cheapskate. Again, it's important to speak up early and give the restaurant a chance to fix the problem; but if that doesn't work, my own policy is to leave no tip at all and write the words "service unacceptable" across the bill.

In the eyes of restaurateurs, some customers fall into the category called "impossible to please." If you have a complaint, be prepared to accept a reasonable solution. And watch out for minefields. It might be wise to order something else if you request the venison steak well-done and the waiter says it might not be tender if it's cooked that way.

Ultimately, it's important to have courage. If something isn't right with your restaurant experience and you say nothing, you're guaranteed to be unhappy as you leave. If you speak up, you may salvage your meal and your evening—and you'll be giving the restaurant a chance to turn a negative experience into a positive one.

Just try it.

**Have you ever complained in a restaurant about the service or food, or both. If yes, what was the reaction? Why should restaurant managers (and other service providers) look on complaints as a "gift"? How does this discussion relate to the Gap model of service quality?**

Source: Adapted from Talin Vartanian "The Case for Complaining in a Restaurant," broadcast on *Marketplace*, Feb. 27, 2002, CBC Television. Copyright © Canadian Broadcasting Corporation. http://www.cbc.ca/consumers/citizentalin/tips_restaurant.html

ited to handling advertising, sales promotion, and some public relations. The "sales force" comprises those people who are in direct contact with customers (for example, the branch managers and tellers in a bank). Except for the people in the marketing department, however, staff members are not hired for their marketing know-how but for their ability to produce services. *Yet the person who produces a service must also be able to market that service.* In most cases, what is needed is not professional salespeople but service workers who sell—in effect, producer-sellers.

The dilemma arises when service firms are insufficiently aware of the need to have personnel who can adequately perform both marketing and service-production functions. Furthermore, when the workload is high, too little time may be spent on marketing—an imbalance that will likely have very serious long-term consequences for the organization.

This overview of services concludes our discussion of products. The reader should remember that the term "product" includes services as well as goods. Life-cycle analysis, as well as product classification systems and other product management processes, can be applied to all products. The next two chapters consider issues concerning price, another element of the marketing mix.

## SUMMARY

A service is a product without physical characteristics—a bundle of performance and symbolic attributes designed to produce consumer want satisfaction. Buyers of services are often buying promises.

Most products have both tangible and intangible attributes. Tangible goods tend to be high in search qualities, mixed goods high in experience qualities, and intangible goods in credence qualities. Marketers of services must try to manage tangibles to convince customers, as these attributes serve as cues to customers about service quality.

Four characteristics of services distinguish them from goods: intangibility, inseparability of production and consumption, heterogeneity, and perishability.

In addition to marketing to target market customers, services often have to be marketed internally to employees. The employees in turn engage in interactive marketing with customers. External marketing, internal marketing, and interactive marketing make up the services marketing triangle.

## KEY TERMS

credence qualities, p. 303
experience qualities, p. 303
inseparability, p. 305
intangible attributes, p. 302
interactive marketing, p. 309

internal marketing, p. 309
search qualities, p. 303
service, p. 302
tangible attributes, p. 302

## INTERACTIVE SUMMARY AND DISCUSSION QUESTIONS

1. A service is a product without physical characteristics—a bundle of performance and symbolic attributes designed to produce consumer want satisfaction. Use banking services to explain this definition.
2. Many products have both tangible and intangible attributes. Select three products not discussed in this chapter, and identify for each both types of attributes.
3. Buyers of services are often buying promises. Explain this statement.
4. Four characteristics of services distinguish them from goods: intangibility, inseparability of production and consumption, heterogeneity, and perishability. Explain each of these characteristics.
5. Suggest some marketing strategies to take account of each of the characteristics listed in question 4.

6. In addition to marketing to target market customers, services often have to be marketed internally. Why?

7. Marketers of services must try to manage tangibles to convince customers about the services. Give some examples.

8. Organizational responsibility for marketing services goes beyond those people who are charged with marketing planning. The person who produces a service must also be able to market that service. Why? How can this requirement be implemented?

9. Describe the last transportation service you purchased. What was your impression of the way it was marketed? How could the firm's marketing effort have been improved?

10. Identify three or four service firms, and propose methods they could use to overcome problems with the perishability of their respective services.

11. Visit Merrill Lynch and Apple Canada on the Web. What differences do you see between the two sites? How do these differences relate to some of the unique qualities of their services?

www.ml.com

www.apple.ca

# Case

## Second Cup Ends Incentive Program

Second Cup has cancelled its Coffee Club card program in Quebec, the first step in a plan to wind down the customer loyalty initiative across the country, the company confirmed recently.

The decision marks the first major strategic change by the specialty coffee retailer since becoming a wholly-owned subsidiary of Cara Operations Ltd., Canada's largest restaurant conglomerate and owner of the Swiss Chalet and Harvey's chains.

It comes as numerous retailers and food-service providers are retooling or dropping older loyalty programs, which do not collect information about the customers who frequent their businesses.

While acknowledging the 20-year-old program was one of the best known of its kind in Canada, Second Cup officials view the cards as outmoded. The card gave a free 12-oz. cup of brewed coffee after six purchases.

Outlets in Quebec stopped giving cards this week and will end the program in about a month's time. Across Canada, the cafés will likely stop accepting the cards by year's end, said Mike Arseneault, director of marketing for the 400-outlet chain.

"We talked to customers and franchisees, and [the card] was pretty low on the list of reasons driving people to come to Second Cup," he said. "It's time to look into new technologies to find ways to reward people for their patronage."

www.secondcup.com

But industry experts cautioned such a move stands to alienate customers.

"The cost of giving someone a free coffee is negligible," said Anthony Stokan, a Toronto retail and marketing consultant, who said customers are most likely to be loyal because of service, product quality, and convenience, but freebies certainly don't hurt.

"I am a great advocate of simple programs that reward consumers without expecting anything in return. It would be remiss of any retailer to say that doesn't drive loyalty from consumers, and there's an inherent risk factor in not rewarding people if you created the expectation in the first place."

Modern loyalty programs are seen by retailers primarily as a way to mine consumers for information about buying preferences. Programs such as Shoppers Drug Mart's Optimum plan track key information about shopping habits.

### You Be the Marketer

1. Is Second Cup making a wise move?
2. How would you predict this action will affect customers' evaluations of their experience at Second Cup?
3. Would you expect overall satisfaction to go down, up, or be unchanged?
4. If you were the national marketing manager for Second Cup, what action would you take?

Source: Excerpted from Hollie Shaw, "Second Cup Winds Down Loyalty Cards, End to Free Coffee," *Financial Post*, Friday, August 2, 2002. http://www.nationalpost.com/financialpost/story.html?id={5591B750-F75E-4CD7-9D84-80B8B7D52021}. Reprinted with permission.

# 13

# UNDERSTANDING PRICING

Japanese electronics and entertainment giant Sony Corp. slashed the U.S. price of its PlayStation 2 video-game machine to $199, underpricing its biggest rival, Microsoft Corp.'s Xbox, by $100.

Sony's popular game console, which has sold more than 30 million worldwide, had been selling in the United States for $299. Sony also lowered the price of the less advanced PS One Console to $49 from $99.

Ken Kutaragi, president of Sony Computer Entertainment, the video-game unit of Sony, said the PlayStation 2 controls 82 percent of the highly sought-after video-game market. The lower price underlines Sony's determination to stay on top of rivals Microsoft and Nintendo.

Sony released PlayStation 2 in late 2000, a full year before Microsoft and Nintendo shipped their versions. More than 1.5 million Xbox machines have been sold in the United States since they arrived in stores in November. Nintendo has sold more than 2.7 million GameCube consoles worldwide, about half of those in Japan.

GameCube sells for $199 in the United States, while Xbox sells for $299.

In Japan, the PlayStation 2 has been selling for $230. Kutaragi said the machine will now go for an "open" price in Japan, meaning it likely will be discounted at some stores.

**Pricing decisions are an extremely important part of the marketing mix. Price has the most immediate and direct impact on overall profitability. It is also the only component of the marketing mix that can be changed quickly. Prices often change over the life cycle of a product. As Sony realizes, many things can affect the appropriateness of a particular price. Along with knowing what the customer is willing to pay, competitive activity, industry capacity, international currency strength, and general economic health, to name but a few factors, can all affect the pricing decision.**

**A price that is well set strengthens a firm's position in the marketplace. Pricing mistakes, on the other hand, can be disastrous.**

---

www.sony.ca

# INTRODUCTION

The first critical element of a firm's marketing mix is the design and management of the goods and services to offer the target market. Price is the second element of the marketing mix. Determining profitable and justified prices is the result of pricing objectives and various approaches to setting prices, the topics of this chapter. This chapter focuses on the economic foundations of pricing. It discusses three basic approaches to establishing a price and also looks at the special situations of industrial pricing and the pricing of public services. The starting place for examining pricing strategy is to understand the meaning of the term *price*.

**price**
The value that a buyer exchanges for a good or service.

**Price** is the value that a buyer exchanges for a good or service. Value is ultimately determined by customers. In earlier times, the price of an acre of land might have been twenty bushels of wheat, three cattle, or a boat. Price is a measure of what one must exchange in order to obtain a desired good or service. When the barter process was abandoned in favour of a monetary system, price became the amount of money required to purchase an item. As David Schwartz has pointed out, contemporary society uses a number of terms to refer to price:

> Price is all around us. You pay *rent* for your apartment, *tuition* for your education, and a *fee* to your physician or dentist.
> The airline, railway, taxi, and bus companies charge you a *fare;* the local utilities call their price a *rate;* and the local bank charges you *interest* for the money you borrow.
> The price for taking your car on the ferry to Prince Edward Island or Vancouver Island is a *toll,* and the company that insures your car charges you a *premium.*
> Clubs or societies to which you belong may make a special *assessment* to pay unusual expenses. Your regular lawyer may ask for a *retainer* to cover her services.
> The "price" of an executive is a *salary;* the price of a salesperson may be a *commission;* and the price of a worker is a *wage.*
> Finally, although economists would disagree, many of us feel that *income taxes* are the price we pay for the privilege of making money.[1]

**utility**
The want-satisfying power of a product or service.

All products have some degree of **utility**, or want-satisfying power. While one individual might be willing to exchange the utility derived from a colour television for a vacation, another may not be willing to make that exchange. Prices are a mechanism that allows the customer to make a decision. In contemporary society, of course, prices are translated into monetary terms. Customers evaluate the utility derived from a range of possible purchases and then allocate their exchange power (in monetary terms) so as to maximize satisfaction. Pricing may be the most complicated aspect of the marketing manager's job. It is somewhat difficult to determine the price needed to realize a profit. But an even greater problem is that of determining a price that customers will respond to positively and that can be maintained in a competitive environment.

Price is fundamental to many aspects of the economic system. Price often serves as a means of regulating economic activity. The employment of any or all of the four factors of production (land, labour, capital, and entrepreneurship) depends on the price received by each.

For an individual firm, prices (along with the corresponding quantity that will be sold) determine the revenue to be received. Prices, therefore, influence a company's profit as well as its use of the factors of production. Early written accounts refer to attempts to develop a fair, or just, price. The "fair price" differs dramatically depending on one's perspective. If you are buying gasoline in Thunder Bay during daylight hours, you will have one set of criteria to judge whether the price is fair. If you are driving late at night on a deserted highway north of Lake Superior, and the tank is nearly empty, you will have a different price perception.

# PRICE DETERMINATION

There are three general approaches to determining price. One is price derivation, which is based on theoretical economic analysis. A second is the cost-plus approach, where the costs of producing the product are determined, and a margin of profit is added on. The third method, discussed in

Chapter 14, is the marketing approach. The marketing approach is built on aspects of the economic-analysis and cost-plus methods, and adds an important marketing dimension to come up with a realistic price.

# PRICE DETERMINATION IN ECONOMIC THEORY

Few businesses follow economic theory strictly in setting prices. Because of this, some students ask why we should bother with reviewing the economic approach to pricing. The reason is that *the concepts of economic price theory are essential to other pricing approaches, and they apply to almost any pricing situation.* These concepts are important building blocks that help us understand what is happening in a particular pricing situation.

The microeconomic approach, or price theory, assumes a profit maximization objective and leads to deriving correct equilibrium prices in the marketplace. Because price theory considers both demand and supply factors it is a more complete analysis than what is typically found in practice.

*Demand* refers to a schedule of the amounts of a firm's product or service that consumers will purchase at different prices during a specific period. *Supply* refers to a schedule of the amounts of a product or service that will be offered for sale at different prices during a specified time period. These schedules may vary for different types of market structures.

## Market Structures

There are four types of market structure: pure competition, monopolistic competition, oligopoly, and monopoly. Very briefly, **pure competition** is a market structure in which there is such a large number of buyers and sellers that no one of them has a significant influence on price. Other characteristics of pure competition include a homogeneous product and ease of entry for sellers, and complete and instantaneous information. This marketing structure is largely theoretical in contemporary society; however, some uncontrolled sectors of the agricultural commodity sector exhibit many of the characteristics of such a market, and provide the closest example of it.

**Monopolistic competition** is also a market structure with a large number of buyers and sellers. However, in this market there is some degree of heterogeneity in good and/or service, that is, customers can distinguish one producer's product from another's. There also is usually geographical differentiation. Because customers can distinguish between the companies, they will form preferences for one company's product or service over another's product or service. The existence of differentiation allows the marketer some degree of control over price. Most retail stores fall into this category, which partially explains why some small retailers can exist with prices 5 to 10 percent higher than their larger competitors.

An **oligopoly** is a market structure in which there are relatively few sellers. Each seller may affect the market, but no one seller controls it. Examples are the car, steel, tobacco, and petroleum-refining industries. High start-up costs create significant entry barriers, making it extremely difficult for new competitors to enter the market. **Oligopsony** is the other side of the coin: a market in which there are only a few buyers.

A **monopoly** is a market structure with only one seller of a product with no close substitutes. Anticombines legislation has tended to eliminate all but *temporary* monopolies, such as those provided by patent protection, and *regulated* monopolies, such as the public utilities (electricity, gas). Regulated monopolies are granted by government in markets where competition would lead to an uneconomic duplication of services. In return for this monopoly, government regulates the monopoly rate of return through regulatory bodies such as the Canadian Transport Commission, the Canadian Radio-television and Telecommunications Commission, the National Farm Products Marketing Council, and provincial public utility regulatory commissions. In recent years even some long-standing monopolies, such as electricity providers, are losing their monopoly status.

**pure competition**
A market structure in which there is such a large number of buyers and sellers that no one of them has a significant influence on price.

**monopolistic competition**
A market structure with a large number of buyers and sellers where heterogeneity in good and/or service and usually geographical differentiation allow the marketer some control over price.

**oligopoly**
A market structure in which there are relatively few sellers.

**oligopsony**
A market in which there are only a few buyers.

**monopoly**
A market structure with only one seller of a product with no close substitutes.

The automobile manufac-
turing industry is an oligopoly: a market structure in
which there are relatively few
sellers.

## Revenue, Cost, and Supply Curves

Economic approaches to pricing focus on the elements of demand, costs, and supply within each of
these market structures. The demand side of price theory is concerned with *revenue curves*. A revenue curve is simply the amount of revenue earned by selling a particular quantity of a product at
a particular price. *Average revenue* (AR) is obtained by dividing *total revenue* (TR) by the *quantity*
(Q) associated with these revenues:

$$AR = \frac{TR}{Q}$$

The plotted average revenue line is actually the demand curve facing the firm. *Marginal revenue*
(MR) is the change in total revenue ($\Delta$TR) that results from selling an additional unit of output
($\Delta$Q). This can be shown as

$$MR = \frac{\Delta TR}{\Delta Q}$$

To complete the analysis, the supply curves must be determined for each of these market situations. A firm's cost structure determines its supply curves. Let us examine each of the cost curves that
apply to price determination.

**Average cost** (AC) is obtained by dividing total cost by the quantity (Q) associated with the total
cost. *Total cost* (TC) is composed of both fixed and variable components. *Fixed costs* are those costs
that do not vary with differences in output, while *variable costs* are those that change when the level
of production is altered. Examples of fixed costs include executive compensation, depreciation, and
insurance. Variable costs include raw materials and the wages paid to production workers.

**Average variable cost** (AVC) is simply the total variable cost (TVC) divided by the related quantity. Similarly, *average fixed cost* (AFC) is determined by dividing total fixed costs (TFC) by the related
quantity. **Marginal cost** (MC) is the change in total cost ($\Delta$TC) that results from producing an additional unit of output ($\Delta$Q). Thus, it is similar to *marginal revenue,* which is the change in total rev-

**average cost**
Obtained by dividing total
cost by the quantity associated with this cost.

**average variable cost**
The total variable cost
divided by the related
quantity.

**marginal cost**
The change in total cost
that results from producing
an additional unit of
output.

Samsung's marginal cost for their microwaves is the cost to them of producing one more microwave oven.

enue resulting from the production of an incremental unit. The point of profit maximization is where marginal costs are equal to marginal revenues.

These cost derivations are shown in the following formulas:

$$AC = \frac{TC}{Q} \qquad\qquad AFC = \frac{TFC}{Q}$$

$$AVC = \frac{TVC}{Q} \qquad\qquad MC = \frac{\Delta TC}{\Delta Q}$$

The resulting *cost curves* are shown in Figure 13.1. The marginal cost curve (MC) intersects the average variable cost curve (AVC) and average cost curve (AC) at their minimum points.

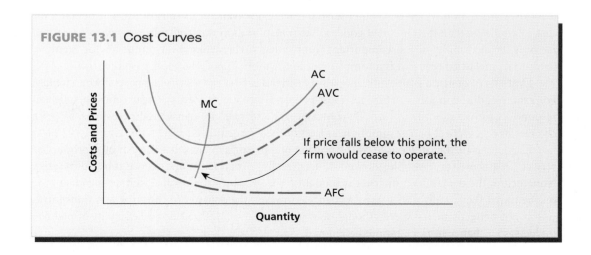

**FIGURE 13.1 Cost Curves**

supply curve

The marginal cost curve above its intersection with average variable cost.

In the short run, a firm will continue to operate even if the price falls below AC, provided it remains above AVC. Why is this rational market behaviour? If the firm were to cease operations after the price fell below AC, it would still have some fixed costs, but *no revenue*. Any amount received above AVC can be used to cover fixed costs. The firm is acting rationally by continuing to produce as long as price exceeds AVC, since this minimizes losses. If price falls below AVC, the firm would cease operations, because continued operation would result in real losses from out-of-pocket costs per unit, with no control of fixed costs. Therefore, the **supply curve**, or the amount of a product that firm is willing to produce, is the marginal cost curve above its intersection with AVC, since this is the area of rational pricing behaviour for the firm.

# The Concept of Elasticity in Pricing Strategy

Although the intersection of demand and supply curves determines the equilibrium price for each of the market structures, the specific curves vary. To understand why, it is necessary to understand the concept of elasticity.[2]

elasticity

A measure of the responsiveness of purchasers and suppliers to changes in price.

**Elasticity** is a measure of the responsiveness of purchasers and suppliers to changes in price. The *price elasticity of demand* is the percentage change in the quantity of a product or service demanded divided by the percentage change in its price. A 10 percent increase in the price of eggs that results in a 5 percent decrease in the quantity of eggs demanded yields a price elasticity of demand for eggs of 0.5.

## Elasticity Terminology

Consider a case in which a 1 percent change in price causes more than a 1 percent change in the quantity supplied or demanded. Numerically, that means an elasticity greater than 1.0. When the elasticity of demand or supply is greater than 1.0, it is termed *elastic* and is considered sensitive to price changes.

If a 1 percent change in price results in less than a 1 percent change in quantity, a good's elasticity of supply or demand will be numerically less than 1.0 and is called *inelastic* and is considered insensitive to price changes. The demand for eggs in the example above is inelastic. Similarly, gasoline prices can fluctuate quite widely; however, the resulting change in total sales is minimal.

An extreme case occurs when the quantity supplied or demanded does not change at all when the price changes. Then the supply or demand is called *perfectly inelastic*.

The case in which a 1 percent change in price results in exactly a 1 percent change in quantity is called *unit* (or *unitary*) *elastic*.

## Determinants of Elasticity

Why is the elasticity of supply or demand high for some goods and services and low for others? What constitutes the specific determinants of demand elasticity?[3]

One factor that determines the elasticity of demand is the availability of substitutes. If a product or service has close substitutes, the demand tends to be elastic. The demand for olive oil, for instance, is more elastic than it would be if other salad oils were not available as substitutes. The demand for cars is less elastic than it would be if good public transportation was available everywhere. A related factor is the availability of more important complements. The demand for motor oil, for example, tends to be inelastic because it is a complement to the more important good, gasoline.

Elasticity of demand is also influenced by whether a product or service is a necessity or a luxury. For example, dining out is a luxury for most people. If restaurant prices increase, most people can respond by eating at home instead. By contrast, eggs and milk are considered necessities, so price changes have less effect on consumption, at least in the short run.

Elasticity is further influenced by the portion of a person's budget that is spent on a product or service. Matches, for example, are no longer really a necessity, and good substitutes exist. Nonetheless, the demand for matches is thought to be very inelastic because people spend so little on them that they hardly notice a price change. However, the demand for housing and transportation is not perfectly inelastic even though they are necessities. Both occupy a large part of people's budgets, so a change in price cannot be ignored.

Elasticity of demand is also affected by the time perspective under consideration. Demand is often less elastic in the short run than in the long run. Consider the demand for home heating fuel. In the short run, when the price goes up, people find it difficult to cut back on the quantity they use. They are accustomed to living at a certain temperature, dressing a certain way, and so forth. Given time, though, they may find ways to economize. They can better insulate their homes, form new habits of dressing more warmly, or even move to a warmer climate.

All the factors mentioned here are only tendencies, yet often the tendencies reinforce one another. The classic case of inelastic demand is salt, which has no good substitute, is a nutritional necessity, and uses a very small part of one's budget. Sometimes, though, the rules just do not seem to fit. Alcohol and tobacco, which are not necessities and do occupy a large share of some personal budgets, also are subject to notoriously inelastic demand.

It is important to understand that there are actually three kinds of elasticity. **Industry or market elasticity**, which we have been discussing, refers to changes in total demand resulting from general changes in price across the industry. Related concepts, which are also important to the marketer, are company, or brand, elasticity and segment elasticity.

**Company elasticity** refers to the sensitivity to changes in price that a particular company or brand faces. Even though the demand for gasoline is very price inelastic, any single retailer's demand is very price elastic. That is, raising a single service station's price even a fraction of a cent above the competition's price will result in significant loss of business. On the other hand, due to a strong reputation, a company such as IBM, for example, may benefit from slightly lower levels of price elasticity than many of its competitors. The result is that IBM can sell its products at a premium. In contrast, one would expect that President's Choice Cola is more price elastic than Coca-Cola.

**Segment elasticity** refers to the sensitivity to changes in price that a particular market segment exhibits. Die-hard audiophiles, for example, tend to be very inelastic in their demand patterns, focusing instead on obtaining the best sound reproduction possible. They represent a particularly attractive segment for stereo manufacturers to target—particularly early in the product life cycle.

**industry or market elasticity**
Refers to changes in total demand resulting from general changes in price across the industry.

**company elasticity**
Refers to the sensitivity to changes in price that a particular company or brand faces.

**segment elasticity**
Refers to the sensitivity to changes in price that a particular market segment exhibits.

## Elasticity and Revenue

There is an important relationship between the elasticity of demand and the way that total revenue changes as the price of a good or service changes. Suppose the city of Montreal wants to find a way to raise more money for its public transportation system. One possible fundraising method is to change the transit fare, but should it be raised or lowered? The correct answer depends on the elasticity of demand for city bus rides. A 10 percent decrease in fares is sure to attract more riders, but unless there is more than a 10 percent increase in riders, total revenue will fall. A 10 percent increase in fares will bring in more money per rider, but if more than 10 percent of the riders are lost, revenue will fall. A price cut will increase revenue only if demand is *elastic,* and a price increase will raise revenue only if demand is *inelastic.*

## Practical Problems in Applying Price Theory

From the viewpoint of the marketer, price theory concepts are sometimes difficult to apply in practice. What are their practical limitations?

1. Many firms do not attempt to maximize profits. Economic analysis is subject to the same limitations as the assumptions on which it is based, and the assumption of profit maximization often does not hold true.
2. It is difficult to estimate demand curves. Modern accounting procedures provide managers with a clear understanding of their cost structure. The manager, therefore, can readily comprehend the supply side of the price equation. But it is difficult to estimate demand at various price levels. Demand curves must be based on market research estimates that are often not as exact as cost figures. Although the demand element can be identified, it is often difficult to measure in the real-world setting.
3. Inadequate training and communications hinder price theory in the real world. Many businesspeople lack the formal training in economics to be able to apply its concepts to their own pricing decisions. On the other hand, many economists remain essentially theorists who devote little

Voir TOUT Montréal avec la Carte touristique
*See ALL of Montréal with the Tourist Card*

En vente d'avril à octobre dans toutes les stations du centre-ville en plus de Sherbrooke,
Mont-Royal, Pie-IX, Viau, Jean-Talon et Longueuil, ainsi qu'au *Bureau d'information
touristique du Vieux-Montréal*, 174, rue Notre-Dame Est (coin Jacques-Cartier)./
*Available from April to October in all downtown metro stations and also at Sherbrooke, Mont-Royal,
Pie-IX, Viau, Jean-Talon and Longueuil stations, and at Tourist Information Office in Old Montreal,
174 East Notre-Dame Street (corner Place Jacques-Cartier).*

En vente toute l'année aux stations Berri-UQAM et Bonaventure.
*Available all year long at Berri-UQAM and Bonaventure metro stations.*

14,00 \$ — Accès illimité au réseau pour 3 jours./
 *Unlimited access to the transit system for 3 days.*
7,00 \$ — Accès illimité au réseau pour 1 jour./
 *Unlimited access to the transit system for 1 day.*

 **STM**
www.stm.info

**Montreal Transit's Tourist Card will be effective if tourists' use of public transit is price elastic.**

interest or effect to real-world pricing situations. This dual problem significantly hinders the use of economic theory in actual pricing practice.[4]

In spite of these problems, it is very useful for pricing decision makers to consider whether demand for their product is elastic or inelastic, what kind of market structure they are operating in, and other related theoretical matters as a starting point for other pricing approaches.

# COST-ORIENTED PRICE SETTING

For many firms, price determination tends to be based on some form of the cost-plus approach.

**Cost-plus pricing** uses some base cost figure per unit to which is added a markup to cover unassigned costs and to provide a profit. The only real difference in the multitude of cost-plus techniques is the relative sophistication of the costing procedures employed. For example, the local clothing store may set prices by adding a 40 percent markup to the invoice price charged by the supplier. This markup is expected to cover all other expenses, as well as permit the owner to earn a reasonable return on the sale of the garments.

In contrast to this rather simple pricing mechanism, a large manufacturer may employ a pricing formula that requires a computer to handle the necessary calculations for a sophisticated costing procedure. But in the end, the formula still requires someone to make a decision about the markup. The clothing store and the large manufacturer may be vastly different with respect to the *cost* aspect, but they are remarkably similar when it comes to the *markup* side of the equation. We will look at mark-ups in a moment, but first let's consider some issues surrounding cost-based pricing.

A major problem associated with cost-oriented pricing is that *costs should not determine prices, since the proper function of cost in pricing is to determine the profit consequences of pricing alternatives.*

**cost-plus pricing**

Pricing technique using base cost figure per unit to which is added a markup to cover unassigned costs and to provide a profit.

That is, costs in the long run only determine the floor for the price. Furthermore, it is possible that costs may be too high and not supportable by the marketplace. Unfortunately, this is not always understood by some companies.

## Full-Cost Pricing

The two most common cost-oriented pricing procedures are the full-cost method and the incremental-cost method. *Full-cost pricing* uses all relevant variable costs in setting a product's price. In addition, it considers an allocation of the fixed costs that cannot be directly attributed to the production of the specific item being priced. Under the full-cost method, if job order 515 in a printing plant amounts to 0.000127 percent of the plant's total output, then 0.000127 percent of the firm's overhead expenses are allocated to this job. This approach therefore allows the pricer to recover all costs plus the amount added as a profit margin.

The full-cost approach has two basic deficiencies. First, it does not consider the demand for the item or its competition. Perhaps no one wants to pay the price that the firm has calculated. Second, any method of allocating overhead, or fixed expenses, is arbitrary and may be unrealistic. In manufacturing, overhead allocations are often tied to direct labour hours. In retailing, the mechanism is sometimes floor area in each profit centre. Regardless of the technique, it is difficult to show a cause-and-effect relationship between the allocated cost and most products.

## Incremental-Cost Pricing

One way to overcome the arbitrary allocation of fixed expenses is by *incremental-cost pricing,* which attempts to use only those costs directly attributable to a specific output in setting prices. For example, consider a small manufacturer with the following income statement:

| | | |
|---|---|---|
| Sales (10 000 units at $10) | | $100 000 |
| Expenses | | |
| Variable | $50 000 | |
| Fixed | $40 000 | $90 000 |
| Net Profit | | $10 000 |

Suppose that the firm is offered a contract for an additional 5000 units. Since the peak season is over, these items can be produced at the same average variable cost. Assume that the labour force would be idle otherwise. To get the contract, how low could the firm price its product?

Under the full-cost approach, the lowest price would be $9 each. This is obtained by dividing the $90 000 in expenses by an output of 10 000 units. The full-cost pricer would consider this a profitless situation. When pricing in this manner, there is a real problem with using full cost. This is set as a floor below which the price will not be allowed to fall. Instead, the type of costs should be understood. Then they can be viewed as somewhat flexible, and serve as a reference point to which flexible markups are added.

The incremental-cost approach, on the other hand, would permit a price of anywhere from $5.01 upward depending on the competition. If competition were strong, a price of $5.10 would be competitive. This price would be composed of the $5 variable cost related to each unit of production, plus a 10 cents per unit contribution to fixed expenses and overhead. With these conditions of sale, note the revised income statement:

| | | |
|---|---|---|
| Sales (10 000 at $10 plus 5000 at $5.10) | | $125 500 |
| Expenses | | |
| Variable (15 000 × $5) | $75 000 | |
| Fixed | $40 000 | $115 000 |
| Net Profit | | $10 500 |

Profits were increased under the incremental approach. Admittedly, the illustration is based on two assumptions: (1) the ability to isolate markets so that selling at the lower price would not affect the price received in other markets, and (2) the absence of certain legal restrictions on the firm. The example, however, does show that profits can sometimes be enhanced by using the incremental approach.

## Limitations of Cost-Oriented Pricing

While the incremental method eliminates one of the problems associated with full-cost pricing, it fails to deal effectively with the basic malady: *cost-oriented pricing does not adequately account for product demand.*

The problem of estimating demand is as critical to these approaches as it is to classical price theory. To the marketer, the challenge is to find some way of introducing demand analysis into cost-plus pricing. A well-reasoned approach to pricing should compare the impact of a pricing decision on total sales receipts, or revenue, and on total costs. It involves the increase or decrease in revenue and costs, not just of the product under consideration, but of the business enterprise as a whole.

## Break-even Analysis: A Useful Tool in Pricing

**break-even analysis**

A means of determining the number of goods or services that must be sold at a given price to generate sufficient revenue to cover total costs.

Although microeconomic approaches to understanding the pricing decision sometimes have limited direct marketing applicability, some of the underlying concepts of pricing theory can be applied in very useful ways. **Break-even analysis** is a means of determining the number of goods or services that must be sold at a given price in order to generate sufficient revenue to cover total costs. Figure 13.2 shows the calculation of the break-even point graphically. The total cost curve includes both fixed and variable segments, and total fixed costs are represented by a horizontal shaded bar. Average variable cost is assumed to be constant per unit as it was in the example used for incremental pricing.

The break-even point is the point at which total revenue (TR) just equals total cost (TC). It can be found by using the following formulas:

$$\frac{\text{Break-even Point}}{\text{(in units)}} = \frac{\text{Total Fixed Costs}}{\text{Per-Unit Selling Price} - \text{Average Variable Cost}}$$

$$= \frac{\text{Total Fixed Costs}}{\text{Per-Unit Contribution to Fixed Cost}}$$

## THE INFORMED CONSUMER

### TO BUY OR LEASE?

As consumers buy any big-ticket items, but especially cars, they are increasingly facing a choice of whether to buy the product outright or to lease it. The advantages of leasing include lower up-front costs and lower monthly payments. On the other hand, if you plan to buy the vehicle when the lease expires, it is almost always cheaper overall to just buy it outright. According to *Consumer Reports*, leasing makes sense if

■ You do not exceed the annual mileage allowance (in Canada, typically 18 000 to 22 000 km per year). Going over results in additional costs charged per kilometre.

■ You do not terminate the lease early—you may risk thousands of dollars in penalties if you do.

■ You keep your vehicle in very good shape. "Excess wear and tear" charges at lease-end can be very expensive.

www.consumerreports.org

■ You prefer to trade in your vehicle every two or three years. If you usually keep a vehicle for more than three years, you're better off buying it from the start.

**What are the advantages to automobile manufacturers of leasing arrangements?**

Source: Based on "To Lease or Not to Lease?" *Consumer Reports* (April 1999), p. 11. © 1999 by Consumers Union of U.S., Inc., Yonkers, NY 10703-1057, a nonprofit organization. Used by permission.

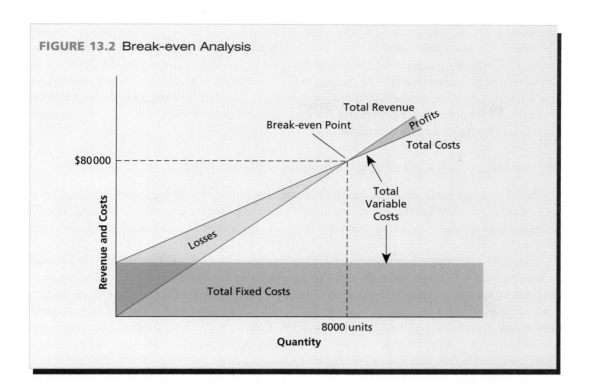

**FIGURE 13.2 Break-even Analysis**

$$\text{Break-even Point (in dollars)} = \frac{\text{Total Fixed Costs}}{1 - \dfrac{\text{Variable Cost per Unit}}{\text{Selling Price}}}$$

In our earlier example, a selling price of $10 and an average variable cost of $5 resulted in a per-unit contribution to fixed costs of $5. This figure can be divided into total fixed costs of $40 000 to obtain a break-even point of 8000 units, or $80 000 in total sales revenue:

$$\text{Break-even Point (in units)} = \frac{\$40\ 000}{\$10-\$5} = \frac{\$40\ 000}{\$5} = 8\ 000 \text{ units}$$

$$\text{Break-even Point (in dollars)} = \frac{\$40\ 000}{1 - \dfrac{\$5}{\$10}} = \frac{\$40\ 000}{0.5} = \$80\ 000$$

Break-even analysis is an effective tool for marketers in assessing the sales required to cover costs and achieve specified profit levels. It is easily understood by both marketing and nonmarketing executives and may assist in deciding whether required sales levels for a certain price are in fact realistic goals. Extending this analysis a bit further, a simple profit breakdown is also shown. If a 10 percent profit on sales was desired, sales of $96 000 would be required. More data would be needed if a return on investment or some other measure was used as a profitability target.

$$\text{Break-even Profit Point (in dollars)} = \frac{\$40\ 000 + 10\% \text{ of Sales } (\$8000)}{1 - \dfrac{\$5}{\$10}} = \frac{\$48\ 000}{0.5} = \$96\ 000$$

Break-even analysis is not without shortcomings. First, the model assumes that costs can be divided into fixed and variable categories. Some costs, such as salaries and advertising outlays, may be either fixed or variable depending on the particular situation. In addition, the model assumes that per-unit variable costs do not change at different levels of operation. However, these may vary as a result of quantity discounts, more efficient use of the workforce, or other economies resulting from increased levels of production and sales. Finally, the basic break-even model does not consider demand. It is a cost-based model and does not directly address the crucial question of whether consumers will actually purchase the product at the specified price and in the required quantities to break even or to generate profits. The challenge of the marketer is to modify break-even analysis and the other cost-oriented approaches to pricing in order to introduce demand analysis. Pricing must be examined from the buyer's perspective. Such decisions cannot be made in a management vacuum in which only cost factors are considered.

## The Dynamic Break-even Concept

**dynamic break-even analysis**
Combines the traditional break-even analysis model with an evaluation of consumer demand.

In Figure 13.2, the break-even analysis was based on the assumption of a constant $10 retail price regardless of quantity. What happens when different retail prices are considered? **Dynamic break-even analysis** combines the traditional break-even analysis model with an evaluation of consumer demand.

Table 13.1 summarizes both the cost and the revenue aspects of a number of alternative retail prices. The cost data are based on the costs used earlier in the basic break-even model. The expected unit sales for each specified retail price are obtained from consumer research. The data in the first two columns of Table 13.1 represent a demand schedule by indicating the number of units consumers are expected to purchase at each of a series of retail prices. This data can be superimposed on a break-even chart in order to identify the range of feasible prices for consideration by the marketing decision maker. This is shown in Figure 13.3.

As Figure 13.3 indicates, the range of profitable prices exists from a low of approximately $8 ($TR_4$) to a high of $12 ($TR_2$), with a price of $10 ($TR_3$) generating the greatest projected profits. Changing the retail price produces a new break-even point. At a relatively high $14 retail price, the break-even point is 4445 units; at a $10 retail price, the break-even point is 8000 units; and at a $6 price, the break-even point is 30 000 units.

The contribution of dynamic break-even analysis is that it forces the pricing decision maker to consider whether consumers are likely to purchase the required number of units of a good or service that will achieve the break-even point at a given price. The analysis demonstrates that a larger number of units sold does not necessarily produce added profits, since—other things being equal—lower prices are necessary to stimulate added sales. Consequently, careful consideration of both costs and consumer demand is necessary in determining the most appropriate price.

## Working with Prices: Markups, Markdowns, and Turnover

In working with prices, marketers often must consider three basic concepts: markups, markdowns, and turnover. An ability to handle these is essential for many day-to-day marketing decisions.

---

**TABLE 13.1 Revenue and Cost Data for Dynamic Break-even Analysis**

| REVENUES | | | COSTS | | | |
|---|---|---|---|---|---|---|
| Price ($) | Quantity Demanded | Total Revenue | Total Fixed Costs ($) | Total Variable Costs ($) | Total Cost ($) | TOTAL PROFIT (OR LOSS) ($) |
| 14 | 3 000 | 42 000 | 40 000 | 15 000 | 55 000 | (13 000) |
| 12 | 6 000 | 72 000 | 40 000 | 30 000 | 70 000 | 2 000 |
| 10 | 10 000 | 100 000 | 40 000 | 50 000 | 90 000 | 10 000 |
| 8 | 14 000 | 112 000 | 40 000 | 70 000 | 110 000 | 2 000 |
| 6 | 26 000 | 156 000 | 40 000 | 130 000 | 170 000 | (14 000) |

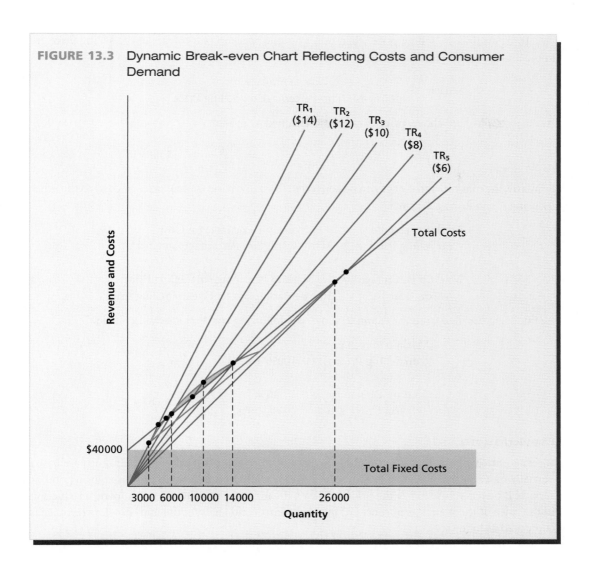

**FIGURE 13.3** Dynamic Break-even Chart Reflecting Costs and Consumer Demand

## Markups

A **markup** is the amount a producer or channel member adds to cost in order to determine the selling price. It is typically stated as a percentage of either the selling price or the cost. The formulas used in calculating markup percentages are as follows:

$$\text{Markup Percentage on Selling Price} = \frac{\text{Amount Added to Cost (the Markup)}}{\text{Price}}$$

$$\text{Markup Percentage on Cost} = \frac{\text{Amount Added to Cost (the Markup)}}{\text{Cost}}$$

Consider an example from retailing. Suppose an item that sells for $1.00 has an invoice cost of $0.60. The total markup is $0.40. The markup percentages would be calculated as follows:

$$\text{Markup Percentage on Selling Price} = \frac{\$0.40}{\$1.00} = 40\%$$

$$\text{Markup Percentage on Cost} = \frac{\$0.40}{\$0.60} = 67\%$$

**markup**
The amount a producer or channel member adds to cost in order to determine the selling price.

To determine the selling price when only cost and markup percentage on the selling price are known, the following formula is used:

$$\text{Price} = \frac{\text{Cost in Dollars}}{100\% - \text{Markup Percentage on Selling Price}}$$

In the example cited above, price could be determined as $1.00:

$$\text{Price} = \frac{\$0.60}{100\% - 40\%} = \frac{0.60}{60\%} = \$1.00$$

Similarly, the markup percentage can be converted from one basis (selling price or cost) to the other by using the following formula:

$$\frac{\text{Markup Percentage}}{\text{on Selling Price}} = \frac{\text{Markup Percentage on Cost}}{100\% + \text{Markup Percentage on Cost}}$$

$$\frac{\text{Markup Percentage}}{\text{on Cost}} = \frac{\text{Markup Percentage on Selling Price}}{100\% - \text{Markup Percentage on Selling Price}}$$

Again, using the data from the example above, the following conversions can be made:

$$\frac{\text{Markup Percentage}}{\text{on Selling Price}} = \frac{67\%}{100\% + 67\%} = \frac{67\%}{167\%} = 40\%$$

$$\frac{\text{Markup Percentage}}{\text{on Cost}} = \frac{40\%}{100\% - 40\%} = \frac{40\%}{60\%} = 67\%$$

## Markdowns

**markdown**
A reduction in the price of an item.

A related pricing issue that is particularly important to retailers is markdowns. Markups are based partially on executive judgements about the prices consumers are likely to pay for a given good or service. If buyers refuse to pay the price, however, the marketer must take a **markdown**, a reduction in the price of the item. For purposes of internal control and analysis, the markdown percentage is computed as follows:

$$\text{Markdown Percentage} = \frac{\text{Markdown}}{\text{"Sale" (New) Price}}$$

Suppose no one is willing to pay $1.00 for an item and the marketer decided to reduce the price to $0.75. The markdown percentage would be

$$\text{Markdown Percentage} = \frac{\$0.25}{\$0.75} = 33\frac{1}{3}\%$$

From a customer's viewpoint, this is only a 25 percent reduction, which is known as the "off-retail percentage." This is the percentage that should be quoted in advertisements. Markdowns are also used for evaluative purposes. For instance, department managers or buyers in a large department store could be evaluated partially on the basis of the average markdown percentage on the product lines for which they are responsible.

## Turnover

**stock turnover**
The number of times the average inventory is sold annually.

All too often, traditional markup and markdown percentages lead to competitive inertia within an industry. Standard percentages are too frequently applied to all items in a given category regardless of factors such as demand.

A method for avoiding competitive inertia is to use flexible markups that vary with **stock turnover**—the number of times the average inventory is sold annually. The figure can be calculated by one of the following formulas. When inventory is recorded at retail:

$$\text{Stock Turnover} = \frac{\text{Sales}}{\text{Average Inventory}}$$

When inventory is recorded at cost:

$$\text{Stock Turnover} = \frac{\text{Cost of Goods Sold}}{\text{Average Inventory}}$$

Store A, with $100 000 in sales and an average inventory of $20 000 (at retail), would have a stock turnover of 5. Store B, with $200 000 in sales, a 40 percent markup rate, and an average inventory of $30 000 (at cost), would have a stock turnover of 4.

| Store A | Store B |
|---------|---------|
| $\dfrac{\text{Stock}}{\text{Turnover}} = \dfrac{\$100\ 000}{\$20\ 000} = 5$ | $200\ 000$  Sales<br>$-\ 80\ 000$  Markup (40 percent)<br>$\$120\ 000$  Cost of Goods Sold<br><br>$\dfrac{\text{Stock}}{\text{Turnover}} = \dfrac{\$120\ 000}{\$30\ 000} = 4$ |

While most marketers recognize the importance of turnover, they often use it more as a measure of sales effectiveness than as a pricing tool. However, it can be particularly useful in setting markup percentages if some consideration is given to consumer demand.

Table 13.2 indicates the relationship between stock turnover and markup. Above-average turnover, such as for grocery products, is generally associated with relatively low markup percentages. On the other hand, higher markup percentages typically exist in such product lines as jewellery and furniture, where relatively lower annual stock turnover is common and inventory and overhead costs must be covered through higher margins.

**TABLE 13.2** Relationship between Markup Percentage and Stock Turnover

| STOCK TURNOVER RATE IN RELATION TO THE INDUSTRY AVERAGE | MARKUP PERCENTAGE IN RELATION TO THE INDUSTRY AVERAGE | PRODUCT EXAMPLE |
|---|---|---|
| High | Low | Soft Drinks |
| Average | Average | Motor Oil |
| Low | High | Sports Cars |

# NEGOTIATED PRICES AND COMPETITIVE BIDDING

So far, this chapter has described the basic considerations for determining price. But, many situations that involve government and business procurement are not characterized by set prices, particularly for nonrecurring purchases such as a defence system for the armed forces. Markets such as these are growing at a fast pace. Governmental units now spend nearly half of Canada's GDP!

**Competitive bidding** is a process by which buyers request potential suppliers to make price quotations on a proposed purchase or contract. **Specifications** give a specific description of the needed item or job that the government or industrial firm wishes to acquire. One of the most important tasks in modern purchasing management is to describe adequately what the organization seeks to buy. This generally requires the assistance of the firm's technical personnel, such as engineers, designers, and chemists.

Competitive bidding strategy should employ the concept of *expected net profit*, which can be stated as

$$\text{Expected Net Profit} = P\ (\text{Bid–Costs})$$

where P = the probability of the buyer accepting the bid.

**competitive bidding**
A process by which buyers request potential suppliers to make price quotations on a proposed purchase or contract.

**specifications**
A specific description of a needed item or job that the buyer wishes to acquire.

Consider the following example. A firm is contemplating submitting a bid for a job that is estimated to cost $23 000. One executive has proposed a bid of $60 000, another, $50 000. It is estimated that there is a 40 percent chance of the buyer accepting bid 1 ($60 000) and a 60 percent chance of the buyer accepting bid 2 ($50 000). The expected net profit formula indicates that bid 2 would be best, since its expected net profit is the higher of the two.

$$\text{Bid 1} \quad \text{ENP} = 0.40\ (\$60\ 000 - \$23\ 000)$$
$$= 0.40\ (\$37\ 000)$$
$$= \$14\ 800$$
$$\text{Bid 2} \quad \text{ENP} = 0.60\ (\$50\ 000 - \$23\ 000)$$
$$= 0.60\ (\$27\ 000)$$
$$= \$16\ 200$$

The most difficult task in applying this concept is estimating the likelihood that a certain bid will be accepted. But this is not a valid reason for failing to quantify one's estimate. Prior experience often provides the foundation for such estimates.

In some cases, industrial and governmental purchasers use **negotiated contracts** instead of inviting competitive bidding for a project. In these situations, the terms of the contract are set through talks between the buyer and the seller. Where there is only one available supplier, or where contracts require extensive research and development work, negotiated contracts are likely to be employed.

Some provincial and local governments permit their agencies to negotiate purchases under a certain limit, say $500 or $1000. This policy is an attempt to reduce costs, since obtaining bids for relatively minor purchases is expensive and there is little prospect of large savings to the agency involved.

In times of inflation, the fear that inflation may have unknown effects on the economic viability of prices has become a major deterrent to companies bidding for or negotiating contracts that take some time to implement. One response has been to include an **escalator clause**[5] that allows the seller to adjust the final price based on changes in the costs of the product's ingredients between the placement of the order and the completion of construction or delivery of the product. Such clauses typically base the adjustment calculation on commodity indices, the cost-of-living index, or a similar indicator. While an estimated one-third of all business-to-business marketers use escalator clauses in some of their bids, these clauses are most commonly used with major projects that involve long time periods and complex operations.

**International pricing** takes all of the foregoing into consideration, as appropriate, but requires additional considerations: exchange risk, price escalation through multiplication of channels, and transportation.

Suppose, after looking at costs and exchange rates, you agree to sell your product for 30 000 rubles to a company in Russia and to deliver it in six months. You could lose a great deal of money if the value of the ruble should fall—say, by 25 percent. In this case, the buyer would pay the amount of rubles agreed to, but you would receive only 75 percent of the value you expected. This is known as **exchange risk**. One way of avoiding this risk is to negotiate the price to be paid in Canadian dollars or some other stable currency. There are several other ways of compensating for this risk, which are beyond the scope of this book.

Selling internationally often requires additional channel members to handle the product in another country, resulting in **price escalation**. If customary margins are given to all channel members, the market price can escalate beyond what is acceptable to final customers. Thus the international marketer must rethink its expected markup and negotiate lower margins with channel members.

Shipping products overseas may be a significant additional cost for many products. As with price escalation, the international marketer cannot just simply add on the increased transportation costs. Innovative solutions to reducing transportation costs and a willingness to absorb some of these costs may be necessary in order to come up with a price that is acceptable in an international setting.

**negotiated contract**
The terms of the contract are set through talks between the buyer and the seller.

**escalator clause**
Allows the seller to adjust the final price based on changes in the costs of the product's ingredients between the placement of the order and the completion of construction or delivery of the product.

**international pricing**
Setting prices to be charged to buyers in other countries taking into consideration exchange risk, price escalation through multiplication of channels, and transportation.

**exchange risk**
The risk of negotiating a price in another nation's currency and finding upon delivery of the product that the currency's value has dropped in relation to your country's currency.

**price escalation**
The increase in final price in a foreign market over a domestic price because of having to pay for the services of additional channel members to get the product to that market.

International pricing is complicated by exchange risk: the possibility that the currency of a buyer's country may drop in relation to the value of currency of the seller's country.

# THE TRANSFER PRICING PROBLEM

One pricing problem that is peculiar to large-scale enterprises is that of determining an internal **transfer price**—the price for sending goods from one company profit centre to another. As a company expands, it usually needs to decentralize management. **Profit centres** are then set up as a control device in the new decentralized operation. Profit centres are any part of the organization to which revenue and controllable costs can be assigned, such as a department.

In large companies, the centres can secure many of their resource requirements from within the corporate structure. The pricing problem becomes what rate Profit Centre A (maintenance department) should charge Profit Centre B (sales department) for the cleaning compound used on B's floors. Should the price be the same as it would be if A did the work for an outside party? Should B receive a discount? The answer to these questions depends on the philosophy of the firm involved.

The transfer pricing dilemma is an example of the variations that a firm's pricing policy must deal with. Consider the case of UDC-Europe, a Universal Data Corporation subsidiary that itself has ten subsidiaries. Each of the ten is organized on a geographic basis, and each is treated as a separate profit centre. Intercompany transfer prices are set at the annual budget meeting. Special situations, like unexpected volume, are handled through negotiations by the subsidiary managers. If complex tax problems arise, UDC-Europe's top management may set the transfer price.

**transfer price**

The price for sending goods from one company profit centre to another.

**profit centre**

Any part of the organization to which revenue and controllable costs can be assigned, such as a department.

# PRICING IN THE PUBLIC SECTOR

Pricing public services has also become an interesting, and sometimes controversial, aspect of contemporary marketing. A good example is the price of tuition for college and university courses. Students have watched with alarm as tuition has risen significantly across Canada in the past several years. They fear that a postsecondary education will become unaffordable. At the same time, though, some commentators argue that tuition has in fact been too low.

Traditionally, government services either were very low-cost or were priced using the full-cost approach: users paid all the costs associated with the service. In some cases there have been attempts to set prices using incremental or marginal pricing, which considers only those expenses specifically associated with a particular activity. However, it is often difficult to determine the costs that should be assigned to a particular activity or service. Governmental accounting problems are often more complex than those of private enterprise.

Another problem in pricing public services is that taxes act as an *indirect* price of a public service. Someone must decide the relative relationship between the direct and indirect prices of such a service. A shift toward indirect tax charges (where an income or earnings tax exists) is generally a movement toward charging on the *ability to pay* rather than on the *use* principle.

The pricing of any public service involves a basic policy decision as to whether the price is an instrument to recover costs or a technique for accomplishing some other social or civic objective. For example, public health services may be priced near zero so as to encourage their use. On the other hand, parking fines in some cities are high so as to discourage the use of private cars in the central business district. Pricing decisions in the public sector are difficult because political and social considerations often outweigh the economic aspects. As governments have cut services or transferred them to the private sector, the pricing problem has been simplified somewhat as tax and public policy considerations have been largely eliminated.

## SUMMARY

Economic approaches to pricing consider supply and demand, marginal revenue, marginal costs, and average revenues and costs. The profit maximizing price is that point where marginal revenue equals marginal costs.

Elasticity of demand is a measure of the responsiveness of buyers to changes in price. Goods can be elastic, or very sensitive to price changes, or inelastic, or not very responsive to price changes.

Cost-plus pricing uses some base cost figure per unit to which is added a markup to cover unassigned costs and to provide a profit. However, costs should not determine prices. The proper function of cost in pricing is to determine the profit consequences of pricing alternatives. Incremental-cost pricing is superior to full-cost pricing in that it gives a more accurate picture of a particular product's contribution to overall profits.

Break-even analysis is a means of determining the number of goods or services that must be sold at a given price in order to generate sufficient revenue to cover total costs.

In international marketing, some important additional considerations that affect pricing are exchange risk, price escalation, and transportation.

Pricing in the public sector is complex, because different constituencies with conflicting wishes and needs are often involved.

# KEY TERMS

average cost, p. 322
average variable cost, p. 322
break-even analysis, p. 328
company elasticity, p. 325
competitive bidding, p. 333
cost-plus pricing, p. 326
dynamic break-even analysis, p. 330
elasticity, p. 324
escalator clause, p. 334
exchange risk, p. 334
industry or market elasticity, p. 325
international pricing, p. 334
marginal cost, p. 322
markdown, p. 332
markup, p. 331

monopolistic competition, p. 321
monopoly, p. 321
negotiated contract, p. 334
oligopoly, p. 321
oligopsony, p. 321
price, p. 320
price escalation, p. 334
profit centre, p. 335
pure competition, p. 321
segment elasticity, p. 325
specifications, p. 333
stock turnover, p. 332
supply curve, p. 324
transfer price, p. 335
utility, p. 320

# INTERACTIVE SUMMARY AND DISCUSSION QUESTIONS

1. One approach to determining price is based on theoretical economic analysis, which uses the concepts of supply and demand. Using these concepts, show how price can be determined theoretically.

2. In the short run, a firm will continue to operate even if a price falls below average cost, provided it remains above average variable cost. Why is this rational market behaviour?

3. Elasticity of demand is a measure of the responsiveness of purchasers and suppliers to changes in price. Explain why it is extremely important to take elasticity of demand into consideration in setting prices.

4. Price theory is very useful in understanding many of the forces in the marketplace that should be considered in setting prices, but are quite difficult to apply in practice. Explain.

5. Cost-plus pricing uses some base cost figure per unit to which is added a markup to cover unassigned costs and to provide a profit. However, costs should not determine prices, since the proper function of cost in pricing is to determine the profit consequences of pricing alternatives. Explain.

6. Explain why incremental-cost pricing is a better procedure than full-cost pricing.

7. Break-even analysis is a means of determining the number of goods or services that must be sold at a given price in order to generate sufficient revenue to cover total costs. Calculate the break-even point in dollars and units for a product with a selling price of $25, related fixed costs of $126 000, and per-unit variable costs of $16.

8. Behind a list price quotation is a number of other prices and price practices, such as market price, cash discounts, trade discounts, and quantity discounts. Explain each in relation to the list price.

9. In international marketing, some important additional considerations that affect pricing are exchange risk, price escalation, and transportation. Explain how each of these can affect the final realized price.

10. Pricing in the public sector is complex, because different objectives and motives are often involved. Describe how this applies in pricing postsecondary tuition.

11. Select five different products that are available through the Web as well as through traditional channels. Are the prices quoted on the Web different from those found in traditional channels?

# Case

## WestJet Taking Wing for Caribbean Hot Spots

WestJet Airlines Ltd. is opening another front in its offensive against Air Canada by launching charter flights to sunshine destinations this winter out of Southern Ontario.

The flights to Cuba and the Dominican Republic are being offered in conjunction with tour operator Signature Vacations Inc., which is responsible for marketing and for booking tickets. Signature will pay WestJet a flat fee for each flight.

But the WestJet imprimatur is central to the project, with the company's regular planes and personnel flying to the Caribbean. As well, WestJet will be a central part of Signature's advertising campaign.

"It will be WestJet-type service, fun and friendly," said spokeswoman Siobhan Vinish.

WestJet has offered charter flights for a couple of years, but this is the first time it will fly to island destinations, and the first time it will offer out-of-country trips from Central Canada.

"No doubt—it is in Air Canada's backyard," said Sam Barone, an independent airlines analyst, adding that the expansion puts WestJet into direct competition with Air Canada Vacations, the charter arm of Air Canada.

Once a week, WestJet will fly from Toronto's Pearson International Airport to Cuba. As well, it will fly weekly to Cuba and the Dominican Republic from Hamilton's John C. Munro International Airport.

The expansion is the latest escalation in the competitive dogfight between WestJet, growing out of its regional roots, and Air Canada, which is trying to adapt its business model to the increasing market dominance of consumers who want cheap no-frills service.

Air Canada has also been busy, launching its Zip Air Inc. subsidiary, which is aimed at serving the no-frills end of the market in Western Canada.

In May 2002, WestJet began flying out of Toronto, supplementing its long-established routes from Hamilton.

WestJet, based in Calgary, acknowledged that the expansion to the Caribbean is part of its move to broaden its competitive scope. Ms. Vinish said the company's Boeing 737-700 planes, which it began acquiring in January 2001, have the range to reach Caribbean destinations. "It's part of the evolution of our company," said Ms. Vinish, adding that the 700 series is able to reach Hawaii from Vancouver.

Signature, headquartered in Toronto, said passengers will be served a cold snack and will have access to a cash bar, a departure from WestJet's usual basic service of a packaged snack and soft drinks.

Mr. Barone predicted that WestJet will keep up the pressure on Air Canada, adding the number of flights from Pearson, in order to compete on convenience as well as price. Also, he said, the western airline will eventually expand to direct flights to the United States, raising the competitive stakes once again. "The next frontier will be a transborder service," he said.

Ms. Vinish said the company hopes to expand to the United States in the next two to three years.

### You Be the Marketer

1. Why is price such an important concern for flights to the Caribbean?
2. Why would WestJet sell their flights to a charter company rather than directly marketing the flights themselves?
3. What action do you think Air Canada will take?

Source: Patrick Brethour, "WestJet Taking Wing for Caribbean Hot Spot," *The Globe and Mail*, September 25, 2002, p. B1. Reprinted with permission from *The Globe and Mail*.

# tango for miles & miles

## {did we mention Aeroplan Miles on every flight}

| from Charlottetown one way fares starting at | $69 Halifax | $129 Montréal | $129 Ottawa | $139 Toronto | $299 Calgary | $349 Vancouver | save $2.50 each way when you book on-line |
|---|---|---|---|---|---|---|---|

Say hello to Tango, the new low-price air service from Air Canada. Book on-line at **www.flytango.com** (and save $2.50 each way), or contact your travel agent or call us at **1-800-315-1390**. Hearing impaired (TTY): 1-800-361-8071. Either way, you'll earn Aeroplan® Miles every time you tango.

**Starting June 22** : Calgary, Halifax, Montréal, Ottawa, Toronto, Vancouver

**say hello to tango. low one way fares. no advance purchase. no saturday night stay. Aeroplan® Miles.**

Air Canada has introduced Tango as a response to price challenges from smaller regional airlines.

# MANAGING THE PRICING FUNCTION

## CHAPTER OBJECTIVES

After reading and studying this chapter, you should be able to

1. Understand the benefits of the marketing approach to pricing.
2. Present a useful model for setting a price.
3. Explain the importance of establishing pricing policies before individual prices are set.
4. Understand and apply skimming and penetration pricing strategies.
5. Describe how prices are quoted.

**A**s much as 40 percent of Air Canada's domestic flight capacity will be provided by discount brands Tango and Zip by the summer of 2003, the Montreal-based carrier said yesterday.

In a conference call to discuss the company's first-quarter loss, chief executive Robert Milton said that Tango, introduced in November, has done better than the airline expected and is even outperforming its regular flights on the same routes.

The purple Tango aircraft achieved a load factor—a measure of seats filled—of 83.4 percent in the first quarter, compared with a 74.6 percent rate for flights on Air Canada's main network.

While the discounted seats obviously bring in less revenue, Milton said that Tango's break-even point "is well below that."

"On comparable domestic routes, Tango is outperforming the regular flights, and that is a real eye-opener for us," Milton told analysts.

"We're absolutely ecstatic by what Tango is doing at this stage."

By this summer, Tango will have 20 planes in the air, accounting for 20 percent of Air Canada's domestic capacity. With approval from Air Canada's pilots' union to expand the company's new Zip no-frills carrier to 20 aircraft, Milton said the two brands could soon account for 40 percent of all domestic capacity.

In a rare admission of admiration for WestJet, Milton said Air Canada has to copy its Calgary rival's success in meeting demand for low-cost travel.

"We're kidding ourselves if we don't look to that model and frankly mimic it."

WestJet—with employee share option plans, no unions, and scheduling and aircraft operations that cut operating costs—has been consistently profitable and is based on the successful business model of Dallas-based Southwest Airlines Co., one of the fastest-growing carriers in the competitive U.S. market.

Source: Excerpted from "Tango Boosts Air Canada: Discount Division Tango is Out-performing Air Canada's Regular Flights," by Allan Swift, *London Free Press*, Friday, May 3, 2002. http://www.canoe.ca/LondonBusiness/ lf.lf-05-03-0078.html. Reprinted with the permission of The Canadian Press.

www.aircanada.ca

# INTRODUCTION

In Chapter 13, we discussed that *price* is the value that a buyer exchanges for a good or service and customers ultimately determine value. Price is a measure of what one must exchange in order to obtain a desired good or service. The previous chapter also outlined the three main approaches to determining a price. Beyond this, however, there are many other pricing issues that the manager must understand—issues with which Air Canada is currently dealing. These include the setting of pricing policies, strategic decisions as to the level at which price should be set, and numerous day-to-day issues in pricing management. These will be the subjects of this chapter.

# MARKETING APPROACHES TO PRICING

Marketing is an eclectic discipline. It draws good ideas from many sources. A *marketing approach to pricing* is no exception. A marketing approach recognizes the numerous valuable concepts developed by economic theory. We discussed several of these concepts in Chapter 13. Especially valuable are the concepts of demand estimation and price elasticity. Cost accounting is also considered essential in pricing. Without a thorough understanding of costs, a firm's pricing policies can soon go awry.

A marketing approach to pricing adds the dimension of *consumer analysis* to the economic and cost analysis. For example, this approach might accept that a profit margin of, say, 35 percent would be desirable for the firm. It also considers potential demand for the product, as well as price elasticity. It goes beyond these considerations, however. The marketing approach asks the question of *how potential consumers would respond* to such a price. Would this price cross some possible psychological threshold and be viewed as much higher than it really is? Or would the proposed price seem so low that it would negatively affect the product's image and sales? The astute marketer asks a host of other questions based on the unique perspective of consumer orientation.

In addition to considering the responses of various consumer segments, the marketing approach to pricing considers competitors individually, in addition to as a whole. In some cases, prior experience will have shown that a key competitor will likely respond in a certain way to any pricing moves. For example, car rental firms have quite a good understanding of their competitors' likely response to any pricing change that they might make. Psychological thresholds of key competitors are also important. A particular competitor might not react to a 3 percent price change, for example, but would react to a 5 percent drop.

## A Pricing Decision Flow Chart

A marketing approach to pricing begins and ends with the company's marketing strategy. The strategy sets the general parameters for pricing decisions (the beginning) and becomes the reference point against which pricing effectiveness is measured (the end) (see Figure 14.1).

### Establish Pricing Objectives

Pricing objectives flow from the marketing strategy. As discussed below, objectives can relate to profits, volume, competition, or prestige. Once pricing objectives have been established, economic, cost, and consumer analyses take place. The economic analysis would include a look at the price elasticity of the product.

### Establish a Price Range

It is helpful to understand the maximum, or ceiling, price and minimum, or floor, price for which a product can be sold. The *ceiling price* comes from the consumer analysis. It is the greatest amount that some segment of the market would be willing and able to pay for this product. The *floor price*, in contrast, is a function of cost. In the short term as discussed in Chapter 13, the firm cannot price

## PRICE WARS

Sometimes, particularly with undifferentiated products, it seems to the marketer that the only way to increase market share is to drop the price. The problem is, competitors are usually in a similar situation. To defend their share, they will also drop prices. If the first company tries again, the situation can very quickly degenerate into a scenario that makes no economic sense. The following news story from March 1999 describes a price war in Britain.

### Battle to Boost Sales Means Loaves Cost Less than Sheep Feed

LONDON: ASDA Group PLC, yesterday, fired the latest shot in a British supermarket price war that has already made sliced bread so cheap some farmers are feeding it to their sheep.

ASDA, the third biggest British food retailer, announced a new "rollback" promotion, cutting more than 1000 prices at its stores. ASDA's move followed rival Tesco PLC's campaign last month, which cut prices on hundreds of lines. Competition between Britain's Big Four supermarkets—Tesco, J. Sainsbury PLC, ASDA, and Safeway PLC—has slashed the price of some everyday foods dramatically.

Tesco's Value Medium Sliced White bread now costs only seven pence a loaf (17¢ Cdn), making it cheaper than conventional wheat feed given to sheep. Farmers, who themselves have been suffering a slump in sheep prices, have been buying up hundreds of loaves from local stores to feed their flocks.

Britain's food retailers are battling to boost sales and profits in a low-growth and low-inflation environment where price competition seems to have heated up since the start of the year.

They are also facing a probe by the Office of Fair Trading, Britain's competition watchdog, which is expected to publish its findings in March 1999. The OFT investigation into the supermarkets' profitability, launched in July 1998, was responding to concerns raised about their buying power from the farming sector and elsewhere.

The analysts said the key question was whether the price cutting was going to get worse. "Either there will be an uneasy peace or it will get more intense," said one.

There are really only two situations in which a company can win a price war. The first is if it has a real cost advantage over the competition. That is, it can produce its product or service at a lower cost than can the competition. The other situation, which is not nearly as attractive, is when one company has significantly greater resources than the competition. In that case the larger company, if it chooses, can simply accept losses on a particular product and wait out the competition, knowing that it can survive longer. This second case can easily attract the attention of market regulators, depending on the precise details of the situation, as it can amount to an abuse of market power and be perceived as an attempt to reduce competition (by driving competition out of business or out of a particular market).

www.asda.co.uk

www.tesco.com

Source: Adapted from Jane Merriman, "British Supermarkets Slash Prices, Shepherds Flock to Bread Aisle," *Financial Post* (March 9, 1999), p. C14. Copyright Reuters Limited 1999. Reuters content is the intellectual property of Reuters. Any copying, republication, or redistribution of Reuters content is expressly prohibited. Reuters shall not be liable for any errors or delays in content, or for any actions taken in reliance thereon.

below its variable cost of production without losing money on each sale. In the longer term, there also has to be some contribution to overhead.

## Establish an Initial Price

Competitive analysis and legal and ethical analysis will almost always result in a price that is somewhere between the floor and the ceiling. All three factors tend to constrain price decisions down from the price ceiling. If we assume a fairly large range between the firm's floor price and what customers will actually pay for the product, competitive action will usually force the firm to drop prices below the ceiling. That is, competitors will see the large difference and choose to offer a lower price to the same market. In the absence of some other advantage, such as recognized quality or a unique patent, the original firm will be forced to lower its prices to retain its share of the market.

Even with distinct advantages over competition, legal or ethical considerations tend to result in an initial price that is below the ceiling price. Interestingly enough, these considerations can also

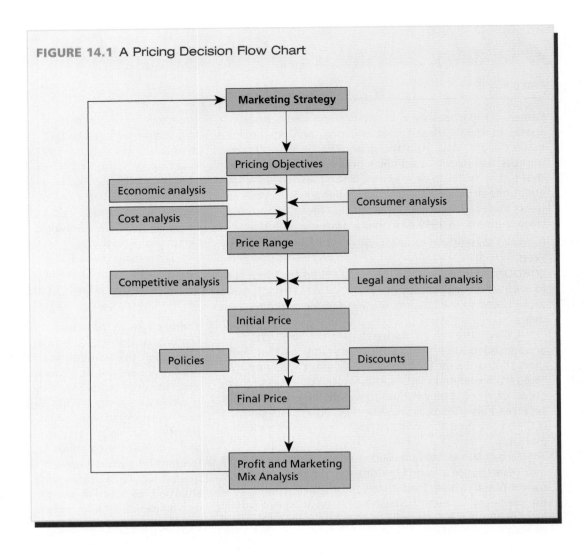

**FIGURE 14.1** A Pricing Decision Flow Chart

result in prices that are higher than the floor price, if it can be demonstrated that the purpose of pricing near cost is primarily to damage competition.

## Establish a Final Price

The final price for which a product is actually sold often will be somewhat different than the initial price. The final price will be affected by the firm's pricing policies regarding skimming, penetration, flexibility, and other issues. Discounts to the trade, freight allowances, and other price promotions will also affect the final price. All of these issues are discussed in this chapter.

## Evaluate Profitability and Marketing Mix Consistency

When the final price has been established, there must be an evaluation process. The first test is to see if the pricing strategy will meet financial goals such as return on investment (ROI), target rate of return on sales, or a payback period. Failure to meet financial goals sends the pricing strategist back to the beginning of the process. In actual practice, the firm will probably have tested the price against its financial goals at several steps along the way. In fact, for new products in particular, it is desirable to make profit plans as early as the concept stage during new-product development. These plans can be updated as the product passes through the development stages.

The second test is to evaluate the selected price in terms of the product, channel, advertising, and personal-selling strategies that will be used in the market segment in question. The role of price in the marketing mix should be specifically identified, and all elements of the mix must blend

## ON-LINE AUCTIONS

Another solution to the pricing problem is to put goods up for auction. At an auction, potential buyers state what they are willing to pay for a good by way of a bidding process. Bids can be open or closed. In open bidding, potential buyers know one another's bids and can adjust their bid, and submit follow-up bids, accordingly. In closed bidding, each buyer submits only one bid and does not know what others are bidding.

Auctions tend to be used in three situations: (1) when a seller needs to dispose of goods quickly and either does not have the time or does not have the means to sell them at a preset price (for example, an estate sale); (2) when a seller has been unable to sell a product at a preset price (for example, a used car with high mileage); or (3) when the object is unique and the seller doesn't know what buyers might be willing to pay for it (for example, fine art).

Several auction houses have sprung up on the Internet, in effect making the entire world part of the bidding audience. Of course, a few bugs must be worked out.

www.ebay.com

Recently, a bed believed to have belonged to Sir John A. Macdonald, Canada's first prime minister, was put up for auction by eBay, an Internet auction house. The owners were no doubt thrilled when the winning bid came in at $400 000 U.S. Thrilled, that is, until it was discovered that the bidder had also purchased a Van Gogh sketch, a 1971 Corvette, a medical centre, and various other things that added up to a bill of about $3.2 million U.S. The problem was, the bidder was only 13 years old—and his allowance wouldn't quite cover his commitments.

**What do you see as some of the advantages and disadvantages of selling goods at auction? Over the Internet?**

Source: For details of this story, see Charlie Gillis, "High-Roller on Internet Auction Site Only 13," *National Post* (April 27, 1999), p. 1, and http://www.canoe.ca/CNEWS/macbed_jun20-cp.html (downloaded June 20, 2002). Internet auction houses such as eBay are becoming popular, but work is still needed to prevent hoax bids.

---

together. Any inconsistencies must be reconciled by altering the price or one of the other elements of the mix.

A low price is appropriate when the product category is at the mature stage in its cycle. A low price may also be appropriate when there is little promotion, the product is mass-produced, market coverage is intense, production is capital-intensive, technological change is slow, the product is needed to complete the product line, few services are offered, the product is disposable, or the life cycle is short.

# PRICE AND THE MARKETING MIX

Just as price is highly important in affecting economic activity, it is a central consideration in developing a marketing mix. A key question when setting a price is "What is the role of price in this marketing mix?" One marketing strategy will assign a major role to price as a means of attracting customers and sales. The discount food chain Save-On Foods is an example. Toward the other end of the spectrum, the marketing strategy of Lexus uses high price as a signal of the value of that fine car. In another marketing mix, price will play a much less important role. It is clear that there are different possible *objectives* for price.

## Pricing Objectives

Pricing flows from the goals of the firm and the marketing organization. Pricing objectives, in turn, shape pricing policies and procedures (see Figure 14.2).

A firm may have as its primary goal becoming the dominant supplier in the domestic market. Its marketing objective might then be to achieve maximum sales penetration in all sales regions. The

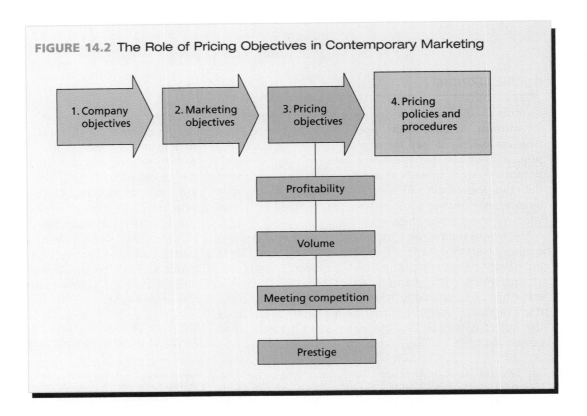

**FIGURE 14.2** The Role of Pricing Objectives in Contemporary Marketing

related pricing objective would be sales maximization (through low prices). These goals and objective might lead to the adopting of a low-price policy implemented by providing the highest cash and trade discounts in the industry.

Pricing objectives vary from firm to firm. In an interesting U.S. study, marketers identified the primary and secondary pricing objectives of their companies. Meeting competitive prices was most often mentioned, but many marketers ranked two profitability-oriented objectives higher: a specified rate of return on investment and specified total profit levels. These two objectives ranked first and second as *primary* pricing objectives. The findings are shown in Table 14.1.

Pricing objectives can be classified into four major groups: (1) profitability objectives, (2) volume objectives, (3) competition-meeting objectives, and (4) prestige objectives. Profitability objectives include profit maximization and target return goals.

## Profitability Objectives

Businesses need to make profits in order to survive. How much profits? In classical economic theory, discussed in Chapter 13, the traditional pricing objective has been to *maximize profits*. In terms of actual business practice, this means that profit maximization would be the basic objective of individual firms.

Profits, in turn, are a function of revenue and expenses:

$$\text{Profits} = \text{Total Revenues} - \text{Total Costs}$$

Revenue is determined by the selling price and the quantity sold:

$$\text{Total Revenue} = \text{Price} \times \text{Quantity Sold}$$

Price, therefore, should be increased up to the point where it causes a disproportionate decrease in the number of units sold. A 10 percent price increase that results in only an 8 percent cut in volume adds to the firm's revenue. However, a 10 percent hike that causes an 11 percent sales decline reduces total revenue.

In terms of the quantity of product that the firm should produce and offer for sale, the point of **profit maximization** is where the addition to total revenue is just balanced by an increase in total cost. This approach is referred to as *marginal analysis*. This is a valuable concept that the reader

**profit maximization**
The point where the addition to total revenue is just balanced by an increase in total cost.

**TABLE 14.1** Primary and Secondary Pricing Objectives of Firms

| | PERCENTAGE OF RESPONDENTS RANKING THE ITEMS | | |
|---|---|---|---|
| PRICING OBJECTIVE | As Primary Objectives | As Secondary Objectives | As Either Primary or Secondary Objectives |
| Meeting competitive price level | 38.3 | 43.0 | 81.3 |
| Specified rate of return on investment | 60.9 | 17.2 | 78.1 |
| Specified total profit level | 60.2 | 17.2 | 77.4 |
| Increased market share | 31.3 | 42.2 | 73.5 |
| Increased total profits above previous levels | 34.4 | 37.5 | 71.9 |
| Specified rate of return on sales | 47.7 | 23.4 | 71.1 |
| Retaining existing market share | 31.3 | 35.9 | 67.2 |
| Serving selected market segments | 26.6 | 39.1 | 65.7 |
| Creation of a readily identifiable image for the firm and/or its products | 21.9 | 41.4 | 63.3 |
| Specified market share | 15.6 | 40.6 | 56.2 |
| Other | 5.5 | — | 5.5 |

should understand. Making it work, however, is not so easy. The basic problem centres on the difficulty of achieving this delicate balance between marginal revenue and marginal cost. As a result, relatively few firms actually achieve the objective of profit maximization. A significantly larger number prefer to direct their efforts toward goals that are more easily implemented and measured.

Consequently, target return objectives have become quite common in industry, particularly among the larger firms where public pressure may limit consideration of the profit maximization objective. Telephone and other utility companies are an example of this phenomenon. **Target return objectives** may be either short-run or long-run goals, and usually are stated as a percentage of sales or investment. A company, for instance, may seek a 15 percent annual rate of return on investment or an 8 percent rate of return on sales. A specified return on investment was the most commonly reported pricing objective in Table 14.1.

Target return objectives offer several benefits to the marketer. (1) They are likely to result in a more stable and planned profit pattern for the company. This contrasts with a profit maximization approach, which can be very unstable. (2) They serve as a means for evaluating performance. (3) They also are designed to generate a "fair" profit, as judged by management, shareholders, and the general public as well. When using such target objectives, management should avoid a short-term perspective. For example, if a product has contributed according to target for a time and now faces price competition, it still could be making a good contribution to overhead and should not be arbitrarily dropped.

**target return objectives** Either short-run or long-run goals, usually stated as a percentage of sales or investment.

## Volume Objectives

Some writers argue that a better explanation of actual pricing behaviour is William J. Baumol's belief that firms attempt to **maximize sales** within a given profit constraint.[1] In other words, they set a minimum floor at what they consider to be the lowest acceptable profit level and then seek to maximize sales (subject to this profit constraint) in the belief that increased sales are more important to the long-run competitive picture. The company will continue to expand sales as long as its total profits do not drop below the minimum return acceptable to management.

**sales maximization** The pricing philosophy analyzed by economist William J. Baumol. Baumol believes that many firms attempt to maximize sales within a profit constraint.

**market share objective**
To control a specific portion of the market for the firm's product.

Another volume-related pricing objective is the **market share objective**—that is, the goal is set to control a specific portion of the market for the firm's product. The company's specific goal can be to maintain or increase its share of a particular market. For example, a firm may want to increase its 10 percent share of a particular market to 20 percent.[2] As Table 14.1 indicates, about two-thirds of all responding firms list retaining existing market share as either a primary or a secondary pricing objective.

Market share objectives can be critical to achieving other objectives. High sales, for example, may mean more profit. The extensive *Profit Impact of Market Strategies (PIMS)* project conducted by the Marketing Science Institute analyzed more than 2000 firms and revealed that two of the most important factors influencing profitability were product quality and a large market share.

### Competition-Meeting Objectives

**status quo objectives**
Objectives based on maintaining stable prices.

www.mlfi.com

**Status quo objectives**—objectives based on maintaining stable prices—are the basis of the pricing philosophy for many enterprises. This philosophy usually stems from a desire to minimize competitive pricing action. Maintaining stable prices allows the firm to concentrate its efforts on nonprice elements of the marketing mix, such as product improvement or promotion. Maple Leaf Foods International de-emphasized price competition and developed an advertising campaign emphasizing product features that differentiated its product, Tenderflake lard, from the competition. As a result, market share and profits increased significantly. The company was even able to raise prices gradually. Status quo objectives remain a significant factor in pricing.

### Prestige Objectives

**prestige objectives**
Establishing relatively high prices in order to develop and maintain an image of quality and exclusiveness.

www.birks.com

Another category of pricing objectives unrelated to either profitability or sales volume is that of prestige objectives. **Prestige objectives** involve establishing relatively high prices in order to develop and maintain an image of quality and exclusiveness. Such objectives reflect marketers' recognition of the role of price in creating an overall image for the firm and its products and services. It appears that Birks and Holt Renfrew follow this strategy. Many manufacturers of luxury products also use prestige pricing to suggest quality. Accordingly the Jaguar XKR convertible is priced at approximately $120 000.

www.holtrenfrew.com

# PRICING POLICIES

Pricing policies are important for properly managing pricing. They provide the overall framework and consistency needed in pricing decisions. A **pricing policy** is a general guideline based on pricing objectives that is intended for use in specific pricing decisions. Pricing policies affect the **price structure**, which is an outline of the selling price and the various discounts offered to intermediaries. Price structure decisions take the selected price policy as a given, and specify the discount structure details. Pricing policies have great strategic importance, particularly in relation to competitive considerations. They are the bases on which pricing decisions are made. Future Shop, for example, has a policy that it will never be undersold and that if a customer buys from the company and then finds a lower price, a portion of the price difference will be refunded.

www.jaguar.ca

**pricing policy**
A general guideline based on pricing objectives that is intended for use in specific pricing decisions.

Many businesses would be well advised to spend more managerial effort in establishing and periodically reviewing their pricing policies. Companies normally give a great deal of thought and planning to engineering, manufacturing, advertising, and sales promotion policies. It is essential that the same kind of careful study and planning be directed toward the formulation of price policies that will best serve the long-run objectives of the business.

**price structure**
An outline of the selling price and the various discounts offered to intermediaries.

International competition is another reason for establishing clearly formulated price policies. For example, in the retailing sector, the incursion of large U.S. low-price competitors has forced Canadian retailers to quickly rethink their pricing practices. Perhaps if Canadian retailers had been more conscious of the potential international competition, they might have established pricing policies and prices that would have made the Canadian market seem less attractive to foreign competitors.

Pricing policies provide a focus in dealing with varied competitive situations. The type of policy depends on the environment within which the pricing decision must be made. The types of policies to be considered are skimming versus penetration pricing, price flexibility, relative price levels, price lining, and promotional prices. They should all be arrived at through an analysis of the role of pricing in the marketing mix as a whole.

## New Product Pricing Policies: Skimming versus Penetration

In pricing new products, the initial price that is quoted for an item may determine whether or not the product will eventually be accepted in the marketplace. The initial price also may affect the amount of competition that will emerge. Consider the options available to a company that is pricing a new product. It may price at the level of comparable products, very high, or very low. Figure 14.3 illustrates that the market is made up of different layers of potential customers with varying degrees of willingness and ability to pay depending on whether prices are higher or lower. This is another way of expressing the downward-sloping demand curve that applies to most products.

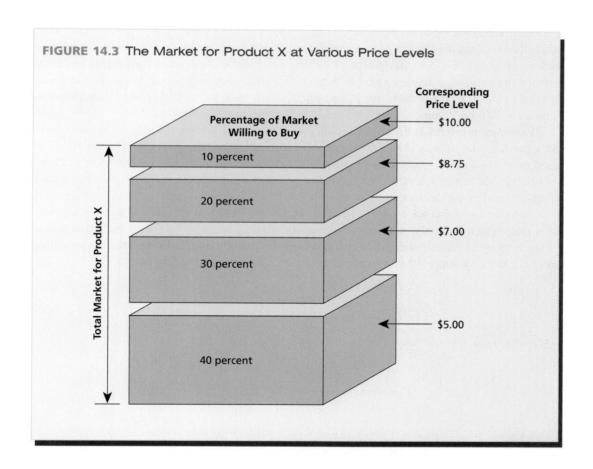

**FIGURE 14.3** The Market for Product X at Various Price Levels

A **skimming pricing** policy chooses a high entry price. The name is derived from the expression "skimming the cream." The plan is to sell first to consumers who are willing to pay the highest price, and then reduce the price (perhaps introduce a less fancy model) and market to the next level, and so on. One purpose of this strategy is to allow the firm to recover its development costs quickly. The assumption is that competition will eventually drive the price to a lower level, as was the case, for example, with compact discs.

**skimming pricing**
Choosing a high entry price; to sell first to consumers who are willing to pay the highest price, and then reduce the price.

A skimming policy, therefore, attempts to maximize the revenue received from the sale of a new product before the entry of competition. Ballpoint pens were introduced shortly after World War II at a price of about $20. Today, the best-selling ballpoint pens are priced at less than $1. Other examples of products that have been introduced using a skimming policy include television sets, videocassette recorders, home computers, and pocket calculators. Subsequent price reductions allowed the marketers of these products to appeal to additional market segments that are more price-sensitive.

A skimming strategy permits the marketer to control demand in the introductory stages of the product's life cycle and to adjust its productive capacity to match demand. A danger of low initial price for a new product is that demand may outstrip the firm's production capacity, resulting in consumer and intermediary complaints and possibly permanent damage to the product's image. Excess demand occasionally results in poor-quality products as the firm strives to satisfy consumer desires with inadequate production facilities.

During the late growth and early maturity stages of the product life cycle, the price is reduced for two reasons: (1) the pressure of competition and (2) the desire to expand the product's market. Figure 14.3 shows that 10 percent of the market for Product X would buy the item at $10, while another 20 percent would buy at $8.75. Successive price declines will expand the firm's market as well as meet new competition.

A skimming policy has one chief disadvantage: it attracts competition. Potential competitors who see the innovating firms make large returns also enter the market. This forces the price even lower than it might have had to be using a different pricing policy under a sequential skimming procedure. However, if a firm has patent protection—as Polaroid had—or a proprietary ability to exclude competition, it may use a skimming policy for a relatively long period. Figure 14.4 indicates that 14.4 percent of the respondents in one pricing study used a skimming policy. Skimming also appears to be more common in business markets than in consumer markets.

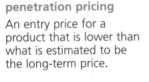

**penetration pricing**

An entry price for a product that is lower than what is estimated to be the long-term price.

**Penetration pricing** is the opposite policy in new-product pricing. It results in an entry price for a product that is lower than what is estimated to be the long-term price. Penetration pricing is used more often in consumer markets. Soaps and toothpastes are often good examples of this kind of pricing. For instance, a new combined shampoo and conditioner could be introduced with a cents-off label to induce consumers to try it.

The premise is that an initially lower price will help secure market acceptance. Since the firm later intends to increase the price, brand popularity is crucial to the success of a penetration policy. One advantage of such a policy is that is discourages competition from entering, since the prevailing low price does not suggest the attractive returns associated with a skimming policy.

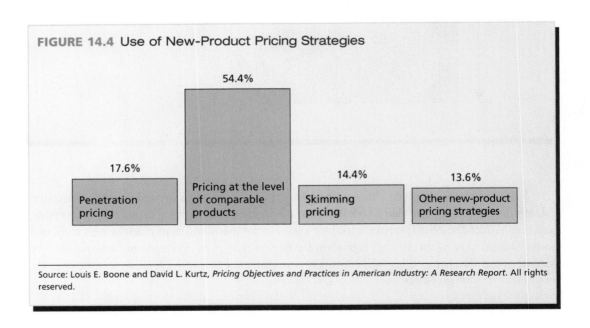

**FIGURE 14.4 Use of New-Product Pricing Strategies**

- 17.6% — Penetration pricing
- 54.4% — Pricing at the level of comparable products
- 14.4% — Skimming pricing
- 13.6% — Other new-product pricing strategies

Penetration pricing is likely to be used in instances where demand for the new product or service is highly elastic and large numbers of consumers are highly price-sensitive. It is also likely to be used in instances where large-scale operations and long production runs result in substantial reductions in production and marketing costs. Finally, penetration pricing may be appropriate in instances where the new product is likely to attract strong competitors when it is introduced. Such a strategy may allow it to reach the mass market quickly and capture a large share of the market before the entry of competitors. With penetration pricing, the marketers will likely forgo some profits, at least in the short run.

The key decision, of course, is when to move the price to its intended level. Consumers tend to resist price increases, so correct timing is essential. The solution depends on the degree of brand loyalty that has been achieved. Brand loyalty must be at the point where a price increase would not cause a disproportionate decrease in customers. A series of modest price changes, rather than a single large hike, also can retain customers. Often, firms will use cents-off deals to enter at a lower price. These can then be phased out more easily.

A firm may, of course, decide to use neither a skimming nor a penetration price. It may try to price a new product at the point where it is intended to sell in the long run. All three new-product pricing strategies are common, but it can be seen from Figure 14.4 that this last strategy was chosen in 54.4 percent of new-product pricing situations.

## Price Flexibility

Marketing executives must also determine company policy with respect to **flexible pricing**. Is the firm going to have just one price or pursue a variable price policy in the market? In general, *one-price policies* characterize situations where mass selling is employed, and *variable pricing* is more common where individual bargaining typifies market transactions, for example, the purchase of a car.

A one-price policy is common in Canadian retailing, since it facilitates mass merchandising. For the most part, once the price is set, managers can direct their attention to other aspects of the marketing mix. Flexible prices, by contrast, are found more in wholesaling and business markets. This does not mean that price flexibility exists only in manufacturing industries. A study of the retail home appliance market concluded that people who had purchased identical products from the same dealer had often paid different prices for them. The primary reasons for the differences were customer knowledge and bargaining strength.[3]

While variable pricing has the advantage of flexibility in selling situations, it may result in conflict with the Competition Act provisions. It may also lead to retaliatory pricing on the part of competitors, and it is not well received by those who have paid the higher prices.

**flexible pricing**
A variable price policy.

## Relative Price Levels

Another important pricing policy decision concerns the relative price level. Are the firm's prices to be set above, below, or at the prevailing market price? In economic theory, this question would be answered by supply and demand analysis. However, from a practical viewpoint, marketing managers *administer* prices. In other words, they subjectively set the markup percentages to achieve the price level desired. The decision maker must still develop a basic policy in regard to relative price levels. A fine clothing store, such as Harry Rosen, would probably have a policy of pricing at a level that is higher than most other clothing retailers. Wal-Mart, on the other hand, emphasizes its everyday low prices.

### THE PRACTISING MARKETER

**NEW-PRODUCT PRICING**

Suppose you are the marketing manager of a large candy manufacturer. Your product development team has just come up with a new type of chocolate bar that tastes very similar to fudge. Consumer taste tests have shown that most consumers have a very pronounced preference for the new bar and would be willing to pay a slightly higher price for it than they pay for regular chocolate bars. The best news is, it's actually cheaper to produce the new bar than regular bars. You are unable to patent the bar but are quite confident that it will take at least a year for your competitors to come up with a similar product. You have ample production capacity to manufacture the new bar. Scale and experience economies are not significant.

**If your regular bars are priced at 90 cents each, what should be the price of the new bar? Explain your answer.**

*Following the competition* is one method of negating the price variable in marketing strategy, since it forces competition to concentrate on other factors. Some firms choose to price below or above competition. These decisions are usually based on a firm's cost structure, overall marketing strategy, and pricing objectives.

The price level decision is distinct from the issue of penetration or skimming pricing in that it relates to the long-term price position of the firm. Penetration and skimming relate more narrowly to a new product being introduced to the marketplace.

## Price Lining

**price lining**

The practice of marketing merchandise at a limited number of prices.

Most companies sell a varied line of products. An effective pricing strategy should consider the relationship among the firm's products rather than view each in isolation. Specifically, **price lining** is the practice of marketing merchandise at a limited number of prices. For example, a clothier might have a $195 line of men's suits and a $325 line. Price lining is used extensively in retail selling. It can be an advantage to both retailer and customer. Customers can choose the price range they wish to pay, and then concentrate on all the other variables, such as colour, style, and material. The retailer can purchase and offer specific lines rather than a more generalized assortment.

Price lining requires that one identify the market segment or segments to which the firm is appealing. For example, a suitcase manufacturer may see its market not as all luggage, but as the "medium-price, hard-side" portion of the luggage trade. The firm must decide how to *line* its product prices. A dress manufacturer might have lines priced $89.95, $159.95, and $199.95. Price lining not only simplifies the administration of the pricing structure, but also alleviates the confusion of a situation in which all products are priced separately. Price lining is really a combined product/price strategy.

One problem with a price-line decision is that once it is made, retailers and manufacturers have difficulty adjusting it. Rising costs, therefore, put the seller in the position of either changing the price lines, with the resulting confusion, or reducing costs by adjusting production, which opens the firm to the complaint that "XYZ Company's merchandise certainly isn't what it used to be!"

## INTERNET IMPACT

### THE INTERNET'S IMPACT ON PRICING

It's possible to buy just about anything on the Internet—used or new. The continued growth of Internet retailing—increasingly dubbed e-tailing—can potentially put price pressure on traditional retail outlets. There are two reasons for this possible pressure.

The first source of price pressure is simply that it is so easy to compare prices on the Internet. Rather than trudging from one store to the next, checking flyers, or spending many happy hours on the telephone, if you start out knowing fairly exactly what you are looking for, you can check out several Internet sites in a matter of minutes.

The second price pressure stems from the fact that several Internet retailers are very aggressively competing on price. Of these, Buy.com currently has the highest profile. They used to advertise the "lowest prices on Earth" and were prepared to sell products at a loss in order to make good on that claim. More recently their advertising has been somewhat more circumspect:

At buy.com, we offer a low price guarantee in all our stores except our Wireless and Clearance stores. If you find a price lower than ours on the Internet, and you meet the eligibility requirements listed below, you may qualify for a price match. (Source:http://www.buy.com/corp/support/guarantees/lowpriceguarantee.asp June 21, 2002)

www.us.buy.com

Whether the company has a viable long-term strategy remains to be seen. In the short term, though, its high visibility and aggressive price stance is almost sure to trim the margins of many retailers to some degree.

**Do conventional retailers have any way of responding to Internet retailers like Buy.com other than simply trying to match prices? If so, how?**

Source: For a more complete discussion of buy.com, see Ross Laver, "Nutty Ideas Worth Billions," *Maclean's* (May 3, 1999), p. 42.

# Promotional Prices

A **promotional price** is a lower-than-normal price used as an ingredient in a firm's selling strategy. In some cases promotional prices are recurrent, such as the annual shoe store sale: "Buy one pair of shoes, get the second for one cent." Or a new pizza restaurant may have an opening special to attract customers. In other situations, a firm may introduce a promotional model or brand to allow it to compete in another market.

Promotional pricing is often seen at the retail level. One type is **loss leaders**, goods priced below cost to attract customers who, the retailer hopes, will then buy other, regularly priced merchandise. The use of loss leaders can be effective, and is a commonly used means of generating business.

> Probably one of the best innovators of this pricing method was Cal Mayne. He was one of the first men to systematically price specials and to evaluate their effect on gross margins and sales. Mayne increased sales substantially by featuring coffee, butter, and margarine at 10 percent below cost. Ten other demand items were priced competitively and at a loss when necessary to undersell competition. Still another group of so-called secondary demand items were priced in line with competition. Mayne based his pricing policy on the theory that the customer can only remember about 30 prices. Keep prices down on these items and the customer will stay with you.[4]

Some studies have indeed reported considerable price confusion on the part of consumers. One study of consumer price recall reported that average shoppers misquoted the price they last paid for coffee by over 12 percent, toothpaste by over 20 percent, and green beans by 24 percent. While some people hit the prices exactly, others missed by several hundred percent.[5] The use of loss leaders is common in several branches of retailing today.

Three potential pitfalls should be considered when one faces a promotional pricing decision:

- The Competition Act may prohibit some types of promotional pricing practices (see Chapter 2).
- Some consumers are little influenced by price appeals, so promotional pricing will have little effect on them.[6]

**promotional price**
A lower-than-normal price used as an ingredient in a firm's selling strategy.

**loss leader**
Goods priced below cost to attract customers.

---

## THE ETHICAL MARKETER

### JOHNSON & JOHNSON'S PRICING PRACTICE

Pricing decisions can raise some complicated ethical issues. Johnson & Johnson managed to touch on at least two problems with one decision when the company priced the drug levamisole, which it sells under the brand name Ergamisol. Levamisole was discovered to be very effective against colon cancer, the second leading cause of cancer-related deaths. Johnson & Johnson priced the product so that a year's supply ended up costing between $1250 and $1500 (U.S.).

No one argued that $1500 was an unreasonable price for a life-saving drug—until one patient noticed that the active ingredients in her cancer drugs were essentially the same as the ingredients in the deworming medicine she used for her sheep. The deworming medicine sold for more like $14. You might say that the sheep hit the fan for Johnson & Johnson about that point, with accusations of price gouging pouring in from all sides.

Johnson & Johnson, which actually has a stellar reputation for ethical conduct, argues (along with every other major pharmaceutical company) that wide margins are necessary on successful drugs because research costs are so high and it takes so long to develop and bring drugs to market. Furthermore, many research streams are dead ends that never return a profit.

**The two issues underlying Johnson & Johnson's dilemma come down to (1) when, if ever, is it ethical to charge different segments different prices for essentially the same product? and (2) is it ethical to take large (or any) margins on products that are necessary to sustain a person's life? What do you think?**

www.johnsonandjohnson.com/home.html

Source: The facts presented in this box are drawn from Robert F. Hartley, *Business Ethics: Violations of the Public Trust* (New York: John Wiley & Sons, 1993), pp. 305–307.

---

- Continuous use of an artificially low rate may result in its being accepted as customary for the product. Bic pens were introduced as a low-price product (with corresponding manufacturing costs). It would be extremely difficult to raise their prices significantly now.

# PRICING PRACTICES

## Psychological Pricing

**psychological pricing**
The use of prices to suggest values of a product or attributes of a product/price offering.

**Psychological pricing** is the use of prices to suggest values of a product or attributes of a product/price offering. Prestige pricing, mentioned earlier in this chapter, is one of many forms of psychological pricing.

The psychology of pricing can be complicated. Professor Lee Kreul has found through research that in restaurant newspaper advertisements for a meal costing less than $7, the price usually ends in 9 (e.g., $4.99). This implies a discount. For meals costing above $7, prices usually end in 5. Professor Kreul believes that as prices go up, the ending number changes because it takes more than one cent to create the discount illusion. Furthermore, people interested in paying more than $7 might think that a price ending in 9 suggests discounts, low quality, or hurried service.[7]

**odd pricing**
Prices are set ending in some amount just below the next rounded number.

**Odd pricing** is a good example of the application of psychological pricing. Prices are set ending in some amount just below the next rounded number. A price of $16.99 is assumed to be more appealing than $17 (supposedly because it is a lower figure).

Originally, odd pricing was used to force clerks to make change, thus serving as a cash control device within the firm.[8] Now it has become a customary feature of contemporary prices. For instance, one discounter uses prices ending in 3 and 7 rather than 5, 8, or 9 because of a belief that customers regard price tags of $5.95, $6.98, and $7.99 as *regular* retail prices, while $5.97 and $6.93 are considered *discount* prices. Obviously, intuition and experience play a part in establishing an odd pricing policy.

## The Price–Quality Concept

One of the most researched aspects of pricing is the relationship between price and the consumer's perception of the product's quality.[9] In the absence of other cues, price is an important factor in the consumer's perception of the product's quality.[10] The higher the price, the better the buyer believes

FÖRBY stool
$4.95
Stackable. Clear-lacquered tubular steel frame with a durable plastic seat. RA Ø35–H44cm
*Maria Vinka*
Maria Vinka, designer

Shop by phone 1 800 661-9807

IKEA 2003

Shop by phone 1 800 661-9807

IKEA furniture and products are priced affordably, for most consumers. To combat the perception that the company's relatively low prices mean lower quality, IKEA's catalogue cover showcases its furniture's quality and workmanship.

the quality of the product to be. One study asked 400 people what terms they associated with the word *expensive*. Two-thirds of the replies were related to high quality, such as *best* and *superior*.[11] The relationship between price and perceived quality is a well-documented fact in contemporary marketing.

Probably the most useful concept in explaining price–quality relationships is the idea of **price limits**.[12] It is argued that consumers have limits within which product quality perception varies directly with price. A price below the lower limit is regarded as too cheap, while one above the higher limit means it is too expensive. Most consumers do tend to set an acceptable price range when purchasing goods and services. The range, of course, varies depending on consumers' socioeconomic characteristics and buying dispositions. Consumers, nonetheless, should be aware that price is not necessarily an indicator of quality. Alberta Consumer and Corporate Affairs summarized seven price–quality research studies, six covering *Consumer Reports* analyses of 932 products between 1940 and 1977, and one for 43 products tested by *Canadian Consumer* between 1973 and 1977. It found that while there was a positive relationship between price and quality, the correlation was low (Spearman rank correlation = .25). In addition, about 25 percent of products tested had a negative price–quality relation. That is, products ranked lower in performance had higher prices than products deemed superior by the Canadian and U.S. consumer testing organizations.[13]

## Unit Pricing

Consumer advocates have often pointed out the difficulty of comparing consumer products that are available in different-size packages or containers. Is an 800 g can selling for 75 cents a better buy than two 450 g cans priced at 81 cents or another brand that sells at three 450 g cans for 89 cents? The critics argue that there should be a common way to price consumer products.

**Unit pricing** is a response to this problem. Under unit pricing, all prices are stated in terms of some recognized unit of measurement (such as grams or litres) or a standard numerical count. There has been considerable discussion about legislating mandatory unit pricing. The Consumers' Association of Canada has endorsed unit pricing, and many of the major food chains have adopted it.

The real question, of course, is whether unit pricing improves consumer decisions. One study found that the availability of unit prices resulted in consumer savings, and that retailers also benefited when unit pricing led to greater purchases of store brands. The study concluded that unit pricing was valuable to both buyer and seller and that it merited full-scale use.[14] Others have questioned the amount of use of unit pricing by consumers.

# PRICE QUOTATIONS

How prices are quoted depends on many factors, such as cost structures, traditional practice in the particular industry, and the policies of individual firms. In this section, we shall examine the reasoning and methodology behind price quotations.

The basis on which most price structures are built is the **list price**, the rate normally quoted to potential buyers. List price is usually determined by one or a combination of the methods discussed in Chapter 13. The sticker prices on new cars are good examples: they show the list price for the basic model, and then add the list price for the options that have been included.

## Discounts, Allowances, and Rebates

The amount that a consumer pays—the **market price**—may or may not be the same as the list price. In some cases, discounts or allowances reduce the list price. List price is often used as the starting point from which discounts that set the market price are derived. Discounts can be classified as cash, trade, or quantity.

**Cash discounts** are those reductions in price that are given for prompt payment of a bill. They are probably the most commonly used variety. Cash discounts usually specify an exact time period, such as "2/10, net 30." This means that the bill is due within 30 days, but if it is paid in 10 days, the

**price limits**
Limits within which product quality perception varies directly with price.

**unit pricing**
Stating prices in terms of some recognized unit of measurement (such as grams or litres) or a stan-

www.consumer.ca

**list price**
The rate normally quoted to potential buyers.

**market price**
The amount that a consumer pays.

**cash discount**
Reduction in price that is given for prompt payment of a bill.

customer may subtract 2 percent from the amount due. Cash discounts have become a traditional pricing practice in many industries. They are legal provided that they are granted to all customers on the same terms. Such discounts were originally instituted to improve the liquidity position of sellers by reducing accounts receivable, lower bad-debt losses, and reduce the expenses associated with collecting bills. Whether these advantages outweigh the relatively high cost of capital involved in cash discounts depends on the seller's need for liquidity as well as alternative sources (and costs) of funds.

**trade discount**

Payment to channel members or buyers for performing some marketing function normally required of the manufacturer.

**Trade discounts**, which are also called functional discounts, are payments to channel members or buyers for performing some marketing function normally required of the manufacturer. These are legitimate as long as all buyers in the same category, such as wholesalers and retailers, receive the same discount privilege. Trade discounts were initially based on the operating expenses of each trade category, but have now become more of a matter of custom in some industries. An example of a trade discount would be "40 percent, 10 percent off list price" for wholesalers. In other words, the wholesaler passes the 40 percent on to his or her customers (retailers) and keeps the 10 percent discount as payment for activities such as storing and transporting. The price to the wholesaler on a $100 000 order would be $54 000 ($100 000 less 40% = $60 000, less 10%). Note the sequence in which the discount calculations are made.

**quantity discount**

Price reduction granted for large purchases.

**Quantity discounts** are price reductions granted for large purchases. These discounts are justified on the grounds that large-volume purchases reduce selling expenses and may shift a part of the storing, transporting, and financing functions to the buyer. Quantity discounts are lawful provided they are offered on the same basis to all customers.

Quantity discounts may be either noncumulative or cumulative. Noncumulative quantity discounts are one-time reductions in list price. For instance, a firm might offer the discount schedule in Table 14.2. Cumulative quantity discounts are reductions determined by purchases over a stated time period. Annual purchases of $25 000 might entitle the buyer to an 8 percent rebate, while purchases exceeding $50 000 would mean a 15 percent rebate. These reductions are really patronage discounts, since they tend to bind the customer to one source of supply.

**trade-in**

Deduction from an item's price of an amount for the customer's old item that is being replaced.

Allowances are similar to discounts in that they are deductions from the price the purchaser must pay. The major categories of allowances are trade-ins and promotional allowances. **Trade-ins** are often used in the sale of durable goods such as cars. They permit a reduction without altering the basic list price by deducting from the item's price an amount for the customer's old item that is being replaced.

**promotional allowance**

Extra discount offered to retailers so that they will advertise the manufacturer along with the retailer.

**Promotional allowances** are extra discounts offered to retailers so that they will advertise the manufacturer along with the retailer. They are attempts to integrate promotional strategy in the channel. For example, manufacturers often provide advertising and sales-support allowances for other channel members. Many manufacturers offer such allowances to retail dealers.

**rebate**

Refund by the seller of a portion of the purchase price.

**Rebates** are refunds by the seller of a portion of the purchase price. They have been used most prominently by car manufacturers eager to move models during periods of slow sales. Manufacturers' rebates are sometimes used to stimulate sales of small appliances such as coffeemakers or hair dryers. Manufacturers' rebate coupons are placed in the retail outlets near the product being promoted.

---

**TABLE 14.2 A Noncumulative Quantity Discount Schedule**

| UNITS PURCHASED | PRICE |
|---|---|
| 1 | List price |
| 2–5 | List price less 10 percent |
| 6–10 | List price less 20 percent |
| Over 10 | List price less 25 percent |

Usually promotional prices are set to attract new customers. This *Realm* magazine promotion rewards subscribers.

## Geographic Considerations

Geographic considerations are important in pricing when the shipment of heavy, bulky, low unit-cost materials is involved. Prices may be quoted with either the buyer or the seller paying all transportation charges or with some type of expense sharing.

A firm's competitiveness often depends on how it handles the costs of transportation. In the extreme case, where the cost of transportation is high compared with the value of the product (e.g., cement), the competitive limits of a firm's territory can easily be defined. In cases where product margins are high or transportation costs are low, market coverage can be extensive. Furthermore, the more differentiated the product, the easier it is for a company to pass along the costs of distribution in the price.

The seller has several alternatives in handling transportation costs. These are FOB plant, uniform delivered price, and zone pricing.

**FOB plant** or *FOB origin* pricing provides a price that does not include any shipping charges. The buyer must pay all the freight charges. The seller pays only the cost of loading the merchandising aboard the carrier selected by the buyer. The abbreviation FOB[15] means *free on board*. Legal title and responsibility pass to the buyer once the purchase is loaded and a receipt is obtained from the representative of the common carrier.

Prices may also be shown as FOB origin—freight allowed. The seller permits the buyer to subtract transportation expenses from the bill. The amount the seller receives varies with the freight charges charged against the invoice. This alternative, called **freight absorption**, is commonly used by firms with high fixed costs (who need to maintain high volume) because it permits a considerable expansion of their market, since a competitive price is quoted regardless of shipping expenses.

The same price (including transportation expenses) is quoted to all buyers when a **uniform delivered price** is the firm's policy. Such pricing is the exact opposite of FOB prices. This system is often compared with pricing a first-class letter, which is the same across the country. Hence, it is sometimes called *postage-stamp pricing*. The price that is quoted includes an *average* transportation charge per customer, which means that distant customers are actually paying a lesser share of selling costs, while customers near the supply source pay what is known as *phantom freight* (the average transportation charge exceeds the actual cost of shipping).

In **zone pricing**, which is simply a modification of a uniform delivered pricing system, the market is divided into different zones and a price is established within each. Canadian parcel post rates depend on zone pricing. The primary advantage of this pricing policy is that it is easy to administer and enables the seller to be more competitive in distant markets. Figure 14.5 shows how a marketer in Winnipeg must divide its market into geographic segments. All customers in zone 1 are charged $10 per unit of freight, while more distant customers pay freight costs based on the zone in which they are located.

**FOB plant**
The buyer must pay all the freight charges.

**freight absorption**
The seller permits the buyer to subtract transportation expenses from the bill.

**uniform delivered price**
The same price (including transportation expenses) is quoted to all buyers.

**zone pricing**
The market is divided into different zones and a price is established within each.

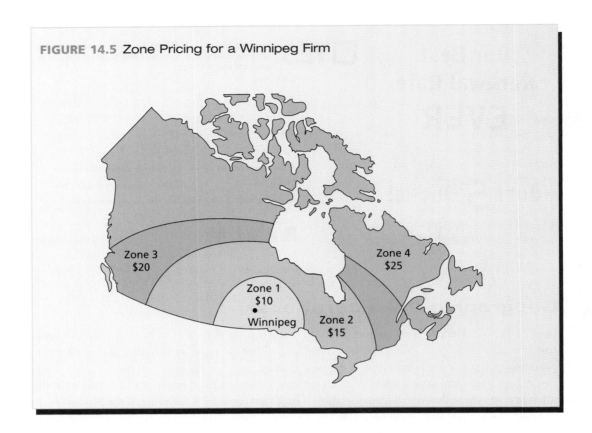

**FIGURE 14.5 Zone Pricing for a Winnipeg Firm**

Zone 3
$20

Zone 4
$25

Zone 1
$10
• 
Winnipeg

Zone 2
$15

## SUMMARY

Pricing objectives must be set before a pricing decision can be made. The four pricing objectives are profitability, volume, meeting the competition, and prestige. When focusing on profitability, firms may attempt to maximize profits, or they may aim for a target return. When concentrating on volume, firms can attempt to maximize sales within a given profit constraint, or they can attempt to maximize market share.

The marketing approach to pricing takes the price theory and cost-accounting approaches to price into consideration, and adds a pragmatic use of consumer analysis as well as a strategic evaluation of likely competitor response.

A pricing policy is a general guideline based on pricing objectives that is intended for use in specific pricing decisions. Pricing policies affect the price structure and provide focus in dealing with varied competitive situations.

New product pricing can either meet competition or use a skimming or penetration price. A skimming policy chooses a high entry price for a new product. A penetration policy chooses a low entry price. Penetration pricing is likely to be used in instances where demand for a new product or service is highly elastic and large numbers of consumers are price-sensitive.

A company's long-term price can be set at, above, or below competition, depending on the rest of the company's marketing mix.

Price lining is the practice of marketing merchandise at a limited number of prices. Psychological pricing is the use of prices to suggest values of a product or attributes of a product/price offering.

Arriving at a final price involves considering a number of other prices and price practices, including market price, cash discounts, trade discounts, and quantity discounts. Price escalation can be an important consideration in long-term contracts. Another set of terms, related to geographical considerations, are FOB plant, freight absorption, uniform delivered price, and zone pricing.

# KEY TERMS

cash discount, p. 355
flexible pricing , p. 351
FOB plant, p. 357
freight absorption, p. 357
list price, p. 355
loss leader, p. 353
market price, p. 355
market share objective, p. 348
odd pricing, p. 354
penetration pricing, p. 350
prestige objectives, p. 348
price limits, p. 355
price lining, p. 352
price structure, p. 348
pricing policy, p. 348

profit maximization, p. 346
promotional allowance, p. 356
promotional price, p. 353
psychological pricing, p. 354
quantity discount, p. 356
rebate, p. 356
sales maximization, p. 347
skimming pricing, p. 349
status quo objectives, p. 348
target return objectives, p. 347
trade discount, p. 356
trade-in, p. 356
uniform delivered price, p. 357
unit pricing, p. 355
zone pricing, p. 357

# INTERACTIVE SUMMARY AND DISCUSSION QUESTIONS

**1.** Pricing objectives must be set before a pricing decision. The four main pricing objectives are profitability, volume, meeting the competition, and prestige. Give one or two product examples for which each objective seems to apply.

**2.** The two main profitability objectives are profit maximization and target return objectives. Explain the advantages and disadvantages of each.

**3.** In the case of volume objectives, some firms attempt to maximize sales within a given profit constraint. Others use a market share objective. Explain the advantages and disadvantages of each.

**4.** Besides trying to make as much money as possible, what are the other advantages of prestige pricing? What are the disadvantages?

**5.** The marketing approach to pricing takes the price theory and cost-accounting approaches to prices into consideration, and adds a pragmatic use of consumer analysis as well as a strategic evaluation of likely competitor response. Your new boss asks you to write a short memo outlining an approach to pricing a new mountain bike. How might the marketing approach to pricing be applied? What are the broad necessary steps that you would recommend?

**6.** A pricing policy is a general guideline based on pricing objectives that is intended for use in specific pricing decisions. Pricing policies affect the price structure. Give an example of the price structure of a product you are familiar with. What is the likely pricing policy for that product?

**7.** Pricing policies provide focus in dealing with varied competitive situations. Explain why it is very important to have a pricing policy in such situations.

**8.** A skimming policy chooses a high entry price. Explain the reasons why a business might choose such a policy. What are the potential disadvantages?

**9.** Penetration pricing is the opposite policy to a skimming policy in new-product pricing. Explain the reasons why a business might choose penetration pricing. What are the potential disadvantages?

**10.** Penetration pricing is likely to be used in instances where demand for a new product or service is highly elastic and large numbers of consumers are highly price-sensitive. Explain.

**11.** A business might set prices relatively higher than those of most competitors. Give an example of such a business, and explain why this might be a good strategy.

**12.** Price lining is the practice of marketing merchandise at a limited number of prices. In what circumstances is such a practice desirable? Why?

**13.** Psychological pricing is the use of prices to suggest values of a product or attributes of a product/price offering. Make a list of as many different examples of psychological pricing as you can think of.

**14.** A set of terms related to geographic considerations are FOB plant, freight absorption, uniform delivered price, and zone pricing. Explain each term.

**15.** From time to time, marketers of gasoline are criticized for raising the price of gas almost simultaneously (suggesting collusion) and raising prices seemingly independent of the cost of oil.
a. Based on your readings, including this chapter, are these accusations justified?
b. Using the Web, research the literature and government investigations of gasoline pricing practices. What conclusions have been drawn with respect to these issues?

## Tom's Place Breaks the Rules

Here's a really bad business idea.

Open a store in the stinkiest part of the city, not far from a shop that offers "live carp." Make sure your aisles are good and cramped, and whatever you do, don't put prices on the goods.

To ruin any hope of success, cram the store with upscale items, specifically designer suits and ties. People who buy expensive clothes would never want to put up with all this nonsense, would they?

You bet they would. Tom Mihalik, proprietor of Tom's Place, a discount men's and women's designer clothing store in the heart of Toronto's odorous Kensington Market, is living proof that a retailer can break almost every rule in the book and still become a roaring success.

His store sells about $8 million worth of designer suits, shirts, jackets, blouses, and ties annually. Sales per square foot, a key measure in retail, top $1000—more than twice the industry average. That's impressive, considering the whole store was pulling in less than $100 000 a year when it opened in the early eighties.

His secrets: offer friendly service, good prices, and a little razzle-dazzle. If you've got those, customers will forgive all sorts of sins.

A visitor quickly learns that there are two prices at Tom's Place—a virtual price, which the salespeople initially quote to customers, and Tom's price.

Does he always offer a discount? "Always, always, always. I never sold anything at the asking price, never," he says.

### You Be the Marketer

1. How do you explain the success of Tom's Place?
2. What pricing policy is Tom Mihalik following?
3. What other changes to the marketing mix would be necessary in order for Tom's Place to charge the premium prices its products would normally command?

Source: Excerpted from John Heinzl, "Tom's Tactics: Low Prices and Larger than Life," *The Globe and Mail* (July 10, 1998), p. B23. Reprinted with permission from *The Globe and Mail*.

# Our Reputation Is Built On Service

For 25 years Flanagan Foodservice has been growing and evolving to meet the changing needs of the foodservice industry. A company that began with one man's dream and dedication has become one of the largest privately owned independent foodservice distributors in Canada.

The basic ingredient of our success is our commitment to provide the best in customer service. From major institutions to intimate restaurants, we have the facilities and industry knowledge to provide the ideal solution. With over 10,000 items you can be sure we have the products to meet your needs. At Flanagan Foodservice, you will find that we have the capabilities of a large operation and the heart of a small business.

Exceptional service is the least we can offer.

**FLANAGAN** 25th ANNIVERSARY FOODSERVICE INC.

Left to right Rick, Dan, Murray and Jeff Flanagan

**Kitchener**
100 Sasaga Drive,
Kitchener ON N2C 2G7
Tel: 519.748.6878
Toll Free: 800.265.6550

**Owen Sound**
2125 12th Avenue, East,
Owen Sound, ON N4K 5P5
Tel: 519.376.8407
Toll Free: 800.265.9690

**Sudbury**
69 Magill St, Walden Business
Park, Lively ON P3Y 1K6
Tel: 705.692.5850
Toll Free: 800.565.5850

## Chapter 15

# CHANNEL AND DISTRIBUTION STRATEGY

## CHAPTER OBJECTIVES

After reading and studying this chapter, you should be able to

1. Discuss channel strategy as one of the elements of the marketing mix.
2. Relate channel strategy to the concept of total customer satisfaction.
3. Explain the role of distribution channels in marketing strategy.
4. Describe the various types of channels of distribution.
5. Outline the major strategy alternatives in using marketing channels.
6. Identify the conditions under which a manufacturer is likely to assume wholesaling functions rather than use independents.
7. Distinguish among merchant wholesalers, agents, and brokers.
8. Identify the major types of merchant wholesalers and instances in which each type might be used.
9. Provide an overview of the many types of wholesaling intermediaries and their functions.
10. Describe conflict and cooperation in the distribution channel.
11. Explain the issues involved in changing from the use of one channel intermediary type to a different type.

Imagine a cupboard filled with 10 000 different products and you will get a sense of what the foodservice industry is partly about. "Foodservice distributors are wholesale companies who sell product to restaurants and institutions," says Justin Sherwood, Vice-president, Foodservice and Ontario Public Policy, at the Canadian Council of Grocery Distributors. A $10-billion-per-year industry, foodservice is "a totally different arm of the food industry, with its own set of unique challenges."

The foodservice industry provides a significant link in the food continuum. Foodservice companies are "the middle men" of the food industry, says Dan Flanagan, president of Flanagan Foodservice Inc. in Kitchener, Ontario. "On the one hand, you've got the restaurant, hospital or institution, and, on the other hand, the manufacturer who makes the product," he says. "Then you've got us, the distributors in the middle, who receive the product from the manufacturer, warehouse it, and accept and deliver orders from customers."

Mr. Flanagan says his company stocks about 12 000 products in warehouses totalling 160 000 square feet; his is a $130-million per year business. Foodservice distributors store everything from pork to prunes, carrots to creamers, pizza to pie filling, Flanagan says. "A restaurant isn't about to get delivery from, say, Heinz, and another from a meat producer and another from a vegetable source. We consolidate. We bring it all in and then ship whatever the restaurant wants in one big order."

"We see ourselves as not just suppliers, but also people who can help our customers improve their business," says Jim Greenwood, president of Gordon Food Services Ontario. "It goes beyond shipping product."

Nonetheless, shipping product is what this industry is basically about. Flanagan Foodservice, for example, distributes from three locations across Ontario using a fleet of more than 40 trucks. Colabor, an integrated marketing and food distribution network operating in Quebec and the Maritimes, distributes approximately 15 000 products, coming from 800 suppliers and manufacturers, to about 30 000 points of sale.

Distributors' warehouses and transportation departments run 24 hours a day. Orders are taken up to 5 p.m. for delivery the next day, says Greenwood. "We haul product all through the night to get to various terminals."

The industry's service level is very high, Mr. Flanagan says, because customers are very demanding. In a business where a restaurant will call up to order 40 racks of lamb for the next day, or when two hotels at opposite ends of the city want their order delivered at 10 a.m. on the same day, there is a lot of pressure to keep everyone happy. "We have to be conscious of our customers' needs and try to fulfill them in an efficient and profitable manner," says Flanagan, adding "It is a daily challenge to put it all together. We have our customers' demands at one end and our suppliers telling us how they're going to do things at the other. It's up to us, stuck in the middle, to make it all work to everybody's benefit."

**This is a good example of the importance and dynamism of this "hidden" aspect of marketing. As we will see in this chapter it is one of the most important aspects of marketing. There are a huge number of channel alternatives available to the marketing planner and the system is quite complex. Experienced marketers know that achieving good distribution for goods and services is one of the most challenging aspects of implementing marketing strategy.**

Source: Excerpted from Marilyn Linton, "Demand Heats Up for Foodservice Distribution," *National Post*, May 27, 2002, p. JV7. Reprinted with permission of the author.

www.flanagan.ca

# INTRODUCTION

In Australia, Gary Jones formed a company to produce and market a line of high-class cosmetics for women and men. Where should they be sold? It was not hard to decide that they should be distributed through high-class department stores and cosmetic stores. Jones then bought a company that produced a standard-quality line of skin care products. The natural distribution outlets for this line were mass marketers such as supermarkets.

How do you get these retailers to carry such products, and how do you distribute these products? Jones could have tried to send salespeople to each outlet and then established a fleet of trucks to deliver the products. However, he knew that a much more efficient system was already available. This was the system of intermediaries (middlemen), such as agents and wholesalers, that would perform the functions of selling, storing, financing, and delivering for him. Such marketing functions always have to be performed, but there is often a choice as to who performs them.

Remarkably, adding more intermediaries to the distribution channel can make distribution more efficient than selling direct. As Figure 15.1 indicates, the number of transactions between manufacturers and their customers is markedly reduced by introducing a wholesaler or retailer.

You can have a great product and a great price, but you will fail unless you have worked out a good channel of distribution strategy that is suited to your available resources, as well as to the nature and value of your product.

In Chapter 1 we saw that marketing creates several types of utility. Marketing channels create time, place, and ownership utility in a direct way. Let's take the example of swimwear. Products for the coming spring and summer have already been produced in the months of December and January, and are en route to retail stores throughout the continent. Information from the marketing department has allowed swimwear manufacturers to identify preferences for new colours, styles, and

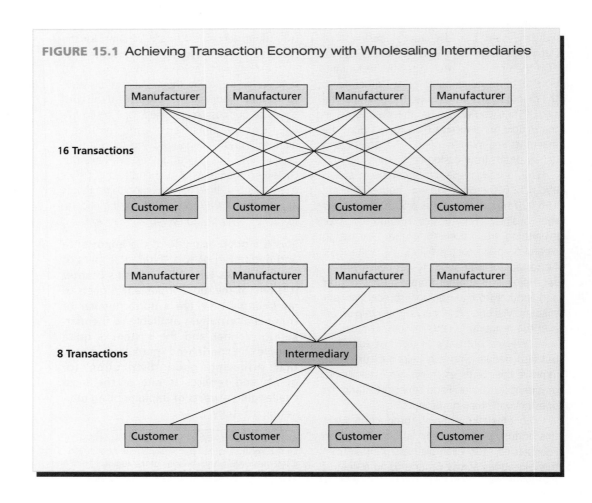

FIGURE 15.1 Achieving Transaction Economy with Wholesaling Intermediaries

16 Transactions

8 Transactions

fabrics and to produce products of the highest quality for each market. However, swimwear of even the highest quality will fail to generate adequate sales unless it is delivered to the right place (place utility), at the right time (time utility), and with appropriate legal requirements (ownership utility). Swimwear that meets consumers' quality expectations is available in the appropriate outlet the first warm day in April, and is accompanied by a sales receipt indicating ownership will be able to provide buyers with form, time, place, and ownership utility—and a little later they'll slip it on, tiptoe across a sunny beach, and dip a pale toe into the chilly water.

A manufacturer of swimwear must therefore work out a clear channel strategy in order for the entire distribution process to work. Let us now consider basic channel strategy as the starting point for a discussion of the distribution function and its role in the marketing mix. An underlying consideration is providing total customer satisfaction. More North American organizations are learning that such an emphasis has a tremendous influence on performance, as measured by cost or customer responsiveness. Products are produced that possess superior technical features and meet the needs and wants of customers, and reach customers through distribution channels.

Carson luggage is made in Ottawa, Staedtler pens and erasers come from Germany, plywood is produced in British Columbia and other provinces, and Timex watches are assembled in Toronto. All are sold throughout Canada. In each case, some method must be devised to bridge the gap between producer and consumer that was discussed in Chapter 1. Distribution channels provide purchasers with a convenient means of obtaining the products that they wish to buy. **Distribution channels** (also called marketing channels) are the paths that goods—and title to these goods—follow from producer to consumer.[1] Specifically, the term *channels* refers to the various marketing institutions and the interrelationships responsible for the flow of goods and services from producer to consumer or industrial user. Intermediaries are the marketing institutions in the distribution channel. A **marketing intermediary** is a business firm operating between the producer and the consumer or business purchaser. The term therefore includes both wholesalers and retailers.

**distribution channels**
The paths that goods—and title to these goods—follow from producer to consumer.

**marketing intermediary**
A business firm operating between the producer and the consumer or business purchaser.

Seeking to increase distribution for a new product.

**Wholesaling** is the activities of intermediaries who sell to retailers, other wholesalers, and business users but not in significant amounts to ultimate consumers. The terms *jobber* and *distributor* are considered synonymous with wholesaler in this book.

Confusion can result from the practices of some firms that operate both wholesaling and retailing operations. Sporting goods stores, for example, often maintain a wholesaling operation in marketing a line of goods to high schools and colleges as well as operating retail stores. For the purpose of this book, we will treat such operations as two separate institutions.

A second source of confusion is the misleading practice of some retailers who claim to be wholesalers. Such stores may actually sell at wholesale prices and can validly claim to do so. However, stores that sell products purchased by individuals for their own use and not for resale are by definition **retailers**, not wholesalers.

# THE ROLE OF DISTRIBUTION CHANNELS IN MARKETING STRATEGY

Distribution channels play a key role in marketing strategy, since they provide the means by which goods and services are conveyed from their producers to consumers and users. The importance of distribution channels can be explained in terms of the utility that is created and the functions that are performed.

## Distribution Channels Perform Important Functions

The distribution channel performs several functions in the overall marketing system.[2] These include facilitating the exchange process, sorting to alleviate discrepancies in assortment, standardizing transactions, holding inventories, assisting in the search process, and transporting materials and finished products.[3]

### Facilitating the Exchange Process

The evolution of distribution channels began with the exchange process described in Chapter 1. As market economies grew, the exchange process itself became complicated. With more producers and more potential buyers, intermediaries came into existence to facilitate transactions by cutting down the number of marketplace contacts. For example, if ten orchards in the Okanagan valley each sell to six supermarket chains, there are a total of 60 transactions. If the producers set up and market their apples through a cooperative, the number of contacts declines to 16 (see Figure 15.1).

### Sorting to Alleviate Imbalances Between Outputs and Consumer Needs

For economic reasons, a producer tends to maximize the quantity of a limited line of products (limited assortment). For example, one manufacturer may produce 10 000 each of a limited line of golf balls. On the other hand, the buyer needs a minimum quantity of a wide selection of alternatives (an assortment of twelve golf balls, one pair of shoes, and one golf jacket). Thus, there is a discrepancy between what one producer has to offer and what the consumers want. **Sorting** is the process that alleviates discrepancies in assortment by reallocating the outputs of various producers into assortments desired by individual purchasers. This is handled by an intermediary such as a wholesaler or retailer that buys large quantities of different goods from several suppliers, and then makes available a customized assortment to fit the needs of its customers.

Figure 15.2 shows an example of the sorting process. First, an individual producer's output is divided into separate homogeneous categories such as the various types and grades of apples. These apples are then combined with the similar crops of other orchards, a process known as *accumulation*. These accumulations are broken down into smaller units or divisions, such as crates of apples. This

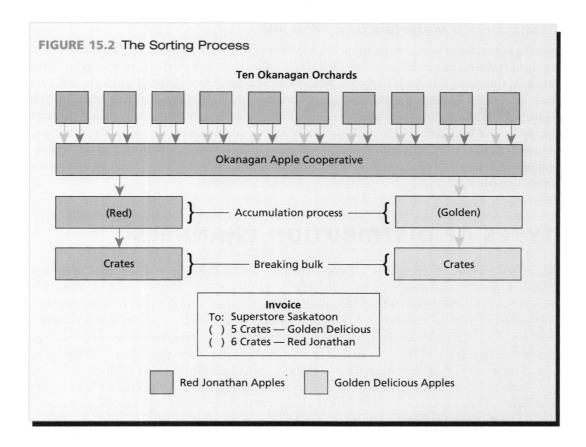

**FIGURE 15.2** The Sorting Process

Ten Okanagan Orchards

Okanagan Apple Cooperative

(Red) } ──── Accumulation process ──── { (Golden)

Crates } ──── Breaking bulk ──── { Crates

**Invoice**
To: Superstore Saskatoon
( ) 5 Crates — Golden Delicious
( ) 6 Crates — Red Jonathan

Red Jonathan Apples     Golden Delicious Apples

is often called *breaking bulk* in marketing literature. Finally, an assortment is built for the next level in the distribution channel. For example, the Okanagan cooperative might prepare an assortment of five crates of Golden Delicious and six crates of Red Jonathan apples for a Superstore supermarket in Saskatoon.

## Standardizing Transactions

If each transaction in a complex market economy were subject to negotiation, the exchange process would be chaotic. Distribution channels standardize exchange transactions in terms of the product, such as grading of apples into types and grades, and the transfer process itself. Order points, prices, payment terms, delivery schedules, and purchase lots tend to be standardized by distribution channel members. For example, supermarket buyers probably have online communications links with the cooperative cited in Figure 15.2. Once a certain stock position is reached, more apples would automatically be ordered from either the cooperative's current output or its cold storage.

## Holding Inventories

Distribution channel members hold a minimum of inventories to take advantage of economies of scale in transporting and to provide a buffer for small changes in demand. This also makes products available to meet changing consumer demand.

## Assisting the Search Process

Distribution channels also accommodate the search behaviour of both buyers and sellers. (Search behaviour was discussed earlier in Chapter 8.) Buyers are searching for specific products and services to fill their needs, while sellers are attempting to find what consumers want. A college student looking for some Golden Delicious apples might go to the fruit section of the Superstore in Saskatoon. Similarly, the manager of that department would be able to provide the Okanagan cooperative with information about sales trends in his or her marketplace.

### Transporting Materials and Products

Storing products in convenient locations for shipment to wholesale and retail establishments allows firms to embody time utility in the product. Place utility is created primarily by transporting the product. Customer satisfaction depends heavily on the reliable movement of products to ensure their availability. Eastman Kodak Company committed a major blunder in the late 1970s when it launched a multimillion-dollar advertising campaign for its new instant camera before adequate quantities had been delivered to retail outlets. Many would-be purchasers visited the stores and, when they discovered that the new camera was not available, bought a Polaroid instead. By providing consumers with time and place utility, physical distribution contributes to implementing the marketing concept.

# TYPES OF DISTRIBUTION CHANNELS

There are four main types of distribution channel: direct, one-step, two-step, and multistep. However, no one marketing channel is superior to all others. The "best" channel for Electrolux vacuum cleaners may be direct from manufacturer to consumer through a sales force of 1000 men and women. The "best" channel for frozen french fries may be from food processor to agent intermediary to merchant wholesaler (a wholesaler who takes title) to supermarket to consumer. The marketing manager must therefore analyze alternative channels in the light of consumer needs and competitive restraints to determine the best channel or channels for the firm's products.

Even when the proper channels have been chosen and established, the marketing manager's channel decisions are not over. Channels, like so many of the other marketing variables, change, and today's ideal channel may prove less effective in a few years.

For example, the typical channel for books has been from publisher/producer to local bookstore and department store. Now the smaller stores are being supplanted by superstores such as Chapters/Indigo, McNally Robinson, and others that carry an extensive range of books plus videos, CDs, and a coffee bar. In addition, books are now widely available through the Internet from such suppliers as Amazon.com and the Internet arm of the likes of Chapters/Indigo.

Figure 15.3 depicts the major channels available for marketers of consumer and business goods. In general, business goods channels tend to be shorter than consumer goods channels because of geographic concentrations of business buyers, a relatively limited number of purchasers, and the absence of retailers from the chain. The term *retailer* refers to the supplier of consumer goods. Service channels also tend to be short because of the intangibility of services and the need to maintain personal relationships in the channel.

www.chapters.indigo.ca

www.mcnallyrobinson.com

www.tupperware.com

www.avon.com

## Direct Channel

The simplest, most direct marketing channel is not necessarily the best, as is indicated by the relatively small percentage of the dollar volume of sales that moves directly *from the producer to the consumer.* Less than 5 percent of all consumer goods are candidates for the producer-to-consumer channel. Dairies, Tupperware, Avon cosmetics, and newspapers are examples of firms whose product moves directly from manufacturer to ultimate consumer. Some products, such as milk, are distributed through retail channels as well. The use of multiple channels is quite common for many products. As the use of the Internet increases, the direct channel will likely become a powerful additional channel. For example, since Dell has been so successful in selling computers directly to consumers both through media advertising and through the Internet, IBM and others have decided that they too will sell directly to customers. Another company offers a bonus of free software for orders placed through the Internet. Airlines have aggressively pushed customers toward online purchasing. Direct channels are much more important in the business goods market, where most major installations and accessory equipment—and many of the fabricated parts and raw materials—are marketed through direct contacts between producer and user. Electronic exchanges facilitate this tendency.

# One-Step Channel (Consumer Goods)

This channel is being used more and more, and in many instances it has taken the place of the traditional channel. When large retailers are involved, they are willing to take on many functions performed by the wholesaler—consequently, goods move *from producer to retailer to consumer*. Costco is a good example. It buys in bulk from the producer and sells to individual customers and business customers. No wholesaler has to be involved. A unique aspect of Costco is that it also acts as a wholesaler. It sells to small retailers who in turn sell to final customers. The system works because these small retailers offer the products at a more convenient time and location.

www.costco.com/home.asp

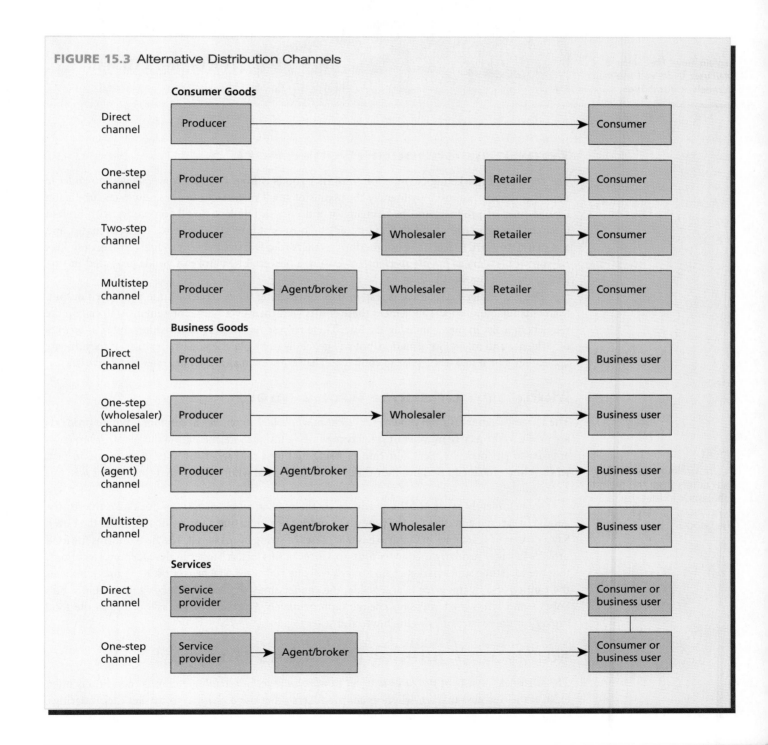

**FIGURE 15.3** Alternative Distribution Channels

Explain how *The Globe and Mail* uses direct and one-step channels of distribution.

## Two-Step Channel (Consumer)

The traditional marketing channel for consumer goods is *from producer to wholesaler to retailer to user.* It is the method used by literally thousands of small manufacturers or companies producing limited lines of products and by as many or more small retailers. Small companies with limited financial resources use wholesalers as immediate sources of funds through their bulk purchases, and as a marketing arm to reach the hundreds of retailers who will stock their products. Smaller retailers rely on wholesalers as *buying specialists* to ensure a balanced inventory of goods produced in various regions of the world.

The wholesaler's sales force is responsible for reaching the market with the producer's output. Many manufacturers also supplement these efforts with their own sales representatives to call on the retailers to assist in merchandising the line. These representatives serve the manufacturer as sources of influence and market information, but will generally not make the sales transaction. If they initiate a sale, they give it to a wholesaler to complete. They are known as *missionary sales representatives.*

## Multistep Channel (Consumer)

**agent**

A wholesaling intermediary that differs from the typical wholesaler in that the agent does not take title to the goods.

The longest channel is *from producer to agent to wholesaler to retailer to consumer.* Where products are produced by a large number of small companies, a unique intermediary—the agent, or broker—appears to perform the basic function of bringing buyer and seller together. **Agents** are, in fact, wholesaling intermediaries, but they differ from the typical wholesaler in that they *do not take title to the goods.*

Agents, merely represent the producer or the regular wholesaler (who does take title to the goods) in seeking a market for the producer's output or in locating a source of supply for the buyer. Say a canner of vegetables in Ontario has 6000 cases of string beans to sell. The firm informs the food brokers (agents) regularly used in various provinces of this fact. A broker in the Maritimes ascertains that the Maritime supermarket chain Sobey's will buy 800 cases. The broker takes the order, informs the canner, and, if the price is acceptable, the canner ships the order to Sobey's. The canner bills Sobey's and sends a commission cheque (approximately 3 percent of the sale price) to the food broker for the service of bringing buyer and seller together.

## Multistep Channel (Business Goods)

This channel consists of *producer to agent to wholesaler to industrial user.* Similar conditions often exist in the business market, where small producers often use a channel to market their offerings.

The agent wholesaling intermediary, often called a manufacturer's representative or manufacturer's agent, is a company that provides an independent sales force for contacting large, scattered wholesalers and some key business buyers. For example, a manufacturer of specialty industrial tapes might use agents to sell to industrial wholesalers and to encourage the wholesaler's sales force to push the product to business users.

## One-Step (Agent) Channel (Business)

Where the unit sale is small, a **merchant wholesaler** must be used to cover the market economically. By maintaining regional inventories, merchant wholesalers can achieve transportation economies by stockpiling goods and making the final small shipment over a small distance. But where the unit sale is large and transportation costs account for a small percentage of the total product costs, the *producer to agent to business user* channel may be employed. The agent wholesaling intermediaries become, in effect, the company's sales force. For example, a producer of special castings might engage agents who are already calling on potential customers with other lines.

**merchant wholesaler**
A wholesaler who takes title to the products carried.

## One-Step (Wholesaler) Channel (Business)

Similar characteristics in the business market often lead to the use of wholesalers between the manufacturer and industrial purchaser. The term **industrial distributor** is commonly used in this market to refer to those wholesalers that take title to the goods they handle. These wholesalers are involved in marketing small accessory equipment and operating supplies, such as building supplies, office supplies, small hand tools, and office equipment.

**industrial distributor**
A wholesaler that operates in the business goods market and typically handles small accessory equipment and operating supplies.

## Direct Channel (Services)

Distributing services to both consumers and business users is usually simpler and more direct than for consumer and business goods. In part, this is due to the intangibility of services; the marketer of services does not often have to worry about storage, transportation, and inventory control. Shorter channels, often direct from service provider to consumer or business user, are typically used.

Many services can be performed only on a direct basis, and personal relationships between performers and users are very important. Consumers tend to remain clients of the same bank, car repair shop, or hairstylist as long as they are reasonably satisfied. Likewise, accounting firms and attorneys are retained on a relatively permanent basis by business buyers.

## One-Step Channel (Services)

When service providers use marketing intermediaries to reach consumers or business users, these are usually *agents or brokers*. Common examples include insurance agents, securities brokers, travel agents, and entertainment agents.

For instance, travel and hotel packages are sometimes created by intermediaries and then marketed at the retail level by travel agents to both vacationers and firms that want to offer employee incentive awards.

## A Special Note on Channel Strategy for Consumer Services

A dominant reason for patronizing many consumer services, such as banks, motels, and car rental agencies, is convenient location. It is absolutely essential to carefully select the retail site. For example, banks locate branches in suburban shopping centres and malls. Automated electronic tellers that enable customers to withdraw funds and make deposits when a bank is closed are a further example of attempting to provide convenience as well as more efficient operations.

## Multiple Channels

As mentioned earlier, a common phenomenon is using more than one marketing channel for similar products. These *multiple channels* (or dual distribution) are used when the same product is marketed through several channels as well as both to the ultimate consumer and to business users. Dial soap is distributed through the traditional grocery wholesaler to food stores to the consumer, but a second channel also exists, from the manufacturer to large retail chains and motels that buy direct from the manufacturer. Competition among retailers and other intermediaries that are striving to expand lines, profitability, and customer service has created these multiple channels.

In other cases, the same product is marketed through a variety of types of retail outlets. A basic product such as a paintbrush is carried in inventory by the traditional hardware store; it is also handled by such nontraditional retail outlets as auto accessory stores, building supply outlets, department stores, discount houses, mail-order houses, supermarkets, and variety stores. Each retail store may use a different marketing channel.

Firestone tires are marketed

1. directly to General Motors, where they serve as a fabricated part for new Chevrolets
2. through Firestone stores, company-owned retail outlets
3. through franchised Firestone outlets
4. from the factory to tire jobbers to retail gas stations

Each channel enables the manufacturer to serve a different market.

## Reverse Channels

**reverse channels**
The paths goods follow from consumer to manufacturer or to marketing intermediaries.

While the traditional concept of marketing channels involves moving products and services from producer to consumer or business user, there is increasing interest in reverse channels. **Reverse channels** are the paths goods follow from consumer to manufacturer or to marketing intermediaries. These channels are normally seen in recycling. For example, metal, paper, and glass are sent back from user to manufacturer for reuse.

Reverse channels increase in importance as raw materials become more expensive, and as additional laws are passed to control litter and the disposal of packaging materials such as soft-drink bottles. For recycling to succeed, four basic conditions must be satisfied:

1. A technology must be available that can efficiently process the material being recycled.
2. A market must be available for the end product—the reclaimed material.
3. A substantial and continuing quantity of secondary product (recycled aluminum, reclaimed steel from cars, recycled paper) must be available.
4. A marketing system must be developed that can bridge the gap between suppliers of secondary products and end users on a profitable basis.[4]

In some instances, the reverse channel consists of traditional marketing intermediaries. In the soft-drink industry, retailers and local bottlers perform these functions. In other cases, manufacturers take the initiative by establishing redemption centres. A concentrated attempt by the Reynolds Metals Company in one area permitted the company to recycle an amount of aluminum equivalent to 60 percent of the total containers marketed in the area. Other reverse-channel participants may include community groups, which organize "cleanup" days and develop systems for rechannelling paper products for recycling, and specialized organizations developed for waste disposal and recycling.

### Reverse Channels for Product Recalls and Repairs

Reverse channels are also used for product recalls and repairs. Ownership of some products (for example, tires) is registered so that proper notification can be sent if there is a product recall. In the case of automobile recalls, owners are advised to have the problem corrected at their dealership. Similarly, reverse channels have been used for repairs to some products. The warranty for a small appliance may specify that if repairs are needed in the first 90 days, the item should be returned to the dealer. After that period, the product should be returned to the factory. Such reverse channels are a vital element of product recalls and repair procedures.

## Facilitating Agencies in the Distribution Channel

A **facilitating agency** provides specialized assistance for regular channel members (such as producers, wholesalers, and retailers) in moving products from producer to consumer. Included in the definition of facilitating agencies are transportation companies, warehousing firms, financial institutions, insurance companies, and marketing research companies.

**facilitating agency**
An agency that provides specialized assistance for regular channel members (such as producers, wholesalers, and retailers) in moving products from producer to consumer.

## The Use of the Internet in Distribution

The use of the Internet in distribution is growing rapidly. Some products are distributed directly *from manufacturer to consumer,* such as software, music, and computers. But other channel configurations seem to be able to make more use of the Internet. This is probably because most producers are not set up to ship directly to the buyer.

The use of the Internet by channel intermediaries is also growing rapidly. This is especially true at the retail level, where everything from books to airline tickets to stocks to bank loans can be obtained through the Internet. This topic will be discussed more extensively in the next chapter.

As we have seen in Chapter 9, business-to-business marketing, suppliers and customers have well-established means of conducting electronic commerce. This can be through the Internet, but it is also possible that they have established other means of direct communication. For example, as components are used by a manufacturer, the supplier is informed electronically, and at a predetermined inventory level the supplier automatically sends components to replenish the manufacturer's inventory.

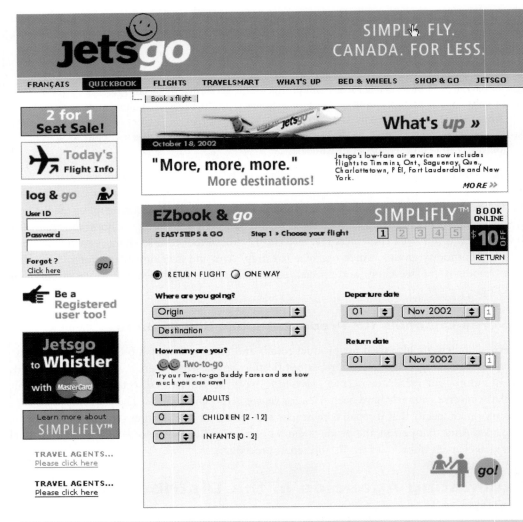

A one-step channel.

## WHOLESALING

Wholesaling is big! Everyone knows that retailing is an important part of the Canadian economy, but most do not realize that wholesaling is equally important. The total operating revenue of wholesaling is larger than retailing, and wholesale trade as a percentage of GDP is approximately the same (6 percent). There are approximately 65 000 wholesale locations in Canada whose sales total $380.7 billion, and employees number 810 000. Figure 15.4 illustrates the relative growth of Gross Domestic Product contributions over the past thirty years for Wholesale, Retail, Manufacturing, and for All Industries. During that period, Wholesale's value-added contribution has increased close to eightfold to $50.3 billion, almost double that of the other categories. Figure 15.5 shows the types and proportion of wholesale customers. Retail and industrial customers are the largest customers.

Wholesalers are more prominent in some distribution channels than others. They are involved in selling to retailers such goods as food, beverages, apparel, and household furnishings. On the other hand, for goods such as metals, machinery and equipment, grain, and petroleum, wholesalers mainly supply industrial and commercial users, farmers, and foreign markets directly. In fact, 65 percent of total wholesale trade activity in Canada does not include retailers.

Wholesaling is the initial marketing institution in many channels of distribution from manufacturers to consumer or business user. Furthermore, there are several different types of wholesaling

**FIGURE 15.4** GDP Growth by Category

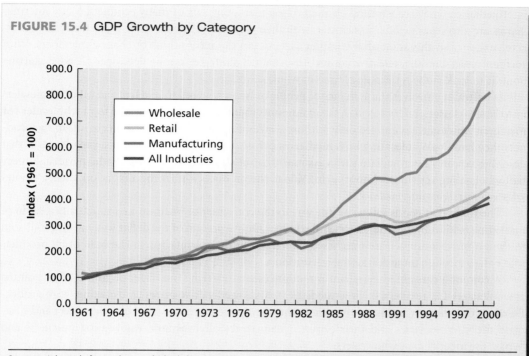

Source: Adapted from data pubished by Statistics Canada Wholesale Statistics, available at this Internet site http://strategis.ic.gc.ca/pics/dm/wholesale-eng.pdf, "Wholesale Trade – Service Industries Overview Series," January 2002. Reprinted with permission of the Minister of Industry Canada.

**FIGURE 15.5** Wholesale Customers Distribution

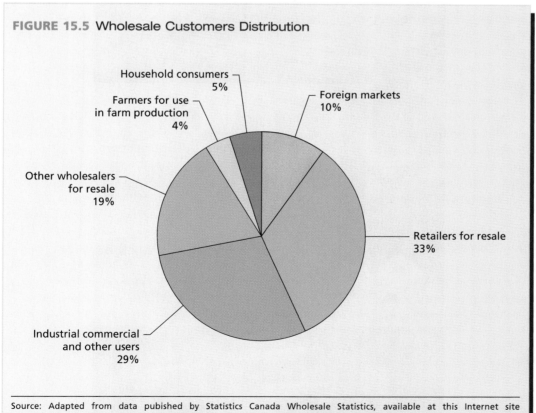

Source: Adapted from data pubished by Statistics Canada Wholesale Statistics, available at this Internet site http://strategis.ic.gc.ca/pics/dm/wholesale-eng.pdf, "Wholesale Trade – Service Industries Overview Series," January 2002. Reprinted with permission of the Minister of Industry Canada.

intermediaries. They are a critical element of the marketing mix of many products. Many intermediaries are also separate business entities with their own marketing mixes. It is essential that a marketer understand this somewhat complex system and the motivations of channel members. With such an understanding, effective competitive channel strategies can be developed. A good starting point is to look at the terminology used in wholesaling.

Wholesaling involves the activities of people or firms who sell to retailers and other wholesalers or to business users, but not in significant amounts to ultimate consumers. The term **wholesaler** (or merchant wholesaler) is applied only to those wholesaling intermediaries who *take title* to the products they handle. **Wholesaling intermediaries** (or wholesaling middlemen) is a broader term that describes not only intermediaries who assume title, but also agents and brokers who perform important wholesaling activities without taking title to the products. Under this definition, then, a wholesaler is a *merchant intermediary*.

The route that goods follow on the way to the consumer or business user is actually a chain of marketing institutions—wholesalers and retailers. Only 3 percent of the dollar value of all goods sold to the ultimate consumer are purchased directly from the manufacturer. The bulk of all products sold passes through these marketing institutions.

A common consumer complaint is that prices are too high. The finger of guilt is often pointed at wholesalers and retailers, the intermediaries who allegedly drive prices up by taking "high profits." Discount outlets such as Costco often claim that their prices are lower since they buy direct and eliminate the intermediaries and their profits. Chain stores often assume wholesaling functions and bypass the independent wholesalers.

Are these complaints and claims valid? Are wholesaling intermediaries anachronisms doomed to a swift demise? Answers to these questions can be formulated by considering the functions and costs of these marketing intermediaries.

**wholesalers**
Wholesaling intermediaries who take title to the products they handle.

**wholesaling intermediaries**
Intermediaries who assume title, as well as agents and brokers who perform important wholesaling activities without taking title to the products.

Catalogue distribution has a long history.

# Wholesaling Functions

A marketing institution will continue to exist only as long as it fulfills a need by performing a required service. Its death may be slow, but it is inevitable if other channel members discover that they can survive without it. Figure 15.6 shows that there are seven possible functions provided by wholesaling intermediaries: buying, selling, storing, transporting, risk taking, financing, and providing market information. It is important to note that numerous types of wholesaling intermediaries exist and that not all of them provide every one of these functions. Producers–suppliers and their customers, who rely on wholesaling intermediaries for distribution, select those intermediaries that provide the desired combination of services.

## Buying and Selling

Buying and selling are two key functions of wholesaling. A product does not move from a producer unless a wholesaler is willing to take the risk of buying a quantity for sale to its customers. Because wholesalers are professional purchasers, they have to be convinced that the product will be accepted by ultimate users. Thus the task of the supplier is to prove the advantages of the product, and how the supplier will support the wholesaler and other resellers with advertising and other marketing functions.

**FIGURE 15.6** Possible Wholesaling Functions for Customers and Producers–Suppliers

**Buying**
Acts as purchasing agent for customers, anticipates customer demands, possesses knowledge of alternative supply sources.

**Selling**
Maintains a sales force to call on customers, thus providing a low-cost method of serving smaller retailers and business buyers.

**Transporting**
Customers receive prompt delivery in response to their demands, reducing their inventory investments. By "breaking bulk" (purchasing in carload or truckload lots, then reselling in smaller quantities), wholesalers reduce overall transportation costs.

**Risk Taking**
Aids producers by evaluating credit risks of numerous distant retail customers and smaller business users. Extending credit to these customers is another form of risk taking. Risk of possible spoilage, theft, or obsolescence is assumed when the wholesaler is responsible for transporting and stocking goods in inventory.

**Storing**
Performs a warehousing function, reduces risk and cost of maintaining inventory for producers, and provides customers with prompt delivery service.

**Providing Marketing Information**
Serves as key marketing research input for producers through regular contact with retail and business buyers. Provides customers with information about new products, technical information about product lines, information on competitive activities and industry trends, and advisory information concerning changes in such areas as pricing and legal rulings.

**Financing**
Aids customers by granting credit that might not be available if they purchased directly from distant manufacturers. Provides financing assistance to producers by purchasing goods in advance of sale and through promptly paying bills.

Once wholesalers agree to carry the product, they implicitly accept the task of selling it to other resellers or users. Wholesalers thus have sales personnel to handle these functions. Because of the large number of products normally carried by a wholesaler, it is difficult for these salespeople to give individual products intensive attention. That is why manufacturers often have their own missionary sales representatives to add to the efforts of the wholesaler's sales force.

## Transporting and Storing Product

Wholesalers transport and store products at locations that are convenient to customers. Manufacturers ship products from their warehouses to numerous wholesalers, who then ship smaller quantities to retail outlets that are convenient to the purchaser. A large number of wholesalers and most retailers assume the inventory function (and cost) for the manufacturer. The retailer benefits from the convenience afforded by local inventories, and the manufacturer's cash needs are reduced since the firm's products are sold directly to the wholesaler or retailer.

At the wholesale level, costs are reduced by making large purchases from the manufacturer. The wholesaler receives quantity discounts from the manufacturer—along with reduced transportation rates, since economical carload or truckload shipments are made to the wholesaler's warehouses. At the warehouse, the wholesaler breaks bulk into smaller quantities and ships to the retailer over a shorter distance than would be the case if the manufacturer filled the retailer's order directly from a central warehouse.

Costs are often lowered when intermediaries are used, since the sales force of the retailer or wholesaler can represent many manufacturers to a single customer. As Figure 15.1 indicates, the number of transactions between manufacturers and their customers is reduced by introducing an intermediary (a wholesaler or retailer). Reduced market contacts can lead to lowered marketing costs. When a wholesaling intermediary is added, the number of transactions in this illustration is reduced from sixteen to eight, thereby creating economies of scale by providing an assortment of goods with greater utility and at lower cost than would be the case without such an intermediary.

## Providing Marketing Information

Because of their central position between the manufacturer and retailers or business buyers, wholesalers serve as important information links. Wholesalers provide their customers with useful information about new products. They also supply manufacturers with information concerning market reception of their product offerings.

## Risk Taking

Wholesalers must evaluate the credit risks of retail customers and business users. Risk is assumed by extending credit to its customers. Wholesalers are also faced with a barrage of new products that they must evaluate to determine the likelihood for market acceptance. In addition, the wholesaler is responsible for transporting goods and stocking them in inventory, as well as assuming the risk of possible spoilage, theft, or obsolescence.

## Financing

Wholesalers provide a financing function as well. Wholesalers often provide retailers with goods on credit. By purchasing goods on credit, retailers can minimize their cash investments in inventory and pay for most of their purchases as the goods are being sold. This allows them to benefit from the principle of *leverage:* a minimum investment inflates their return on investment. For example, a retailer with an investment of $1 million and profits of $100 000 will realize a return on investment (ROI) of 10 percent. But if the necessary invested capital can be reduced to $800 000 through credit from the wholesalers, and if the $100 000 profits can be maintained, the retailers ROI increases to 12.5 percent.

Wholesalers of goods for the business market provide similar services. In the steel industry, intermediaries called metal service centres currently market approximately one-fifth of the steel shipped by Canadian mills. Such a centre may stock as many as 6500 items for sale to many of the thousands of major metal users who buy their heavy-usage items in large quantities directly from the steel mills, but who turn to service centres for quick delivery of special orders and other items in small quantities. While an order from the mills may take 90 days to be delivered, a service centre can usually deliver within 24 to 48 hours. Such service reduces the investment needed in stock.

## Distribution Channel Functions Can Be Assumed by Other Channel Members

While wholesaling intermediaries often perform all seven of the above functions for their producer, retailer, and other wholesale clients, these functions could be performed by other channel members. Manufacturers may choose to bypass independent wholesaling intermediaries by establishing networks of regional warehouses, maintaining large sales forces to provide market coverage, serving as sources of information for their retail customers, and assuming the financing function. In some instances, they may decide to push the responsibility for some of these functions through the channel on to the retailer or the ultimate purchaser. Large retailers who choose to perform their own wholesaling operations face the same choices.

A fundamental marketing principle is that *marketing functions must be performed by some member of the channel; they may be shifted, but they cannot be eliminated.* Either the large retailers such as Wal-Mart who bypass the wholesaler and deal directly with the manufacturer will assume the functions previously performed by wholesaling intermediaries, or these functions will be performed by the manufacturer. Similarly, a manufacturer who deals directly with the ultimate consumer or with industrial buyers will assume the functions of storage, delivery, and market information previously performed by other marketing intermediaries. Intermediaries themselves can be eliminated from the channel, but the channel functions must be performed by someone.

The potential gain for the manufacturer or retailer who might be considering bypassing wholesaling intermediaries can be estimated from the profit structure of the wholesaling industry. After-tax profitability runs about 1.7 percent on income, and 11.4 percent on equity.[5] These amounts could theoretically be saved *if* channel members performed the wholesale functions as efficiently as independent wholesaling intermediaries. Such savings could be used to reduce retail prices, to increase the profits of the manufacturer or retailers, or both. In general, profit levels are low. High turnover is therefore a necessity to provide adequate returns on investment.

## Types of Wholesaling Intermediaries

As mentioned previously, various types of wholesaling intermediaries are present in different marketing channels. Some provide a wide range of services or handle a broad line of products, while others specialize in a single service, product, or industry. Table 15.1 classifies wholesaling intermediaries based on two characteristics: *ownership* (whether the wholesaling intermediary is independent, manufacturer-owned, or retailer-owned) and *title flows* (whether title passes from the manufacturer to the wholesaling intermediary or not). There are, in turn, three basic types of ownership: (1) independent wholesaling, which can involve either merchant wholesalers (who do take title to goods) or agents and brokers (who do not);[6] (2) manufacturer-owned sales branches and offices; and (3) retailer-owned cooperatives and buying offices.

### Manufacturer-Owned Facilities

Increasing volumes of products are being marketed directly by manufacturers through company-owned facilities. There are several reasons for this trend: some products are perishable, some require complex installation or servicing, others need more aggressive promotion, and still others are high-unit-value goods that the manufacturer wishes to control through the channel directly to the purchaser. Among the industries that have largely shifted from using independent wholesaling intermediaries to using company-owned channels are paper, paint, lumber, construction materials, piece goods, and apparel manufacturers.[7] More than 50 percent of all business goods are sold directly to users by the manufacturer, and slightly more than one-third of *all* products are marketed through manufacturer-owned channels.

www.walmart.com

**TABLE 15.1** Categorizing Wholesaling Intermediaries

**Classification Based on Ownership of the Intermediary**
- Independent wholesaling intermediaries
- Manufacturer-owned sales branches and offices
- Retailer-owned cooperatives and buying offices

**Classification Based on Title Flows**
- Merchant wholesalers (take title)
- Agents and brokers (do not take title)

# INTERNET IMPACT

## HOW THE INTERNET AFFECTS THE MUSIC INDUSTRY'S DISTRIBUTION CHANNELS

Recently, the music industry has come face to face with the Internet—and it's scared. New formats for storing music, especially the one called MP3, make it a snap to share over the Net recordings that can be played, in full stereo, on PCs with speakers, in regular CD players, and on Walkman-like devices designed for MP3. Last year listeners downloaded literally billions of songs from Web sites and paid for next to none of them.

Welcome to yet another chapter of "The Internet Changes Everything." This particular one is a profile of two men on opposite ends of the music business spectrum: Val Azzoli, co-chairman and co-CEO of $700-million-plus-a-year Atlantic Group, which sells the work of artists like Hootie & the Blowfish, Jewel, and Sugar Ray; and Michael Robertson, CEO of a privately held Web site called MP3.com, which gives away digitized songs by artists you've mostly never heard of and yet is perhaps the key company in this digital revolution. The men have never met; they are two of the many people, at companies ranging from Real Networks in Seattle and Microsoft in Redmond, Washington, to IBM in Armonk, New York, and Bertelsmann in Germany, who are either defending against or promoting this new technology.

The problem the $38-billion-a-year recording industry faces is that the ability to ship music directly may shift the balance of economic power. If artists can deliver to fans via the Net, who needs labels and distributors? The threat is nascent—North Americans spent almost nothing on downloaded music last year and just $134 million on CDs ordered via the Web vs. nearly $14 billion on tunes bought in stores. But there is evidence of change: The Recording Industry Association of America says MP3 piracy may have

helped drive a slight decline in music sold to the 15–24 age group in the past two years. "The barbarians are at the gate," says Robert Goodale, CEO of Ultrastar, a New York firm that helps artists connect with fans and promote music on their own Web sites. "They're in the moats, and they're climbing up the sides of the castle."

www.mp3.com

The Attila the Hun of this latest digital revolution is a blond, baby-faced 31-year-old named Michael Robertson, CEO of MP3.com. "We're working for a higher purpose," he says, earnest as a preacher. "We're providing artists with an option besides the traditional industry route—an avenue in which they have control of their destiny and keep ownership of their work."

Robertson's business consists of a site, www.mp3.com, where you can click on any of several thousand recordings and download it onto your computer's hard drive. At that point the song is, for all intents and purposes, yours to listen to on your computer's speakers or your stereo system, to transfer to an MP3 player like the Diamond Rio (a machine the RIAA would like to ban, but that's sold in places like CompUSA for $200), or to post to a pirate Web site where thousands of your best friends can share them. The songs on MP3.com are not pirated, unlike many of the music files available on the Net—artists place their music here as a way of introducing listeners to their work.

**Is this approach to distribution "piracy"? What do you think will be its impact on other channels of distribution?**

Source: Excerpted from Jodi Mardesich, "How the Internet Hits Big Music," *Fortune* (May 10, 1999), pp. 96–98. Reprinted with permission.

This does not mean that independent wholesalers are being squeezed out. Their numbers remain in the thousands, and their volume of trade in the billions of dollars. Table 15.2 shows a summary outline of manufacturer-owned facilities.

**TABLE 15.2** Manufacturer-Owned Facilities

| MANUFACTURER-OWNED FACILITIES | DESCRIPTION |
| --- | --- |
| Sales branch | Manufacturer-owned facility that carries inventory and processes orders to customers from available stock. |
| Public warehouses | Independently owned storage facilities. Manufacturer rents space to store inventory for shipment by the warehouse to customers in the area. Warehouse will break bulk (divide up a carload), package inventory, and fill orders. |
| Trade fairs | Manufacturers in a particular industry display their wares at some temporary venue for visiting retail and wholesale buyers, e.g., Montreal Toy Show. |
| Merchandise mart | Permanent exhibition at which manufacturers rent showcases for product offerings, e.g. Taipei, World Trade Centre. |

### Independent Wholesaling Intermediaries

As has been mentioned earlier, there are many independent wholesaling intermediaries. They perform vital functions in the marketing of goods and services, and their role and categorization should be understood clearly. These intermediaries may be divided into two categories: merchant wholesalers, which take title to the products, and agents and brokers, which may take possession of the products, but do not take title to them. Merchant wholesalers account for approximately 85 percent of all sales handled by independent wholesalers. As Figure 15.7 indicates, they can be further classified as full- or limited-function wholesalers. Table 15.3 shows a summary outline of independent wholesaling intermediaries.

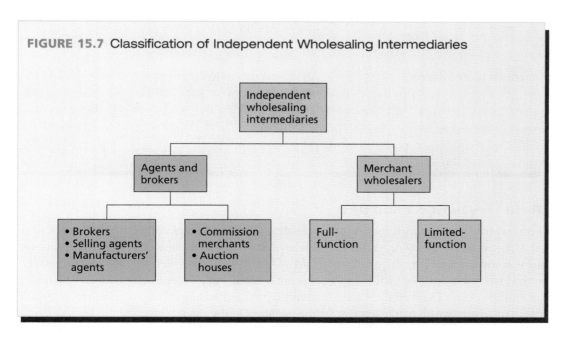

**FIGURE 15.7** Classification of Independent Wholesaling Intermediaries

**TABLE 15.3** Independent Wholesaling Intermediaries

| INDEPENDENT WHOLESALING INTERMEDIARIES | DESCRIPTION |
| --- | --- |
| **MERCHANT WHOLESALERS** | Full-function merchant wholesalers provide a complete assortment of services for retailers or business purchasers. Have own sales force, make deliveries, and extend credit. Common where retailers are small and carry more inexpensive items. |
| rack jobber | This wholesaler provides the racks, stocks the merchandise, prices the goods, and refills the shelves (e.g., housewares and books in a supermarket). |
| cash-and-carry wholesaler | Performs most wholesaling functions except financing and delivery. Costco acts as a cash- and-carry wholesaler for many small retailers and restaurants. |
| truck wholesaler/truck jobber | Carries products needing frequent replenishment (e.g., bread and potato chips, and supply items for service stations). |
| drop shipper | Takes orders from customers and places them with producers, which then ship directly to customers. Take title but never physically handle products (e.g., bulky items such as coal and lumber). |
| direct-response wholesaler | Limited function merchant wholesaler that relies on catalogues to contact outlying retail or industrial customers (e.g., hardware, cosmetics, jewellery). |
| **AGENTS AND BROKERS** | In contrast with merchant wholesalers, agents and brokers never take title to the products they handle. Main function to bring together buyers and sellers. |
| commission merchant | Takes possession of agricultural products and acts as the producer's agent at a central market. Has power to set prices. |
| auction house | Brings buyers and sellers together and allows buyers to inspect merchandise before the bidding process. Used in selling art, used cars, flowers, and fruit. |
| selling agents | Responsible for total marketing for a firm's product line. Used in textile, coal, sulphur, and lumber industries. |
| manufacturers' agent | An independent salesperson (or company with a sales force) who works for several manufacturers of related but non-competing products. Shared selling costs make it possible for a small producer to have representation. Also used by some large companies because of their contacts and expertise in a market. |

### Retailer-Owned Facilities

Retailers have also assumed numerous wholesaling functions in attempting to reduce costs or to provide special services. Independent retailers have often banded together to form buying groups to achieve cost savings through quantity purchases. Other groups of retailers have established retailer-owned wholesale facilities by forming a cooperative chain. IGA (Independent Grocers Alliance) is an example. Large chain retailers often establish centralized buying offices to negotiate large-scale purchases directly with manufacturers for the members of the chain.

This summary of channel intermediaries could have been expanded significantly, for this is an important and complex topic. It is important for you to learn the names and functions of these intermediaries in order to take advantage of the many possibilities that exist in developing an appropriate channel strategy. For example, the set of channel distribution options for a newly developed lightweight hair dryer would likely be quite different depending on whether Black and Decker or a new start-up venture had developed it. Reputation and resources would make it much easier for Black and Decker to get the product into the traditional channels. The new company would probably have to use one of the channel intermediaries.

www.blackanddecker.com

# Vertical Marketing Systems

Some channel members, and even entire channels of distribution, act quite independently. They have no formal long-term ties to others in the channel, but build relationships with buyers or sellers in an autonomous fashion.

More commonly, intermediaries have found it desirable to form a **vertical marketing system**. A vertical marketing system (VMS) is a network of channel intermediaries organized and centrally managed to produce the maximum competitive impact. In such a system, the coordination of the various channel members can produce operating efficiencies, deep market penetration, and greater profits. Vertical marketing systems produce economies of scale through their size and the elimination of duplicated services. There are three types of VMS: corporate, administered, and contractual. They are summarized in Table 15.4.

**vertical marketing system**

A network of channel intermediaries organized and centrally managed to produce the maximum competitive impact.

## Corporate System

When there is single ownership of all stages of the marketing channel, a *corporate vertical marketing system* exists. Holiday Inn owns a furniture manufacturer and a carpet mill. Bata Shoes owns a retail chain of shoe stores. Many McDonald's food outlets are corporate-owned.

**TABLE 15.4 Three Types of Vertical Marketing Systems**

| TYPE OF SYSTEM | DESCRIPTION | EXAMPLES |
| --- | --- | --- |
| Corporate | Channel owned and operated by a single organization | Bata Shoes<br>Firestone<br>Sherwin-Williams<br>Singer<br>McDonald's (partial) |
| Administered | Channel dominated by one powerful member that acts as channel captain | Kodak<br>General Electric<br>Corning Glass |
| Contractual | Channel coordinated through contractual agreements among channel members | Wholesaler-Sponsored Voluntary Chain<br>  IGA<br>  Canadian Tire<br>  Independent Druggists Alliance (IDA)<br>  Allied Hardware<br>Retail Cooperative<br>  Associated Grocers<br>Franchise Systems<br>  McDonald's (partial)<br>  Century 21 Real Estate<br>  AAMCO Transmissions<br>  Coca-Cola bottlers<br>  Ford dealers |

## Administered System

Channel coordination is achieved through the exercise of economic and "political" power by a dominant channel member in an *administered vertical marketing system.* Canadian General Electric has a network of major appliance dealers who aggressively display and promote the line because of its strong reputation and brand. Although independently owned and operated, these dealers cooperate with the manufacturer because of the effective working relationships enjoyed over the years and the profits to be realized from selling the widely known, well-designed, broad range of merchandise. Dominance can come from the retail end of the channel too. Wal-Mart and Sears dominate their suppliers, and their demands on suppliers and other intermediaries result in powerful retail operations.

## Contractual System

The most significant form of vertical marketing is the *contractual vertical marketing system.* It accounts for nearly 40 percent of all retail sales. Instead of the common ownership of channel components that characterizes the corporate VMS or the relative power relationships of an administered system, the contractual VMS is characterized by formal agreements between channel members. In practice, there are three types of agreements: the wholesaler-sponsored voluntary chain, the retail cooperative, and the franchise.

### WHOLESALER-SPONSORED VOLUNTARY CHAIN

The wholesaler-sponsored voluntary chain represents an attempt by the independent wholesaler to preserve a market for the firm's products by strengthening the firm's retailer customers. To enable the independent retailers to compete with the chains, the wholesaler enters into a formal agreement with a group of retailers whereby the retailers agree to use a common name, standardize their facilities, and purchase the wholesaler's products. The wholesaler often develops a line of private brands to be stocked by the members of the voluntary chain. A common store name and similar inventories allow the retailers to achieve cost savings on advertising, since a single newspaper advertisement promotes all retailers in the trading area. IGA, with a membership of approximately 800 food stores, is a good example of a voluntary chain.

### RETAIL COOPERATIVES

A second type of contractual VMS is the retail cooperative, which is established by a group of retailers who set up a wholesaling operation to compete better with big chains. A group of retailers purchase shares of stock in a wholesaling operation and agree to purchase a minimum percentage of their inventory from the firm. The members may also choose to use a common store name, such as Home Hardware, and develop their own private brands in order to carry out cooperative advertising.

Buying groups like wholesaler-sponsored chains and retail cooperatives are not a new phenomenon in the Canadian distribution industry. They date back at least 50 years, some having evolved from the cooperative movement of the early years of the century. Under the Competition Act, suppliers may charge different prices for different volumes of purchases as long as these prices are available to all competing purchasers of articles of like quantity and quality. And suppliers have done so; it is common practice to offer volume rebates. Thus, buying groups improve the small retailers' bargaining position with their suppliers, thus increasing competition for their large rivals.

In some cases, buying groups have failed because of difficulties with organization and management. In others, the buying group concept has worked very well, with some groups now as large as the chains. The chains themselves have now formed their own buying groups. Recently, five of these large buying groups in the food industry represented some 14 000 stores and accounted for about 85 percent of all retail food sales in Canada.[8] This development leads to the concern that while buying groups may improve the balance of market power in some areas, there is a possibility of abuse of power in others.

### FRANCHISES

**franchise**
An agreement whereby one firm (franchisee) agrees to meet the operating requirements of a successful business (franchisor) in return for the right to carry the name and products of the franchisor.

A third type of contractual VMS is the **franchise**. A franchise is an agreement whereby one firm (franchisee) agrees to meet the operating requirements of a successful business (franchisor) in

return for the right to carry the name and products of the franchisor. The franchisee pays a predetermined royalty on sales to the franchisor. In addition, the franchisee typically receives a variety of marketing, management, technical, and financial services in exchange for a specified fee. KFC started out by franchising its stores, but the company now has the resources to pay for and manage its own stores. Thus it has more control over operations.

Although franchising attracted considerable interest beginning in the late 1960s, the concept actually began 100 years earlier when the Singer Company established franchised sewing-machine outlets. Early impetus for the franchising concept came after 1900 in the automobile industry. The soft-drink industry is another example of franchising, but in this case the contractual arrangement is between the syrup manufacturer and the wholesaler–bottler.

The franchising form that created most of the excitement both in retailing and on Wall Street since the late 1960s was the retailer franchise system sponsored by the service firm. McDonald's Corporation is an excellent example of such a franchise operation. McDonald's brought together suppliers and a chain of hamburger outlets. It provided a proven system of retail operation (the operations manual for each outlet weighs over 1 kg) with a standardized product and ingenious promotional campaigns. This enabled lower prices to be offered to customers through the franchisor's purchasing power on meat, buns, potatoes, napkins, and other supplies. In return, the franchisee pays a fee for the use of the name (over $150 000 for McDonald's) and a percentage of gross sales. Other familiar examples include Tim Hortons, Avis, Pizza Hut, and Weight Watchers.

In some countries, adjustments to the North American marketing plans have been made to match local needs. Although their menu is rigidly standardized in Canada, McDonald's executives approved changes to the menu in outlets in France. KFC replaced french fries with mashed potatoes to satisfy its Japanese customers.

Although many franchises are profitable, the infatuation with the franchising concept and the market performance of franchise stocks have lured dozens of newcomers into the market who have failed. Lacking experience and often with a well-known celebrity's name as their sole asset, many of these firms have disappeared almost as quickly as they entered the market.

The median investment for a franchise varies tremendously from one business area to another. A pet-sitting franchise might sell for as low as $9500, whereas a restaurant franchise will

www.kfc.com

www.mcdonalds.com

Harvey's is one of many franchises in Canada.

# THE PRACTISING MARKETER

## INVESTIGATE BEFORE YOU INVEST IN A FRANCHISE!

Purchasing a franchise is a major investment decision and not every franchise is ideal for every individual. The Canadian Franchise Association (CFA) recommends that you ask a number of questions when considering this enterprise. They have prepared a comprehensive checklist of questions that you should consider when purchasing a franchise. The following is a sample of the questions available with the purchase of the CFA "Info Kit."

### Investigate the Franchisor (Identity and Experience)
• Who are the key individuals associated with the franchisor, including all shareholders, officers, and directors?
• How many years has the franchisor been operating?
• How many franchises does the franchisor have?

### Franchisor Relations With its Franchisees
• How does the franchisor select prospective franchisees? Have your qualifications been reviewed?
• How does the franchisor monitor franchisee operations? Does the franchisor periodically inspect all of the franchisees?
• Does the franchisor solicit franchisee input into marketing strategies, new product development, etc.?

### Required Investment
• How much is the initial franchise fee?
• Is there a deposit?
• How much is refundable? Under what circumstances?

### Franchised Product or Service
• What makes the franchisor's product/service unique?
• How long has the product/service been on the market?
• What products must be purchased from the franchisor or designated supplier?

### Sales Territory and Location
• Is your franchise territory exclusive? If not exclusive, is there any territorial protection?

• Will there be other outlets opening near your territory?
• Does the franchisor sell its products through other channels? If so, what are these channels?

www.cfa.ca

### Questions to Ask Current Franchisees
• What was your total investment for the franchise?
• Did the franchisor provide effective, thorough training? How long was the training?
• How long did it take for you to receive a reasonable salary?

### The Contract
• Are the franchise, the location, and the territory clearly described in the contract?
• Does the contract clearly describe the duration, type, and cost of the training to be provided by the franchisor?
• What type of records and reports are you required to provide to the franchisor?

### Franchisor's Support Service
• Will the franchisor choose the site or assist you in selecting the appropriate one for your business?
• Does the franchisor build the premises? If not, does the franchisor specify the design of premise's layout and displays?
• What continuing management assistance will you receive?

**What does this range of questions tell you about being a franchisee?**

Source: "Investigate Before You Invest in a Franchise," http://www.cfa.ca/investigate.html, June 10, 2002. Reprinted with permission of the Canadian Franchise Association.

---

likely average over $250 000. In 1999 the average franchise fee was $23 213, and the average investment paid by Canadian franchisees for their franchise (building, supplies, etc.) was $166 603.[9] The great bulk of the nation's franchises are in the "traditional" franchise areas such as car dealers, service stations, and soft-drink bottlers. Figure 15.8 shows a summary of Canadian franchise facts.

Despite the many franchise opportunities available, there are few specific regulations with respect to the proper disclosure of information to prospective franchisees. It is worthwhile to evaluate the opportunity carefully before investing.

The foregoing discussion has shown that vertical marketing systems, whether in the form of corporate, administered, or contractual systems, have become a dominant factor in the consumer goods sector of the Canadian economy. Over 60 percent of the available market is currently in the hands of retail components of VMS.

**FIGURE 15.8** Canadian Franchise Facts, 1999

| Industry Size | |
|---|---|
| Number of franchisors reported by Francon | 1326 |
| Number of corporate owned units | 10084 |
| Number of franchised units | 65725 |
| **Canadian industry total units** | **75809** |

*Did you know that a Canadian franchise opens every two hours, 365 days a year?*

| Company Size | |
|---|---|
| Average corporate units per franchisor | 7.7 |
| Average franchised units per franchisor | 50.7 |
| Average franchisor unit size | 58.4 |

The average number of years in business for a Canadian franchisor is 20.7 years.

The average franchise fee for a Canadian franchisor is $23213.

The average investment paid by Canadian franchisees for their franchise is $166603. This does not include any financing that a franchisee might obtain.

Restaurant categories control over 18000 outlets in Canada.

*Burgers, casual dining, chicken, coffee, bakery and donuts, family dining, fast food, ice cream, yogurt and candy, pizza, sandwiches, and Tex Mex.*

| | |
|---|---|
| Miscellaneous products and services | 9755 units |
| Automotive products and services | 5695 units |

Source: Francon Canada Web site, "Canadian Franchise Facts, 1999" page (http://www.francon.com/CDNFACTS.htm), downloaded June 10, 2002. Reprinted with permission.

# CHANNEL STRATEGY AND MANAGEMENT DECISIONS

Marketers face several channel strategy decisions. The selection of a specific distribution channel is the most basic of these, but the level of distribution intensity and the issue of vertical marketing systems must also be addressed (see Figure 15.9).

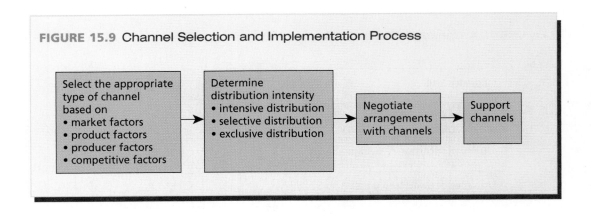

**FIGURE 15.9** Channel Selection and Implementation Process

## Select the Appropriate Distribution Channel

What is an appropriate marketing channel if you want to sell bottled water to Japan? What makes a direct channel (manufacturer to consumer) best for the Fuller Brush Company? Why do operating supplies often go through both agents and merchant wholesalers before being purchased by an industrial firm? Why do some firms employ multiple channels for the same product? The firm must answer many such questions when it determines its choice of marketing channels. The choice is based on an analysis of the market, the product, the producer, and various competitive factors. Each is often of critical importance, and all are often interrelated.

### Market Factors

A major determinant of channel structure is whether the product is intended for the consumer or the business market. Business purchasers usually prefer to deal directly with the manufacturer (except for supplies of small accessory items), but most consumers make their purchases from retail stores. Products sold to both business users and the consumer market usually require more than one channel.

The geographic location and the needs of the firm's potential market also affect channel choice. Direct sales are possible when the firm's potential market is concentrated in a few regions. For example, industrial production tends to be concentrated in a relatively small geographic region, making direct contact possible. The small number of potential buyers also increases the feasibility of direct channels.

On the other hand, consumer goods are purchased by every household everywhere. Since consumers are numerous and geographically dispersed, and purchase a small volume at a given time, intermediaries must be employed to market products to them efficiently.

In Canada, population distribution is an extremely influential factor in channel decisions. For example, the markets for fishing nets are on the two coasts, with smaller markets on the Great Lakes, Lake Winnipeg, and a few other large lakes. The Rockies and the Canadian Shield effectively divide markets and strongly affect channels of distribution. Our relatively smaller and widely dispersed centres of population tend to result in less specialized wholesaling and retailing institutions than in the United States and other developed, heavily populated countries. This may limit the range of channel opportunities available to the marketing manager.

Order size will also affect the marketing channel decision. Manufacturers are likely to employ shorter, more direct channels in cases where retail customers or business buyers place relatively small numbers of large orders. Retail chains often employ buying offices to negotiate directly with manufacturers for large-scale purchases. Wholesalers may be used to contact smaller retailers.

Shifts in consumer buying patterns also influence channel decisions. As newer retail forms such as Superstore, Costco, and Toys Я Us have become more popular, manufacturers have had to shift their emphasis to distribute products through these channels as well.

Market factors and buyer expectations are equally important to consider in developing international distribution and channel structures. For example, in Japan many more channel intermediaries

www.toysrus.com

are typically used. In the distribution of soap, for instance, the product goes from manufacturer to large wholesaler to smaller wholesaler to very small wholesaler, and finally to the retailer.

## Product Factors

Product characteristics also play a role in determining optimum marketing channels. *Perishable products,* such as fresh produce and fruit, and fashion products with short life cycles, *typically move through relatively short channels* direct to the retailer or to the ultimate consumer. Old Dutch Potato Chips are distributed by company salespeople–truck drivers direct to retail shelves. Each year, Hines & Smart Corporation ships over 2 million kg of live lobsters by air, in specially designed insulating containers, directly to restaurants and hotels throughout North America.

Complex products, such as custom-made installations or computer equipment, are typically sold direct from the manufacturer to the buyer. As a general rule, *the more standardized a product, the longer the channel will be.* Such items will usually be marketed by wholesalers. Also, products that require regular service or specialized repair services usually avoid channels that employ independent wholesalers. Cars are marketed through a franchised network of regular dealers whose employees receive regular training on how to service their cars properly.

Another generalization concerning marketing channels is that *the lower the unit value of the product, the longer the channel.* Convenience goods and business supplies with typically low unit prices are frequently marketed through relatively long channels. Installations and more expensive business and consumer goods go through shorter, more direct channels.

## Producer Factors

Companies with adequate resources—financial, marketing, and managerial—will be less compelled to use intermediaries in marketing their products. A financially strong manufacturer can hire its own sales force, warehouse its products, and grant credit to the retailer or consumer. A weaker firm relies on intermediaries for these services (although some large retail chains may purchase all of the manufacturer's output, making it possible to bypass the independent wholesaler). Production-oriented firms may be forced to use the marketing expertise of intermediaries to replace the lack of finances and management in their organization. In the international marketplace, producers often rely on intermediaries because they know the market better, and it is usually cheaper than setting up a new distribution system.

A firm with a broad product line is better able to market its products directly to retailers or business users, since its sales force can offer a variety of products to customers. Larger total sales allow the selling costs to be spread over a number of products and make direct sales more feasible. The single-product firm often discovers that direct selling is an unaffordable luxury.

The manufacturer's need for control over the product will also influence channel selection. If aggressive promotion for the firm's products at the retail level is desired, the manufacturer will choose the shortest available channel. For new products, the manufacturer may be forced to implement an introductory advertising campaign before independent wholesalers will handle the item.

## Competitive Factors

Some firms are forced to develop unique marketing channels because of inadequate promotion of their products by independent intermediaries. Avon concentrated on house-to-house selling rather than being directly involved in the intense competition among similar lines of cosmetics in traditional channels. This radical departure from the traditional channel resulted in tremendous sales by the firm's thousands of neighbourhood salespeople. Similarly, Honeywell discovered that its home security system was being inadequately marketed by the traditional, wholesaler-to-retailer channel and switched to a direct-to-home sales force.

Table 15.5 summarizes the factors that affect the choice of optimal marketing channels and shows the effect of each characteristic on the overall length of the channel.

**TABLE 15.5** Factors Affecting Choice of Distribution Channels

| FACTOR | CHANNELS TEND TO BE SHORTER WHEN |
|---|---|
| **Market Factors** | |
| Consumer market or business market | Users are in business market |
| Geographic location of target market | Customers are geographically concentrated |
| Customer service needs | Specialized knowledge, technical know-how, and regular service needs are present |
| Order size | Customer places relatively small number of large orders |
| **Product Factors** | |
| Perishability | Products are perishable, either because of fashion changes or physical perishability |
| Technical complexity of product | Products are highly technical |
| Unit value | Products have high unit value |
| **Producer Factors** | |
| Producer resources—financial, managerial, and marketing | Manufacturer possesses adequate resources to perform channel functions |
| Product line | Manufacturer has broad product line to spread distribution costs |
| Need for control over the channel | Manufacturer wants to control the channel |
| **Competitive Factors** | |
| Need for promotion to channel members | Manufacturer feels that independent intermediaries are inadequately promoting products |

## Determine Distribution Intensity

Adequate market coverage for some products such as fine furniture could mean one dealer for each 50 000 people. On the other hand, Procter & Gamble defines adequate coverage for Crest toothpaste as almost every supermarket, discount store, drugstore, and variety store, plus many vending machines.

### Intensive Distribution

**intensive distribution**

A form of distribution that attempts to provide saturation coverage of the potential market.

www.timex.com

Producers of convenience goods that attempt to provide saturation coverage of their potential markets are the prime users of **intensive distribution**. Soft drinks, bread, candy, and chewing gum are available in convenient locations to enable purchasers to buy with a minimum of effort.

Bic pens can be purchased in thousands of retail outlets in Canada. TMX Watches of Canada Ltd. uses an intensive distribution strategy for its Timex watches. Consumers may buy a Timex in many jewellery stores, the traditional retail outlet for watches. In addition, they may find Timex in discount stores, variety stores, department stores, hardware stores, and drugstores.

Mass coverage and low unit prices make the use of wholesalers almost mandatory for such distribution. An important exception to this generalization is products sold and delivered on a direct-to-customer basis. For example, Avon operates direct to the consumer through a nationwide network of neighbourhood salespeople who purchase directly from the manufacturer, at 60 percent of the retail price, and service a limited area with cosmetics, toiletries, jewellery, and toys. Other examples are Tupperware, Mary Kay, and other multilevel marketing companies.

It must be remembered that while a firm may want intensive distribution, the retailer or industrial distributor will carry only products that sell in enough volume to make a profit. If demand is low, the producer may have to settle for less than complete market coverage.

## Selective Distribution

As the name implies, **selective distribution** involves the selection of a small number of retailers to handle the firm's product line. This can work *if* consumers are willing to shop around for the product category. By limiting its retailers, the firm may reduce its total marketing costs, such as those for sales force and shipping, while establishing better working relationships within the channel. This practice may also be necessary to give the retailers an incentive (through having a product available to a limited number of sellers) to carry the product and promote it properly against many competing brands. Cooperative advertising (where the manufacturer pays a percentage of the retailer's advertising expenditures and the retailer prominently displays the firm's products) can be used to mutual benefit. Marginal retailers can be avoided. Where product service is important, dealer training and assistance is usually forthcoming from the manufacturer. Finally, price cutting is less likely, since fewer dealers are handling the firm's line.

## Exclusive Distribution

When manufacturers grant exclusive rights to a wholesaler or retailer to sell in a geographic region, they are practising **exclusive distribution**, which is an extreme form of selective distribution. The best example of exclusive distribution is the automobile industry. For example, a city of 100 000 might have a single Toyota dealer or one Cadillac agency. Exclusive distribution arrangements are also found in the marketing of some major appliances and in fashion apparel. Powerful retailers may also negotiate to acquire exclusive distribution.

Some market coverage may be sacrificed through a policy of exclusive distribution, but this is often offset through the development and maintenance of an image of quality and prestige for the products, with more active attention by the retailer to promote them, and the reduced marketing costs associated with a small number of accounts. Producers and retailers cooperate closely in decisions concerning advertising and promotion, inventory to be carried by the retailers, and prices.

### THE LEGAL PROBLEMS OF EXCLUSIVE DISTRIBUTION

The use of exclusive distribution presents a number of potential legal problems. Three problem areas exist: exclusive dealing, tied selling, and market restriction. Each will be examined briefly.

Press the accelerator of the 911 Turbo and what happens next is astonishing. The raw surge of power. The incredibly honed balance. Yes, it's crazy to take automotive achievement to such an extreme. That may be the best reason of all. Contact us at 1-800 PORSCHE or porsche.com.

**Keeps the logical side of the brain pinned to the back of your skull.**

PORSCHE

A product appropriate for exclusive distribution.

**exclusive dealing**
An arrangement whereby a supplier prohibits a marketing intermediary (either a wholesaler or, more typically, a retailer) from handling competing products.

**Exclusive dealing** prohibits a marketing intermediary (either a wholesaler or, more typically, a retailer) from handling competing products. Through such a contract, the manufacturer is assured of total concentration on the firm's product line by the intermediaries. For example, an oil company may consider requiring all dealers to sign a contract agreeing to purchase all of their accessories from that company.

The legal question is covered in Part IV of the Competition Act, which prohibits exclusive dealing by a major supplier if it is likely to

1. Impede entry into or expansion of a firm in the market.
2. Impede introduction of a product into or expansion of sales of a product in the market.
3. Have any other exclusionary effect in the market, with the result that competition is or is likely to be lessened substantially.[10]

**tied selling**
An arrangement whereby a supplier forces a dealer who wishes to handle a product to also carry other products from the supplier or to refrain from using or distributing someone else's product.

A second problem area is **tied selling**. In this case, a supplier forces a dealer who wishes to handle a product to also carry other products from the supplier or to refrain from using or distributing someone else's product. Tied selling is controlled by the same provision as exclusive dealing.

The third legal issue of exclusive distribution is the use of **market restriction**. In this case, suppliers restrict the geographic territories for each of their distributors. The key issue is whether such restrictions substantially lessen competition. If so, the Restrictive Trade Practices Commission has the power to order the prohibition of such practices. For example, a *horizontal territorial restriction*, where retailers or wholesalers agree to avoid competition in products from the same manufacturer, would likely be declared unlawful.

**market restriction**
An arrangement whereby suppliers restrict the geographic territories for each of their distributors.

## Negotiate with Channels

Having gone through the channel selection process, you may not be able to get the channel that you have so carefully selected for your new line of hair dryers. Consider the situation of the buyer for a large and successful drugstore chain such as London Drugs or Shoppers Drug Mart. Will the buyer automatically stock your new dryer? Not likely, because she or he is faced with a fixed amount of shelf space, of which a certain proportion is already allocated and filled with eleven different dryers. There is never vacant shelf space. To get your product on the shelf, you have to make it so attractive to the buyer that she or he will remove some other product to make space. *If* the buyer does so, it will usually be because you make it profitable to do so.

Normally this is done through offering a good profit margin and promising to affect demand through a strong advertising campaign. It is easier to persuade the buyer that you can do this if you are a well-established supplier such as Black and Decker and have already developed a good relationship with the channel. If you are a new company, your negotiations may well fail, and you will have to turn to other outlets or a different channel arrangement. That is why it is so important to understand the various channel options.

## Support the Channel

After a channel of distribution has been set up, the job is not done. Since channels carry many products, they normally do not have time or motivation to pay special attention to your product. Thus it is important to support the channel members' activities through regular calls on channel members, missionary selling, advertising, and other methods. This combination of activities helps to move the product, and as it moves, channels will be happy to carry and support your product, and perhaps other products of yours.

# LEADERSHIP AND COOPERATION IN THE CHANNEL

Leadership and cooperation in the marketing channel are necessary for successfully implementing marketing strategy. Channel leadership is a function of one's power within the distribution channel, and the most powerful often becomes the dominant and controlling member of the channel—the **channel captain**. Historically, the role of channel captain belonged to the manufacturer or wholesaler, since retailers tended to be both small and locally oriented. However, retailers are increasingly taking on the role of channel captain as large retail chains assume traditional wholesaling functions and even dictate product design specifications to the manufacturer. For example, Loblaws Supermarkets in Canada has developed a line of products called President's Choice. Sainsbury's in Britain has its own lines of products as well. Costco has an ever-expanding line of its own Kirkland branded products.

**channel captain**
The most dominant member of the distribution channel.

---

# THE PRACTISING MARKETER

## DISTRIBUTION IS EVERYTHING (ALMOST)

After 112 years of selling mostly sugar water, Coca-Cola Co. is making plans to peddle plain water in plastic bottles.

The soft-drink giant expects to introduce in select markets its own brand of purified bottled water, according to people familiar with the plans. A leading candidate for the brand's name is Dasani. The water will come from the tap or wells, be purified, and then have minerals added, which Coke will sell to its franchised bottlers.

A nationally branded water by Coca-Cola has been the subject of intense speculation in the beverage industry. Many industry executives say that Coke can't wait any longer, given the explosive growth of bottled water in the past few years. Coke officials reason that if consumers are going to drink bottled water, they might as well drink a Coke product.

Furthermore, several Coke bottlers have been urging Coke to market a national brand of water so they don't have to sell a hodgepodge of little-known waters. Currently, Coke bottlers sell a variety of bottled waters, which they make a significant profit on. Several have said they are willing to pay a royalty to Coke if it puts marketing muscle behind a bottled water.

"It's no longer a question of if, but when," said one person familiar with Coke's plans. Others, however, cautioned that several details need to be ironed out and that may have some bearing on a final decision by Coca-Cola chairman M. Douglas Ivester.

Coca-Cola sells a bottled water called BonAqua in several overseas countries. Thanks to health-minded consumers, the bottled water business is now a business worth $4 billion (U.S.) a year, up from $2.65 billion in 1990. Sales of plastic bottles of water, popular because of their convenience, have been the biggest winners, increasing 28 to 30 percent for the past couple of years. PepsiCo Inc. jumped into the water business with its Aquafina brand, first test-marketed in 1994, and the sheer power of Pepsi's vast distribution system has already made Aquafina the top-selling water brand in convenience and gas stores.

For Coke, however, dipping its toe in the water business has been a source of internal debate for years. The biggest obstacle has been financial. Coca-Cola makes its money by selling concentrate to bottlers, independent companies (franchisees) that add water and carbonation to the drinks and distribute them. But with water, Coke can't sell any syrup. Indeed, Mr. Ivester said in June that bottled water is a "tricky subject—we have to be careful that we don't replace high-margin soft drinks with low-margin water."

www.coca-cola.com

The mineral packets Coke plans to sell the bottlers would take the place of concentrate and make the venture more financially feasible. The minerals could include small amounts of potassium and magnesium, and would make water taste better, industry executives said. The purification process of reverse osmosis removes all taste from water and gives it a bland flavour, says James Stevens, a veteran bottled water executive and former chief operating officer of Coca-Cola Enterprises Inc., Coca-Cola's largest bottler.

One plus for Coke is that consumers seem far more accepting of purified water over spring water; that makes it easier to create a national brand. Coke has been wary of spring water, because it could mean relying on an outside company to bottle it at the source, according to Mr. Stevens. A bottled-water venture doesn't need to be expensive for Coke. It could vault to the top tier, thanks to its far-flung distribution system. "They'll have a big advantage," said Mr. Stevens.

**Explain why franchisees are ready to pay Coke to put out a bottled water when they could easily produce one themselves. What does this article illustrate about the concept of "channel captains"?**

Source: Adapted from Nikhil Deogun, "Coke to Peddle Bottled Water," *The Wall Street Journal* in *The Globe and Mail* (November 3, 1998), p. B12. Reprinted with permission of *The Wall Street Journal*. Copyright © 1998 Dow Jones & Company, Inc. All Rights Reserved Worldwide.

---

Distribution channels must be organized and regarded as a systematic cooperative effort if operating efficiencies are to be achieved. In a sense, the forward-thinking organizations are those that form strategic alliances among channel members in order to take advantage of the competitive attributes each possesses. These alliances include direct channel participants as well as facilitating agencies such as transportation companies, legal organizations, and the like. No longer is it likely that completely independent channel players will dominate the competition in globally oriented industries. Organization and cooperation between independent entities within the channel is a must today.

Cooperation and mutual understanding based on enlightened self-interest are far from the reality of channel relations, according to numerous authors. Instead, many channel relationships are marked by intense rivalry and conflict.

**Channel conflict** can evolve from a number of sources. For example, a manufacturer of cough lozenges may have planned that its product display would be placed near the cash register to encourage impulse purchases. Many retailers might be unwilling to do this because of many other items taking up the same space. In other situations, a manufacturer might wish certain market information from retailers, but they may not be interested in cooperating. A wholesaler may find that it is being bypassed by a retailer that buys direct from a manufacturer. Manufacturers may wish to dictate the resale prices of their merchandise. These may be lower or higher than the prices that retailers feel are appropriate to their circumstances.

Channel relationships are dynamic. Just when channel procedures and relationships seem to be sorted out, a competitive action by some channel member upsets the balance, and a whole series of countermoves are triggered to adjust to the changing competitive situation. It is this continuing process that results in the evolution of new and improved channel forms to serve consumer needs.

The study of channels of distribution, and the changes that continually occur, can be fascinating. After this rather extensive overview of channel and distribution strategy, the next two chapters will look more closely at retailing and the process of logistics and supply chain management.

**channel conflict**
Rivalry and conflict between channel members because of sometimes different objectives and needs.

## SUMMARY

The number of actual transactions in an economic system that is comprised of manufacturers and customers can be reduced significantly by inserting one or more intermediaries between the manufacturer and the consumer.

The distribution channel performs several functions in the overall marketing system. These include facilitating the exchange process, sorting, standardizing transactions, holding inventories, assisting in the search process, and transporting.

Channels can be categorized as multistep, two-step, one-step, and direct. In the multistep channel, the product moves from producer to agent/broker to wholesaler to retailer to consumer. An increasingly common phenomenon is the use of more than one marketing channel for similar products.

The term *wholesaler* is applied only to those wholesaling intermediaries that take title to the products they handle. The term *wholesaling intermediary* is a broader term that also includes others who perform important wholesaling activities. These are merchant wholesalers, agents, and brokers.

Trade fairs are periodic shows at which manufacturers in a particular industry display their wares for visiting buyers. International marketers make much use of trade fairs, which work well in certain domestic situations as well.

A manufacturers' agent is essentially an independent salesperson who works on a commission basis for a number of manufacturers of related but noncompeting products. Companies employ manufacturers' agents when they do not have enough sales in an area to warrant having their own sales force, or when they want a special push on certain product lines.

Distribution intensity for various products ranges from intensive to selective to exclusive.

A vertical marketing system (VMS) is a network of channel intermediaries that is organized and centrally managed to produce the maximum competitive impact. The types are corporate, administered, and contractual.

A franchise is an agreement whereby one firm (franchisee) agrees to meet the operating requirements of another successful business (franchisor) in return for the right to carry the name and products of the franchisor.

Channels and channel relationships change. A marketing institution will continue to exist only as long as it fulfills a need by performing a required service. This means that changes in power and function will gradually change over time.

## KEY TERMS

agent, p. 370

auction house, p. 382

broker, p. 382

cash-and-carry wholesaler, p. 382

channel captain, p. 393

channel conflict, p. 394

commission merchant, p. 382

direct-response wholesaler, p. 382

distribution channels, p. 365

drop shipper, p. 382

exclusive dealing, p. 392

exclusive distribution, p. 391

facilitating agency, p. 373

franchise, p. 384

industrial distributor, p. 371

intensive distribution, p. 390

manufacturers' agent, p. 382

market restriction, p. 392

marketing intermediary, p. 365

merchandise mart, p. 381

merchant wholesaler, p. 371

public warehouse, p. 381

rack jobber, p. 382

retailer, p. 366

reverse channels, p. 372

sales branch, p. 381

selective distribution, p. 391

selling agent, p. 382

sorting, p. 366

tied selling, p. 392

trade fairs, p. 381

truck wholesaler, p. 382

vertical marketing system, p. 383

wholesalers, p. 376

wholesaling, p. 366

wholesaling intermediaries, p. 376

## INTERACTIVE SUMMARY AND DISCUSSION QUESTIONS

1. The distribution channel performs several functions in the overall marketing system. These include facilitating the exchange process, sorting, standardizing transactions, holding inventories, assisting in the search process, and transporting. Provide an example of each function.

2. In the multistep channel, the product moves from producer to agent/broker to wholesaler to retailer to consumer. Describe how this works, and the names of intermediary companies, using some product you are familiar with.

3. An increasingly common phenomenon is the use of more than one marketing channel for similar products. In what ways could multiple channels produce channel conflict? Be specific.

4. The term *wholesaler* is applied only to those wholesaling intermediaries that take title to the products they handle. The term *wholesaling intermediary* is a broader term that also includes others that perform important wholesaling activities. Differentiate among merchant wholesalers, agents, and brokers.

5. A marketing institution will continue to exist only as long as it fulfills a need by performing a required service. Does this mean that large retailers will gradually take over from wholesalers and put them out of business? Explain.

6. The number of actual transactions in an economic system comprised of manufacturers and customers can be *reduced* significantly by inserting one or more intermediaries between the manufacturer and the consumer. Explain.

7. Wholesaling intermediaries can be classified based on ownership of the intermediary and on title flows. Assuming that the independent wholesaling intermediary was the first type established in the

"ownership" category, discuss the reasons why the other two types in that category might have emerged.

8. Match each of the products in the first column with the most appropriate wholesaling intermediary:

_____ groceries      a. drop shipper

_____ potato chips      b. truck wholesaler

_____ coal      c. auction house

_____ grain      d. manufacturers' agent

_____ antiques      e. full-function merchant wholesaler

     f. commission merchant

9. Merchant wholesalers take title to products. Agents and brokers may take possession, but do not take title to products. Why is the operating-expense ratio of the merchant wholesaler higher than that of a typical agent or broker?

10. Comment on the following statement: Drop shippers are one type of merchant wholesaler that are good candidates for elimination. All they do is process orders. They don't even handle the goods.

11. The term *broker* also appears in the real-estate and securities fields. Are such brokers identical to the agent wholesaling intermediaries described in this chapter? Explain.

12. Trade fairs are periodic shows at which manufacturers in a particular industry may display their wares for visiting buyers. Explain how an international marketer of agricultural machinery might make use of a trade fair.

13. A manufacturers' agent is essentially an independent salesperson who works on a commission basis for a number of manufacturers of related but noncompeting products. Under what circumstances would a company employ manufacturers' agents?

14. Distribution intensity for various products ranges from intensive to selective to exclusive. Which degree of distribution intensity is appropriate for each of the following?

a. *Maclean's* magazine

b. Caterpillar bulldozers

c. Mercury outboard motors

d. Dove soap

e. Cuisinart food processors

f. Kawasaki motorcycles

g. Waterford crystal

15. Would your answers in question 14 change if your target market was China? If so, how?

16. A vertical marketing system (VMS) is a network of channel intermediaries organized and centrally managed to produce the maximum competitive impact. Distinguish among the following types of VMS: corporate, administered, and contractual.

17. A franchise is an agreement whereby one firm (franchisee) agrees to meet the operating requirements of another successful business (franchisor) in return for the right to carry the name and products of the franchisor. What advantages does franchising offer the small retailer?

18. Why would any manufacturer deliberately choose to limit market coverage through a policy of exclusive coverage?

19. Assume you are planning to set up a retail business (of your choice) on the Internet. Use the Web to locate suitable wholesalers that would supply products. Report on your findings.

## Atrium Biotechnologies Inc.

Traditional wisdom says that when you have a breakthrough product you market it to the world. Atrium Biotechnologies Inc. has taken a different tack. When the Quebec City pharmaceutical company develops an active ingredient for use in cosmetics or nutritional products, it offers customers exclusivity. "As a small Canadian company, our greatest challenge is attracting the interest of multinationals," says Atrium president Richard Bordeleau. "We need to give them incentives from a marketing or commercial standpoint."

The strategy has worked well, particularly in the cosmetics industry, where one breakthrough can give a company a huge advantage. If Atrium develops a new anti-wrinkle product or eye cream, says Bordeleau, the firm will sell it to just three to five non-competitive cosmetics companies. "We'll offer them six months' to two years' exclusivity before we'll take the product to other companies."

Atrium chooses customers based on their distribution channels and target markets. "We might go to one direct-marketing company, such as Avon, which has selective markets and won't be competing with higher-priced brand names such as Chanel and Lancôme," he says. Atrium also looks for geograph-ically disparate clients; selling to Japanese giant Kanebo, for instance, won't bother U.S.-based Estée Lauder.

www.atrium-bio.com

The approach helped Atrium penetrate a new niche market last year: "corrective cosmetics" for people with severe skin problems. Atrium beat out three European pharmaceutical companies for a contract to develop an active ingredient for an international cosmetics firm, says Bordeleau. "We won the race because we agreed not to promote our technology to the company's two main competitors."

Still, Bordeleau admits his approach works best when dealing with clear market segmentation. "We're in a very competitive industry, where breakthrough innovations are the key to success," says Bordeleau. "If we offer a product to the whole industry, the big guys will pass. By offering exclusivity, we now have some of the biggest cosmetic multinationals interested in co-developing products with us."

### You Be the Marketer

1. Explain why their system of "exclusivity" seems to work.
2. What are the disadvantages of this approach?
3. Is this a viable long-term strategy? Why or why not?

Source: Adapted from "Atrium Biotechnologies Inc." from http://www.profitguide.com/profit100/2002/features.asp?ID=943, June 2, 2002. Reprinted with permission from *Profit: The Magazine for Canadian Entrepreneurs.*

# La SENZA

Lingerie retailer La Senza has established a competitive edge over the mass merchants by bringing glamour to underwear shopping.

## Chapter 16

# THE MANY FACES OF RETAILING: IN-STORE, DIRECT, AND INTERNET

## CHAPTER OBJECTIVES

After reading and studying this chapter, you should be able to

1. Explain the role played by retailing in the marketing mix.
2. Outline the decision framework for retailing.
3. Distinguish between limited-line retailers and general-merchandise retailers.
4. Identify and explain each of the six bases for categorizing retailers.
5. Identify the major types of mass merchandisers.
6. Discuss the opportunities and challenges of retailing through the Internet.
7. Contrast the three types of planned shopping centres.
8. Identify new trends in retailing.

**H**ow often would a company abandon its well-known corporate name for that of one of its subsidiaries? In May 2001, management decided to drop Suzy Shier as its corporate title and opted instead for La Senza Corp., the name of its popular lingerie chain because it had been so successful. This heralded the beginning of a major overhaul for the company. The company is now focusing on underserved markets and the brands that offer the best chance for expansion beyond Canada.

Lingerie retailer La Senza has established a competitive edge over the mass merchants by bringing glamour to underwear shopping. At the La Senza lingerie store in Toronto's Eaton Centre, the aisles were ablaze with undergarments in vibrant tangerines and fuchsias, animal prints and florals.

It was, and is, a great time to be selling lingerie in Canada. The C$1 billion market has been increasing by 8–10 percent per year, according to Laurence Lewin, La Senza's president, and roughly $1 of every $5 spent on fashion today goes toward a lingerie or nightwear purchase.

Whereas underwear was a functional purchase 20 years ago—"like men buying a white shirt" as Lewin put it—the category has since become more glamorous, varied, and fun.

"Women enjoy buying lingerie today: it's a fun buy, a fashion buy and it feels great—more so than buying a skirt or blouse," Lewin said. La Senza has made the most of this and has aggressively expanded its niche to become the country's largest specialty lingerie/nightwear chain in sales and market share, with approximately C$200 million in annual sales.

Beginning with four stores in 1990, the company progressed to 85 in 1993, and today has 188 Canadian units under the La Senza and silk and satin banners. In addition, it has 25 locations of a new tween-age (8 to 14) concept called La Senza Girl. La Senza has established a strong competitive position by providing a more attractive store ambience and better service than the mass merchants, while keeping the price point low.

"Our success is related to the intimate feel and personalized shopping which customers enjoy in our stores," Lewin said. "We try to have a high standard of store fittings and design to give our stores an expensive feel, but we stay in a moderate price range."

Close attention to pricing is vital in the current shopping environment, pointed out David Howell, vice president of NPD.

Tom Leung, partner with Vancouver retail consultancy Thomas Consultants, describes La Senza's management as "very good operators." He said the company was perceptive in identifying a gap in merchandise offerings at Canadian malls several years ago and developing a concept to fill it.

**Retailing is very dynamic. Competition is tough, and management must always be alert to new trends, to competitive actions as well as changes in consumer attitudes and shopping behaviour. The retailer is the final distributor in the channel of distribution. It is essential in marketing planning that an effective interface with retailers be considered. La Senza is a good example of the way that changes and opportunities occur in retailing.**

Source: Adapted from Susan Thorne, "Canada's Secret," www.ICSC.ORG (Website of International Council of Shopping Centres) Nov. 2001; Steve Match, "Retailer's Makeover Paying Off," *Financial Post*, April 17, 2002, p. IN1; and Marina Strauss, "La Senza Beats Forecasts In Tough Market," *The Globe and Mail*, Wednesday, April 10, 2002, www.globeandmail.com.

www.lasenza.com

# INTRODUCTION

Retailing is a vital part of the Canadian economy. Look around as you travel to and from school. You will probably see fast-food restaurants, such as Wendy's and Tim Hortons, convenience stores such as 7-Eleven and Mac's, and local corner stores. As well, there may be car dealerships and shopping centres. You might also pass some retailers that don't sell physical products but instead provide services, such as movie rentals.

Because retailers sell the products created by others to the ultimate consumers, retailers are the final link in the marketing channel. In a very real sense, retailers *are* the marketing channel for most consumers, since consumers have little contact with manufacturers and almost none with wholesaling intermediaries. The services provided—location, store hours, quality of salespeople, store layout, Web site, selection, and returns, among others—often figure even more importantly than the physical product in buying decisions.

Retailers are both customers and marketers in the channel. They market goods and services to ultimate consumers and also are the consumers for wholesalers and manufacturers. Because of their critical location in the channel, retailers may perform an important feedback role in obtaining information from customers and transmitting it to manufacturers and other channel members.

Retailing is the "last step of the marketing channel" for the consumer-goods manufacturer. Whether the manufacturer has established a company-owned chain of retail stores or uses several of the thousands of retail stores in Canada, the success of the entire marketing strategy rides on the decisions of consumers in the retail store.

**retailing**
All the activities involved in selling goods and services to the ultimate consumer.

**Retailing** may be defined as all the activities involved in selling goods and services to the ultimate consumer. Retailing involves not only sales in retail stores, but also several forms of nonstore retailing. These include telephone and direct-response sales (e.g., Internet selling), automatic merchandising, and direct house-to-house solicitations by salespeople.

# EVOLUTION OF RETAILING

www.hbc.com

Early retailing in Canada can be traced to the voyageurs, to the establishment of trading posts by the Hudson's Bay Company and others, and to pack peddlers who literally carried their wares to outlying settlements. After the trading post days, the Hudson's Bay and other retailers evolved into the institution known as the *general store*. The general store was stocked with general merchandise to meet the needs of a small community or rural area. Here customers could buy clothing, groceries, feed, seed, farm equipment, drugs, spectacles, and candy. The following account provides a good description of this early retail institution:

> The country store was in many respects a departmental store on a small scale, for a well-equipped store contained a little of everything. On one side were to be seen shelves well filled with groceries, crockery-ware, and a few patent medicines, such as blood purifiers, painkillers, and liniments; on the other side, a well assorted stock of dry goods, including prints, woollens, muslins, calico, cottons, etc. At the back, a lot of hardware, comprising nails, paints, oils, putty, glass, and garden tools, as well as an assortment of boots and shoes—from the tiny copper-toe to the farmer's big cowhide. In the back room, at the rear end of the store, were to be found barrels of sugar and New Orleans molasses, crates of eggs, and tubs of butter and lard. With this miscellaneous mixture—tea, coffee, dry goods, codfish, and boots and shoes—the odour of the country store was truly a composite one, and trying to the olfactory organs of the visitor. The country merchant was usually a man in good circumstances, for he was obliged in most cases to give a year's credit, the farmers paying their bills in the fall of the year, after the "threshing" or the "killing"; their only source of revenue at any other time being from butter and eggs, which their wives took to the country store, usually once a week, and exchanged for store goods. Perhaps there was no more popular place of meeting than the country store.[1]

The basic needs that caused the general store to develop also doomed this institution to a limited existence. Since the general store owners attempted to satisfy the needs of customers for all types of "store-bought" goods, they carried a small assortment of each good. As the villages grew, the size of the market was large enough to support stores specializing in specific product lines, such as groceries, hardware, dry goods, and drugs. Most general stores either converted into more specialized limited-line stores or closed. But the general store did, and in some rural areas still does, fill a need for its customers. General stores are still operated profitably in less developed countries, where income levels cannot support more specialized retailers, and in a few isolated parts of Canada as well.

## The Importance of Retailing

Retailing is the face of marketing for many people. It is the end-point of most marketing activities. Every day we pass through this important marketing institution. It is impossible to consider marketing strategy without taking into consideration the retailing dimension. Because retailers are seen everywhere every day we sometimes take retailing for granted. However, the introduction of your new product will likely fail if you have not taken into consideration the complex and sometimes expensive process required to get it stocked in appropriate retail outlets.

Retailing can also be a rewarding and challenging career. The type of person needed to manage a retail store would have to combine the skills of many of the following: marketer, fashion expert, financial analyst, personnel manager, logistics manager, information system manager, economist, and accountant. With decisions to be made in all of these areas, in a fast-paced, ever-changing environment it is clear that retailing is worth considering. Starting salaries for managers are competitive, and in the longer run, can be quite satisfactory.

## Innovation and Competition in Retailing

Retailing is an extremely competitive industry. A major determinant of success is to develop a *differential advantage* over competitors. Without a sustainable differential advantage, no retailer will last for long. Therefore, retailing is one of the most dynamic components of the economic system. As consumers, we see these changes occurring almost on a daily basis, yet we often do not think about the retail warfare going on around us.

Retailing operations are remarkable illustrations of the marketing concept in operation. Retail innovations often develop as attempts to better satisfy particular consumer needs, or to make the enterprise more competitive.

As consumers' needs and lifestyles change, institutions emerge to meet this demand. The supermarket appeared in the early 1930s to meet consumer desires for lower prices. Its success was enhanced by the fact that cars and good roads were commonly available. Convenience food stores such as 7-Eleven meet the need today for readily available basic products at all hours. Superstores and membership and warehouse clubs such as Costco serve consumers who want low prices and are willing to travel significant distances, as well as give up services.

www.7-eleven.com

www.homedepot.com

Large-format specialty stores such as Home Depot are a particularly potent competitor, because they provide low prices and breadth and depth of merchandise, as well as services. Department stores provide a wide variety of other products and services to meet other customer needs. The once-powerful Eaton's department store failed to do this and the company (but not its brands) is now history. Vending machines, door-to-door retailers, and mail-order retailing offer buyers convenience. Planned shopping centres provide a balanced array of consumer goods and services and include ample parking for their customers.

## The Wheel-of-Retailing Hypothesis

M.P. McNair attempted to explain the patterns of change in retailing through what has been termed the **wheel of retailing**. According to this hypothesis, new types of retailers gain a competitive foothold by offering lower prices to their customers through the reduction or elimination of services. Once they are established, however, they evolve by adding more services, and their prices gradually rise. Then they become vulnerable to a new low-price retailer that enters with minimum services—and the wheel turns.

**wheel of retailing**
Hypothesized process of change in retailing, which suggests that new types of retailers gain a competitive foothold by offering lower prices through the reduction or elimination of services; but once established, they add more services and their prices gradually rise, so that they then become vulnerable to a new low-price retailer with minimum services—and the wheel turns.

A room screaming for personality.
Faux plaster texture like the
expert in the orange apron showed me.

Potential is a wonderful thing.

The evolution of "big box" stores such as Home Depot has been a significant trend.

Faux plaster technique in *Fox Hollow*. Hallway in *Khaki Shadow*. Back wall in *Light Lichen*. Ceiling in *Caprice*. Trim in *Dry Fern*.

Most of the major developments in retailing appear to fit the wheel pattern. Early department stores, **chain stores**, supermarkets, and discount stores all emphasized limited service and low prices. In most instances, price levels have gradually increased as services have been added.

There have been some exceptions, however. Suburban shopping centres, convenience food stores, and vending machines were not developed on a foundation of low-price appeals. However, the wheel pattern has been present often enough in the past that it should serve as a general indicator of future developments in retailing.

# MARKETING STRATEGY IN RETAILING

The retailer's decision-making process, like the producer's and wholesaler's, centres on the three fundamental steps of (1) analyzing, evaluating, and ultimately selecting a *target market*, (2) analyzing the strengths and weaknesses of competitors, and (3) developing a *marketing mix* designed to satisfy the chosen target market profitably. In other words, the retailer must develop a product offering to appeal to the chosen consumer group, set prices, and choose a location and method of distribution. Finally, the retailer has to develop a marketing communications strategy (Figure 16.1).[2]

## Conduct Target Market Research and Analysis

Target market analysis is essential in retailing. Canada's retail establishments are involved in developing specific marketing mixes to satisfy chosen market segments. For example, a retailer planning to establish a new cosmetics and skin care store recognizes a great deal of existing competition.

**chain store**

Group of retail stores that are centrally owned and managed and that handle the same lines of products.

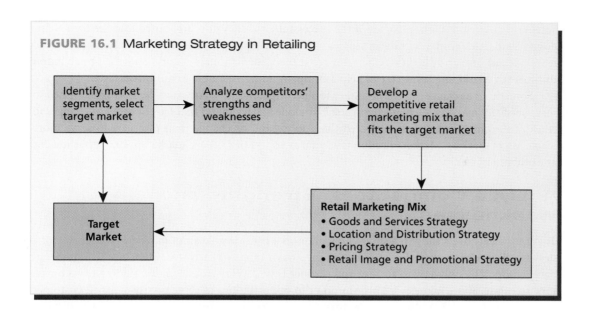

**FIGURE 16.1** Marketing Strategy in Retailing

Identify market segments, select target market → Analyze competitors' strengths and weaknesses → Develop a competitive retail marketing mix that fits the target market

Target Market ← **Retail Marketing Mix**
• Goods and Services Strategy
• Location and Distribution Strategy
• Pricing Strategy
• Retail Image and Promotional Strategy

Success will be greatly affected by how well she identifies the needs of potential customers. Like other marketers, retailers must start by selecting the target market to which they wish to appeal. Marketing research is often used in this aspect of retail decision making. For example, retailers entering new countries, or even new markets in the same country, have been surprised that the target market of their home location apparently does not exist in the new location. Canadian Tire expanded to the larger U.S. market with the purchase of White Stores, Inc., but found U.S. market

www.canadiantire.com

Prepare to start a new habit.

Chicken BLT Salad

Wendy's® New Garden Sensations™   We've Raised The Bar On Salads.

**Retail changes often develop from attempts to better satisfy particular consumer needs or to make the enterprise more competitive.**

acceptance of virtual carbon copies of the successful Canadian store so limited that the firm abandoned that market after significant losses. Marks and Spencer, one of Britain's most successful retailers, had similar difficulties when it entered the Canadian market and finally had to abandon this market. Marketing research can help a company adjust to a new environment faster.

Sometimes a retailer finds it necessary to shift target markets. For example, stores established to serve specialty markets, such as skiers or snowmobilers, have found that lack of snow or changes in consumer recreation habits have forced them to expand or change their offerings to serve more viable target markets. Market selection is as vital an aspect of retailers' marketing strategy as it is for any other marketer.[3]

## Analyze Competitors' Strengths and Weaknesses

To set up a new dress shop in a shopping mall takes a considerable amount of nerve. In fact strong nerves will not be enough. Every shopping mall has a range of such stores that will be significant competitors. The only way to survive and prosper is to develop a clear understanding of competitors' strengths and weaknesses. This can point to opportunities to serve poorly-satisfied customer needs and indicate strengths of competitors. Can you overcome such strengths, or will it be like hitting your head against the wall?

An analysis of competitors' strengths and weaknesses, as well as an understanding of your target market, provide a foundation for developing a retail marketing mix, and for differentiating your retail operation. These processes will be discussed next.

## Develop a Marketing (Retail) Mix That Fits the Target Market

The retail mix is comprised of the following elements: decision about goods and services, prices, location and distribution, and retail image and promotion. The objective is to blend these elements to provide a unique offering to the market.

### Goods and Services Strategy

Retailers must also determine and evaluate their offerings with respect to the following:

- general goods/services categories
- specific lines
- specific products
- inventory depth
- inventory breadth (range of assortment)

These decisions are determined by the size of the retailer, as well as whether the store tends to concentrate on convenience, shopping, or specialty goods. Other marketing factors can influence goods and/or service offerings. For instance, Toys Я Us distinguishes itself by specializing and providing great breadth and depth of assortment at low prices.

Product strategy evolves to meet competition and changing consumer needs. The success of Loblaws' Superstores forced Safeway to develop its large Food for Less establishments. On a more limited scale, a decision by Tim Hortons to provide a new menu line would likely have to be matched by Robins if the new Tim Hortons line proved to be popular.

### Pricing Strategy

Pricing is another critical element of the retailing mix. The essential decisions concern relative price levels. Does the target market want service and high quality, high-priced merchandise (as offered by Holt Renfrew), or lower-priced items (as offered by Zellers)? Price is such an important variable in the retail marketing mix that it continually drives the establishment of new types of retail operations, such as Costco. These will be discussed in more detail later.

www.safeway.com

www.timhortons.com

Other pricing decisions concern markups, markdowns, loss leaders, odd pricing, and promotional pricing. The retailer is the channel member with direct responsibility for the prices paid by consumers. As Chapters 13 and 14 pointed out, the prices that are set play a major role in buyer perceptions of the retail market.

## Location and Distribution Strategy

Real-estate professionals often say that there are three critical factors for establishing a retail establishment: "Location, location, location." A store must be in an appropriate location for the type and price of merchandise carried. Small service outlets such as dry cleaners have discovered that there is a difference between being on the "going to work" side of a busy street and the "going home" side. Other retailers have found success in small strip-type neighbourhood shopping centres that are close to where people live. These centres continue to flourish despite the advent of larger suburban community shopping centres.[4]

**Retail trade area analysis** refers to studies that assess the relative drawing power of alternative retail locations. For example, shoppers might be polled as to where they live, how they get to the stores they shop at, how long it takes, how often they shop, and the like. Similarly, the credit charges of an existing store might be plotted to show what its service area is.

Another technique to use is retail gravity theory, sometimes called Reilly's law after its originator, William J. Reilly.[5] The **law of retail gravitation**, originally formulated in the 1920s, delineates the retail trade area of a potential site on the basis of distance between alternative locations and relative populations. That is, shoppers are attracted approximately in direct proportion to the population of the two cities and in inverse proportion to the square of the distance from these two cities to the intermediate place. The formula is

**retail trade area analysis**
Studies that assess the relative drawing power of alternative retail locations.

**law of retail gravitation**
Principle that delineates the retail trade area of a potential site on the basis of distance between alternative locations and relative populations.

$$\text{Breaking point in km from A} = \frac{\text{km between A and B}}{1 + \sqrt{\dfrac{\text{Population of B}}{\text{Population of A}}}}$$

Assume a retailer is considering locating a new outlet in Town A or Town B, which are located 60 km from each other. The population of A is 80 000 and the population of B is 20 000. One question that concerns the retailer is where people living in a small rural community located on the highway between the two towns 25 km from Town B are likely to shop.

According to the law of retail gravitation, these rural shoppers would most likely shop in Town A even though it is 10 km farther away than Town B. The retail trade area of A extends 40 km toward B, and the rural community is located only 35 km away.

$$\text{Breaking point in km from A} = \frac{60}{1 + \sqrt{\dfrac{20\,000}{80\,000}}} = \frac{60}{1 + \sqrt{.25}} = \frac{60}{1.5} = 40$$

The formula can be applied inversely to find Town B's trade area, yielding a figure of 20 km, which falls 5 km short of the rural community:

$$\text{Breaking point in km from B} = \frac{60}{1 + \sqrt{\dfrac{80\,000}{20\,000}}} = \frac{60}{1 + \sqrt{4}} = \frac{60}{3} = 20 \text{ km}$$

The complete trade area for A or B could be found by similar calculations with other communities.

The application of this technique is limited in an area of urban sprawl, regional shopping centres, and consumers who measure distances in terms of travel time.

## OTHER DISTRIBUTION DECISIONS

Retailers are faced with a variety of other distribution decisions, largely in order to ensure that adequate quantities of stock are available when consumers want to buy. The definition of "adequate" will vary with the service strategy of the retailer. In many traditional retail situations, since the cost of carrying inventory is high, a high-margin, full-service retailer will likely have a greater depth and range of merchandise than a low-margin, limited-time, high-volume outlet. This generalization does not hold in the case of some large-format specialty stores, such as Office Depot or Staples.

### Retail Image and Promotional Strategy

**retail image**

The consumer's perception of a store and of the shopping experience it provides.

**Retail image** refers to the consumer's perception of a store and of the shopping experience it provides.[6] Promotional strategy is a key element in determining the store's image with the consumer. Another important element is the amenities provided by the retailer—the so-called atmospherics.

Promoting a store with screaming headlines about fantastic once-in-a-lifetime sale prices creates a substantially different image from that using a subdued, tasteful illustration of obviously stylish, elegant clothing. Similarly, walking into a discount store filled with the smell of caramel popcorn produces an image that is dramatically different from that of entering a beautifully carpeted boutique.

Regardless of how it is accomplished, the objective of retailer promotional strategy should be to align the consumer's perception of the store with other elements of the retailing mix: retail image should match the target market that is selected.

## Differentiate Store from Competitors

Differentiation is a key factor in competitive strategy.[7] Retailers can differentiate themselves in many ways. However, three elements—price, location, and store atmosphere and service—are typically used to differentiate stores from the competitors in the same strategic group. The **differentiation triangle** is shown in Figure 16.2.

Changes in these elements do not transform a store from one type to another (e.g., a convenience store to a department store). Yet the way the elements are used is important, since they give

**differentiation triangle**

Differentiation of a retail store from competitors in the same strategic group through price, location, and store atmosphere and service.

Marks & Spencer had a loyal customer core of mostly expatriate Britons, but failed to market itself to others in Canada.

## A FAILURE IN GLOBAL MARKETING

Highly successful British retailing institution Marks & Spencer PLC packed up its food and clothing and left Canada in 1999 after years of failing to connect to Canadian tastes. Marks & Spencer Canada Inc. closed all 38 stores in the country and laid off about 900 employees. Parent company Marks & Spencer PLC estimated that leaving Canada cost about $60 million.

"I think the brand ... never really found its niche in the Canadian market," David Stewart, president and chief executive officer in Canada for the company's last two years, said in an interview.

"It was a British concept that was imported and assumed to work in Canada. I put together a North American management team that tried to change it. But [it was] far too late.... There [was] too much to rejig."

Marks & Spencer, known fondly by many for its quality underwear, turned a profit only three times since it set up shop in Canada in 1973: in the 1992–93 year and twice in the 1980s. It had a loyal customer core of mostly expatriate Britons, but never bothered to market itself to others in Canada, observers say.

"They were viewed as being terribly unfashionable," said retail consultant John Williams of J.C. Williams Group Ltd. in Toronto. "[They] had a dowdy image. They were insensitive to the needs of Canadian consumers."

The plans to close [came] amid heated competition among clothing retailers, especially since department store chains such as The Bay moved more into apparel. The arrival of giant discounter Wal-Mart Canada Inc. in 1994 and other U.S.-based big-box category killers also squeezed virtually all rivals.

You cannot assume that a product or concept that works in your country will work in another.

www.walmart.com

www.marksandspencer.com

Source: Adapted from Marina Strauss, "Marks & Spencer to Leave Canada," *The Globe and Mail* (April 29, 1999), p. B1. Reprinted with permission from *The Globe and Mail*.

---

**FIGURE 16.2** Differentiation Triangle: Avenues for Differentiation Within Strategic Groups

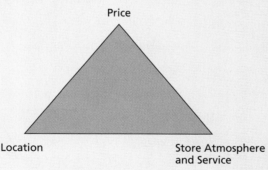

Source: Adapted from *Retail Management*, 2nd ed. by Avijit Ghosh, pp. 59–60. Copyright © 1994. Reprinted with permission of South-Western, a division of Thomson Learning: www.thomsonrights.com. Fax 800-730-2215.

---

the customer reasons to choose one store over another. For example, location is very important, as we have already discussed.

Price is a powerful tool in the retail mix. It is not always the differentiating factor, but retailers must understand when it does play that role. In such a circumstance, retailers are finding that they cannot "play around" with discounting. Price cuts must be truly significant in order to compete with other retailers who have also chosen price as a means of differentiation.

## DO RETAIL BRANDS TRAVEL?

In presenting one face to the world, a company risks presenting the wrong face to entire nations.

Conventional wisdom holds that a great retail brand must present one face to the world—a consistent image that defines the product wherever consumers find it. But retail chains have found that although they can hang out their signs anywhere, consumers respond differently in every country. Understanding those differences is the key to building a successful retail brand across borders.

Our survey of 40 retail grocery and clothing brands in France, Germany, and the United Kingdom* shows the importance of tailoring a product's image to each national market. As retailers such as Aldi, Tesco, and Zara move into new territory, they may have to define themselves not once but many times over. Retailers that rely on a single brand formula can find themselves forced out of some markets, as Eddie Bauer, Marks & Spencer, and Wal-Mart can attest.

By comparing more than 1500 consumers' ratings of how well the stores performed with the store choices these consumers actually made, we found that what they say and what they do are not always identical. Customers tend, for example, to say that they don't shop in particular stores because their friends do, but their friends' shopping choices turn out to be powerful motivators. Customers also overstate the importance of certain issues. In choosing grocery stores, for example, German shoppers are less influenced by the range of products stocked than they claim to be, so retailers that spend heavily to offer a wide product range might achieve better results by investing, for example, in more targeted marketing to boost a store's attractions for affinity customers (described below).

As retail chains attempt to go global, they will have to pay greater attention to such market nuances. Large advertising expenditures and a global brand are not enough. In presenting one face to the world, a company risks presenting the wrong face to entire nations.

**How do you account for such differences in customer behaviour?**

**Exhibit A: What Do European Consumers Value?**

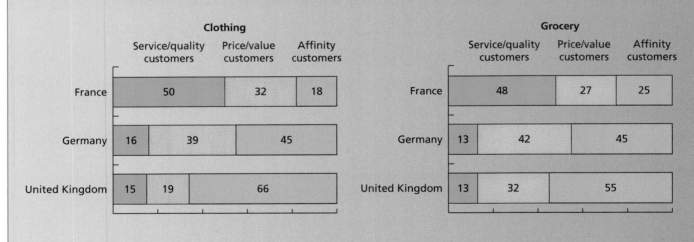

| Clothing | Service/quality customers | Price/value customers | Affinity customers |
|---|---|---|---|
| France | 50 | 32 | 18 |
| Germany | 16 | 39 | 45 |
| United Kingdom | 15 | 19 | 66 |

| Grocery | Service/quality customers | Price/value customers | Affinity customers |
|---|---|---|---|
| France | 48 | 27 | 25 |
| Germany | 13 | 42 | 45 |
| United Kingdom | 13 | 32 | 55 |

Stores can also differentiate by improving store atmosphere and customer service. Unfortunately, many retailers have ignored this element's potential and allowed service quality to deteriorate in the pursuit of cost savings. As manufacturers and other service providers are learning to emphasize total quality in their products, retailers also need to reevaluate the quality of their service.

# CATEGORIZING RETAILERS

The nation's retailers come in a variety of forms. Since new types of retail operations continue to evolve in response to the changing demands of their markets, no universal classification has been devised. The following characteristics or bases can be used in categorizing them:

- shopping effort expended by customers
- services provided to customers
- product lines
- location of retail transactions
- form of ownership
- margin and turnover

Any retailing operation can be classified using each of these six bases. A 7-Eleven store may be classified as a convenience store (category 1), self-service (category 2), relatively narrow product lines (category 3), in-store retailing (category 4), a member of a corporate chain (category 5), and high margin/high turnover (category 6). Figure 16.3 illustrates the bases for classifying retail operations. Note that the categories are not absolute. The most exclusive specialty store carries handkerchiefs, and many supermarkets have gourmet food departments.

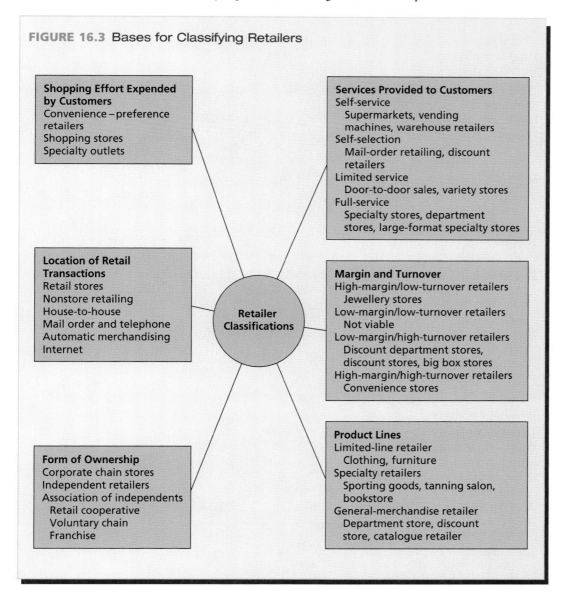

**FIGURE 16.3** Bases for Classifying Retailers

**Shopping Effort Expended by Customers**
Convenience–preference retailers
Shopping stores
Specialty outlets

**Services Provided to Customers**
Self-service
   Supermarkets, vending machines, warehouse retailers
Self-selection
   Mail-order retailing, discount retailers
Limited service
   Door-to-door sales, variety stores
Full-service
   Specialty stores, department stores, large-format specialty stores

**Location of Retail Transactions**
Retail stores
Nonstore retailing
House-to-house
Mail order and telephone
Automatic merchandising
Internet

**Margin and Turnover**
High-margin/low-turnover retailers
   Jewellery stores
Low-margin/low-turnover retailers
   Not viable
Low-margin/high-turnover retailers
   Discount department stores, discount stores, big box stores
High-margin/high-turnover retailers
   Convenience stores

**Retailer Classifications**

**Form of Ownership**
Corporate chain stores
Independent retailers
Association of independents
   Retail cooperative
   Voluntary chain
   Franchise

**Product Lines**
Limited-line retailer
   Clothing, furniture
Specialty retailers
   Sporting goods, tanning salon, bookstore
General-merchandise retailer
   Department store, discount store, catalogue retailer

# In-Store Retailing Today

Retailing is carried on within stores, and without. By far, most retailing occurs in and through stores. The most commonly used method of categorizing retailers is to consider the product lines they handle. Grouping retailers by product lines produces three major categories: limited-line retailers, specialty retailers, and general-merchandise retailers. Because retailing is so dynamic, the significance of the various categories has changed over time. Some have nearly vanished, other exciting types have arisen to change the retailing landscape. Table 16.1 shows retail trade for various types of outlets. From this it can be seen that Canadians spend the most on food and automobiles.

**TABLE 16.1** Retail Trade[1]

| | 1997 | 1998 | 1999 | 2000 | 2001 |
|---|---|---|---|---|---|
| | | | $ THOUSANDS | | |
| **Canada** | **237 836 642** | **246 674 830** | **260 779 457** | **277 033 166** | **289 129 995** |
| **Food** | 55 949 491 | 57 664 384 | 58 889 235 | 61 090 154 | 63 651 604 |
| Supermarkets and grocery stores | 51 655 381 | 53 346 164 | 54 500 310 | 56 592 005 | 58 858 418 |
| All other food stores | 4 294 110 | 4 318 220 | 4 388 925 | 4 498 149 | 4 793 186 |
| **Drug and patent medicine stores** | 12 297 715 | 12 944 258 | 13 334 755 | 13 498 880 | 14 415 892 |
| **Clothing** | 13 384 977 | 13 950 453 | 14 422 357 | 15 278 251 | 15 868 022 |
| Shoe stores | 1 649 767 | 1 704 158 | 1 714 375 | 1 769 716 | 1 772 121 |
| Men's clothing stores | 1 569 634 | 1 581 640 | 1 536 280 | 1 531 380 | 1 421 283 |
| Women's clothing stores | 4 335 286 | 4 405 600 | 4 504 777 | 4 627 375 | 4 773 872 |
| Other clothing stores | 5 830 290 | 6 259 055 | 6 666 925 | 7 349 780 | 7 900 746 |
| **Furniture** | 11 605 367 | 12 536 204 | 13 654 313 | 15 158 799 | 16 364 383 |
| Household furniture and appliance stores | 9 305 441 | 10 107 335 | 11 082 142 | 12 276 135 | 13 254 137 |
| Household furnishings stores | 2 299 926 | 2 428 869 | 2 572 171 | 2 882 664 | 3 110 246 |
| **Automotive** | 93 323 871 | 94 980 648 | 102 315 054 | 111 051 131 | 115 523 830 |
| Motor vehicle and recreational vehicle dealers | 62 767 698 | 64 458 096 | 69 376 278 | 73 104 031 | 76 617 532 |
| Gasoline service stations | 16 928 075 | 16 186 761 | 18 000 463 | 22 363 631 | 22 414 833 |
| Automotive parts, accessories & services | 13 628 098 | 14 335 791 | 14 938 313 | 15 583 469 | 16 491 465 |
| **General merchandise stores** | 26 182 665 | 27 956 026 | 29 989 514 | 31 297 287 | 32 293 926 |
| **Other retail stores** | 25 092 557 | 26 642 858 | 28 174 229 | 29 658 662 | 31 012 337 |
| Other semi-durable goods stores | 8 187 560 | 8 217 439 | 8 492 872 | 8 720 757 | 8 952 480 |
| Other durable goods stores | 6 008 252 | 6 750 354 | 7 060 211 | 7 459 808 | 7 694 405 |
| All other retail stores | 10 896 745 | 11 675 065 | 12 621 146 | 13 478 097 | 14 365 452 |

[1] Seasonally adjusted.

Source: Adapted from the Statistics Canada publication "Market Research Handbook," Catalogue No. 63-224, 1998, page 122. Reprinted with permission of the Minister of Industry Canada.

## Limited-Line Retailers

A large assortment of a single line of products or a few related lines of products are offered in **limited-line stores**. Their development parallelled the growth of towns when the population grew sufficiently to support them. These operations include such retailers as furniture stores, hardware stores, grocery stores and supermarkets, appliance stores, and sporting goods stores. Examples of limited-line stores include Sherwin-Williams (paint), House of Teak (furniture), Radio Shack (home electronics), Pegabo and Bata (shoes), Calculator World (electronic calculators), Gap (ready-to-wear), and Chapters/Indigo (books).

These retailers choose to cater to the needs of a specific target market—people who want to select from a complete line in purchasing a particular product. The marketing vice president of a limited-line firm might summarize the limited-line retailer's strategy this way: "Canadian Tire can show customers 5 types of safety boots, but we can show them 25."

**limited-line store**
Retailer that offers a large assortment of a single line of products or a few related lines of products.

### SUPERMARKETS

The supermarket concentrates mainly on a single line—groceries—but this line contains many different products.

A **supermarket** can be defined as a large-scale, departmentalized retail store offering a large variety of food products such as meats, produce, dairy products, canned goods, and frozen foods in addition to various nonfood items.

Vigorous competition is a way of life for supermarkets. One Ontario supermarket attempted to increase its share of the market through a well-publicized price-cutting program. The ramifications were quickly felt in other areas of the country where branches of competing chains operate. Retaliation by other supermarkets was swift, and temporary price cuts ensued—as well as reductions in profits. Supermarket profits average only about 1 percent of sales after taxes. However, a high turnover of 20–26 times per year provides attractive returns on investment.

With a razor-thin profit margin, supermarkets compete through careful planning of retail displays in order to sell more merchandise per week and reduce the amount of investment in inventory. Product location is studied carefully in order to expose the consumer to as much merchandise as possible (and increase impulse purchases). In an attempt to respond to the tendency of consumers to eat many of their meals outside the home, supermarkets feature their own delicatessens and bakeries.

Nonfood products such as toiletries, magazines, videos, over-the-counter drugs, prescription pharmaceuticals, and small kitchen utensils are carried for two reasons: (1) consumers have displayed a willingness to buy such items in supermarkets, and (2) supermarket managers like these items because they have a higher profit margin than the food products. Nonfood sales have grown substantially as a percentage of supermarket sales.

The trend in this category is toward larger stores. Many of these, such as Loblaws' Superstores, carry a variety of other merchandise, such as clothing, hardware, and gift items.

**supermarket**
Large-scale, departmentalized retail store offering a large variety of food products such as meats, produce, dairy products, canned goods, and frozen foods in addition to various nonfood items.

## Specialty Retailers

A **specialty store** typically handles only part of a single line of products. However, this narrow line is stocked in considerable depth. Such stores include meat markets, shoe stores, bakeries, furriers, and luggage shops. Although some of these stores are operated by chains, most are run as independent small-scale operations. The specialty store is perhaps the greatest stronghold of the independent retailer, who can develop expertise in providing a very narrow line of products for his or her local market.

Specialty stores should not be confused with specialty goods, for the specialty store typically carries convenience and shopping goods. The label "specialty" comes from the practice of handling a specific, narrow line of merchandise.

**specialty store**
Retailer that handles only part of a single line of products.

## General-Merchandise Retailers

### DEPARTMENT STORES

The department store is actually a series of limited-line and specialty stores under one roof. A **department store**, by definition, is a large retailer that handles a variety of merchandise that may

**department store**
Large retailer that handles a variety of merchandise.

ARMANI COLLEZIONI  BURBERRY  CANALI  DOLCE & GABBANA  ESKANDAR  GIORGIO ARMANI
GUCCI  HUGO BOSS  JIL SANDER  PIAZZA SEMPIONE  PRADA  RALPH LAUREN BLACK LABEL  ST. JOHN  ZEGNA SPORT

COMPLIMENTARY PERSONAL SHOPPING

## HOLT RENFREW

QUEBEC  MONTREAL  OTTAWA  TORONTO  CALGARY  EDMONTON  VANCOUVER  WWW.HOLTRENFREW.COM

**This ad attracts attention, then subtly reinforces Holt Renfrew's world-class image by listing the prestige brands it carries.**

include apparel and accessories, home furnishings, cosmetics, housewares, and appliances. It serves the consumer by acting as a one-stop shopping centre for almost all personal and household items.

A distinguishing feature of the department store is indicated by its name. The entire stock is *organized around departments* for the purposes of service, promotion, and control. A general merchandising manager is responsible for the entire store's product planning. Reporting to the merchandising manager are the buyers who manage each department. The buyers typically run the departments almost as independent businesses and are given considerable discretion in merchandising and layout decisions. Acceptance of the retailing axiom that "well-purchased goods are half sold" is indicated in the department manager's title of *buyer*. The buyers, particularly those in charge of high-fashion departments, spend a considerable portion of their time making decisions concerning the inventory to be carried in their departments.

Today, almost every urban area in Canada has one or more department stores associated with its downtown area and its major shopping areas. Department stores have had a major impact in many cities.

The impact of department stores on urban life is not confined to Canada. Such stores are, of course, widespread in the United States. European shoppers associate London with Harrod's and Paris with Au Printemps. Australians associate Melbourne and Sydney with Cole/Meyers.

Department stores are known for offering their customers a wide variety of services such as charge accounts, delivery, gift wrapping, and liberal return privileges. In addition, approximately 50 percent of their employees and some 40 percent of their floor space are devoted to nonselling activities. As a result, department stores have relatively high operating costs, averaging between 45 and 60 percent of sales.

Department stores have faced intense competition in the past 30 years. Their relatively high operating costs make them vulnerable to other retailing types such as discount stores and "big box" warehouse stores (discussed later in this section). In addition, department stores are often located in downtown business districts and experience the problems associated with limited parking, traffic congestion, and urban migration to the suburbs.

Successful department stores have displayed a willingness to adapt to competition and changing consumer desires. Reducing prices through lowering service levels has been one notable response by some department stores. (However, reduced service takes away some of the competitive advantage of a department store.) Also, department stores have followed the movement of the population to the suburbs by opening major branches in outlying shopping centres.

## INTERNET IMPACT

### INTERNET SUCCESS LEADS TO BRICKS AND MORTAR

Here's a switch: an Internet store successful enough to move into the bricks-and-mortar arena.

Originally created as an e-commerce and catalogue operation, justwhiteshirts.com has opened its first downtown Toronto store and raised $1.8 million to continue its retail expansion across Canada. Not bad for a seven-year-old outfit that was originally conceived only to sell 100% cotton dress shirts for men. Now it sells everything from dress pants and ties to cologne and shaving cream, under the brand name "Just." This past May, justwhiteshirts.com also introduced a women's line.

www.justwhiteshirts.com

President and CEO Leon Goren planned to open more Toronto locations and then look at opening stores in its second and third best-selling markets, Calgary and Vancouver. Justwhiteshirts.com has operated a retail store at its Toronto head office since 2000, raking in $1.4 million in sales annually although it's located outside of the downtown core. Goren says the aim is to "fit in between" Harry Rosen, also a provider of men's dress shirts, and Banana Republic, which he says he admires for its unisex demographic and comfortable atmosphere. Justwhiteshirts.com's main customer has traditionally been men earning a salary of over $75 000, although that is starting to change.

But can justwhiteshirts.com succeed in the fiercely competitive bricks-and-mortar retail landscape? The on-line business currently accounts for 30% of its revenue, but as stores start opening Goren believes that will fall to 15 or 20%.

"Roughly 90% of Canadians will not shop using mail order or e-commerce. They like the act of shopping," he says. "Of that 10%, we've done a good job of marketing to them. Now we're opening up our concept to a wider audience." He adds the multi-channel model, made up of mail order, online and now the stores, gives it various ways to cross-sell and promote.

Success on the Internet led to the establishment of bricks-and-mortar stores.

Justwhiteshirts.com's "sizable" advertising budget will continue to focus on traditional media, says Goren, with ads running in newspapers like *The Globe and Mail* and a radio campaign on 680 News.

**What do you think of the company putting an increasing emphasis on bricks-and-mortar operations instead of building on their proven formula of marketing through the Internet?**

Source: Adapted from Chris Daniels, "Here's a Switch: An Internet Store Successful Enough to Move into the Bricks-and-Mortar Arena," *Marketing Magazine*, Jan. 7, 2002. Reprinted with permission.

## VARIETY STORES

variety store
Retailer that offers an extensive range and assortment of low-priced merchandise.

Retailers that offer an extensive range and assortment of low-priced merchandise are called **variety stores**. Two examples are Fields and Stedmans. Most of the products carried by these stores are quite basic. Consumers seldom have strong preferences for particular brands. Thus stores can carry a limited range in each product line without losing potential customers. The nation's variety stores account for only about 0.64 percent of all retail sales. Variety stores have steadily declined in popularity. Many have evolved into or have been replaced by other retailing categories such as discounting.

## MASS MERCHANDISERS

mass merchandiser
Retailer that concentrates on high turnover of items, emphasizes lower prices than department stores, and offers reduced services.

Mass merchandisers are direct competitors of department stores. **Mass merchandisers** concentrate on high turnover of items, emphasize lower prices than department stores, and offer reduced services. Typically, they give considerable attention to small appliances, hardware, automotive products, and sporting goods in addition to apparel.

Canadian Tire is an example of a mass merchandiser. Other major types of mass merchandisers are discount houses, hypermarkets, and catalogue retailers.

## DISCOUNT HOUSES

discount house
Retailer that, in exchange for reduced prices, does not offer such traditional retail services as credit, sales assistance by clerks, and delivery.

The birth of the modern **discount house** came at the end of World War II when a New York operation named Masters discovered that a very large number of customers were willing to shop at a store that did not offer such traditional retail services as credit, sales assistance by clerks, and delivery, in exchange for reduced prices. Within a very brief period, retailers throughout the country followed the Masters formula and either changed over from their traditional operations or opened new stores dedicated to discounting. At first the discount stores were primarily involved with selling appliances, but they have spread into furniture, soft goods, drugs, and even food.

The new discounters operated large stores, advertised heavily, and emphasized low prices on well-known brands. And consumers, who had become accustomed to self-service by shopping at supermarkets, responded in great numbers to this retailing innovation.

As the discount houses moved into new product areas, a noticeable increase in the number of services offered as well as a corresponding decrease in the discount margin became evident. Carpeted floors appeared in some discounters' stores, credit became increasingly available, and many discounters even quietly dropped the term *discount* from their name. This is an example of the wheel of retailing discussed earlier.

Wal-Mart has renewed the competitive challenge. Wal-Mart generates differential price advantage through great purchasing power and efficiencies in distribution. In addition to low prices, it competes by offering extra services. Zellers and Canadian Tire are two major retailers that are being especially challenged by Wal-Mart. Kmart and Woolco, which both had a long history, were unable to meet the competition and failed in Canada.

membership and warehouse club
Very large, warehouse-type retail store that offers low prices because of its no-frill format and paid membership requirement.

Two new formats have evolved in the discount store category.[8] These are membership and warehouse clubs and large-format specialty stores. An example of a **membership and warehouse club** is Costco. Customers must purchase a membership card (about $35) before they can enter the store. The stores are often located in an industrial subdivision and are constructed like warehouses, with steel walls and roofs and cement floors. They range in size from 9000 to 12 000 m$^2$. Customers vie with forklift trucks in the aisles, as all merchandise is stored on tall metal shelving.

Large-size packaging, in most instances, requires the buyer to purchase a supply that will last several months. There is no service, and prices are low enough that many small businesses are seen buying merchandise for resale. These warehouses are having a sizable impact on the retail market, as well as on the market share of traditional retailers.

large-format specialty store
Large, warehouse-type retail store that specializes in selling a great variety of one category of merchandise at very low prices.

Another new threat to existing retailers is the development of very large specialty retailers. **Large-format specialty stores** can be of similar size to warehouse clubs. They are known as *category killers*. The characteristics of these stores give some reasons for this name:

1. They are very large and specialize in one type of merchandise. Each store has a huge variety to choose from.

2. They use low-cost, warehouse-type building structures.
3. They sell a very large volume of merchandise at very low prices. The average gross margin is approximately 8 percent.
4. Their average sales per square metre are $4300—about twice as much as traditional retailers.
5. These new retailers offer a great deal of service. Consider Home Depot, for example. It looks like a warehouse, has a huge selection of hardware and building items, and even offers "how-to" sessions taught by professionals.
6. These category killers locate in a free-standing suburban location. This gives them 35 to 50 percent lower location costs than in the downtown area. Other costs are often much less than in more congested retail areas.

Another example of a large-format specialty store is Chapters/Indigo, a bookstore stacked with 100 000 different types of books. Included is live children's entertainment and a cappuccino bar with a reading room. Yet another example is Petsmart, a pet supply store of 1800 m$^2$. This is about ten times larger than typical stores. It carries 6500 products to keep animals happy, healthy, and fashionable.

Because of their size and the warehouse-type facility, these two types of retailers are also known as *big box retailers*. The development of these two types of discount operations is a classic example of retailers seeking a differential advantage. In the case of the category killers, they are very strong on at least two aspects of the differential triangle: price and service. Consumers have ready access to virtually anything they want in a particular category without shopping around—and likely at a lower price. Selection plus service at a low price is a hard combination for traditional retailers to beat.

Groupings of two or more large-format retailers in the same areas are known as **power nodes**. These have a large drawing power and are pulling consumers away from traditional shopping areas.

Established retailers are scrambling to compete. Canadian Tire, for example, is increasing the size of its stores and adopting a warehouse format. It has also announced new lower prices.

**power node**
Groupings of two or more large-format retailers that result in large customer drawing power.

## HYPERMARKETS

These giant mass merchandisers operate on a low-price self-service basis and carry lines of soft goods, hard goods, and groceries. **Hypermarkets** are sometimes called superstores, although this latter term has also been used to describe a variety of large retail operations.[9] The *hypermarché*, or hypermarket, began in France and has since spread to a limited degree to Canada and the United States. The Hypermarché Laval outside Montreal was the first to open and had 19 500 m$^2$ of selling space (eleven to fifteen times the size of the average supermarket) and 40 checkouts. A typical hypermarket is like a shopping centre in a single store. It sells food, hardware, soft goods, building materials, auto supplies, appliances, and prescription drugs, and has a restaurant, a beauty salon, a barber shop, a bank branch, and a bakery. Many of these superstores are currently in operation throughout the world. It appears that they are more popular in Europe than in North America. This is likely because North America already had many large, well-developed shopping centres before the hypermarket concept arrived.

**hypermarket**
Mass merchandiser that operates on a low-price, self-service basis and carries lines of soft goods, hard goods, and groceries.

## OFF-PRICE RETAILERS

Off-price retailers specialize in selling manufacturers' excess stocks of brand-name merchandise at a discount. **Off-price retailers** stock designer labels or well-known products and sell at prices that approximate wholesale. One of the keys to their success is the ability of buyers to find and take advantage of special price offers from manufacturers that are selling excess merchandise. Winners is an example of such a retailer.

**off-price retailer**
Retailer that specializes in selling manufacturers' excess stocks of brand-name merchandise at a discount.

## RECYCLED MERCHANDISE RETAILERS

Interest in recycled merchandise, such as castoff clothes, furniture, and other products, is growing. There are several different types of **recycled merchandise retailers**: pawn shops, thrift shops, and flea markets. Another version is the recycled discount store typified by Value Village. Value Village arranges with the Tuberculosis Society to pick up castoff merchandise from households and purchases this merchandise for resale from the Society. Specialty versions of recycled merchandise retailers have emerged, offering children's clothes, outerwear, and other merchandise.

**recycled merchandise retailer**
Retailer that sells castoff clothes, furniture, and other products.

## LIQUIDATORS

There are thousands of retailers in the marketplace, and some do not make it. Even successful retailers often have lines of products that they don't want to carry any longer, or they have broken lots of merchandise they want to get rid of. The result is a great deal of products that need to be disposed of. **Liquidators** are specialty retailers who either come into a bankrupt store and handle the closeout, or who buy the entire lot and sell it in their own stores. Liquidation World is a chain of liquidators that is spreading across the country. Buying products for approximately 30 cents on the dollar, the liquidator can offer good value to customers and still be profitable.

## CATALOGUE RETAILERS

These retailers mail catalogues to their customers and operate from a showroom displaying samples of their products. **Catalogue retailers** fill orders from a backroom warehouse. Price is an important factor for catalogue store customers, and low prices are made possible by few services, storage of most of the inventory in the warehouse, reduced shoplifting losses, and handling of products that are unlikely to become obsolete, such as luggage, small appliances, gift items, sports equipment, toys, and jewellery. (Mail-order catalogue retailing is discussed later in this chapter.)

# Nonstore Retailing and Direct Marketing

While the overwhelming majority of retail sales occur in retail stores, nonstore retailing is important for many products. Nonstore retailing includes direct house-to-house sales, mail-order retailing, and automatic merchandising machines. These kinds of sales account for about 1.7 percent of all retail sales.

## House-to-House Retailing

One of the oldest marketing channels was built around direct contact between the retailer–seller and the customer at the home of the customer—**house-to-house retailing**. It provides convenience for the consumer and allows the manufacturer to control the firm's marketing channel. House-to-house retailing is a minor part of the retailing picture, with less than 1 percent of all retail sales.

House-to-house retailing is conducted by a number of different merchandisers. Manufacturers of such products as bakery and dairy products and newspapers use this channel. Firms whose products require emphasis on personal selling and product demonstrations may also use it. Such products and services include, for example, cosmetics (Avon), vacuum cleaners (Electrolux), household brushes (Fuller Brush Company), encyclopedias (World Book), and insurance.

Some firms—such as Tupperware and Stanley Home Products—use a variation called *party-plan selling*, where a customer gives a party and invites several neighbours and friends. During the party, a company representative makes a presentation of the product, and the host or hostess receives a commission based on the amount of products sold.

The house-to-house method of retailing would appear to be a low-cost method of distribution. No plush retail facilities are required, no investment in inventory is necessary, and most house-to-house salespeople operate on a commission basis. In fact, this method is an extremely high-cost approach to distribution. Often the distribution cost of a product marketed through retail stores is half that of the same product retailed house-to-house. High travel costs, the problems involved in recruiting and training a huge sales force that generally has a high turnover, nonproductive calls, several layers of commissions, and the limited number of contracts per day result in high operating expenses.

## MULTILEVEL MARKETING

Another version of house-to-house retailing is **multilevel marketing**. This type of marketing depends heavily on the personal influence network of consumers and "positive thinking" techniques. Many different products are sold, from burglar alarms to cosmetics to "wellness" products such as vitamins and meal supplements. Examples of such companies are Amway and Shaklee.

The system depends on a network of people.[10] As many as possible are recruited to sell the products to friends, family, and acquaintances. In return, the salesperson, or "independent distributor," gets a commission. But the real money comes in when the salesperson recruits others who become distributors.

In return for bringing in new people—known in the business as "down-liners"—the recruiter receives a cut of all of their sales. If these new people also recruit, they get a cut of that too. Commissions can travel five or six layers up the network of distributors, depending on the company's policy. A key to making the system work is to keep all the people involved highly motivated. Consequently, a regular series of local and district motivational meetings are a standard requirement.

Critics say multilevel marketers flog a deck of dreams that is stacked against the people who buy it. But supporters see it as an entrepreneurial opportunity that is open to anyone and requires little start-up capital.

Federal regulations require multilevel marketers to disclose realistic earnings forecasts for distributors. For example, Interior Design Nutritional, a spinoff of Nu Skin International, reports that 70 percent of participants earn an annual average of $2000, and according to Amway Canada, the average monthly compensation is $61.[11] This is not much. New candidates are recruited on the basis of the opportunity of earning much more.

## THE ETHICAL MARKETER

### AMWAY'S NEW METHOD OF RECRUITING REPRESENTATIVES

Mr. Davies shakes hands as he strides to the front of a curious crowd that has gathered at the Embassy Suites hotel into a well-practised presentation meant to motivate and excite his audience about an amazing business opportunity. The hook comes about a third of the way through his routine. "Internet. E-commerce. Cybermall." He punches out the words, as if each one held the key to a better life. "We know that E-commerce is the way to go," he continues, holding up a copy of *Fortune* magazine emblazoned with the latest trendy E-term. "All you have to do is plug people into the Internet and you'll get paid for it.... Even Martha Stewart is going on-line."

Eventually, the important details begin to surface. After more than an hour of patient listening, the young, fidgety audience of about 150 discovers that Mr. Davies is a senior distributor and recruiter for multilevel marketing company Amway Corp. Clearly disappointed, most of the room clears during a ten-minute break. "Sounds like a pyramid scheme to me," says one twenty-something who decides he's wasted his time. Still, the buzzwords lured him to the meeting, and showing up is the first step to becoming a new recruit in the multilevel marketing operation.

Amway is seeking a new way of recruiting representatives. Ken Wong, associate professor of marketing and business strategy at Queen's University in Kingston, Ontario, says "The fact that you have the Internet out there, there's always going to be people trying to take advantage of it. People are lured by the seeming magic and ease of making money through E-commerce [and] a chance to be on the leading edge of technology."

Multilevel marketing is often equated—mistakenly—with illegal pyramid schemes, in which participants make money solely by signing up new members. Multilevel marketers survive by recruiting a large stable of independent sales representatives who, like most salespeople, earn a commission for the products they sell. Unlike most salespeople, however, these reps also make money from new members. They get a percentage of the revenue that their own recruits generate—and so on, in a top-down structure that resembles a pyramid. Start early enough in the process and have the persistence to stay in the game, and the rewards grow exponentially. Amway is hoping the lure of the Internet will get more people into the game.

Companies such as Amway are not doing anything wrong, says Mr. Wong. Nonetheless, he calls such operations "deceptive" because they feed off the innocent and the naive. "The challenge you face if you're an Amway or someone else is that at some point, you run out of recruits ... you start to exhaust the market," says Mr. Wong, explaining that pyramid-like schemes by nature begin to collapse once a market is saturated.

**What do you think of this method of direct marketing and recruiting?**

www.amway.com

Source: Adapted from Tyler Hamilton, "Sold on the Web," *The Globe and Mail* (March 11, 1999), pp. T1 and T3. Reprinted with permission from *The Globe and Mail*.

About 750 000 Canadians are involved full- or part-time in one or more of the 300 to 400 multilevel marketing companies starting up, progressing, or fizzling out in this country at any given time, according to federal government figures. Although 70 percent of these companies collapse before they are eight months old, it is a multibillion-dollar industry that spans the continent and is rapidly going global. The Better Business Bureau receives between 5000 and 7000 industry-related complaints every year. Most are from people who have stockpiled product they purchased in an effort to keep their sales quotas up, and then could not unload. Others paid substantial fees to become distributors only to find the job was not the paved road to prosperity they were led to expect.

### Mail-Order Retailing

**mail-order merchandiser**
Retailer that offers its customers the option of placing merchandise orders by mail, by telephone, or by visiting the mail-order desk of a retail store.

The customers of **mail-order merchandisers** can place merchandise orders by mail, by telephone, or by visiting the mail-order desk of a retail store. Goods are then shipped to the customer's home or to the local retail store.

Many department stores and specialty stores issue catalogues to seek telephone and mail-order sales and to promote in-store purchases of items featured in the catalogues. Among typical department stores, telephone and mail-generated orders account for 15 percent of total volume during the Christmas season.

Mail-order selling began in Canada in 1894 when Eaton's distributed a slim 32-page booklet to rural visitors at the Canadian National Exhibition in Toronto. That first catalogue contained only a few items, mostly clothing and farm supplies. Simpsons soon followed, and mail-order retailing became an important source of products in isolated Canadian settlements.

Even though mail-order sales represent only a small percentage of all retail sales, this type of retailing is an important channel for many consumers who want convenience and a large selection of colours and sizes.

www.sears.ca

Sears is the one major mail-order catalogue marketer left in Canada. Sales have been strong. Sears now has over 2100 catalogue sales offices across Canada and produces 22 catalogues a year, with a combined distribution of 45 million.

Mail-order houses offer a wide range of products—from novelty items (Regal Gifts) to sporting equipment (S.I.R. and L.L. Bean). The growing number of women who work outside the home, increasing time pressures, and a decline in customer service in some department stores seem to be good signs for the success of catalogue sales.

### Automatic Merchandising

*Automatic vending machines*—the true robot stores—are a good way to purchase a wide range of convenience goods. These machines accounted for over $424.5 million in sales in Canada.[12] Approximately 213 000 vending machines are currently in operation throughout the country.

While automatic merchandising is important in the retailing of some products, it represents less than 1 percent of all retail sales. Its future growth is limited by such factors as the cost of machines and the necessity for regular maintenance and repair. However, with the possibility of credit card readers in these machines, a wide variety of additional, more expensive products can be sold.

Automatically vended products are confined to convenience goods that are standardized in size and weight, with a high rate of turnover. Prices for some products purchased in vending machines are higher than store prices for the same products.

## Retailing Through the Internet: E-commerce and E-tailing

As a result of the Internet we are in the midst of a sea-change from gravitational commerce, demarcated by its time and location constraints upon customers, to a business environment that will also make significant use of digital commerce. Digital commerce is almost entirely free of time and location constraints.[13] As a result, we will increasingly see procurement and consumption happening anytime, anywhere. Figure 16.4 illustrates this important shift.

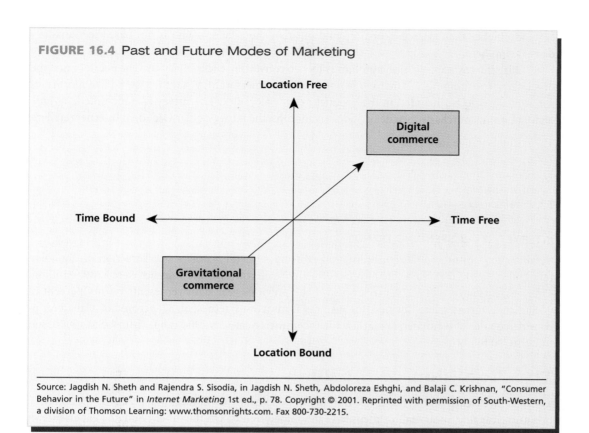

**FIGURE 16.4** Past and Future Modes of Marketing

Location Free

Digital commerce

Time Bound ← → Time Free

Gravitational commerce

Location Bound

Source: Jagdish N. Sheth and Rajendra S. Sisodia, in Jagdish N. Sheth, Abdoloreza Eshghi, and Balaji C. Krishnan, "Consumer Behavior in the Future" in *Internet Marketing* 1st ed., p. 78. Copyright © 2001. Reprinted with permission of South-Western, a division of Thomson Learning: www.thomsonrights.com. Fax 800-730-2215.

## E-tailing in Canada: The Current Situation

A study from Royal Bank of Canada carried out by Ipsos-Reid, a large marketing research organization, showed that Canadian families are making major lifestyle changes in response to the wave of new communications technologies entering their homes. The daily lives of Canadian families are more and more influenced by communications technologies. A computer with Internet access is fast becoming an appliance on which the household depends, rather than the 'nice to have' console it used to be.

- The personal computer is now considered the communications nerve centre in the home.
- Two-in-three Canadian households (67 percent) have a personal computer and almost half (47 percent) of Canadian Internet-using families have more than one computer. Twenty percent of all families with home Internet access have computers that have been networked.
- Taking all household members into account, the average family is spending slightly more than 32 hours online per week. This translates into over 1600 hours per family in one year. [14]

Another study shows that fully half of Canadian Internet users have bought goods or services from a retail Web site in the past six months.[15] "While Canadians' online spending is rising, so too is their use of the Internet to read up on products before buying them in a store. About 15% of online Canadians claim they use the Internet to research more than half of all their offline purchases," said David Stark, public affairs director of NFO CFgroup. The survey found that the biggest selling point for online shopping is its 24/7 convenience, while the biggest concern of online Canadians is the fear of credit card fraud.

Aside from security concerns, the survey uncovered other factors that affect online sales. Three in ten online Canadians say that, within the past six months, they did not complete a purchase after initially clicking on an item that they fully intended to buy. While the reasons for shopping cart abandonment online are varied, shipping is often the culprit. Either shoppers discover that the shipping costs are higher than expected, or they find out that the e-tailer—who is not based in Canada—doesn't ship here.

"Shipping costs are a major stumbling block to converting clicks into sales. The per item method of charging for shipping and delivery is not what consumers want. What they would like most is for shipping costs to be included in the product price," said Stark. The survey also identified, by incidence of online purchasing in the previous six months, the most popular Canadian Internet retailers:

1. chapters.indigo.ca—25%
2. sears.ca—23%
3. Columbiahouse.ca—17%
4. ticketmaster.ca—17%
5. futureshop.ca—12%

### INTERNET RETAIL SPENDING TRENDS

Retailing on the Internet is significant, and growing, but still is only a small fraction of Canadian retail sales. As of 2000, the value of retail Canadian sales through the Internet were $889.9 million. This was an increase of $279.3 million over the previous year. This represents twenty percent of Canadian Internet sales. Business-to-business transactions represent 80 percent of Canadian e-commerce sales.[16] Estimates of world wide e-commerce sales in 2004 range from US$1400 billion to US$6790 billion.[17]

## The Realities of E-tailing

The evidence clearly shows that a vast number of people have computers and are using the Internet. It is also clear that about half of them have purchased online. On the other hand, the experience of the business community is that **e-tailing** has been a disappointment to many. There have been many dot.com seller failures and many bricks-and-mortar retailers who rushed into e-tailing and have had to scale back their activities because of limited results.

There are still rich possibilities for e-tailing. The Internet has become not only an information source and a means of communication, but also an important business tool. Wise use of the Internet in retailing is one area that can be greatly facilitated through careful planning. For example, Bolen's Books in Victoria set up a home page for the purpose of retailing its line of books. Within a year of starting to retail on the Internet, the company had covered the costs of setting up and running the system. It now receives orders from around the world. Blaney's Travel agency publishes special travel deals on the Internet in order to generate new clients. It offers its travel services to anyone logging onto its home page. These are but two examples of the thousands of firms retailing through the Internet.

The applications seem to be limited only by the creativity of the company. However, in spite of the possibilities and promise of e-tailing the retailing world has come to realize that success might not be as simple as first thought. A closer look at the issue is warranted. What are the conditions that promote and inhibit retailing through the Internet?

In order for an Internet operation to displace a traditional retail channel it must become a credible substitute for the functions of a traditional channel intermediary. Furthermore, it must be able to dominate the current performance of a traditional channel intermediary. Unfortunately, to this date, most existing Internet operations have failed to provide sufficient benefits to make this come about. To be successful, the online shopping experience must be at least as positive as shopping in a conventional store. In the conventional store consumers experience personal service, entertainment, social interaction, "hands-on" experience with the product, and a nice outing. Another factor affecting Internet retailing is ease of use. Because of forgotten passwords, bad connections, misunderstood user interfaces, and other glitches many customers do not find online shopping to be very easy.

Another significant challenge is the method and cost of delivery of products. For example, consider the experience of Shopping Alternatives, a company providing home shopping services to supermarket chains. It charged a $9 delivery fee to the customer and an $8 fee to the supermarket to

**e-tailing**
Retailing via the Internet.

provide the service. It cost the retailer approximately $5 to collect, can, bag and store the selected items. Therefore it cost the retailer $13 to serve the home shopper.[18] Or, if the cost of delivery is passed on to the consumer, such a cost can be a detriment to the purchase. Another disadvantage from the retailer's point of view is that all prices become very public, and competition tends to push prices to the lowest common denominator.

Where will be the greatest possibilities of success in virtual retailing? It will be where firms can leverage the unique aspects of electronic commerce to benefit consumers. Peterson et al.[19] suggest that consumers are more likely to search for product information, make a brand selection, and acquire the product or service on the Internet when the value proposition is intangible or informational. In the case of tangible products, purchasing on the Internet will be more likely when such products can be easily evaluated using online information. Dell Computer and Gateway 2000 are examples.

### BENEFITS OF INTERNET RETAILING

Internet retailing provides a considerable number of benefits to both consumers and retailers. Consumers enjoy the benefit of convenience—they can shop 24 hours a day from their own homes. Price competition is another benefit for consumers. Studies have shown that products in certain retail categories, especially mid- to high-priced commodity-oriented items, sell for lower prices online than in traditional stores.[20] Comparison shopping is easy and fast. This could bring about a shift in power from retailer to consumer because the consumer will have more information about prices and products.

Selection is another advantage. Consumers can find a much broader and deeper selection of items on the Internet. The vast selection on booksellers' Web sites is a good example. Customization can also be obtained in some Internet purchasing. For example, Dell Computers' Internet site allows customers to custom design the exact computer system that matches their needs and budget.

www.dell.com

We invite you to become clients of the oldest, established travel agency in Victoria.

**BLANEY'S TRAVEL**

Providing top

quality service to

business and

vacation travellers

since 1945

920 Douglas Street
Victoria, BC  V8W 2C1
Tel: (250) 382-7254
blaneys@blaneystravel.com
**www.blaneystravel.com**

**Blaney's has developed a list of customers who pay close attention to their regular e-mail special offers.**

Information is perhaps the most important benefit to consumers. The Internet provides businesses with a low-cost means of disseminating all types of business information. However, when customers log on to a site, they have very high expectations. Thus great care must be taken by the firm to build a proper site. For example a well-known sports equipment company may produce a great number of camping products; however, if the information provided on its Web site is very limited, the potential buyer will not be able to make an informed choice.

The Internet serves as a communication tool between consumers and retailers. A continuing dialogue can be maintained before and after a product purchase, which can help to create a very high level of customer satisfaction. Similarly, a retailer can undertake online surveys and feedback forums that facilitate developing databases on customers' ideas, attitudes, and product preferences.

Retailers can likewise benefit by optimizing their inventory management practices through connections with suppliers and agreements to keep retailers supplied with a steady flow of merchandise rather than a few large lots. In the case of online retailing, the Internet can provide a very efficient and profitable means of processing orders. Potential cost savings can be achieved through lower inventory, transaction costs, easier customer service, and lower administration and communication costs.

## SUCCESSFUL RETAIL CATEGORIES SOLD ON THE INTERNET

Products that are best suited for selling on the Internet have the following characteristics:

- They are sold in fragmented markets and involve substantial comparison shopping.
- They have relatively low shipping costs.
- They do not require a physical inspection before a purchase is made.

Figure 16.5 shows the relative potential of various products to be sold on the Internet.

## THE IMPORTANCE OF BRANDING

Strong brand-name recognition may be even more important in Internet retailing than traditional retailing. Customers are more comfortable ordering products with familiar names and characteristics. This applies to store branding as well as to product branding.

## DEMOGRAPHIC CHARACTERISTICS OF INTERNET USERS

Internet users are, in general, above-average spenders. They also tend to be highly educated people, 18–44 years of age, high-income earners, and white-collar workers. The 12 to 24-year-old segment

**FIGURE 16.5** Potential of Products to Be Sold on the Internet

| Relative Potential | Retail Categories |
|---|---|
| High | Insurance/financial services<br>Computer hardware/software<br>Travel services<br>Books, magazines, music/videos<br>Flowers, gifts, greeting cards<br>Office supplies |
| Moderate | Cars<br>Sporting goods<br>Consumer electronics/appliances<br>Food and beverages<br>Collectibles<br>Apparel, shoes, accessories<br>Health and beauty products |
| Low | Toys and games<br>Tools/home improvement products<br>Home furnishings |

is also a very attractive target market given its large size, technological sophistication, and willingness to make Internet purchases. Male Internet users have traditionally outnumbered female users. However, this is changing.

## THE FUTURE OF INTERNET RETAILING

Computers are found in virtually every business and in a large number of homes. The number of home computers is growing rapidly, and it is expected that within a short time most homes will have one. Bill Gates, CEO of Microsoft, and others in the industry have predicted that as these homes get hooked up to digital information links, it will be only a matter of time before the computer, telephone, television, and online information services converge into a single system for handling all home entertainment, education, information, and communication needs.

If you want to watch a movie, play a computer game, buy the latest music recording by your favourite artist, or acquire some new software, you will just dial in to the information highway over the phone line or cable and download whatever product or service you want, charging the cost to a debit or credit card.

The ultimate mix of computer technology, consumerism, and television, however, would come with use of the shopping channel, where consumers could design "virtual shopping malls" in which they were the only customers. These would work by having the consumer designate which shops he or she would like to frequent (from either an on-screen or published catalogue). The system would then respond by displaying a video game–style representation of a mall with shop fronts. The consumer would then use the handheld controller to "walk through" the custom-designed on-screen malls, stopping at the shops whose goods he or she might be interested in buying.

The on-screen shop fronts, when entered, would be replaced with an on-screen catalogue of the goods available in that shop. By pointing at the picture of any item, consumers will be able to get detailed information on it, including price, warranty details, and estimated delivery times.

Will such a system really exist someday? A skeptic would say that predictions of computer retailing have been made for over 30 years. The theme is the same—only the format of the implementation varies. On the other hand, we are much closer to the interactive link described above. It is happening, so a more relevant question is how many people will use such a system?

The Canadian Government "Strategis" site has a range of useful documents about e-commerce. Examples include (1) "ebiz.enable," an e-business portal designed specifically to guide commercial organizations through the issues and options encountered in implementing e-business strategies; (2) Electronic Commerce in Canada, which provides access to numerous resources on the electronic commerce industry in Canada; (3) e-Team Canada: The Canadian E-Business Opportunities Roundtable is a private-sector led initiative for accelerating Canada's participation in the Internet economy; (4) Net Gain: Doing Business on the Internet; and (5) Retailing on the Internet: A Guide, which provides you with a framework for understanding and exploring the Internet's potential as a retail channel. These may be found at http://strategis.ic.gc.ca.

w w w
www.strategis.ic.gc.ca

# SHOPPING CENTRES

A **planned shopping centre** is a group of retail stores planned, coordinated, and marketed as a unit to shoppers in a particular geographic trade area. These centres followed population shifts to the suburbs and focused on correcting many of the problems involved in shopping in the downtown business districts. Ample parking and locations away from downtown traffic congestion appeal to the suburban shopper. Additional hours for shopping during the evenings and on weekends facilitate family shopping.

planned shopping centre
Group of retail stores planned, coordinated, and marketed as a unit to shoppers in a particular geographic trade area.

## Types of Shopping Centres

There are three types of planned shopping centres. The smallest and most common is the *neighbourhood shopping centre,* which most often comprises a supermarket and a group of smaller stores, such as a drugstore, a laundry and dry cleaner, a small appliance store, and perhaps a beauty shop and barbershop. Such centres provide convenient shopping for perhaps 5000 to 15 000 shoppers who live within a few minutes' commuting time of the centre. These centres typically contain five to fifteen stores whose product mix is usually confined to convenience goods and some shopping goods.

*Community shopping centres* typically serve 20 000 to 100 000 people in a trade area extending a few kilometres in each direction. These centres are likely to contain 15 to 50 retail stores, with a branch of a local department store or a large variety store as the primary tenant. In addition to the stores found in a neighbourhood centre, the community centre is likely to have additional stores featuring shopping goods, some professional offices, and a bank branch.

The largest planned centre is the *regional shopping centre,* a giant shopping district of at least 30 000 m² of shopping space, usually built around one or more major department stores and containing as many as 300 smaller stores. To be successful, regional centres must be located in areas where at least 150 000 people live within a 30-minute drive of the centre. Characteristically, they are temperature-controlled, enclosed facilities. The regional centres provide the widest product mixes and the greatest depth of each line.

www.westedmonton mall.com

Such a centre is West Edmonton Mall, located in west Edmonton. Said to be the largest shopping centre in the world, West Edmonton Mall is located in a densely populated area and is easily accessible to both cars and pedestrians. Catering to a range of suburban clientele, the stores at this mall offer a variety of quality merchandise to their customers. Because of its unique features, such as an amusement park, wave pool, skating rink, and hotel, this mall also counts on tourist traffic.

Planned shopping centres account for approximately 40 percent of all retail sales in Canada. Their growth has slowed in recent years, however, as the most lucrative locations are occupied and the market for such centres appears to have been saturated in many regions. Recent trends have moved toward building smaller centres in smaller cities and towns.

# SCRAMBLED MERCHANDISING

**scrambled merchandising**

The retail practice of carrying dissimilar lines to generate added sales volume.

You will not be surprised that a characteristic of retailing is the steady deterioration of clear-cut delineations of retailer types. Anyone who has attempted to fill a prescription recently has been exposed to the concept of **scrambled merchandising**—the retail practice of carrying dissimilar lines to generate added sales volume. The large mass-merchandising drugstore carries not only prescription and proprietary drugs, but also gifts, hardware, housewares, videos, magazines, grocery products, garden supplies, even small appliances. Gasoline retailers sell bread and milk; supermarkets carry antifreeze, televisions, cameras, and stereo equipment.

Scrambled merchandising was born out of retailers' willingness to add dissimilar merchandise lines in order to offer additional high-profit lines, as well as to satisfy consumer demands for one-stop shopping. It complicates manufacturers' channel decisions, because attempts to maintain or increase a firm's market share mean, in most instances, that the firm will have to develop multiple channels to reach the diverse retailers handling its products. On the other hand, customers benefit from increased availability, and retailers benefit from additional sales.

This chapter has described some aspects of the many faces of retailing. As this is the end of the marketing channel that handles millions of products and services, a vast array of retailers can be categorized in several different ways. A basic characteristic of retailing is change. New retail forms are continually emerging. Existing retailers gradually adjust to meet the new competition. If they cannot adjust, they disappear.

World-famous West Edmonton Mall is a complete shopping and entertainment experience.

## SUMMARY

Retailing is big business and a vital part of the national economy. It is comprised of many different types of operations, ranging from fast-food restaurants to convenience stores to department stores to some services to Internet retailers.

The wheel-of-retailing hypothesis postulates that new types of retailers gain a competitive advantage by offering lower prices to their customers through reducing services. Gradually they add services and increase prices, opening the door to new low-cost retailers entering the market.

The retailer's decision process centres on developing a retail marketing strategy that includes the following steps: (1) identify market segments and select a target market; (2) analyze competitors' strengths and weaknesses; and (3) develop a competitive retail marketing mix that fits the target market.

The elements of a retail marketing mix are: (a) goods and service strategy; (b) location and distribution strategy; (c) pricing strategy; and (d) retail image and promotional strategy.

Differentiation is a key factor in competitive strategy. The differentiation triangle has the following elements: price, location, and store atmosphere and service.

The law of retail gravitation (Reilly's law) delineates the retail trade area of a potential site on the basis of distance between alternative locations and relative populations.

Retailers can be classified in six different ways: (1) shopping effort expended by customers, (2) services provided to customers, (3) product lines, (4) location of retail transactions, (5) form of ownership, and (6) margin and turnover.

As a result of the Internet we are in the midst of a change from gravitational commerce, demarcated by its time and location constraints upon customers, to a business environment that will also make significant use of digital commerce. However, in order for an Internet operation to displace a traditional retail channel it must become a credible substitute for the functions of a traditional channel intermediary.

## KEY TERMS

catalogue retailer, p. 416

chain store, p. 402

department store, p. 411

differentiation triangle, p. 406

discount house, p. 414

e-tailing, p. 420

house-to-house retailer, p. 416

hypermarket, p. 415

large-format specialty store, p. 414

law of retail gravitation, p. 405

limited-line store, p. 411

liquidator, p. 416

mail-order merchandiser, p. 418

mass merchandiser, p. 414

membership and warehouse club, p. 414

multilevel marketing, p. 416

off-price retailer, p. 415

planned shopping centre, p. 423

power node, p. 415

recycled merchandise retailer, p. 415

retail image, p. 406

retail trade area analysis, p. 405

retailing, p. 400

scrambled merchandising, p. 424

specialty store, p. 411

supermarket, p. 411

variety store, p. 414

wheel of retailing, p. 401

## INTERACTIVE SUMMARY AND DISCUSSION QUESTIONS

1. The retailer's decision process centres on analyzing and selecting a target market and developing a marketing (or retailing) mix designed to satisfy that market. Compare and contrast the marketing mix with the retailing mix.
2. The law of retail gravitation (Reilly's law) delineates the retail trade area of a potential site on the basis of distance between alternative locations and relative populations. Assume that a large-format specialty retailer is considering opening an outlet in Town A, population 144 000. The retailing firm wants to know how far its trade area would extend toward Town B (population 16 000), 72 km away. Apply the law of retail gravitation to the retailer's problem. What other factors should be taken into consideration in this location decision?
3. The differentiation triangle has the following elements: price, location, and store atmosphere and service. Explain the importance of this triangle in considering a retailer's competitive options.
4. There are three types of retailers if classified by shopping effort: convenience–preference stores, shopping stores, and specialty retailers. In which of these types would the following products likely fit?
   a. Kodak film
   b. *Foundations of Marketing* textbook
   c. computer paper
   d. fax machine
   e. leather slippers
   f. Cartier watch
   g. picture framing
5. Some examples of general-merchandise retailers include department stores, variety stores, mass merchandisers, and discount houses. If you were marketing a new line of perfume, which of these outlets would you choose to use first? Why?
6. Large-format specialty stores can be of similar size to warehouse clubs. They are known as category killers. Explain why.
7. There are relatively few large warehouse and membership clubs in each community, yet the significance of this type of retail operation to retail competition in general is great. How can this be?

8. Multilevel marketing has several distributor levels, makes use of a personal influence network, and promises great rewards to those who work hard. What is your evaluation of these promised rewards?

9. Chain stores are groups of retail stores that are centrally owned and managed and that handle the same lines of products. Illustrate how the chain store concept results in powerful competition.

10. The wheel-of-retailing hypothesis postulates that new types of retailers gain a competitive advantage by offering lower prices to their customers through reducing services. Gradually they add services and increase prices, opening the door to new low-cost retailers entering the market. List several examples of the wheel of retailing in operation. Can you list examples that do not conform to this hypothesis?

11. What is your assessment of the future of e-commerce or "e-tailing"?

12. Write a brief report comparing, contrasting, and evaluating five different retailing Web sites.

# Case

## The Lookers–Morrison Deal

In London, the supermarket chain, W.M. Morrison, has edged out its larger rivals at the wire by setting up a joint venture enabling shoppers to buy cars at their local store.

It will be the first time British customers have been able to shop for a car in this way. Other chains are thought to be waiting for the European Union to overturn rules that state cars can only be sold through approved dealerships.

Morrison announced a joint venture with Lookers, a motor dealership, allowing cars to be sold in its shops. The deal pre-empts moves in the EU to liberalize the motor market and remove a "block exemption" to competition rules that has given manufacturers and approved dealerships a stranglehold over the car market.

Supermarkets and virtual retailers are not able to offer cars because existing regulations require dealers to provide repair services. The deal between Morrison and Lookers could be the first step toward cheaper cars and parts. "We will be offering special deals on cars initially through Morrisons. It may lead to cheaper parts in time," said a spokesman for Lookers.

The block exemption has been constantly challenged on the basis that manufacturers have been using their networks to maintain high prices in certain parts of the EU. However, the European Commission challenged such thinking, warning that allowing supermarkets and Internet dealers to sell cars might in the long term reduce consumer choice and lead to price increases.

The Commission is understood to fear supermarkets could use their bulk buying power and high volume capacity to raise prices. Lookers has set up computer terminals in three Morrison outlets where customers can browse the Internet, arrange a test drive, and choose a car.

www.lookers.plc.uk

www.morrisons.plc.uk

### You Be the Marketer

1. Evaluate the belief statements of the EU about the effects of such an arrangement.
2. Does it make sense that this deal "may lead to cheaper parts in time."
3. What are the steps that Morrison would have to undertake in order for this venture to be a success?
4. Would you buy a car at such an outlet?

Source: Kate Burgess, "U.K. Grocer Adds Cars to Its Lineup," in *National Post*, May 7, 2002, p. FP16. Reprinted with permission of *The Financial Times*.

Seven-Eleven Japan is one of the most innovative companies
in the management of its supply chain.

## Chapter 17

# SUPPLY CHAIN AND LOGISTICS MANAGEMENT

## CHAPTER OBJECTIVES

After reading and studying this chapter, you should be able to

1. Relate supply chain management to the other variables of the marketing mix.
2. Explain the role of supply chain and logistics management in an effective marketing strategy.
3. Describe the objectives of logistics.
4. Identify and compare the major components of the logistics system.
5. Discuss some of the basic concepts involved in making transportation decisions.
6. Relate the major transportation alternatives to such factors as efficiency, speed, dependability, and cost.
7. Discuss the problem of suboptimization in logistics.

In the midst of the Asian economic crisis, one shining star has bewildered investors and has beaten all odds by posting record profits. Seven-Eleven Japan, a major retail chain in that country, has been so successful that its stock value appreciation in recent years has even surpassed that of Dell Computer, a darling of Wall Street.

Interestingly, Seven-Eleven Japan and Dell Computer represent two of the most innovative companies in the management of their supply chains. They both have created new ways to operate their supply chains, defined new rules of the game, and maintained supply chain excellence as part of their strategic competitive edge. They are among the leaders in successfully integrating their supply chains.

The results that supply chain leaders like Seven-Eleven Japan and Dell have achieved are clearly impressive. Cost reduction is one highly desirable result but not the only one. Supply chain integration also creates profits, increases market share, strengthens competitive position, and enhances the value of the company.

In today's environment, customers are less forgiving of poor customer service and more demanding of customized products or services. Information integration is the foundation of broader supply chain integration. For companies to coordinate their material, information, and financial flows, they must have access to information reflecting their true supply chain picture at all times. Without information integration, few gains can be made in overall supply chain integration.

Similarly, through extensive collaboration with its suppliers and its stores, Seven-Eleven Japan created new, highly customized products. The company also replenished stores rapidly to meet the personal needs of many customer segments in different locations and at different times of the day or week. Such a high degree of customization (almost like a one-to-one marketing effort) enhances customer relationships. In fact, it is a key factor behind the success of Seven-Eleven Japan.

For most companies, the biggest opportunities lie outside of the four walls of the manufacturing plant. Key questions are: Where do you source your materials? Where do you process or convert them? What channels of distribution do you use? How do you build a strong relationship with your suppliers and customers? How do you get direct information from your end-consumers? What logistics structure should you impose? How do you coordinate your information flows and systems globally? And how do you set up incentive systems for all of your partners in the supply chain to optimize overall performance?

The field of competition has now shifted to management of the global supply chain. A well-orchestrated, tightly integrated supply chain is crucial to the competitiveness of an enterprise.

**This story illustrates the type of planning that goes on daily in the movement of materials and goods from original source to manufacturer to distributor to customer. People are often amazed when they find out that a courier package sent from Fredericton via FedEx goes first to a massive distribution centre in the southern United States, where it is sorted along with thousands of other packages, and ends up in Edmonton, on schedule, the next morning. It happens because someone has carefully worked out the most efficient way.**

Source: Excerpted from Hau L. Lee, "Creating Value Through Supply Chain Integration," *Supply Chain Management Review*, Sept/Oct 2000, http://www.scmr.com. Reprinted with permission of Reed Business Information.

www.dell.com

www.sej.co.jp

# INTRODUCTION

It is essential to select the right channel of distribution. It is equally important to work out how to physically distribute products. An example of not-so-efficient distribution occurred when the U.S. armed forces were preparing for the Gulf War in Kuwait (Desert Storm) in 1990. It took over five months to build up the force, and the order-delivery time for spare supplies was 26 days. Half of the 40 000 containers of equipment shipped went unused because soldiers did not know what equipment was in what container. With a better distribution system in 1995, it took only a month to have the Bosnia force in place, and the order-delivery time was seven days.[1]

"Impressive," you say, "but what's that got to do with me?" Distribution affects you every time you go shopping. How many times have you gone to a store and found that the product you wanted was out of stock? For you it was an annoyance. For that retailer, and perhaps the producer, the accumulated out-of-stock situations represent a tremendous loss of business. This loss may be permanent because you and other consumers went somewhere else and never came back.

One of the reasons for the past success of The Gap is because it dramatically shortened the delivery time of its clothing. Products that are moving quickly can be replenished at the retail level before current supplies run out, so sales are not missed. Similarly, hot new items can be distributed from central supply depots to catch new fashion waves.

The Gap, as well as cotton producers, clothing manufacturers, and other middlemen are links in a chain that supplies the needs of final consumers. This is known as a **supply chain**. A supply chain is a network of facilities and distribution options that performs the functions of procurement of materials, transformation of these materials into intermediate and finished products, and the distribution of these finished products to customers.[2] (See Figure 17.1.)

Figure 17.1 shows an example of a supply chain. Materials flow downstream, from raw material sources through a manufacturing level transforming the raw materials to intermediate products (also referred to as components or parts). These are assembled on the next level to form products.

www.gap.ca

**supply chain**

A network of facilities and distribution options that performs the functions of procurement of materials, transformation of these materials into intermediate and finished products, and the distribution of these finished products to customers.

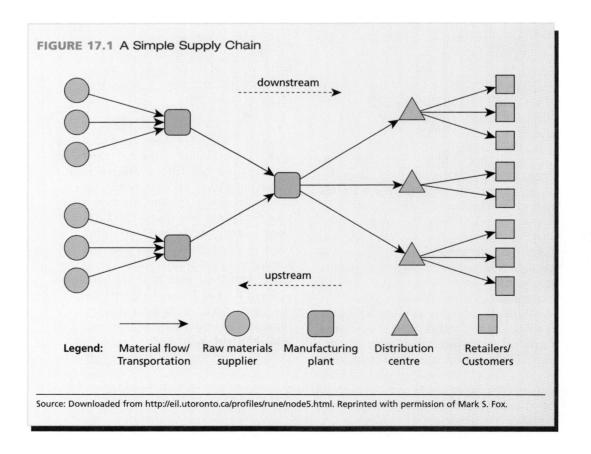

**FIGURE 17.1 A Simple Supply Chain**

Legend:
→ Material flow/Transportation
○ Raw materials supplier
▢ Manufacturing plant
△ Distribution centre
▫ Retailers/Customers

Source: Downloaded from http://eil.utoronto.ca/profiles/rune/node5.html. Reprinted with permission of Mark S. Fox.

The products are shipped to distribution centres and from there on to retailers and customers. These are part of the downstream flow. Information, market intelligence, and cash flow both downstream and upstream. Specifically, there are seven key elements that are involved in a supply chain:

- Supply
- Production
- Inventory
- Location
- Transportation
- Information, and
- Customer needs

An efficient supply chain can make a huge difference to the availability and cost of products. It is vital in the creation of a competitive advantage. This has led to efforts to integrate and manage the supply chain as effectively as possible. **Supply chain management** is the systematic, strategic coordination of the traditional business functions and the tactics across these business functions within a particular company and across businesses within the supply chain for the purposes of improving the long-term performance of the individual companies and the supply chain as a whole.[3]

Effective management coordinates all the different pieces of this chain to produce and supply as quickly as possible without losing any of the quality or customer satisfaction, while still keeping costs down.

The first step is either the decision to produce a line of products, or the obtaining of a customer order. This is followed by production, storage, and distribution of products and supplies to customers. Included in this supply chain process are customer orders, order processing, inventory, scheduling, transportation, storage, and customer service.

**supply chain management (SCM)**
The systematic, strategic coordination of the traditional business functions and the tactics across these business functions within a particular company and across businesses within the supply chain for the purposes of improving the long-term performance of the individual companies and the supply chain as a whole.

Companies can rely on Demand Solutions Canada for supply chain management.

A key to the success of a supply chain is the speed at which these activities can be accomplished. Reduced inventories, lower operating costs, product availability, and customer satisfaction are all benefits that grow out of effective supply chain management.

Managing the supply chain requires an understanding of demand patterns, service level requirements, distance considerations, cost elements, and other related factors. These factors are highly variable in nature and this variability needs to be considered during the supply chain analysis process. The interplay of these complex considerations has a significant bearing on the outcome of the supply chain management efforts and the competitive effectiveness of a firm.

Since the goal of supply chain management is to build flexible and efficient supply chains, manufacturers need to forge close, long-term ties with their suppliers. They must work hand in hand to refine products and components, respond to shifts in demand, unclog bottlenecks, and share sensitive information. Research into supply chain management by Chrysler and Ford[4] suggests that the most effective alliances with external suppliers are built on four pillars:

www.chrysler.com

www.ford.com

- *Power balancing.* Instead of using their buying leverage to extract crippling concessions from small suppliers, purchasing managers balance their contracts so that neither manufacturer nor supplier is highly dependent on the other.
- *Co-specialization.* As they try to balance power, purchasing managers also try to achieve a degree of mutual dependence in their alliances. A supplier might have a factory make parts that work exclusively in one car model, or the carmaker might adapt one of its assembly lines to fit a particular supplier's needs. Often, a manufacturer will decide on "preferred suppliers" for a particular component, which encourages them to move beyond manufacturing and contribute to the design and engineering of components.
- *Target costing.* The cooperative approach extends to pricing as well. Instead of the adversarial system of competitive bidding for contracts, the purchasing managers set target costs based on the manufacturer's goal for the final selling price of the car. Open communication encourages suppliers to engage in joint problem solving, leading to more efficient design and production.
- *Personal ties.* Personal ties among managers are often what keeps alliances productive. One way these can be created is through establishing joint teams to solve problems. This not only improves the flow of information but also encourages each side to feel comfortable with the other. Alliances built along these lines enable manufacturers and suppliers to cooperate closely and share information openly.

From this example of supply chain management in the automotive industry, we can see how the possibilities of developing strong supply chain relationships in other spheres of business are inviting.

## Logistics: The Critical Element in Supply Chain Management

**logistics**

That part of the supply chain process that plans, implements, and controls the efficient, effective forward and reverse flow and storage of goods, services, and related information between the point of origin and the point of consumption in order to meet customers' requirements.

Every item consumed in daily living is affected by logistics. **Logistics** is that part of the supply chain process that plans, implements, and controls the efficient, effective forward and reverse flow and storage of goods, services, and related information between the point of origin and the point of consumption in order to meet customers' requirements.[5]

## Distinguishing Between Logistics and Supply Chain Management

Logistics is the critical element in supply chain management. There is considerable confusion over the difference between these two terms. Supply chain management is focused on the *integration of all business processes* that add value for customers. Logistics on the other hand, is focused on *moving and storing activities* as products and information wind their way through the supply chain to customers. Thus, supply chain management is a broader, integrative discipline that includes the coordination of several business processes in addition to logistics.[6]

## Thanks to logistics, lobsters can fly.

To places like Paris, Munich and Tokyo. And hundreds of cities in between. But rather than wings, they're powered by the magic of logistics. A science so capable, it can send 5.5 million live lobsters airborne every year.

Just ask the world's largest exporter of live lobster, Clearwater Fine Foods in Bedford, Nova Scotia. "Lobsters are like eggs—an accident waiting to happen," sighs Clearwater distribution director Ron Carter, a Professional Logistician (P.Log.). Preventing mishaps is why Clearwater's lobsters spend several days in an Olympic-sized pool to relax after they're caught, and before being stored for up to a year in vast arrays of capsule hotel rooms called "dry land pounds" flushed with sea water straight from the Atlantic.

When they're ready to be air freighted, the lobsters are packed in 30-pound styrofoam trays and wrapped in sea-soaked newspaper, a process which provides them with enough oxygen to survive the journey—usually to a linen-clad table in an elegant setting.

Having a ready supply of premium, hard-shell lobster in and out of season calls for the kinds of organizational skills only professional logisticians can provide. Which is why Clearwater relies so heavily on people like Ron Carter.

Professional logistics is helping a growing number of Canadian companies, some of which (Canadian Tire, IBM, Nabisco and Xerox Canada, to name a few) have enrolled as corporate members of the Canadian Professional Logistics Institute, the national governing body dedicated to teaching, developing and promoting logistics.

To find out how your business can also benefit from corporate membership in the Logistics Institute, perhaps you should call us today. We could be just the lift you need.

CANADIAN PROFESSIONAL LOGISTICS INSTITUTE
10 King Street East, 4th Floor, Toronto, Ontario M5C 1C3
Tel: (416) 363-3005   Fax: (416) 363-5598
e-mail: loginfo@istar.ca   website: www.loginstitute.ca

**Logistics. The driving force of human achievement.**

**Efficient logistics make possible sales of perishable goods far from the source of supply.**

As our previous examples illustrated, logistics is a process that can be honed to a high level of efficiency. Logistics has stolen the limelight in business, according to a Logistics in Canada survey conducted by KPMG and *Materials Management* magazine.[7] Companies have proven not only that capabilities in logistics can increase their competitiveness, but that savings in costs go right to the bottom line of the company.

www.kpmg.ca

# LOGISTICS

The study of logistics is one of the classic examples of the systems approach to business problems. The basic notion of a logistics system is that it is a set of interrelated parts. The word "system" is derived from the Latin word *systema,* which means an organized relationship among components. In a system, each component must function properly if the system is to be effective and the organizational objectives are to be achieved. A system thus may be defined as an organized group of parts or components linked together according to a plan to achieve specific objectives. The logistics system contains the following elements:

- *Customer service.* What level of customer service should be provided?
- *Transportation.* How will the products be shipped?
- *Materials handling and protective packaging.* How do we develop efficient methods of handling products in the factory, warehouse, and transport terminals?
- *Order processing.* How should orders be handled?
- *Inventory control.* How much inventory should be maintained at each location?
- *Warehousing.* Where will the products be located? How many warehouses should be used?

A simple but powerful concept is that these components are interrelated, and *decisions made in one area affect the relative efficiency of other areas.* For example, you might be able to reduce transportation costs by using low-cost, relatively slow water transportation, but this will probably reduce customer service and may increase inventory costs, since the firm may be required to maintain larger inventory levels to compensate for longer delivery times. The logistics manager must balance each component so that no single aspect is stressed to the detriment of the overall distribution system.

## The Objective of Logistics

In logistics management, the customer is king. The first question is what level of service is necessary to get and keep the customer's business. The objective of a firm's logistics system is to produce a specified level of customer service while minimizing the costs involved in physically moving and storing the product from its production point to the point where it is ultimately purchased. For example, Dell must determine how long a customer is willing to wait for delivery after placing an order for a new computer. Next day delivery by air might be nice but would require extra inventory and higher delivery costs. If most customers do not require this level of service it would be foolish to provide it.

To achieve this, the logistics manager makes use of three basic concepts that are vital to effective logistics management: (1) the total-cost approach, (2) the avoidance of suboptimization, and (3) the use of cost tradeoffs.

### Total-Cost Approach

**total-cost approach**
Holds that all relevant factors in physically moving and storing products should be considered as a whole and not individually.

The **total-cost approach** holds that all relevant factors in physically moving and storing products should be considered as a whole and not individually. Thus, each element of the logistics system listed above should be included. All of these cost items must be considered as a whole when attempting to meet customer service levels at minimum cost. Management might therefore choose a faster but more expensive transportation mode if the cost of warehousing and materials handling could be reduced beyond the higher cost of transportation.

### The Problem of Suboptimization

**suboptimization**
A condition in which the manager of each logistics function attempts to minimize costs, but due to the impact of one logistics task on the others, the results are less than optimal.

Although the total-cost approach requires that all logistics elements must be considered as a whole rather than individually, sometimes this does not happen. **Suboptimization** is a condition in which the manager of each logistics function attempts to minimize costs, but due to the impact of one logistics task on the others, the results are less than optimal. Consider a football team that is made up of several talented individuals who seldom win games. Team members hold league records in a variety of skills: pass completions, average distance gained per rush, blocked kicks, and average gains on punt returns. Unfortunately, however, the overall ability of the team to accomplish the organizational goal—scoring more points than its opponents—is rarely achieved.

Why does suboptimization occur frequently in logistics? The answer lies in the fact that each separate logistics activity is often judged by its ability to achieve certain management objectives, some of which are at cross-purposes with other objectives. Sometimes departments in other functional areas take actions that cause the logistics area to operate at less than full efficiency. Psychological factors often come into play here. For example, a product manager might think, "Cartons are bought out of my department's budget, so we'll buy only standard, nonreinforced ones. We don't care if the warehouse staff complain—breakages are their problem, not ours. We'll look good because this department kept costs down." Counteracting this type of attitude is the responsibility of top management, who must convince junior management that they are serious about *total* cost—which means not complaining about the cost of cartons to one department head and complaining about breakages to the other.

Effective management of the logistics function may result in some costs increasing in order to reduce total costs. This means some cost tradeoffs may be required. Of course, reducing any logistics cost assumes that the level of customer service will not be sacrificed.

## Cost Tradeoffs

The third fundamental concept of logistics is the use of **cost tradeoffs**. This approach assumes that some functional areas of the firm will experience cost increases while others will have cost decreases. The result will be that total logistics costs will be minimized, while at no time is the established level of customer service sacrificed. By thinking in terms of a total system and the cost tradeoffs shown in Figure 17.2, management should minimize the total of these costs rather than attempt to minimize the cost of each component.

For example, the Gillette Company, the world's largest producer of safety razors, was faced with an ever-expanding assortment of products due to its expansion into a broad range of toiletry products. To produce good customer service, Gillette shipped by air freight, but this proved to be very expensive. Through a detailed study of its distribution system, Gillette discovered that its problem was inefficient order processing. By simplifying the paperwork involved, the company was able to reduce the time required to process new orders. Gillette was then able to return to lower-cost surface transportation and still meet previous delivery schedules. The cost tradeoff here was that the order-processing costs increased and transportation costs decreased, and the net result was that total logistics costs decreased.

The integration of these three basic concepts—the total-cost approach, the avoidance of suboptimization, and the use of cost tradeoffs—forms what can be referred to as the **logistics concept**. It should be noted that the real uniqueness of the logistics concept is not in the individual functions, since each function is performed anyway. Rather, this uniqueness stems from the integration of all of these functions into a unified whole, the objective of which is providing an established level of customer service at the lowest possible distribution costs.

**cost tradeoffs**

Approach that assumes that some functional areas of the firm will experience cost increases while others will have cost decreases.

www.gillette.com

**logistics concept**

The integration of the total-cost approach, the avoidance of suboptimization, and the use of cost tradeoffs.

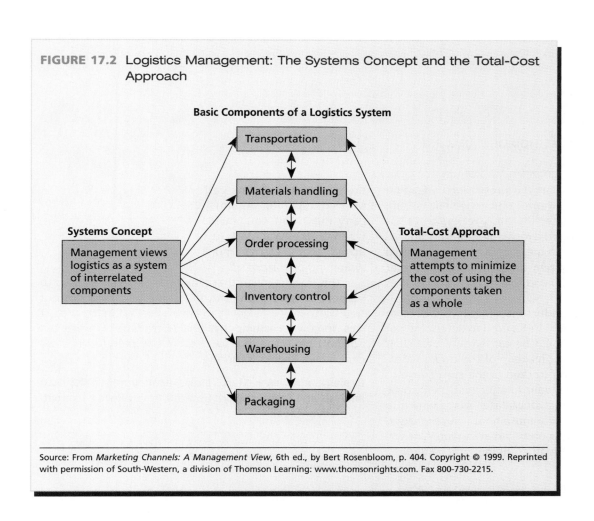

**FIGURE 17.2  Logistics Management: The Systems Concept and the Total-Cost Approach**

**Basic Components of a Logistics System**

- Transportation
- Materials handling
- Order processing
- Inventory control
- Warehousing
- Packaging

**Systems Concept**

Management views logistics as a system of interrelated components

**Total-Cost Approach**

Management attempts to minimize the cost of using the components taken as a whole

Source: From *Marketing Channels: A Management View*, 6th ed., by Bert Rosenbloom, p. 404. Copyright © 1999. Reprinted with permission of South-Western, a division of Thomson Learning: www.thomsonrights.com. Fax 800-730-2215.

## Customer Service

The role logistics activities play in providing customer service is critical. Robert Woodruff, former president of The Coca-Cola Company, emphasized the role of logistics in his firm's success when he stated that his organization's policy was to "put Coke within arm's length of desire." Having its products available everywhere is one of The Coca-Cola Company's greatest strengths.

Customer service standards are the quality-of-service levels the firm's customers will receive. Companies should set goals and define acceptable performance for the quality of service that they expect to deliver. For example, a customer service standard of one firm might be that 60 percent of all orders will be shipped within 48 hours after they are received, 90 percent in 72 hours, and all orders within 96 hours. Setting the standards for customer service to be provided is an important marketing channel decision. FedEx has a policy of answering the phone after the first ring.

Achieving an optimum logistics system is no simple matter. Markets can be spread over a region, a province, a country, and even the world. This complex and expensive process has been passed by some companies to **third-party logistics providers**. These are specialist firms that perform virtually all of the logistical tasks that manufacturers or other channel members would normally perform themselves. More and more companies are turning over their logistics decisions to such specialist firms. With third-party logistics, a company can partner with an organization that can fulfill requirements from storage to transportation. This allows the client company to focus on its core business. An example of a third-party logistics provider is Canada Messenger, which has developed a sophisticated distribution and warehouse system that can handle the logistical tasks for its clients.

www.fedex.com

**third-party logistics provider**
Specialist firm that performs virtually all of the logistical tasks that manufacturers or other channel members would normally perform themselves.

## Transportation

www.tc.gc.ca/en/menu.htm

How will the products be shipped, and by what carrier? The transportation system in Canada is a regulated industry, much like the power industry. The federal and provincial governments perform both promotional and regulatory functions to maintain a viable Canadian transportation system.

---

## THE CANADIAN MARKETPLACE

### "TRAITING": WAL-MART'S METHOD OF MANAGING INVENTORY

Another reason that Wal-Mart has grown into a leading position in retailing is its inventory management system. Wal-Mart's use of sophisticated inventory technologies has permitted the chain to look beyond the more traditional "merchandising by region to merchandising by individual store." Wal-Mart uses a system called *traiting* to look at both the customers' makeup and their buying preferences at individual stores.

Traiting indexes the product movement at each store with the store's market traits. This is used to determine not only if a given product should be carried in a particular store given the demographic makeup of the trading area, but also where it should be stocked in the store's layout. Traiting permits a store manager to alter total shelf space allotments based on product flow data. That's why in a rural area Wal-Mart may carry more hardware and do-it-yourself merchandise, and in an urban area Wal-Mart will stock more fax paper and other home office supplies.

Likewise, a store in one part of a metropolitan area may carry more golf equipment, whereas the Wal-Mart just across town carries more swimming pool supplies.

This doesn't mean that only sales data can be used to support carrying a product. If a store manager finds out that Garth Brooks is going to have a concert in the area, it is reasonable to assume that 1000 Garth Brooks T-shirts will not only be in the manager's store but every other store near where Brooks is touring.

www.walmart.com

**Explain how Wal-Mart makes consumer behaviour analysis and logistics work together to produce a competitive advantage.**

Source: From *Retailing*, 3rd ed., by Patrick Dunne and Robert F. Lusch, p. 16. Copyright © 1999. Reprinted with permission of South-Western, a division of Thomson Learning: www.thomsonrights.com. Fax 800-730-2215.

---

Transport Canada, a government agency within the federal bureaucracy, supports technological developments associated with the airways, waterways, and highways in Canada.

The Canadian Transport Commission (CTC), an agency of the federal government, is responsible for the air, rail, pipeline, and inland water components of the transportation industry. Each province has a transportation regulatory agency whose functions are equivalent to those of the CTC. In general, the purpose of government intervention in the transportation sector is to assure the development of a sound, efficient transportation infrastructure while protecting the public against abusive tactics.

## Classes of Carriers

Three legal forms of transportation carriers exist to provide linkages between the various channel members: common, contract, and private. **Common carriers** must "hold themselves out" to serve the general public for a fee. They must receive appropriate regulatory authority to perform transport service, and must adhere to guidelines and rules as to rate setting, mergers, application of accounting procedures, and financial dealings. Although common carriers provide transportation services between each of the marketing channel intermediaries, they most frequently operate among manufacturers, wholesalers, and retailers moving goods of high value.

**Contract carriers** do not offer their services to the public at large. Rather, they enter into contractual arrangements with select customers. All rates and charges are included in the contractual instrument, along with additional terms and conditions associated with providing service. Although regulatory requirements for contract carriers are significantly fewer than for common carriers, rules and standards are in effect at both the federal and provincial levels of government to delineate the scope of their authority to provide transportation services. Contract carriers tend to operate between raw material suppliers and manufacturers, and between manufacturers, rather than among wholesalers, retailers, and final customers, since they tend to be commodity and final goods consolidators rather than break-bulk operators.

**Private carriers** are not providers of transportation for a market fee. Instead, they provide transportation services for a particular firm and may not solicit other transportation business. The test to determine whether a carrier is a private or a for-hire carrier is to ask whether the primary business is transportation or not. Legal status depends on the percentage of revenues from transportation activities or the ratio of transportation to nontransportation-related assets. Owing to the exclusive nature of their operations, and the fact that transportation is incidental to the main operations of the firm, private carriers are not subject to economic regulation by either the federal or the provincial governments. They are, however, subject to federal and provincial safety regulations, as are others who use transportation facilities.

There are five major transportation alternatives, referred to as *modes*, that link the various channel intermediaries. These are *railways, trucking companies, water carriers, air freight,* and *pipelines.* Railways are the largest transporters (as measured by tonne-kilometres of freight) and are considered the most efficient land mode in moving bulk commodities over long distances. They are readily available in most locations in North America, although line abandonment has considerably reduced the operating systems of the major rail carriers over the past three decades. Likewise, railways are quite flexible in that many different commodities, raw materials, liquids, grains, and finished goods can be safely and efficiently moved.

Trucking companies compete with railways in several product categories. However, where speed, flexibility, and frequency of service are important, motor carriers often outperform rail carriers. The truck shows its inherent advantage in moving high-valued goods short to intermediate distances. While the rate per tonne-kilometre is often greater for motor than for rail carrier, the service advantages provided by truck often more than compensate for the added expenditures. Furthermore, the variety of available trucking technologies provides the shipper with a broad array of options in transporting goods to market. No other mode rivals trucking in the range of transportation options.

Water carriers are much like rail carriers in that they tend to perform best in moving bulky, low-value commodities long distances. Whether along the inland waterway system, the Great Lakes, or in international commerce, water carriers tend to carry bulk cargoes at rather low speeds. They do have

**common carrier**
Transportation carrier that provides service to the general public, and is subject to regulatory authority including fee setting.

**contract carrier**
Transportation carrier that serves only customers it has contracts with. Contracts include rates to be charged.

**private carrier**
Transportation carrier that provides transportation services for a particular firm and may not solicit other transportation business.

The size of this centre signifies the importance of logistics to CN.

the advantage in international commerce of moving freight of all kinds as no other mode can, given present technologies. Rates per tonne-kilometre tend to be lowest for this mode, reflecting in part the relatively low value per unit of weight of cargoes typically carried by water. The exception to this general case is container service for medium- to high-value goods. Container ships provide manufacturers with the opportunity of extending market channels to locations that are quite distant from sourcing and producing sites. The presence of scale economies in production and distribution permit effective competition with local production.

Air freight is often referred to as "premium transportation" because of the high-cost–high-service nature of the mode. Speed is the single most important factor in selecting air over other freight carriers, and the rate per tonne-kilometre tends to be among the highest of all modes. Cut flowers from southern U.S. growing fields, fresh seafood from Vancouver, and component parts urgently needed for a downed assembly line in Ontario are examples of the types of goods often moved by air freight carriers. In recent years, the demand for expedited small parcel and parcel post service has exploded, and companies like Emery Worldwide and FedEx have developed as a response to this demand.

Pipeline transportation is the mode least likely to be used within a marketing channel except in specific industries such as oil extraction and refining and coal extraction, and in industries where raw commodities can be pulverized into small pellets or a powder, mixed with water, and transported in suspension.

## THE CANADIAN MARKETPLACE

### THE GIANTS—CANADA'S HISTORIC PORTS

It's the stuff of lore: Explorer Alexander Mackenzie traveled from Canada's Northwest to Montreal by canoe, carrying furs destined for the London markets. In 1792, Mackenzie was the first European to cross North America by land. He dreamed of trading between Europe and Asia, across the oceans and across Canada.

In 1809, John Molson launched British North America's first steamship, the *Accommodation*. And in the mid-nineteenth century, Halifax's Samuel Cunard transformed his father's timber export business into what would become a storied name in passenger lines.

Today our ports are healthier than ever. More natural resources, agricultural products, and manufactured goods flow through them than ever before. For example, in 2001, Vancouver, the country's largest port, and number one in North America in foreign exports, handled 72.8 million tonnes of cargo. Modern ports are vital for a healthy economy. They are essential for efficient logistics of many goods.

Moving goods more quickly and cheaply requires dedicated bulk-cargo terminals, and up-to-date container facilities and tracking systems. Ports, terminal operators, and railways are investing hundreds of millions of dollars to expand their container business.

Source: Excerpted from Gordon Bowness, "The Giants," *R.O.B. Magazine*, April 2002, p. 56. Reprinted with permission of the author.

## Multimodal Transportation

Since the various modes of transportation have advantages and disadvantages, it is logical that a combination of modes may meet established customer service standards at the lowest cost. Companies such as Canadian Pacific have, for many years, responded to the need for combined modes by providing ocean and rail transportation.

## Inventory Control

How much inventory should be maintained at each location? Inventory control analysts have developed a number of techniques that aid the logistics manager in effectively controlling inventory costs. The most basic is the **economic order quantity (EOQ)** model. This technique emphasizes a cost tradeoff between two fundamental costs involved with inventory: inventory holding costs and order costs. As Figure 17.3 indicates, these two cost items are then "traded off" to determine the optimum order quantity of each product.

No aspect of logistics strategy has experienced the changes brought about by acceptance of the total quality management (TQM) philosophy as much as inventory practice and policy. Once it is recognized that significant resources are often tied up in inventory, it should come as no surprise that great distribution cost savings have accrued from minimizing inventory holding costs. Many firms have capitalized on this simple idea with the implementation of **just-in-time (JIT)** inventory systems. The basic idea is to identify stock levels that meet peak efficiency minimums and to trade off higher transportation expenditures for reduced inventory holding expenditures.

The concept can be visualized in the following illustration. Imagine a young couple entering a car dealership in Calgary. They have a vague idea of the features they would like to have in their dream car and have sought out the services of an informed representative to assist them in their purchase decision. The representative activates her computer and asks the young couple for the specific features they would like in their car: exterior and interior colours, fabric type, stereo system, wheel type, suspension, and so forth. As the couple discusses the various options, the representative enters the information into the computer. Once the features have all been selected, she pushes a button and a simulated version of the car with the designated features appears on the monitor.

Assuming the couple agrees on the features and a transaction occurs, the representative activates an order to the manufacturer, which contacts various component suppliers and assembly plants to ship parts for the car. An order is sent to the battery manufacturer, the stereo manufacturer, the engine manufacturer, and to all other component suppliers that contribute to producing the ordered

www.emeryworldwide.com
/eww/emerweb

www.cp.ca

**economic order quantity (EOQ)**

A model that emphasizes a cost tradeoff between inventory holding costs and order costs.

**just in time (JIT)**

An approach to minimizing inventory costs through identifying minimal inventory levels and arranging with suppliers to replenish stocks just in time to be used in production.

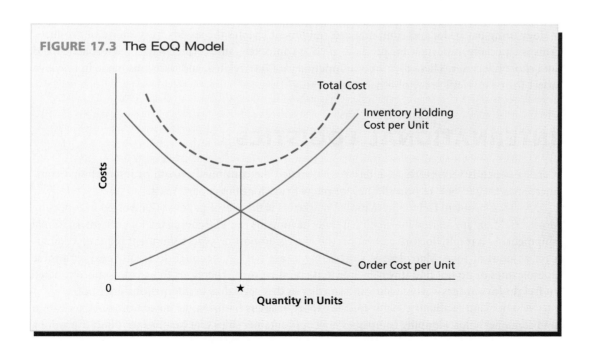

**FIGURE 17.3** The EOQ Model

car. From the subassembly plants, the various components are produced and then shipped to the next unit in the manufacturing chain just in time for their use.

The important point is that inventories are not held in large amounts anywhere in the manufacturing or marketing channel. Instead, upon receiving the order, the subassembler produces the component and transports it in minimum efficient lot sizes to the next assembler in the channel. The JIT method results in significant reductions in inventory costs even though transportation costs may increase. Just as important as reducing inventory costs, however, are the gains from reductions in setup and changeover times in procedures and equipment modifications, in more rapid response to changes in market conditions, and in the increased awareness of total quality management by using the most recent technologies in producing component parts.

## Protective Packaging and Materials Handling

How do we develop efficient methods of handling products in the factory, warehouse, and transport terminals? All the activities associated with moving products among the manufacturer's plants, warehouses, wholesalers, retailers, and transportation company terminals are called *materials handling*. Two important processes are combining as many packages as possible into one load (**unitization**) and combining several unitized loads (**containerization**). These have revolutionized the materials handling field. The materials handling system must be thoroughly coordinated for plants and warehouses that service the various channel intermediaries to perform effectively.

## Order Processing

Businesses today expect not only that orders will be processed quickly and efficiently, but that information regarding the status of the order will be readily available. Online ordering and computer tracking makes this possible. Such information systems also enable the supplier to be more efficient.

## Warehousing

Where will the products be stored? How many warehouses should be used? Warehouses lend themselves exceptionally well to automation, with the computer as the heart of the operation. **Distribution warehouses** are designed to assemble and then redistribute products, whereas **break-bulk warehouses** receive consolidated shipments from a central distribution centre, and then distribute them in smaller shipments to individual customers in more limited areas. Another type of warehouse, the **storage warehouse**, stores products for moderate to long periods of time in an attempt to balance supply and demand for producers and purchasers. Automated warehouse technology using bar codes and computerized equipment enables the speedy turnaround of products. This is especially important for products such as computer games, which have high initial demand and short life cycles. These distribution functions are interrelated, and decisions made in one area affect the relative efficiency of other areas.

# INTERNATIONAL LOGISTICS

Canada depends very much on international trade. The continued growth of international commerce has created new responsibilities for many firms' logistics departments.

A major problem facing international marketers is the pile of paperwork involved in exporting products. Many specialized international trade documents must be completed for each international shipment. As a result, documentation for the average import or export shipment requires a significant amount of time. Many logistics departments are not large enough to readily deal with these complexities or do not find it worthwhile to do on their own. Therefore, this work is subcontracted to **freight forwarders**—wholesaling intermediaries that specialize in international logistics.

A significant facilitating factor for the export business has been the advent of containerization and container ships. Shipping companies now use container ships that can make a round trip among

Halifax, Bremerhaven, and Rotterdam in fourteen days. Only four days are needed for each crossing of the Atlantic, and another six for the three port calls. This speed allows Canadian exporters to provide competitive delivery schedules to European markets. Similar procedures are followed for other foreign destinations.

The largest volume of Canadian shipments, however, still comprises agricultural products and raw materials (lumber and minerals). The importance of these basic commodities to Canada has resulted in specialized, complex systems at various ports for handling them.

## SUMMARY

Every item consumed in daily living is affected by logistics. Logistics is the process of managing and implementing the physical movement of products from source to place of use.

To obtain efficiencies and gain competitive advantage, it is necessary to consider and manage the entire supply chain. Supply chain management is the systematic, strategic coordination of the traditional business functions and the tactics across these business functions within a particular company and across businesses within the supply chain for the purposes of improving the long-term performance of the individual companies and the supply chain as a whole. It involves the coordination of the flow of materials and products from the source of raw materials to the production line, and ultimately to the consumer. It includes managing information, cash, and process/work flows.

The study of logistics is one of the classic examples of the systems approach to business problems. The goal of a logistics system is to produce a specified level of customer service while minimizing the costs involved in physically moving and storing the product from its production point to the point where it is ultimately purchased. The logistics system consists of six elements: (1) customer service, (2) transportation, (3) inventory control, (4) protective packaging and materials handling, (5) order processing, and (6) warehousing. These elements are interrelated and must be balanced for a distribution system to run smoothly.

Three basic concepts of the systems approach—the total-cost approach, the avoidance of suboptimization, and cost tradeoffs—combine to form the logistics concept.

The logistics manager has available five transportation alternatives: railways, motor carriers, water carriers, air freight, and pipelines. Multimodal transportation systems are available and increasingly used.

Efficient international logistics allows a firm to compete more effectively in foreign markets.

## KEY TERMS

break-bulk warehouse, p. 442
common carrier, p. 439
containerization, p. 442
contract carrier, p. 439
cost tradeoffs, p. 437
distribution warehouse, p. 442
economic order quantity (EOQ), p. 441
freight forwarder, p. 442
just in time (JIT), p. 441
logistics, p. 434

logistics concept, p. 437
private carrier, p. 439
storage warehouse, p. 442
suboptimization, p. 436
supply chain, p. 432
supply chain management (SCM), p. 433
third-party logistics provider, p. 438
total-cost approach, p. 436
unitization, p. 442

# INTERACTIVE SUMMARY AND DISCUSSION QUESTIONS

1. Some say that logistics has been one of the last areas in most companies to be carefully studied and improved. How can this be explained?
2. Outline the basic reasons for the increased attention to logistics and supply chain management.
3. The logistics system contains the following elements: customer service, transportation, inventory control, protective packaging and materials handling, order processing, and warehousing. Explain how specifying a level of customer service can affect each of the other elements.
4. Customer service standards are an essential element in developing a logistics plan. Who should be ultimately responsible for determining the level of customer service? Why?
5. What are the basic objectives of logistics?
6. The five main transportation modes are railway, motor carrier, water carrier, air freight, and pipelines. Outline the basic strengths and weaknesses of each mode of transport.
7. Legal forms of transportation carriers can be categorized as common, contract, and private. In what circumstances would each be used?
8. Under what circumstances are freight forwarders used?
9. Suggest the most appropriate transportation mode for each of the following products, and defend your choices:
   a. iron ore
   b. crude oil
   c. Dash detergent
   d. orchids
   e. heavy earth-moving equipment
   f. lumber
10. The location of distribution warehouses has a significant bearing on costs and customer service. What factors should be considered in locating a new warehouse?
11. Economic order quantity emphasizes a cost tradeoff between two fundamental costs involved with inventory: inventory holding costs and order costs. Explain how EOQ works.
12. Describe how the notion of a cost tradeoff should be applied to the elements of the logistics system listed in question 3.
13. Select two companies such as Wal-Mart and FedEx. Using the Internet, research how an emphasis on logistics and supply chain management have contributed to their success.

www.walmart.com

www.fedex.com

## Moving an Airport Overnight

In the wee hours of the morning on July 5, 1998, Hong Kong made history by carrying out the largest peacetime movement of men and equipment. In just seven hours, Kai Tak, the world's third busiest international passenger airport, was moved to its new home 30 km west to Chek Lap Kok on Lantau Island.

"The relocation operation involved the movement of equipment, vehicles, personnel, and aircraft from Kai Tak to Chek Lap Kok over a 90-day period, culminating in the overnight closure of operations at Kai Tak and the opening of Hong Kong's new international airport seven hours later," says Michael Winarick, a retired British Army colonel who planned the logistics of the airport move.

Equipment to be moved ranged from small tractors, to an entire aero engine.

On move night, there were 1000 vehicle movements, 70 barges transporting heavier loads through Victoria Harbour, and 30 airliners. The heaviest item was an aircraft recovery vehicle big enough to haul a disabled Boeing 747 from the runway.

To help control traffic, 1000 police officers were called in that evening. "The move, without doubt the largest in Hong Kong history, included the separate relocation of 72 business partners and 13 government departments," Winarick says. The airport's business partners involved in the move included government departments, airlines, and airport operators, including ramp and cargo handlers, base and line maintenance operators, retail outlets, and airline caterers.

A number of government departments and external agencies helped move-night organizers with things such as traffic control, permits for unlicensed vehicles to travel on public roads, and permits for those vessels entering the marine exclusion zones around both airports.

Because the two airports are so close together, air traffic control concerns dictated that both airports could not be open at the same time, so Kai Tak had to close before Chek Lap Kok could open, leaving Hong Kong without an airport for seven hours. "The need to ensure the cohesion necessary, the tight time schedule on move night, and the discipline so important for ingress and egress at each airport necessitated a military-style operation," says Winarick.

www.hkairport.com/welcome/main/index.htm

Kai Tak's geographical location in the densely populated Kowloon district of Hong Kong, the fact that the move was scheduled during typhoon season, and part of the route was over one of the world's longest suspension bridges, Tsing Ma, were some of the unique problems faced on move night. When implementing the changeover, two movement control centres were set up, one at each airport.

A computer program was designed and developed to monitor the real-time movement details during move night and track the actual move against planned parameters.

The move was a resounding success, Winarick says. All essential equipment was in place to allow operations to begin at 6:30 A.M. at the new airport. During the transfer, there were no major hold-ups. One piece of equipment was delayed 35 minutes, as its blown tire was replaced while on the Tsing Ma bridge.

### You Be the Marketer

1. Is this an example of supply chain management or logistics?
2. What would have been the implications if this had not gone off as planned?
3. What parallels are there between the process described above, and the manufacturing of a new car?
4. What parallels are there between the process described above, and a major department store such as Sears getting ready for the Christmas rush?

Source: Adapted from Sherry Butt, "Hong Kong's Flight Plan," *Calgary Sun,* Resource and Supply Chain Management Supplement (January 1999), p. 8. Reprinted with permission of the *Calgary Sun.*

## Everyone will notice the 260 horsepower G35.

How do you rewrite the history of the sports sedan? Start with the heart-stopping power of a class-leading DOHC V6 engine. Then master it with breakthrough aerodynamic design that produces an unheard of zero front lift that maximizes your connection with the road. With a race-inspired driver's cockpit, state-of-the-art 3D Birdview™† navigation system and a spacious leather interior, driving becomes an unparalleled sensory experience. Amazingly well-equipped from $38,900. **The new G35. *Now* you're driving.**

*Accelerating the future*

**INFINITI**

# MARKETING COMMUNICATIONS STRATEGY

How does an advertising campaign get developed? What is the thinking process behind some of the advertisements we see every day? John Roumelis, an Account Director at advertising agency TBWA\Chiat\Day in Toronto tells the following interesting story about developing a marketing communications strategy for a new car.

There are so many vehicles in the marketplace that not even the keen automotive marketers can speak knowledgeably about them all. Throw your typical consumer into this sea of products, add a high-ticket price, and it can take them awhile to zone in on their purchase (or lease)— usually six months from the time they started looking.

That's not your average impulse buy. The challenge for a manufacturer is what to stand for and how to stand out.

Enter the G35, Infiniti Canada's new high performance luxury sedan. It had the makings of a flagship product but how could we get people to listen? Intenders of certain European brands often don't consider anything else. Add the noise of heavy competitive activity and it can be a daunting task.

We decided to be aggressive. A high-performance luxury sedan in an extremely competitive segment necessitated an aggressive stance. We would launch the G35 with the media weight deserving of flagship status. We selected a complementary mix of media including newspaper, selective magazine, outdoor, and unprecedented online advertising.

Our media research indicated that the luxury automotive buyer is a heavy newspaper reader. Newspaper automotive supplements are also cited among consumers as an important source for staying in tune with retail market opportunities.

Standing out and being noticed in newspaper meant paying a premium to ensure greater registration with four-colour, full-page executions. We weren't just competing for share of voice with competitors, we were competing with the editorial [content as well]. We needed compelling ads.

The creative had to be aggressive while maintaining a level of sophistication consistent with the Infiniti brand.

We [also] had to attract the European car enthusiasts where performance was a key motivator in their purchase decision. Since we felt the 260 horsepower G35 could outperform its key competitors, our objective was to position the Infiniti G35 as an awe-inspiring performance vehicle. The clearest way to communicate this was through power—an elegant, witty and smart expression of power. We had multiple executions with tremendous stopping power (no pun intended) so that anyone who saw the ads would know exactly what the G35 and Infiniti stood for. The Infiniti G35 exceeded its sales target by 57 percent. The G35 more than delivered on its brand promise. A promise that a multimedia campaign with an emphasis on newspaper helped us fulfill.

**An attention-getting advertising campaign used in a creative way to transmit a message—that is the essence of marketing communications. And the variations that people think up are endless. This is what makes marketing communications one of the most interesting and exciting elements of the marketing mix.**

Source: Excerpted from John Roumelis, "How to Get Noticed...Fast," *Marketing*, April 2002, p. 26.

www.Infiniti.ca

# INTRODUCTION

You have come up with a wonderful product. You have determined the market segment that it will serve, appraised customer needs, analyzed competitors' offerings, and defined a positioning strategy. How then should your product's advantages be communicated to the target audience?

A vast array of communication alternatives are available. How about direct mail (is it really "junk," as some people claim?) or celebrity advertising? Perhaps the main communication message should be carried by salespeople. But that might cost too much. On the other hand, why waste money by not spending enough on marketing communications? How much *is* "enough"?

These few questions just scratch the surface of the many issues involved in developing and implementing a marketing communications strategy. It is an exhilarating and creative process that requires tough thinking and a very systematic approach. This chapter and the next will introduce the domain of marketing communications.

**Marketing communications**, the fourth variable in the marketing mix, is defined as all activities and messages that inform, persuade, and influence the consumer in making a purchase decision. Figure 18.1 depicts the relationship between a firm's marketing communications strategy and the other elements of the overall marketing plan.

**marketing communications**

All activities and messages that inform, persuade, and influence the consumer in making a purchase decision.

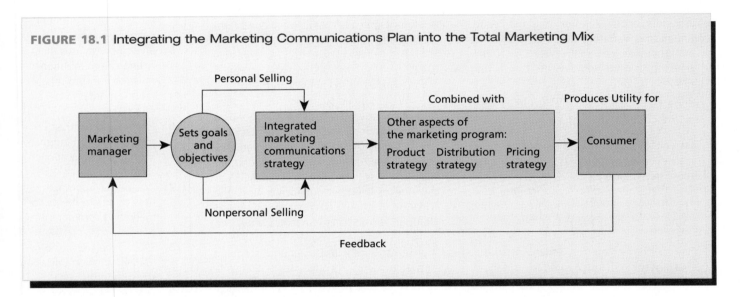

**FIGURE 18.1** Integrating the Marketing Communications Plan into the Total Marketing Mix

The marketing manager sets the goals and objectives of the firm's communications approach in accordance with overall organizational objectives and the goals of the marketing plan. Then, based on these goals, the various elements of marketing communications—advertising, personal selling, sales promotion, publicity, and public relations—are formulated in a coordinated plan. This plan, in turn, becomes an integral part of the total marketing strategy for reaching selected consumer segments. Finally, the feedback mechanism, in such forms as marketing research and field reports, closes the system by identifying any deviations from the plan and by suggesting modifications or improvements.

# INTEGRATED MARKETING COMMUNICATIONS (IMC)

The foregoing approach is also known as integrated marketing communications (IMC). Formerly, a significant number of firms tended to view the elements of the promotion mix individually, each with its own plans and tactics for influencing the target market. For example, advertising was managed separately from the sales promotion, publicity, and direct marketing functions.

Today it is recognized that the vast array of communication alternatives should be integrated to create the greatest impact. The integrated marketing communications approach looks at company information outputs from the customer's perspective. It recognizes that the customer develops an understanding of the company or the product through a *combination* of many sources: advertising, the Internet, direct mail, billboards, and coupons. In addition, the IMC concept includes all of the other ways that customers learn about the company and product, such as packaging, displays, and sales literature. All communications must be integrated so that the customer receives a unified message. Such communications are coordinated with other elements of the marketing mix to create synergistic effects.

**Integrated marketing communications (IMC)** has been defined by the American Association of Advertising Agencies as a concept of marketing communications planning that recognizes the added value of a comprehensive plan that evaluates the strategic role of a variety of communication disciplines—for example, general advertising, direct response, sales promotion, and public relations—and combines these disciplines to provide clarity, consistency, and maximum communications impact.[1]

An integrated, comprehensive plan is more difficult to achieve than it sounds. A large number of people within the firm are involved, each with somewhat different responsibilities and perspectives. Furthermore, good information is necessary. An important integrating factor is the availability of high-quality customer databases that contain not only customer names and addresses, but also demographic data, lifestyle information, and brand preferences. Database marketing has been discussed in earlier chapters. Valid information about customers creates a good picture of their needs and wants, making it easier to focus and integrate all of the elements of the communications mix. Toyota, for example, has developed a database of its car buyers. The data can be used not only for product, distribution, and pricing planning, but also to develop an integrated marketing communications plan that supports and enhances the other elements of the marketing mix.

Developing an integrated marketing communications program is a detailed and complex process. As will be shown in this chapter, many decisions have to be made about the role and importance of each promotional element, and how these decisions will fit together to best communicate with target customers.

**integrated marketing communications (IMC)**

A comprehensive marketing communications plan that takes into consideration all the communication disciplines being used and combines them to provide clarity, consistency, and maximum communications impact.

www.toyota.ca

# THE COMMUNICATIONS PROCESS

Figure 18.2 shows a generalized communications process using terminology borrowed from radio and telecommunications.[2] The sender is the *source* of the communications system, since he or she seeks to convey a *message* (a communication of information or advice or a request) to a *receiver* of the communication. The message must accomplish three tasks to be effective:

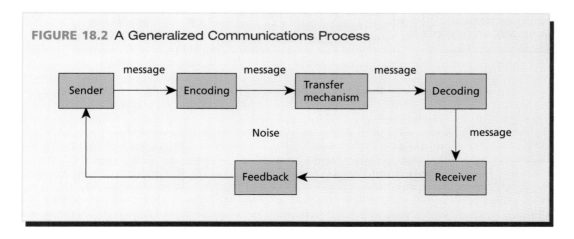

**FIGURE 18.2 A Generalized Communications Process**

1. It must *gain the attention* of the receiver.
2. It must *be understood* by both the receiver and the sender.
3. It must *stimulate* the needs of the receiver and *suggest* an appropriate method of satisfying these needs.[3]

The message must be *encoded,* or translated into understandable terms, and transmitted through a communications medium or transfer mechanism. *Decoding* is the receiver's interpretation of the message. The receiver's response, known as *feedback,* completes the system. Throughout the process, *noise* can interfere with the transmission of the message and reduce its effectiveness.

In Figure 18.3, the generalized communications process is applied to marketing communications. The marketing manager is the sender in the system. The message is encoded in the form of sales presentations, advertisements, displays, or publicity releases. The *transfer mechanism* for delivering the message may be a salesperson, print or electronic advertising media, direct mail, the Internet, or a public relations channel.

The *decoding* step involves the consumer's interpretation of the sender's message. This is the most troublesome aspect of marketing communications, since consumers often do not interpret a promotional message in the same way as its sender does. Because receivers are likely to decode messages based on their own frames of reference or individual experiences, the sender must be careful to ensure that the message is properly encoded to match the target audience. If the message is decoded properly, there is a greater chance of a positive consumer *response*—an attitude change or decision to purchase.

*Feedback* is information about the receiver's response to the message. The response may take the form of attitude change, purchase, or nonpurchase. In some instances, a firm may use marketing communications to create a favourable attitude toward its new products or services. Such attitude changes may result in future purchases. In other instances, the objective of the communication is to stimulate consumer purchases. Such purchases indicate positive responses to the firm, its product/service offerings, its distribution channels, its prices, and its promotion. Even nonpurchases can serve as feedback to the sender. They may result from ineffective communication in that the message was not believed, not remembered, or failed to persuade the receiver that the firm's products or services are superior to its competitors. Feedback can be obtained from advertising research, field sales reports, or an analysis of inventory movements.

*Noise* represents interference at some stage in the communications process. It may result from such factors as competitive promotional messages being transmitted over the same communications channel, misinterpretation of a sales presentation or an advertising message, receipt of the promo-

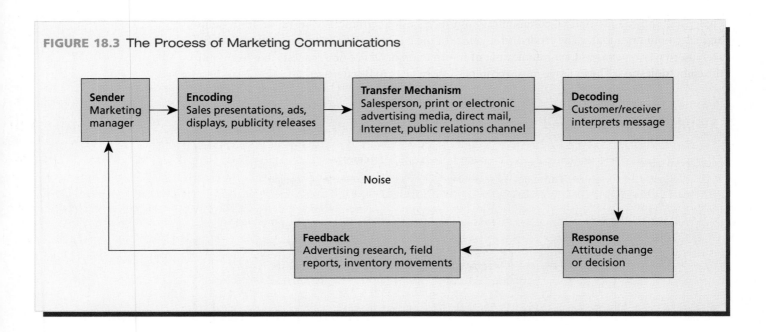

FIGURE 18.3 The Process of Marketing Communications

tional message by the wrong person, or random noise factors, such as people conversing—or leaving the room—during a television commercial.

Table 18.1 illustrates the steps in the communications process with three examples of promotional messages. Although the types of promotion vary from a highly personalized sales presentation to such nonpersonal promotion as a two-for-one coupon and television advertising, each form of promotion goes through each stage in the communications model.

**TABLE 18.1** Examples of Marketing Communications

| TYPE OF PROMOTION | SENDER | ENCODING | TRANSFER MECHANISM | DECODING BY RECEIVER | RESPONSE | FEEDBACK |
|---|---|---|---|---|---|---|
| Personal selling | Canon Office Equipment | Sales presentation on new model office copier | Canon sales representative | Office manager and employees in local firm discuss Canon sales presentation and those of competing suppliers | Order placed for Canon copier | Information that customers are reacting positively to the message |
| Two-for-one coupon (sales promotion) | Wendy's Hamburgers | Wendy's marketing department and advertising agency | Coupon inserted in weekend newspaper | Newspaper reader sees coupon for hamburger and saves it | Hamburgers purchased by consumers using the coupon | Information that customers are reacting positively to the message |
| Television advertising | Movie producer | Advertisement for a new movie is developed by the producer's advertising agency | Network television during programs with high percentage of viewers in target market | Audience sees ad but few decide to go to the movie | Small number of movie tickets purchased | Communication failed to interest and motivate the target market |

# THE MARKETING COMMUNICATIONS MIX

Similar to the marketing mix, in planning marketing communications, numerous variables must be considered and blended together. The **marketing communications mix** is a subset of the marketing mix that blends personal selling and nonpersonal communication (including advertising, sales promotion, public relations, sponsorship marketing, and point-of-purchase communications) by marketers in an attempt to accomplish information and persuasion objectives. Figure 18.4 illustrates this relationship.

Personal selling and advertising are generally the most significant elements of the mix, since they usually account for the bulk of a firm's marketing communications expenditures. However, in any individual company, marketing planners may gain a competitive advantage by emphasizing other elements of the communications mix. A discussion of each of these elements is presented in Chapter 19. Only brief definitions will be given here to set the framework for the overall discussion of marketing communications.

## Personal Selling

**Personal selling** may be defined as a seller's promotional presentation conducted on a person-to-person basis with the buyer. It is a direct face-to-face form of promotion. Personal selling was also the original form of promotion. Twenty-six percent of all jobs are in sales and service.

**marketing communications mix**
The blend of personal selling and nonpersonal communication (including advertising, sales promotion, public relations, sponsorship marketing, and point-of-purchase communications) by marketers in an attempt to accomplish information and persuasion objectives.

**personal selling**
A seller's promotional presentation conducted on a person-to-person basis with the buyer.

**FIGURE 18.4** The Marketing and Marketing Communications Mixes

**Marketing Mix**
Product
Price
Distribution
Marketing communications

**Marketing Communications Mix**
Personal selling
Nonpersonal communication
• Advertising
• Sales promotion
  –point-of-purchase communications
• Public relations
  –sponsorship marketing
• Publicity

## Nonpersonal Communication

Nonpersonal communication is divided into advertising, sales promotion, and public relations. Advertising is usually regarded as the most important of these forms.

**advertising**

Paid nonpersonal communication through various media by business firms, nonprofit organizations, and individuals who are in some way identified with the advertising message and who hope to inform or persuade members of a particular audience.

**Advertising** is paid nonpersonal communication through various media by business firms, nonprofit organizations, and individuals who are in some way identified with the advertising message and who hope to inform or persuade members of a particular audience.[4] It involves the mass media, such as newspapers, television, radio, magazines, and billboards. Business realizes the tremendous potential of this form of communication, and advertising has become increasingly important in marketing. Mass consumption makes advertising particularly appropriate for products that rely on sending the same message to large audiences.

Ford Motor Company sponsors the annual "One of a Kind Christmas Show and Sale" in Toronto, Ontario.

**Sales promotion** includes "those marketing activities, other than personal selling, mass media advertising, and publicity, that stimulate consumer purchasing and dealer effectiveness, such as displays, shows and expositions, demonstrations, and various nonrecurrent selling efforts not in the ordinary routine."[5] Sales promotion is usually practised together with other forms of advertising to emphasize, assist, supplement, or otherwise support the objectives of the promotional program. It is growing in importance.

**Point-of-purchase communications** includes a variety of materials that are designed to influence buying decisions at the point of purchase. Examples are displays, posters, signs, packaging, and even brand names.

**Public relations** is a component of marketing communications that focuses on creating favourable attention and word of mouth among various publics—including the organization's customers, suppliers, shareholders, and employees; the government; the general public; and the society in which the organization operates. Public relations programs can be either formal or informal. Every organization, whether or not it has a formalized, organized program, must be concerned about its public relations. Publicity generated by such activities can have very positive effects on consumers' product and company knowledge.

**Sponsorship marketing** is the practice of promoting the interests of a company and its brands by associating the company or a brand with a specific event (such as a hockey tournament or festival) or charitable cause (such as the United Way).

# FACTORS AFFECTING USE OF MARKETING COMMUNICATIONS MIX ELEMENTS

How can a marketer know which of the communications mix elements to use? Precise quantitative measures to determine the effectiveness of each component of the communications mix in a given market segment are not generally available. Thus, choosing a proper mix of communications elements is one of the most difficult tasks facing the marketing manager. Some of the key factors that affect the choice of mix elements are (1) the objectives of the marketing plan, (2) the actions of competitors, (3) the nature of the market, (4) the nature of the product, (5) the product's stage in the product life cycle, (6) price, and (7) funds available.

## Objectives of the Marketing Plan

The first consideration in developing a communications mix is the objectives of the marketing plan. As outlined in Chapter 5, the marketing plan makes specific decisions about each element of the marketing mix. The *role* that marketing communications should play in that plan has to be clearly defined. Is its role to provide supplemental support to an aggressive pricing strategy, for example, or will marketing communications be used to promote product features? If promoting product features, what are the best ways to communicate the message?

## Actions of Competitors

Considering competitors' actions is important in developing marketing strategy, and it is of critical importance to understand the communications program of competitors. The marketer must decide whether to match competitors' communications mix or to develop a different mix that counters the competition's strategy more effectively.

## Nature of the Market

The marketer's target audience has a major impact on what type of communications mix elements will work best. In cases where there is a limited number of buyers (as, for example, with a manufacturer of printing presses), personal selling may prove highly effective. However, markets that are characterized by a large number of potential customers scattered over a large geographic area may make the cost of contact by personal salespeople prohibitive; in such instances, marketers may make extensive use of advertising (as, for example, is done for Kodak film).

The type of consumer also affects the marketing communications mix. A target market that is made up of business purchasers or retail and wholesale buyers is more likely to require personal selling than one consisting of ultimate consumers. Also, because the value of their purchases is significant, it is economically feasible to use personal selling.

## Nature of the Product

Another important factor in determining an effective marketing communications mix is the product itself. Highly standardized products with minimal servicing requirements are less likely to depend on personal selling than are higher-priced custom products that are technically complex and require servicing. Consumer goods are more likely to rely heavily on advertising than are business goods.

Within each product category, marketing communications mixes vary. For instance, in business marketing, installations typically involve a heavy reliance on personal selling compared with the marketing of operating supplies. Convenience goods rely heavily on manufacturer advertising, and personal selling plays a role only in getting the product distributed.

On the other hand, personal selling is often more important in marketing shopping goods, and both personal selling and nonpersonal selling are important in marketing specialty goods. Finally, personal selling is likely to be more important in marketing products that are characterized by trade-ins.

## Stage in the Product Life Cycle

The marketing communications mix must also be tailored to the stage in the product life cycle. In the introductory stage, heavy emphasis is placed on personal selling to inform the marketplace of the merits of the new product and to gain distribution. Salespeople contact marketing intermediaries to secure interest and commitment to handle the new product. Trade shows and exhibitions are frequently used to inform and educate prospective dealers and ultimate consumers. Any advertising at this stage is largely informative, and sales promotional techniques, such as samples and cents-off coupons, are designed to influence consumer attitudes and stimulate initial purchases.

As the product moves into the growth and maturity stages, advertising becomes more important in attempting to persuade consumers to make purchases. Personal-selling efforts continue to be directed at intermediaries in an attempt to expand distribution. As more competitors enter the marketplace, advertising stresses product differences in an attempt to persuade consumers to purchase the firm's brand. Reminder advertisements begin to appear in the maturity and early decline stages. Sponsorship marketing may be used at this time.

## Price

The price of the product is a sixth factor in the choice of marketing communications mix elements. Advertising is a dominant mix component for low-unit-value products due to the high costs per contact involved in personal selling. The cost of a sales call by an intermediate level sales representative, for example, has been estimated at nearly $93, excluding overhead costs.[6] As a result, it has become unprofitable to promote lower-value products through personal selling. Advertising, by contrast, permits a low promotional expenditure per sales unit since it reaches mass audiences. For low-value consumer products, such as chewing gum, soft drinks, and snack foods, advertising is the only feasible means of promotion.

## Funds Available

A very real barrier to implementing any marketing communications strategy is the size of the budget. If a 30-second television commercial costs a packaged-goods company $100 000 to shoot, and one 30-second showing nationally during a special event costs $6000 or more, television advertising is costly. Even though the message is received by millions of viewers and the cost per contact is relatively low, such an expenditure for just one showing would exceed the entire promotional budget of thousands of firms.

For many new or smaller firms, the cost of national mass advertising is prohibitive, so they are forced to seek less expensive, and possibly less efficient, methods. One common approach involves using smaller, local media. Neighbourhood retailers may not be able to advertise in metropolitan newspapers or on local radio and television stations; apart from personal selling, therefore, their limited promotional budgets may be allocated to an eye-catching sign, one of the most valuable promotional devices available to small retailers, or local circulation of handbills. A well-designed Web site is another reasonably priced option.

Table 18.2 summarizes the factors that influence the determination of marketing communications mix elements for a marketing program.

**TABLE 18.2** Factors That Influence the Marketing Communications Mix

| FACTOR | EMPHASIS ON | |
| --- | --- | --- |
| | Personal Selling | Advertising |
| Objectives of the Marketing Plan | Affects all decisions in the mix | |
| Actions of Competitors | Decide whether to match competitors and/or to develop a different mix | |
| **Nature of the Market** | | |
| Number of buyers | Limited number | Large number |
| Geographic concentration | Concentrated | Dispersed |
| Type of customer | Business purchaser | Ultimate consumer |
| **Nature of the Product** | | |
| Complexity | Custom-made, complex | Standardized |
| Service requirements | Considerable | Minimal |
| Type of good | Business | Consumer |
| Use of trade-ins | Trade-ins common | Trade-ins uncommon |
| Stage in the Product Life Cycle | Introductory and early growth stages | Latter part of growth stage and maturity and early decline stages |
| Price | High unit value | Low unit value |
| Funds Available | Affects all decisions in the mix | |

# MARKETING COMMUNICATIONS STRATEGY—PULL OR PUSH?

Broadly speaking, there are two marketing communications policies that may be employed: a pulling strategy and a pushing strategy. A **pulling strategy** is a promotional effort by the seller to stimulate final-user demand, which then exerts pressure on the distribution channel. The plan is to build consumer demand for the product by means of advertising so that channel members will have to stock the product to meet that demand. If a manufacturer's advertising efforts result in shoppers

**pulling strategy**

A promotional effort by the seller to stimulate final-user demand, which then exerts pressure on the distribution channel.

requesting the retailer to stock an item, they will usually succeed in getting that item on the retailer's shelves, since most retailers want to stimulate repeat purchases by satisfied customers. For example, grocery retailers are unwilling to stock a new product unless the manufacturer mounts a significant advertising and promotional program. They realize that it is necessary to pull the product through the channel.

A pulling strategy may be required to motivate marketing intermediaries to handle a product when they already stock a large number of competing products. When a manufacturer decides to use a pulling strategy, personal selling is often largely limited to contacting intermediaries, providing requested information about the product, and taking orders. Advertising and sales promotion are the most commonly used marketing communications elements in a pulling strategy.

By contrast, a **pushing strategy** relies more heavily on personal selling. Here, the objective is the promotion of the product first to the members of the marketing channel, who then participate in its promotion to the final user. This can be done through personal-selling efforts by the firm's sales force, cooperative advertising allowances, trade discounts, and other dealer supports. Such a strategy is designed to produce marketing success for the firm's products by motivating representatives of wholesalers or retailers to spend a disproportionate amount of time and effort in promoting these products to customers. For example, a lawn mower manufacturer may decide to provide high margins plus other incentives to dealers to encourage them to push their brand rather than competitors' brands. Thus money is spent in this way rather than on extensive advertising.

While pulling and pushing are presented here as alternative policies, it is unlikely that many companies will depend entirely on either strategy. In most cases, marketers employ a mixture of the two.

## Timing

In situations where both advertising and personal selling are used, timing is another factor to consider in developing a marketing communications strategy. Figure 18.5 shows the relative importance of advertising and selling in different periods of the purchase process. During the pre-transactional period (before the actual sale), advertising has been found to be more important than personal selling. It is often argued that one of the primary advantages of a successful advertising program is that it sensitizes prospects to the product, and it assists the salesperson in

**pushing strategy**
The promotion of the product first to the members of the marketing channel, who then participate in its promotion to the final user.

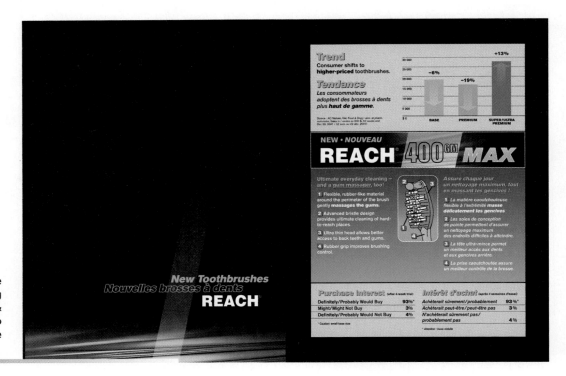

A pushing strategy: These carefully designed selling sheets assist Johnson & Johnson's representatives to promote this product to the trade.

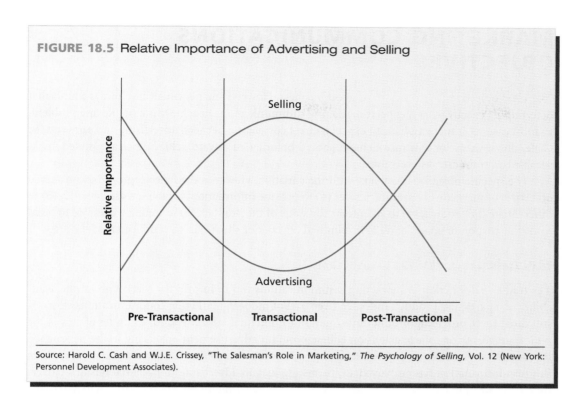

**FIGURE 18.5** Relative Importance of Advertising and Selling

Source: Harold C. Cash and W.J.E. Crissey, "The Salesman's Role in Marketing," *The Psychology of Selling*, Vol. 12 (New York: Personnel Development Associates).

approaching the prospect. Personal selling becomes more important than advertising during the transactional phase of the process. In most situations, personal selling is the actual mechanism for closing the sale. In the post-transactional stage, advertising regains primacy in the communication effort. It serves as an affirmation of the customer's decision to buy a particular good or service, as well as a reminder of the product's favourable qualities, characteristics, and performance.

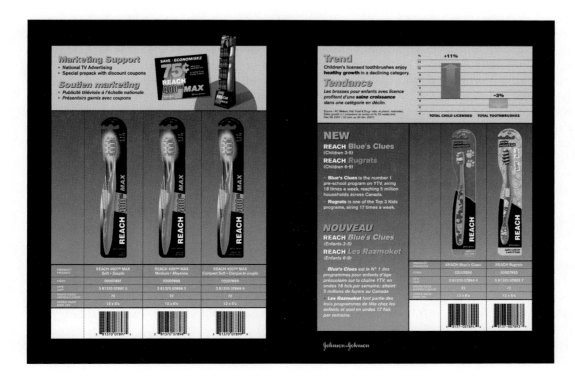

© Johnson & Johnson Inc. 2002

# MARKETING COMMUNICATIONS OBJECTIVES

"Set clear objectives" is an axiom of good business. However, management has always found that determining exactly what it expects marketing communications to achieve is a perplexing problem. In most cases, it is too simplistic to expect a direct correlation between advertising and sales results. Generally, strategy for this mix element should be oriented toward achieving clearly stated, measurable communications objectives.

The specific objective must vary with the situation. However, the following can be considered objectives of marketing communications: (1) to provide information, (2) to increase demand, (3) to differentiate the product, (4) to accentuate the value of the product, (5) to stabilize sales, (6) to build a positive corporate image, and (7) in a limited number of situations, to produce sales.

## Providing Information

The traditional function of marketing communications was to inform the market about the availability of a particular product. Indeed, a large part of modern marketing communications efforts is still directed at providing product information to potential customers. An example of this is the typical university or college extension course program advertisement appearing in the newspaper. Its content emphasizes informative features, such as the availability of different courses. Southam Business Information has employed an interesting idea in advertising to potential business advertisers. The ad shows the back of a station wagon covered with bumper stickers, and then makes the point "To communicate effectively, deal with one idea at a time." The ad educates potential advertisers and shows how Southam can help.

## THE ETHICAL MARKETER

### BID TO TEAR DOWN SEXIST ADS

In Australia, the government of the state of Victoria is planning a crackdown on outdoor advertising it says exploits women.

The government has announced it will develop a charter to reduce sexist billboard advertising following criticism of negative images of women on some ads.

Minister for Women's Affairs Mary Delahunty said compliance with the charter would be selection criteria for advertising agencies to bid for state contracts.

"The guidelines, to be introduced in January next year, will cover outdoor advertising campaigns by all government departments, statutory authorities and agencies, including advertising on public transport and bus shelters," Ms. Delahunty said in a statement.

The minister said advertising agencies and billboard contractors would be invited to develop and sign the charter in a commitment to the positive portrayal of women in outdoor advertising.

"The portrayal of women in the media and advertising is a powerful contributor to how women view themselves and other women," she said.

The guidelines have been developed following complaints about a spate of advertising campaigns showing women in provocative poses.

Ads by Chiko Roll, Windsor Smith shows, and Chivas Regal whisky have all raised the ire of women's groups.

Windsor Smith is under investigation by the Australian Standards Bureau for one advertisement that shows a topless man being caressed from behind by a woman wearing a low top and long boots.

Ms. Delahunty said today other professional bodies, such as advertising agencies, would be invited to develop and sign the charter.

The government would also develop a self-regulating service to judge advertisements against the charter, she said.

**Do women need protecting? Has the government gone too far?**

Source: Steven Moynihan, "Bid to Tear Down Sexist Ads," *The Age* http://www.theage.com.au/articles/2002/06/18/1023864418133.html, June 18, 2002. Reprinted with permission.

The informative function often requires repeated customer exposures. For instance, "in a ... study concerning customer acceptance of a new durable good, it was found that ... at least several months were required after introduction (and accompanying promotion) before consumers became generally aware of the item and somewhat familiar with its characteristics."[7]

## Increasing Demand

The primary objective of most marketing communications efforts is to increase the demand for a specific brand of product or service. This can be shown by using the familiar demand curves of basic economics (see Figure 18.6). Successful promotion can shift demand from schedule 1 to schedule 2, which means that greater quantities can be sold at each possible price level. Procter & Gamble has done this successfully with its Tide detergent.

www.pg.com

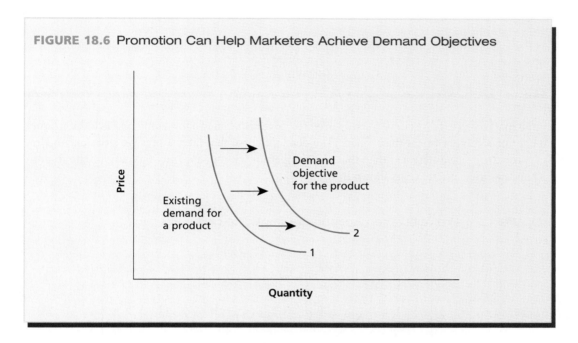

**FIGURE 18.6** Promotion Can Help Marketers Achieve Demand Objectives

## Differentiating the Product

Product differentiation is often an objective of the firm's marketing communications efforts. Homogeneous demand, represented by the horizontal line in Figure 18.7, means that consumers regard the firm's product as no different from that of its competitors. In such cases, the individual firm has no control over such marketing variables as price. A differentiated demand schedule, in contrast, permits more flexibility in marketing strategy, such as price changes.

For example, McCain, a producer of frozen vegetables, advertises the dependable high quality and good taste of its products. This differentiates these products from others. Consequently, some consumers who want these attributes are willing to pay a higher price for McCain than they would for other brands. Similarly, the high quality and distinctiveness of Cross pens are advertised, resulting in Cross's ability to ask for and obtain a price that is 100 times that of some disposable pens.

With the exception of commodities, most products have some degree of differentiation, resulting in a downward-sloping demand curve. The angle of the slope varies somewhat according to the degree of product differentiation.

www.mccain.com

## Accentuating the Value of the Product

Marketing communications can point out important features of a product to buyers, thereby accentuating the value of the product. The good or service might then be able to command a higher price

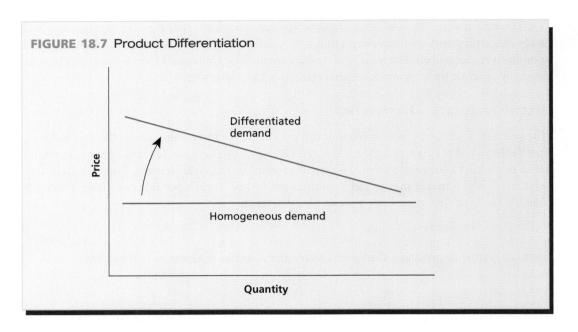

**FIGURE 18.7** Product Differentiation

in the marketplace. For example, status-oriented advertising may allow some retail clothing stores to command higher prices than others. The demand curve that faces a prestige store may be less responsive to price differences than that of a competitor without a quality reputation. The responsiveness to price differences is shown in Figure 18.8.

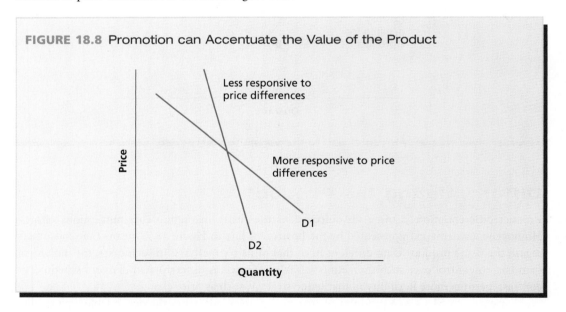

**FIGURE 18.8** Promotion can Accentuate the Value of the Product

## Stabilizing Sales

A company's sales are not uniform throughout the year. Fluctuations can occur for cyclical, seasonal, or other reasons. Reducing these variations is often an objective of the firm's marketing communications strategy.

Other objectives of stabilizing sales are to create brand loyalty and to increase repeat purchases. These advertising objectives are two of the most important purposes of promotional activity.

## Building Positive Corporate Image

A positive corporate image provides a great deal of assurance to potential and actual customers. A product may be chosen because of the perceived company image, and repeat purchases can also be enhanced when customers are satisfied that they are dealing with a good company. Thus, building a positive corporate image is another common communications objective that is often combined with other communication objectives.

## Producing Sales

In a limited number of situations, marketing communications are the direct cause of a sale. One example is a direct marketing campaign that offers a product for sale. This might be done through direct mail or the Internet. If consumers respond with orders, the cause-and-effect relationship between the message and the response is clear. TV, radio, and newspaper advertising that offers various items on sale can also bring a flow of purchasers. Note that producing sales is only one of the legitimate expectations for marketing communications, and is not considered the predominant one.

# ADVERTISING PLANNING

Advertising plans provide the framework for properly implementing marketing communications strategy. Advertising planning begins with effective research. Information from research allows management to make strategic decisions, which are then translated into tactical execution, budgeting, copywriting, scheduling, and the like. Finally, there must be some feedback mechanism for measuring the effectiveness of the advertising. The elements of advertising planning are shown in Figure 18.9.

There is a real need to follow a sequential process in making advertising decisions. Novice advertisers are often guilty of being overly concerned with the technical aspects of designing adver-

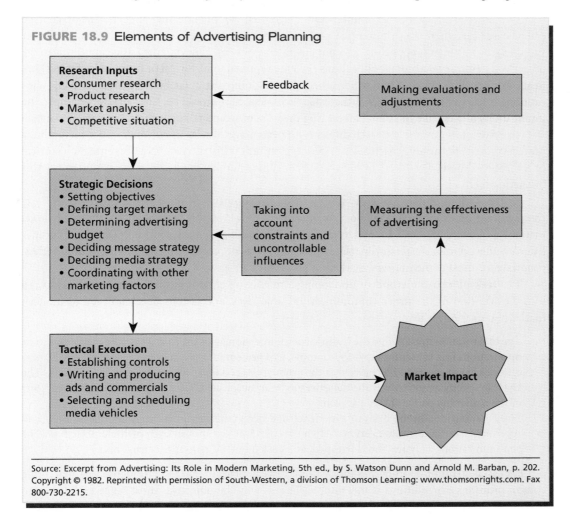

FIGURE 18.9 Elements of Advertising Planning

Source: Excerpt from Advertising: Its Role in Modern Marketing, 5th ed., by S. Watson Dunn and Arnold M. Barban, p. 202. Copyright © 1982. Reprinted with permission of South-Western, a division of Thomson Learning: www.thomsonrights.com. Fax 800-730-2215.

tisements while ignoring the more basic steps, such as market analysis. The type of advertisement that is employed in any particular situation is largely related to the planning phase of this process.

# BUDGETING FOR MARKETING COMMUNICATIONS EFFORTS

Marketing communications budgets can differ not only in amount but also in composition. Business-to-business marketers generally invest a larger proportion of their budgets in personal selling than in advertising, while the reverse is usually true of most consumer-products producers.

## How Much Should Be Spent on Marketing Communications?

Theoretically, the optimal method of determining how much to spend on marketing communications (known as a marketing communications budget) is to expand it until the cost of each additional increment equals the additional incremental revenue received. In other words, the most effective allocation procedure is to increase expenditures until each dollar of expense is matched by an additional dollar of profit. This procedure—called *marginal analysis*—results in the maximization of the input's productivity. The difficulty arises in identifying this optimal point. In practice, doing so is virtually impossible.

The common methods of determining a marketing communications budget are percentage of sales, fixed sum per unit, meeting competition, and the task-objective method.

*Percentage of sales* is a very common (but dangerous) way of allocating budgets. The percentage can be based on either past (for example, previous-year) or forecasted (current-year) sales. While the simplicity of this plan is appealing, it is not an effective way of achieving the basic communications objectives. Arbitrary percentage allocations (whether applied to historical or future sales figures) fail to allow the required flexibility. Furthermore, such reasoning is circular, because the advertising allocation is made to depend on sales, rather than vice versa, as it should be. Consider, for example, the implications of a decline in sales—advertising investment would fall just when it was needed most.

The *fixed sum per unit* approach differs from percentage of sales in only one respect: it applies a predetermined allocation to each sales or production unit. This also can be set on either a historical or a forecasted basis. Producers of high-value consumer durable goods, such as cars, often use this budgeting method.

Another traditional approach is simply to match competitors' outlays—in other words, *meet competition*—on either an absolute or a relative basis. However, this kind of approach usually leads to a status quo situation at best, with each company retaining its market share. Meeting the competition's budget does not necessarily relate to the objectives of promotion and, therefore, seems inappropriate for most contemporary marketing programs.

The **task-objective method** of developing a marketing communications budget is based on a sound evaluation of the firm's communications objectives, and is thus better attuned to modern marketing practices. It involves two sequential steps:

1. The organization must define the realistic communication goals the firm wants the marketing communications mix to accomplish—for example, a 25 percent increase in brand awareness, or a 10 percent rise in consumers who realize that the product has certain specific differentiating features. The key is to specify quantitatively the objectives to be accomplished. They then become an integral part of the marketing communications plan.
2. The organization, on the basis of experience and expert advice, must determine the amount and type of marketing communications activity required to accomplish each of these objectives. The communications activities thus identified, and costed out, determine the firm's budget.

A crucial assumption underlies the task-objective approach: that the productivity of marketing communications expenditures is measurable. That is why the objectives must be carefully chosen,

<div class="margin">

**task-objective method**

A sequential approach to allocating marketing communications budgets that involves two steps: (1) defining the realistic communication goals the firm wants the marketing communications mix to accomplish, and (2) determining the amount and type of marketing communications activity required to accomplish each of these objectives.

</div>

### CONSUMERS CAN AFFECT ADVERTISING

Bunny lovers have forced a major automotive company to withdraw an advertising campaign that depicts a domestic rabbit being released into a forest—an act they say would, in real life, have resulted in the animal's death.

Subaru's ad for its Forester SUV shows a mother and daughter apparently rescuing a cuddly rabbit from a classroom and releasing it into a wooded setting.

The problem with the ad, as bunny advocates across North America quickly and vociferously pointed out, is that the rabbit shown was clearly not a cottontail or wild rabbit, a breed capable of surviving in the wilderness. Rather, the fluffy grey-coloured animal with a white nose and white paws was a domestic rabbit, ill-equipped to survive for any amount of time on its own.

"We were horrified," said Margo DeMello, executive director of the House Rabbit Society, whose 10 000-strong membership aims to advocate and educate North Americans about rabbits. "That rabbit would have been savaged in no time ... He was being released almost certainly to his death."

But even the rabbit enthusiasts are amazed at how promptly their concerns were heeded.

"We're not an animal rights group or anything," said Ms. DeMello, from her home in Berkeley, California. "We rescue rabbits that have been abandoned and educate the public about rabbit care, so this doesn't fit into what we normally do."

She said what made the ad particularly troubling for so many of her group's members was that it came at a time when they are already dealing with so many cases of domestic bunnies being abandoned in the woods after families tire of them as Easter presents. Ms. DeMello's pets, Pammy and Jessie, are two such rescued bunnies.

www.houserabbits.com

"We really need to let people know that releasing domestic bunnies into the wild is not at all appropriate," she said.

The group's letter-writing campaign to Subaru last week used words such as "cruel" and "death sentence" to describe the scene that was being depicted.

In its response to the complaints, Mike Darling, the company's vice-president of marketing, explained that the advertising spot, called Outside the Box, aimed to show the admirable release of a wild cottontail.

"Unfortunately, the message yielded an unintended conclusion, that being a domestic rabbit was released into the wild," said Mr. Darling. "Critics were a relatively small but passionate group, and, quite frankly, we have other things to attend to and do not need the distraction."

In a letter to the House Rabbit Society, Mr. Darling said the company "has long been a friend of the environment and related causes" and in no way condones the release of domestic animals into the wild.

**This story shows that advertisers do listen to comments about their advertising. Can you think of current campaigns about which you might express your opinion to the advertiser?**

Source: Anne Marie Owens, "Doomed Bunnies, Sex, Violence Aren't Big Winners," *National Post*, June 17, 2002, p. 1. Reprinted with permission.

quantified, and coordinated with the rest of the marketing mix. Generally, an objective like "We wish to achieve a 5 percent increase in sales" is an ill-conceived marketing objective, because a sale is the culmination of the effects of *all* elements of the marketing mix. A more appropriate advertising objective might be "To make 30 percent of the target market aware of the facilities available at our health spa."

# MEASURING THE EFFECTIVENESS OF MARKETING COMMUNICATIONS

It is widely recognized that part of a firm's marketing communications effort is ineffective. John Wanamaker, a successful nineteenth-century retailer, once observed, "I know half the money I spend on advertising is wasted; but I can never find out which half."

Measuring the effectiveness of marketing communications is an extremely important research question, particularly among advertisers. Studies aimed at this measurement objective face several

**direct-sales results test**

A test that attempts to ascertain for each dollar of promotional outlay the corresponding increase in revenue.

major obstacles, among them the difficulty of isolating the effect of the marketing communications variable.

Most marketers would prefer to use a **direct-sales results test** to measure the effectiveness of marketing communications. Such a test attempts to ascertain for each dollar of promotional outlay the corresponding increase in revenue. The primary difficulty involves controlling the other variables that operate in the marketplace. A $1.5 million advertising campaign may be followed by an increase in sales of $20 million. However, this shift may have more to do with a sudden price hike by the firm's leading competitor than with the advertising expenditure. Therefore, advertisers are turning to establishing and assessing achievable, measurable objectives.

With the increasing sophistication of marketing analysts, analytical techniques, and computer-based marketing information systems, banks of historical data on marketing communications expenditures and their effects are being subjected to ever more scrutiny. More and more is being learned about measuring and evaluating the effects of marketing communications activity. While the technical literature in marketing reveals much of what is happening in this critical area, firms are reluctant to release much of this information. Not only do they wish to keep their proprietary information about how the market works to themselves for competitive reasons, but they do not want competitors to know the methods and decision routines used in planning marketing communications activity.

Other methods of assessing marketing communications effectiveness include inquiries about the product, about changes in attitudes toward the product, and about improvements in public knowledge and awareness. One indicator of probable advertising effectiveness is the elasticity or sensitivity of sales to marketing communications based on historical data concerning price, sales volume, and advertising expenditures.

It is difficult for the marketer to conduct research in a controlled environment like other disciplines can set up. The difficulty of isolating the effects of marketing communications causes many to abandon all attempts at measurement. Others, however, turn to indirect evaluation. These researchers concentrate on quantifiable factors, such as recall (how much is remembered about specific products or advertisements) and readership (the size and composition of the audience). But it remains difficult to relate these variables to sales. Does extensive ad readership actually lead to increased sales? Another problem is the high cost of research. To assess the effectiveness of marketing communications expenditures correctly may require a significant investment.

# THE VALUE OF MARKETING COMMUNICATIONS

Various aspects of marketing communications have often been the target of criticism. A selection of these includes the following:

- "Advertising contributes nothing to society."
- "Most advertisements and sales presentations insult my intelligence."
- "Promotion 'forces' consumers to buy products they cannot afford and do not need."
- "Advertising and selling are economic wastes."
- "Salespeople and advertisers are usually unethical."

Consumers, public officials, and marketers agree that all too often many of these complaints are true. Some salespeople do use unethical sales tactics. Some product advertising is directed at consumer groups that can least afford to purchase the particular item. Many television commercials are banal and annoying.

While such components of the marketing communications mix as advertising can certainly be criticized on many counts, it is important to remember that marketing communications play a crucial role in modern society. This point is best explained by looking at the importance of marketing communications on the business, economic, and social levels.

## Business and Nonprofit Enterprise Importance

Marketing communications is essential for both profit and nonprofit organizations, both large and small. The long-term rise in outlays for advertising and other communications elements is well documented and certainly attests to management's faith in this element of the marketing communications mix. It is difficult to conceive of an enterprise that does not attempt to promote its goods or services in some way or another. Most modern institutions simply cannot survive in the long run without communicating with their market.

Nonbusiness enterprises also recognize the importance of this variable. The Canadian government is consistently one of the largest advertisers in Canada, promoting many programs and concepts. Religious organizations have also acknowledged the importance of promoting what they do. Even labour organizations have used marketing communications channels to make their viewpoints known to the public at large. In fact, advertising now plays a larger role in nonprofit organizations than ever before.

## Economic Importance

Advertising has assumed a degree of economic importance, if for no other reason than that it is an activity that employs thousands of people. More importantly, however, effective advertising has allowed society to derive the benefits of learning about new products and new ways of doing things. This can set many economic activities into motion. Advertising creates awareness around the world and stimulates global trade.

Marketing communications strategies that increase the number of units sold permit economies in the production process, thereby lowering the production costs assigned to each unit of output. Lower consumer prices then allow these products to be available to more people. Similarly, advertising subsidizes the informational content of newspapers and the broadcast media. In short, advertising pays for many of the enjoyable entertainment and educational aspects of contemporary life, as well as lowers product costs.

## Social Importance

Criticism such as "Most advertising messages are tasteless" and "Advertising contributes nothing to society" disregard the foregoing economic facts. Furthermore, they ignore the fact that no commonly accepted set of standards or priorities exists within our social framework. We live in a varied economy that is characterized by consumer segments with differing needs, wants, and aspirations. What is tasteless to one group may be quite informative to another. Advertising is faced with an "averaging" problem that escapes many of its critics. The one generally accepted standard in a market society is freedom of choice for the consumer. Consumer buying decisions eventually determine what is acceptable practice in the marketplace.

**Dramatizing the career possibilities generated from an education at Ryerson.**

Advertising has become an important factor in the campaigns to achieve such socially oriented objectives as stopping smoking, promoting family planning, encouraging physical fitness, eliminating drug abuse, and supporting countless benevolent causes. Advertising performs an informative and educational task that makes it extremely important in modern society. As with everything else in life, it is how one uses advertising, not advertising itself, that can be criticized.

## SUMMARY

Today it is recognized that the vast array of communications alternatives should be integrated to create the greatest impact. Integrated marketing communications is a comprehensive marketing communications plan that takes into consideration all the communication disciplines being used and combines them to provide clarity, consistency, and maximum communications impact.

A generalized model of the communications process includes the following elements: sender, encoding, transfer mechanism, decoding, and receiver. The marketing communications mix comprises the following elements: personal selling and nonpersonal communication (which comprises advertising, sales promotion, public relations, and publicity).

The factors that influence the use of marketing communications mix elements are the nature of the market, nature of the product, product's stage in the product life cycle, price, and funds available.

A pulling strategy is a promotional effort by the seller to stimulate final-user demand, which then exerts pressure on the distribution channel. A pushing strategy is the promotion of the product first to the members of the marketing channel, who then participate in its promotion to the final user.

Six different types of objectives are the focus of different marketing communications strategies: (1) to provide information, (2) to increase demand, (3) to differentiate the product, (4) to accentuate the value of the product, (5) to stabilize sales, and (6) to produce sales. The last objective is significant, but is not the most important one for most companies.

The common methods of determining the amount of money to be spent on marketing communications are percentage of sales, fixed sum per unit, meeting competition, and the task-objective method.

Marketing communications is sometimes maligned. However, three categories of contributions are made by this part of the marketing mix: business importance, economic importance, and social importance.

## KEY TERMS

advertising, p. 452
direct-sales results test, p. 464
integrated marketing
   communications (IMC), p. 449
marketing communications, p. 448
marketing communications mix, p. 451
personal selling, p. 451

point-of-purchase communications, p. 453
public relations, p. 453
pulling strategy, p. 455
pushing strategy, p. 456
sales promotion, p. 453
sponsorship marketing, p. 453
task-objective method, p. 462

## INTERACTIVE SUMMARY AND DISCUSSION QUESTIONS

**1.** A generalized model of the communications process includes the following elements: sender, encoding, transfer mechanism, decoding, and receiver. Using this model, explain how a sales presentation could be structured to make it work better. Using this model, show how a sales presentation could become ineffective.

2. The marketing communications mix comprises the following elements: personal selling and non-personal communication (which comprises advertising, sales promotion, public relations, and publicity). Using Xerox copiers as an example, propose a realistic communications mix, and explain how it should blend with the rest of the marketing mix.

3. The factors that influence the use of marketing communications mix elements are the nature of the market, nature of the product, product's stage in the product life cycle, price, and funds available. If CD players are in the late growth stage of the product life cycle, what would be an appropriate type of advertising message for a CD player manufacturer?

4. A pulling strategy is a promotional effort by the seller to stimulate final-user demand, which then exerts pressure on the distribution channel. A pushing strategy is the promotion of the product first to the members of the marketing channel, who then participate in its promotion to the final user. Would you use a pushing strategy for introducing a new line of drinks that would compete with products such as Clearly Canadian? Explain.

5. Six different types of objectives are the focus of different marketing communications strategies: (1) to provide information, (2) to increase demand, (3) to differentiate the product, (4) to accentuate the value of the product, (5) to stabilize sales, and (6) to produce sales. Give examples of situations in which each type of objective would be appropriate.

6. Explain the effects of advertising being used to shift the demand curve to the right.

7. The common methods of determining the amount of money to be spent on marketing communications are percentage of sales, fixed sum per unit, meeting competition, and the task-objective method. Discuss the pros and cons of the percentage-of-sales method.

8. A new store that features specialty music geared to the 35–45 age group is about to open. Describe exactly how the store could establish a communications budget using the task-objective method.

9. Marketing communications is sometimes maligned. However, three categories of contributions are made by this part of the marketing mix: business importance, economic importance, and social importance. Defend the proposition that marketing communications offers a significant social contribution.

10. Select two products that are widely advertised. Find advertisements for these products in the traditional media and on the Web. What conclusions can you make about Web advertising?

# Case

## 'Made in Canada' Label

In June 2002 the Canadian government proposed an unprecedented five-year $8.1 billion agriculture package to overhaul the way governments support farmers.

The policy was designed to replace year-to-year emergency bailouts with a strategy to ensure the long-term financial survival of farms.

A large portion of the spending was intended to make Canada the first country to market its food production around the world as environmentally friendly and unimpeachably safe to human health. The government hoped that by branding 'Made in Canada' food as the highest quality, farmers will draw premium prices and win new markets among increasingly discerning consumers. Sixty percent of Canadian agricultural products are exported to the United States. Under the plan, producers will participate in labeling, certification, and tracing regimes, that will allow consumers to track a piece of meat or produce to a farm, and assure themselves the farming procedures met strict standards.

Some 85 percent of the cost will be split 60–40 by the federal and provincial governments and follows a year of consultation with farmers and the provinces.

The federal contribution of $3.4 billion over five years was expected to be matched by a provincial share of $2.9 billion to fund promotion of food safety, environmental stewardship, scientific research, and spending on skills training and new technologies.

The government will support farmers looking for innovative uses of crops, such as turning plants into clean fuels. Farmers seeking to acquire business skills in finance and marketing will also receive support.

The five-plank Agriculture Policy Framework was aimed at ending decades of crisis management, which saw the government topping up more than $1 billion in annual agriculture spending.

### You Be the Marketer

1. Evaluate the strategy of using advertising to create a brand preference for Canadian agricultural products.
2. What type of advertising campaign might be appropriate for this purpose?
3. What type of advertising media should be used?
4. Can they afford the media you propose?
5. Do you know of other countries that have followed this advertising approach?

Source: Excerpted from Luiza Chwialkowska, "Vanclief to Unveil Plan for Long-term Survival," *National Post*, June 20, 2002, p. A14. Reprinted with permission.

An ad designed to increase awareness, as well as newsstand sales, of Canadian magazines.

## Chapter 19

# INTEGRATED MARKETING COMMUNICATIONS APPLICATIONS

## CHAPTER OBJECTIVES

After reading and studying this chapter, you should be able to

1. Identify the categories of advertisements.
2. Identify and discuss the main advertising media.
3. Describe the process of creating an advertisement.
4. Explain public relations and its functions.
5. Discuss sales promotion and its various elements.
6. Classify the three basic types of selling.
7. Outline the seven steps in the sales process.
8. Specify the functions of sales management.

**W**hat are the elements of a good advertising campaign? The program developed by the Canadian Magazine Publishers Association is a good example of an unusual, but creative approach. As strange as it sounds the "Canadian Mountain Kangaroo" and a team of sled-pulling poodles are two of the animal anomalies featured in their $5.5-million marketing effort.

Featuring the tag line "It's not the same if it's not Canadian," the French- and English-language "Genuine Article" campaign features ads in 185 magazines and on leading specialty channels, including Bravo!, WTN, and HGTV. The four-month campaign also features a direct mail component and a newsstand promotion with Coca-Cola and Hachette Distribution Services (HDS), which operates the magazine retail stores—the Great Canadian News Company, Maison de la Presse, and the airport Relay Stores.

The ads were created by Toronto advertising agency Shop One company (formerly Ranscombe & Co.), while Tattoo Direct + Digital is handling the DM component—a discounted "order two, get one free" subscription offer being sent to one million Canadian households. Tattoo is also involved in the newsstand promotion, which features backer cards and window posters in about 1500 retail outlets across the country.

"It's a good solid marketing campaign," says CMPA president Mark Jamison, calling it "the most comprehensive campaign ever undertaken by Canadian publishers. The industry's buying in big time."

Each of the ads in the campaign features an unusual variation on a typically Canadian theme. For example, the print ad "Sled Poodles" depicts a dogsled being pulled by a group of reluctant French poodles instead of the traditional huskies.

One of the TV ads shows Animal Kingdom-type documentary footage of the "Canadian Mountain Kangaroo," which is referred to as the country's "largest big-game animal," while the other spot matches the audio play-by-play of Paul Henderson's famous goal against the Soviet Union in the 1972 Summit Series with video footage of soccer-playing elephants.

All of the ads direct people to the "Genuine Article" Web site (www.genuinearticle.ca), where they can find content and subscription information for more than 300 Canadian magazines.

Jamison says the new campaign's objectives include increasing awareness, as well as newsstand and subscription sales, of Canadian magazines and raising the profile of Canadian magazines among advertisers and creatives.

First conceived about two years ago, the campaign was precipitated by "the overwhelming impact foreign titles have on the Canadian market," explains Jamison. "Canadians will buy Canadian magazines if they can find them, because they're about them, for them and by them. The issue has always been, where can they get their hands on them?"

Participating magazines will also display an icon resembling a wax seal and containing the phrase "genuine article" on their covers. At Selected HDS retail outlets (about 250), people purchasing magazines bearing this "seal" will receive a free bottle of Coca-Cola's new Diet Coke with Lemon.

**The extensive use of different types of advertising media is particularly noteworthy in this advertising effort. The campaign also does a nice job of incorporating and making use of the Internet, which is used as a source of considerable extra information.**

Source: Adapted from Chris Powell, "CMPA Launches $5.5M Ad Effort," *Marketing Magazine*, April 2002, p. 4. Reprinted with permission of *Marketing Magazine*.

www.cmpa.ca

# INTRODUCTION

Time is money. Consider the advertising industry: major advertisers routinely spend thousands of dollars for 30 or 60 seconds of air time. Advertisers want to convince you that their car will make your driving easier, their clothes will make you more attractive, and they offer many other ways to improve your whole life. They buy over $9 billion worth of advertising each year in this process. This includes spending on television (the number one medium by sales), radio, newspapers, magazines, billboards, telephone directories, direct mail, Web advertising, and many other media.

Marketing communications efforts constantly change and evolve. With the advent of the Internet, a new and important advertising medium has emerged. The opening story illustrates how advertising can be used in many types of media including on the Internet. Advertising is becoming an integral part of Internet activity, just as it is of television, newspapers, radio, and so on. The range of marketing communications options is vast.

The previous chapter introduced the topic of marketing communications strategy, communication theory and the communications process, the marketing communications mix, and the process of advertising planning. You now know that the objectives of marketing communications are to provide information, stimulate demand, differentiate the product, accentuate the value of the product, stabilize sales, or, in some cases, actually produce sales. This chapter will discuss the major advertising media and illustrate the main marketing communications applications: advertising, publicity, sales promotion, and personal selling.

# ADVERTISING

If you wanted to be the next prime minister of Canada, you would need to communicate with every possible voting Canadian. If you invented a new computer game and went into business to sell it, your chances of success would be slim without informing and persuading children and young people of its uniqueness. In both these situations you would discover, as have countless others, that you would need to use advertising to communicate with buyers or voters. In the previous chapter, advertising was defined as paid nonpersonal communication through various media by business firms, nonprofit organizations, and individuals who are in some way identified with the advertising message and who hope to inform or persuade members of a particular audience.

Today's widespread markets make advertising an important part of business. Since the end of World War II, advertising and related expenditures have risen faster than gross domestic product and most other economic indicators. Furthermore, about 45 500 people were employed in advertising in 1998, according to the Statistics Canada Web site.

Three advertisers—General Motors of Canada, BCE Inc., and the government of Canada—spent more than $89 million each for advertising in 1998.[1] It is particularly noteworthy that federal and provincial governments are such a major force in Canadian advertising. The federal government more than doubled its total spending since 1993. Total Canadian advertising media expenditures in 2000 were about $10.3 billion. This means that about $330 is spent on advertising each year for every person in Canada.

When considered on a sector basis, retail, automotive, and business equipment and services are the three biggest advertising spenders. Table 19.1 ranks the top ten industry sector advertisers in Canada. When the two categories of automotive advertising are combined, the automotive industry becomes the largest advertiser.

Advertising expenditures as a proportion of sales vary among industries and companies. Wide differences exist among industries. Advertising spending can range from 0.2 percent (as is the case with iron and steel foundries) to more than 7 percent of sales (as in the soap and detergent industry). Cosmetics companies are often cited as an example of firms that spend a high percentage of their funds on advertising and promotion.

www.statcan.ca/english/
Pgdb/Economy/Finance/
fin11.htm

www.gmcanada.com

**TABLE 19.1** The Top Ten Advertising Sectors in Canada, 2001

| RANK | SECTOR | EXPENDITURES ($) |
|------|--------|------------------|
| 1 | Retail | 997 261 000 |
| 2 | Automotive: Cars; Mini Vans; Trucks; Vans; Dealer | 918 069 000 |
| 3 | Food | 367 684 000 |
| 4 | Entertainment | 350 814 000 |
| 5 | Financial Services and Insurance Services | 319 020 000 |
| 6 | Local Automotive Dealer Advertising | 318 679 000 |
| 7 | Travel and Transportation | 241 485 000 |
| 8 | Restaurants and Catering Services | 233 162 000 |
| 9 | Telecommunications | 212 010 000 |
| 10 | Media | 202 364 000 |

Source: Copyright © Nielsen Media Research Limited, 2002. Reprinted by permission.

Sophisticated advertisers increasingly depend on research to understand the markets that they are attempting to reach. Originally, advertising research dealt primarily with media selection and the product. Then, advertisers became increasingly concerned with aiming their messages more specifically through determining the appropriate demographics (such characteristics as the age, gender, and income level of potential buyers). Now, understanding consumer behaviour has become an important aspect of advertising strategy. As discussed in Chapter 3, psychographics can be useful in describing potential markets for advertising appeals. Increased knowledge of such factors as lifestyle and personal attitudes has led to improved advertising decisions.

The emergence of the marketing concept, with its emphasis on a company-wide consumer orientation, saw advertising take on an expanded role as marketing communications assumed greater importance in business. Advertising provides an efficient, inexpensive, and fast method of reaching consumers. Its extensive use now rivals that of personal selling. Advertising has become a key ingredient in effectively implementing the marketing concept.

## The Advertising Campaign: Integrated Marketing Communications

A company that develops a marketing communications strategy often does not restrict its plan to advertising alone. Just as a military campaign combines many elements in a strategic effort to meet objectives, the elements of the communications mix are blended to provide maximum consumer impact. As an example of a complete advertising campaign, suppose that we are planning an advertising campaign for the opening of a new women's fashion store in downtown Calgary.

To announce the opening of the new store, we could use a variety of advertising media, including local magazines, public transit posters, billboards, radio, newspapers, direct mail, and public relations. We might arrange for Calgary issues of *Flare* and

## THE ROOTS OF MARKETING

### SOME EARLY ADVERTISING METHODS

Some form of advertising aimed at boosting product sales has probably existed since the development of the exchange process.[2] Most early advertising was vocal. Criers and hawkers sold various products, made public announcements, and chanted advertising slogans like this one (now familiar to many as a nursery rhyme):

One-a-penny, two-a-penny, hot-cross buns
One-a-penny, two for tuppence, hot-cross buns

Signs were also used in early advertising. Most were symbolic and identified products and services. In Rome, a goat signified a dairy; a mule driving a mill, a bakery; a boy being whipped, a school.

Later, the development of the printing press greatly expanded advertising's capability. A 1710 advertisement in the *Spectator* billed one tooth powder as "the Incomparable Powder for cleaning of Teeth, which has given great satisfaction to most of the Nobility and Gentry in England."

THREE THINGS I'VE LEARNED
*Martin Brodeur*

1: Keep your ego in check.

2: Know your opponents.

3: Never go up a size in the off-season.

Martin Brodeur, goaltender for the New Jersey Devils, is wearing Canali. In appreciation of his appearance here, a donation has been made on Mr. Brodeur's behalf to the Martin Brodeur Centre. For our complete interview with Martin Brodeur, visit www.harryrosen.com.

**HARRY ROSEN**

MAKE A STATEMENT.

MONTREAL • OTTAWA • TORONTO • WINNIPEG • CALGARY • EDMONTON • VANCOUVER • www.harryrosen.com

A marketing communications strategy is often not restricted to advertising alone. In this ad for Harry Rosen, consumers are told that a charitable donation has been made in appreciation of Martin Brodeur's participation. They are also invited to read an interview with Martin Brodeur on the company's Web site.

## THE CANADIAN MARKETPLACE

### ADVERTISING INDUSTRY JARGON

**Above-the-Line** Advertising that uses catchy, creative techniques and often appeals to the subconscious.

**AIDA** Attention, interest, desire, and action: the classic model of how advertising works.

**AM Drive, PM Drive** Radio time slots.

**Below-the-Line** Less creative advertising, such as sales promotions and direct marketing.

**Bounce Back** Any ad campaign that asks you to fill in a personal information card and send it back.

**Cost per Thousand (CPM)** The cost, per 1000 people reached, of buying advertising space in a given medium.

**Full-Service Agency** An advertising agency that handles all aspects of the advertising process, from planning to placement. May handle other aspects of marketing communication and public relations as well.

**HH Share** The percentage of total households that own a TV or radio and are tuned in to a program.

**In-Home** Advertising on broadcast and cable television and the Internet.

**Interstitial Ad** An ad that pops up between loading Internet pages.

**Market Blitz** A short but broad campaign that uses a lot of repetition over different advertising media.

**Narrowcasting** Using a broadcast medium to appeal to audiences with special interests.

**Out-of-Home** Radio and outdoor advertising.

**Premium** An item offered free or at a low price as an incentive to purchase the advertised product or service.

**Skyscraper Ad** Tall vertical Internet ad.

**Tombstone Ad** An ad without pictures.

**Vertical Publications** Publications whose editorial content deals with the interests of a specific industry, such as Infectious Wastes News.

*Maclean's* to include special sections with a mix of ads and "advertorials" (advertisements that look like editorials). Radio stations could be used first for "teaser" ads, which are designed to stimulate interest but not reveal the sponsor, and then for "launch" or opening ads. Furthermore, the sales staff could be encouraged to verbally emphasize the special appeals chosen for the campaign.

In addition, we could send a direct mailing to 20 000 households that have demographic characteristics approximating our target market. Moreover, we could establish a Web site that contains up-to-the minute reports on fashion trends, and has links to selected fashion magazines and other sites of interest to the fashion-conscious woman. This Web site would be promoted in our advertisements.

Next, we could design a distinctive and eye-catching shopping bag that customers will be proud to carry their purchases in. Finally, in order to get some free media publicity, we could invite the mayor, a group of dignitaries, and the media to a ribbon-cutting ceremony followed by a reception.

## Creating an Advertisement

A major step in the advertising process is developing and preparing an advertisement. As discussed in the previous chapter the process is as shown in Figure 19.1.

The advertisement should flow logically from this carefully executed strategic process.

This step should thus be a complementary part of the marketing mix, with its role in total marketing strategy carefully determined. For example, a reminder-oriented advertising campaign would not be the best way to introduce a new product. In addition, major factors to consider when preparing an advertisement are its creativity, its continuity with past advertisements, and possibly its association with other company products.

What should an advertisement accomplish? Regardless of the exact appeal that is chosen, an ad should (1) gain attention and interest, (2) inform or persuade, and (3) eventually lead to buying action.

Gaining attention should be productive. That is, the reason for gaining consumers' attention should be to instill some recall of the product. Consider the case of The Gillette Company, which had a chimpanzee shave a man's face in a commercial. After tests in two cities, one Gillette man observed, "Lots of people remembered the chimp, but hardly anyone remembered our product. There was fantastic interest in the monkey, but no payoff for Gillette."[3] The advertisement gained the audience's attention, but it failed to lead to buying action. An ad that fails to gain and hold the receiver's attention is ineffective.

Together, information and persuasion are the second factor to consider when creating an advertisement. For example, insurance ads typically specify the features of the policy and may use testimonials to persuade prospects.

www.gillette.com

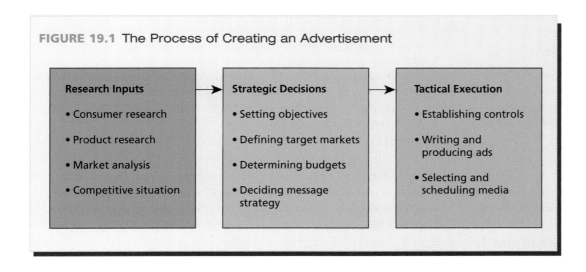

FIGURE 19.1 The Process of Creating an Advertisement

| Research Inputs | Strategic Decisions | Tactical Execution |
|---|---|---|
| • Consumer research | • Setting objectives | • Establishing controls |
| • Product research | • Defining target markets | • Writing and producing ads |
| • Market analysis | • Determining budgets | • Selecting and scheduling media |
| • Competitive situation | • Deciding message strategy | |

Stimulating buying action is often difficult, however, since an advertisement cannot actually close a sale. Nevertheless, if the first steps have been accomplished, the advertising has likely been worthwhile. Too many advertisers fail to suggest how receivers of the message can buy the product if they so desire.

## Categories of Advertisements

www.coca-cola.com

www.pepsiworld.com

www.mcdonalds.com

There are two basic types of advertisements: product and institutional. Product advertising can be subdivided into informative, persuasive, and reminder-oriented categories.

**Product advertising** deals with the nonpersonal selling of a particular good or service. It is the type we normally think of when the subject of advertising comes up. **Institutional advertising**, by contrast, is concerned with promoting a concept, idea, or philosophy, or the goodwill of an industry, company, or organization. It is often closely related to the public relations function of the enterprise.

### Informative Product Advertising

All advertising seeks to influence the audience, as does any type of communication. **Informative product advertising** seeks to develop demand through presenting factual information on the attributes of the product or service. For example, an advertisement for a new hydrogen fuel cell car would attempt to persuade through citing the various unique product or service features of that car, as well as providing assurances of satisfaction. Informative product advertising tends to be used in promoting new products, to announce their availability and characteristics that will satisfy needs. Thus it is often seen in the introductory stages of the product life cycle.

### Persuasive Product Advertising

In **persuasive product advertising**, the emphasis is on using words or images to try to create an image for a product and to influence attitudes about it. In contrast to informative product advertising, this type of advertising contains little objective information. Coca-Cola and Pepsi use persuasive techniques in their lifestyle advertisements featuring a group of happy people enjoying the product. Persuasive advertising is generally used more in the growth and maturity stages of the product life cycle.

### Reminder-Oriented Product Advertising

The goal of **reminder-oriented product advertising** is to reinforce previous promotional activity by keeping the product or service name in front of the public. It is used in the maturity period as well as throughout the decline phase of the product life cycle. An example of a reminder-oriented advertising campaign is Maytag's lonely service repairman series. The signs on the boards of hockey arenas are other examples of reminder-oriented advertising. Figure 19.2 illustrates the general relationship between the type of advertising and the stage of the life cycle.

### Retail Advertising

Retail advertising is the advertising done by stores that sell goods or services directly to consumers. Retail advertising accounts for a sizable portion of total advertising expenditures. Supermarkets advertise weekly specials, restaurants and fast-food chains promote the quality of their products, and lawyers advertise such services as handling accident claims.

The quality of retail advertising varies greatly. Some, like that of McDonald's, is created by professionals and generally follows the procedures described previously. Other retail advertising, like much local automobile dealer advertising, appears to be slapped together by rank amateurs. Because retail advertising is frequently prepared without the benefit of professional advertising experience or adequate research, there is considerable scope for improving the effectiveness of such advertising.

One aspect of advertising that involves a retailer–manufacturer relationship is **cooperative advertising**. This involves the sharing of advertising costs between the retailer and the manufacturer.

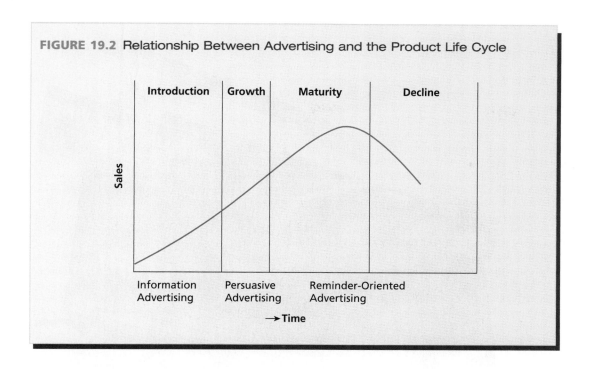

**FIGURE 19.2** Relationship Between Advertising and the Product Life Cycle

For example, Maple Leaf Foods may pay 50 percent of the cost of a 50 cm$^2$ area of a supermarket chain's weekly newspaper ad that features one or more of Maple Leaf's products.

Cooperative advertising benefits both retailer and manufacturer. It permits the retailer to secure additional advertising that it would not otherwise have. The manufacturer benefits from having retailers share in advertising costs. In addition, retailers that have invested in the advertisement will not only carry the manufacturer's product but also try to be sure of having enough in stock to satisfy demand.

### Institutional Advertising

As mentioned earlier, institutional advertising seeks to increase public knowledge of a concept, idea, philosophy, industry, or company. For example, egg marketers have run a series of advertisements on the desirability of eating eggs. Similarly, the dairy industry has extolled the value of butter through a long-running series of advertisements. When the oil industry was experiencing some unfavourable publicity, it decided that it had a positive story to tell. It increased its advertising budget to educate the public about the industry's contributions to society. Other firms, such as Volvo, have continuously advertised their innovativeness and reliability.

## Techniques for Delivering Advertising Messages

Advertising messages are delivered using many classic techniques. The structure of the message; the use of various appeals, such as humour, sex, and fear; and the use of comparative advertising are examples.

### Structure

Since readers tend to skim advertising, a number of subheadings that summarize the entire message are usually an advantage. Because of many competing stimuli, it is necessary to attract the audience's attention. Bold headlines, colour, sound effects, louder sound during a television commercial, and unusual images are only a few of the methods used by advertisers.

The LCBO, in partnership with Mothers Against Drunk Driving (MADD) Canada, recently unveiled a three-dimensional (3-D) billboard with an actual crashed car and the message "Drinking and Driving is no Accident".

## Use of Humour, Sex, and Fear

Most people say they love humour in advertising, and many think that all advertisements should use this technique. Unfortunately, with advertising, it is not that simple. Even advertising humour classics, such as those developed by Alka Seltzer a few years ago, failed. Humour must not detract from the central message the advertiser wishes to deliver. Also, many attempts at humour in advertising are not that funny. The bottom line in advertising is to communicate the advertiser's message.

In order to gain attention, some advertisers use sexual images. It is now believed that unless such images are used in a setting that is natural to the product, this approach does not help. Furthermore, society has become resistant to advertisers who seem to be exploiting people in their advertising. For example, women's groups have objected to the brewing industry about their thinly disguised sex/lifestyle ads. A classic longitudinal study of the effects of erotic content on brand recall showed that as erotic content increases, the probability of people correctly recalling the associated brand decreases.[4]

Fear is another technique used in advertising. Advertisers sometimes appeal to people's fear of social stigma in their ads for deodorants, breath sweeteners, and dandruff treatments. Antidrinking advertisements showing powerful images of fatal car crashes have been created to limit drinking by young people. Life insurance companies sometimes use the fear of dying or of leaving loved ones uncared for in their advertising appeals. Research has shown that fear appeals can be effective unless the appeal is so strong that individuals psychologically repress the message because it disturbs them too much. A very important consideration is to determine what the target audience actually fears. Car crash pictures may not seem personally relevant unless a young driver knows someone who has suffered from a major accident. And pictures of a lung cancer operation may be less threatening to a young person than a message showing that smokers have trouble dating.

## SEX, VIOLENCE AREN'T BIG WINNERS

Sex apparently doesn't sell, a new study says.

Researchers have found that people who watched violent or sexually explicit programs on television were far less likely to remember the contents of commercials than those who watched more neutral programming.

The study, published in the latest issue of the *Journal of Applied Psychology*, says people who viewed sexual or violent shows recalled 67 percent less than others when quizzed about brand names immediately after watching TV and 60 percent less than others when they were asked again a day later. The experiment, involving 324 adults, was meant to reflect "average North American TV viewers," and randomly assigned them to watch either sexual, violent, or neutral programming.

In each session, viewers were exposed to the same nine advertisements, peddling products ranging from breakfast cereal to laundry detergent, and then quizzed about the brand names they recalled.

Only those who had watched the neutral programming could demonstrate a significant recall of the advertised products, the researchers found.

The sexual and violent programming impaired memory for men and women of all ages, regardless of whether they liked programs containing sex and violence, the study said.

"It flies in the face of the belief that sex sells," said Brad Bushman, a psychology professor at Iowa State University who led the research team.

"If I were an advertiser, it would certainly change my mind about what kinds of shows I sponsor."

He said that although the findings may come as a surprise to advertisers, they were not particularly surprising to the research team, which had done previous work into how violent programming affects memory.

"The same reason that violence impairs memory should also apply to sex—it is the same kind of physiological arousal that decreases attention," said Dr. Bushman.

Put simply, sex and violence tend to consume all of the viewer's attention, leaving little or no room for retaining other information, such as the content of commercials.

Another possibility, the study suggests, is that sexual and violent programs prompt the viewer to have sexual and violent thoughts, which in turn reduces the chance that they will remember anything about the commercials.

**Do you agree with these conclusions?**

Source: Anne Marie Owens, "Sex, Violence Aren't Big Winners," *National Post*, June 17, 2002. Reprinted with permission.

## Comparative Advertising

**Comparative advertising** makes direct promotional comparisons with competitive brands. The strategy is best employed by firms that do not lead the market.

Companies used to be afraid to mention the name of their competitor's product because that was thought to be a "free" reminder about that product, sometimes going to ridiculous lengths. For example, a salesperson would refer only to "that other product" or use some other euphemism. Everyone listening immediately substituted the competing brand for the euphemism.

This is seen both in personal selling and in advertising. Many advertisers are now choosing to compare their products directly with those of competitors. The comparison can sometimes take the form of an attack on the competition.

Comparative advertising can be challenged in the courts, as was the case when Robin Hood Multifoods compared a pie crust made with its shortening to one made with Maple Leaf Foods Inc. Tenderflake and Gainsborough lard. The court ordered Robin Hood to pull its ads because they would "have the effect of diminishing Maple Leaf's reputation and lead to a loss of goodwill as well. They tend to create the impression that [Maple Leaf's] product will be a misshapen pie and not a normal pie."[5]

Advertisers sometimes get carried away using the comparative approach. During the 1993 federal election campaign, the Conservatives used an advertisement emphasizing Jean Chrétien's partially paralyzed mouth. The outcry among all Canadians caused the ad to be pulled after only one day.

**comparative advertising**
Advertising that makes direct promotional comparisons with competitive brands.

www.robinhood.com

www.mapleleaf.com

Marketers who contemplate using comparative advertising should ensure that they can prove their claims, because such advertising has the potential of producing lawsuits. From a long-run perspective, advertisers need to decide whether a more solid product and company image can be created with a message devoted to communicating about and positioning a product in its own right, or by comparing the product with others.

These are a few examples of the many technical issues in creating advertising messages. Creating messages is serious business—thousands of messages are wasted every day because advertisers use worn-out phrases and unimaginative messages.

Table 19.2 provides a summary of important points made by the famous William Bernbach concerning advertising messages.

## Using Celebrities to Promote the Company and Its Products

Even though Wayne Gretzky has retired, his name continues to be associated with several different products. Some of the corporate names that have sought his endorsement are the Hudson's Bay Co., Post Cereals, McDonald's, Canadian Imperial Bank of Commerce, Zurich Financial Services Group, Tylenol, and Campbell Soup. Many companies believe that **celebrity marketing**—having celebrities lend their name and influence to the promotion of a product—is worth the cost of paying the celebrity for his or her endorsement of the product. These marketers feel that there will be a positive association between the public acceptance of the celebrity and the acceptance of their product. Advertisers hope that the characteristics celebrities represent—beauty, courage, talent, athletic ability, and sex appeal—will create a positive image for their brand. If consumers like the celebrity, they may like the brand. Well-liked Bill Cosby is perfect for endorsing Jell-O.

**celebrity marketing**

Having celebrities lend their name and influence to the promotion of a product.

---

**TABLE 19.2** Important Points about Advertising Messages

1. Crash through the wall! Not to be different is virtually suicide.
2. Impressions outweigh numbers.
   - Nobody counts the number of ads you show, they just remember the impressions you make.
   - Make your ad so provocative, so artful, that it is many times more effective than your competitors'.
3. Create personality.
   - Differentiate your ad from the competition's, and produce individuality.
4. Don't waste the reader's time.
   - Don't just get attention with an easy, irrelevant gimmick. Make sure the attention-getting element stems from your product.
5. Make your ads memorable.

Source: Adapted from William Bernbach, address to Western Region Annual Meeting, American Association of Advertising Agencies, Pebble Beach, CA, November 13, 1965.

While the risk is perhaps not too great, if the celebrity falls out of favour, the company has to try to quickly dissociate itself from that person. This happened to Hertz when O.J. Simpson was accused of murdering his ex-wife.

Celebrity marketing can be expensive. Nora beverages of Mirabel, Quebec, uses role model marketing instead. **Role model marketing** associates a product with the positive perception of a type of individual or a role. Nora sells its Naya brand bottled water in almost 3000 vending machines across North America. In one campaign, it placed 40 machines along Los Angeles County beaches—an unusual locale for the units. The company also donated $185 000 to help operate these beaches. In exchange, the company was allowed to advertise on lifeguard stands ("Naya—made when the world was still pure") and put its logo on the time and temperature blackboards. The role model association here was with 150 healthy-looking lifeguards. Lifeguards are held in high esteem—they take care of their bodies, and it is assumed that they are concerned about nutrition.[6] As the cost of celebrity marketing increases and the availability of suitable celebrities decreases, role model marketing is a useful alternative.

A version of role model marketing is known as **buzz marketing**. In this case, a marketer gives a significant person in a social system a product to use. The hope is that others will see and want to buy the product. For example, the maker of a special brand of athletic shoes has a designated representative who goes to high school and college basketball games to find outstanding players. These players are then interviewed to determine whether they have a pleasant outgoing personality. Those that are selected are given a pair of the latest shoes and asked to wear them extensively.

**role model marketing**
Marketing technique that associates a product with the positive perception of a type of individual or a role.

**buzz marketing**
Giving a significant person in a social system a product to use in the hope that others will see and want to buy the product.

## Media Selection

One of the interesting phenomena in the world of high-tech recorded music is the small but significant group of consumers who prefer vinyl records to CDs. They argue that the music on vinyl is "warmer" and not as "antiseptic" as on CDs. Suppose you want to advertise to these people. A mass television campaign might reach them, but you would waste your message on most of the audience. The proper approach would be to find an advertising medium that is more focused on that group. Perhaps you could reach them through an audiophile magazine, or through the Internet.

One of the most important decisions in developing an advertising strategy is media selection. A mistake at this point can cost a company literally millions of dollars in ineffectual advertising. Media strategy must achieve the communications goals mentioned earlier.

Research should identify the target market, determine its size and characteristics, and then match the target with the audience and effectiveness of the available media. The objective is to achieve adequate media coverage without advertising beyond the identifiable limits of the potential market. Finally, alternative costs are compared to determine the best possible media purchase.

There are many types of advertising media, and the characteristics of some of the more important ones will be considered here. The advantages and disadvantages of each are shown in Table 19.3 and discussed briefly below. Net advertising revenues by medium are shown in Figure 19.3.

### Television

Television is the largest advertising medium. It now accounts for about 26 percent of total advertising volume. Since 1991, it has grown by 22 percent. Television advertising can be divided into three categories: network, national spot, and local spot. The Canadian Broadcasting Corporation, the Canadian Television Network, and Global Television are the three national networks. Network advertising usually accounts for over two-thirds of the total television advertising expenditures. A national "spot" refers to non-network broadcasting used by a general advertiser. For example, Black & Decker might choose to place an advertisement in several cities across the country without buying time from a television network. Local spots, primarily used by retailers, consist of locally developed and sponsored commercials. Television advertising offers the following advantages: impact, mass coverage, repetition, flexibility, and prestige. Its disadvantages include the temporary nature of the message, high costs, high mortality rates for commercials, some evidence of public distrust, and lack of selectivity.

www.cbc.ca

## TABLE 19.3 Advantages and Disadvantages of Various Advertising Media

| MEDIUM | ADVANTAGES | DISADVANTAGES |
|---|---|---|
| **Television Advertising** | • Demonstration ability<br>• Intrusion value<br>• Ability to generate excitement<br>• One-on-one reach<br>• Ability to use humour<br>• Effective with salesforce and trade<br>• Ability to achieve impact | • Rapidly escalating cost<br>• Erosion of viewing audiences<br>• Audience fractionalization<br>• Zipping and zapping<br>• Clutter |
| **Newspaper Advertising** | • Audience in appropriate mental frame to process messages<br>• Mass audience coverage<br>• Flexibility<br>• Ability to use detailed copy<br>• Timeliness | • Clutter<br>• Not a highly selective medium<br>• Higher rates for occasional advertisers<br>• Mediocre reproduction quality<br>• Complicated buying for national advertiser<br>• Changing composition of readers |
| **Radio Advertising** | • Ability to reach segmented audiences<br>• Intimacy<br>• Economy<br>• Short lead times<br>• Transfer of imagery from TV<br>• Use of local personalities | • Clutter<br>• No visuals<br>• Audience fractionalization<br>• Buying difficulties |
| **Magazine Advertising** | • Some magazines reach large audiences<br>• Selectivity<br>• Long life<br>• High reproduction quality<br>• Ability to present detailed information<br>• Authoritative conveying of information<br>• High involvement potential | • Not intrusive<br>• Long lead times<br>• Clutter<br>• Somewhat limited geographic options<br>• Variability of circulation patterns by market |
| **Direct Mail** | • Selectivity<br>• Intense coverage<br>• Speed<br>• Flexibility of format<br>• Complete information<br>• Personalization | • High cost per person<br>• Dependence on quality of mailing list<br>• Consumer resistance |
| **Internet Advertising** | • Ability to reach segmented audiences<br>• Ability to change message quickly<br>• High user interest in medium<br>• Use of colour and limited motion graphics<br>• Ability to bridge to extensive message and to advertiser's Web site<br>• Can close a sale and take order | • Limited initial message length<br>• Clutter<br>• Uncertain effectiveness of new medium<br>• Consumer resistance<br>• Concern about security of information |
| **Outdoor Advertising** | • Broad reach and high frequency levels<br>• Geographic flexibility<br>• Low cost per thousand<br>• Prominent brand identification<br>• Opportune purchase reminder | • Nonselectivity<br>• Short exposure time<br>• Difficult to measure audience size<br>• Environmental problems |

Source: Adapted from *Advertising, Promotion, and Supplemental Aspects of Integrated Marketing Communications* 4th ed., by Terrance A. Shimp. Copyright © 1997, pp. 324–325. Reprinted with permission of South-Western, a division of Thomson Learning: www.thomsonrights.com. Fax 800-730-2215.

## FIGURE 19.3 Net Advertising Revenues by Medium

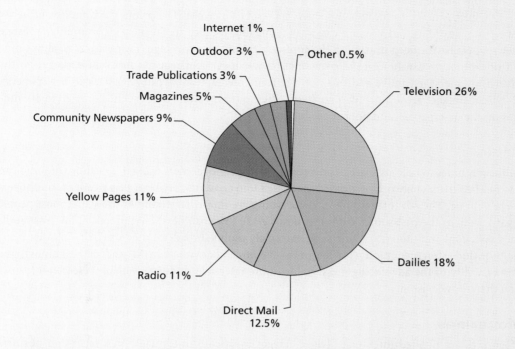

- Internet 1%
- Outdoor 3%
- Other 0.5%
- Trade Publications 3%
- Magazines 5%
- Television 26%
- Community Newspapers 9%
- Yellow Pages 11%
- Radio 11%
- Direct Mail 12.5%
- Dailies 18%

Source: Canadian Media Directors' Council, *Media Digest*, 1998–99, p. 11. Publication can be accessed on-line at http://www.marketingmag.ca. Data compiled from Statistics Canada, CRTC, CNA, CCNA,/Les Hebdos du Québec, Magazines Canada, CARD, CAN, TeleDirect, Canada Post, IAB and industry estimates.

# THE CANADIAN MARKETPLACE

## THE MATHEMATICS OF SPONSORING TELEVISION SPORTS

Recently a $600-million ABC/ESPN television deal was signed with the National Hockey League. Experts have done the math on the deal, and the numbers still don't make any sense. ESPN and ESPN2 are paying $70 million a season for a total of 130 games. The revenue required for ESPN to break even is difficult to determine, because subscription rates contribute to its revenue, and rates can be hiked.

ABC's financial commitment is more straightforward. It ponied up $50 million a year for the rights to 16 to 20 games (four to seven in the regular season; one a week in the playoffs, the entire final).

Generally, a hockey game produces about 56 commercial spots 30 seconds in length. Over 20 games, that adds up to 1120 spots. ABC, to make back its $50-million investment, will need to charge more than $45 000 a spot over 20 games (assuming the Cup final goes a full seven games).

But the most money that Fox Sports ever received for a 30-second spot in a Cup final was $45 000. Regular season ads sell for only $25 000. So how can ABC even come close to breaking even?

Said one television insider, "The ABC offer was based less on business than emotion. Disney wanted to knock off Fox and I think Michael Eisner's love for hockey had a lot to do with the price that was paid." Eisner is the chairman/CEO of the Disney Co., which owns ABC/ESPN and the NHL's Anaheim Mighty Ducks.

**Consider how this insight into the mathematics of commercial television might apply to the advertising rights for other programs.**

www.espn.go.com

www.abc.go.com

www.nhl.com

Source: Adapted from "William Houston's World of Television and Radio Sports," *The Globe and Mail* (August 29, 1998), p. A24. Reprinted with permission from *The Globe and Mail*.

## Newspapers

Newspapers are approximately the same as television in size as an advertising medium. About 28 percent of Canada's total advertising revenues are spent on newspaper advertising. Dailies account for 19 percent and community newspapers represent 9 percent. The primary advantages of newspapers are flexibility (advertising can vary from one locality to the next), community prestige (newspapers have a deep impact on the community), intense coverage (in most places, about nine out of ten homes can be reached by a single newspaper), and reader control of exposure to the advertising message (unlike audiences of electronic media, readers can refer back to newspapers). The disadvantages are a short lifespan, hasty reading (the typical reader spends only 20 to 30 minutes on the newspaper), and poor reproduction.

## Radio

Radio continues to hold its share of advertising revenue. Advertisers using the medium of radio can also be classified as network or local advertisers. Radio accounts for about 11 percent of total advertising volume. The advantages of radio advertising are immediacy (studies show that most people regard radio as the best source for up-to-date news); low cost; flexibility; practical, low-cost audience selection; and mobility (radio is an extremely mobile broadcast medium). Radio's disadvantages include fragmentation (for instance, Montreal has fifteen AM and FM stations), the unavailability of the advertising message for future reference, and less available research information than for television.

## Magazines

Magazines are divided into such diverse categories as consumer magazines, farm and business publications, and directories. They account for about 8 percent of all advertising. The primary advantages of magazine advertising are selectivity of target markets, quality reproduction, long life, the prestige associated with some magazines, and the extra services offered by many publications. Canadian consumer magazines have pioneered many controlled distribution techniques. Our postal code system, with its six-digit forward sortation area (FSA) and local delivery unit (LDU), can be linked with census data at the enumeration area (EA) level to produce well-defined circulation clusters based on demographics, life cycles, or other interest–activity profiles. The primary disadvantage is that magazines lack the short-term flexibility of newspapers, radio, and television.

## Direct Mail

Direct mail is a very significant advertising medium. It now accounts for 13 percent of advertising revenues. Sales letters, postcards, leaflets, folders, broadsides (which are larger than folders), booklets, catalogues, and house organs (periodicals issued by an organization) are all forms of direct-mail advertising. The advantages of direct mail include selectivity, intensive coverage, speed, format flexibility, complete information, and the personalization of each mailing piece. Direct-mail purchasers also tend to be consistent buyers by mail. A disadvantage of direct mail is its high cost per reader. Direct-mail advertising also depends on the quality of the mailing list. Often those unfamiliar with the effectiveness of direct mail condemn it all as "junk mail." They are very surprised to find that many people respond positively to such advertising. In fact, marketing research surveys consistently show a majority who say they prefer to receive it. Effectively used, direct mail is a successful and lucrative marketing tool. Direct mail can be used for many purposes, including informative, persuasive, and reminder-oriented advertising. However, a major function is to generate direct orders. Direct response marketing is further discussed later in this chapter.

## Internet Advertising

Internet advertising is growing, but at 1 percent it is still a small proportion of Canadian advertising media. Internet advertising can be used for informative, persuasive, and reminder-oriented advertising. It is also a useful means of direct marketing. Currently, one of its most effective uses is to provide information. Through the Internet we can look up virtually any company and any product and get much useful information that would otherwise take days to acquire.

Many realize that there is *potential* in Internet advertising, but there has been a great deal of scepticism and uncertainty as to where its value lies beyond making information readily available. AC Nielsen, a large marketing research organization, undertook one of the most extensive studies ever conducted of the value of online advertising. They isolated the effects from online ad banner exposure so they could precisely quantify its value. They focused on the effects of a single ad banner exposure. Their research demonstrates that online advertising is an effective branding tool. Because of the research expertise of this organization the results are very significant.

They carefully measured the effectiveness across twenty-four advertisements for the fourteen leading brands in Australia. Their results concluded that online advertising caused: [7]

www.acnielsen.com

- 8% increase in intent to purchase
- 6% increase in top-of-mind (unaided first mention) brand awareness
- 1.4% increase in aided brand awareness
- 30% increase in ad recall
- Statistically significant improvements in ten out of fifteen measures of brand image. These increases are tangible evidence of the value and importance of online advertising.

DoubleClick is a company that specializes in Internet advertising. It is an ad-sales network that represents more than 70 sites on the Internet. One of the strengths of a company like this is that it can deliver just those parts of the vast Internet audience most valuable to an advertiser. If an advertiser wants to reach women, they can offer advertising box or banner space on the Web site of clients such as foodtv.com, an offshoot of cable television's Food Network.

www.doubleclick.com

If customers want even more precise targeting, such companies can often oblige. One advertising manager wants to reach people in one city, but not the nearby suburbs of a neighbouring city, where his cellular-phone company can't deliver service. No problem. In the brief moment when Internet users wait for a Web page to be delivered to their screen, DoubleClick's computers can identify the area code being serviced. People in the selected area code would get the company ad; those elsewhere wouldn't. The customer has been targeted before he knows it.

E-mail is another form of Internet advertising. Most people have access to e-mail and as a result, the idea of sending advertising messages by e-mail is very appealing. It is not so appealing to many receivers of such e-mail messages. It is easy and cheap to obtain a list of thousands of e-mail addresses. The resulting "Spam" is highly resented by most receivers.

Another, more acceptable type of e-mail advertising is *permission-based* e-mail. When Internet surfers sign up for some service, or buy a product, they are normally asked whether they would like to receive other messages about related topics or items. If they agree, a much more valuable mailing list is created. One study indicated that 88 percent of consumers have made purchases as a result of permission-based e-mail.[8]

As with the use of other advertising media, there are specialist companies that can handle or facilitate this type of Internet advertising.

As discussed more fully in the Business-to-Business and Retailing chapters, companies are finding that e-commerce is not a magic bullet. However, they are learning the limitations and real advantages of using the Internet. Its use in advertising will continue to be significant, and will be increasingly efficient.

An important aspect of advertising on the Web is the ability to measure Web site traffic and verify how many ad impressions are delivered. Good progress has been made toward providing more measurement and independent auditing services as well.

In summary, we have seen that the advantages of Internet advertising are:

- Target market selectivity
- Tracking—how much users interact with them.
- Deliverability and flexibility—information is delivered 24 hours a day 7 days a week.
- Interactivity—you can interact directly with a company in ordering or other communication without leaving your computer.

## A SUCCESS STORY

### Nike Canada—Instructor Network Program Web Site

**Client:**
NIKE Canada for its NIKE Fitness brand

**Agency:**
CyberSight (now ninedots)

**Background:**
NIKE offers fitness instructors a discount on products in order to promote the products within their fitness classes. To accomplish this, NIKE has traditionally distributed a print catalogue to instructors who would manually fill out an order form and fax it to NIKE to place an order. NIKE wanted to bring this process online.

**Objectives:**
• Facilitate the process for fitness instructors to order product from NIKE by eliminating the need to manually fill out the order form, make the calculations, and fax the form to NIKE.
• Reduce the printing, production, distribution and internal labour costs associated with the print catalogue.
• Increase the number and dollar value of the orders received from fitness instructors.
• Grow the user database to collect consumer marketing insight and develop a relationship marketing program.

**Strategy/Execution:**
• ninedots designed and built a Web site for the fitness instructor industry to facilitate the ordering process, thereby increasing orders.
• The program offers discount rates for NIKE products to registered fitness instructors in return for their promoting these products to their clients.
• All existing users of the print catalogue were notified by letter of the switch to online ordering. Interested fitness instructors used a general password to initially log in to the site and then were able to personalize their password for future visits.
• The site allows users to choose categories from the home page for footwear, apparel, and accessories, for men or women. Users can then browse and choose their items that have individual pop-ups showing more detail.
• The chosen items are then automatically placed in the order form, the total is calculated with the appropriate taxes, and the user can choose whether to pay by Visa or MasterCard.
• For security purposes, a NIKE representative contacts the user by phone to obtain the credit card information after the order is placed.
• The user-centric design provides an easy and rich user experience. Next steps for NIKE will be to expand the site to include more items and make the site full e-commerce enabled.

**Results:**
• The printing and distribution costs associated with the printed catalogue were immediately saved.
• Orders were placed online within hours of the site going live and the number of orders is on target to exceed orders placed versus last year.
• Verbal and e-mail feedback from users has been extremely positive.

**Timelines:**
• The initial campaign ran from April to July 2001 and repeats over the same time every year.

www.nikeinp.ca

www.ninedots.com

Source: Nike Canada: Instructor Network Program Web site (http://www.iabcanada.com/iab/success_nike.shtml). Courtesy of Nike Canada.

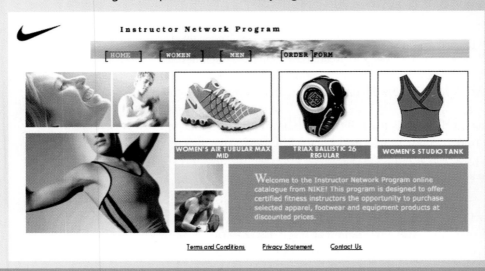

■ Integration—This chapter has given several examples of how easily Internet advertising can be integrated with other elements of the promotion mix.

As the Web moves into living rooms and hotel rooms, advertiser interest in Web advertising will grow with the expanded target audience. Internet advertising has become an advertising medium that can provide unique opportunities for the advertiser.

## Outdoor Advertising

Posters (commonly called billboards), painted bulletins or displays (such as those that appear on building walls), and electric spectaculars (large, illuminated, and sometimes animated signs and displays) make up outdoor advertising. Accounting for 3 percent of advertising volume, this form of advertising has the advantages of quick communication of simple ideas, repetition, and the ability to promote products that are available for sale nearby. Outdoor advertising is particularly effective in metropolitan and other high-traffic areas. Disadvantages of the medium are the brevity of its message and public concern over aesthetics; however, a simple message can be extremely powerful.

Selecting outdoor advertising media presents many opportunities and challenges. Aside from the main media categories listed above, many others can serve an important role in communicating with selected target markets. Table 19.4 lists the main categories. Within each category there are often several companies that provide media opportunities. For example, eight firms provide supermarket advertising services, and two handle washroom advertising. Details on these and other media can be found in the Canadian Media Directors' Council, *Media Digest* at http://www.marketingmag.ca.

### TABLE 19.4 Other Advertising Media

| | |
|---|---|
| Aerial advertising | Programs (for theatres, concerts, trade shows, etc.) |
| Airport display advertising | Receptacle advertising |
| Bar, restaurant, and hotel advertising | Religious publications |
| Brochure advertising | Scholarly publications |
| Cable advertising | Shopping centre advertising |
| Campus advertising | Sports advertising (e.g., rinkboard panels) |
| Closed-circuit advertising | Stadium advertising |
| Coupon advertising | Supermarket advertising |
| Directories, annuals, and almanacs | Tabletop advertising (e.g., tent cards) |
| Elevator advertising | Theatre screen advertising |
| Exhibition centre advertising | Truck advertising |
| Farm publications | University and school advertising |
| Medical advertising | Video screen advertising |
| Mobile signage | Washroom advertising |
| Mural signage | Yellow pages/telephone directory advertising |
| Parking lot advertising | |
| Product postcard service | |

## Organizing the Advertising Function

While the ultimate responsibility for advertising decisions often rests with top marketing management, how the advertising function is organized varies among companies. A producer of a technical industrial product may be served by a one-person operation primarily concerned with writing copy for trade publications. A consumer-goods company, on the other hand, may have a large department staffed with advertising specialists.

The advertising function is usually organized as a staff department reporting to the vice president (or director) of marketing. The director of advertising is an executive position that heads the functional activity of advertising. The individual filling this slot should not only be a skilled and experienced advertiser, but also be able to communicate effectively within the organization. The success of a firm's promotional strategy depends on the advertising director's willingness and ability to communicate both vertically and horizontally. The major tasks typically organized under advertising include advertising research, art, copywriting, media analysis, and, in some cases, sales promotion.

## THE PRACTISING MARKETER

### REACH WOMEN BY FEATURING DAD

Advertisers have long targeted mothers in their ads, spurred by surveys that suggest moms make the majority of spending decisions. But a plethora of new ads are targeting them in a different way, through dads.

From the latest Canadian Tire spots featuring dads in the traditional way used by many advertisers—sharing fun outdoor moments with the kids—to those that attempt to present them in a more modern way such as a Toyota spot with a dealer getting his toddler dressed, or a recent Scotiabank ad that had a young father bathing his baby while chatting with his wife about RRSPs.

The Scotiabank ad had the roles reversed from more traditional ads: a father cared for the baby while he and his wife chatted about her father's advice that they contribute to their RRSPs.

"That particular ad was one of the best-recalled we've ever had," said Rick White, vice-president, marketing, with Scotiabank in Toronto, "We know we hit a nerve." He attributes its success to the modern theme that Mom and Dad are happy to share the responsibilities at home. "It was just positioning Dad in a respectful role."

Canadian Tire, a retailer famous for heartwarming images of Dad in its TV spot—its most memorable was a 1991 spot called "Bike Story," which told the tale of a little boy who dreams of owning the bike from the Canadian Tire catalogue and then sees his dream come true thanks to Dad—is still using dads extensively in its campaigns, leveraging the image of what might be called "weekend moments" between Dad and kids.

The latest campaign, "Let's Get Started" has Dad's schedule chock full of trips to Canadian Tire and spare time playing croquet with his small daughter and another Dad on a fishing trip with a young son.

"Very much where we're going [with this advertising] is parents with kids," said Eymbert Vaandering, vice-president, marketing, Canadian Tire Retail. "We're obviously very famous for ads that show Dad's roles in the world. Obviously Dad is a big part of our heritage and strength, but we also want to talk to Mom."

McDonald's ran an ad that told the story of a female doctor working the night shift who comes to her car in the morning to find a note from her husband and kids asking her to meet them at McDonald's for breakfast. That role reversal of Mom as the busy professional and Dad as the caretaker is an attempt to make ads that feel real.

**Can you think of other similar campaigns? How do you respond to this approach?**

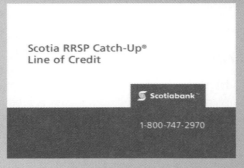

Scotia RRSP Catch-Up® Line of Credit

Ⓢ Scotiabank

1-800-747-2970

This ad has the roles reversed from more traditional ads. Its success fits the modern theme that Mom and Dad are happy to share the responsibilities at home.

www.canadiantire.ca

www.scotiabank.com

Source: Adapted from Susan Heinrich, "Father Figures More Prominent in Ad Campaigns," *Financial Post*, April 22, 2002, p. FP6. Reprinted with permission.

## Advertising Agencies

Many advertisers also use an independent advertising agency. The **advertising agency** is a marketing specialist firm that assists the advertiser in planning and preparing its advertisements.

The first advertising agents were simply newspaper space salespeople. They went from company to company selling the idea of advertising products in the paper. Since many of their potential clients knew little about advertising, some salespeople began to offer additional services, such as artwork and copywriting. The need for these services grew, and advertising agencies evolved as a result.

Within such organizations exists a cross-section of talents. There are creative people who dream up an advertisement or advertising campaign. They or others may write the copy for the advertisement, and still others are involved in producing artwork or commercials. Media specialists in the agency know the many media types and select and schedule ads to reach the right target market. Another group of people who call on clients and liaise between clients, the creative group, and the production people in the agency are known as account executives.

There are several reasons why advertisers use an agency for at least a portion of their advertising. Agencies are typically staffed with highly qualified specialists who provide a degree of creativity and objectivity that is difficult to maintain in a corporate advertising department. In some cases using an agency reduces the cost of advertising, since the agency does not require many of the fixed expenses associated with internal advertising departments. Effective use of an advertising agency requires a close relationship between advertiser and agency.

> **advertising agency**
> A marketing specialist firm that assists the advertiser in planning and preparing its advertisements.

## Assessing the Effectiveness of an Advertisement

For many firms, advertising represents a major expenditure, so it is imperative to determine whether a campaign is accomplishing its promotional objectives. Determining advertising's effectiveness, however, is one of the most difficult undertakings in marketing. In consists of two primary elements—pretesting and post-testing.

### Pretesting

**Pretesting** is the assessment of an advertisement's effectiveness before it is actually used. It includes a variety of evaluative methods. For example, to test magazine advertisements, the ad agency Batten, Barton, Durstine & Osborn cuts ads out of advance copies of magazines and then "strips in" the ads it wants to test. Interviewers later check the impact of the advertisements on the readers who receive free copies of the revised magazine. Television advertisements can be pretested before airing by measuring the responses of a representative sample of prospective customers. Many other techniques are used for pretesting advertising.

> **pretesting**
> The assessment of an advertisement's effectiveness before it is actually used.

### Post-Testing

**Post-testing** is the assessment of advertising copy after it has been used. Pretesting is generally a more desirable testing method than post-testing because of its potential cost savings. But post-testing can be helpful in planning future advertisements and in making adjustments to current advertising programs.

In one of the most popular post-tests, the *Starch Readership Studies,* interviewers ask people who have read selected magazines whether they have read various ads in them. A copy of one of the magazines is used as an interviewing aid, and each interviewer starts at a different point in the magazine. For larger ads, respondents are also asked about specifics such as headlines and copy. All readership or recognition tests assume that future sales are related to advertising readership.

Regardless of the exact method used, marketers must realize that pretesting and post-testing are expensive and must, therefore, be used as effectively as possible.

> **post-testing**
> The assessment of advertising copy after it has been used.

## DIRECT RESPONSE ADVERTISING WORKS

ING Direct, the small but fast-growing virtual bank, launches its third in a series of direct response television ads today, a format typically used by low-budget infomercials and dating hotlines, that has shown it can work for financial institutions as well.

Direct response ads—so called because they invite a call to action with product testimonials and telephone numbers across the screen—might be an unlikely strategy for a bank that has spent extensively to build a reputable brand.

But it's one that's been more successful at bringing in new customers than any of its recent campaigns.

"Had we realized the power in them we would have started them sooner," said Stacey Grant-Thompson, senior vice-president of marketing with ING Direct, which now has some 500 000 clients in Canada and $5 billion in deposits.

The first direct response campaign launched last summer highlighted ING's Investment Savings Account. The results, when compared with those of a traditional branding campaign, were surprising.

"When we compared our results [with those from a year earlier] we more than doubled our qualified leads and nearly doubled the clients we acquired," said Ms. Grant-Thompson. "As a result, [we were] able to grow the business much more quickly than we had been, and we spent much less per client."

Throughout the 60-second spot, a toll-free number appeared at the bottom of the ad along with the company's Web site address. By using a different telephone number for each network on which the ads ran, ING was also able to measure the effectiveness of each placement, thus increasing the effectiveness of their media buy.

Adrienne Simmons, a research executive with Kubas Consultants in Toronto, said a direct response format works well because [they] have given customers everything they need to pick up the phone.

**This campaign worked well. Think of other direct response television advertisements. What is your perception of the image of the advertisement and the company sponsor?**

www.ingdirect.com

## Direct Response Marketing

Marketers have increasingly used various advertising media to make a selling offer directly to the target market. The results of these direct marketing efforts have been so impressive that this practice has grown steadily. **Direct response marketing** is an interactive system of marketing that uses one or more advertising media to effect a measurable response directly to the advertiser, not to an intermediary as in the case of general product advertising.

**direct response marketing**

An interactive system of marketing that uses one or more advertising media to effect a measurable response directly to the advertiser.

Two distinguishing words are *measurable* and *response*. Direct response marketing uses various media such as the Internet, catalogues, direct mail, magazines, television, radio, and newspapers to make a specific offer. The purpose of this offer is to elicit a direct positive response (usually, an order). This contrasts with general advertising for the purpose of creating an image, or communicating for some other purpose.

Direct response marketing anticipates a relatively immediate response (sale) that can be measured against the marketing effort. For example, a television offer of a special CD set might encourage buyers to phone an 800 number or write in to order it and charge it to their credit card. If the campaign costs $70 000 and orders amount to $200 000, the marketer can take other costs into consideration and readily calculate whether or not the direct marketing effort was profitable. As another example, Tilley Endurables elicits direct orders for its Tilley hat and other casual clothing in *The Globe and Mail* and other print media along with a number of other direct marketers. As mentioned earlier, Dell Computers, a manufacturer, has enjoyed phenomenal success through direct response marketing. America OnLine (AOL) and other Internet providers are other examples. Direct response marketing and general advertising are compared in Table 19.5.

Much direct marketing is done through direct mail. Computerization has made this medium extremely versatile, and direct mail can be very focused. For example, you receive a personalized

**TABLE 19.5** Comparison of Direct Response Marketing and General Advertising

| DIRECT RESPONSE MARKETING | GENERAL ADVERTISING |
|---|---|
| Selling to individuals. Customers are often identifiable by name, address, and purchase behaviour. | Mass selling. Buyers are identified as broad groups sharing common demographic and psychographic characteristics. |
| Products may have added value or service. | |
| Distribution is an important product benefit. | Product benefits do not always include convenient distribution channels. |
| The medium is the marketplace. | The retail outlet is the marketplace. |
| Marketer controls product until delivery. | Marketer may lose control as product enters distribution channel. |
| Advertising is used to motivate an immediate order or inquiry. | Advertising is used for cumulative effect over time to build image, awareness, loyalty, or benefit recall. Purchase action is deferred. |
| Repetition is used in ad. | Repetition is used over time. |
| Consumers feel a high perceived risk— product is bought unseen. Recourse is distant. | Consumers feel less risk—have direct contact with the product and direct recourse. |

Source: Reprinted from Bob Stone, *Successful Direct Marketing Methods*, 5th ed. (Lincolnwood, IL: NTC Publishing Group, 1994). Used with permission of NTC/Contemporary Publishing Group, Inc. Copyright The McGraw-Hill Companies, Inc.

letter inviting you to purchase a mobile phone contract. Another arrives announcing a special concert featuring the music you like. These letters were aimed directly at you because you subscribe to a financial magazine or order CDs regularly from a club by mail.

Information about potential mail recipients is so important that an industry has evolved to collect and rent databases. These not only provide names and addresses, but also past purchase behaviour.[9] List houses, or list brokers, specialize in collecting lists and keeping them up to date. A direct marketer must find the right combination of lists to use. This may be done by going directly to the list rental division of major publications or organizations, or to a broker that specializes in selecting lists. About 2000 lists are for rent in Canada.

Lists from many sources are combined, and duplicate names are removed. Renting lists generally costs 5 or 6 cents a name. Those who rent their lists usually insist on approving samples of the material that will be mailed. The renter agrees to one use per rental.

Mailing lists never enter the possession of the renter. Rather, the provider sends a computer tape or disks via the broker to one of several businesses that specialize in combining computer lists and generating labels, envelopes, and customized letters. It is at this stage that duplicates and those on various "do-not-mail" lists are removed. Labels and materials then move on to a mailing house, which stuffs the envelopes and puts them in the mail. List specialists also exist for Internet addresses. Currently, such lists are generally quite cheap. However, costs will rise as the target audience is refined and made more specific.

The range of products offered by direct marketing is large, ranging from computers (sold by Dell) to tax preparation to pest control and many other services. But not everyone prefers to buy directly from manufacturers—many consumers enjoy shopping and browsing in person.

Want a *sure way* to get your advertising through the door?

Target your market with *Unaddressed Admail*™

You want to be sure that your potential customers welcome your advertising into their home or business. So don't get lost in the clutter of weekend flyers, mass advertising distribution and newspaper inserts. Choose Unaddressed Admail, Canada Post's most cost-effective direct mail service.

Delivered along with the regular mail, Unaddressed Admail lets you maximize your advertising dollars. It gives you the flexibility to hand-pick exactly which areas you want to cover – that's as small as one letter carrier route (approximately 500 addresses). Or is as far-reaching as all of Canada. So your brochure, flyer, sample or catalogue gets right into the hands of your very best potential customers.

The results? More visibility. More impact. More response.

For more information on Unaddressed Admail and other Canada Post Marketing and Selling solutions, call **1-866-511-3135** to talk to a professional at the Canada Post Business Sales Centre, your dedicated source for business products and services.
*www.canadapost.ca/admail*

™ Trade-mark of Canada Post Corporation.

From anywhere...to anyone

**Direct mail is important to Canada Post as well as to advertisers.**

A problem with direct response marketing is that because consumers have difficulty avoiding and ignoring it, there is a fair amount of animosity toward its continuous flow. In addition, privacy sometimes becomes an issue. This writer recently received a letter that said, "You have more than 15 000 frequent-flyer air mile points. You can increase them by accepting our offer." How did the direct marketer know how many points I had? Why did the airline company release this information? Direct marketers may learn about consumer purchase behaviour from the list categories they purchase, but they should be careful not to make consumers feel that their privacy has been compromised.

Direct response marketing is used successfully in a growing number of applications and is an important part of marketing. The main threat to its viability is negative public reaction to the intrusiveness of this medium (especially direct mail). Despite a rather small and vocal consumer group that opposes direct response marketing, it continues to thrive.

## SALES PROMOTION

In addition to advertising, sales promotion is another type of nonpersonal selling. It does not have as high a profile as some other marketing communications activities, but is extremely important. As advertising media become more cluttered with competing messages, marketers are turning to an increased use of sales promotion. A study of marketing communications expenses of Canadian packaged goods companies showed that sales promotion accounted for about half as much as advertising expenditures.[10] As we learned in Chapter 18, sales promotion may be defined as the use of incentives to stimulate consumers to purchase a product or deal with a supplier. It includes such activities as point-of-purchase advertising; specialty advertising; samples, coupons, and premiums; loyalty points; deals; rebates; and contests. More than one of these options may be used in a single promotional strategy, but probably no promotional strategy has ever used all the options in a single program. While they are not mutually exclusive, sales promotion methods are generally employed on a selective basis.

Sales promotion techniques may be used by all members of a marketing channel—manufacturers, wholesalers, and retailers—and are typically targeted at specific markets. For example, a manufacturer such as Texize Corporation might combine trial sample mailings of a new spot remover to consumers with a sales contest for wholesalers and retailers who handle the new product. In both instances, the sales promotion techniques are designed to supplement and extend the other elements of the firm's promotional mix.

## Point-of-Purchase Advertising

Displays and demonstrations that seek to promote the product at a time and place closely associated with the actual decision to buy are called **point-of-purchase advertising**. The in-store promotion of consumer goods is a common example. Such advertising can be extremely useful in carrying forward a theme developed in another element of promotional strategy. A life-sized display of a celebrity used in television advertising, for instance, can become a realistic in-store display. Displays also serve as an effective attention-getter and reminder.

## Specialty Advertising

**Specialty advertising** is a sales promotion medium that uses useful articles to carry the advertiser's name, address, and advertising message to reach target customers. The Roots of Marketing box illustrates that this is one of the oldest marketing practices.

Examples of contemporary advertising specialties carrying a firm's name include calendars, pencils, pens, paperweights, matchbooks, mugs, coasters, pocket diaries, shopping bags, memo pads, balloons, measuring sticks, key rings, glasses, and hundreds of other items.

## Samples, Coupons, Premiums, Deals, Rebates, and Loyalty Programs

The distribution of samples, coupons, and premiums is one of the best-known sales promotion techniques. Sampling involves giving away a free item in an attempt to obtain consumer acceptance. This may be done door to door, by mail, through demonstrations, or as an insertion into packages containing other products. Sampling is especially useful in promoting new products.

Coupons offer a discount, usually some specified price reduction, on the next purchase of a product. Coupons are readily redeemable with retailers, who also receive a handling fee. Mail, magazines, newspapers, package insertions, and in-store displays are standard methods of distributing coupons.

Premiums, bonus items given free with the purchase of another product, have proven effective in getting consumers to try a new product or a different brand. Service stations, for example, use glassware, ice scrapers, and beach balls to convince noncustomers to patronize their station. Premiums are also used to encourage response to direct-marketing offers. The value of premium giveaways runs into millions of dollars each year.

Deals to consumers are price reductions designed to encourage trial use of a product or to counteract a competitor's promotion. Deals are also commonly used to encourage retailers to stock enough merchandise. For example, Old Dutch might offer retailers one free case of potato chips with every dozen purchased. The retailers then benefit from selling this "100 percent profit" case of chips. The manufacturer also gains because the deal encourages retailers to stock lots of product. Deals are short-term in nature.

**point-of-purchase advertising**
Displays and demonstrations that seek to promote the product at a time and place closely associated with the actual decision to buy.

**specialty advertising**
Sales promotion medium that uses useful articles to carry the advertiser's name, address, and advertising message.

## THE ROOTS OF MARKETING

### SPECIALTY ADVERTISING TRACED TO THE MIDDLE AGES

Specialty advertising has been traced to the Middle Ages, when wooden pegs bearing the names of artisans "were given to prospects to be driven into their walls and to serve as a convenient place upon which to hang armour."[11] Undoubtedly, many earlier marketers followed similar practices.

Rebates have several uses. In some cases, they are used to encourage consumers to purchase. For example, Kodak offered a $4 rebate to consumers who purchased a package of five films. The consumer had to mail in a form and proof of purchase. Rebates are also used to induce channel member loyalty to a manufacturer. A carpet manufacturer keeps track of the number of metres of carpeting sold by a retailer during the year, and provides a rebate of 25, 35, or 40 cents per metre depending on whether the retailer sells up to one of three preset targets.

**Loyalty programs** stimulate repeat purchases. Similar in concept to rebates, some businesses assign points, based on value, to every purchase. The points are automatically posted by computer after each purchase. After a customer has accumulated a certain number of points, they may be used to purchase products. Zellers Club Z points are an outstanding example. Club Z now has over 10 million members and an incredible reach of 65 percent of all Canadian households.[12] The introduction of Club Z points was a major factor in making Zellers one of the leading retailers in the country and Club Z one of the most successful reward clubs in North America. Strategic alliances have been established with AT&T Canada and CIBC. Now certain purchases from these organizations translate into Club Z points.[13] Airline companies such as Air Canada have also created a great deal of loyalty with their frequent-flyer air-mile programs. Grocery retailers almost force customers to join their loyalty group because they offer deep price cuts on selected items to members.

## Contests

Firms may sponsor contests to attract additional customers, offering substantial cash or merchandise prizes to call attention to their products. The number of such contests is almost infinite. A company might consider employing a specialist in developing this type of sales promotion because of the variety and complexity of schemes available.

## Trade Shows

A small machinist company in central Manitoba invented a machine to hold, dispense, and measure heavy rolls of carpeting. This was an excellent product with worldwide potential. How could this firm with little marketing experience, no sales force, and no international experience distribute its product? A series of trade shows was the answer that resulted in sales and interested dealerships in several different countries.

A **trade show** is an organized exhibition of products based on a central theme. The theme might be Canadian manufactured products, agricultural products, or toys, for example. The trade show is held in a centre that is accessible to buyers and runs for a specified number of days. Each exhibitor rents display space and has personnel available to answer questions. Trade shows are organized by trade associations, businesses, and governments (to promote products in another country). For example, the Canadian government organizes an annual trade show of Canadian agricultural machinery in Dubbo, Australia. It also organizes the rental of enough space for several Canadian companies that might be interested in joining to form a Canadian presence at other trade shows.

# PUBLIC RELATIONS AND PUBLICITY

**Public relations**, or PR, is the component of marketing communications that focuses on fostering goodwill between a company and its various publics. PR efforts are aimed primarily at consumers, employees, suppliers, stockholders, governments, the general public, labour groups, and citizen action groups.[14]

Public relations can be integrated with advertising and other elements of the promotion mix to accomplish objectives other than goodwill. It can also increase brand awareness, build favourable attitudes toward a company and its products, and encourage purchases.

Public relations involves a number of functions and activities, including: (1) providing advice to executives on the impact of their actions on the public; (2) producing publications, such as

**loyalty program**
A program that gives rewards, such as points or free air miles, with each purchase in order to stimulate repeat business.

w w w
www.zellers.ca

**trade show**
An organized exhibition of products based on a central theme.

**public relations**
The component of marketing communications that focuses on fostering goodwill between a company and its various publics.

brochures for stockholders and newsletters for employees; and (3) **publicity**, which is very important. The PR team should be monitoring the current company image and should feed this back to management. Publicity involves disseminating positive information about company activities and products, or overcoming negative attention. Publicity is not paid advertising—it is accomplished through contact with the news media, through news releases, and through press conferences.

Publicity depends on some characteristic, activity, or event to make it "newsworthy" and to stimulate media attention. In North America, over 100 000 media editors are constantly searching for news and public interest stories, including stories about interesting new products, product uses, and services.

The publicity campaign for the Furby toy is a classic example of the power of publicity. Planned almost a year before, the campaign was orchestrated with the advertising and promotion campaign to peak in December. The ultimate sales response was overwhelming.

Publicity is also generated with attention-getting activities. Kellogg's uses a larger-than-life mascot of Tony the Tiger for appearances at public venues. "Kids go nuts—they love the characters," says Carol Reader, product manager for children's cereals at Kellogg Company. "This is a very inoffensive way to remind people about a product."[15]

Publicity has a number of advantages and disadvantages. One advantage is its greater credibility because the information is perceived to be offered by an unbiased source (the media). Another advantage is that coverage often occurs with great speed, which is further enhanced by word of mouth. The public interest generated can often be considerably greater than could be created with an advertising campaign. If an editor thinks your message is newsworthy and runs it, others are likely to pick it up, and terrific momentum can occur.

The disadvantage of publicity is that it is out of the control of the marketer in terms of execution or timing. Thus, it is not possible to count on the fact that there will be any publicity at all, what actually will be said about the product, or when this might happen. Even if the story is run, the marketer

**publicity**
Normally unpaid communication that disseminates positive information about company activities and products.

www
www.kelloggs.com

---

## THE ETHICAL MARKETER

### SALES PROMOTION GONE WRONG?

Clothing maker Abercrombie & Fitch Co. said yesterday it was pulling a new line of Asian-themed T-shirts after Asian-American groups complained they were a blatant example of racist stereotyping.

The shirts, which retail for $25, hit the shelves this week and carry caricatures of slant-eyed Asians in conical hats along with such slogans as "Wong Brothers Laundry Service: Two Wongs can make it white" and "Wok-n-Bowl—Chinese food and bowling."

"It is not and never has been our intention to offend anyone," Abercrombie spokesman Hampton Carney said.

"These graphic T-shirts were designed with the sole purpose of adding humour and levity to our fashion line. Since some customers have been offended by their content, we are pulling these shirts from our stores."

Asian-American groups in California reacted with anger this week after the shirts appeared in local Abercrombie stores. Local activists said their cartoonish representation of Asian figures carried a racist message.

"This is really blatant. It is just like the 1800s said Rev. Norman Fong, program director at San Francisco's Chinatown Community Development Center. "The company has been totally insensitive, and people are pretty upset."

Mr. Carney said the popular youth clothing maker had believed the shirts might appeal to Asian-American consumers, and was surprised by the hostile reception they received.

"The thought was that everyone would love them, especially the Asian community. We thought they were cheeky, irreverent and funny and everyone would love them. But that has not been the case."

Abercrombie & Fitch, based in New Albany, Ohio, has been the target of consumer complaint before.

In 1998, Mothers Against Drunk Driving protested a two-page advertising spread entitled "Drinking 101" that contained recipes for alcoholic drinks, while other parents have complained the company frequently features overtly sexy photos in its advertising layouts.

**Do you agree that the T-shirt slogans were insensitive? Why do you think the company would produce something that might possibly offend?**

Source: "Abercrombie Incurs Asian Wrath," *The Financial Post*, April 19, 2002, p. FP3. Copyright © 2002 Reuters. Reuters content is the intellectual property of Reuters. Any copying, republication or redistribution of Reuters content is expressly prohibited. Reuters shall not be liable for any errors or delays in content, or for any actions taken in reliance thereon.

cannot be sure what will be said. Furthermore, each medium is likely to try covering the topic from a different angle. Photos and videotapes provide some control because they cannot be so readily edited.

The process of gaining publicity is a delicate one that requires good relationships with the media. The marketing company's publicist prepares a kit with a write-up, or press release, on the product and any other relevant materials such as pictures, videotapes, and other background information. The objective is to present the message as conveniently as possible without removing the possibility for the media to create their own angle on the story. Some media will publish the press release as it is, while others never do so because they view it as advertising. Many times, marketers will provide a spokesperson that the media can build the story around.

Publicity can also be generated through publicity stunts or giving the product away to celebrities. Tilley advertises that its sports clothing is worn by Sir Edmund Hillary, the first man to climb Mt. Everest. Products are often given away to charities or to be won as contest prizes. In the case of some products, such as cars and computer software, the product is lent to media specialists on the topic so that they can try it and write about it.

The media are very aware of the publicity objectives of marketers, and they are sensitive to being manipulated. Therefore, they are usually very careful about promoting performance superiority claims. Thus, marketers should supply them with independent test performance results if available.

# PERSONAL SELLING

Personal selling was defined in Chapter 18 as a seller's promotional presentation conducted on a person-to-person basis with the buyer. Selling is an inherent function of any business enterprise. Accounting, engineering, personnel management, and other organizational activities are useless unless the firm's product can be sold to someone. Thousands of sales employees bear witness to the importance of selling in the Canadian economy. While advertising expenses in the average firm may represent from 1 to 3 percent of total sales, selling expenses are likely to equal 10 to 15 percent of sales. In many firms, personal selling is the single largest marketing expense.

As Chapter 18 pointed out, personal selling is likely to be the primary component of a firm's marketing communications mix when customers are concentrated geographically; when orders are large; when the products or services are expensive, technically complex, and require special handling; when trade-ins are involved; when channels are short; and when the number of potential customers is relatively small.

www.avon.com

In instances where personal selling is the primary component of a firm's marketing mix, advertising may be used in a support role to assist the salespeople. Much of Avon's advertising is aimed at assisting the neighbourhood salesperson by strengthening the image of Avon, its products, and its salespeople. Table 19.6 summarizes the factors that affect personal selling's importance in the overall marketing communications mix.

## Categories of Selling

The sales job has evolved into a professional occupation. Today's salesperson is more concerned with helping customers select the correct product to meet their needs than with simply selling whatever is available. Modern professional salespeople advise and assist customers in their purchase decisions. Where repeat purchases are common, the salesperson must be certain that the buyer's purchases are in his or her best interest, or else no future sales will be made. The interests of the seller are tied to those of the buyer. This is another example of the importance of relationship marketing discussed in earlier chapters.

Not all sales activities are alike. While all sales activities assist the customer in some way, the exact tasks that are performed vary from one position to another. Three basic types of selling can be identified: (1) order processing, (2) creative selling, and (3) missionary selling.

Most sales jobs do not fall into any single category. Instead, we often find salespeople performing all three types of selling to a certain extent. A sales engineer for a computer firm may be doing 50

**TABLE 19.6** Factors Affecting the Importance of Personal Selling in the Promotional Mix

| | PERSONAL SELLING IS LIKELY TO BE MORE IMPORTANT WHEN | ADVERTISING IS LIKELY TO BE MORE IMPORTANT WHEN |
|---|---|---|
| **Consumer is** | geographically concentrated, relatively small in number | geographically dispersed, relatively large in number |
| **Product is** | expensive, technically complex, custom-made, requires special handling, frequently involves trade-ins | inexpensive, simple to understand, custom-made, requires special handling, frequently involves trade-ins |
| **Price is** | relatively high | relatively low |
| **Channels are** | relatively short | relatively long |

percent missionary selling, 45 percent creative selling, and 5 percent order processing. In other words, most sales jobs require staff to engage in a variety of sales activities. However, most selling jobs are classified on the basis of the primary selling task that is performed. We will examine each of these categories.

## Order Processing

**Order processing** is most often typified by selling at the wholesale and retail levels. Salespeople who handle this task must do the following:

1. *Identify customer needs.* For instance, a soft-drink route salesperson determines that a store that normally carries inventory of 40 cases has only 7 cases left in stock.
2. *Point out the needs to the customer.* The route salesperson informs the store manager of the inventory situation.
3. *Complete or write up the order.* The store manager acknowledges the situation, the driver unloads 33 cases, and the manager signs the delivery slip.

Order processing is part of most selling jobs, but becomes the primary task in a routine or repeat buying situation when needs can be readily identified and then acknowledged by the customer. Getting business is more a matter of trading on the reputation of the company, which the customer has already decided to deal with.

**order processing**
Selling at the wholesale and retail levels; involves identifying customer needs, pointing out these needs to the customer, and completing the order.

## Creative Selling

**Creative selling** is much more demanding. Often, customers first have to be found, then helped to make a purchase decision. When a considerable degree of analytical decision making on the part of the consumer is involved in purchasing a product, the salesperson must skillfully solicit an order from a prospect. To do so, creative selling techniques must be used. New products often require a high degree of creative selling. The seller must make the buyer see the worth of the item. Creative selling may be the most demanding of the three selling tasks.

An example of how a sales job evolves into creative selling is found in one chemical company. Originally, selling chemicals was a relatively straightforward job. The salesperson was assigned a territory and dispatched to tap every possible customer. She or he was told little about the division's goals or about the profitability of the list of products. Salespeople's marching orders were uncomplicated: sell all you can, as fast as you can.

But the salesperson's job has become much more complex. Now the company tells salespeople: "Don't just sell—we need information. What do our customers need? What is the competition

**creative selling**
Selling that involves making the buyer see the worth of the item.

doing? What sort of financial package do we need to win the order?" Salespeople also are expected to mediate disputes between the credit department and slow-paying customers and to sort out customer complaints concerning the company's products. They must keep informed of fast changes in both government regulations and world chemical markets. In short, the salesperson's job requires applying informed management skills to solving customers' problems.

### Missionary Selling

**Missionary selling** is an indirect type of selling; people sell the goodwill of a firm and provide customers with technical or operational assistance. For example, a toiletries company salesperson may call on retailers to look after special promotions and overall stock movement, although a wholesaler is used to take orders and deliver merchandise. In more recent times, technical and operational assistance, such as that provided by a systems specialist, have also become a critical part of missionary selling.

## Characteristics of Successful Salespeople

The saying "Salespeople are born, not made" is untrue. Most people have some degree of sales ability. Each of us is called upon to sell others our ideas, philosophy, or personality at some time. However, some individuals adapt to selling more easily than others. Selling is not an easy job; it involves a great deal of hard work. Many college and university graduates find it an extremely rewarding and challenging career.

Effective salespeople are self-motivated individuals who are well-prepared to meet the demands of the competitive marketplace. The continuing pressure to solve buyers' problems requires that salespeople develop good work habits and exhibit considerable initiative.

Successful salespeople are not only self-starters, they are also knowledgeable businesspeople. Salespeople are also in the peculiar position of having their knowledge tested almost continually, so sales success is often a function of how well a salesperson can handle questions. Salespeople must know their company, their products, their competition, their customers, and themselves. They must also be able to analyze customer needs and fit them with products and services that satisfy those needs.

## The Sales Process

The sales process involves seven steps. While the terminology may vary, most authorities agree on the following sequence:

1. prospecting and qualifying
2. approach
3. presentation
4. demonstration
5. handling objections
6. closing
7. follow-up

### Prospecting and Qualifying

**Prospecting**—identifying potential customers—is difficult work that often involves many hours of diligent effort. Prospects may come from many sources: previous customers, friends and neighbours, other vendors, nonsales employees in the firm, suppliers, and social and professional contacts. New sales personnel often find prospecting frustrating, since there is usually no immediate payoff. But without prospecting, there are no future sales. Prospecting is a continuous process because there will always be a loss of some customers over time, a loss that must be compensated for with new customers or the discovery of potential customers who have never been contacted. Many sales management experts consider prospecting to be the very essence of the sales process.

**Qualifying**—determining that the prospect is really a potential customer—is another important sales task. Not all prospects are qualified to become customers. Qualified customers are people with both the money and the authority to make purchase decisions. A person with an annual income of $25 000 may wish to own a $70 000 car, but this person's ability to actually become a customer must be questioned.

## Approach

Once the salesperson has identified a qualified prospect, he or she collects all available information relative to the potential buyer and plans an **approach**—the initial contact between the salesperson and the prospective customer. All approaches should be based on comprehensive research. The salesperson should find out as much as possible about the prospect and the environment in which the prospect operates.

approach
The initial contact between the salesperson and the prospective customer.

## Presentation

When the salesperson gives the sales message to a prospective customer, she or he makes a **presentation**. The seller describes the product's major features, points out its strengths, and concludes by citing illustrative successes. The seller's objective is to talk about the product or service in terms that are meaningful to the buyer—that is, to discuss benefits rather than technical specifications. Thus, the presentation is the stage where the salesperson relates product features to customer needs. The presentation should be clear and concise, and should emphasize the positive.

presentation
The act of giving the sales message to a prospective customer.

## Demonstration

**Demonstration** can play a critical role in a sales presentation. A demonstration ride in a new car allows the prospect to become involved in the presentation. It awakens customer interest in a way no amount of verbal presentation can. Demonstrations supplement, support, and reinforce what the salesperson has already told the prospect.

The key to a good demonstration is planning. A unique demonstration is more likely to gain a customer's attention than a "usual" sales presentation. But such a demonstration must be well planned and executed if a favourable impression is to be made. The need for the salesperson to check and recheck all aspects of the demonstration before delivering it cannot be overemphasized.

demonstration
Actions that supplement, support, and reinforce what the salesperson has already told the prospect.

## Handling Objections

A vital part of selling involves handling objections. It is reasonable to expect a customer to say, "Well, I really should check with my family," "Perhaps I'll stop back next week," or "I like everything except the colour." A good salesperson, however, should use each **objection** as a cue to provide additional information. In most cases, an objection such as "I don't like the bucket seats" is really the customer's way of asking what other choices or product features are available. A customer's question reveals an interest in the product. It allows the seller an opportunity to expand a presentation by providing additional information.

objection
Reveals a customer's interest in a product and can be used as a cue to provide additional information.

## Closing

The moment of truth in selling is the **closing**, for this is when the salesperson asks the prospect for an order. A salesperson should not hesitate during the closing. If he or she has made an effective presentation based on applying the product to the customer's needs, the closing should be the natural conclusion.

A surprising number of salespeople have a hard time actually asking for an order. But to be effective, they must overcome this difficulty.

closing
The act of asking the prospect for an order.

## Follow-Up

The post-sales activities that often determine whether a person will become a repeat customer constitute the sales **follow-up**. To the maximum extent possible, sales representatives should contact their customers to find out if they are satisfied with their purchases. This step allows the salesperson to psychologically reinforce the buyer's original decision to buy. It gives the seller an opportunity,

follow-up
The post-sales activities that often determine whether a person will become a repeat customer.

in addition to correcting any sources of discontent with the purchase, to secure important market information and to make additional sales. Car dealers often keep elaborate records on their previous customers. This allows them to remind individuals when they might be due for a new car. One successful travel agency never fails to telephone customers on their return from a trip. Proper follow-up is a logical part of the selling sequence.

## Managing the Sales Effort

**sales management**
Securing, maintaining, motivating, supervising, evaluating, and controlling the field sales force.

The selling function is made effective through **sales management**, which involves securing, maintaining, motivating, supervising, evaluating, and controlling the field sales force. The sales manager is the link between the firm and the marketplace through the sales force. The sales manager has a challenging task that involves interpreting and implementing company strategy through a diverse group of sales representatives. Similarly, since the sales force also represents the customers, the sales manager must represent customers' and sales representatives' needs and concerns to senior management.

The sales manager performs seven basic managerial functions: (1) recruitment and selection, (2) training, (3) organization, (4) supervision, (5) motivation, (6) compensation, and (7) evaluation and control. Each of these is an elaborate and demanding task; unfortunately, describing them in detail is beyond the scope of this book. An interested reader can refer to many books on sales management.

## SUMMARY

This chapter has discussed the major advertising media and has illustrated the main marketing communications applications: advertising, sales promotion, public relations and publicity, and personal selling.

Today's widespread markets make advertising an important part of business. Advertising expenditures as a proportion of sales vary among different industries and companies because of the different role that advertising plays in the different marketing mixes.

There are four basic types of advertising: informative product advertising, persuasive product advertising, reminder-oriented product advertising, and institutional advertising.

Cooperative advertising involves the retailer and the manufacturer sharing advertising costs. Comparative advertising makes direct promotional comparisons with competitive brands.

Celebrity marketing is the process of engaging celebrities to lend their names and influence in promoting a product. Role model marketing associates a product with the positive perception of a type of individual or role.

Advertisements have to be created with both the consumer and the advertising medium in mind. Selecting advertising media is an important task that enables the marketer to precisely direct the message. Television and newspapers are the most important advertising media, followed by direct mail.

Direct response marketing is an interactive system of marketing that uses one or more advertising media to effect a measurable response or transaction at any location.

Sales promotion includes such activities as point-of-purchase advertising; specialty advertising; samples, coupons, premiums, deals, rebates, loyalty programs; contests; and trade shows.

Public relations is the component of marketing communications that focuses on fostering goodwill for the company. One aspect of PR is publicity, which is normally unpaid communication that disseminates positive information about company activities and products.

The three basic types of selling are order processing, creative selling, and missionary selling. The sales process involves seven steps: prospecting and qualifying, approach, presentation, demonstration, handling objections, closing, and follow-up.

There are a growing number of useful Web sites that can provide further insight on the topics discussed in this chapter. Web sites such as those for the Ad Age Group, the Ad Council, *Adweek* magazine, and the University of Texas at Austin Department of Advertising are good places to start.

www.adage.com

www.adcouncil.org

www.adweek.com

www.advertising.utexas.edu/world/inde.html

# KEY TERMS

advertising agency, p. 489

approach, p. 499

buzz marketing, p. 481

celebrity marketing, p. 480

closing, p. 499

comparative advertising, p. 479

cooperative advertising, p. 476

creative selling, p. 497

demonstration, p. 499

direct response marketing, p. 490

follow-up, p. 499

informative product advertising, p. 476

institutional advertising, p. 476

loyalty program, p. 494

missionary selling, p. 498

objection, p. 499

order processing, p. 497

persuasive product advertising, p. 476

point-of-purchase advertising, p. 493

post-testing, p. 489

presentation, p. 499

pretesting, p. 489

product advertising, p. 476

prospecting, p. 498

public relations, p. 494

publicity, p. 495

qualifying, p. 498

reminder-oriented product advertising, p. 476

role model marketing, p. 481

sales management, p. 500

specialty advertising, p. 493

trade show, p. 494

# INTERACTIVE SUMMARY AND DISCUSSION QUESTIONS

1. Advertising expenditures as a proportion of sales vary among different industries and companies because of the different role that advertising plays in the different marketing mixes. Rank the following industries in terms of proportionate advertising expenditures (1 = lowest proportion), and then explain your reasoning.
___ Soap/detergent ___ Chemicals ___ Restaurant

2. Advertising is the most important component in the marketing mix for positioning a product. A product can be positioned by attributes, price/quality, competitor, application, product user, and product class. Give an example of each.

3. There are four basic types of advertising: informative product advertising, persuasive product advertising, reminder-oriented product advertising, and institutional advertising. What type of advertising would you recommend for Ford Motor Company? For Compaq computers? For Mohawk gas? Explain your reasoning.

4. Television is the second-largest advertising medium. Television advertising can be divided into three categories: network, national spot, and local spot. When would each be used, and who would be the likely users?

5. "The final step in the advertising process is the development and preparation of an advertisement." Outline the earlier steps.

6. Cooperative advertising involves the sharing of advertising costs between the retailer and the manufacturer. Develop an argument favouring or opposing the use of cooperative advertising by a marketer who is currently preparing an advertising plan. Make any assumptions that are necessary.

7. Comparative advertising makes direct promotional comparisons with competitive brands. Suggest a list of conditions under which a company should consider using comparative advertising.

8. The famous advertiser and head of DDB Advertising Agency, William Bernbach, said about advertising, "You must crash through the wall." Explain and elaborate on the meaning of this statement.

9. Direct marketing is an interactive system of marketing that uses one or more advertising media to effect a measurable response or transaction at any location. Compare and contrast this with general advertising.

10. Publicity is generating awareness about a product beyond regular advertising methods. Discuss the advantages and limitations of using publicity.

11. Develop a plan for a publicity campaign for a newly opened dry cleaner in a strip mall near a residential neighbourhood.

**12.** Celebrity marketing is the process of engaging celebrities to lend their names and influence in promoting a product. Role model marketing associates a product with the positive perception of a type of individual or role. Give an example of a role model marketing campaign.

**13.** Sales promotion includes such activities as point-of-purchase advertising; specialty advertising; samples, coupons, premiums, deals, rebates, and loyalty programs; contests; and trade shows. Sales promotion seems to be growing at the expense of advertising. How can this be?

**14.** The three basic types of selling are order processing, creative selling, and missionary selling. Give an example of each.

**15.** The expression "Salespeople are born, not made" is untrue. Explain why.

**16.** The sales process involves seven steps: prospecting and qualifying, approach, presentation, demonstration, handling objections, closing, and follow-up. Distinguish between the sales process and a sales call.

**17.** Select three products of interest. Find a Web advertisement, a TV advertisement, and a print advertisement for each. Compare them and write an evaluation of their estimated role and value in marketing the products.

## Fujifilm

"Don't Say Cheese," the latest campaign for the Fujifilm digital camera plays on the idea that taking pictures should be spontaneous and creative not stilted and

www.fujifilm.ca

posed. "We're asking consumers to step back, stop worrying about obtaining the perfect or conventional picture and start spontaneously experimenting with their surroundings—from family and friends to pets and old deck shoes," said Tim Berry, VP and GM, Marketing with Fuji Photo Film Canada Inc. The campaign builds on last year's "Open Your Eyes" theme and includes both television and print elements done by John St., a

Toronto-based ad shop. The print ad uses a montage of candid pictures set above the "Don't Say Cheese" tagline to convey the idea that digital cameras allow budding photographers to capture anything they like and then be selective about what they print.

### You Be the Marketer

Review the advertisement and evaluate it. Among other things you might want to consider:

- The layout of the ad
- The information portrayed
- The message delivered
- The creativity of the ad
- The value of the ad to Fujifilm

Source: "Ad Review: Pretty Ad Comes up Short on Selling the Product," *The Financial Post*, May 27, 2002. Reprinted with permission.

A company with a global vision.

# GLOBAL MARKETING

Global business is the life blood of Acadian Seaplants Limited of Dartmouth, Nova Scotia. It has found an exclusive niche market in Japan for its cultivated seaweeds, which it has been exporting to that country for over eight years.

For a company engaged primarily in the cultivation, processing, and development of value-added seaweed and seaweed-based products, it was no accident to target Japan where 15 percent of the Japanese diet is seaweed.

Market and product research was key to the operation. "This is one of the facts we discovered during our extensive market research," says company Chairman and Founder, Louis Deveau. "We had one of our people spend six months in Japan, studying conditions and requirements for our products—with good assistance there from Canada's Trade Commissioner Service."

With confirmation that Japan was indeed looking for cultivated seaweed, Acadian's unique cultivated pink seaweed, called Aka Hana-nori, was first introduced to the Japanese food market in the middle 1990s. Based on its success, the company soon produced green (Ao Hana-nori) and the first-ever yellow (Kiku Hana-nori).

With an emphasis on quality it has achieved worldwide distribution and recognition as a diversified manufacturer of innovative and top quality products.

Acadian's seaweeds are grown on land in outdoor growing ponds containing purified seawater, under quality-controlled conditions.

The company received a Canada Export Award in 1996 and more recently the 2001 Canadian Innovation Award for Technology.

About 98 percent of Acadian's products—which include feed additives, fertilizers, animal feed, and ingredients for health and beauty products and the brewing industry—are exported to over 65 countries.

"These unique seaweed food products from Canada have met with exceptional Japanese market acceptance and demand," explains Hiroki Nakamoto, the company's Sales and Marketing Manager—Food Division. "As a matter of fact, when it comes to demand, we sell absolutely everything we can grow to Japan."

The products are sold for use in retail grocery products, restaurants, hotels, convenience stores, and institutional food services (hospitals, universities). Uses range from seaweed salads to sashimi garnishes and soup ingredients.

## Ingredients for Success

Nakamoto, who makes frequent trips to Japan, calling on customers and investigating new markets, is also quick to emphasize quality. "When it comes to selling products abroad, especially food, it has to be of the highest quality," he insists. "Other ingredients include good market research, strong customer relations, understanding market structures and regulations, and specific requirements such as food certifications."

What better proof than Acadian's resounding success in Japan?

**Acadian Seaplants Limited is just one of thousands of companies who have found success through global marketing. Through careful planning and follow-through they have been able to carve out a very successful business in a difficult, but rewarding marketplace.**

Source: "A Niche Market Worth Cultivating," *CanadExport*, (Department of Foreign Affairs & International Trade), Volume 20, No. 5, March 15, 2002, p. 10. Reproduced with the permission of Her Majesty the Queen in Right of Canada, as represented by the Minister for International Trade, 2002.

www.acadianseaplants.com

# INTRODUCTION

Without international trade Canada would be an out-of-date backwater. International trade is vital to a nation and its business for several reasons. International business expands the market for a country's or firm's products and thus makes possible further production and distribution economies. An added benefit to an exporting firm that has global trade experience is that it can compete more effectively with foreign competitors who enter this market at a later date. Furthermore, international involvement is the only way many firms can survive in the competitive world marketplace. Global marketing can also mean more jobs at home. It is estimated that some 11 000 new jobs are supported by every billion export dollars.

International marketing is growing rapidly. It not only is good for business, but also provides tremendous career opportunities for marketing graduates who are willing to become involved in doing business in an unfamiliar culture.

www.gm.com

www.pwrm.com

Some Canadian companies depend heavily on their ability to sell their products abroad. For companies like Acadian Seaplants Limited, General Motors, Bombardier, Alberta and Southern Gas, and others, the majority of sales dollars come from customers in other countries. Many smaller companies have also discovered the value of selling into international markets. Indeed, some companies, like high-tech Power Measurement Ltd. of Victoria, British Columbia, would find it difficult to survive without international sales. For such companies, the Canadian market may not even be large enough for their specialized products.

Business is now international. Whether you are a farmer, a small local retailer, a wholesaler, or one of the established Canadian telecommunications companies, you will be affected by global competition. International goods, services, and competitors are found in virtually every aspect of the Canadian (and every other country's) economy. In developing business strategy, this international dimension must be as carefully considered as the domestic environment.

Some 2 million Canadians—1 in 5 of the labour market—work in areas that are directly or indirectly related to export trade. Thus, there is a good chance that every single Canadian has a close connection with export trade through family or friends. Thirty cents of every dollar of our gross national product (GNP) comes from our exports.

Our exports pay for the things we import to meet our high standard of living expectations—our morning orange juice, fresh vegetables in winter, wool and cotton clothes, TV sets, some cars, and some computers. On another level, exports not only provide jobs, they also pay for the interest and dividends on foreign investment, for the deficit on tourism, for access to foreign technologies, and for the borrowing that different levels of government use to finance our economic development.

In other words, foreign trade is important to Canada from both the *exporting* and the *importing* viewpoints. International trade is more important to the economy of some countries than others. In addition to Canada, countries such as the United Kingdom, Belgium, the Scandinavian countries, and New Zealand also heavily depend on international trade. On the other hand, although the United States is both the largest exporter and the largest importer in the world, its exports account for only about 7.7 percent of its gross national product. Compare this with the percentages for Belgium (88 percent) and Germany (33 percent). Canadian exports account for about 44 percent of our GNP. Canada's leading trading partners are shown in Table 20.1. The United States is clearly our chief trading partner, supplying about 76 percent of our imports and buying about 79 percent of our exports.

There are both similarities and differences between international and domestic marketing. This chapter examines characteristics of the global marketplace, environmental influences on marketing, and the development of an international marketing mix. Most of this chapter considers global marketing from the perspective of a company. However, we will first introduce the basic concepts of international trade from a nation's point of view.

## TABLE 20.1 Canadian Imports and Exports of Goods on a Balance-of-Payments Basis

| | 1996 | 1997 | 1998 | 1999 | 2000 | 2001 |
|---|---|---|---|---|---|---|
| | | | $ MILLIONS | | | |
| **Exports to:** | **280 079.3** | **303 378.2** | **326 180.7** | **365 233.2** | **422 558.7** | **413 109.8** |
| United States[1] | 222 461.3 | 242 542.3 | 269 335.8 | 309 193.7 | 359 551.2 | 351 085.0 |
| Japan | 12 423.4 | 11 925.5 | 9 639.9 | 9 552.0 | 10 312.3 | 9 362.8 |
| United Kingdom | 4 608.5 | 4 689.5 | 5 235.0 | 5 672.2 | 6 700.4 | 6 454.0 |
| Other European Economic Community countries | 12 796.3 | 13 260.4 | 13 758.4 | 13 653.5 | 15 408.6 | 15 453.2 |
| Other OECD[2] | 5 087.8 | 8 849.0 | 8 889.9 | 8 986.5 | 10 171.1 | 10 296.3 |
| Other countries[3] | 22 702.0 | 22 111.6 | 19 321.6 | 18 175.4 | 20 415.2 | 20 458.4 |
| | | | | | | |
| **Imports from:** | **237 688.6** | **277 726.5** | **303 378.0** | **326 843.7** | **363 281.3** | **350 502.8** |
| United States[1] | 180 010.1 | 211 450.8 | 233 759.1 | 249 331.2 | 267 674.5 | 255 086.9 |
| Japan | 7 227.4 | 8 711.0 | 9 663.3 | 10 588.8 | 11 713.9 | 10 585.0 |
| United Kingdom | 5 581.1 | 6 126.5 | 6 083.1 | 7 689.3 | 12 256.7 | 11 830.2 |
| Other European Economic Community countries | 14 994.7 | 18 112.9 | 19 149.0 | 20 739.4 | 21 171.2 | 23 212.2 |
| Other OECD[2] | 9 040.6 | 11 376.7 | 11 392.4 | 13 253.0 | 18 946.7 | 18 609.8 |
| Other countries[3] | 20 834.6 | 21 948.7 | 23 331.2 | 25 242.0 | 31 518.3 | 31 178.8 |
| | | | | | | |
| **Balance** | **42 390.7** | **25 651.7** | **22 802.7** | **38 389.5** | **59 277.4** | **62 607.0** |
| United States[1] | 42 451.2 | 31 091.5 | 35 576.7 | 59 862.5 | 91 876.7 | 95 998.1 |
| Japan | 5 196.0 | 3 214.5 | -23.4 | -1 036.8 | -1 401.6 | -1 222.2 |
| United Kingdom | -972.6 | -1 437.0 | -848.1 | -2 017.1 | -5 556.3 | -5 376.2 |
| Other European Economic Community countries | -2 198.4 | -4 852.5 | -5 390.6 | -7 085.9 | -5 762.6 | -7 759.0 |
| Other OECD[2] | -3 952.8 | -2 527.7 | -2 502.5 | -4 266.5 | -8 775.6 | -8 313.5 |
| Other countries[3] | 1 867.4 | 162.9 | -4 009.6 | -7 066.6 | -11 103.1 | -10 720.4 |

[1] Includes also Puerto Rico and Virgin Islands.
[2] Organisation for Economic Co-operation and Development excluding the United States, Japan, United Kingdom and the other European Economic Community countries.
[3] Countries not included in the European Economic Community or the OECD.

Source: Adapted from the Statistics Canada Web site http://www.statcan.ca/English/Pgdb/gblec02a.htm. Reproduced with permission of the Minister of Industry.

# MEASURING A COUNTRY'S INTERNATIONAL TRADE ACTIVITY

Since imports and exports are important contributors to a country's economic welfare, governments and other organizations are concerned about the status of various components of international marketing. The concepts of balance of trade and balance of payments are a good starting point for understanding international business.

## Balance of Trade

A nation's **balance of trade** is determined by the relationship between a country's exports and its imports. A favourable balance of trade (trade surplus) occurs when the value of a nation's exports exceeds its imports. This means that, other things being equal, new money would come into the country's economic system via the sales abroad of the country's products. An unfavourable balance

**balance of trade**
The relationship between a country's exports and its imports.

of trade (trade deficit), by contrast, results when imports exceed exports. The net money flow would then be outward, other things being equal.

On the whole, Canada has maintained a favourable balance of trade. However, as Table 20.1 shows, Canada has a large positive balance with the United States that masks negative balances with a number of other trading partners.

## Balance of Payments

A country's balance of trade plays a vital role in determining its **balance of payments**, the flow of money into or out of a country. However, other factors are also important. A favourable balance of payments (or "current account") indicates that there is a net money inflow; an unfavourable balance of payments means that there is a net money outflow from the country.

The balance of payments is also affected by such factors as tourism, interest on foreign borrowings, military expenditures abroad, investment abroad, and foreign aid. A money outflow caused by these factors may exceed the money inflow from a favourable balance of trade and leave a nation with an unfavourable balance of payments.

Figure 20.1 shows that Canada has had a positive merchandise trade balance. However, because of a negative non-merchandise balance, the overall balance of payments has been mostly negative since 1987, until 1999. Thus, for most of this period, Canadian residents spent more than they earned abroad.

## Exchange Rate Adjustments

When the real value of a currency is out of line with international currencies in terms of relative buying power, the **exchange rate**, the rate at which a nation's currency can be exchanged for other

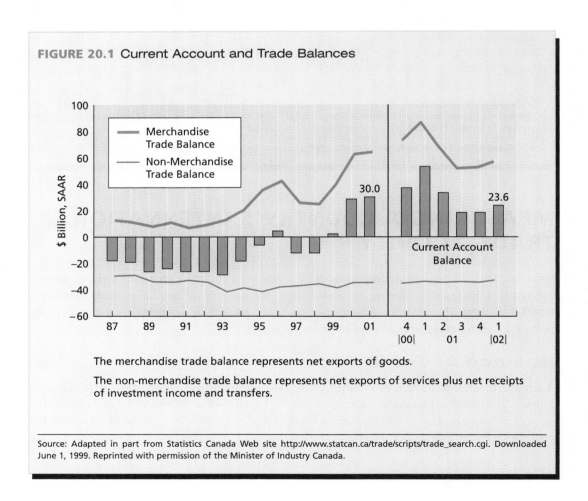

**FIGURE 20.1** Current Account and Trade Balances

The merchandise trade balance represents net exports of goods.

The non-merchandise trade balance represents net exports of services plus net receipts of investment income and transfers.

Source: Adapted in part from Statistics Canada Web site http://www.statcan.ca/trade/scripts/trade_search.cgi. Downloaded June 1, 1999. Reprinted with permission of the Minister of Industry Canada.

### HOW THE EURO IS HAVING AN IMPACT ON TRAVELLING ABROAD

Once upon a time, travellers in Europe going from country to country needed to develop a strategy for paying for their dinners.

One could get a fistful of cash, no small thing in Italy where, in early November last year, a meal that cost the equivalent of $75 in Canadian funds was presented as a bill for 101 000 lira.

Or one could have used traveller's cheques sold with a typical 1-percent service charge and cashed for variable rates of exchange in various businesses.

Finally, it would have been possible to risk paying with a credit card at an exchange rate not known at the time of purchase but seldom as good as a rate one can get with careful currency shopping at competing banks.

Today, the monetary landscape has changed, for since January 1, 2002, the euro, worth about $1.55 in Canadian funds, has become legal tender in a dozen countries: Austria, Belgium, Finland, France, Germany, Greece, Ireland, Italy, Luxembourg, the Netherlands, Portugal, and Spain. By virtue of being accepted in those countries, it is also the common currency of San Marino, Andorra, Monaco, and the Vatican, which, encapsulated within Rome, is going along with monetary union.

With one currency, most of Europe is now in the single currency zone.

The exceptions are EU member holdouts Denmark, Sweden, and Britain. As well, Switzerland, which is not in the EU, retains its franc. The traveller's nightmare of converting from, say, Canadian dollars to sterling, then leftover pounds to francs, then converting remaining French money to deutsche marks and watching buying power shrivel from handling fees and exchange spreads is over.

The transactions costs of handling European money are a fraction of what they were.

Consistent euro pricing across Europe has made it easy to compare prices in one country to another. For instance, a Big Mac in Greece costs 2.11 euros, compared to the 4.60 euros price for the same product from a McDonald's outlet in Ireland.

There is not much worry that anyone is going to cross distant borders to scarf down burgers, but price transparency should affect consumers' buying patterns for costly durable goods.

Price gaps may close most rapidly in businesses where shaving input prices may make the difference between profit and loss. Managers know their costs and should shop their raw materials or components carefully.

The single currency reduces transaction costs and so reduces input prices. That downward pressure on prices should eventually work through to equalize many retail prices.

Some price gaps will probably not change. Trains cost more in Amsterdam than in Lisbon, a reflection of varying real income levels and different numbers of stops, stations, and running costs. Anyway, transparent or not, taking the Metro in Paris is a decision that should have nothing to do with the price of the U-bahn in Berlin.

**What are the implications of the existence of the euro currency for a Canadian company that exports products to several different European countries?**

Source: Excerpted from "How The Euro Is Having An Impact On Traveling Abroad," *The Globe and Mail*, Tuesday, May 14, 2002, p. F3.

currencies or gold, may change. (See the Practising Marketer box for an unusual but practical example.) Some countries try to fix the exchange rate. In Canada we have a floating rate. Fluctuations in the exchange rate have a significant impact on both the balance of trade and the balance of payments. Because of this, government policy may lead to efforts to stem significant fluctuations by buying or selling foreign—for example, U.S.—currency.

**Devaluation** occurs when a nation reduces the value of its currency in relation to gold or some other currency. Devaluation of the dollar has the effect of making Canadian products less expensive abroad and trips to Canada cheaper for foreign visitors, thus enhancing export trade. On the other hand, imports are more expensive. As a result, importing and cross-border shopping become much less attractive. **Revaluation**, a less typical case, occurs when a country adjusts the value of its currency upward. This makes imports cheaper and exports more expensive. Either of these actions may force firms to modify their world marketing strategies.

**devaluation**
Situation in which a nation reduces the value of its currency in relation to gold or some other currency.

**revaluation**
Situation in which a country adjusts the value of its currency upward.

## The Case for Open Trade[3]

It is better for a country to be open to, and to facilitate trade with, other countries. Open trade between countries benefits those countries, including consumers and business in general. There is a strong case for an open trading system. One piece of evidence is the experience of world trade and economic growth since World War II. Since that time, tariffs have fallen steeply and now average less than 4 percent in industrialized countries. During the first decades after the war, world economic growth averaged about 5 percent per year, a high rate that was partly the result of lower trade barriers. World trade grew even faster, averaging about 8 percent during the period. There is a definite statistical link between freer trade and economic growth.

There are strong reasons for the link. All countries, including the poorest, have assets—human, industrial, natural, financial—that they can employ to produce goods and services for their domestic markets or to compete overseas. We can benefit when these goods and services are traded. Simply put, the principle of *comparative advantage* (discussed in more detail in a later section) says that countries prosper most by taking advantage of their assets in order to concentrate on what they can produce best, and then by trading these products for products that other countries produce best.

Firms do exactly that quite naturally on the domestic market. But what about the international market? Most firms recognize that the bigger the market, the greater their potential—they can expand until they are at their most efficient size, and they can have access to large numbers of customers.

## Will Trade Take Away from a Nation's Self-Sufficiency?

The Pacific island republic of Nauru has only a few thousand people but one of the richest deposits of phosphate in the world. New Zealand has a very productive sheep and cattle industry. Singapore has about 4 million people crowded into a small area. However, it has become one of the largest ports in the world, and has specialized in being a financial and information centre for the entire region. Kuwait has rich oil fields but few other industries or resources. Should these countries try to diversify their product base in order to increase their self-sufficiency?

The economic argument is that nations are usually better off specializing in certain products or marketing activities. By doing what they do best, nations are able to exchange products for foreign-made goods they need. Nauru could attempt to develop a tourist trade, but it has opted to specialize in phosphate mining. This allows the country a higher standard of living than would be possible through diversified business enterprises.

Nevertheless, a nation should not necessarily remain fixated on producing certain products or services. Just as the ability to compete well in certain products can shift from company to company, the same can happen between countries. Over time, countries (and their businesses) need to evolve from a pure commodity approach in order to become more efficient in world trade, and thus create more economic opportunity for their people.

For example, if "specialization" means selling nonrenewable resources, a country could find itself without a specialty and have a devastating balance of trade when these resources diminish.

Canada faces this problem to some degree. For example, it has quite a high volume of trade with Japan and has generally maintained a positive balance of trade with that country. The problem for Canada is that it sells Japan mostly raw materials (coal, wood, pulp, softwood lumber, precious metals, fish, and wheat) while importing manufactured goods from Japan (cars, computers, telecommunications equipment, and photographic products). Canada is not likely to run out of its resources because most are renewable. The problem is that this trade does not create as many jobs as secondary manufacturing. The challenge is to expand exports of finished goods that create more jobs at home.

Specialization by countries sometimes produces odd situations. A classic example is the many Canadian tourist souvenirs and flags for sale in Canada that are made in China or some other country. Similarly, a number of "Buy Canadian" stickers can be found on the rear bumpers of Subarus and Toyotas.

## Comparative Advantage: Trade Is Beneficial

Understanding the concepts of absolute and comparative advantage is important to the study of global trade. These important concepts explain why all countries can benefit from trade.

### Absolute Advantage

A nation has an **absolute advantage** in the marketing of a product if it is the sole producer or can produce a product for less than anyone else. Since few nations are sole producers and economic conditions rapidly alter production costs, examples of absolute advantage are rare. However, suppose country A is better at making tractors, and country B is better at making computers. Clearly, both would benefit if A specialized in tractors and B specialized in computers, and then they traded. This is a case of absolute advantage.

**absolute advantage**
A nation has an absolute advantage in the marketing of a product if it is the sole producer or can produce a product for less than anyone else.

## Comparative Advantage

**comparative advantage**

A nation has a comparative advantage if it can produce a given product more efficiently per unit of output than it can produce other products.

What if a country is bad at making everything? Will trade drive all producers out of business? The answer is no. The reason is the principle of comparative advantage, one of the most powerful concepts in international trade. A nation has a **comparative advantage** if it can produce a given product more efficiently per unit of output than it can produce *other* products.

According to the principle of comparative advantage, countries A and B still stand to benefit from trading with each other even if A is better than B at making everything. The concept of comparative advantage, although a bit complicated, explains why it is beneficial for all nations to trade with one another. Comparative advantage is a *relative* concept. In comparison with country B, what goods should country A trade?

If A is far better at making tractors and only slightly better at making computers, then A should still invest resources in what it does best—making tractors—and export the product to B. B should still invest in what it does best—making computers—and export that product to A, even if it is not as efficient as A. Both would still benefit from the trade. A country does not have to be best at anything to gain from trade. That is comparative advantage.

Country A should produce and trade those products that it can. Thus, if country A produces tractors more efficiently per unit of output than it can produce other products, it should concentrate on producing tractors.

Country A should also buy products that it might produce, but less efficiently, from country B. A should do this even if it could produce these products more efficiently than country B. In total, A's outputs will be maximized by concentrating on its most efficiently produced product. This is because A's total productive capacity is fixed, and thus should be devoted to products that it makes most efficiently.

Country B has a comparative advantage in the product that it trades to country A because it is the one that B is most efficient at producing. Trade can be beneficial to both countries regardless of absolute costs. Nations will usually produce and export those goods in which they have the greatest comparative advantage and import those items in which they have the least comparative advantage (or the greatest comparative disadvantage).

Figure 20.2 suggests how the comparative advantage concept works for Canada. The export commodities tend to be those in which there is a comparative advantage. Being an industrialized nation with ample natural resources, Canada tends to export manufactured items, such as cars and machinery, and natural resources, such as grain, wood, and ores. By contrast, countries with lower-cost labour tend to specialize in products that require a significant labour content, such as textiles, shoes, and clothing.

Despite the principle of comparative advantage, there are noneconomic reasons for not specializing in certain items. Some countries refuse to specialize their productive efforts because they want to be self-sufficient. The Communist nations typically followed this pattern, to their disadvantage and downfall. It gradually became clear that it is impossible for a country to be fully self-sufficient. Self-sufficiency is also motivated by security concerns and the desire for high national status. Still other nations adopt the self-sufficiency viewpoint only for certain commodities that they regard as important to their long-run development. For instance, a country might choose to maintain self-sufficiency in weapons production for defence reasons.

# GOING INTERNATIONAL: HOW CAN A COMPANY GET INVOLVED?

There are a variety of approaches to global marketing that can be seen. Some firms do not get involved at all. Others export occasionally when an order happens to arrive from overseas or possibly when they have some excess product. Both of these could be classified as "not-committed approaches."

Among firms committed to international business, Warren Keegan has identified four different approaches: ethnocentric, polycentric, regiocentric, and geocentric.[4]

**FIGURE 20.2** Leading Commodities in Canadian Foreign Trade

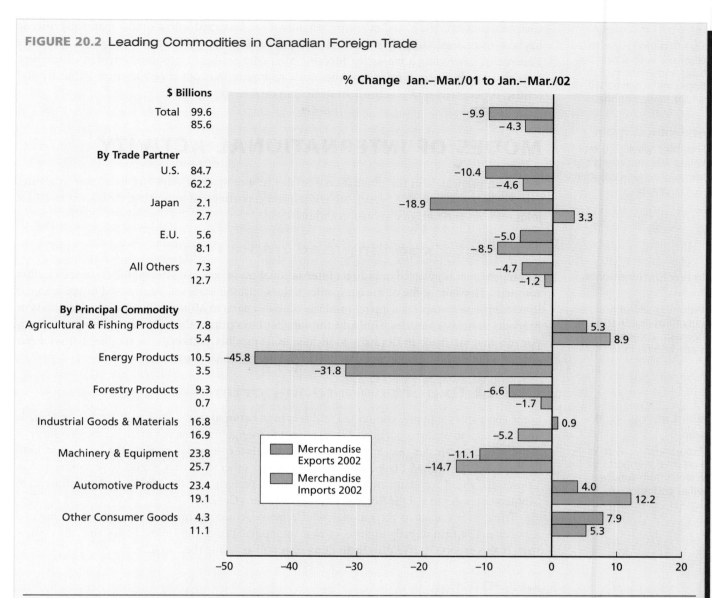

% Change  Jan.–Mar./01 to Jan.–Mar./02

| $ Billions | | |
|---|---|---|
| **Total** | 99.6 | –9.9 |
| | 85.6 | –4.3 |
| **By Trade Partner** | | |
| U.S. | 84.7 | –10.4 |
| | 62.2 | –4.6 |
| Japan | 2.1 | –18.9 |
| | 2.7 | 3.3 |
| E.U. | 5.6 | –5.0 |
| | 8.1 | –8.5 |
| All Others | 7.3 | –4.7 |
| | 12.7 | –1.2 |
| **By Principal Commodity** | | |
| Agricultural & Fishing Products | 7.8 | 5.3 |
| | 5.4 | 8.9 |
| Energy Products | 10.5 | –45.8 |
| | 3.5 | –31.8 |
| Forestry Products | 9.3 | –6.6 |
| | 0.7 | –1.7 |
| Industrial Goods & Materials | 16.8 | 0.9 |
| | 16.9 | –5.2 |
| Machinery & Equipment | 23.8 | –11.1 |
| | 25.7 | –14.7 |
| Automotive Products | 23.4 | 4.0 |
| | 19.1 | 12.2 |
| Other Consumer Goods | 4.3 | 7.9 |
| | 11.1 | 5.3 |

Merchandise Exports 2002
Merchandise Imports 2002

Source: Adapted in part from the Statistics Canada Web site http://www.statcan.ca/trade/scripts/trade_search.cgi. Reprinted with permission of the Minister of Industry Canada.

A company that is **ethnocentric** assumes that its way of doing business in its home market is the proper way to operate, and tries to replicate this in foreign markets. As the previous discussion has shown, such an inflexible approach is likely to severely inhibit the effectiveness of a firm's efforts in another country.

The opposite of the ethnocentric approach is the **polycentric** approach. Companies that are polycentric assume that every country is different and that a specific marketing approach should be developed for each separate country. This attitude certainly overcomes the inflexibility of ethnocentricity. For many firms, being insightful enough to see the pitfalls of the ethnocentric approach and being willing to adapt have become the foundation of success and are cause for some pride. Such an approach can be more costly, however, because the marketing must be custom-tailored to each individual country.

As business has become more global in its orientation, managers have found that it is not always necessary to develop a separate plan for each country. A **regiocentric** approach recognizes that coun-

**ethnocentric company**
Firm that assumes that its way of doing business in its home market is the proper way to operate, and tries to replicate this in foreign markets.

**polycentric company**
Firm that assumes that every country is different and that a specific marketing approach should be developed for each separate country.

tries with similar cultures and economic conditions can be served with a similar marketing mix. As has been mentioned earlier, in the case of some products it is possible to take a **geocentric** approach. This means developing a marketing mix that meets the needs of target consumers in all markets. Note that this is different from an ethnocentric approach. Depending on the circumstances, polycentric, regiocentric, and geocentric strategies can each be appropriate.

# MODES OF INTERNATIONAL ACTIVITY

Firms can participate in the international market in a number of ways and to a lesser or greater extent. The simplest level of participation is indirect exporting and importing; the highest levels are joint ventures and foreign production and marketing.

## Indirect Exporting and Importing

A company that is involved in **indirect international trade** does not attempt to buy or sell in other countries. However, some of the companies it does business with will be involved in exporting or importing. For example, a supplier produces and sells parts to Monarch Pumps, which markets its products in many countries. Similarly, the supplier buys from a Canadian distributor some components that are made in Germany to include in its product. Although the supplier has no direct contact with foreign firms, it is a vital part of the international market.

## Direct Exporting and Importing

Some companies are more committed to **direct international trade**. They may produce in Canada and then seek to export a portion of their output to foreign markets. For example, the developer of a software program for managing trucking distribution companies markets the product in both Canada and the United States, and considers which other countries would have similar needs. Conversely, an oil company imports crude oil from Venezuela or the Middle East to refineries in Montreal in order to sell the finished product in eastern Canada.

Triple E, a Canadian recreational vehicle manufacturer, is involved in both importing and exporting. The firm directly imports certain components from the United States and other countries. It also exports its RVs directly to Europe, as well as selling them in Canada.

## Licensing

**Licensing** allows a firm in another country to produce and sell a product for a fee paid to the licensing company. For example, the Canadian inventor of a commercial trash compactor displays her product at a trade show. Among the visitors to her booth is a Taiwanese businessman. Impressed with the product, he offers to produce and sell it in Taiwan under licence. The licence agreement gives him the know-how and legal right to produce the compactor in Taiwan at a set fee per unit. This saves the Canadian inventor a great deal of trouble. However, normally the return on licences is quite low, and it may be difficult to monitor patent control.

## Joint Venture

In an international **joint venture**, a company sets up a business in a foreign market by going into partnership with a local enterprise. Such an arrangement allows for financial risk to be shared and reduces the problems inherent in doing business in a foreign country, because the partner can supply knowledge of local marketing and production practices. More specifically, the partner can supply knowledge of the market itself (local tastes and preferences) and established relationships with local organizations (wholesalers, retailers, government agencies, banks) and customers. A joint venture requires a much greater commitment of resources than importing, exporting, or licensing. General Motors and Suzuki, in Ingersoll, Ontario, is an example of an international joint venture.

In China, a country of great potential but high risk, nearly 50 000 joint ventures were established in the first fifteen years after China started allowing them.[5]

## Foreign Production and Marketing

**Direct investment** in another country requires the greatest commitment to global enterprise. In such an enterprise, a firm invests in facilities, staff, and marketing programs in a foreign market without a local partner. If the enterprise is successful, the rewards do not have to be shared, and the business can operate freely without the need to make decisions jointly with a foreign partner. Canadian auto-parts manufacturer Magna International has such an operation in Mexico.

**direct investment**
The ownership and management of production and/or marketing facilities in a foreign country.

## Multinational Enterprise

A company that handles its own foreign production and marketing may be, or could become, a **multinational corporation** (MNC). An MNC produces and markets in several countries; it has a world orientation rather than loyalty to any one country. Thus, it chooses to produce in whichever country happens to be the best for the job. An MNC's marketing strategies in various countries are often similar or interrelated, and may follow a common theme.

Alcan Aluminum is a multinational corporation headquartered in Canada, but its products can be found around the world. The company has branches in many world markets. With approximately 80 percent of its sales originating outside Canada, the company must think in global rather than domestic terms.

**multinational corporation (MNC)**
A corporation that produces and markets goods and services in several countries.

w w w

www.alcan.com

# STARTING INTERNATIONAL OPERATIONS: STRATEGIC EXPORT PLANNING

Before deciding to "go international," a company needs to ensure that it has the following elements: a strong senior management commitment, adequate resources, a viable product, and strategic planning.

## Management Commitment

Developing and implementing a strategic plan for an international venture requires a substantial investment of financial and human resources for a considerable period before any profits are seen. Therefore, it is crucial that senior management be committed to an international venture before embarking on it.

## Adequate Resources

Before making any decision to export, a company needs to thoroughly review its domestic performance and capabilities. For example, sales profit margins and prices should be compared with those of the industry. If competitors are already exporting, this is a positive sign that there may be a good opportunity in the international market.

The company's own resources should be thoroughly assessed. Does it have the financial and human resources to research foreign markets? Does it have the production capacity to ensure prompt deliveries when orders come in? Reliability is one of the most essential requirements for success in selling internationally.

## Planning Should Be Part of Corporate Strategy

Export strategy should be part of overall corporate strategy. The company must be clear about its expectations of an international venture as well as fully aware of its own limitations. For example, if the company is not prepared to spend the time and money to research the market and to adapt and produce the proper type and quantity of products, then it should not be considering the export market.

Once management decides to examine the feasibility of an international venture, it should begin by scanning possible markets. Countries first considered would normally be those that are geographically close, similar in language and culture, or familiar to company officials. The preliminary scanning should include factors such as market size, political and economic stability, competition, distribution, and profit potential. This initial survey provides management with the information to select the four or five most likely markets for further analysis.

# CONSIDER KEY ENVIRONMENTAL AND MARKET VARIABLES

While some Canadian firms have never ventured outside their own domestic market, others have discovered the challenges as well as the payoffs of marketing abroad. In some ways, marketing in Malaysia is very similar to marketing in Canada. That is, the marketing principles discussed in this book apply everywhere. However, the economic environment and culture often result in significant differences in the implementation of a marketing plan.

Market size, for example, means different things in different countries. Thailand has a population almost twice as large as Canada's. However, its potential market for many products is quite small, since the per capita income is only about $3100, compared with Canada's $33 000. On the other hand, there could well be a very profitable market niche of well-to-do customers in Thailand.

## Buyer Behaviour

There are many influences on buyer behaviour. Some of these, as discussed in Chapters 2 and 8, represent components of the external environment, as well as cultural and individual elements. In international marketing, the culture of the country is a key factor.

## What Is Culture?

**culture**

An integrated system of learned behaviour patterns that are distinguishing characteristics of the members of any given society.

**Culture** is defined as an integrated system of learned behaviour patterns that are distinguishing characteristics of the members of any given society. It includes everything that a group thinks, says, does, and makes—its customs, language, material artifacts, and shared systems of attitudes and feelings.[6]

Culture therefore defines social structure, decision-making practices, and communication styles. It dictates behaviour, etiquette, and protocol and impacts everyone. It influences how we act and respond.

Because the culture of other countries is not the same as ours, we can easily make serious mistakes when visiting, or trying to do business in another country. Consider these situations caused by cultural misunderstandings:

**Misunderstanding # 1:** Leslie Whitman meets with Mohammed Sulaiman, a client in Malaysia. After a productive first meeting, Leslie warmly clasps Said's hand with two hands, emphasizing the depth of their mutual goodwill. For reasons Whitman never understands, Said is never again as cordial. Why not?

In Malaysia, and throughout the Muslim world, the left hand is considered to be unclean. By grasping Said with his left hand Whitman sent an extremely offensive message.

**Misunderstanding # 2:** Alex McClellan arrives in Mexico City to meet with a new client. Despite arriving at the specified appointment time Alex has to wait for 45 minutes before getting in to see the client. Alex is further frustrated because instead of getting down to business the Mexican spends time in small talk, then suggests lunch, and after that wants to show her the historical and cultural highlights of the city. What is happening?

Alex comes from Canada, a task-centred culture. The Mexican's culture values social activity and development of relationships highly, and wishes to establish a relationship before deciding whether or not to do business.

These are just two of dozens of misunderstandings that have occurred in attempting to transact international business. In such situations individuals have been frustrated or less successful because they had an imperfect understanding of another culture. Cultural differences can have great impact. Careful preparation can prepare one to avoid embarrassment and make the best of such situations.

## Avoiding Misunderstandings

In international settings business gifts are commonly given, but the process and circumstances are very different from country to country. In Latin America, it is customary to present business gifts only after negotiations have been completed. Also, gifts that bear logos are considered cheap. On the other hand, business transactions can suffer if gifts are deemed too personal. Business visitors to the Arab world should understand that Arabs believe their public image to be greatly enhanced by lavish gift giving. The giver who pays tribute to an Arab's honour and enhances that person's self-esteem presents the most successful gift.

The cultural nuances cannot be underestimated. In Japan, for instance, it is wise not to say "no" when asked a question. When a Japanese client asks if it is possible to modify a particular product, it may be better to say, "I'll think about it" or "Let me get back to you in a few days." Marketers must be careful that their marketing strategies comply with local customs, tastes, and buying practices.

In some cultures, long-term relationships are very important. When, for example, Nortel Networks became the first non-Japanese telecommunications company to make a major sale to Nippon Telegraph and Telephone with a $250-million seven-year deal, it was the culmination of a four-year marketing effort. Much of this effort was "trust-building" work. The company president alone made eleven trips to Japan within a space of six months.

## The Elements of Culture

In the study of culture there are characteristics known as *cultural universals*. These characteristics are manifestations of the way of life for a group of people. They include such elements as bodily adornments, courtship, etiquette, family, gestures, joking, mealtimes, music, personal names, status differentiation, and trade.[7] The common denominators for learning about and understanding these cultural universals are known as the elements of culture:

- Language
  - Verbal
  - Nonverbal
- Religion
- Values and attitudes
- Manners and customs
- Material elements
- Aesthetics
- Education
- Social institutions

Life and business are incorporated within the local pattern of each of these elements. Edward Hall has called these the "hidden language" of foreign cultures.[8]

Using nonverbal language as an example, consider body language. Different cultures vary in the amount of personal space they find comfortable. Latin Americans and Arabs like to stand close to people they are speaking with. Canadians like a greater distance. Therefore, Canadians would likely find themselves backing away from a Latin American in a conversation. This might be taken as a negative reaction.

Space does not permit a similar discussion for each of the other elements of culture, but a similar set of challenges and opportunities will be found for each one.

This analysis shows that culture is like an iceberg—only the tip can be seen. There is a remaining huge portion of the iceberg hidden below the surface that can cause great difficulties for a person or firm involved in international business.

Venturing into different cultures without adequate preparation can be just as dangerous as a ship manoeuvring icy waters without charts, hoping to be lucky enough to avoid hitting an iceberg. The difference is that the ship will know immediately when it hits an iceberg. Unsuspecting companies may never realize they hit an iceberg but they will, nevertheless, feel the impact. It appears in the form of delayed or abandoned projects, misunderstood communications, frustrated employees, and a loss of business and reputation. The costs of cultural myopia and the inability to adjust can be staggering.[9]

## Economic and Societal Factors

International marketing is also affected and influenced by economic and societal factors. The economic status of some countries makes them less (or more) likely candidates for international business expansion. Nations with lower per capita income may still represent a market but packaging may have to change (for example, sizes may have to be much smaller). Wealthier countries can prove to be prime markets for the products of many Canadian industries, particularly those involved with consumer goods and advanced business products, but there are frequently wealthy market segments to be found in less well-off countries.

Many products have failed abroad simply because the producing firm tried to use the same marketing strategy that was successful at home. Consider an advertising strategy based primarily on using print media that features testimonials. Such a campaign would have dim prospects in a less developed nation with a high degree of illiteracy. Other marketing practices can be transferred successfully. It all depends—and that is why a systematic market assessment is even more important in marketing to another country than in your own market, where you have knowledge and experience.

## THE PRACTISING MARKETER

**LICENSING A PRODUCT AND CULTURAL ADAPTATION OF LINGERIE RETAILING**

La Senza is a successful Canadian lingerie retail chain. It markets its products in interesting and dramatic fashion. For example, at the lingerie store in Toronto's Eaton Centre, the aisles are ablaze with undergarments in vibrant tangerines and fuchsias, animal prints, and florals.

La Senza has extensive overseas sales via licensed operating agreements in the United Kingdom, Malaysia, and several Arab countries. Interestingly, the Middle East has responded strongly to the specialty retailer's concept, despite deeply entrenched conservative traditions in some parts of the region. La Senza's presence in Saudi Arabia sparked more requests from neighbouring countries, leading to operations in Kuwait, Oman, Qatar, and Lebanon. A first Moroccan store was opened recently, and the company also recently signed an agreement with a licensee for Egypt.

Laurence Lewin, La Senza's president, explained that while Muslim dress codes require women to be covered up in public in black hooded robes in most of these countries, demand for fashion, including lingerie, is very strong and taste in undergarment fashions is similar to that of North America. "Internationally, women like the same merchandise by and large," he explained, "and under those black outer gowns, the women in Saudi Arabia are every bit as fashionable as women in New York City or London. But there are cultural and religious differences—that's why local involvement is vital." In Saudi Arabia, for example, only men are allowed to work in stores, so all staff in La Senza outlets are male. There are no fitting rooms and no pictures of merchandise or models on storefronts.

www.lasenza.ca

**How would licensing be particularly helpful in adapting the marketing approach in this setting?**

Source: Adapted from Susan Thorne, "Canada's Secret," www.ICSC.ORG Website (International Council of Shopping Centres), Nov. 2001; Steve Match, "Retailer's Makeover Paying Off," *Financial Post*, April 17, 2002, p. IN1; and Marina Strauss, "La Senza Beats Forecasts In Tough Market," *The Globe and Mail*, Wednesday, April 10, 2002, at globeandmail.com.

North American products do not always meet the needs of foreign consumers. Products that are strongly culture-bound are usually the most difficult to market globally. Foods, for example, have widely different acceptance levels in different countries. Some Canadians find many Asian foods too "adventurous." People from other cultures, on the other hand, find some Canadian foods very boring. Similarly, products that are used in the course of daily living are often difficult to transfer to another country because ways of doing things are different. Until recently, washing machines in Europe operated differently from those in North America. Therefore, for a company from either continent to just export its product to the other would have not been very successful, because consumers would not be familiar with the washing process. Likewise, a North American laundry detergent (which does not contain perborate) may not satisfy Europeans who are used to washing their laundry at near-boiling temperatures.

## Political and Legal Factors

The international marketer may find that the political environment of another country requires some modifications in the ways of doing business. For example, China is a socialist, centrally

---

## THE PRACTISING MARKETER

### DO YOUR HOMEWORK BEFORE YOU LEAVE CANADA

About five years ago, Barbara Barde waltzed into the offices of a Japanese television company armed with a program already in production, but in need of investment to complete. She met with the boss, who was a model of Japanese civility.

Her pitch was a flop.

"I really thought it was a good idea and they should put money into it," she says. "I think ... they thought I hadn't paid my dues in their marketplace. They didn't know me."

In retrospect, Ms. Barde, 51, founder of Toronto-based Up Front Entertainment Inc., says her idea could have been a winner if she had done more research, spent more time with her prospective Japanese partner, and learned a little more about the person she would be meeting.

But the experience also taught her something about exporting. "You could see he was fairly uncomfortable about doing business with me. I have no doubt it was based on gender."

A federally commissioned survey of female business owners engaged in exporting suggests her experience is not isolated. Beyond Borders: Canadian Businesswomen in International Trade reports there is a host of gender issues that affect the way women do business at home and internationally.

However, the study revealed that among the 254 business operators surveyed, international marketing is generally considered to be the biggest obstacle to breaking into foreign markets. The women said the cost of developing new markets, obtaining information, setting up distribution channels, coping with government regulations, and finding partners were their biggest challenges.

Cultural issues and not being taken seriously were most often cited as problems, the report says.

"Cultural challenges were most often cited in the context of business transactions in Asia, the Middle East, South Africa, India and South America," according to the report.

### HOW TO GO GLOBAL

Female business owners offer tips for clearing the gender hurdle:

- Build owner credibility first.
- Work with Canadian trade commissioners to be introduced to potential clients.
- Avoid personal or phone contact in certain countries.
- Use e-mail only with certain customers.
- Have a male employee handle certain client companies.
- Avoid some social events.
- Change business cards to indicate clearly the owner's position.
- In some cases, lay down the law that customers must deal with the female business owner.

Source: Beyond Borders.

**Why do you think that aspects other than gender showed up as the most important obstacles when breaking into new markets?**

Source: Adapted from Dawn Walton, "Female Exporters Face Gender Factor," *The Globe and Mail* (March 10, 1999), p. B9. Reprinted with permission from *The Globe and Mail*.

---

planned economy. Companies wishing to do business there must obtain permission from several layers of government. Doing business in another country means that a company is a guest in that country. Success requires recognizing the political priorities of the host.

International relations can also affect business activities. For example, during the Bosnian crisis, the Canadian government, as well as others, would not allow its country's firms to do business with Serbia. Similarly, the United States has a long-standing trade embargo against Cuba. It has even tried to prosecute firms from Canada and other countries that trade with Cuba.

Each country has evolved a legal system that reflects the values of its culture. As in Canada, most countries have many laws that control the way business is done. For example, Malaysia has laws against cigarette advertising, but the cigarette companies have found a way around these laws by adding other products, such as clothing, to their line. Then they prominently advertise brand names such as Marlborough, ostensibly to promote the other products. A different set of rules can be found in Canada, where a third of a cigarette package must be in black and white, with the words "Smoking can kill you" printed on it.

Canadians marketing food products in the United States find that the requirements for stating the contents are different and more strict than in Canada. All commercials in the United Kingdom and Australia must be cleared in advance. In The Netherlands, ads for candy must also show a toothbrush. Some nations have **local content laws** that specify the portion of a product that must come from domestic sources. This may force a manufacturer to ship a product unassembled and to have the assembly done in the host country. These examples suggest that managers involved in international marketing must be well-versed in legislation that affects their specific industry.

The legal environment for Canadian firms operating abroad can be divided into three dimensions:

- Canadian law
- international law
- laws of host nations

## Canadian Law

International business is subject to various trade regulations, tax laws, and import/export requirements. One significant provision in the Competition Act exempts from anticombines laws groups of Canadian firms that act together to develop foreign markets. An example is the cartel of Canadian uranium producers, which is designed to increase prices received in international markets. The intent of allowing this is to give Canadian industry economic power equal to that possessed by foreign cartels. A **cartel** is the monopolistic organization of a group of firms. Companies operating under this provision must not reduce competition within Canada and must not use "unfair methods of competition." It is hard to say whether companies can cooperate internationally and remain competitive without some cooperation in the domestic market. Canadian law also restricts the export of certain strategic goods, such as sophisticated computer technology, atomic components, and military hardware, to certain countries.

## International Law

International law can be found in the treaties, conventions, and agreements that exist among nations. Canada has many **friendship, commerce, and navigation (FCN) treaties**. These treaties address many aspects of commercial relations with other countries, such as the right to conduct business in the treaty partner's domestic market, and they constitute international law.

Other international agreements concern international standards for various products, patents, trademarks, reciprocal tax treaties, export control, international air travel, and international communications. For example, the leading nations of the world established the International Monetary Fund, which facilitates foreign exchange transactions among nations to conduct international trade.

**local content laws**
Laws specifying the portion of a product that must come from domestic sources.

**cartel**
The monopolistic organization of a group of firms.

**friendship, commerce, and navigation (FCN) treaties**
Treaties that address many aspects of commercial relations with other countries; such treaties constitute international law.

### SOLVING DISPUTES WITH CHINA'S BUSINESS PARTNERS

When making a deal in the international marketplace it is essential to specify the jurisdiction where disputes are to be settled. For example, what do you do if you have a legal dispute with a Chinese company? Can you really feel comfortable that the Chinese legal system will use similar legal processes to those of the West?

Investors encouraged by China's entry to the World Trade Organization, but still mistrustful of its legal system, can use Hong Kong to resolve any business disputes arising in the mainland.

In Australia to promote Hong Kong's common law system, Justice Secretary Elsie Leung said many investors wrongly believed that mainland disputes could only be settled on the mainland.

"I think that if the foreign investor is given a choice (of venue) they would most probably decide on Hong Kong rather than the mainland."

The mainland legal system has lacked transparency, neutrality and finality, although further reform has been promised with China's WTO entry. Ms. Leung urged investors and mainland partners to stipulate in their contracts that any dispute arising from mainland business activities be settled in Hong Kong courts under Hong Kong law.

**Why might dispute settlement be more reliable in Hong Kong than in China?**

Source: Excerpted from Bernard Lane, "HK Law Suits Chinese Investors," *The Australian*, February 25, 2002, p. 33. Reprinted with permission.

### Laws of Host Nations

The legal requirements of host nations affect foreign marketers. For example, some nations limit foreign ownership in their business sectors. Global marketers obey the laws and regulations of the countries within which they operate. The amount and type of advertising allowed are also prescribed by law in many countries. A host of other trade regulations must be understood and met by the foreign marketer. Australia's competition watchdog (The Australian Competition and Consumer Commission) blocked a plan by The Coca-Cola Company to buy soft drink brands from Cadbury Schweppes PLC. It ruled that the merger would result in a market structure where the leading carbonated drinks in almost every category would be controlled by The Coca-Cola Company.

www.cadbury
schweppes.com

# DEVELOP A MARKETING MIX APPROPRIATE TO THE GLOBAL SETTING

A fundamental marketing principle is that the marketing mix must be designed to meet the needs of the target market. This holds whether the marketing is done in Canada or a foreign market. Thus, depending on the international situation, some marketing elements may be relatively unchanged, whereas others require significant modification.

Some products seem to be "global" products, and virtually the same marketing mix can be used everywhere. Examples are Levi jeans, Coca-Cola, Rolex watches, and most business products. In these cases, a universal comprehension of the product exists or has been developed through international media, or there are common behaviour patterns between countries. A computer is not "culture-bound," whereas a food item, or the place and method of serving it, could be very much an acquired preference that is moulded by culture. For example, many Germans accustomed to heavy, dark bread might find Canadian mass-produced bread unappetizing. It seems that "culture-boundness" is a function of time. Products that have been around the longest, like food and articles of clothing, are the most culture-bound. New products, like computers and cell phones, are less culture-bound.

www.us.levi.com

Adaptation is required for many products—and for managerial styles. Let us consider a few examples of adaptations to the marketing mix.

An analysis that considers the market, product, price, marketing communications, and distribution is the next step. Examples of the relevant issues for each factor follow.

## Analysis of the Market

Market analysis is an important step in developing any marketing plan. In the global context these are some of the important considerations:

# THE PRACTISING MARKETER

## MCDONALD'S FOR MANY CULTURES

McDonald's has arrived in India. It set up shop in a fairly low-key manner and abandoned the Big Mac. In fact, it serves a chicken burger, potato cutlets, and some other items unheard of at any other McDonald's outlet in the world.

www.mcdonalds.com

To understand McDonald's strategy, one has to understand more about the environment and culture of India. There is a common myth in the West that India is a vegetarian country.

Actually, the majority of Indians are nonvegetarian, including Hindus. But, as with certain lobby groups in the West, the vegetarian segment in India is a very vocal and powerful minority. Such groups have also lashed out against foreign companies with claims of the damage these companies are doing to the livestock population and to the health of the people by serving meat.

So, there was a potential danger that McDonald's new outlets would be picketed as "disseminators of dangerous foreign culture" and "vendors of holy cows."

McDonalds then offered Maharaja Macs (mutton burgers). However, because of low sales the fast food giant has now discontinued any mutton burgers in its outlets. The Maharaja Mac (which originally had two mutton cutlets) is now replaced by chicken cutlets and is repositioned as Chicken Maharaja Mac.

Meanwhile, in Jerusalem the Big Macs were kosher, but there was hardly a kippah in sight as McDonalds opened the world's first kosher store at the Harel shopping mall in Mevasseret Zion.

The illuminated menu on the McDonald's wall looked much like those in the other 18 outlets the American fast-food chain has opened throughout Israel—except that this menu listed no cheeseburgers, milk shakes, or sundaes. According to Omri Padan, McDonald's Israeli licensee, all the Israeli outlets use kosher ingredients. At Pesach, buns are made with potato flour and Chicken McNuggets are coated with matzah meal.

McDonald's has customized its menu in many areas. There is the "Kiwi Burger" in New Zealand with beets, fried egg, and the rest of a usual hamburger. In Brazil, they

There's a little M in everyone

serve expresso-type coffee and have coffee machines arranged through the restaurant rather than serving it at the counter. (Brazilians like their coffee at the end of a meal, and hot….) In France, McDo (as the French call it) serves beer.

Think about it. A McDonald's that doesn't serve a Big Mac or a small Mac, but is quietly widening its outlet base in many different cultures. The question to ask ourselves: Is the burger really McDonald's core value, or is it something much stronger, that allows such changes in strategy without hurting the brand?

**McDonald's has been famous for its standardization and reliability. Do you see these adaptations as eroding or changing McDonald's image?**

Source: Adapted from communications from Larry Grant, http://www.larrygrant.net, to GINLIST@LIST.MSU.EDU. Reprinted with permission. Jacques Chevron, jacques@jrcanda.com to GINLIST@LIST.MSU.EDU, and from Meena Nichani, Mumbaiour Bureau (Thursday, January 10, 2002, 12:51:30 a.m.).

- What are the tariff barriers, import quotas, and internal taxes for the product?
- What is the size and the sector of the market that will purchase the product?
- What is the long-term potential, based on future growth, for each sector?
- Who are the major competitors, and what is their market share? Is the market politically and economically stable?

## Product Decisions

Customer expectations define quality and value, and those expectations are not always the same as they are in Canada. Nortel Networks learned that lesson after it sold its SL-1 telephone answering and switching system to a large Japanese department store. Among the features of the product is one called "music on hold." Both Japanese and North American customers are familiar with this. However, familiarity and expectations are two different things. The Japanese *expect* to hear music under all circumstances while waiting to be connected. The SL-1 gave them music while they waited to be connected to a particular department, but if that call was transferred to somebody else, no music would play. As a result, the Japanese callers assumed they had been disconnected and they hung up. Rather than trying to reshape the listening habits of 130 million Japanese, the company redesigned its system to meet Japanese expectations.

Government-established product standards often differ among countries. Host-country standards obviously must be met. For example, a Canadian marketer of packaged food products must meet specific nutritional label information requirements of the host country. Similarly, electrical products must meet varying codes from country to country. Germany, for example, has very rigid requirements for products such as fax machines that are connected to the telephone system. Thus, well-known brands accepted in Canada may not be allowed in Germany.

The export viability of the product should be determined by considering the following factors:

- Who will use the product?
- Who will make the purchasing decisions in the foreign country?
- Will the product be purchased throughout the year or on a seasonal basis?
- From whom is the product being purchased now?
- Will the product have to be modified to adapt to specific market nuances or regulations? If so, what will this cost?
- Is the product easy to ship? Are there any special handling costs?
- Is the product competitive on the basis of price, quality, and delivery?

## Pricing Decisions

When exporting, a cost-plus approach to pricing can quickly destroy potential opportunities. This is because more intermediaries are often required. If all these intermediaries take a standard markup based on a percentage of the cost they pay, the resulting price increase can be so large that the product is priced out of the foreign market. Table 20.2 shows an example of how a product that retails for $10.01 in Canada could end up being priced at $18.30 in a foreign market if a simple cost-plus pricing approach is used. This could well make the product uncompetitive in the foreign market. This problem can be avoided by reconsidering the internal costing system, as well as whether the standard markups are necessary in this situation.

Because exchange rates fluctuate, marketers must be careful to consider whether the price that they are asking for will be enough at the time of delivery. The currency of the deal might devaluate, thus possibly wiping out all profits. Because of this, a stable, commonly traded currency such as U.S. dollars may be chosen as the currency of payment.

If a country has limited foreign exchange reserve, it may not be able to afford to pay for a product in foreign currency. It is sometimes necessary to think about payment in different terms. For example, Nortel Networks sometimes agrees to accept payment in kind from customers. "Deals often hinge on how willing companies are to set aside more cherished commercial practices and accept

## TABLE 20.2 How Prices Can Mount When Exporting to a Foreign Market

| | DOMESTIC EXAMPLE | FOREIGN EXAMPLE (IMPORTER AND WHOLESALER IMPORTING DIRECTLY) |
|---|---|---|
| Manufacturing net | $5.00 | $5.00 |
| Transport, c.i.f.[a] | n.a. | 1.10 |
| Tariff (20 percent c.i.f. value) | n.a. | 1.22 |
| Importer pays | n.a. | 7.32 |
| Importer margin when sold to wholesaler (25% on cost) | n.a. | 1.83 |
| Wholesaler pays landed cost | 5.00 | 9.15 |
| Wholesaler margin (33⅓% on cost) | 1.67 | 3.05 |
| Retailer pays | 6.67 | 12.20 |
| Retail margin (50% on cost) | 3.34 | 6.10 |
| Retailer price | 10.01 | 18.30 |

[a] c.i.f. = cost, insurance, and freight

payment in the form of copper, sugar cane, bamboo, rice, or even a boatload of figs," says the vice-president of marketing of a large Canadian exporting company.

### Key Pricing Questions

■ What is the profitability at various pricing levels?
■ Can the pricing match or better the competition and still have a healthy profit margin?
■ If pricing cannot match the competition, can the product still sell because of product superiority, ability to deliver, and after-sales servicing?

## Marketing Communications

In Canada, sales representatives sometimes try to develop rapport with a client by asking about his or her family. In Saudi Arabia, this could be taken as an insult. Advertising messages also vary from country to country. In France, sexually explicit advertising is more common than in Canada, and the British tend to use more humour.

The newly promoted global advertising manager for a brand of toothpaste for children was puzzled. The company's highly successful ad campaign, which had boosted sales in Canada, the United States, Europe, and Australia, was not well received by the folks in the Bangkok office. "Too American" they kept repeating. So, the manager showed them the French and British versions of the campaign. Still, the Bangkok staff was uneasy, and, as politely as their Thai upbringing allowed, told the manager that the campaign would not work in their country. It had to do with the "pat on the head" that appeared in a scene that closed all commercials in the campaign. This gesture was meant to express the parents' appreciation of their child's good brushing with the toothpaste. But one does not touch the head of another person in many Asian countries. Thus, to make the communication successful, a different way of showing approval had to be found.

Because communication is so entwined with culture, the subtle nuances that make messages acceptable or unacceptable should be, at least, monitored by a local communicator before use. Preferably, local communicators should develop the message so that it accords with pre-established company strategy.

## Important Marketing Communication Questions

- Is the product "culture bound?"
- What are the types and costs of advertising in the individual markets, and which are best suited to the needs of the product?
- What are the advertising practices of competitors? What percentage of their gross profit goes into advertising, and what media do they advertise in?
- Where and when do trade fairs and exhibitions take place, and what opportunities exist for participating in them?

# Distribution Decisions

Distribution is one of the major problems in developing and implementing a marketing plan for a foreign market. This is especially true of exporting—the logistics of moving products are often very complicated. Fortunately, service firms called freight forwarders specialize in distribution and can be counted on to help solve the physical distribution problem. Obviously, both the service provided and the transportation add to the cost structure and must be reflected in the price or compensated for by reducing other costs.

Another problem is deciding which channels of distribution to use. The system may be quite different from what the Canadian marketer is accustomed to. In some countries, it may be difficult to find the necessary wholesaling intermediaries. In Japan, the opposite is true: channels of distribution normally consist of many layers of wholesalers that sell the product to others of their kind, that finally sell it to the retailer. As in the domestic market, the marketer has to solve the problem of how to persuade the channels to carry and promote the product.

## Key Distribution Questions

- What methods of distribution are available in the country, and which is the most reliable and cost-efficient?
- What markups are normally sought by intermediaries in the industry?
- Who are the main importers; what are their reputations, capabilities, and financial strengths?
- What types of carriers are needed? What are the transportation costs? How frequent and reliable are the various modes of transportation?
- Is there an agent capable of providing satisfactory technical services?

From the foregoing discussion, it is clear that the marketing mix is likely to require some adaptation before success in the foreign market can be achieved. An attitude of openness and flexibility is essential.

As well, a diligent search for information is required. Some of this information is available from provincial business and trade departments as well as Foreign Affairs and International Trade Canada. After gleaning as much information as possible in Canada, it is very important for the marketer to make a trip to the target country to size up the situation.

After an analysis that takes the foregoing factors into consideration, the business will be in a better position to decide whether it should proceed with an international venture. Such an appraisal also provides the groundwork for developing the company strategy that is necessary to enter the foreign market. It is a challenging task. However, those who proceed in a systematic fashion generally find that going international is worthwhile.

Companies who want international success must be willing to adapt their products and marketing strategies to the needs of the customer and the attitudes and business practices of the country they are operating in, no matter how demanding these may be.

If that means having to make major and costly product modifications to meet the technical requirements and customer expectations, so be it.

If it means investing years of time and money in order to build trust and establish a presence to win that first contract, then that too has to be done.

## THE PRACTISING MARKETER

### TO BRIBE, OR NOT TO BRIBE

Canadian corporate executives are an honest bunch who generally shy away from bribing officials when they do business in foreign lands, according to a new international survey.

But others aren't so pure, and bribery of public officials is a way of life for multinationals seeking deals in the developing world, according to the survey by Transparency International, a nonprofit group based in Berlin.

Russian, Chinese, Taiwanese, and South Korean companies are the most likely to use bribes to win contracts overseas, the survey found. Among developed companies, the top bribe-payers are found in Italy, Japan, and the United States.

Canada ranks fifth among the countries with the most honest business people, behind Australia, Sweden, Switzerland, and Austria.

Bribery is most common in public works, arms, and oil and gas sectors, the survey found.

To compile the figures, Transparency International hired Gallup to poll 835 businesspeople, accountants and bankers in 15 emerging countries, including Argentina, Brazil, India, Indonesia, Mexico, South Africa, and Thailand.

"We cannot continue to only talk about the bribe-takers," Frank Vogl, the vice-chairman of Transparency International, said in an interview from Washington yesterday. "We have to look at the bribe-makers."

www.transparency.org

"These figures are really shocking," Mr. Vogl added. "We're not talking about a morality issue. We're talking about people breaking the law. If there was a high-profile prosecution of a bribe-payer in Europe, the U.S. or Japan, that would send a signal." Canada has been a leader in the fight against global bribery. Action by Parliament in 2000 led to the ratification of the Anti-Bribery Convention of the Organization for Economic Co-operation and Development, since ratified by 33 other countries. The convention says those who pay bribes face jail time.

The problem is "nobody is enforcing it," says Mr. Vogl.

**Why is bribery a problem? Can Canadian businesses be successful without bribery?**

Source: Peter Kuitenbrouwer, "To Bribe or Not to Bribe," *National Post*, May 15, 2002, p. FP5. Reprinted with permission.

---

If it means applying a sensitive understanding of cultural behaviour, such as learning the language, then that must be done as well.

And if it means fashioning an appealing cooperative marketing package that maximizes the benefits of the products you sell, that must be done.

Only by embracing these kinds of value-charged initiatives can you hope to surmount the complex barriers and challenges of international marketing. Companies that do will find themselves well on the way to global competitive success. Companies that don't will sadly discover their respective customers don't care about their work.[10]

# CANADIAN GOVERNMENT ASSISTANCE TO EXPORTERS

Exporting is of great importance to a country. It creates jobs and helps bring about a positive balance of trade, thus making the entire economy more prosperous. Consequently, governments have active programs to help companies become more active in the global marketplace. Provincial governments provide information and guidance to businesses and have even set up foreign trade offices in major markets such as Japan, Hong Kong, and Britain.

The Canadian government has trade officers in every embassy and consulate around the world. These people seek out opportunities for Canadian goods and services and send this information back to Canada. They also help Canadian businesspeople make the right contacts when travelling abroad. Furthermore, trade officers may arrange trade shows that demonstrate Canadian products. For example, in Australia, a large Canadian agricultural equipment show is held in Dubbo, a big agricultural town.

In Canada, Foreign Affairs and International Trade Canada has trade officers in many major cities; these individuals facilitate export planning by Canadian firms and connect them with the overseas consulates. Their offices are also good sources of secondary data concerning exporting and various countries. The Internet is also proving to be a useful source of data on global marketing planning.

Through Foreign Affairs and International Trade Canada offices, the Canadian government administers various travel support programs in the form of loans to firms that need to go to a foreign market to initiate trade. If the venture is successful, the loan must be paid back.

Export Development Canada (EDC) is a Canadian Crown corporation that provides financial services to Canadian exporters and foreign buyers in order to facilitate and develop export trade. It does this through a wide range of insurance, guarantee, and loan services not normally provided by the private sector. Through its export financing programs, EDC extends to the Canadian exporter's foreign buyer the medium- or long-term financing required to purchase Canadian goods or services.

With EDC's accounts receivable insurance, Canadian firms can protect their export sales against nonpayment by foreign buyers for up to 90 percent of the value of their sales. EDC's insurance essentially transfers the foreign buyer's risk to EDC, enabling the exporter to make more sales in more countries. Up to 85 percent of the Canadian portion of an export deal can generally be financed. Once the Canadian exporter has fulfilled the terms of the commercial contract and has provided the appropriate documentation, EDC pays the exporter on behalf of the foreign buyer/borrower. Exporters in other countries have access to similar support facilities from their governments through Export Credit Agencies.

EDC thus assumes all subsequent payment risk and collects payments from the borrower over the life of the loan. EDC's export financing services include direct loans; lines of credit and protocols, which are streamlined financing facilities set up between EDC and a foreign bank; note purchase agreements, under which the EDC buys promissory notes issued by foreign banks to Canadian

www.dfait-maeci.gc.ca/
menu-e.asp

www.edc.ca

Chances are your buyer's in our database of 70 million.

**EDC's online services – manage your credit risk, fast.**

Export Development Canada (EDC) offers a complete online solution for exporters looking to reduce their credit risk. With a single visit to our website, you can assess and protect against risk quickly and conveniently with the following products:

**EXPORT *Check*** – Promptly determine your buyer's credit profile before you close the deal by accessing our database of more than 70 million buyers in over 100 markets. We'll provide an EDC assessment of insurability as well as reports with detailed credit information (through Dun & Bradstreet).

**EXPORT *Protect*** – You can insure a single transaction for up to 90% of your losses if a foreign buyer doesn't pay. It's quick and convenient coverage at the click of a mouse.

**Economic Reports** – Gauge opportunities in more than 200 markets. Benefit from our foreign market expertise with these regularly updated reports that help you monitor global political and economic events.

**EXPORT *Able?*** – Considering exporting? Not sure if you're ready? We've developed a tool to help you gauge your level of export readiness and address any questions and concerns you may have.

To take advantage of these online services, visit us at **www.edc.ca/e-services**

**EDC**
Export Development Canada
Exportation et développement Canada

**Realize a World of Opportunity**

The Export Development Corporation facilitates trade by backing financial transactions of exporting companies.

exporters for the purchase of Canadian goods or services; and specialized credits. EDC facilitates this by (normally) assuming the commercial and political risks, including insolvency or default by the buyer and blockage of funds in a foreign country.

EDC will also make long-term loans to foreign buyers of Canadian capital goods and services. Funds are disbursed directly to Canadian suppliers on behalf of the borrower, in effect providing the exporters with cash sales. EDC policy is to achieve maximum private-sector involvement in export financing; it therefore provides 100 percent guarantees to banks and financial institutions to facilitate the exporters' banking arrangements.

# INTEGRATION OF WORLD MARKETS

One country would find it difficult to produce all the goods and services it needed, so international trade occurs. Nevertheless, every country tends to jealously protect its own producers and markets. This results in a maze of laws, tariffs, and restrictions that need to be overcome by trading firms.

Over the years, all nations have recognized that there is a need for an open trading system based on multilaterally agreed-upon rules. Protectionism leads to bloated and inefficient companies and can, in the end, lead to factory closures and job losses. Consequently, in 1948 many countries negotiated a General Agreement on Tariffs and Trade (GATT), which was revised periodically. However, in 1995, after a massive set of negotiations (known as the Uruguay Round because that country was the host), the World Trade Organization was established to do much more than the GATT. A major objective of the WTO is to reduce protectionism.

The **World Trade Organization (WTO)** is an international organization that deals with the rules of trade between nations. The WTO agreements are the legal rules for international commerce and trade policy. The agreements have three main objectives: to encourage free trade, to further open international trade through negotiation, and to provide a way to settle disputes between countries.[11]

## Principles of the Trading System

Five fundamental principles run throughout all WTO agreements and form the foundation of the multilateral trading system. Trade should be

1. *Without discrimination*—a country should not discriminate between its trading partners (they are all, equally, granted "most-favoured-nation" or MFN status); and it should not discriminate between its own and foreign products, services, or nationals (they are given "national treatment").
2. *Freer*—with barriers coming down through negotiation.
3. *Predictable*—foreign companies, investors, and governments should be confident that trade barriers (including tariffs, nontariff barriers, and other measures) should not be raised arbitrarily; more and more tariff rates and market-opening commitments are "bound" in the WTO.
4. *More competitive*—by discouraging "unfair" practices such as export subsidies and dumping products at below cost to gain market share.
5. *More beneficial for less developed countries*—by giving them more time to adjust, greater flexibility, and special privileges.[12]

## Trade Agreements

Some countries decide to go further and make agreements to open their borders for trading with one another. The North American Free Trade Agreement (NAFTA) among Canada, the United States, and Mexico is an example of this. Even though inter-country trade was very large, each country agreed that it would be to the advantage of all to further simplify and extend the process.

Different types of arrangements are used to achieve greater economic integration. The simplest approach is a **free trade area**, within which participants agree to free trade of goods and services among themselves. Normally such agreements are phased in over a period of time to allow companies in both countries to adjust. NAFTA is an example.

**free trade area**
Area established by agreement among two or more nations within which participants agree to free trade of goods and services among themselves.

A **customs union** establishes a free trade area, plus a uniform tariff for trade with nonmember nations. The European Community (EC), comprising Belgium, Britain, Denmark, France, Germany, Greece, Ireland, Italy, Luxembourg, Portugal, The Netherlands, and Spain, is the best example of a customs union.

As these nations gained experience, they went further and formed a **common market**. The common market is a customs union that also allows factors of production such as labour, capital, and technology to flow freely among members. Thus there are no restrictions on immigration and cross-border investment. Under a common market, this mobility of production factors allows them to be employed most productively.

In 1993, these nations went beyond a common market to form an **economic union**. The European Union (EU) officially came into being January 1, 1994. It goes beyond a common market and also requires members to harmonize monetary policies, taxation, and government spending. In addition, most member countries use a common currency. The euro has been established and is being phased into use by EU members. The individual countries give up control of the value of their currency and social programs to some degree. A final step in this evolution would be a political union. The community has expanded to 15 member nations and is growing.

The European Union (EU) has resulted in a trading bloc that is unparallelled in history. It now constitutes a giant single market of nearly 400 million consumers. The rest of the world watches it with fascination and some nervousness. Some nations worry that the EU could turn into Fortress Europe, slamming the door on trade with its members.

The **North American Free Trade Agreement (NAFTA)** started with the Canada–U.S. **Free Trade Agreement (FTA)**. It reinforced the long-term trading relationship between Canada and the United States. Each country has traditionally been the other's biggest customer. NAFTA includes Mexico and builds on the trading and other relationships among the three countries.

In the world marketplace, the United States has been the target of many trading countries. This has resulted in serious negative trade balances for the United States. Gradually that country began to put significant restrictions on trade, restrictions that threatened Canadian business as well. In addition, the United States arbitrarily made judgements about whether Canadian firms were trading "fairly." The potential of greater access to the U.S. and Mexican markets, as well as the potential of further restrictions and arbitrary decisions encouraged Canada to negotiate the Free Trade Agreement, which had been under discussion.

All tariffs were scheduled to be gradually eliminated according to a timetable over a ten-year period. Companies can now bid on government procurement projects worth $25 000 (U.S.) or more in other countries. This now gives companies in each country access to government business through NAFTA. A Trade Commission was created to supervise the agreement. As well, a dispute settlement mechanism and panels of individuals to settle disputes were established.

NAFTA has created hardships for some industries as companies settle their operations in one country or another. On the other hand, it presents great opportunities for others who seek them out. The concept is now well enough accepted by the three member nations that further expansion is being undertaken. Canada has established a similar relationship with Chile, which is expected to become the fourth member of NAFTA, and other South American countries will be added as they develop economically and politically.

The evolution of the European Union and NAFTA has made other nations, such as Japan and other Asian countries, somewhat concerned about the possible negative effects of trading blocs on those on the outside. Asia Pacific countries have formed a working group called the Asia Pacific Economic Council (APEC) to consider economic matters. Canada and the United States are members of this group. It is too soon to tell whether APEC will develop into a trading bloc as well. There are a number of other regional trade agreements among the nations of the world.

The global marketplace is dynamic and exciting. It is clear that the growth of most firms will depend on some involvement in foreign marketing. The movement toward globalization of business is accelerating, and this will create many opportunities for the student of marketing who wants to be part of the world marketplace.

**customs union**
Agreement among two or more nations that establishes a free trade area, plus a uniform tariff for trade with nonmember nations.

**common market**
A customs union that also allows factors of production such as labour, capital, and technology to flow freely among members.

**economic union**
A common market that also requires members to harmonize monetary policies, taxation, and government spending. In addition, a common currency is used by members.

**North American Free Trade Agreement (NAFTA)**
The agreement establishing a free trade area among Canada, the United States, and Mexico that followed the FTA.

**Free Trade Agreement (FTA)**
The agreement establishing a free trade area between Canada and the United States that preceded NAFTA.

## Trade Restrictions

**tariff**

A tax levied against products imported from abroad.

Assorted trade restrictions can greatly affect world trade. These restrictions are most commonly expressed through tariffs. A **tariff** is a tax levied against products imported from abroad. Some tariffs are based on a set tax per unit. Others are figured on the value of the imported product. Tariffs may be classified as either revenue or protective tariffs. *Revenue tariffs* are designed to raise funds for the government. Most of the Canadian government's revenue in the early years of Confederation came from this source. *Protective tariffs* are designed to raise the price of imported goods to that of similar domestic products or higher. In the past, it was believed that a country should protect its infant industries by using tariffs to keep out foreign-made products. Some foreign goods would still enter, but the addition of a high tariff payment would make the domestic products competitive. Protective tariffs are usually higher than revenue tariffs. Different interest groups argue about whether or not tariffs should be raised to protect employment and profits in domestic Canadian industry. It is debatable whether, in the long run, such a goal is obtainable through tariff protection.

**import quota**

A limit set on the amount of products that may be imported in a certain category.

There are other forms of trade restrictions. An **import quota** sets a limit on the amount of products that may be imported in a certain category. One country may use unofficial quotas to limit imports. When Canadian hog farmers began to take over the U.S. Midwest market, U.S. officials "discovered" that Canadian meat might have certain additives that might be "harmful" and, therefore, restricted imports. The objective of import quotas normally is to protect local industry and employment and preserve foreign exchange. There are sometimes other motives. Russia stopped issuing import licences for U.S. poultry and placed a temporary ban on poultry imports. This was a move to pressure U.S. producers to divulge what antibiotics, preservatives, and other substances are used.

**embargo**

A complete ban on importing a particular product.

The ultimate form of a quota is an **embargo**, a complete ban on importing a particular product. When British cattle began to suffer from mad cow disease, the whole world shuddered at the thought of humans contracting the disease. Therefore, most countries placed an embargo on British beef until they could be sure that it was safe.

**exchange control**

Requirement that firms gaining foreign exchange by exporting must sell their foreign exchange to the central bank or agency, and importers must buy foreign exchange from the same organization.

Foreign trade can also be regulated by exchange control through a central bank or government agency. **Exchange control** means that firms gaining foreign exchange by exporting must sell their foreign exchange to the central bank or agency, and importers must buy foreign exchange from the same organization. The exchange control authority can then allocate, expand, or restrict foreign exchange according to existing national policy.

## Dumping—A Marketing Problem

In a battle between shoe manufacturers and retailers, Revenue Canada sided with Canadian manufacturers and imposed dumping charges on imported women's footwear from low-cost overseas producers. It was expected that between $22 million and $41 million in dumping charges would be imposed. Importers, including retailers, contended that most of the new charges will be passed on to consumers through price increases of up to 30 percent. Canadian shoe manufacturers argued that this estimate was much exaggerated.

**dumping**

Practice of selling products at significantly lower prices in a foreign market than in a nation's own domestic market.

The term **dumping** is applied to situations in which products are sold at significantly lower prices in a foreign market than in a nation's own domestic market. If foreign goods sell in Canada for substantially lower prices than Canadian products, the likely consequence is a loss of jobs here. Canada Customs investigates alleged cases of dumping. If there is a preliminary determination of dumping, the Deputy Minister submits the finding to the Anti-Dumping Tribunal. The tribunal must make an inquiry within 90 days and issue a finding as to whether dumping is causing or likely to cause national injury to the production in Canada of like goods. This may lead to the imposition of anti-dumping duties by Customs and Excise. The tariff charge is designed to protect Canadian business and employment by raising the product's price up to what it sells for in its home market.

Some critics have argued that fear of the dumping procedure and its tariff causes many foreign markets to keep their export prices higher than would normally be the case. The result, it is argued, is higher prices for the Canadian consumer. It is likely that dumping will remain a controversial topic in international trade for some time. Periodically, it is expected that countries will invoke dumping claims to protect industries that are suffering from international competition. International trade-regulating bodies, such as the World Trade Organization, will then have to resolve the issue.

# THE INTERNET AND GLOBAL BUSINESS

The Internet has proven to be a valuable tool in global business. The major ways that it can be applied are gathering information, communication, and e-business.

## Gathering Information

This book has stressed the idea that to make good marketing decisions you need to have good information. Guessing as to the nature of the market, or the likely response to a product or marketing communications is just not good business practice.

The need for information is even greater when making decisions about the international marketplace. Today, fortunately, the Internet can play an important role in gathering information. There are several types of information that can be readily collected at the home office, just sitting in front of a computer.

1. *Country data.* Country data includes information about size of market, income levels, and infrastructure. This can be found through the host country's statistical Web site as well as through Web sites of the United Nations, World Bank, and other economic agencies.
2. *Competitor information.* Using one of the many search engines it may be possible to learn what competing products are available, as well as which companies will be likely competitors.
3. *Pricing information.* Using search engines and e-mail.
4. *Finding partners and distributors.* The distribution system in another country can be very different, and sometimes quite complex. An early understanding of that system before entering that country is critical.

## Communication

As every student knows, the Internet makes written communication easy. Companies can communicate with their branches and their clients on the other side of the world as easily as if they were next door. Furthermore, while telephone rates have been generally falling, the use of the Internet for telephone communications and facsimile transmissions is also an option to make such communication even cheaper. Many countries throughout the world are embracing the Internet as an efficient and cost-effective method of communication, a new way of accessing markets and consumers, and an unlimited source of information.

## E-Business

If you can't find the right snowboard in your home country try one of the Internet shopping malls, or other retailers. A friend in Australia looked locally for a book but couldn't find it so ordered one through Amazon.com.

A large range of different types of merchandise is marketed around the world on the Internet. For some businesses the Internet will enable them to go global without leaving home. Companies can target customers around the globe without the costly headaches that often scare them away from the international marketplace.

Perhaps more significant will be the use of the Internet in business-to-business marketing. As discussed in Chapter 9 there are several types of vertical Web communities. A B2B electronic exchange is one example. This is an organized group of buyers and sellers from a specific industry linked together electronically. Electronic exchanges benefit buyers and sellers through the close linkage that they achieve. For example, a business purchaser might post a request for quotations for 1000 automotive CD players. An attachment would include drawings and precise specifications. The posting would be placed through an Internet exchange network operated by the company (if the business is large enough) or by other providers. On the closing date, the purchaser would review the quotations that had been received from around the world, and would then issue the purchase order electronically. All other parts of the transaction, except physical delivery and handling, would be handled electronically, including the relaying of information to relevant units of the organization. The CD players would arrive on the production line in the right quantities and at the specified delivery times.

The range of possibilities for the use of the Internet in global marketing is extensive. It is clearly one of the areas of business that will benefit most from this technology. However, although helpful, in most cases the Internet will not take the place of travel to personally observe and understand markets. Furthermore, business relationships need to be developed on a personal basis. The Internet is a means of making business practices more effective.

## SUMMARY

Global business is one of the most important economic activities for Canada. It expands the market for a country's or firm's products. Some 11 000 new jobs are supported by every billion export dollars.

A nation's balance of trade is determined by the relationship between its exports and its imports. If a nation exports more than it imports, it has a favourable balance of trade. However, because of foreign travel and interest payments, the overall balance of payments may be negative.

Devaluation occurs when a nation reduces the value of its currency in relation to gold or some other currency. If a currency is devalued, it makes exports cheaper to other nations and imports more expensive to the importing country.

The concept of comparative advantage explains why it is beneficial for all nations to trade with one another. The concept says that countries prosper most by taking advantage of their assets in order to concentrate on what they can produce best, and then by trading these products for products that other countries produce best.

Four different approaches to involvement in international business are ethnocentric, polycentric, regiocentric, and geocentric. An ethnocentric approach is likely to be the least effective.

Firms can participate in the international market in a number of ways and to a lesser or greater extent. The lowest level of participation is indirect exporting and importing; the highest levels are joint ventures and foreign production and marketing.

In international marketing, understanding the culture of the country is a key factor. Culture is defined as an integrated system of learned behaviour patterns that are distinguishing characteristics of the members of any given society.

The legal environment for Canadian firms operating abroad can be divided into three dimensions: Canadian law, international law, and the laws of host nations. All three are significant and must be understood and followed by the international marketer.

The marketing mix in the global context could be similar to that at home, but is likely to be different because of the need to adjust to the environment in a foreign market.

For most countries, and especially Canada, international trade is essential to long-term prosperity and jobs. Canada's national policy promotes international trade wherever possible.

GATT was an international trade agreement to gradually lower tariffs among countries. It has been replaced with the World Trade Organization (WTO), the international body that deals with the rules of trade between nations. The WTO agreements have three main objectives: to encourage free trade, to further open international trade through negotiation, and to provide an impartial means of settling trade disputes between countries.

World markets are being drawn together through various treaties among nations. Four significant types of trading arrangements have emerged: free trade area, customs union, common market, and economic union. The European Union is an economic union, making it one of the most powerful trade arrangements in the world.

Dumping is a situation in which products are sold at significantly lower prices in a foreign market than in the producing nation's own domestic market. Countries try to penalize dumping because it creates unfair competition for their businesses.

The Internet has proven to be a valuable tool in global business. The major ways that it can be applied are gathering information, communication, and e-business.

## KEY TERMS

absolute advantage, p. 511

balance of payments, p. 508

balance of trade, p. 507

cartel, p. 520

common market, p. 529

comparative advantage, p. 512

culture, p. 516

customs union, p. 529

devaluation, p. 509

direct international trade, p. 514

direct investment, p. 515

dumping, p. 530

economic union, p. 529

embargo, p. 530

ethnocentric company, p. 513

exchange control, p. 530

exchange rate, p. 508

Free Trade Agreement (FTA), p. 529

free trade area, p. 528

friendship, commerce, and balance of trade navigation (FCN) treaties, p. 520

geocentric company, p. 514

import quota, p. 530

indirect international trade, p. 514

joint venture, p. 514

licensing, p. 514

local content laws, p. 520

multinational corporation (MNC), p. 515

North American Free Trade Agreement (NAFTA), p. 529

polycentric company, p. 513

regiocentric company, p. 514

revaluation, p. 509

tariff, p. 530

World Trade Organization (WTO), p. 528

## INTERACTIVE SUMMARY AND DISCUSSION QUESTIONS

1. Global business is one of the most important economic activities for Canada. Why is it important to Canadian firms? To the Canadian economy?

2. A nation's balance of trade is determined by the relationship between its exports and its imports. If a nation exports more than it imports, how can it have a negative balance of *payments*?

3. Is the marketing mix in the global context likely to be different from that in the domestic context?

4. Devaluation occurs when a nation reduces the value of its currency in relation to gold or some other currency. Explain how devaluation is likely to affect trade.

5. The concept of comparative advantage explains why it is beneficial for all nations to trade with one another. Comparative advantage is a *relative* concept. In *comparison with* nation B, what goods should nation A trade?

6. GATT was an international trade agreement to gradually lower tariffs among countries. The World Trade Organization is a much broader international trade-facilitating body. Why is international trade so important?

7. Dumping is a situation in which products are sold at significantly lower prices in a foreign market than in the producing nation's own domestic market. If countries are seeking to lower tariffs, and therefore prices, isn't dumping a good thing? Why or why not?

8. The legal environment for Canadian firms operating abroad can be divided into three dimensions: Canadian law, international law, and the laws of host nations. What do Canadian law and international law have to do with business a Canadian company conducts in another country?

9. The concept of the marketing mix applies in international marketing just as it does in domestic marketing. However, marketing in a foreign country may not be the same as in Canada, even for the same product. Explain when it would be similar and when it might be different.

**10.** Four different approaches to involvement in international business are ethnocentric, polycentric, regiocentric, and geocentric. Explain each of these approaches.

**11.** World markets are being drawn together through various treaties among nations. Four significant types of trading arrangements have emerged: free trade area, customs union, common market, and economic union. Differentiate among the four.

**12.** Trade restrictions such as import quotas and embargoes may be employed to restrict or to stimulate international marketing activities. Why might a country do each of these, and what would be the effect?

**13.** Comment on the following statement: "It is sometimes dangerous for a firm to attempt to export its marketing strategy."

**14.** Give an example—hypothetical or actual—of a firm for each of the following approaches to international marketing. How would the marketing mix compare with that used in the home market?
a. exporting in response to external demand
b. ethnocentric approach
c. polycentric approach
d. regiocentric approach
e. geocentric approach

**15.** The following business opportunity was listed in *CanadExport*:

> Singapore—a services and supplies company wishes to import *water treatment products for the pharmaceutical, food and beverages industries.* Contact Randy Yang, Marketing Manager, Jelen Supplies and Services, Singapore.
> Tel. _____; Fax_____; Telex_____.

Assume that you work for a company that supplies such products. Outline the possible opportunities that such a venture might bring to your firm, and then list the possible problems. What steps should be taken to fully follow up on this advertisement?

**16.** Assume that you market a product in Canada on which there is a 20 percent U.S. tariff for such products coming from Canada and a 25 percent Canadian tariff for products coming from the United States. In two years the product will be tariff-free under the terms of NAFTA. What are the challenges and opportunities of such a change? What should your company do in anticipation of the change?

**17.** Assume that your company makes high-quality tennis, badminton, and squash racquets. It is considering the possibility of marketing them in Malaysia. Using the Internet, determine whether there would be a market for your products. Also, find out whether any restrictions or conditions have to be met to enter the Malaysian market.

## Artisan's Link

Artisan's Link is an organization currently helping Mexican artisans to market handicrafts in the United States. Approximately half of the artisans it works with are located in the U.S., the other half are in Mexican border towns. Artisan's Link wants to set up a U.S. and Canadian distribution network.

All of their products are traditional Latin American and Indian crafts. These crafts are often created in the artisan's home, then purchased by Artisan's Link for distribution. English is not the first language of any of the artisans, many of whom are Spanish speakers. As a result, Artisan's Link is the only opportunity for the artisans to sell outside their culture.

Artisan's Link has identified three possible channels of distribution for their products:

1. Direct mail order from distribution centres set up in the U.S. Artisan's Link would own and run the centres and be responsible for order-taking.
2. Sell to direct mail merchandisers. Artisan's Link will ship to the merchandiser's warehouses, at which point the merchandisers will take title and be responsible for selling the crafts.
3. Sell to specialty retail stores. These could be art/craft retail stores, galleries, department stores, or Mexican craft stores.

Artisan's Link needs to set up its distribution system. When making this decision as to which of these three options is the best for this organization, the management needs to keep the following in mind:

www.peoplink.com

- Many of the products being sold are fragile (pottery or hand-painted woodwork) or may be protected by import quotas (textiles, art, or embroidered goods).
- These products would be covered under the appropriate NAFTA regulations.
- Many mail merchandisers and retailers require a steady shipment of goods. Because individuals in their homes make most of the crafts, there is no way to guarantee quality or quantities. At any given time there could be a shortage of the good being made, and many of the goods are unique. If there is a great demand for a good, it is doubtful the artisans could keep up with the production. Artisan's Link controls the supply and demand, and is responsible for deciding which products will be made and in what quantity, before they are offered to the distribution channels.

### You Be the Marketer

1. What would the best distribution channel(s) be? Why?
2. What possible problems and/or barriers might there be in entering the market?
3. How would you position this product?
4. What are the possible market segments?
5. Would these segments be different for the U.S., Mexico, and Canada?
6. How would you promote these products?
7. What should the image be? Why?

Source: Virginia Yonkers, *Using Case Studies to Teach EFL Business English.* From Virginia Gorman Yonkers' *Independent Professional Project for MA Teaching*, School for International Training, Brattleboro, Vermont, January 1998.

Children's Television Workshop, creators of *Sesame Street*, is a worldwide nonprofit organization dedicated to children's education. They recently introduced their newest Muppet character, Kami, designed to raise AIDS awareness among children in South Africa.

## Chapter 21

# NOT-FOR-PROFIT MARKETING

## CHAPTER OBJECTIVES

After reading and studying this chapter, you should be able to

1. Outline the primary characteristics of nonprofit organizations that distinguish them from profit-seeking organizations.
2. Show that marketing applies to nonprofit organizations in the same way it does to businesses.
3. Identify the main categories of marketing in nonprofit settings.
4. Apply the marketing mix to nonprofit settings.

The first HIV-positive Muppet recently joined the cast of *Sesame Street* in South Africa to educate children about the deadly virus that infects more than 10 percent of the country.

Kami, a mustard-coloured female character, was introduced on *Takalani Sesame* in September 2002.

Kami will associate freely with the show's other characters as a way to fight stereotypes and dispel myths about people living with the virus, said Yvonne Kgame of the South African Broadcasting Corp., which airs the program.

"We want to build hope and address the issues of stereotypes against HIV," Kgame said. "It's about instilling positive attitudes toward people HIV-infected."

Story lines for the character will confront serious issues about HIV in a way that is appropriate for its viewing audience of young children.

"It will have, in a childlike manner, open discussions about sexuality, HIV and AIDS, and death and dying," Kgame said. "The reality is that children as young as they are affected very closely by HIV/AIDS. They experience death and dying of people very close to them."

With more than 4.7 million people living with HIV, South Africa has the world's largest population infected with the virus. Despite this, there is a crushing stigma surrounding the virus in the country.

---

Source: Adapted from "HIV-positive Muppet added in S. Africa," July 12, 2002, http://www.canoe.ca/Television/jul12_muppets-ap.html. Reprinted with permission of The Associated Press.

www.scienceinafrica.co.za/
2002/august/muppet.htm

# INTRODUCTION

Too often, people look at the *advertising* that is done by nonprofit organizations (NPOs)[1] and equate it with marketing. By now, the reader will realize that marketing is much more than just advertising or selling. Marketing involves applying the entire marketing mix in accordance with a well-planned marketing strategy.

At first glance, an HIV-positive Muppet character may seem to have nothing at all to do with marketing. But, in fact, it is a very creative example of social marketing—a particular kind of nonprofit marketing that we will discuss in more detail below.

In Chapter 1, marketing was defined as the process of planning and executing the conception, pricing, promotion, and distribution of ideas, goods, and services to create exchanges that satisfy individual and organizational objectives. Although much of the text up to now has concentrated on organizations that operate for profit, the activities of the Children's Television Workshop, the producers of Sesame Street, are as representative of modern marketing activities as are the marketing programs of IBM, Wendy's, and Maple Leaf Foods. Our definition of marketing is sufficiently comprehensive to encompass nonprofit as well as profit-seeking organizations.

**nonprofit organization (NPO)**
Organization whose primary objective is something other than returning a profit to its owners.

A substantial portion of our economy is composed of **nonprofit organizations (NPOs)**—those whose primary objective is something other than returning a profit to their owners. An estimated one of every ten service workers and one of six professionals are employed in the nonprofit sector. The nonprofit sector includes thousands of religious organizations, social service organizations, museums, libraries, colleges and universities, symphony orchestras and other music organizations, and organizations such as government agencies, political parties, and labour unions.

Nonprofit organizations can be found in both public and private sectors of society. In the public sector, federal, provincial, and local governmental units and agencies whose revenues are derived from tax collection have service objectives that are not keyed to profitability targets. One part of Foreign Affairs and International Trade Canada, for instance, provides services that facilitate exports of Canadian products. A provincial department of natural resources regulates conservation and environmental programs. The local animal control officer enforces ordinances that protect both people and animals.

Some public-sector agencies may be given revenue or behaviour goals. An urban-transit system might be expected to pay a great deal of its costs out of revenues, for example. But society does not expect these units to routinely produce a surplus that is returned to taxpayers.

The private sector offers an even more diverse array of nonprofit settings. Art institutes, churches, labour unions, private schools, the United Way, the Rotary Club, and the local country club all serve as examples of private-sector, nonprofit organizations. The diversity of these settings suggests how pervasive organizational objectives other than profitability really are in a modern economy.

The market offering of the nonprofit organization is frequently more nebulous than the tangible goods or service provisions of profit-seeking firms. Table 21.1 lists social issues and ideas, ranging from family planning to using motorcycle helmets, that represent the offerings made by some nonprofit organizations to their publics.

The diversity of these issues suggests the size of the nonprofit sector and the marketing activities involved in accomplishing the objectives of these organizations. They are different from their profit-seeking counterparts in a number of ways.

# CHARACTERISTICS OF NONPROFIT ORGANIZATIONS

Nonprofit organizations have a special set of characteristics that affect their marketing activities. Like the profit-oriented service offerings discussed in Chapter 12, the product offered by a nonprofit organization is often intangible. A hospital's diagnostic services exhibit marketing problems similar to those inherent in marketing a life insurance policy.

**TABLE 21.1** Social Issues Marketed by Nonprofit Organizations

| | | |
|---|---|---|
| Abortion rights | Fire prevention | 911 (emergency number) |
| Affirmative action | Fluoridation | Nonsmokers' rights |
| Alcoholism control | Forest fire prevention | Nuclear energy |
| Birth defects | Foster parenthood | Physical fitness |
| Blood | Fraternal organizations | Police, support of |
| Blue laws | Free enterprise | Pollution control |
| Buy Canadian goods | Freedom of the press | Population control |
| Cancer research | French immersion | Prison reform |
| Capital punishment | Gay rights | Religion |
| CARE packages | Housing cooperatives | Right to life |
| Carpooling | Legalized gambling | Save the whales |
| Child abuse | Literacy | Seatbelt use |
| Child adoption | Littering prevention | Solar energy |
| Consumer cooperatives | Mass transportation | STD hotline |
| Crime prevention | Mental health | Suicide hotline |
| Drunk driving | Metric system | Tax reform |
| Energy conservation | Military recruiting | UNICEF |
| Euthanasia | Motorcycle helmets | United Way |
| Family planning | Museums | |

Source: Most of these issues are listed in Seymour H. Fine, *The Marketing of Ideas and Social Issues* (New York: Praeger, 1981), pp. 13–14. Copyright © 1981 by Praeger Publishers, New York. Reprinted by permission of Greenwood Publishing Group, Inc., Westport, CT.

A second feature of nonprofit organizations is that they must deal with multiple publics. As Professor Philip Kotler points out,

> Nonprofit organizations normally have at least two major publics to work with from a marketing point of view: their clients and their funders. The former pose the problem of resource allocation and the latter, the problem of resource attraction. Besides these two publics, many other publics surround the nonprofit organization and call for marketing programs. Thus a college can direct marketing programs toward prospective students, current students, parents of students, alumni, faculty, staff, local business firms, and local government agencies. It turns out the business organizations also deal with a multitude of publics but their tendency is to think about marketing only in connection with one of the publics, namely their customers.[2]

A customer or service user may have less influence than a customer of a profit-seeking (or for-profit) firm. A government employee may be far more concerned with the opinion of a member of the Cabinet than with that of a service user. Furthermore, nonprofit organizations often possess some degree of monopoly power in a given geographical area. As an individual, a person might object to the local United Way's inclusion of a crisis centre among its supported agencies, but as a contributor who accepts the merits of the United Way appeal, this same person recognizes that a portion of total contributions will go to the agency in question.

Another problem involves the resource contributor, such as a legislator or a financial backer, who interferes with the marketing program. It is easy to imagine a political candidate harassed by financial supporters who want to replace an unpopular campaign manager (the primary marketing position in a political campaign).

Perhaps the most commonly noted feature of the nonprofit organization is its lack of a **bottom line**, which refers to the overall-profitability measure of performance. That is, nonprofit organizations have goals other than profit. While a nonprofit organization may attempt to maximize its return from a specific service, less measurable goals such as service level standards are the usual substitute for an overall evaluation. The net result is that it is often difficult to set marketing objectives that are in line with overall organizational goals.

**bottom line**
The overall-profitability measure of performance.

The United Way, like other nonprofit organizations, is responsible not only to its service users (clients) but also to it funders (those whom the organization must attract for donations).

Another characteristic is the lack of a single clear organizational structure. Nonprofit organizations refer to constituencies that they serve, but these are often considerably less exact than the shareholders of a profit-oriented corporation. Nonprofit organizations often have multiple organizational structures. A hospital might have an administrative structure, a professional organization consisting of medical personnel, and a volunteer organization that dominates the board of trustees. These people may sometimes work at cross-purposes and not be totally in line with the marketing strategy that has been devised.[3]

A final characteristic of the nonprofit sector is that it is sometimes inefficient. Often two or more NPOs work toward the same "cause." For example, there may be several affirmative-action groups. Religious organizations, many with very similar objectives, abound and overlap. This could be seen as a duplication or multiplication of efforts. Clearly, however, there is competition in many cases, and the competition is not only to win a larger portion of the client target market. In fundraising, the same types of NPOs sometimes compete for donor support. In addition, competition for personnel, such as fundraisers, occurs.

While the above factors may also characterize some profit-oriented organizations, they are certainly prevalent in nonprofit settings. These characteristics affect the implementation of marketing efforts in such organizations and must be considered in the development of an overall strategy.

# TYPES OF NONPROFIT MARKETING

Although nonprofit organizations are at least as varied as profit-seeking organizations, it is possible to categorize them based on the type of marketing each requires. The three major types of marketing among NPOs are person marketing, social marketing, and organization marketing.

**THE UNITED WAY'S STATEMENT OF PRINCIPLES FOR DONORS' RIGHTS**

The donor participates in the very essence of our mission and purpose, exercises rights, prerogatives, and fundamental privileges that must be recognized at all times and without reservation.

www.uwc-cc.ca

This document was approved by the membership of United Way of Canada–Centraide Canada at its March 1998 Annual General Meeting. Member United Ways–Centraides are expected to comply with these guidelines. These guidelines were developed for United Ways–Centraides in Canada.

- The right to be informed of the organization's mission and purpose and to become a member of the organization if the donor so wishes;
- The right to know the identity of the organization's officers and members of the Board of Directors and to expect that they act with the greatest transparency, integrity, and discernment in implementing the organization's mission and purpose for the best interests of the community;
- The right to have access to the organization's annual financial statements and to easily obtain a copy;
- The right to know how donations, directly or indirectly contributed to the organization, are distributed, and to

be assured that donated funds are used as intended by the donor;

- The right to be treated with consideration and respect by the organization and to receive appropriate acknowledgment and recognition;
- The right to confidentiality regarding personal information about donors and facts about their donations;
- The right to expect that all relationships between the organization's representatives and the donor will be professional in nature;
- The right to be informed of the exact nature of the relationship that exists between fundraisers and the organization;
- The right to expect that the organization will not share or sell a mailing list that includes the donor's name, without providing the donor with a meaningful opportunity to decline;
- The right to ask questions of the organization and to expect prompt, truthful, and complete answers in an easy-to-understand manner.

**Why might the United Way have decided that a statement of principles of donors' rights was necessary?**

Source: United Way, "Statement of Principles for Donors' Rights," www.unitedway.ca/english/docs/principles_of_donors_rights.html, downloaded June 15, 1999. Reprinted with permission.

## Person Marketing

**Person marketing** refers to efforts designed to cultivate the attention, interest, and preference of a target market toward a person.[4] This type of marketing is typically employed by political candidates and celebrities.

Leadership campaigns for political parties are good examples of person marketing. Serious contenders conduct research into the various voter segments and develop strategies to reach them. Similarly, in a profit-seeking setting, various musicians are carefully marketed to subsegments of the total market. The marketing mix for marketing Shania Twain is different from that for Céline Dion.

**person marketing**
Efforts designed to cultivate the attention, interest, and preference of a target market toward a person.

## Social Marketing

The second type of nonprofit marketing deals with causes and social issues rather than an individual. **Social marketing** refers to "the analysis, planning, execution, and evaluation of programs designed to influence the voluntary behaviour of target audiences in order to improve their personal welfare and that of society."[5]

Social marketing is distinct from other forms of marketing, including other forms of nonprofit marketing, in that its goal is explicitly and singularly to work to the benefit of the target audience by influencing the target audience's behaviour.

The importance of wearing sunscreen is an idea currently being marketed in several countries. Anti-smoking marketing programs have been so successful that many people have quit smoking, and legislation has been passed that forbids smoking in public places.

**social marketing**
The analysis, planning, execution, and evaluation of programs designed to influence the voluntary behaviour of target audiences in order to improve their personal welfare and that of society.

You don't have to give up a great looking lawn when you reduce or eliminate pesticides. There are many effective natural alternatives. And by going natural, rain runoff from your lawn won't carry pesticides to rivers and Lake Ontario — our drinking water source. For more, visit our web site, or call for your free copy of *The Green Guide to a Healthy Lawn.*

*Using* **TOO MANY PESTICIDES?**
Call 416-397-LAWN
www.city.toronto.on.ca/pesticides

TORONTO

**What are the social marketing objectives for this advertisement from the City of Toronto?**

## Organization Marketing

**organization marketing**
Attempts to influence others to accept the goals of, receive the services of, or contribute in some way to an organization.

The third type of nonprofit marketing, **organization marketing**, attempts to influence others to accept the goals of, receive the services of, or contribute in some way to an organization. Included in this category are mutual benefit organizations, such as churches, labour unions, and political parties; service organizations, such as colleges, universities, hospitals, and museums; and government organizations, such as military services, police and fire departments, the post office, and local communities.[6]

# UNDERSTANDING OF MARKETING BY NONPROFIT ORGANIZATIONS

Nonprofit organizations often have too limited an understanding of marketing. In many cases, marketing is taken to mean simply marketing communications. Developing a well-thought-out marketing strategy, as well as considering other components of the marketing mix—product development, distribution, and pricing strategies—have too often been largely ignored. Marketing,

# THE PRACTISING MARKETER

## DO CANADIAN ANTI-SMOKING SPOTS SEND WRONG SIGNAL?

Which is the more persuasive anti-smoking ad?

A spot that shows figure skater Elvis Stojko twirling across the ice and saying he's grateful he never started smoking?

Or an ad that shows graphic images of a 31-year-old mother dying from emphysema, interspersed with pictures of her two distraught daughters?

The first is a Government of Canada ad that aired during the Winter Olympics. The second is a U.S. spot from the Massachusetts Department of Public Health.

They aren't even in the same league, says Garfield Mahood, executive director of the Non-Smokers' Rights Association. The same is true of other U.S. and Canadian anti-smoking ads, he says.

"The stuff that's been produced here, compared with the United States, is absolute pablum," says Mr. Mahood, who just released a scathing report on Canada's $28-million tobacco-control mass-media campaign of the past year.

He's not the only anti-tobacco advocate who thinks so. Canada's anti-smoking ads are, for the most part, weak and ineffective weapons in the war against tobacco, critics say. They are urging Health Canada to adopt U.S.-style advertising that features more graphic images of tobacco's destructiveness and is far more critical of the industry.

"The Stojko thing is a waste of time," says Marty Rothstein, a marketing consultant and former president of the Heart and Stroke Foundation of Ontario. Ads featuring role models encouraging young people not to smoke aren't effective, he says.

That ad and others illustrate that the government has "decided to cut a very down-the-middle-of-the-road approach" with anti-tobacco ads.

Another major shortcoming of Canada's anti-smoking ads is that they don't do enough to expose the tobacco industry's role in contributing to addiction and death, critics say.

"Denormalizing" the industry—that is, stripping it of legitimacy in the eyes of consumers—is a key component of U.S. anti-smoking ad campaigns, such as the one featuring Pam Laffin, the mother who developed emphysema at 24 and died at 31, leaving behind daughters aged 9 and 12.

The stark images of Ms. Laffin, with tubes in her nose and wearing an oxygen mask, are accompanied by hard-hitting voice-overs.

"The tobacco industry is spending millions telling us about all the things they do for kids. But they never bother to mention all the things they take away," one ad says, as the camera focuses on Ms. Laffin.

The goal is to expose the hypocrisy of the U.S. tobacco industry's efforts to rehabilitate its image by donating funds to various causes.

Denormalization is vital for a couple of reasons, anti-tobacco advocates say. First, it helps smokers understand the tobacco industry's role in getting them hooked, which may cause some to become outraged enough to consider quitting.

Second, singling out the tobacco industry lays the foundation for legislative reform aimed at reducing tobacco use.

Health Canada officials insist their ads include denormalization messages. For instance, a recent ad that aimed to underline the dangers of light and mild cigarettes depicted bottles of cyanide and other deadly chemicals. The voice-over said: "No one would label a hazardous product like this light or mild, except the tobacco industry."

As well, Canadian anti-tobacco ads sometimes use stark, disturbing images to make their point, says Hélène Goulet, director-general of the tobacco control program at Health Canada.

She cites a dramatized spot in which dead bodies in a morgue wear toe tags numbered 44,998, 44,999 and 45,000—a reference to the number of Canadians who die each year in Canada from smoking-related illnesses.

"We had a lot of telephone calls following that ad," she says. Some people supported the ad for its frankness, while others thought it was too morbid. "But that means they remembered it."

Health Canada has run graphic U.S. ads in the past, such as the acclaimed spot featuring Debi, who smokes through a hole in her throat. But it would be a mistake to air only shocking ads, because the public would learn to tune them out, she says.

"You have to have a mixture of messages, a mixture of types of ads, a mixture of themes," she says.

Anti-tobacco advocates agree that a mixture of ads works best—namely, those focusing on denormalization, on the dangers of second-hand smoke, and on encouraging people to seek help in quitting.

**What do you think? Which ads are the most effective? How do these examples relate to the discussion of fear appeals in Chapter 19?**

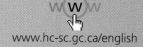

www.no-smoke.org

www.hc-sc.gc.ca/english

Source: Excerpted from John Heinzl, "Do Canadian Anti-smoking Spots Send Wrong Signal?" *The Globe and Mail*, Friday, July 12, 2002, p. B9. Reprinted with permission from *The Globe and Mail*.

considered and practised merely as aggressive promotion, is a short-lived, surface-level solution to a variety of organizational problems and objectives. For instance, one university decided to "adopt marketing" and thought it was doing so by planning to release balloons containing scholarship offers. And a "marketing planning" conference for a private school consisted mainly of developing new slogans for advertisements.

Professor Seymour H. Fine conducted a survey of nonprofit organizations to assess the degree of marketing sophistication present. His findings, illustrated in Table 21.2, revealed that many respondents were unaware of, or at least reluctant to admit, the presence of marketing efforts in their organization. Although this study was done some time ago, it is fair to say that nonprofit appreciation of the benefits of marketing still lacks that of profit-oriented firms.

Nonprofit organizations need to take the time to develop a comprehensive marketing approach. One university, for example, conducted a comprehensive marketing audit that designated strong and weak areas in its product mix (program offerings). It was then possible to develop strategies after the basic parameters of market, resources, and mission had been identified and analyzed.

**TABLE 21.2** Responses of Selected Nonprofit Organization Representatives

| NONPROFIT ORGANIZATION | RESPONSE TO THE QUESTION "DO YOU HAVE A MARKETING DEPARTMENT OR EQUIVALENT?" |
|---|---|
| Public health service official | "Marketing fluoridation is not a function of government — promotion and public awareness is." |
| Administrator of regional women's rights group | "We have never thought of ourselves as marketing a product. We have people who are assigned equal pay for work of equal value as their 'item.'" |
| Group crusading for the rights of the left-handed | "Don't understand the term [marketing]; we do lobbying, letter writing to appropriate government and commercial concerns." |
| A national centre for the prevention of child abuse | "We disseminate information without the marketing connotation. Besides, demand is too great to justify marketing." |
| Recruiting officer | "Not applicable." |

Source: Adapted from Seymour H. Fine, *The Marketing of Ideas and Social Issues* (New York: Praeger, 1981), p. 53. Copyright © 1981 by Praeger Publishers, New York. Used by permission of Greenwood Publishing Group, Inc., Westport, CT.

# IMPORTANCE OF MARKETING TO NONPROFIT ORGANIZATIONS

Marketing as a recognized function is a late arrival to managing nonprofit organizations. The practices of improved accounting, financial control, personnel selection, and strategic planning were all implemented before formal marketing planning. Nevertheless, nonprofit organizations have begun to accept marketing enthusiastically. For example, university administrators attend seminars and conferences to learn how to better market their institutions.

Marketing's rise in the nonprofit sector could not be continued without a successful track record. While it is often more difficult to measure results in nonprofit settings, marketing can already point to examples of success. The Church of the Nazarene in Canada, for instance, has used a telemarketing campaign called "Phones for You" to develop a target clientele interested in supporting the start of new churches. And one art gallery's marketing analysis resulted in defining two distinct market segments it should serve. Marketing is increasingly an accepted part of the operational environment of successful nonprofit organizations. Table 21.3 presents a hypothetical job description for a marketing director at a university.

# DEVELOPING A MARKETING STRATEGY

The need for comprehensive marketing planning and control rather than a mere increase in marketing communications expenditures has already been noted. Substantial opportunities exist for effective, innovative strategies, since there has been little previous marketing effort in most nonprofit settings.

---

**TABLE 21.3** Job Description: Director of Marketing for a University

**Position Title:** Director of Marketing

**Reports to:** A vice-president designated by the president

**Scope:** University-wide

**Position Concept:** The director of marketing is responsible for providing marketing guidance and services to university officers, school deans, department chairpersons, and other agents of the university

**Functions:** The director of marketing will
1. Contribute a marketing perspective to the deliberations of the top administration in its planning of the university's future
2. Prepare data that might be needed by any officer of the university on a particular market's size, segments, trends, and behavioural dynamics
3. Conduct studies of the needs, perceptions, preferences, and satisfaction of particular markets
4. Assist in the planning, promotion, and launching of new programs
5. Assist in the development of communication and promotion campaigns and materials
6. Analyze and advise on pricing questions
7. Appraise the workability of new academic proposals from a marketing point of view
8. Advise on new student recruitment
9. Advise on current student satisfaction
10. Advise on university fundraising

**Responsibilities:** The director of marketing will
1. Contact individual officers and small groups at the university to explain services and to solicit problems
2. Rank the various requests for services according to their long-run impact, cost-saving potential, time requirements, ease of accomplishment, cost, and urgency
3. Select projects of high priority and set accomplishment goals for the year
4. Prepare a budget request to support the anticipated work
5. Prepare an annual report on the main accomplishments of the office

**Major Liaisons:** The director of marketing will
1. Relate most closely with the president's office, admissions office, development office, planning office, and public relations department
2. Relate secondarily with the deans of various schools and chairpersons of various departments

---

Source: Philip Kotler, "Strategies for Introducing Marketing into Nonprofit Organizations," *Journal of Marketing* (January 1979), p. 42. Reprinted with permission by the American Marketing Association.

## Marketing Research

Many decisions in nonprofit settings (as well as in business) are based on little, if any, research. For example, numerous Canadian art galleries arbitrarily establish programs and schedules with little or no reference to audience marketing research.

Adequate marketing research can be extremely important in a variety of nonprofit settings. Resident opinion surveys in some cities have proven valuable to public officials.[7] Analyzing projected population trends has led school boards to build new schools and to phase out others.

## Product Strategy

Nonprofit organizations face the same product decisions as profit-seeking firms. They must choose a product, service, person, idea, or social issue to be offered to their target market. They must decide whether to offer a single product or a mix of related products. They must make product identification decisions. The fact that the United Way symbol and the Red Cross trademark are as familiar as the golden arches of McDonald's or the Shell logo illustrates the similarity in the use of product identification methods.

A common failure among nonprofit organizations is assuming that heavy promotional efforts can overcome a poor product strategy or marketing mix. For example, some liberal arts colleges tried to use promotion to overcome their product mix deficiencies when students became increasingly career-oriented. Such promotions often met with limited success: successful institutions adjust their product offerings to reflect customer demand.

www.redcross.ca

Emily's mother was one of them.

Mothers Against Drunk Driving (MADD), recognized throughout North America by its red ribbon campaign, is also known for its dramatic television commercials.

# Pricing Strategy

Pricing is typically a very important element of the marketing mix for nonprofit organizations.

Pricing strategy can be used to accomplish a variety of organizational goals in nonprofit settings. These include

- *Profit maximization.* While nonprofit organizations by definition do not cite profitability as a primary goal, there are numerous instances in which they do try to maximize their return on a single event or a series of events. The $1000-a-plate political fundraiser is an example.
- *Cost recovery.* Some nonprofit organizations attempt to recover only their actual cost of operating. Mass transit, colleges, and airports are common examples. The amount of recovered cost is often dictated by tradition, competition, or public opinion.
- *Providing market incentives.* Other nonprofit groups follow a penetration pricing policy or offer a free service to encourage increased usage of the product or service. The Saskatoon Symphony's policy of setting its subscription prices for a series of concerts well below the normal individual ticket price is intended to increase overall attendance at performances. Many performing arts organizations follow similar pricing approaches.
- *Market suppression (demand deterrance).* Price is sometimes used to discourage consumption. In other words, high prices are used to accomplish social objectives and are not directly related to the costs of providing the product or service. Illustrations of suppression include tobacco and alcohol taxes, parking fines, tolls, and gasoline excise taxes.[8]

# Distribution Strategy

Distribution channels for nonprofit organizations tend to be short, simple, and direct. If intermediaries are present in the channel, they are usually agents, such as an independent ticket agency or a specialist in fundraising. Even so, there are opportunities for creativity. Each summer the Victoria Symphony rents a barge and performs from Victoria's harbour, while the audience sits on lawn chairs or blankets on the banks. Organizers estimate that attendance ranges up over 40 000.

Nonprofit organizations often fail to exercise caution in planning and executing the distribution strategy. For example, organizers of recycling centres sometimes complain about lack of public interest when their real problem is an inconvenient location or lack of adequate drop-off points. In a number of cities, this problem has been solved by dropping blue boxes off at people's homes. By contrast, some public agencies, like health and social welfare departments, have set up branches in neighbourhood shopping centres to be more accessible to their clientele. Nonprofit marketers must carefully evaluate the available distribution options if they are to be successful in delivering their products or in serving their intended consumers.

# Marketing Communications Strategy

It is common to see or hear advertisements from nonprofit organizations such as educational institutions, churches, and public service organizations.

## THE PRACTISING MARKETER

### IT SEEMED LIKE A GOOD IDEA ...

Call it a failed experiment in charity. You'll see plenty of people dropping donations into the collection boxes scattered around Almudena Cathedral in Madrid. But hardly anyone stops at the credit-card machine by the doorway—people prefer handing over money the old-fashioned way.

The cathedral, which sits next to the Royal Palace, opened in 1993 after 110 years of construction, but its interior is still unfinished. Hoping to increase donations, the church had the credit-card machine installed last year, but fewer than a dozen people a month have used it.

Well, it sounded like a good idea: the machine was proposed by a credit-card company, which figured that since credit cards were so popular in Spain—outpacing even personal cheques as the preferred method of payment—people would take to the cash-free charity box.

It's scheduled to be removed shortly. Just hope church officials resist the remote-videocam-confessional-booth idea.

**Why might visitors to a cathedral be reluctant to use credit cards to make contributions? How might market research have prevented this mistake from happening?**

Source: "Church Disses Credit," *Time Digital* (May 24, 1999), p. 7. Copyright © TIME Inc. Reprinted with permission.

Marketing communications are affected by a variety of factors, including relative involvement in the nonprofit setting, pricing, and perceived benefits.[9] But overall, marketing communications are seen by many nonprofit managers as the primary solution to their marketing problems. As noted earlier, this view is often naive, but it does not diminish the importance of this mix element in a nonprofit setting.

All types of marketing communications elements have been used. The Canadian Armed Forces has used television advertising to attract recruits. Fundraising for some support groups for the handicapped is done through personal selling over the telephone. Volunteers are an essential part of the marketing program for many nonprofit organizations. They are used to "sell" (canvass) by phone or in person. Such individuals pose a significant "sales management" problem. With a paid sales force, it is easy to demand certain behaviour on the part of personnel or to provide various financial incentives to affect their behaviour. Similar methods are not as readily available with volunteers. Other stimulation and incentives, such as public recognition or receptions, are used as substitutes. Even so, it is unlikely that the same effects can be achieved.

Advertising is a desirable marketing communications option. However, because the cost of media is high, fundraising drives often rely on publicity and public relations efforts, such as appearances on TV talk shows, to promote their product. Many church groups find that community service projects not only help them fulfill their mandate of ministry to their community but will often result in favourable publicity in local media.

# THE FUTURE OF NONPROFIT MARKETING

While marketing has gained increasing acceptance in the nonprofit sector of society, it is still viewed with suspicion by some of the people involved. The heavy emphasis on marketing communications

www.recruiting.dnd.ca

Lizard, public zoo

Roy Watson, homeless

- climate-controlled habitat

- medical care

- fresh food from Africa

**Many NPOs are making effective use of advertising.**

is one reason. Marketing efforts in nonprofit organizations often lack the sophistication and integration found in the marketing of profit-oriented industries. Marketing is too often seen as the "quick-fix" solution to a more basic problem. To combat this, nonprofit marketers must market their own discipline in a realistic and socially responsible manner. The client must be helped to understand the opportunities, benefits, behaviour modifications, and commitment involved in adopting the marketing concept in a nonprofit setting.

## SUMMARY

A nonprofit organization is one whose primary objective is something other than returning a profit to its owners. The marketing mix is just as applicable to not-for-profit marketing as it is to for-profit marketing.

The special characteristics of nonprofit organizations are as follows:

- often intangible product
- often dealing with multiple publics
- customer may have less influence than a customer of a profit-seeking organization
- lack of a bottom line
- lack of a single clear organizational structure
- inefficient operation

Three types of marketing among NPOs are person marketing, social marketing, and organization marketing. Market suppression, or demand deterrence, is sometimes practised in nonprofit marketing.

## KEY TERMS

bottom line, p. 539

nonprofit organization (NPO), p. 538

organization marketing, p. 542

person marketing, p. 541

social marketing, p. 541

## INTERACTIVE SUMMARY AND DISCUSSION QUESTIONS

1. A nonprofit organization is one whose primary objective is something other than returning a profit to its owners. Give an example of other core objectives that such organizations could have.
2. Explain how each of the following special characteristics of nonprofit organizations might affect the way nonprofit organizations practise marketing.
   a. often intangible product
   b. often dealing with multiple publics
   c. customer may have less influence than a customer of a profit-seeking organization
   d. lack of a bottom line
   e. lack of a single clear organizational structure
   f. inefficient operation
3. Three types of marketing among NPOs are person marketing, idea marketing, and organization marketing. For which of these would the application of marketing principles be the most difficult? Explain.
4. The marketing mix is just as applicable to not-for-profit marketing as it is to for-profit marketing. Would there be any differences in applying the marketing mix in the case of not-for-profit marketing? Use examples to explain your answer.
5. Market suppression, or demand deterrence, is sometimes practised in nonprofit marketing. Give examples of this. Which of the elements of the marketing mix would most likely be applicable in accomplishing market suppression?

6. Cite several examples of circumstances in which penetration pricing might be practised by public utilities.
7. How would you assess the marketing performance of the following?
   a. your college or university
   b. Canadian Postal Workers Union
   c. Planned Parenthood
   d. the re-election committee of a local politician
8. Outline the marketing program of your college or university. Make any reasonable assumptions necessary. Where are the major strengths and weaknesses of the current program? What recommendations would you make for improvement?
9. Why might there be a greater tendency for a nonprofit organization to define marketing inaccurately?

10. Visit the Web sites of two nonprofit organizations and two for-profit organizations. How are they similar? How are they different? What do you think accounts for the differences?

## Canada's Image in the U.S.

Most American business managers know Canada is a compelling place to invest—it just takes time to convince them of that before they get here.

That was the reaction of several economists and academics Monday to a poll that suggests Canada wouldn't make a short list of attractive countries to invest for several reasons, including a perception that corporate tax rates are too high.

"It shows it really does take a long time to change impressions," said Doug Porter, an economist at BMO Nesbitt Burns. "Even though Canadian taxes have been coming down—especially on the corporate level—for the past couple of years, they are either in line or below U.S. levels. It takes time for that to really make an impression, not just outside of Canada but even inside Canada."

The survey, conducted for the Canadian government by U.S. marketing company Wirthlin Worldwide, suggests 49 percent of the American managers surveyed didn't even mention Canada or gave little consideration to Canada as a place to invest.

High taxes were cited as a chief reason despite falling corporate tax rates in Canada. The Quebec sovereignty issue was raised even though it's hardly been a hot issue in the country for several years. And the East Coast was pegged by some managers as "economically depressed" and at "almost poverty level."

Hurt feelings aside, reaction was muted because the survey only focused on managers in the biotechnology, information, and communication technology sectors, and only those located in Boston and Dallas—two American hotbeds for those sectors.

The study, which was not released publicly likely due to some inflammatory remarks about Quebec and Atlantic Canada, focused on those fast-growing areas since the federal government wanted to investigate why Canada is lacking in direct foreign investment in those sectors.

A broader survey would show, however, that American businesses, particularly large manufacturers such as the Big Three carmakers—GM, Ford, and DaimlerChrysler—do value Canada as a place to set up shop.

"You'd get a much different picture from U.S. managers who think about these decisions and actually know that Canada is an attractive place to do business," said Tony Frost, a business professor at the University of Western Ontario in London, Ontario.

"Cost-wise, we're definitely cheaper," Frost added, noting that the low Canadian dollar keeps labour costs down, while

health care coverage and a knowledgeable workforce also contribute.

www.bmonesbittburns.com

The responses of the high-tech and biotech business managers may suggest Canada needs to do a better job marketing itself, said Frost, especially when it comes to promoting the country's low tax rates.

Ottawa has been reducing corporate tax levels since 2000 and will continue to bring them down through to 2006.

"Typically in the U.S., the general notion of Canada is that it's a high-tax country," he said. "When you show [Americans] the data on corporate income tax rates, they're stunned."

"Communicating the message . . . We need to do a much better job."

The country may need to better educate its American neighbours about fiscal policy inroads, said BMO's Porter.

"Maybe that's the main message here, that policymakers should not assume that the job has been done," he said.

"And it's important to keep some controls on the spending side so that there's still room to reduce taxes further," he added. "I still think that's very important in keeping Canada competitive."

Outside of taxation, concerns about Atlantic Canada when considering the country as a place to invest would be "complete idiocy," said Peter Dungan, an economist and professor with the University of Toronto.

"There are high-tech firms in the East Coast, so these guys haven't done their homework," he said. "But why does that matter? Why does that stop somebody putting something in B.C.?"

One executive with a media buying company that deals with American clients looking to advertise here said some outdated views about Atlantic Canada and the Quebec independence movement should come as no surprise.

"Even though we are their largest trading partner, it's only once they come to the point where they're doing business in Canada that they need to understand the basics of Canadian geography," said Mark Sherman of Montreal-based Media Experts.

"Canada is a foreign territory. For a kid going to school, they learn probably as much about Canada as they do France."

### You Be the Marketer

1. What type of not-for-profit marketing is involved in this case?
2. What action can various levels of government in Canada take to address the image problem?

---

*Source:* "Canadian Image Outdated in U.S., Investment Suffers Because of Misconceptions," *The StarPhoenix* (Saskatoon), Tuesday, July 9, 2002. Reprinted with the permission of The Canadian Press.

# A Note on the Case Method

What is a case? It is a description of a specific situation or incident that usually requires a decision. It normally includes more than the bare facts of the situation. Varied opinions of individuals involved in the case and background information to which the real decision maker in the case might have access are also provided.

A case puts you in the role of the decision maker. Solving a case is like working with the problems that people in actual business situations encounter.

In some ways, the case method of learning is more difficult than the lecture method. Instead of casting the facts into some suitable semipermanent pedagogical order, the instructor assumes the difficult task of helping students meet new and different problems. The instructor's task becomes one of fostering a facility for approaching and handling new and unstructured situations. The students often find initial difficulties:

> Instead of beginning with…textbook…principles …the student is given a pedestrian description of how the Ward Machine Company put a mechanical shaver on the market.

> The initial atmosphere of the classroom does little to restore a feeling of certainty. The behaviour of the professor is strangely disconcerting. There is an absence of professorial dicta, a surprising lack of "answers" and "cold dope" which the student can record in his notebook; rather he is asked what he thinks, what he would do, what problems he feels are important.[1]

Despite these difficulties, experience indicates some strong arguments in favour of the case method.

First, it challenges you to use and develop your own insight and knowledge in a realistic situation.[2] Second, as you genuinely apply yourself to the analysis of cases, you will develop abilities to deal successfully with new management problems as they occur in the business world. Thus, your transition from the world of formal education will be easier. Third, the case method gives you an opportunity to experiment with various ways of using your knowledge of the basic principles of the field you are studying.[3]

## PREPARING A CASE

Preparing a case requires some diligence. It is not enough to skim the case once or twice and then come to class and "shoot from the hip" (or lip), or write down the first solution that comes to mind. Rather, the solution is a progressive process through a methodical and systematic analysis that provides great challenge and interest.

You should read the case several times, starting first with a quick skim to get the overall feel of the situation. Then read it again in more detail as you learn more facts and begin to think about the various aspects of the case. There are several possible approaches to successful case analysis. One alternative is presented below. Use it, but do not try to follow every point slavishly. You are not being asked to "fill in the blanks," but to analyze the case intelligently, using your own judgement and analytical skills fully.

## SUGGESTIONS FOR DEVELOPING CASE SOLUTIONS

A case solution should be organized into five parts:
1. Summary of Important Facts
2. Problem
3. Analysis
4. Conclusion
5. Recommendations

### Summary of Important Facts

There are two possible methods of making this summary. You should probably use the first method until you have developed some competence in logically outlining the facts in a case. Then the briefer summary (described in number 2 below) will suffice. The alternative methods are as follows:
1. Outline in logical order the important facts given in the case.
   a. Do not merely list miscellaneous facts in the order given in the case.
   b. Organize your outline in logical fashion under a few main headings. Possible groupings include nature of the company and its products; competitive situation; market for the product; channels of distribution; pricing policies; organization of sales department; policies relating to management of salespeople, and so on.
2. Prepare a concise, one-paragraph summary giving a brief picture of the company and the factors that gave rise to the problem to be solved.

### Problem

Clearly and concisely state the problem that is to be solved.
1. This may be an exact restatement of the problem given at the end of a case, or
2. The problem may be given to you by your instructor, or

---

Source: R.H. Evans and M.D. Beckman, *Cases in Marketing: A Canadian Perspective* (Toronto: Prentice-Hall, 1972).

[1] Donald R. Scheen and Philip A. Sprague, "What Is the Case Method?" In *The Case Method at the Harvard Business School*, ed. Malcolm P. McNair (New York: McGraw-Hill, 1954), p. 78.

[2] Charles I. Gragg, "Because Wisdom Can't Be Told," in *The Case Method at the Harvard Business School*, ed. Malcolm P. McNair (New York: McGraw-Hill, 1954), pp. 2–7.

[3] John T. Gullahorn, "Teaching by the Case Method," *School Review* (January 1959), pp. 448–60.

3. You may have to use your own powers of discernment in order to pick out the main problem, because it is not stated in so many words.

## Analysis

1. This is the crucial segment in the development of a case. You should make a detailed analysis, leading to your decision and recommendations. You should organize it in accordance with the basic issues or factors in the case.
2. In your analysis, it is necessary and important to consider the weakness of your decision. Consider and present arguments on both sides of the major issue involved.
3. Analytical arguments should be based on the facts of the case, as well as on logical and clear-cut reasoning.
4. State clearly any assumptions you make, and give your reasons for making them.
5. Where possible, "push your pencil" and make use of the data. Make creative use of all possible information in the case.
6. Use an objective, unemotional approach in your analysis. This does not mean that you may not be persuasive in your methods of presentation. In fact, you may do an effective "selling" job in your presentation. A logical grouping of related points will help, as will full development of each point. Give your analysis depth as well as breadth; substantiate major points with minor points. Be sure that you cover each point adequately with explanations or evidence.

## Conclusion

The conclusion should summarize briefly the arguments used in the development of the case analysis. In a written report it is inadequate to simply state "the arguments above warrant …" It is too much to expect the reader to think back and perhaps reread the report to discover what the arguments were.

## Recommendations

State in point form the course of action you believe to be the most sound solution, based on your exhaustive analysis of all alternative possibilities.

Common difficulties encountered in case analysis are:

1. Students at first have a tendency to repeat the statements in the problem book without reorganizing them and relating them to the problem. Thus the report becomes simply a rehash of the problem. To avoid this the student should keep in mind at all times what the problem is and should constantly think, "What has this to do with the problem?" It is wise also to close the book while writing the report, referring to it only in order to get the accurate facts.
2. Statements of conclusions may be presented without the reasoning that leads to them. So far as the reader is concerned such statements are simply snap judgements and have no more validity than the flipping of a coin. All statements must be substantiated by the evidence. A conclusion may be stated at the beginning or at the end of the evidence, but in either case it is necessary to show how the evidence connects with the conclusion. This is done by the use of connectives—"because," "the reason is," and "it follows that."
3. It is tempting to neglect to present evidence that is adverse to the conclusion in the report. However, since the report is to lead to executive action, both sides must be considered and carefully weighed one against the other. Here again, the proper use of connectives is helpful. Such connectives as "notwithstanding," "in spite of," and "be that as it may" indicate that the argument given is subordinate to some other.
4. Students often fail to carry through the argument to a logical conclusion. This indicates lazy thinking. The careful reader or listener wonders, "So what?" indicating that the analyst has failed to show the pertinence of some statement to the problem solution.
5. Students may fall into using generalizations when specific statements can be made. Most material in the problems is specific and applies to this particular problem. There is no point in making it general and thus weakening the argument.
6. Students often use their personal attitudes as an argument. Statements such as "I firmly believe" or "It is my considered opinion" are pompous excuses for real arguments.
7. Students sometimes come up with the conclusion and recommendation that the firm should do the "best thing under the circumstances." Such a recommendation is simply passing the buck and would indicate to the employer a refusal to take responsibility. The reader or listener wants you to decide, not sit on the fence.

# Case 1

## Computers for the Blind

### SITUATION SUMMARY

Entrepreneurs, Dr. Roman Gouzman and Dr. Igor Karasin, had developed a system to enable blind people to use a computer to feel representations, including maps and fine art. They called their innovation the Virtual Touch system for the blind, and they applied to the U.S. Patent Office for a patent. The patent was issued in June 1999; however, the commercialisation of an invention was quite complex.

### THE FIRM

It was in 1996 that Dr. Gouzman and Dr. Karasin created VirTouch Ltd., the purpose of which was to market their Virtual Touch System. The firm was established in the framework of the Jerusalem Software Incubator, and in 1998, VirTouch graduated as a full-fledged high-tech new venture. It built its reputation as a beta-site (testing ground) for Microsoft technology development. In Jerusalem, the capital city of Israel, the Chief Scientist of the Israel Ministry of Industry and Trade endorsed the firm.

### THE ENVIRONMENT FOR ENTERPRISE IN ISRAEL

With more than 80 venture capital firms in Israel, finance is seldom problematic in Israel. Furthermore, special financial incentives are available for firms that contribute to employment and to exports.

The state offers tax-free investment grants, and a variety of R & D grants. Among these are R & D grants for the development of innovative products (50% of approved expenditures) and R & D grants for new ventures (66% of approved expenditures). In addition, assistance is available to train employees and to reduce the cost of rent. As well, the government provides market research grants and subsidies toward the preparation of business plans. The Marketing Encouragement Fund, for instance, gives financial support to enterprises seeking to enlarge their international marketing efforts.

Complementing the many grants, loans are also readily available. There are several loan funds in Israel, involving $150 million. These include government loan funds, philanthropic loan funds, and private loan funds.

Israel is the only country to have free trade agreements with Canada, the European Union, Turkey, and the United States. On March 6, 2000, Israel signed a free trade agreement with Mexico. Israel also has preferential customs agreements and double taxation agreements with other countries.

### THE PRODUCT

The Virtual Touch System included a device, which functions as a tactile display, providing resolution close to the maximum limit of a finger's perception. Three dimensions also allow for the representation of colours. The system displays Braille, and also easy-to-feel Latin characters.

The user can navigate the cursor to transform images, as well as to capture illustrations and to play computer games. The system thus helps develop spatial awareness and related motor skills. Consequently, it makes possible, to the blind, career options in virtual arts as well as computer science.

The Virtual Touch System includes educational materials to teach algebra, astronomy, chemistry, geography and geometry. A special programme allows the user to learn specific routes, e.g. how to walk from home to the post office.

### THE MARKET

The Virtual Touch System was introduced at the July 1998 National Federation of the Blind Convention, which took place in Dallas, Texas. Later that year, the system was demonstrated at a convention in Minneapolis, Minnesota, and in 1999, at California State University. Potential users expressed enthusiasm with the system, and prospects for sales seemed promising.

Furthermore, there was a large potential market for the system. There were 17 million visually-impaired people in the industrialised world. In the United States, half a million of these were already computer users. It was felt that a large demand could arise for the Virtual Touch System world-wide.

Just as Louis Braille introduced, in 1829, a tactile system of reading and writing for the blind, the inventors of the Virtual Touch System intended to open the computer graphic world, to the visually-impaired, simultaneously enhancing the spatial awareness of users.

### ASSIGNMENT

Serve as consultant for the Virtual Touch system. What are your recommendations regarding production, pricing, promotion and distribution?

This case was written by **Professor Leo Paul Dana**, University of Canterbury, New Zealand. It is intended to be used as the basis for class discussion rather than to illustrate either effective or ineffective handling of a management situation. The case was compiled from published sources. © 2001 LP Dana, University of Canterbury, Christchurch, New Zealand. Distributed by The European Case Clearing House, England and USA. North American phone: + 1 781 239 5884, fax: + 1 781 239 5885, e-mail: ECCHBabson@aol.com. Rest of the World, phone + 44 (0) 1234 750903, fax: +44 (0)1234 751125, e-mail: ECCH@cranfield.ac.uk. All rights reserved. Printed in UK and USA. Web Site: http://www.ecch.cranfield.ac.uk.

## Sound Tech

Sound Tech is a manufacturer of high-quality sound systems. Products include receivers, amplifiers, tape decks, and other associated products. These are distributed nationwide through all the major retail outlets. The company regularly advertises its products through network television and consumer and trade magazines. The advertising strategy is not only to create brand awareness, but to cultivate brand preference for the Sound Tech product line.

Adrienne Stezenko, the marketing manager for Sound Tech, as a member of the Academy of Marketing Science, received her regular copy of the *Marketing Science News*. As she leafed through it, she found herself reading the article reproduced below. As she did so, she had a feeling of threat, excitement, and challenge. This new way of managing marketing communications was certainly different from the way the company now tried to promote its products, and it put current methods into question.

On the other hand, the article made a lot of sense, and she could see a great number of possibilities for developing an even stronger marketing communications mix.

### INTEGRATED MARKETING COMMUNICATIONS

### What Is IMC?

To those involved in the teaching and research of advertising and promotion, "IMC" (Integrated Marketing Communications) has become a familiar term. Readers of the advertising and promotions literature might already have noted the prolific work on the topic from Professor Don Schultz of Northwestern University's Medill School of Journalism. Don is one of the leading proponents of this new concept, and recently acted to replace Medill's Advertising program with a Department of Integrated Marketing Communications.

To new initiates, IMC consists of the familiar promotional mix augmented by a new twist: the key premise of IMC is that the promotional mix should be used in a synergistic fashion and that every element depends on every other element for successful marketing results from promotional programs. This view was engendered by the advent of new-age media and market/audience fragmentation. In many marketing programs, it has become difficult to achieve objectives using the traditional network TV buys. Niche media have been utilized to supplement flagging mainstream media; moreover, a key aspect of IMC in the Schultz tradition is a keen focus on database marketing. In this view, nothing makes promotion more effective than knowing who the audience is. Once this knowledge is gained, many mass-exposure media are made obsolete and individual exposures can be achieved in a direct fashion.

### How Is It Different from "Marketing Communications?"

It would appear to be the focus on the uses of market databases and direct media that differentiates Integrated Marketing Communications from the more basic concept of "marketing communications." The previous view was that advertising (or PR, or sales, or sales promotion) was more effective when used in concert with the other elements of the promotions mix; each reinforced the other and brought additional reach and frequency to a campaign. The modern view has gone a step further and added a new element to the mix: [This is] characterized loosely as "telecommunications" in order to encompass the full range of the emerging "new media."

In modern marketing, advertising products on network TV is becoming passé. Indeed, television now means far more than [CBC, CTV,] ABC, CBS, and NBC. It means a full range of highly targeted cable niches, making rifle-like targeting all the more possible. Of course, this puts a substantial burden on media planners.

Naturally, there has always been an incredible range of magazines that served much the same rifle-targeted audience. However, added to this mix is the wide-open possibility of broadband telecommunications. Fledgling efforts at marketing through the Internet have been recently noted and will no doubt grow in the near future. This is the future of promotional communications. It seems likely that mass exposure as a means of promotion will have to be rethought.

### "MASS" MARKETS OF THE FUTURE

Perhaps we will still have mass exposure capabilities, but they will be "summated mass" rather than "simultaneous mass" audiences. Consider the recently discussed possibilities of individually tailored entertainment and shopping services at home via the emerging broadband net: in the future, people are likely to choose what entertainment to view when they want to view it, choosing from digitally scored and manipulated archives. They may not even go out to the store for some portion of their consumer purchases: the shop-at-home services available on cable now are just the tip of the iceberg so far as future capabilities are concerned. It may not be much longer that we can count on the type of mass tune-in audiences to expose themselves to a particular program all at once. Instead, we'll have to reach them one by one.

Source: Prepared by M. Dale Beckman, Faculty of Business, University of Victoria. Based on Thomas E. Stafford, "New Issues in Marketing: Integrated Marketing Communications," *Academy of Marketing Science Newsletter* 16:3 (July 1995), p. 5. Reprinted by permission of Academy of Marketing Science, University of Miami, Coral Gables, FL.

## NEW USES FOR FAMILIAR TOOLS

As many have noted in the mainstream press, the computer-guided nature of interactive communications that we are likely to see in the near future will be a two-way street: the audience members can choose what they want when they want it, but the media will be able to fully monitor and archive records of these choices. Schultz's database approach is likely to become part of a powerful new marketing toolbox, given such potential media capabilities. Indeed, if media and purchase behaviour through media can be closely monitored via the computer-mediated interactive mechanism, the well-developed tools of choice modelling—previously limited to analysis of scanner data—will have a new dramatic application in the near future.

So when Don Schultz suggests that the old ways of marketing through the promotional mix are gone, he has a point that bears consideration. We are designing this transition as it takes place before us. Although it is difficult to predict with accuracy exactly what will change, and which form innovation will take, it can be predicted with some certainty that changes will take place. Scholars of the discipline, and marketers everywhere, would do well to begin considering the part they can play in shaping this still-malleable future of a critical element of the marketing mix.

## DISCUSSION QUESTIONS

1. Work out a detailed communications mix for Sound Tech based on the concepts outlined in the above article. Provide some concrete examples of how the company might apply them.

2. How practical and relevant are these new ideas for Sound Tech?

## Bribery in Calgary?

Sue's supervisor looked at her in surprise, obviously taken aback. "Wher… wha…what did you…?" He paused and started again, more calmly, "Who have you been talking to?"

Sue was a recent B.Comm. graduate; she had just celebrated her 22nd birthday, and was six months into her job with a major consumer foods company. She was working in the company's regional office in Calgary. The other employees in the office were in their 30s or early 40s and tended to treat Sue a bit like their kid sister—a role she didn't particularly mind because she was learning a lot and no one ever seemed to object to her many questions.

She had had a conversation the other day that left her quite puzzled. So she explained her question to her supervisor, Jeff. "Well, I was talking to a friend of mine who works at another consumer foods company and she says they bribe people. She says everyone does it—it's the only way the sales reps can get their products displayed in stores. I told her that our company doesn't do things like that and that during my orientation we were told specifically that we don't bribe people. She just looked at me and laughed. So how about it Jeff, do we bribe people?"

Jeff paused again and then said, "Come with me Sue." Together they went to see Bill, the accounts manager.

"Now ask Bill what you asked me."

Sue repeated her story for the accounts manager and then concluded with the same direct question, "So how about it Bill? Do we bribe people?"

Bill leaned back in his chair and smiled benignly. "Bribe is really a nasty word," he said. "We don't bribe people. What we do is build rapport." He reached out and picked up a stuffed toy trade character that was associated with one of the company's most popular products.

"You see this guy? Well I know that the manager of one of my retail accounts has a 1-year-old at home who would just love this thing—so I gave him one. I did that because I'm the manager's friend; I want to do him a favour. And later, when I need some end-of-aisle display space in this manager's store, I know I'll get it—because he's my friend and he wants to do me a favour. That's not a bribe; that's building rapport."

Sue didn't say anything, but as she left the account manager's office, she wasn't so sure Bill had given her a satisfactory answer.

### DISCUSSION QUESTIONS

1. Is Sue's company bribing the retail managers?
2. Who is being hurt by this activity?
3. What should Sue do?

---

Source: Prepared for the textbook by John M. Rigby. This case is based on a true incident. It is intended purely as a basis for classroom discussion.

# Case 4

## Mid-West Petroleum

Brian watched with carefully concealed surprise as the new area rep for Mid-West Petroleum, a major international oil company, left his office. Brian lived in a small western city, and had come from a sales rep position with Southern Oil to take over as the commercial cardlock agent for Mid-West about five years ago. During that time his agency's sales volume had grown steadily, exceeding both his own and Mid-West's projections.

Brian attributed the cardlock's growth to the personal attention he gave his major accounts and the careful service and support he gave all his customers. Nevertheless, in his efforts to attract new accounts, and keep established accounts satisfied, pricing was always a key issue. Major accounts could be won or lost on a price differential of as little as a half-cent per litre. When a pricing proposal for a large account was being written up, Brian usually had to consult with Mid-West Petroleum to arrive at a final price that was acceptable to the company but that Brian thought could win the contract.

Tyler Ward, the new area rep for Mid-West, had joined the company about eight months ago after a successful career at Southern. In fact, Brian and Tyler had worked together at Southern before Brian had taken over the commercial cardlock.

Brian knew Tyler was a little aggressive, but still was surprised by what had just happened. As he and Tyler chatted, mixing together small talk and business, Tyler walked over to Brian's computer and logged on to the Web.

"Take a look at this, Brian," he said, "I think you'll like it." He then proceeded to log on to Southern's supposedly secure Web page. With a few clicks he called up Southern's confidential price list for all its commercial fuels. "They still have the same password as when I worked for them," Tyler explained.

As he got up to leave, Tyler commented, "Well, there's one company that won't beat us on price."

Brian sat at his desk for several minutes wondering what use, if any, to make of the new tool Tyler had given him.

### DISCUSSION QUESTIONS

1. Was it unethical for Tyler to give Brian Southern's Web site password?
2. Would it be unethical for Brian to access the site and use the information to help put together price proposals?
3. Does Southern bear any responsibility?
4. In general, what obligation does an employee have to his or her former company?

---

Source: Prepared for the textbook by John M. Rigby. This case is based on a true incident, although names have been changed throughout. It is intended purely as a basis for classroom discussion.

# Republic Industries Inc.

In addition to the Chevys, Fords, and Toyotas its stores sell, an American company, AutoNation, has been considering whether to offer a house-brand car.

The idea isn't as far-fetched or as frivolous as it may sound. Certainly cars are in a different league from the soda pop that Wal-Mart, Kmart and others sell under private labels, or even the washers and vacuums that Sears sells under its Kenmore name. But for the first time, the conditions may now exist for a retailer to try the same idea with cars and trucks.

"The question isn't if we could do it, but would we want to do it," says H. Wayne Huizenga, chairman and co-chief executive officer of Republic Industries Inc., the parent of the rapidly expanding AutoNation chain of car stores.

Mr. Huizenga, the former Blockbuster video king, says Republic has been weighing whether to develop its own private-label car ever since certain car makers—which he won't identify—began approaching his company. According to some industry analysts, the automakers' pitch is that AutoNation buy up their excess capacity and sell the vehicles under its own brand.

Of all the unconventional ideas bubbling around the auto-retailing revolution, this is one of the most intriguing. Outside consolidators such as Mr. Huizenga for the past four or five years have been experimenting with setting up big chains of vehicle retailers, hoping to create economies of scale. Automakers also are trying to rethink how their dealer networks operate.

If automakers and retailers succeed in slashing some of the 25 to 30 percent of the price of a car that is tied up in marketing and distribution, the revolution would benefit consumers. AutoNation and others are also trying to shorten, simplify, and make the consumer buying experience more transparent.

How would a house-brand car fit with those aims? Theoretically, it could provide the retailer an exclusive, special-value product to entice customers. And a big enough order of such cars could certainly give a manufacturer a profitable way of employing some of its capacity.

"AutoNation could tell a manufacturer which it sells a lot of cars for already that it would take 10 percent of production if it could specify certain features on the car that make the car exclusive to AutoNation," says Jay Houghton, marketing manager at consultant A.T. Kearney in Detroit. "The idea wouldn't be that far removed from what car companies already do by licensing popular brands such as Eddie Bauer or Coach leather goods."

"For somebody looking for basic transportation, a private-label car would definitely be appealing," says William Pochiluk, the president of Coopers & Lybrand Consulting's AutoFacts unit in Westchester, Pennsylvania. "It's a legitimate concept that can't be taken lightly."

Among the conditions that make a private-label car something worth considering now is that there are loads of excess capacity sloshing around the world auto industry. The increasing modularization of vehicle manufacturing is making it easier to cobble together a special vehicle. And consumers are showing an almost unending desire for new brands.

Perhaps even more important, Republic is the closest any auto retailer has yet come to achieving the critical mass that would be required. Since it got rolling in auto trade seventeen months ago, Republic has become the largest new-car franchise owner in the United States with about a 1 percent share of the $330-billion (US)-a-year new-car market. That is the biggest share controlled by a single retailing organization. At any one time, Mr. Huizenga has about 88 000 cars for sale on his new- and used-car lots.

The idea wouldn't be to go into competition with the Big Three or to try to strong-arm manufacturers with Republic's buying clout, Mr. Huizenga says. "We want good relationships with existing manufacturers," he says. "We don't want them saying, 'Hey, those guys are competitors.'"

U.S. automakers are reluctant to discuss the idea of AutoNation or anyone else offering a house-brand car, largely because all three of them see building up their own brands as a key to seizing a competitive advantage. Neither Chrysler Corp. nor General Motors Corp. would comment on the subject. At Ford Motor Co., spokesman Ken Zino acknowledged that "the market is so competitive, and excess capacity is such a big issue that we wouldn't rule out somebody doing it." But, he added, "we wouldn't have any interest in doing it."

Industry experts point to South Korean automakers as the most likely to be involved in producing house-brand vehicles. They have lots of excess capacity and, in the United States, their brands aren't well enough established that producing vehicles to sell under some other company's label would weaken them.

Mr. Huizenga and co-CEO Steve Berrard like the idea of working more closely with manufacturers to help create cars in the future. This would help fulfil the executives' goal of making AutoNation a retail outlet to which consumers can turn for anything having to do with cars—from buying gasoline to renting cars to buying a new car over the Internet.

## DISCUSSION QUESTIONS

1. What do you think of Mr. Huizenga's idea?
2. Relate this proposal to the text discussion on channels of distribution.

Source: Fara Waner, "AutoNation Is Considering Offering a House-Brand Car — Republic Industries' Chain Would Tap Auto Makers' Excess Capacity," *The Wall Street Journal* in *The Globe and Mail*, (July 21, 1998), p. B12. Reprinted by permission of *The Wall Street Journal*. Copyright © 1998 Dow Jones & Company, Inc. All Rights Reserved Worldwide.

# Case 6

Richard Ivey School of Business
The University of Western Ontario

## Consumer Sales Promotion: Winners & Losers[1]

Consumer sales promotions are used to acquaint new users with a brand, to load existing users, and to maintain interest in the brand on the part of the salesforce, the retailers and the consumers. Most consumer promotions are accompanied by a trade promotion to encourage retail display, co-operative advertising in flyers and newspapers, or on Web sites, price featuring, or any combination of these activities.

Consumer sales promotions place top emphasis on achieving short-term sales targets at retail. Consumer sales promotions generally are conceived by product managers and executed by a company salesforce or broker. The basic concept of the sales promotion will be important in securing salesforce support and, ultimately, sales. But it is not always easy to identify a winning promotion before it is conducted.

The following four cases are based on actual proposals for sales promotions. Two of the four were considered successful by the manufacturer, and the other two were judged unsuccessful. Consider the characteristics of each promotion and the surrounding circumstances. Evaluate, and see if you can uncover the successful ones. Then, generalize about the factors that are important for "successful" promotions.

### AMCREW STYLING GEL

To kick off the summer of 2000 hair-care promotions program for Ontario, Canada, Megan Russell, brand manager of Amcrew Hair Styling Products, was preparing to launch the annual Amcrew styling gel consumer promotion. Amcrew was a national brand of hair-care products that included shampoos, conditioners and hair styling products in its lineup.

The market for hair styling products was very fragmented, and no single manufacturer held more than 20 per cent of the category. Hair sprays (aerosol and non-aerosol), styling gels and styling mousse products (in that order of market share) were the most popular products and accounted for the majority of this category.

Amcrew was a well-known styling gel used by men, and it met a different consumer need than the Amcrew styling mousse and Amcrew hair spray product lines. Russell had decided to run a national eight-week on-pack bonus. Russell chose to offer consumers a 20-millilitre sample bottle of Amcrew's "Refresh" shampoo with the purchase of every bottle of Amcrew styling gel. Each sample was valued at $0.79 retail, but would cost Russell only $0.15 (with an additional $0.20 per bottle in costs to package the sample onto the gel bottle). A 150-gram bottle of Amcrew sold at regular price for $3.29 (an average retail price between the drug, food, and mass merchandiser channels), and a 300-gram bottle sold for $5.99. Although sales for all men's hair styling products had been down slightly in recent months, a similar annual bonus promotion had been run successfully on Amcrew for more than 10 years. Russell believed that consumers expected a promotion this year and that response again would be good.

In addition to maintaining the Amcrew existing franchise, Russell had other objectives for this promotion. These were: to build trade inventories; to increase short-term volume sold; and to load the consumer. To aid the consumer promotion in achieving these objectives, Russell planned to give the retailers a descriptive flyer about the promotion. Also, she would offer the retailers five per cent off the regular case price in hopes of having the retail price reduced, and an additional five per cent would be offered in an effort to obtain display activity and/or co-operative advertising in flyers. Russell knew that the usual offer to the trade was between 15 per cent to 20 per cent, but she believed that Amcrew's strong franchise would enable her to be successful in offering less. In total, the promotion was likely to cost $94,500. This total included the cost of the shampoo sample, the flyer, incremental packaging and physical distribution costs, but not the trade price cuts. The cost to produce the flyer would be covered in a miscellaneous budget.

The 150-gram bottle was packed 24 to a case and the 300-gram bottle was packed 12 to a case. Russell forecast that sales for the promotional period would be 15,000 cases split evenly between the two sizes. Without the promotion, she judged that Amcrew sales would be 10,900 cases. In calculating this, Russell considered that it was unlikely that there would be any competitive promotions during her planned promotional period. The contribution rate for products of this type was about 45 per cent, and retail margins were about 35 per cent. No pre-testing had been done for the promotion, other than a successful history of promotions on this brand.

**Ken Mark** prepared this case under the supervision of Professor Robert Fisher solely to provide material for class discussion. The authors do not intend to illustrate either effective or ineffective handling of a managerial situation. The authors may have disguised certain names and other identifying information to protect confidentiality.

[1] This case is based upon "Pick a Winner Consumer Sales Promotions"—#9A83A013, written by Kenneth G. Hardy with the assistance of Lisa Symons and John Kennedy.

## SKIPTREE PEANUT BUTTER

Trevor Thompson, product manager for Skiptree Peanut Butter, had developed an "instant win" sales promotion for the year 2000. The instant win certificate for Fischer toys and games would be placed between the lid and the cardboard insert on the 500-gram, one-kilogram, and 1.5 kilogram sizes of Skiptree Peanut Butter. Any certificates showing three identical animal figures would entitle the bearer to $12 off selected Fischer games. As Fischer had approached Skiptree for this promotion, Thompson expected that the cost of the creation of the Fischer coupon, insertion and redemption would be covered by Fischer as part of its promotional campaign.

Thompson had several reasons for wanting to run this national 12-week promotion. December was usually a low-volume period with unpromoted sales for all sizes estimated at 700,000-kilograms, and Thompson thought he could offset the seasonal downturn with the promotion. Further, instant win campaigns were becoming the most favored type of promotion among many product managers. Over all, Thompson thought the promotion would "increase short term volume, build trade inventories, increase the interest of the salesforce, and get display activity." Because this type of promotion had been used successfully in the company several times in the recent past, Thompson decided that it would not be necessary to supplement it with any point-of-purchase material. Although no major competitive activity was expected during the planned promotional period, Thompson was wary of a rumored Kraft new-flavor launch. (However, as a result of no announced competitive activity as of yet, Thompson did not believe he necessarily had to meet the general trade expectation of a 10 per cent discount on promotions like this one.)

The peanut butter market in Canada was dominated by Kraft, which held 39 per cent of the market. There was a very strong brand loyalty amongst Kraft consumers, but multiple brand switching was usual amongst consumers of lesser brands. As the third major producer in terms of sales, Skiptree Peanut Butter held a 10 per cent market share. The average price paid to the manufacturer for Skiptree Peanut Butter was $1.15 per kilogram, and the manufacturer's contribution margin was $0.56 per kilogram. The trade usually made a 35 per cent margin over the retail selling price. Generally, the composition of sales was as follows:

| Package Size | Per cent of Sales | Packages per Case |
|---|---|---|
| 500 g (new) | 4 | 24 |
| 1 kg | 40 | 12 |
| 1.5 kg | 40 | 12 |
| 2 kg | 15 | 6 |
| 3 kg | 1 | 6 |

To supplement the consumer promotion, Thompson was planning to offer retailers case allowances on three of the promoted sizes. The trade would get a promotional allowance (different from a trade discount) of $3 off per case of the one-kilogram jar of peanut butter, $2.50 off per case of the 1.5-kilogram size, and $2.50 off per case of the new 500-gram jar. Over and above these allowances, another $15,000 would go to the trade as a one-time incentive for their support of the promotion (this promotion was slated to run in the important pre-Christmas season). Total sales for the promotion were forecast at one million kilograms. Additional promotion costs came to $45,000, not including trade discounts. It was expected that 20 per cent of the incremental sales would come from the 500-gram size, 50 per cent from the one-kilogram size, and 30 per cent from the 1.5-kilogram size. There had been no pretesting on this promotion.

## SILHOUETTE'S CUSTOM PLUS DISPOSABLE RAZORS

Silhouette's marketing plan called for a consumer promotion to be run on its Custom Plus disposable razors in the spring. The product manager responsible for disposable razors, Andrew Smith, had considered several promotions and had decided on a bonus pack. He would offer seven razors for $3.59, which was the regular price for five Custom Plus disposable razors. This bonus package would be sold nationally for 12 weeks. Smith had chosen this promotion over others in order to "increase consumer trial, pre-empt the competition (defend against competitive sales promotions), and increase short-term volume." Smith expected that the added value of the promotional package would be the main reason for extra sales.

The disposable razor market was very competitive (wide variety of choices), and consumers were believed to be price sensitive. Silhouette had put Custom Plus on the market in 1998 as an upgrade to their Close Shaves version dating back to the earlier 1980s. Since its introduction, Silhouette had managed to grow the Close Shaves (of which Custom Plus was the premium stock keeping unit [SKU]) brand to 25 per cent of the disposable market (where Bic was a major competitor) by the start of 2000.

In this type of market, Smith was always concerned about competitive activity. He strove to at least maintain existing market position. The competitive promotion that particularly concerned Smith was an economy-size package of 10 disposable razors for only $4.99 that a major competitor was expected to introduce. The same competitor usually offered a five-pack for $2.99. Consequently, Smith intended to enhance the Custom Plus bonus pack with special artwork and packaging. The only incentive he was planning to offer retailers was a promotional allowance of $2 per case. There would be 20 packages in a case.

He had budgeted the cost of the case allowance portion of the promotion at $45,000, but did not count the loss from the reduced price or artwork costs. On a regular non-promoted pack, this product had a contribution rate of about 35 per cent and a retail margin of 35 per cent. A special flag on the package would read "Buy 5, Get 2 Extra!". Artwork for the special pack was estimated to cost $0.25 per package. Smith expected that both the salesforce and the retailers would be enthusiastic about the promotion because of the consumer value of the bonus. As a result, he anticipated sales of the promotional package to be 22,500 cases plus 10,000 cases of the regular pack, as compared to 24,000 cases that he would sell without the promotion.

## TOTALRINSE ORAL ANTISEPTIC

Janice Wong, product manager responsible for TotalRinse oral antiseptic, had just completed the plans for an eight-week national consumer promotion to be run in the early spring of 2000. The target for the promotion was existing users of TotalRinse mouthwash. The promotion consisted of an on-pack $2 mouthwash coupon offer. To receive the $2 coupon, the consumer would have to buy a one-litre bottle of TotalRinse at an average price of $3.49 (an average price among the drug, food and mass merchandiser channels), cut the offer off the package, put a stamp on the envelope, and mail it to Werner-Lombard Inc. Werner-Lombard would then mail a coupon worth $2 to the consumer, who could redeem it on the next purchase of any size of TotalRinse.

TotalRinse shared the majority of the market with Procter & Gamble's Scope mouthwash. Although TotalRinse enjoyed strong consumer loyalty, it had seen its share of the market slowly eroded by Scope, and by some lesser brands. In addition, Werner-Lombard had launched TingleMint, a new, mint-flavored version of TotalRinse which grew rapidly to equal TotalRinse's market share. Consequently, the primary objective of this promotion was "to defend against the competition." Wong also aimed to load the consumer, thereby maintaining current TotalRinse users and building trade inventories.

Wong expected sales during the promotion would reach 325,000 litres, of which approximately two-thirds would be in the one-litre size. There would be 12 one-litre bottles per case, and this size was sold only during promotions. Regular sizes were 750-millilitres, 500-millilitres, and 250-millilitres. The 500-millilitres size usually accounted for over half of the regular TotalRinse volume.

On the one-litre size, Wong was planning to offer retailers case allowances of $2.50 per case plus $1.50 extra per case on orders exceeding 300 cases. She expected about two-thirds of the one-litre sales would be below the under-300 case order price, giving them a discount of $2.50. Wong had budgeted a max-

imum of $60,000 to cover coupon redemptions. This cost included the retailer's handling charge of $0.15 for every coupon redeemed, her projected handling costs of $1.50 per redemption for mailing, postage and the costs of redeemed coupons.

Other than Scope's promotional activity and the regular trade deals, Wong expected there would be very few competitive promotions. She expected to receive the maximum amount of support for this type of promotion from both the Werner-Lombard salesforce, and from the food, drug and mass merchandise retailers. In the absence of any competitive sales promotion, Wong believed that she might expect to sell about 160,000 litres at an average retail price of $3.65 per litre. At this pricing, the contribution rate was about 30 per cent after average retail margins of 35 per cent. The one-litre promotion would have a retail margin (before trade allowances) of 35 per cent, and a company contribution of 22 per cent.

This specific promotion had not been pretested, but many coupon promotions had been run on TotalRinse. Wong had considered complementing the program with advertising, but had decided that her budget was not sufficient to cover an extra $40,000 in either television copy (five-second tag) or advertising on direct-to-consumer campaigns run by retailers.

## Greenpeace Finland (A)

In June 1995 Mr. Matti Ikonen, the person responsible for the Greenpeace Finland forest campaign, was trying to decide how to deal with the negative publicity Greenpeace was receiving in the Finnish media concerning forest issues.

### BACKGROUND

Greenpeace Finland was founded in 1989 and was later listed in the Association Register in Finland. Greenpeace Finland, along with the 30 other national Greenpeace organizations, acted much like a franchise of Greenpeace International. Greenpeace International was dedicated to maintaining the world ecological balance and world peace. For Greenpeace the main issues were ozone depletion and toxic chemicals, protection of biodiversity and the proliferation of nuclear energy and weapons. It had concentrated its action on more specific areas, i.e. nuclear tests, whales and endangered forests. Greenpeace financed its activities with membership fees and donations from private persons. It did not accept donations from governments and companies.

Greenpeace Finland had basically the same goals as Greenpeace International, but in the context of Finland. Greenpeace Finland started with nuclear energy issues in 1989. Forest issues became of current interest in 1992 when the general assembly of Greenpeace International decided to expand the Greenpeace rain forest campaign to all endangered forests. Forestry and nuclear energy were thus the focus of Greenpeace Finland's limited resources.

Greenpeace Finland was located in the residential area of Kruunuhaka in the center of Helsinki and had seven employees, of whom four worked full-time. The work was divided between the Executive Director of Greenpeace Finland, who was generally responsible for activities and press releases, two persons responsible for forestry, one person responsible for nuclear energy, one person responsible for fund raising, a bookkeeper and an office assistant.

In 1995 Greenpeace Finland had 12,000 supporting members, but it aimed to increase and stabilize its membership at around 20,000 to become financially independent. A few hundred members participated in its activities occasionally and around 50 members participated regularly on a weekly basis. Some 20 members participated in Greenpeace's environmental campaigns. Greenpeace's income in 1994 was FIM 2.5 million and its expenditures FIM 2.3 million, which meant that its turnover was lower than in 1993. The decrease was especially

### TABLE 1. Greenpeace Finland

| | INCOME 1993 | | INCOME 1994 | |
|---|---|---|---|---|
| | FIM 1000 | % | FIM 1000 | % |
| Membership fees | 1278.5 | 48.25 | 1035.8 | 40.92 |
| Donations | 652.8 | 24.64 | 420.1 | 16.60 |
| International support | 476.9 | 18.00 | 842.1 | 33.27 |
| Selling of GP articles | 218.8 | 8.26 | 216.8 | 8.57 |
| Other | 22.6 | 0.85 | 16.3 | 0.64 |
| **Total** | 2649.5 | 100.00 | 2531.1 | 100.00 |

| | EXPENDITURES 1993 | | EXPENDITURES 1994 | |
|---|---|---|---|---|
| | FIM 1000 | % | FIM 1000 | % |
| Campaign work | 679.3 | 25.65 | 691.7 | 29.71 |
| Information | 574.1 | 21.67 | 521.3 | 22.39 |
| Fund raising | 753.4 | 28.44 | 407.3 | 17.49 |
| Administration + Rents | 420.9 | 15.89 | 479.2 | 20.58 |
| GP articles for sale | 165.3 | 6.24 | 170.8 | 7.34 |
| Other | 55.7 | 2.10 | 57.9 | 2.49 |
| **Total** | 2648.7 | 100.00 | 2328.2 | 100.00 |

clear in donations and membership fees while international support increased. Table 1 shows Greenpeace Finland's income and expenditures for 1993 and 1994.

Until 1997, Greenpeace Finland was to receive an important share of its income from Greenpeace International. After 1997 it was gradually expected to contribute up to 40 per cent of its income to Greenpeace International. Greenpeace Finland was not allowed to accept corporate sponsorship, because Greenpeace International found corporate sponsorship incompatible with the organization's mission. Greenpeace Finland obtained its income mainly from members in the form of membership fees and donations. The acquisition of donations and even new members was connected with financial activities and its cost was substantial.

### GREENPEACE'S COMPETITORS

Greenpeace Finland as well as Greenpeace International were competing for a market share in the ideological NP (non-profit) sector. Their competitors were mostly other NPOs (nonprofit organizations), e.g. Luontoliitto (Nature union) and WWF in Finland. Greenpeace had to channel people's opinion through the organization and get new members, possibly convincing them to choose Greenpeace instead of another organization. In the case of NPOs and their members, it was not only a question of competition within a single field such as culture or environment. Because of the voluntary nature of NPO activities, people used NPOs' services in their free time, and may thus not only choose between, for example, different environmental organizations, but also between all other NPOs. A sports event can, for example, compete with an environmental event.

Generally, all three Finnish environmental organizations, i.e. Greenpeace Finland, Luontoliitto and WWF Finland, had lost some members and financial support. Nevertheless, the loss was biggest for Greenpeace, possibly in part because it did not accept financial support from companies or the government. Another reason might have been that Greenpeace either did not want to compromise with its goals or was inflexible. Greenpeace differed from the Finnish Luontoliitto, for example, in that Greenpeace demanded a fundamental change in the forest industry, while Luontoliitto worked with single forest actions for certain endangered forests. Also, Greenpeace was an international organization and Greenpeace Finland was located in Helsinki, whereas Luontoliitto was a Finnish organization and had activities all over Finland.

## THE ROLE OF PUBLICITY

The primary aim of both Greenpeace Finland and Greenpeace International was not to be profitable in the economic sense but to address ecological issues. Greenpeace needed, however, more financial resources to accomplish its mission.

Greenpeace won support with environmental actions and statements in order to create a positive image of the organization through the media. People would then channel their environmental concerns through Greenpeace and give the organization their financial and moral support. Greenpeace's viability depended to a great extent on media publicity.

Greenpeace Finland had been very visible in the media thanks to its forest actions. For example, Greenpeace claimed that large Finnish paper companies used raw material from clear cuts and old forests, activities which, according to Greenpeace, were significantly weakening the biodiversity of Finnish forest areas.

Forestry issues were very important and sensitive in Finland because a very large part of the population received their income directly or indirectly from the forest industry.

Greenpeace had received both positive and negative publicity related to its forest actions. However, in the summer of 1995, according to Mr. Matti Ikonen, who was responsible for Greenpeace Finland's forestry campaign, the Greenpeace forest campaign was receiving more negative publicity than ever before.

## THE 290-YEAR-OLD STUMP

On June 9, 1995 the tabloid *Ilta-Sanomat* had a hostile headline and article against Greenpeace, which launched a series of other negative articles and letters to editors.

Mr. Matti Ikonen and a group of activists visited a logging area in Northern Karelia at the end of May. Ikonen and the activists took a tree stump from a cut area in a state forest and claimed that it was 290 years old. They aimed to use it in their campaign against clear cutting. They wanted to show the representatives of a large Finnish pulp and paper company Enso-Gutzeit, that the company was using old trees from clear-cut areas as raw material. Their aim was to stop this practice. The stump was also shown to Enso-Gutzeit's German customer to persuade them to influence Enso-Gutzeit and to get publicity for Greenpeace.

Mr. Ikonen and the activists loaded the stump on a trailer, but their car and trailer got stuck and they had to ask a local farmer to pull them free with his tractor. Mr. Ikonen lied to the farmer and explained that they had taken the stump as part of a prank. This was perhaps how the journalists learned where the stump came from.

One week after Greenpeace had shown the stump to the representatives of Enso-Gutzeit, *Ilta-Sanomat* had a hostile headline: "Greenpeace's stump is a fake." The article said that Greenpeace had claimed that the stump was from a clear cut, but according to the local director of the State Forest Administration, it was instead from a tree that had fallen across a road during a storm. The local director also claimed that the stump was somewhat younger than Greenpeace's estimate. The State Forest Administration demanded compensation from Greenpeace for the "stolen" stump. According to Mr. Ikonen, Greenpeace received a bill for FIM 1,500, of which only FIM 30 was for the stump. The remainder covered administrative costs.

## CONSEQUENCES OF THE ARTICLE

*Ilta-Sanomat*'s article launched a series of other negative articles and letters to editors even in respected papers, which caused some harm for Greenpeace Finland. Matti Ikonen said that the articles had damaged Greenpeace's image. He said that the tabloid *Ilta-Sanomat* had a strong anti-Greenpeace policy. However, there was no reaction from Enso-Gutzeit to this incident in the media, and Mr. Ikonen thought that the tabloid would have liked to see the relationship between Greenpeace and the paper industry became even more strained than it was.

A few members contacted Greenpeace and said that they would quit the organization because they could not accept Greenpeace's forest policy. Ikonen also felt that the forest fundraising campaign initiated before the stump incident might suffer because of the negative publicity Greenpeace had received in connection with the incident.

## Kellogg's Indian Experience

*"Our only rivals are traditional Indian foods like idlis and vadas."*
—Denis Avronsart, Managing Director, Kellogg India.

### A FAILED LAUNCH

In April 1995, Kellogg India Ltd. (Kellogg), received unsettling reports of a gradual drop in sales from its distributors in Mumbai. There was a 25% decline in countrywide sales since March 1995, the month Kellogg products had been made available nationally.

Kellogg was the wholly-owned Indian subsidiary of the Kellogg Company based in Battle Creek, Michigan. Kellogg Company was the world's leading producer of cereals and convenience foods, including cookies, crackers, cereal bars, frozen waffles, meat alternatives, pie crusts, and ice cream cones. Founded in 1906, Kellogg Company had manufacturing facilities in 19 countries and marketed its products in more than 160 countries. The company's turnover in 1999-00 was $7 billion. Kellogg Company had set up its 30th manufacturing facility in India, with a total investment of $30 million. The Indian market held great significance for the Kellogg Company because its US sales were stagnating and only regular price increases had helped boost the revenues in the 1990s.

Launched in September 1994, Kellogg's initial offerings in India included cornflakes, wheat flakes and Basmati rice flakes. Despite offering good quality products and being supported by the technical, managerial and financial resources of its parent, Kellogg's products failed in the Indian market. Even a high-profile launch backed by hectic media activity failed to make an impact in the marketplace. Meanwhile, negative media coverage regarding the products increased, as more and more consumers were reportedly rejecting the taste. There were complaints that the products were not available in many cities. According to analysts, out of every 100 packets sold, only two were being bought by regular customers; with the rest 98 being first-time buyers. Converting these experimenters into regular buyers had become a major problem for the company.

By September, 1995, sales had virtually stagnated. Marketing experts pointed out various mistakes that Kellogg had committed and it was being increasingly felt that the company would find it extremely difficult to sustain itself in the Indian market.

### THE MISTAKES

Kellogg realized that it was going to be tough to get the Indian consumers to accept its products. Kellogg banked heavily on the quality of its crispy flakes. But pouring hot milk on the flakes made them soggy. Indians always boiled their milk unlike in the West and consumed it warm or lukewarm. They also liked to add sugar to their milk. When Kellogg flakes were put in hot milk, they became soggy and did not taste good. If one tried having it with cold milk, it was not sweet enough because the sugar did not dissolve easily in cold milk. The rice and wheat versions did not do well. In fact, some consumers even referred to the rice flakes as rice corn flakes.

In early 1996, defending the company's products, Managing Director Avronsart said, "True, some people will not like the way it tastes in hot milk. And not all consumers will want to have it with cold milk. But over a period of time, we expect consumer habits to change. Kellogg is a past master at the art, having fought—and won—against croissant-and-coffee in France, biscuits in Italy and noodles in Korea."

A typical, average middle-class Indian family did not have breakfast on a regular basis like their Western counterparts. Those who did have breakfast, consumed milk, biscuits, bread, butter, jam or local food preparations like idlis, parathas etc. According to analysts, a major reason for Kellogg's failure was the fact that the taste of its products did not suit Indian breakfast habits. Kellogg sources were however quick to assert that the company was not trying to change these habits; the idea was only to launch its products on the health platform and make consumers see the benefit of this healthier alternative. Avronsart remarked, "Kellogg India is not here to change breakfast habits. What the company proposes is to offer consumers around the world a healthy, nutritious, convenient and easy-to-prepare alternative in the breakfast eating habit. It was not just a question of providing a better alternative to traditional breakfast eating habits but also developing a taste for grain based foods in the morning."

Another mistake Kellogg committed was on the position front. The company's advertisements and promotions initially focussed only on the health aspects of the product. In doing this, Kellogg had moved away from its successful 'fun-and-taste' positioning adopted in the US. Analysts commented that this positioning had given the brand a 'health product' image, instead of the fun/health plank that the product stood on in other markets. (In the US for instance, Kellogg offered toys and other branded merchandise for children and had a Kellogg's fan club as well.)

Another reason for the low demand was deemed to be the premium pricing adopted by the company. At an average cost of Rs 21 per 100 gm, Kellogg products were clearly priced way

This case was written by **A. Mukund**, Icfaian Centre for Management Research (ICMR). It is intended to be used as the basis for class discussion rather than to illustrate either effective or ineffective handling of a management situation. The case was compiled from published sources. © 2002, A Mukund, Icfaian Centre for Management Research (ICMR), Hyderabad, India. Distributed by The European Case Clearing House, England and USA. North America, phone: + 1 781 239 5884, fax: + 1 781 239 5885, e-mail: ECCHBabson@aol.com. Rest of the World, phone + 44 (0) 1234 750903, fax: +44 (0)1234 751125, e-mail: ECCH@cranfield.ac.uk. All rights reserved. Printed in UK and USA. Web Site: http://www.ecch.cranfield.ac.uk.

above the product of its main competitor, Mohan's Cornflakes (Rs 16.50 for 100 gm). Vinay Mohan, Managing Director, Mohan Rocky Springwater & Breweries, the makers of Mohan's cornflakes, said, "Kellogg is able to cater only to the A-Class towns or the more affluent consumers whereas Mohan's caters to the mass market." Another small-time brand, Champion, was selling at prices almost half of that of Kellogg. This gave the brand a premium image, making it seem unattainable for the average Indian consumer. According to one analyst, "When Kellogg tried a dollar-to-rupee pricing for its products, the company lost out on getting to the mass consumer." Even the customers at the higher end of the market failed to perceive any extra benefits in Kellogg's products. A Business Today report said that like other MNCs, Kellogg had fallen into a price trap, by assuming that there was a substantial latent niche market in India for premium products.

In most Third World countries pricing is believed to play a dominant role in the demand for any product. But Kellogg did not share this view. Avronsart said, "Research demonstrates that to be well accepted by consumers even the most nutritious product must taste good. Most consumers view quality as they view taste, but with a very high standard. We approach pricing on a case-to-case basis, always consistent with the total value delivered by each product." He also said, "Local brands are selling only on the price platform. We believe that we're demanding the right price for the value we offer. If the consumer wants duality, we believe he can afford the price." Thus, it was not surprising that the company went ahead with its plans for increasing the price of its products by an average of 18% during 1995-98.

Before the product was made available nationally in March, 1995, the demand from Mumbai had been very encouraging. Within a year of its launch in Mumbai, Kellogg had acquired a 53% market share. Following this, the company accelerated its national expansion plans and launched the product in 60 cities in a 15-month period. However, Kellogg was surprised to see the overall demand tapering off considerably. A Mumbai based Kellogg distributor explained, "Why should somebody sitting in Delhi be deprived of the product? So there was considerable movement from Mumbai to other parts of the country." As the product was officially launched countrywide, the company realized that the tremendous response from the Mumbai market was nothing but the 'disguised demand' from other places being routed through Mumbai.

Kellogg had also decided to focus only on the premium and middle-level retail stores. This was because the company believed that it could not maintain uniform quality of service if it offered its products at a larger number of shops. What Kellogg seemed to have overlooked was the fact that this decision put large sections of the Indian population out of its reach.

## SETTING THINGS RIGHT

Disappointed with the poor performance, Kellogg decided to launch two of its highly successful brands—Chocos (September 1996) and Frosties (April 1997) in India. The company hoped to repeat the global success of these brands in the Indian market. Chocos were wheat scoops coated with chocolate, while Frosties had sugar frosting on individual flakes. The success of these variants took even Kellogg by surprise and sales picked up significantly. (It was even reported that Indian consumers were consuming the products as snacks.) This was followed by the launch of Chocos Breakfast Cereal Biscuits.

The success of Chocos and Frosties also led to Kellogg's decision to focus on totally Indianising its flavors in the future. This resulted in the launch of the Mazza series in August 1998— a crunchy, almond-shaped corn breakfast cereal in three local flavors— 'Mango Elaichi,' 'Coconut Kesar' and 'Rose.' Developed after a one-year extensive research to study consumer patterns in India, Mazza was positioned as a tasty, nutritional breakfast cereal for families. Kellogg was careful not to repeat its earlier mistakes. It did not position Mazza in the premium segment. The glossy cardboard packaging was replaced by pouches, which helped in bringing down the price substantially.

The decision to reduce prices seemed to be a step in the right direction. However, analysts remained skeptical about the success of the product in the Indian market. They pointed out that Kellogg did not have retail packs of different sizes to cater to the needs of different consumer groups. To counter this criticism, the company introduced packs of suitable sizes to suit Indian consumption patterns and purchasing power. Kellogg introduced the 500gm family pack, which brought down the price per kg by 20%. Also, Mazza was introduced in 60gm pouches, priced at Rs 9.50.

Kellogg's advertising had not been very impressive in the initial years. Apart from 'Jago jaise bhi, lo Kellogg's hi,' the brand had no long-term baseline lines. Later, Kellogg attempted to Indianise its campaigns instead of simply copying its international promotions. The rooster that was associated with the Kellogg brand the world over was missing from its advertisements in India. One of its campaigns depicted a cross section of individuals ranging from a yoga instructor to a kathakali dancer attributing their morning energy and fitness to Kellogg. The advertisement suggested that cornflakes could be taken with curds, honey, and banana.

In April 1997, Kellogg launched 'The Kellogg Breakfast Week,' a community-oriented initiative to generate awareness about the importance of breakfast. The program focussed on prevention of anemia and conducted a series of nutrition workshops activities for both individuals and families. The program was launched in Chennai, Delhi and Mumbai. The company tied up with the

Indian Dietetic Association (IDA) to launch a nation-wide public-service initiative to raise awareness about iron deficiency problems. Nutritionists and dieticians from the country participated in a day-long symposium in Calcutta to deliberate on the causes and impact of anemia caused by iron deficiency. This program was in line with the company's global marketing strategy which included nutrition promotion initiatives such as symposiums, educative programs and sponsorship of research.

Emphasizing Kellogg's commitment to nutrition education, Avronsart remarked, "Product modification, particularly the addition of iron fortification in breakfast cereals is how Kellogg responds to the nutritional needs of the consumers. In this spirit, Kellogg India is taking a major step to improve the nutritional status of consumers in the country, the specific opportunity being iron fortification for which we have undertaken major initiatives to promote the awareness of the importance of iron in the diet."

Kellogg also increased its focus on promotions that sought to induce people to try their product and targeted schools across the country for this. By mid-1995, the company had covered 60 schools in the metros. In March, 1996, the company offered specially-designed 50 gm packs free to shoppers at select retail stores in Delhi. This was followed by a house-to-house sampling exercise offering one-serving sachets to housewives in the city. The company also offered free pencil-boxes, water bottles, and lunch boxes with every pack. Plastic dispensers offering the product at discounted rates were also put up in petrol pumps, supermarkets, airports, etc.

Kellogg identified distribution as another major area to address in order to increase its penetration in the market. In 1995, Kellogg had 30,000 outlets, which was increased to around 40,000 outlets by 1998. Avronsart said, "We have increased our reach only slightly, but we are not enlarging our coverage." Considering that it had just one plant in Taloja in Maharashtra, the company was considering plans to set up more manufacturing units.

Kellogg's also began working towards a better positioning plank for its products. The company's research showed that the average Indian consumer did not give much importance to the level of iron and vitamin intake, and looked at the quantity, rather than the quality, of the food consumed. Avronsart commented, "The Kellogg mandate is to develop awareness about nutrition. There is a lot of confusion between nourishment and nutrition. That is something that we have to handle." Kellogg thus worked towards changing the positioning of Chocos and Frosties—which were not positioned on the health platform but, instead, were projected as 'fun-filled' brands.

Kellogg then launched the Chocos biscuits, claiming that cereals being a 'narrow category,' the foray into biscuits would create wider awareness for the Kellogg brand. Biscuits being a mass market product requiring an intensive distribution network, Kellogg's decision to venture into this competitive and crowded market with stalwarts like Britannia, Parle and Bakeman, was seen as a bold move not only in India, but also globally. Avronsart said, "We are ready to develop any food based on grain and nutrition that will satisfy consumer needs."

## THE RESULTS

In 1995, Kellogg had a 53% share of the Rs 150 million breakfast cereal market, which had been growing at 4-5% per annum till then. By 2000, the market size was Rs 600 million, and Kellogg's share had increased to 65%. Analysts claimed that Kellogg's entry was responsible for this growth. The company's improved prospects were clearly attributed to the shift in positioning, increased consumer promotions and an enhanced media budget. The effort to develop products specifically for the Indian market helped Kellogg make significant inroads into the Indian market.

However, Kellogg continued to have the image of a premium brand and its consumption was limited to a few well-off sections of the Indian market. The company had to face the fact that it would be really very difficult to change the eating habits of Indians. In 2000, Kellogg launched many new brands including Crispix Banana, Crispix Chocos, Froot Loops, Cocoa Frosties, Honey Crunch, All Bran and All Raisin. Kellogg also launched 'Krispies Treat,' an instant snack targeted at children. Priced on the lower side at Rs 3 and Rs 5, the product was positioned to compete against the products in the 'impulse snacks' category. According to some analysts, the introduction of new cereals and the launch of biscuits and snacks could be attributed to the fact that the company had been forced to look at alternate product categories to make up for the below-expectation performance of the breakfast cereal brands.

Kellogg sources however revealed that the company was in India with long-term plans and was not focusing on profits in the initial stages. In Mexico the company had to wait for two decades, and in France nine years, before it could significantly influence local palates. With just one rival in the organized sector (Mohan Meakins) and its changed tactics in place, what remained to be seen was how long it would take Kellogg to crack the Indian market.

## DISCUSSION QUESTIONS

1.  What were the reasons behind the poor performance of Kellogg in the initial stages? Do you agree that a poor entry strategy was responsible for the company's problems? Give reasons to support your answer.
2.  Analyze Kellogg's efforts to revamp its marketing mix and comment on the initiatives taken regarding each element of the marketing mix.
3.  Do you think the company's decision to launch biscuits and snacks was a right one? Give reasons for your answer.

# Case 9

## Omega Paw Inc.

Michael Ebert, president of Omega Paw (Omega) and inventor of the "Self-Cleaning Litter Box," reflected on the progress of his St. Mary's, Ontario-based company. In September 1996, after being in business for just over a year, Omega had reached a sales level of $1 million. Ebert knew that with Omega's current resources, the company could potentially target a much larger market. His goal was to "grow the business quickly", and in order to achieve these goals, Ebert knew Omega would have to expand its marketing initiatives and consider alternative channels of distribution.

### THE CAT OWNERS MARKET

In the mid-1990s, North America was home to approximately 66 million cats — 60 million in the United States and six million in Canada. In 1996, approximately 33 per cent of the ten million households in Canada had, on average, two cats. The cat population had risen by seven per cent between 1994 and 1996, and was estimated to continue growing at an annual rate of four per cent for the next few years. A survey conducted by the American Pet Products Manufacturers Association, Inc. cited, as reasons for the growth, the increased trend in apartment and, more recently, condominium living. In addition, the survey pointed to the ever-increasing mobility of the workforce, the rising average age of the Canadian population (the typical cat owner was older than other pet owners), and the ease of care and maintenance for cats relative to other popular pets as reasons for the continued growth.

The typical cat owner spent approximately $520.00 annually on his or her feline pet. Forty-four per cent was spent on food and 23 per cent on veterinarian visits. Cat supplies, such as litter, litter boxes, bowls, etc., accounted for 13 per cent of the yearly budget while 20 per cent was spent on flea and tick supplies, grooming, and toys. Just over 50 per cent of owners bought presents for their cats of, which the majority (88 per cent) were purchased and given during the Christmas season.[1]

### OMEGA PAW'S CONSUMER GROUPS

Based on experience and knowledge, Omega Paw had divided cat owners into three main consumer groups. The first group, five per cent of the total cat owner market was the "new pet owner". These were consumers who had just acquired a cat or a kitten and who needed all the applicable pet care and maintenance products. They often did their own pet and product research, wanted good quality, long-lasting products and usually purchased items at the local pet stores or at the veterinarian's office.

The "existing cat owner," 80 per cent of the total cat owner market, was the second identifiable market. Having owned cats for some time, these consumers were experienced at caring for their cats and were well stocked with the traditional cat care and maintenance supplies. They purchased their cat products at a variety of locations such as pet stores, the veterinarian's office, household supply stores, and grocery stores.

The remaining 15 per cent of the cat owner market was labelled as the "gray zone." Most of this segment lived in the country and owned a variety of 'outdoor' pets such as dogs and cats. Cats in this segment were not only one of many pets, but were also free to roam outside and, as a result, the owners usually did not concern themselves with purchasing specific cat products other than cat food.

### THE "SELF-CLEANING LITTER BOX"

Two years ago, Ebert's brother and sister-in-law had gone on holidays leaving Ebert to care for their cats. "There's got to be a better way," Ebert had thought as he held his nose while cleaning the cats' litter box. By September 1996, not only had Ebert "found a better way" by inventing a self-cleaning litter box, but he had set up a new company to distribute this product and other pet care products through pet store distribution channels all across North America.

The "Self-Cleaning Litter Box" was a moulded plastic box with rounded edges that allowed the cat to enter and leave through a large opening at the side. The box was available in two sizes, and the larger size was ideally suited for large or multiple cats. To clean the litter box, the cat owner would first roll the box onto its back, allowing all of the litter to pass through a filter screen and collecting any clumped litter separately in a long, narrow tray. The owner would then roll the box back to its normal position and allow the clean litter to flow back through the filter to the litter tray. At this point, the narrow tray could be

---

**Jannalee Blok** prepared this case under the supervision of Elizabeth M.A. Grasby solely to provide material for class discussion. The authors do not intend to illustrate either effective or ineffective handling of a managerial situation. The authors may have disguised certain names and other identifying information to protect confidentiality.

[1] "1996-1997 APPMA National Pet Owners Survey" Revised—American Pet Products Manufacturers Assoc., Inc.

[2] All prices are in Canadian dollars unless noted otherwise.

[3] American distributors and pet stores required the same markup as distributors and pet stores in Canada. (Distributors required 40 per cent markup on MSP. Pet stores required 100 per cent markup on DSP.)

[4] Wal-Mart and Kmart each had 2,200 stores in the United States alone.

[5] "hard goods"—generally more durable products giving benefit to the consumer over an extended period of time.

removed by its handle, and the used cat litter could be dumped out. Exhibit 1 illustrates the simplicity of the process: roll back, roll forward, remove the tray and dump the waste.

## THE COMPETITION

### Direct Competition

The first of three main North American competitors, the "Everclean Self Scoop Litter Box", was an open litter box with rounded edges. In order to clean it, the rounded cover had to be attached and the box rolled. This allowed clean litter to fall through the filters and collected the clumped litter in the top half of the box. Following this, the entire top of the box was taken off, carefully maneuvered over a garbage can, and then angled so that the litter clumps would fall into the garbage. When finished, the top of the box was left detached, and had to be stored until the next cleaning.

First Brands Corporation, the manufacturer of the "Everclean Self Scoop Litter Box," retailed its product for between $53 and $63[2]. It spent a lot of money advertising to pet stores via trade magazines, and had North American-wide distribution. First Brands also manufactured well-known home, automotive, and pet-care products, and recently reported annual sales revenues of just over $1 billion.

The second direct competitor, "Quick Sand", used a series of three trays — each with slanted slots on the bottom of the tray. These trays were layered in such a way that the slanted slots of the top and bottom were going in the same direction, and the slanted slots of the middle tray were facing the opposite direction. This layering technique formed a solid bottom to the litter box and prevented the clean litter from filtering through the trays prematurely. In order to clean the litter box, the first tray was lifted and sifted. Clean litter filtered down to the second tray leaving the clumped litter in the top tray. The used litter was deposited into the garbage and the empty tray was replaced under the bottom until the process needed to be repeated.

The whole box required carrying and emptying which was awkward, and trays had to be replaced underneath each other with care so that litter did not leak out onto the floor. However, "Quick Sand" was competitively priced at $29 retail. In addition, it was shorter in length than other litter boxes and, as a result, was easier to place in a secluded spot. Introduced in March 1995, the product was endorsed by Dini Petty, a Canadian morning talk show host. It did not receive much attention, however, until Smart Inventions, an American company, bought the product in 1996 and launched an extensive media campaign. They spent between $200,000 to $300,000 per week for six months, and gained exposure throughout Canada and the United States.

The last main competitor, "Lift & Sift", was very similar to the "Quick Sand" product. It was priced at $29 and also used the three-tray method. In addition, both products incorporated easy-to-follow directions as part of their packaging design. While "Lift & Sift" had been on the market for three years, it had limited advertising exposure. However, in 1996 it benefited from "Quick Sand's" extensive advertising, and actually beat it into mass distribution outlets like Wal-Mart.

### Indirect Competition

Despite the increasing number of "owner-friendly" cat litter boxes, many cat owners continued to favor the basic model. These products retailed for $10 to $15, were sold at numerous locations, and represented the majority of the litter box market (approximately 90 per cent). Although cat litter boxes could be purchased in a variety of colors and sizes, compared to the more recent offerings they were awkward, messy, and smelly.

At the other end of the spectrum, a product named "Litter Maid" had also made its way into the market. With the aid of electric eyes and an automatic sifting comb, this computerized self-cleaning litter box combed through the litter, collected the waste and deposited it into a container at one end of the tray. The electric eyes reacted quickly and the litter box was cleaned within minutes of the cat leaving the box, thereby eliminating almost any odor. Its hassle-free process, benefits, and one-year manufacturer's warranty had all been heavily advertised on TV and in national magazines. "Litter Maid" could be purchased via mail order for $199.00 U.S.

## FROM AUGUST 1995 TO PRESENT

Ebert realized that with such heavy competition, Omega would have to think carefully about its marketing campaign. Specifically, as it attempted to expand distribution, it would have to think carefully of the company's success and failures over the past year.

In August 1995, after four months of advertising the "Self-Cleaning Litter Box" via magazine advertisements (mail-order) and TV commercials, Omega pre-sold 2,500 units. These units were shipped to the customers as the orders came in; however, production problems with the initial moulds caused delays and, instead of the actual product, Omega had to send out letters stating that the product would be ready in a few weeks' time.

In late August 1995, the management group at Omega decided to end the "direct to customer" mail-order experiment, and instead to target pet stores via distributors. Omega contacted Canadian Pet Distributors (CPD) in Cambridge, Ontario, who responded favorably and picked up the "Self-Cleaning Litter Box" line immediately. CPD distributed nationally and required a 40 per cent markup on the manufacturer's selling price; the pet stores, in turn, required a 100 per cent markup on the distributor's selling price.

CPD continued to sell Omega's prototype to pet stores in Canada from August through to December 1995. However, the initial run of products was not yet perfect and, as a result, slightly 'dented' Omega's reputation. When asked why Omega continued to sell these prototype products, Ebert answered, "at that point we were happy to sell to anyone."

By December 1995, the 'new and improved' "Self-Cleaning Litter Box" was ready. Omega sold it for $18. The variable costs for each box were $6.00 for production, $1.50 for shipping, and $1.38 for packaging. Since CPD only sold in Canada, Omega started looking for a distributor in the United States. After being introduced to the product at a trade show that Omega's management had attended, six of seven distributors contacted picked up the product right away. Interestingly, this favorable response made Omega the only 'self-cleaning' litter box on the U.S. market in late 1995.

By January 1996, the management at Omega realized that they could not possibly continue their direct selling technique to the many potential pet store distributors across America. Instead, they chose to utilize the skills and industry contacts of manufacturer representatives. Manufacturer representatives required six per cent commission (on the MSP), and in return added Omega's product line to their existing product line portfolio for sale to pet store distributors across America.[3]

Throughout 1996, Omega continued to attend U.S. industry pet trade shows. The manufacturer representatives were working out very well for Omega and had secured 60 distributors across North America. By September 1996, Omega had sold approximately 50,000 "Self-Cleaning Litter Boxes' totalling $1 million in sales.

## ALTERNATIVES FOR THE FUTURE

After being in business for just over a year, Omega had reached impressive sales levels. Ebert hoped to continue this favorable trend, and aspired to reach sales of $1.7 million by the company's December 1996 fiscal year end, $3 million by December 1997, and $5.7 million by December 1998. He knew that such aggressive growth would not be easy, and wondered "Where do we go from here? Should we continue as we are, increase our penetration into pet stores, revisit mail order channels, pursue mass markets, or expand into grocery stores?"

Ebert wondered what changes to the existing strategy would be necessary to achieve market penetration and increased sales. Should Omega consider using different advertising mediums to attract attention, or should it simply increase the amount of existing advertising? Ebert knew of two or three good trade magazines that offered a one-shot deal (one month / one issue) at a cost of $3,000 to $4,000 including a one-time production fee. However, he wondered if there were any other creative marketing initiatives that could help increase sales among pet stores.

A mail order/TV campaign would cost $20,000 for an initial run. This cost included producing the commercial, a 1-800 phone number, the hiring of a company to answer the calls, and another company to collect the money. As a result of previous difficulties with mail order, a trial run would be conducted. Since Americans tended to be more receptive to mail order than Canadians, the trial would be launched on national television in the United States, and would initially run for a two-week period. Then, if the trial went well, the TV campaign would continue. Ebert noted that under this alternative, Omega would produce and ship the product directly to the customer.

If Omega sold its "Self-Cleaning Litter Box" to mass distribution outlets such as Wal-Mart or Kmart,[4] it would cost an estimated $50,000 for additional tooling, different packaging and increased advertising. If this option was pursued, Ebert wondered what changes would have to be made to the product, and how this might affect the product's selling price, image, and promotional plans.

If mass distribution outlets were pursued, there was also the decision of which trade route to use. With small to medium-sized accounts, Omega could continue using its existing manufacturer representatives to sell to the different stores. However, with large accounts, called "house" accounts, Omega would have to sell directly to the specific mass distribution buyers. The product would then be shipped by the buyers to store distribution centres, and only then would it be sent out to the individual stores. In addition to the added complexity of this trade route, Ebert was especially concerned about meeting the demands of buyers who required a 40-per cent markup (on the MSP), ample quantities, and on-time deliveries.

With 80,000 grocery stores in the United States alone, this relatively untapped market had considerable potential. However, if grocery store placement was pursued, Ebert knew the demands on Omega would be many.

In order to sell to grocery stores, Omega had to sell through a national broker, a regional broker, the distribution centres, and finally the grocery stores. The members of this trade channel respectively required the following:

- The greater of a four per cent margin on the MSP, or a $2,000 monthly retaining fee (national broker);
- A four per cent margin on the MSP (regional broker);
- A 20 to 25 per cent markup on the MSP (distribution centres); and
- A 40 per cent markup on the distributors' selling price (grocery stores).

In addition to the required margin, grocery stores wanted 10 per cent for co-operative advertising and for setting up point-of-purchase displays. Omega estimated a further cost of $3 to produce each of these displays.

Before he could seriously pursue this option, Ebert questioned whether the grocery industry was ready to accept "hard-good"[5] products. He knew some of the more aggressive stores, approximately 10 per cent, were expanding their pet sections, but would customers be willing to make an impulse buy of $30 as part of their weekly grocery shopping? It was evident that this distribution option had high potential, but Ebert questioned whether or not he wanted to be the one to develop it.

## DECISION TIME

Omega had achieved considerable success to date, and the company's current financial resources and production capabilities positioned it well to service a larger market. A marketing budget of $100,000 was available and the manufacturing facilities had a capacity of 3,500 units per week. With all of this in mind, and the options to consider, Ebert wondered what decisions he should make to best position Omega Paw for the future.

Exhibit     1

OMEGA   PAW'S   "SELF-CLEANING    LITTER    BOX"

## Evergreen Trust

Sylvianne Lafontaine, Director of Marketing for Evergreen Trust (ET) reflected on the challenges facing her:

> Historically, ET has never had a marketing nor sales function . . . these are recent phenomena . . . while sales have become quite entrenched in the trust company model, Marketing has not. Our unit has not undertaken the full scope of its marketing responsibilities . . . What should we do to meet ET's objectives?

In early May 1994, she was getting ready for upcoming meetings on marketing planning. Previously known as Brown Trust, ET was now a division of Evergreen Bank (EB), a national chartered bank in Canada. There had been a recent series of acquisitions of trust companies by the Canadian chartered banks; Brown had been acquired by EB just a couple of years ago. Sylvianne had joined the ET team in 1993 having previously worked in retail apparel sales. This was her first time through the planning cycle with ET and she was anxious to do well in the eyes of her superior, the president of ET. She felt she faced a number of major challenges: firstly, to establish the role of marketing in ET; secondly, to help ET be more accepted as a part of EB; and thirdly, to help move ET from its currently unprofitable start-up mode to a profitable operation.

Sylvianne had a small team of five recent "hires" who worked on a variety of tasks ranging from preparing and delivering educational sessions for EB's retail bankers, developing promotional material, to handling calls from the media about ET. She decided she would have to take responsibility for gathering whatever information was required and then for deciding on how to make a plan. She had read many articles on marketing planning, but still she wondered how to prepare for the meetings that would be held during the next month to begin the 1995 ET strategic plan.

## THE ET PLANNING PROCESS

The ET planning process began in March with Strategic Planning by the ET president. This work led to mission statements and high level financial targets which were shared with the functional areas such as Marketing. Marketing Planning began in May and was to culminate in June in a plan and a detailed budget presentation. During July and August there were usually several iterations of this process. By early November it was expected that there would be an approved marketing plan with a tactical plan to be ready by the end of December. The fiscal period was November to October.

Sylvianne began by accumulating all the documents she had that looked at all relevant to a strategic plan. She had inter-office memos about visions and missions, lists of objectives and goals, and lots of outlines of actions to be taken, by whom and when. The pile on her desk rose a good four inches from the surface. The overall ET vision was "To be regarded as the best provider of personal trust services in Canada." The latest ET mission statement was "To provide profitably high quality trust and investment services primarily to wealthy individuals through personnel committed to the highest professional standards." The long term objectives included the following: "To have $20 billion of assets under administration by 1998, to have two per cent of EB's three million customer base also as ET customers by 1998" and "To achieve a ROE of 12 per cent as soon as possible."

## THE TRUST BUSINESS

A trust company was a provincially regulated financial institution that could offer both retail (i.e. individual) and commercial financial services. Trust companies operated out of store fronts, called branches, which in many ways resembled chartered bank branches. In recent years, trust companies had been very aggressive in their efforts to be regarded as alternatives to the banks for accounts and other financial services. What was unique about trust companies was their "fiduciary capabilities". These included stock transfer, executor services, asset distribution, and trustee services. Trust companies provided a wide range of individually tailored services from simple will preparation to complex multi-generational trusts. Services were provided on a fee-for-service basis; these fees were usually based on the dollar value of the assets involved, or as they say "under administration". There were two types of business for a trust company: immediate fee business, such as investment management, and deferred fee business, such as being named as the executor of a will. The latter resulted in fee income only for the year in which the service was provided while the former resulted in a stream of earnings over several years.

## PROSPECTS AND CLIENTS

The potential for ET seemed promising to Sylvianne. Canadians were aging, living longer and becoming more

Professor Michael R. Pearce prepared this case solely to provide material for class discussion. The authors do not intend to illustrate either effective or ineffective handling of a managerial situation. The authors may have disguised certain names and other identifying information to protect confidentiality.

affluent with about one trillion dollars in wealth estimated to be inherited by Canadians in the next decade. This transfer of wealth combined with the dilemmas of aging baby boomers caught between their aging parents and their university aged children, many without jobs, suggested to her a growing market for asset administration and investment management services. ET was not interested in everyone, however, and had targeted those individuals with at least $300,000 in investable assets as their prime prospects. About 10 per cent of EB's client base fit this description. The typical ET client was over 55, female, a long-term EB client, conservative in investments, and concerned about making the right financial choices for herself or her relatives. There were a wide variety of clients ranging from individuals too busy to manage their money, the elderly who were starting to lose their faculties, through to inheritors of all ages. Affluent EB customers, on average, had relationships with three major financial institutions at a time, and almost half had dealings with a trust company. American research had indicated that the average trust client stayed with that organization for 17 years.

Based on some limited focus group work and comments from staff, Sylvianne characterized the typical ET client as wanting the following:

- Advice.
- Access to a broad range of investment vehicles — Canadian and foreign.
- Sound investments for capital protection, safe income generating investments for retirement purposes and security/peace of mind.
- Professional estate management.
- Reasonable access to the account relationship/product expert.
- Personalized service by experienced personnel, easy access to personnel, accurate communications.
- Continuity of relationship.
- Staff to take time to explain everything so client understands.
- Frequent meetings.

Sylvianne also noted that ET's limited research had revealed some of the reasons why prospects apparently did not become ET clients, such as:

- Several did not know what a trust company could do.
- Many expressed surprise that EB had a trust company operation — they'd never heard of ET nor had they ever heard of Brown Trust.
- Some individuals felt there was no need for professional asset distribution services if the assets were to be distributed on death and no long-term management was

required; there were few beneficiaries; and if the estate was not particularly large or complex.
- Some individuals felt they could look after their own financial affairs.
- Some individuals were content with their existing relationships with other professionals such as a lawyer or accountant.
- Some believed that trust companies were not for "ordinary" people.
- Some were concerned that they would lose total control of their money.

## COMPETITORS

There were many competitors for ET. Sylvianne drew a little chart to show the array that faced ET prospects:

| | Asset → Management | Asset → Protection | Asset Distribution |
|---|---|---|---|
| Service/ Product | Investment Mgmt Mutual Funds RRSP's/RRIF's Pension Plans | Trusts Estate Planning Insurance | Estate Administration |
| Suppliers | Trust Cos/"Banks" Mutual Funds Cos Portfolio Managers Insurance Cos Brokers | Trust Cos | Trust Cos Lawyers |

The major competitors included Royal Trust (part of Royal Bank), CIBCTrust (part of CIBC), and Canada Trust. ET faced formidable competition in Sylvianne's view. They were offering some trust services at lower prices and outspending ET on all major media. EB was strongest in Western Canada and had only recently begun an aggressive expansion program in the populous East; so, ET was just beginning to get exposure in Toronto, Montreal and other major markets in the East. Deregulation in the financial services market was expected to continue, further blurring the lines between trust companies, banks, brokers, and others. In such an environment, Sylvianne expected all competitors to become more assertive with their advertising and promotional campaigns and to target the same customer as ET with packaged products.

## PROJECTED ET PERFORMANCE FOR 1994

For the current year, best estimates indicated that ET would have about 790 clients. EB bankers were expected to refer about 2000 customers and ET officers to convert about 40 per cent of those to ET clients. Of these clients, about 80 per cent were expected to be "immediate fee" clients. They were predicted to have average assets of about $450,000. ET would realize an average blended fee of one per cent on these assets during the year with an average variable cost of service provided (including sales commissions) of 0.4 per cent. Analysts were predicting that immediate fee clients would continue to have a yearly transaction of the same size for the lifetime of their relationship with ET. About 20 per cent of the clients gained in 1994 were expected to become "deferred fee" clients in their tenth year of relationship with ET, that is in 2004. In that year, about 70 per cent of them would provide a fee of five per cent on their average assets of $550,000 while 30 per cent would continue to provide a fee of five per cent, per year, for years 11 to 17. In each instance, the variable cost of services provided was expected to be about 0.3 per cent. "Fixed costs" included all sorts of items under the general headings of General and Administrative and Marketing. Marketing costs for 1994 were budgeted at $700,000 while G&A were budgeted at $7.8 million. Sylvianne had been told to ignore inflation in her planning, but to use an interest rate of 10 per cent in any present value calculations.

## THE EB REFERRAL SYSTEM

The current regulations under the Bank Act prevented ET from directly contacting EB's customer base. It was somewhat confusing as to what could and couldn't be done. For example, ET personnel could only speak with EB customers after a referral from EB personnel (there were 50 field officers to meet with prospects), but ET could send direct mail to EB customers. This meant that ET was very dependent on the EB retail branch system to generate qualified leads for ET staff to meet. Sylvianne had discovered this was not an easy task. Everybody involved with the EB retail delivery network claimed to be excessively busy with other priorities; further, Sylvianne knew many of them simply didn't accept that providing referrals to ET was an important part of their job. She had tried to get an objective of one referral per month per branch (there were 700 branches) established, but she knew she had no authority to impose this. ET sales data indicated that at the moment a small number of

bankers accounted for the majority of referrals received. Branch bankers had been exposed to promotional material and in some cases seminars explaining ET, but Sylvianne knew there was much to do by her team on this issue of internal marketing. She had learned that some EB bankers did not know their customers well enough to know who to refer to ET and that some were uncomfortable at the prospect of asking customers about other assets and their plans for the future. As a consequence, there was minimal visibility of ET in the EB branches.

## CONCLUSION

Sylvianne wanted to move quickly to address the challenges facing her. She mused:

> There is no model for a bank owned trust company to pursue its destiny . . . everything the marketing unit has developed has been from the embryonic stage. It is so difficult to plan six months before the fiscal year, in a dynamic changing business, within an even more dynamic, changing organization. How can we best work with each other when there are dependencies among all of our jobs, but we can't identify them effectively; i.e. where does marketing end and field sales begin? How can we work together, efficiently and productively? How can we get the integration and flexibility we need?

Sylvianne wondered how to start. There seemed to be so many questions, so many directions to go. Should she begin by revisiting the mission statement? Should she argue for a separate or combined identity with EB and what would either approach mean? Which prospects in particular should be sought? How could referrals be encouraged? Should she engage in market research and if so, what? Should she be involved in decisions such as which products should be offered? What about customer service standards? There seemed to be so many questions. In fact, she wondered what exactly should the ET marketing team be doing to help grow ET profitably?

## Tucows Inc.

In 1992, a bank loans officer, John Nemanic, and an electronics technician, Bill Campbell, decided to open up a computer store in Toronto. The business grew to three locations. Campbell also had operated, since 1986, an on-line bulletin board service. This business, too, grew so that by 1995 it became an Internet service provider, Internet Direct. The following year, they approached Scott Swedorski, who was running a Web site located in Michigan that distributed software through downloads. Swedorski complained that he had difficulty getting fast downloads to his customers. Swedorski's company was called TUCOWS, an acronym for "The Ultimate Collection of Winsock Software." The collection was largely a number of utilities that ran on the Windows operating system. Utilities programs are those that deal with the operating system directly and make the operation of computers more efficient. As a result of these discussions, Nemanic and Campbell purchased Swedorski's on-line business and the Web site, Tucows.com, and moved the business to Toronto.

To solve Swedorski's problem, Nemanic, Campbell, and Web master Greg Weir devised a system of mirror Web sites. A mirror site is a Web site that is owned by an Internet service provider. A mirror site for Tucows holds a duplicate of everything that is on Tucows' main Web site in Toronto. The process requires the person who wishes to download software to choose the site nearest to him or her. For example, if the customer lives in Australia, that person would choose the country and then the Web site in the city nearest to him or her. This would speed up the transfer of data because the call does not have to go across the Pacific Ocean to Toronto. The concern of having to contact Toronto from Australia is that the telephone lines can carry only a limited amount of information. The downloaded software would then have to take its turn with other information that is going down the telephone lines, thus slowing the downloading process. But when the connection is made to a site based in Australia, the download becomes relatively quick. This program was later enhanced by the marketing team of Ross Rader and Denzil Solomon and became known as the Tucows ISP Advantage Program. This program currently consists of more than 900 ISPs worldwide.

Because Internet Direct and the on-line business grew so quickly, Nemanic and Campbell decided to split the company in two: one for the Internet service provider and the other to distribute software on-line. This on-line software digital distributor became Tucows.com Inc.

### EARLY DEVELOPMENTS

When Tucows.com first started, it needed to determine who its true customers were. At the time, it was felt that the true Internet user, also known as the early adopter, would be its target market. For this group, it had software that included browsers, e-mail, FTP, and HTML programs. When Tucows first started, it worked closely with its developers. Software appeared on its site through submissions of independent suppliers. An editorial group reviewed and rated the product. The developer of the software was in charge of determining the price of the product.

One issue that occurred in the early development stage was advertising. The management of Tucows wanted to advertise in magazines, but, initially, it did not have the cash to pay for magazine advertisements. It resolved this issue by bartering with magazines. These publications would advertise their magazines on Tucows' Web site in return for advertising in each of the magazines. This allowed Tucows to conserve valuable cash for other things that needed to be developed. Another way in which the company was able to promote its business was to run features in magazines. For example, an article would be provided to magazines that featured current favourite programs. The article would mention that it was brought to the reader by Tucows.

The final way in which Tucows was able to promote itself was to appear on Web sites. Part of the arrangement with its mirror sites was that each site would include a banner advertisement for Tucows. A banner is a small advertisement that appears on one part of the screen on a Web site. People visiting these mirror sites would then become familiar with Tucows by reading the banner advertisement. When an Internet service provider became a mirror site, the value of that site would also increase because people would visit this mirror site to get software that Tucows was offering.

### RECENT DEVELOPMENTS

More recently, Tucows' mix of software titles has changed. The company started adding games as well as a line of software aimed at everyone from casual computer users to programmers. The type of software has changed also. While the company started by selling software for the Windows and Macintosh operating systems, it has also added software for the Linux operating system and for use on palmtops. More recently, management has been interested in selling office productivity products, such as word processors, spreadsheets, and presentation software. Much of this software was added through requests from its customers, and was not always part of a larger plan to interest a broad range of customers.

Software, however, is only one of many items that Tucows offers. The others are advertising, digital certificates, and domain name registration (OpenSRS). It is the largest wholesale supplier of domain name registration in the world. More than 5,000 ISPs, web-hosting firms, and others use Tucows for regis-

Source: Prepared for the textbook by David Parker.

tration. Internet advertising has been sold on the basis of the number of people who view a page, or click-throughs, as the industry calls it. The price is generally $25 per thousand click-throughs. Currently, the price is suggested by the Audit Bureau of Circulations, which also audits the company's circulation, or number of impressions. Now, there is the pressure to price advertising on the basis of actual purchases when the customer connects directly to an advertiser.

With the addition of new software, the previous method of pricing based on the direction of the developer was no longer possible. Tucows had grown to an important site that attracted a lot of views from customers. A view occurs when a Web page is visible on the screen of the person using the computer. Tucows took the position that because its Web site has lots of traffic, developers should accept a lower price for their products. However, much higher volumes would offset this lower price. Overall, the developer, and Tucows, would realize much greater revenue. Very recently, the company introduced pay-per-click pricing for authors promoting their software.

## NEW MARKETS

Tucows content business now faces three major considerations: (1) new markets, (2) new advertising revenue models, and (3) the Tucows name.

The management believes there is continuing opportunity to provide promotion and distribution services to shareware and independent software developers. Linux and PDA-software are geared for the more technically inclined, a group often referred to as computer geeks. However, games and themes are of interest to those who are not technically inclined. These two groups pull the product selection in completely different directions. But management feels that sticking to the current group of customers will limit future growth. Some facts about the Web site are summarized in Exhibit 1.

There are some problems with expanding the selection of products. First, if the company were to promote its site more aggressively to newcomers to the Internet, there would be a concern about the amount of help that these new customers would require. For example, a customer who is not familiar with downloading files might download the file to his computer, but then not be able to find it. Further, once it was downloaded, he might not know how to run it so that it expands properly and becomes a useful program. The navigation around the site would have to be quite simple. Customers who are familiar with Web sites understand how they work. Management was concerned that if too much instruction were included in the Web site, its more experienced customers would feel insulted because the instructions talk down to them.

Many people do not want to buy software without first seeing how it works. Tucows wanted to allow customers to try

## EXHIBIT 1   CHARACTERISTICS OF THE TUCOWS.COM WEB SITE

- 80 million page views per month
- 5.2 million downloads per month
- Six million unique visitors per month
- 1200 affiliates in 75 countries
- 30 000 software titles and eight software libraries
- 1.2 million downloads per month of themes and games
- Close to half a million PDA application downloads per month
- 250 000 Linux application downloads per month

software for a limited time period to see whether it fit their needs. Some software would become inoperable after the trial period. However, some software relied on the honour system. So the second issue that Tucows faced was how to package this software.

The last issue facing the management was the name of the Web site. The advantages of the Tucows name were that the name was widely recognized among its current customers and it also gave a friendly, accessible feel to the company, much like Gateway Computer. Gateway started in Iowa, and although it is now located in San Diego, it still ships its computers with cow designs printed on the outside of its boxes, something it started when it was located in the American Midwest. Tucows is located in downtown Toronto.

But the name also posed some significant disadvantages. Among them were that new customers had to know how to spell Tucows. Variations on this included "2cows," "Twocows," and "Toocows." This problem was further complicated by the fact that Tucows had rights only to the "Tucows.com" name. Since other organizations had rights to similar names, this meant that customers might be led to other Web sites. Tucows has taken advantage of American law that prevents people and organizations from staking out Web site addresses that are similar to other addresses for the sole purpose of taking advantage of a better-known Web site. The organization that records names that end in ".com" is based in Virginia and is subject to American legislation. The management of Tucows has needed to draw up letters from lawyers to seek the cooperation of these other businesses. In some cases, they may have to go to court to get the rights to similar Web site addresses.

Another disadvantage with the name was that the "w" in "Tucows" stands for Winsock, which refers to the Windows operating system. Management felt that it might discourage potential customers from visiting the Web site because of the mistaken impression that it sells only Windows-based software. This will be particularly problematic if the company is going to pursue Linux-based software. Many Linux software developers have a passionate dislike for Microsoft.

## DISCUSSION QUESTIONS

1. Do you feel that there is likely a huge market for Tucows to pursue? How would you ensure that your intuition about the size of any potential market could be verified?

2. If you were the marketing manager for Tucows, how would you expand the company's offering? Take a look at the Tucows Web site at http://www.tucows.com. Do you feel that the company has already expanded into the area to capture the two new user groups it wants?

3. If you were to expand the selection of software from what is currently offered, how would you ensure that you did not lose the current customers?

# Case 12

## Mobile Climate Control Industries Inc.

In 1975, Gunnar and Marianne Mannerheim were interested in starting a business in their home country of Sweden. Gunnar was a heating, ventilating, and air conditioning (HVAC) engineer who installed ventilating equipment for buildings. Marianne had studied business at university. She had also acquired other language skills when she studied outside of Sweden. The couple had hoped to start a business in the HVAC industry and take advantage of their combined expertise and experience. Operating their own business was attractive because there was always the challenge of solving new problems.

However, they faced a few obstacles before they started. First, they did not have any money. The Swedish government at the time did not provide entrepreneurs with grants to help start small businesses. Loans were available, but they were difficult to obtain. Their business would not have qualified for any loans. Second, they did not have an identified market. Third, they did not have equipment or a place for operating their business. In short, they had nothing.

It was through Marianne's father that they found their first market. He was a representative for a German company that made cooling systems. This company made air conditioners for cars and large cooling systems for factories. When Marianne's father represented this company, he received inquiries from logging firms about cooling units for their logging machines. These logging companies had started to put cabs on their machines. The German company was not interested in pursuing this business, in large part because the market was small. The Mannerheims took the opportunity to follow it up. They felt that the logging industry was a niche that had not yet been satisfied and that they could turn it into a profitable business. They decided to sell their products not as a luxury, but as a necessity, reflecting the general Swedish mentality of being more environmentally aware and more conscious of employee safety and comfort than in other countries. The Mannerheims also recognized that they happened to be at the right place at the right time.

The Mannerheims started a small company that they named Klimatsystem AB. Because it was so small, the German parts company for whom Marianne's father worked dealt with them as an unimportant customer. As a result, there was an understanding that the equipment it supplied Klimatsystem was for off-road vehicles only. The parts could not be used for automobiles. Further, Klimatsystem could not export any air-conditioning systems that used the German company's air-conditioning parts. The German manufacturer was impor-

tant to Klimatsystem because it supplied the heating coils, the evaporator coils, and valves. At the time, there was not a great demand for air conditioning in cars, unlike the situation in North America. Consequently, this German company was one of the few manufacturers of vehicle air-conditioning parts in Europe and the only one in Germany.

One key item needed for manufacturing is money, primarily to purchase machines and buildings. During the start-up period, however, Klimatsystem suffered from a shortage of money. This prevented the company from being as big as the owners would like, and projects were chosen one at a time to ensure that the company had the money to meet the costs of production and the ability to complete the contract. But little by little, the company grew. After a few years, the owners bought a poultry farm and turned it into a factory. They did the renovations themselves. After eight and a half years of work, the company employed about twenty people and captured 83 percent of the Swedish market.

It was at this time that the owners faced a problem. They wanted to increase the size of the company, but they were constrained. First, they could not really enlarge the Swedish market because they had almost all of it. And second, they couldn't export because of the understanding with the German manufacturer. They felt that they had three choices: (1) They could be content with their business and live in relative prosperity knowing that the company's market would continue to be profitable at least for the foreseeable future. (2) They could try to make the parts that were now being purchased from the German manufacturer. (3) They could sell the business and set up a new one.

For the Mannerheims the first option was not attractive. They could not just stay put, as they knew they would soon become bored with running the business. They needed the challenge of solving new problems. Further, they looked at trying to make the parts themselves, but quickly realized that they did not have the capital needed to invest in the machinery. Even after eight and a half years of operating the business, the German company was still the only practical source for parts. Finally, they decided to sell their business and move to North America. They chose Canada because it was supportive of business, but also because it, like Sweden, had the logging business that had provided the customers for Klimatsystem. They named their new business Mobile Climate Control.

In 1982, they set up their business out of their house in Thornhill, Ontario. They started to pursue opportunities in the off-road sector. The state of the industry in Canada was behind that in Sweden. While there were cabs on logging machines, the air-conditioning units were not as advanced as those built by Klimatsystem in Sweden. The growth in sales was about 30 to 35

Source: Prepared for the textbook by David Parker.

percent per year. This occurred despite the fact that they went against two large competitors: Red Dot Corporation, a company based in Seattle, and Bergstrom Inc., a company based in Rockford, Illinois.

At the same time, the company was extending its market into other areas. One of these came about through an exhibition at which they had a booth. The company was displaying its air-conditioning systems when someone from Nova Bus, a large bus manufacturer based in St. Eustache, Quebec, asked whether Mobile Climate Control could develop defrosters for the drivers' compartment of Nova's buses. The defroster was to be a custom design made especially for Nova Bus. The price to Nova Bus would be about $1000 each. The management of Mobile Climate Control agreed.

This new opportunity came at the point that Mobile Climate Control faced the first of two large challenges and opportunities. The first of these came with concerns about chlorofluorocarbons (CFCs). In 1978, the United States government banned the use of CFCs for almost all aerosol containers. By 1988, Du Pont, the largest producer of CFCs, agreed to phase out its brand, Freon, by 2000. Finally, there was a worldwide agreement to end the use of CFCs in most countries by 2000, which was later amended in 1995. All countries are planning to end the use of CFCs by 2010, if they have not already done so.

Mobile Climate Control was using compressors that could not handle the new refrigerant. However, both Carrier and Thermo King, both large competitors for Mobile Climate Control in the bus air-conditioning business, had piston-driven compressors that also could not handle new refrigerants very well. The first thing that the managers of Mobile Climate Control had to do was to find a new compressor.

The second opportunity again came from Nova Bus. This time, the request was for a rooftop heating unit to heat the passenger compartment of buses. Each of these units would cost Nova Bus about $4000. The management of Mobile Climate Control again agreed. They could see that this had the potential to be a large market and decided to design an air-conditioning unit for the same bus, even though Nova Bus did not request it. Each of these units would be priced between $10 000 and $12 000.

In North America, the significant market for buses is the United States. However, purchases of transit vehicles fall under the requirements of the Buy America Act. This act states that purchases made or subsidized by the United States government must prefer American manufacturers. More specifically, the goods purchased or subsidized must be substantially made in the United States. Manufacturers of buses outside the United States can be considered, but only if their prices are at least 6 percent cheaper than those made in the United States. Even if products made outside the United States are cheaper, the purchase must receive approval before it can be made. This is a par-

ticular problem for Mobile Climate Control because while there are few contracts for air-conditioning units in existing buses, there may be bus manufacturers located in the United States that want air-conditioning units. If Mobile Climate Control were to supply units made outside of the United States, it is possible that American-made buses would not be considered as being substantially made in the United States.

Very briefly, an air-conditioning unit consists of a series of coils and a pump, or compressor. The coils contain refrigerant. This refrigerant is forced through a small opening, called an orifice. When it goes through the orifice, the refrigerant evaporates, cooling the surrounding area. It is very similar to the cooling feeling you get when rubbing alcohol evaporates on your skin. When the refrigerant is entirely evaporated, the compressor applies so much force to the refrigerant that it again becomes a liquid, only to repeat the cycle again. Most air-conditioning compressors use a piston to compress the refrigerant. This design of the compressor does not handle non-CFC refrigerants very well. The search for a new compressor led the company to a manufacturer in England. This manufacturer had the rights to a compressor that worked on a rotary basis. The compressor creates pressure through centrifugal action by rotating a wheel with collapsible fins within an elliptical cylinder. Four factors recommended this compressor. First, it had only one major moving part, thereby reducing maintenance costs and breakdowns considerably. Second, the compressor was much smaller than any other compressor used in the market, allowing it to be installed in tight spaces. Third, it could handle any refrigerant, including ammonia. And finally, it had years of extremely reliable service in high-speed Swedish trains.

The management of Mobile Climate Control believed that they had found a new marketing niche, namely supplying buses with air conditioners for American municipal transit authorities and the coach business. The buses would use Mobile Climate Control's heating and air-conditioning units that used the new English compressor. The management felt that its experience in Sweden on high-speed trains would convince potential customers of the reliability of the compressor. The only problem that the company faced was how it was going to bring all these pieces together to go after its market.

In order to satisfy the requirements of the Buy America Act, management realized that it would have to purchase the patents to the compressor and build a factory in the United States to make the air-conditioning units. The problem was that the patents were going to cost $1.2 million and the factory in the United States was going to cost more than $5 million (US). Further, it would require 100 employees to run it. The only contract the company was sure of getting for this facility was supplying the U.S. Army with two prototype mobile heaters with a total value of $250 000 (US). There was the hope for more heaters should the prototypes prove to be successful. The revenue for the company was $10.8 million with after-tax income of $1.6 million. The company did not have the cash to finance either undertaking.

## DISCUSSION QUESTION

1. Assume that you are the marketing manager of this company. Would you recommend proceeding with developing the HVAC product line for buses? Would you complete only part of the venture — say, only the acquisition of the patents and rights for the compressor? Or would you recommend that the Mannerheims sell the business and, with the proceeds, start a new business?

## Canadian Novelty Printing

Andy Cook, newly appointed President and CEO of Canadian Novelty Printing's Canadian operations, located in Brampton, Ontario, faced the following problem: company profits and the number of active distributors that remain with the company had been steadily declining during the last few years. After reviewing the situation, Andy wondered what action he should take next.

### INDUSTRY OVERVIEW

The World Federation of Direct Selling Associations estimated that 1998 Canadian retail sales by direct selling sources amounted to $1.6 billion. The percentage of sales by major product groups was as follows: home and family care products (cleaning, cookware, and cutlery, etc.), 11 percent; personal care products (cosmetics, jewellery, and skin care, etc.), 30 percent; services and miscellaneous, etc., 14 percent; wellness products (weight loss, vitamins and nutritional supplements, etc.), 36 percent; and leisure items (books, toys and games, etc.), 9 percent. Canadian retail sales by direct selling sources are expected to experience an average annual growth rate of 10 to 15 percent over the next five years.

The locations of these sales that were sold by an estimated 1.3 million distributors, reported as a percentage of sales dollars, were as follows: in the home, 75 percent; in the workplace, 10 percent; over the phone (in a follow-up to a face-to-face solicitation), 11 percent; and at temporary or other locations (fair, exhibition, shopping mall, etc.), 4 percent.

The sales strategies used to generate sales varied considerably. The methods used to generate sales, as a percentage of sales dollars, were as follows: individual one-to-one selling, 65 percent; party-plan or group selling, 29 percent; and customers placing an order directly to the firm (following a face-to-face solicitation), 6 percent.

### CANADIAN NOVELTY PRINTING: GENERAL COMPANY BACKGROUND

Canadian Novelty Printing (CNP) was started in 1946, with a $1000 investment, by Rick Baily, a young Canadian entrepreneur. Mr. Baily was intrigued by the idea of manufacturing and selling personalized business cards and stationery to the expanding market for these products in Canada.

Some of the first products offered by CNP included personalized business cards and office stationery. Over the years,

however, additional products were added to CNP's product line, including office furniture, office supplies, personalized apparel, unique value-priced gift items, books, and motivational artwork.

CNP was a subsidiary of a publicly traded company incorporated under the laws of the Province of Ontario, Canada. The registered office of CNP was located in Brampton, Ontario, Canada.

### CANADIAN OPERATIONS

During 1999, CNP had an established Canadian network of 156 000 active distributors who marketed and sold the company's products to individuals and small businesses across Canada from 44 distribution centres.

### PRODUCTS AND NEW PRODUCT DEVELOPMENT

#### Products

Historically, CNP was known for a product line that focused primarily on quality personalized business cards and stationery. However, over the last few years CNP had expanded its product line to include such items as office furniture, office supplies, personalized apparel, unique value-priced gift items, books, and motivational artwork. CNP selected products that were competitively priced for the quality that they offered.

#### New Product Development

Over the years new products had been added to enrich CNP's product line. These items were added based on management's belief that customers wanted a wider range of products to choose from. New product ideas were derived from a number of sources, including existing distributors, customers, management, and various other CNP personnel.

Purchase volumes were based on estimated demand for products according to seasonal market consumption patterns. For instance, business cards and stationery sold more rapidly during the first few months of the year, whereas novelty gift items and personalized apparel sold more rapidly during the busy Christmas season.

### COMPANY STRUCTURE

#### General Workforce

CNP employed approximately 100 people in a variety of general functions, including administration, marketing, information systems, and operations. There were no collective-bargaining agreements in effect. The company enjoyed excellent ongoing

Source: Joseph J. Schiele prepared this case for the Direct Selling Education Foundation of Canada, solely to provide material for class discussion. The author did not intend to illustrate either effective or ineffective handling of a managerial situation. The author may have disguised certain names and other identifying information to protect confidentiality. The Direct Selling Education Foundation of Canada prohibits any form of reproduction, storage or transmittal of this material without its written permission. To order copies or request permission to reproduce materials, contact the Direct Selling Education Foundation of Canada, 190 Attwell Drive, Unit 630, Etobicoke, Ontario, Canada, M9W 6H8, Tel: (416) 679-8555, Fax: (416) 670-1568. Copyright © 1999, Direct Selling Education Foundation of Canada.

relations with employees. Employees received competitive benefit and compensation packages.

## Senior Management

CNP was managed by Andy Cook, President and CEO; Paul Haesler, Senior Vice President and Chief Financial Officer; Chris Lauterbach, Senior Vice President Operations; Mary Steeds, Senior Vice President Marketing and Sales; and Christine Martini, Senior Vice President Merchandising. CNP senior management had spent most of their careers working in a direct marketing environment. They had come to believe from both their formal education and many years of practical work experience that the success of any direct marketing company was the result of an effective marketing plan. In order to be successful, CNP senior management believed that they needed to continually recruit and retain distributors who were highly motivated to improve their customer base.

## Distribution Centre Managers and Staff

Each of CNP's 44 distribution centres employed a manager, an assistant manager, and various general support staff. The people employed within these distribution centres usually had distribution backgrounds. They had acquired their expertise from years of managing the flow of product from suppliers to distributors. Their jobs typically involved stock-keeping and order-filling. The people employed within each distribution centre had little or no marketing experience and could be seen as an operationally focused workforce.

## SALES AND MARKETING

### Sales

The company's products were sold and distributed through a marketing system consisting of approximately 156 000 active distributors. Distributors were independent contractors who purchased products directly from the company for their own use and for resale to other consumers. Sales revenues were generated from four distinct segments:

1. Self Buyer–Family Buyer

   The self buyer–family buyer segment represented approximately 30 percent of sales revenues. These distributors were people who shared CNP product catalogues with friends and family members. They used their status as distributors to either take advantage of the discounts offered on purchases for themselves or pass these discounts along to their friends and family members. The average annual amount spent by each self buyer–family buyer distributor was $135 per year.

2. Direct Seller Representative

   The direct seller representative segment represented approximately 40 percent of sales revenues. These distributors were people who saw themselves as independent business owners who actively distributed CNP product catalogues and recruited customers in order to make more sales and earn larger commission incomes for themselves. The average annual amount spent by each direct seller representative distributor was $1900 per year.

3. Noncatalogue Retail

   The noncatalogue retail segment represented approximately 19 percent of sales revenues. These were both distributors and nondistributors who purchased heavily discounted items that were advertised through flyers and various mailings and sold through the 44 retail distribution centres.

4. Fundraising

   The fundraising segment represented approximately 11 percent of sales revenues. These distributors were people who used the products sold by CNP to support fundraising activities. These items included personalized apparel, pins and key chains, and other similar items such as personalized coffee mugs or cups. The average annual amount spent by each fund-raising distributor was $2000 per year.

### Marketing

CNP employed a system that enabled distributors to become involved on a part- or full-time basis. CNP concentrated its efforts on encouraging individuals to develop their own business, at their own pace, without the costly expense inherent in franchise operations or other start-up enterprises. CNP gave individuals the opportunity to go into business without significant risk, yet offered them significant upside potential, albeit wholly dependent on their own efforts.

The company's ability to increase sales was significantly dependent on its ability to attract, motivate, and retain distributors and its ability to offer products and services that were well suited to the needs of their customers. Management attempted to do this through a catalogue marketing program that it believed was superior to programs offered by other network marketing companies. Typically, CNP product catalogues were mailed to distributors, who circulated these catalogues to small businesses, friends, family members, and the like in order to generate sales. Distributors could advertise through classified ads, hold home parties where information on the company and its products could be disseminated, go door to door, or contact people through phone solicitation.

Customers would place their orders through distributors, who would then contact a distribution centre where orders could be filled, picked up, and delivered to customers. Money for each order was collected directly from each customer by the respective distributor. This system allowed an individual distributor to leverage his or her time, talent, and energy to earn commissions from sales to all of the people who were introduced to company product lines. These methods had proved to be a simple and effective distribution model for CNP.

The marketing program offered by CNP provided financial incentives for distributors to earn income based on the retail markup on product sales. Distributors purchased product from the company and resold the product at retail prices to consumers. The difference between the price paid by the distributor and the retail price was a distributor's profit or compensation. As a distributor sold more product, the discounts offered would increase accordingly. These discounts ranged from 10 percent for cumulative sales under $250 to 50 percent for cumulative sales above $15 000. Three years ago, in an attempt to motivate sales, changes were made to the discount structure for distributors. Level 1 discounts were reduced from 20 to 10 percent and top-level discounts were raised to as high as 50 percent. (Exhibit 1 provides the new discount structure that corresponded to respective sales levels.)

| EXHIBIT 1 | Revised Distributor Discount Structure | | |
|---|---|---|---|
| DISCOUNT LEVEL | SALES VOLUME | OLD DISCOUNT (%) | NEW DISCOUNT (%) |
| 1 | $1–$249 | 20 | 10 |
| 2 | $250–$499 | 20 | 20 |
| 3 | $500–$999 | 30 | 30 |
| 4 | $1 000–$2 999 | 35 | 35 |
| 5 | $3 000–$7 499 | 40 | 40 |
| 6 | $7 500–$14 999 | 40 | 45 |
| 7 | Over $15 000 | 45 | 50 |

Source: Internal company documents.

## COMPETITION

CNP competed with many companies marketing products similar to those marketed and sold by the company. It also competed directly with other direct marketing companies for the recruitment of distributors.

Not all competitors sold all the types of products marketed by CNP. Some competitors had more focused lines, others more varied lines. For example, some competitors were known for and were identified by the personalized stationery that they sold, while others were known for and identified by a wide array of product lines.

Another source of competition in the sale and distribution of CNP products was from direct retail establishments such as large retailers, independents, and noncategory stores.

There were also many other companies with which CNP competed for distributors. (Exhibit 2 provides an outline of direct marketing companies with whom CNP competed for product sales and distributors, including details on product lines offered, discounts offered, distributor support, and new distributor promotional programs.)

## FUTURE OUTLOOK

The company believed that its success to date was due to its reputation for quality products and services offered, in-stock first-

time delivery of items, its familiar quality product line, such as personalized business cards and stationery, and its appeal to distributors as a business opportunity for those interested in establishing their own direct sales business.

The company's primary objective for the future was to increase sales and profitability by capitalizing on its operating strengths in order to become a leading distributor of consumer products in each of its markets. The company intended to do this by introducing new products, attracting new distributors, and increasing company awareness and loyalty. (Exhibit 3 provides sales and earnings projections for the next three years.)

## CURRENT SITUATION

### Sales Trends

Over the last three years the financial performance of the company had shown a steady decline despite attempts to enrich catalogue offerings and adjust discount structure for distributor segments (Exhibit 4 provides financial results for the past four years.)

### Declining Distributor Base

During the last three years the total number of CNP distributors had declined from 180 000 to 156 000 distributors (Exhibit 4 provides distributor levels for the past four years.)

### Stock-outs and Other Inventory Problems

Over the last four years the number of stock-keeping units for CNP products had increased from 3700 to over 7900 units. Management believed that this increase might have contributed to stock-outs and the problems associated with managing the larger inventory levels needed to meet customer demand. During the last two years distribution centres had been unable to provide in-stock first-time delivery of items for 75 percent of orders.

### Mandate for Turnaround

Due to the losses experienced during the last few years, CNP's parent company decided to change CNP's status as an operating subsidiary to a discontinued operation. Unless Andy could find a way to turn the company around, CNP's parent company would be forced to either sell off or close CNP permanently.

### Other Problems Encountered

Management believed that there were other factors that might have contributed to the decline in sales and distributor levels over the last few years. These factors included a mail strike two years ago that prevented the timely delivery of CNP product catalogues and advertisements, and a rise in inflation that caused significant price increases.

## DECISION

Having reviewed the key information that he felt relevant, Andy wondered what action he should take next.

**EXHIBIT 2**     CNP Competition and Related Attributes

| COMPANY AND ATTRIBUTES | PRODUCT LINE | DISCOUNT STRUCTURE | DISTRIBUTOR SUPPORT | NEW DISTRIBUTOR PROMOTIONAL PROGRAMS |
|---|---|---|---|---|
| CNP | Personalized business cards and stationery, office furniture and supplies, apparel, unique value-priced gift items, books, and motivational artwork. | 10–50 percent discounts on cumulative annual sales volumes. | Support was offered through a 1-800 telephone line, regular noncatalogue flyers, and newsletters. | There was an additional 10 percent discount offered to new distributors as well as free information packages and starter coupons for various products. |
| Company A | Over 5000 brand-name products from over 300 various companies plus thousands of private label products. | 30 percent discounts on items as well as commissions from a distributor's down-line sales network plus 3–25 percent discounts on certain sales items. | Support was offered through product guarantees, written business plans, brochures, and interviews with successful distributors. | There were no special programs. New distributors had to purchase a sales starter kit for approximately $200. |
| Company B | Wide range of cosmetic products including makeup, perfumes, fashion items, jewellery, vitamins, toys, games, compact discs, and videos. | 10–50 percent based on current order volumes plus special discounts on special items. | Support was offered through district managers, a contact person who assisted distributors with questions and training meetings, conferences, and various brochures. | Occasionally the $20 sign-up fee for new representatives was waived or discounted. |
| Company C | Various office products including novelty gift items, supplies, and stationery. | 30 percent based on current sales order. | Support was offered through written material, regular sales training from supervisors, and an extensive distributor support network. | There were no special programs. New representatives had to purchase a sales starter kit for approximately $45. |
| Company D | Plastic household products and toys. | 25–35 percent discounts on current orders. | Support was offered through regular sales and information session meetings, and phone consultation with other distributors. | Many programs existed, including product incentives and new distributor parties. New distributors had to purchase a sales starter kit for approximately $125. |
| Company E | Office business cards and stationery. | 50 percent discount off retail on all orders. | Support was offered through extensive sales and product-related training sessions. | There were no special programs. |
| Company F | Household consumable food items, laundry and cleaning products, and personal health products. | 28–48 percent discounts based on current orders. | Support was offered through local meetings, conferences, and conventions. An area supervisor was also available for consultation. | There were no special programs. New distributors had to purchase a sales starter kit for approximately $99. |

Source: Internal company documents.

**EXHIBIT 3** Three-Year Sales Forecast

|  | CURRENT YEAR ($000 000 CDN.) | 1ST YEAR ENDED ($000 000 CDN.) | 2ND YEAR ENDED ($000 000 CDN.) | 3RD YEAR ENDED ($000 000 CDN.) |
|---|---|---|---|---|
| Sales | $63.0 | $69.3 | $79.7 | $91.7 |
| Earnings Before Tax | (6.7) | (1.0) | 5.1 | 9.8 |

Assumptions:

a. 1st Year Ended: sales grow by 10 percent; margin at 49 percent; expenses reduced by $3.4 million.

b. 2nd Year Ended: sales grow by 15 percent; margin at 50 percent; expenses grow by 2 percent.

c. 3rd Year Ended: sales grow by 15 percent; margin at 51 percent; expenses grow by 3 percent.

Source: Internal company documents.

**EXHIBIT 4** Comparative Results Prior Four Years Ended

|  | 4TH YEAR ENDED ($000 000 CDN.) | 3RD YEAR ENDED ($000 000 CDN.) | 2ND YEAR ENDED ($000 000 CDN.) | CURRENT YEAR ENDED ($000 000 CDN.) |
|---|---|---|---|---|
| Sales | $69.2 | $72.3 | $70.6 | $63.0 |
| Cost of Goods Sold | 31.1 | 35.1 | 36.1 | 32.8 |
| Gross Margin | 38.1 | 37.2 | 34.5 | 30.2 |
| Operating Expenses | 34.1 | 35.6 | 41.1 | 36.9 |
| Earnings Before Taxes | 4.0 | 1.6 | (6.6) | (6.7) |
| Number of Distributors | 172 000 | 180 000 | 176 000 | 156 000 |

Source: Internal company documents.

# Notes

## Chapter 1

1. Peter F. Drucker, *The Practice of Management* (New York: Harper and Row, 1954), p. 37.
2. Richard P. Bagozzi, "Marketing as an Organized Behavioral System of Exchange," *Journal of Marketing* (October 1974), p. 77. Further work by Bagozzi on this subject appears in "Marketing as Exchange," *Journal of Marketing* (October 1975), pp. 32–39, and in "Marketing as Exchange: A Theory of Transactions in the Market-place," *American Behavioral Scientist* (March–April 1978), pp. 535–36.
3. Richard P. Bagozzi, "Marketing as an Organized Behavioral System of Exchange," p. 77.
4. Wroe Alderson, *Marketing Behavior and Executive Action* (Homewood, IL: Irwin, 1957), p. 292.
5. "AMA Board Approves New Marketing Definition," *Marketing News* (March 1, 1985), p. 1.
6. Many discussions of this topic have suggested that marketing passed through a series of "eras": product, sales, and market orientations. However, Ronald A. Fullerton shows that there is little historical support for the concept of progression through various eras in his article "How Modern Is Modern Marketing? Marketing's Evolution and the Myth of the 'Production Era,'" *Journal of Marketing* (January 1988), pp. 108–25.
7. Henceforth, the term "product" will apply to both goods and services, except as otherwise noted. The marketing principles that apply to products normally apply to services as well.
8. Theodore Levitt, *Innovations in Marketing* (New York: McGraw-Hill, 1962), p. 7.
9. Ajay K. Kohli and Bernard J. Jaworski, "Market Orientation: The Construct, Research Propositions, and Managerial Implications," *Journal of Marketing* (April 1990), pp. 1–18; Bernard J. Jaworski and Ajay K. Kohli, "Market Orientation: Antecedents and Consequences," *Journal of Marketing* (July 1993), pp. 53–70.
10. Mansour Javidan and John Rigby, *Marketing*, Proceedings of the Annual Conference of the Administrative Sciences Association of Canada, Vol. 11, Part 3, pp. 147–56.
11. Edna Buchanan, "Lucky Luciano," *Time* 152:23 (December 7, 1998), p. 130.
12. "AMA Board Approves New Marketing Definition," p. 1.

## Chapter 2

1. For a detailed discussion of how to create an effective environmental scanning system, see Peter R. Dickson, *Marketing Management*, 2nd ed. (Fort Worth, TX: Dryden Press, 1997), pp. 93–109.
2. Simon Tuck, "Toys in the Hood," *The Globe and Mail* (February 18, 1999), p. T1.
3. Erika Rasmusson, "Wanted: Profitable Customers," *Sales and Marketing Management* (May 1999), pp. 28–34.
4. Andrew Van Velzen, "Secular Society Gave Couple Their Niche: The Wedding Business," *The Globe and Mail* (August 14, 1989), p. C1.
5. Many economists argue that society is capable of preventing future depressions through the intelligent use of various economic policies. Thus, a recession is followed by a period of recovery.
6. The concept of environmental forecasting is examined in T.F. Mastri, "Environmental Forecasting," *Fairleigh Dickinson University Business Review* (Winter 1973), pp. 3–10.
7. Interesting articles related to this topic include Philip Kotler and Sidney J. Levy, "Demarketing, Yes, Demarketing," *Harvard Business Review* (November–December 1971), pp. 74–80; David W. Cravens, "Marketing Management in an Era of Shortages," *Business Horizons* (February 1974), pp. 79–85; A.B. Blankenship and John H. Holmes, "Will Shortages Bankrupt the Marketing Concept?" *MSU Business Topics* (Spring 1974), pp. 13–18; Philip Kotler, "Marketing during Periods of Shortages," *Journal of Marketing* (July 1974), pp. 20–29; Zohrab S. Demirdjian, "The Role of Marketing in an Economy of Affluence and Shortages," *Business and Society* (Spring 1975), pp. 15–21; Nessim Hanna, A.H. Kizilbash, and Albert Smart, "Marketing Strategy under Conditions of Economic Scarcity," *Journal of Marketing* (January 1975), pp. 63–67; Sunier C. Aggarwal, "Prepare for Continual Materials Shortages," *Harvard Business Review* (May–June 1982), pp. 6–10; Joseph Deutsch, "Effects of a Public Advertising Campaign on Consumer Behavior in a Demarketing Situation," *International Journal of Research in Marketing* 2:4 (1985), pp. 287–90; and Guprit S. Kindra, "Demarketing Inappropriate Health Care Consumption," *Journal of Health Care Marketing* 15:2 (Summer 1995), pp. 10–14.
8. John Kohut, "Competition Body Charges NutraSweet with Monopolizing Canadian Market," *The Globe and Mail* (June 2, 1989).
9. Adapted from Drew Fagan, "Tribunal Sours NutraSweet's Success," *The Globe and Mail* (October 5, 1990).
10. Consumer and Corporate Affairs, personal communication.
11. Consumer and Corporate Affairs, *Misleading Advertising Bulletin* (July–September 1986), p. 11.
12. Alan Toulin, "Pulling Cuban Pajamas Leaves Wal-Mart Exposed," *Financial Post* (March 4, 1997), p. 3.

## Chapter 3

1. See Scott M. Smith and Leland L. Beik, "Market Segmentation for Fund Raisers," *Journal of the Academy of Marketing Science* (Summer 1982), pp. 208–16.

2. CANSIM I Series 01, Table #510005 "Estimates of Population, Canada, Provinces and Territories." From http://dc2.chass.utoronto.ca/cgi-bin/cansim2/getSeriesData.pl?s=v1&b=&c=&f-plain

3. This section relies heavily on Harry H. Hiller, *Canadian Society: A Sociological Analysis* (Scarborough, ON: Prentice-Hall, 1976), pp. 13–37.

4. Statistics Canada, *Canada Year Book 1999*, p. 51.

5. Statistics Canada, *Annual Demographic Statistics, 1998*, Catalogue No. 91-213-XPB, p. 3.

6. Statistics Canada, Population by Mother Tongue, 1996 Census, http://www.statcan.ca.

7. T.R. Weir, "Population Changes in Canada, 1867–1967," *Canadian Geographer* 2:4 (1967), p. 198.

8. From www12.statcan.ca/english/census01/products/standard/popdwell/Table-UR-PS.cfm.

9. *Annual Demographic Statistics, 1998*, p. 27. Calculated from Table 3.2.

10. Larry H. Long, "On Measuring Geographic Mobility," *Journal of the American Statistical Association* (September 1970).

11. Kenneth Runyon, *Consumer Behavior* (Columbus, OH: Merrill, 1980), p. 35.

12. *Annual Demographic Statistics, 1998*, p. 14.

13. Statistics Canada, *Canada at a Glance, 1999*, Catalogue No. 12-581-XPE, p. 6.

14. These examples are from an earlier life-cycle study—see William D. Wells and George Gubar, "Life Cycle Concept in Marketing Research," *Journal of Marketing Research* (November 1966), p. 362; see also Frederick W. Derrick and Alane K. Lehfeld, "The Family Life Cycle: An Alternative Approach," *Journal of Consumer Research* (September 1980), pp. 214–17; Robin A. Douthitt, "Family Composition, Parental Time, and Market Goods: Life Cycle Trade-Offs," *Journal of Consumer Affairs* 24:1 (Summer 1990), pp. 110–33; Rob Lawson, "Patterns of Tourist Expenditure and Types of Vacation Across the Family Life Cycle," *Journal of Travel Research* 29:4 (Spring 1991),

pp. 12–18; and Fabian Linden, "Welcome to the Middle Ages," *Across the Board* 28:7 (July–August 1991), pp. 9–10.

15. Statistics Canada, *Market Research Handbook, 1999*, Catalogue No. 63-224-XPD, p. 36.

16. Statistics Canada, *Changes in Income in Canada, 1970–1980*, Catalogue No. 99-941.

17. For a complete discussion of the Environics segments see Michael Adams, *Sex in the Snow: Canadian Social Values at the End of the Millennium* (Toronto: Viking, 1997).

18. John J. Burnett, "Psychographic and Demographic Characteristics of Blood Donors," *Journal of Consumer Research* (June 1981), pp. 62–86; Mary Ann Lederhaus and Ronald J. Adams, "A Psychographic Profile of the Cosmopolitan Consumers," in *Proceedings of the Southwestern Marketing Association*, eds. Robert H. Ross, Frederic B. Kraft, and Charles H. David (Wichita, KS: Southwestern Marketing Assoc., 1981), pp. 142–45; J. Paul Merenski, "Psychographics: Valid by Definition and Reliable by Technique," *Developments in Marketing Science*, ed. Venkatakrishna V. Bellur (Miami Beach: Academy of Marketing Science, 1981), pp. 161–66; Jack A. Lesser, "The Generalizability of Psychographic Market Segments across Geographic Locations," *Journal of Marketing* 50:1 (January 1986), pp. 18–27; "Psychographics Help Marketers Find and Serve New Market Segments: Scenario for Setting Psychographics to Work," *Marketing News* 21:9 (April 24, 1987), pp. 4–5; and Rebecca Piirto, "Clothes with Attitude," *American Demographics* 12:10 (October 1990), pp. 10, 52, 54.

19. Daniel Yankelovich, "New Criteria for Market Segmentation," *Harvard Business Review* (March–April 1964), pp. 83–90.

20. Peter R. Dickson, *Marketing Management*, 2nd ed. (Fort Worth, TX: Dryden Press, 1997), p. 190.

21. Peter R. Dickson, *Marketing Management*, p. 187.

22. Statistics Canada, Population by Mother Tongue, 1996 Census, http://www.statcan.ca.

## Chapter 4

1. This section is based on materials written by J.D. Forbes, University of British Columbia.

2. "Small Clothes Are Selling Big," *Business Week* (November 16, 1981), pp. 152, 156.

3. Joseph P. Guiltinan, Gordon W. Paul, and Thomas Madden, *Marketing Management, Strategies, and Programs*, 6th ed. (New York: McGraw-Hill, 1997).

4. A similar analysis is suggested in Robert M. Fulmer, *The New Marketing* (New York: Macmillan, 1976), pp. 34–37; Philip Kotler, *Marketing Management: Analysis, Planning, Implementation, and Control*, 7th ed. (Englewood Cliffs, NJ: Prentice-Hall, 1991), pp. 263–86; E. Jerome McCarthy and William D. Perreault, *Basic Marketing: A Global Managerial Approach*, 11th ed. (Homewood, IL: Irwin, 1993), pp. 81–104; and Roger Brooksbank, "The Anatomy of Marketing Positioning Strategy," *Marketing Intelligence and Planning* 12:4 (1994), pp. 10–14.

5. "Properly Applied Psychographics Add Marketing Luster," *Marketing News* (November 12, 1982), p. 10.

6. Victoria Burrus, "A Burning Ambition," *The Globe and Mail* (August 8, 1994), p. B4.

7. Source: www.cfmmajestic.com/IR.

## Chapter 5

1. For a more detailed discussion, see Yoram Wind and Thomas S. Robertson, "Marketing Strategy: New Directions for Theory and Research," *Journal of Marketing* (Spring 1983), pp. 12–15.

2. George S. Day and Robin Wensley, "Assessing Advantage: A Framework for Diagnosing Competitive Superiority," *Journal of Marketing* (Summer 1983), p. 82.

3. This story was related by Mr. Birney during a visit to an MBA class at the University of Manitoba.

4. This list of questions is adapted from O.C. Ferrel, Michael D. Hartline, George H. Lucas, Jr., and David Luck, *Marketing Strategy* (Fort Worth, TX: Dryden Press, 1999), p. 43.

5. Peter Chandler, "Strategic Thinking," *Business Victoria* (May 1994), p. 7.

6. Alfred R. Oxenfeld and William L. Moore, "Customer or Competitor: Which Guideline for Marketing?" *Management Review* (August 1978), pp. 43–48.

7. Benson P. Shapiro, "Getting Things Done," *Harvard Business Review* (September–October, 1985), p. 28.

## Chapter 6

1. Adapted from William A. Brand, "Use the Right Measures to Track Marketing Performance," *Sales and Marketing Management in Canada* (February 1988), p. 33.

2. Adapted from Howard Schlossberg, "Customer Satisfaction Serves and Preserves," *Marketing News* (May 28, 1990), p. 8.

3. This section is based on Charlotte Klopp and John Sterlicchi, "Customer Satisfaction Just Catching on in Europe," *Marketing News* (May 28, 1990), p. 5.

4. Downloaded from www.infoquestcrm.com, May 22, 2002.

5. P.M. Dawkins and F.F. Reichheld, "Customer Retention as a Competitive Weapon," *Directors and Boards* (Summer 1990), pp. 42–47.

6. Francis Buttle and Rizal Ahmad, "Loving, Retaining and Losing Customers—How National First Bank Retains Its Corporate Direct Customers," in *Market Relationships*, Track 1, ed. Per Andersson (Stockholm: European Marketing Academy, 1998), p. 241.

7. Robert C. Blattberg, *Chain Store Age* 74 (January 1998), pp. 46–49.

8. This section is based on Jac Fitz-enz, *Benchmarking Staff Performance* (San Francisco: Jossey-Bass Publishers, 1993), pp. 8–17.

9. Rahul Jacob, "TQM, More than a Dying Fad?" *Fortune* (October 18, 1993), p. 67.

10. George Day, "CSC Index" presentation at ASAC Conference, Lake Louise, May 1993.

11. Based on Robert C. Camp, *Benchmarking: The Search for Industry Best Practices that Lead to Superior Performance* (Milwaukee: ASQC Quality Press, 1989), p. 4.

12. Katherine Doherty, "Pillsbury Measures Customer Service," *U.S. Distribution Journal* 223:12 (December 15, 1996), p. 10.

13. James T. Rothe, Michael G. Harvey, and Candice E. Jackson, "The Marketing Audit: Five Decades Later," *Journal of Marketing Theory and Practice* (Summer 1997), pp. 1–16.

14. C. Grönroos, "Relationship Marketing: The Strategy Continuum," *Journal of the Academy of Marketing Science* 23:4 (April 1995), pp. 252–54.

15. John Berry, "Marketing Automation Gives CRM a Lift," downloaded March 20, 2001, jb@empnet.com.

16. Ivan Snehota and Magnus Soderlund, "Relationship Marketing—What Does It Promise and What Does It Deliver?" in *Market Relationships*, Track 1, ed. Per Andersson (Stockholm: European Marketing Academy, 1998), p. 313.

17. "Relationship Marketing," *Chain Store Age Executive with Shopping Centre Age* 74:7 (July 1998), p. 4B.

18. This section is based on Thomas Stewart, "Brace for Japan's New Strategy," *Fortune* (September 21, 1992), pp. 63–68.

## Chapter 7

1. Official definition of the American Marketing Association.

2. John A. Gardner, "Marketing Research in Canada," in *Cases and Readings in Marketing*, ed. R.H. Rotenberg (Toronto: Holt, Rinehart and Winston, 1974), p. 221.

3. Bertram Schoner and Kenneth P. Uhl, *Marketing Research: Information Systems and Decision Making* (New York: Wiley, 1975), p. 199.

4. Source: Adapted with permission from the Gillette Web sites www.gillette.com/company/

ataglance.html and www.gillette.com/company/mission.html.

5. "Marketing Intelligence Systems: A DEW Line for Marketing Men," *Business Management* (January 1966), p. 32.

6. "Marketing Management and the Computer," *Sales Management* (August 20, 1965), pp. 49–60; see also Leon Winer, "Putting the Computer to Work in Marketing," *Pittsburgh Business Review* (November–December 1972), pp. 1–5ff; and "Computer-Assisted Marketing," *Small Business Reports* 14:5 (May 1989), pp. 76–78.

## Chapter 8

1. This definition is adapted from James F. Engel, Roger D. Blackwell, and Paul W. Miniard, *Consumer Behavior*, 7th ed. (Hinsdale, IL: Dryden Press, 1993), p. 4.

2. See Kurt Lewin, *Field Theory in Social Science* (New York: Harper and Row, 1964), p. 25; see also C. Glenn Walters, "Consumer Behavior: An Appraisal," *Journal of the Academy of Marketing Science* (Fall 1979), pp. 237–84.

3. "Learning How to Please the Baffling Japanese," *Fortune* (October 5, 1981), p. 122.

4. Adapted from Engel, Blackwell, and Miniard, *Consumer Behavior*, 7th ed., p. 63.

5. Statistics Canada, *Canada Year Book 1999*, Catalogue No. 11-402-XPE, p. 99.

6. Statistics Canada, *Market Research Handbook, 1999*, Catalogue No. 63-224-XPB, p. 104.

7. Royal Commission on Bilingualism and Biculturalism.

8. Del I. Hawkins, Kenneth A. Coney, and Roger J. Best, *Consumer Behavior: Implications for Marketing Strategy*, 5th ed. (Homewood, IL: Irwin, 1992), pp. 137–38. The quotation is adapted from S.E. Asch, "Effects of Group Pressure upon the Modification and Distortion of Judgments," in E.E. MacCoby et al., eds., *Readings in Social Psychology* (New York: Holt, Rinehart and Winston, 1958), pp. 174–83.

9. Bruce Carroll, Compusearch Web site (www.polk.ca), August 8, 1999.

10. Carroll, Compusearch Web site, August 8, 1999.

11. Gillian Rice, "Lifestages," *Academy of Marketing Science News* 2 (October 1990), p. 4.

12. Engel, Blackwell, and Miniard, *Consumer Behavior*, 7th ed., pp. 176–82; see also Wilson Brown, "The Family and Consumer Decision Making," *Journal of the Academy of Marketing Science* (Fall 1979), pp. 335–43; Gary L. Sullivan, "The Family Purchase Decision Process: A Cross-Cultural Review and Framework for Research," *Southwest Journal of Business and Economics* 6:1 (Fall 1988), pp. 43–63; Erich Kirchler, "Spouses' Joint Purchase Decisions: Determinants of Influence Tactics for Muddling through the Process," *Journal of Economic Psychology* 14:2 (June 1993), pp. 405–38; and John B. Ford, "Perception of Marital Roles in Purchase Decision Processes: A Cross-Cultural Study," *Journal of the Academy of Marketing Science* 23:2 (Spring 1995), pp. 120–31.

13. A.H. Maslow, *Motivation and Personality* (New York: Harper and Row, 1954), pp. 370–96.

14. A.H. Maslow, *Motivation and Personality*, p. 382; see also George Brooker, "The Self-Actualizing Socially Conscious Consumer," *Journal of Consumer Research* (September 1976), pp. 107–12; and James Rada, Jr., "What Makes Buyers Buy?" *American Salesman* 40:2 (February 1995), pp. 16–19.

15. E.E. Lawlor and J.L. Suttle, "A Causal Correlational Test of the Need Hierarchy Concept," *Organizational Behaviour and Human Performance* 3 (1968), pp. 12–35; see also Jerry L. Gray and Frederick A. Starke, *Organizational Behavior: Concepts and Applications*, 3rd ed. (Columbus, OH: Merrill, 1988), pp. 25–29; and James L. Gibson, John M. Ivancevich, and James H. Donnelly, Jr., *Organizations: Behavior, Structure, Processes*, 7th ed. (Homewood, IL: Irwin, 1991), pp. 102–105.

16. George Katona, *The Powerful Consumer* (New York: McGraw-Hill, 1960), p. 132; see also Engel, Blackwell, and Miniard, *Consumer Behavior*, 7th ed., pp. 490–91.

17. John Brooks, "The Little Ad That Isn't There," *Consumer Reports* (January 1958), pp. 7–10; see also Del Hawkins, "The Effects of Subliminal Stimulation on Drive Level and Brand Preference," *Journal of Marketing Research* (August 1970), pp. 322–26; and Kathryn T. Theus, "Subliminal Advertising and the Psychology of Processing Unconscious Stimuli: A Review of Research," *Psychology and Marketing* 11:3 (May–June 1994), pp. 271–90.

18. See James H. Myers and William H. Reynolds, *Consumer Behaviour and Marketing Management* (Boston: Houghton Mifflin, 1967), p. 14.

19. Richard P. Barthol and Michael J. Goldstein, "Psychology and the Invisible Sell," *California Management Review* (Winter 1959), p. 34.

20. One researcher reports that some overt behaviour in pathologically prone individuals can be influenced if they appeal to the appropriate unconscious wish: see Jack Saegert, "Another Look at Subliminal Perception," *Journal of Advertising Research* (February 1979), pp. 55–57.

21. Stuart Henderson Britt, "How Weber's Law Can Be Applied to Marketing," *Business Horizons* (February 1975), pp. 21–29.

22. Learning is perhaps the most thoroughly researched field in psychology, and several learning theories have been developed. For a discussion of these theories, see Engel, Blackwell, and Miniard, *Consumer Behavior*, 7th ed., pp. 425–55.

23. This section is based on Michael L. Rothschild and William C. Gaidis, "Behavioral Learning Theory: Its Relevance to Marketing and Promotion," *Journal of Marketing* (Spring 1981), pp. 70–78.

24. See J.P. Liefeld, "Problem Recognition," in *Consumer Decision-Making: An Annotated Bibliography* (Ottawa: Consumer and Corporate Affairs, 1979).

25. B.M. Campbell, "The Existence of Evoked Set and Determinants of Its Magnitude in Brand Choice Behavior," in John A. Howard and Lonnie Ostrom, eds., *Buyer Behavior: Theoretical and Empirical Foundations* (New York: Knopf, 1973), pp. 243–44.

26. For a thorough discussion of purchase location, see David L. Loudon and Albert J. Della Bitta, *Consumer Behavior: Concepts and Applications*, 3rd ed. (New York: McGraw-Hill, 1988), pp. 631–51.

27. These categories were originally suggested in John A. Howard, *Marketing Management Analysis and Planning* (Homewood, IL: Irwin, 1963); the discussion here is based on Donald R. Lehmann, William L. Moore, and Terry Elrod, "The Development of Distinct Choice Process Segments over Time: A Stochastic Modelling Approach," *Journal of Marketing* (Spring 1982), pp. 48–50.

## Chapter 9

1. Dartnell Corporation, "Dartnell's 30th Sales Force Compensation Survey" (Palm Beach Gardens, FL, 1999).

2. Dartnell Corporation, "Dartnell's 30th Sales Force Compensation Survey" (Palm Beach Gardens, FL, 1999).

3. The development of the new type of pole and the problems involved in its adoption are described in Arch G. Woodside, "Marketing Anatomy of Buying Process Can Help Improve Industrial Strategy," *Marketing News* (May 1, 1981), Section 2, p. 11.

4. Government of Canada, Contracts Canada, http://contractscanada.gc.ca/en/buying-e.htm#00, June 4, 2002.

5. Oracle Web site (www.oracle. com), March 22, 2000.

6. www.rbc.com, June 5, 2002.

7. Thomas F. Siems, "B2B E-Commerce: Why the New Economy Lives," *Southwest Economy*, (Federal Reserve Bank of Dallas), Issue 4, July/August 2002, p. 1.

8. Charles Phillips and Mary Meeker, "The B2B Internet Report: Collaborative Commerce." Equity

Research, Morgan Stanley Dean Witter, April 2002.

9. Scot Alaniz and Robin Roberts, "E-Procurement: A Guide to Buy-Side Applications," Stephens Inc. Internet Research, December 27, 1999.
10. Siems, *op. cit.*
11. Steve Butler, *eMarketer*, www.emarketer.com, June 19, 2000.

## Chapter 10

1. Committee on Definitions, *Marketing Definitions: A Glossary of Marketing Terms* (Chicago: American Marketing Association, 1960), pp. 9–10.
2. "A Worldwide Brand for Nissan," *Business Week* (August 24, 1981), p. 104.
3. David Aaker and Erich Joachimsthaler, *Brand Leadership* (New York: The Free Press, 2000).
4. Meir Statman and Tyzoon T. Tyebjee, "Trademarks, Patents, and Innovation in the Ethical Drug Industry," *Journal of Marketing* (Summer 1981), pp. 71–81.
5. Bill Abrams, "Brand Loyalty Rises Slightly, but Increase Could Be Fluke," *Wall Street Journal* (February 7, 1982).
6. David Aaker and Erich Joachimsthaler, *Brand Leadership* (New York: The Free Press, 2000), have a very insightful but much more complex typology in their description of brand architecture.
7. Frances Phillips, "Private Label Appliances Vie with National Brands," *Financial Post* (August 13, 1983).
8. *Market Research Facts and Trends* (November–December 1989), p. 1.
9. "Packaging Linked to Ad's Effect," *Advertising Age* (May 3, 1982), p. 63.
10. Bill Abrams and David P. Garino, "Package Design Gains Stature as Visual Competition Grows," *Wall Street Journal* (August 6, 1981).
11. Patricia Lush, "Tide's In, Plastic's Out in Environmentally Safer Pouches," *The Globe and Mail* (September 6, 1989).
12. Robert Ball, "Warm Milk Wakes Up the Packaging Industry," *Fortune* (August 7, 1982), pp. 78–82.
13. This discussion relies on Patrick E. Murphy and Ben M. Enis, "Classifying Products Stategically," *Journal of Marketing* (July 1986), pp. 24–42. Note that these authors argue that their classification system can be applied equally well to business products.

## Chapter 11

1. http://www.bombardier.com.
2. Bill Abrams, "Despite Mixed Record, Firms Still Pushing for New Products," *Wall Street Journal* (November 12, 1981).
3. A good summary of the product life cycle is contained in George S. Day, "The Product Life Cycle: Analysis and Application Issues," *Journal of Marketing* (Fall 1981), pp. 60–67; see also Gerald J. Tellis and C. Merle Crawford, "An Evolutionary Approach to Product Growth Theory," *Journal of Marketing* (Fall 1981), pp. 125–32.
4. This section relies on George S. Day, "The Product Life Cycle," pp. 60–65.
5. Ben M. Enis, Raymond LaGrace, and Arthur E. Prell, "Extending the Product Life Cycle," *Business Horizons* (June 1977), pp. 45–56.
6. William Qualls, Richard W. Olshavsky, and Ronald E. Michaels, "Shortening the PLC: An Empirical Test," *Journal of Marketing* (Fall 1981), pp. 76–80.
7. For a further discussion of fashions and fashion life cycles, see Avijit Ghosh, *Retail Management*, 2nd. ed. (Fort Worth TX: Dryden Press, 1994), pp. 340–42, or Patrick Dunne and Robert F. Lusch, *Retailing*, 3rd. ed. (Fort Worth TX: Dryden Press, 1999), pp. 339–47.
8. Enis, LaGrace, and Prell, "Extending the Product Life Cycle."
9. Gail Bronson, "Baby Food It Is, but Gerber Wants Teen-Agers to Think of It as Dessert," *Wall Street Journal* (July 17, 1981).
10. http://www.wto.org/wto/statis/stat.htm.
11. "The Money-Guzzling Genius of Biotechnology," *The Economist* (May 13, 1989), p. 69.
12. David S. Hopkins, *New Product Winners and Losers* (New York: Conference Board, 1980); see also "Booz Allen Looks at New Products' Role," *Wall Street Journal* (March 26, 1981).
13. Abrams, "Despite Mixed Record," p. 25.
14. Robert Cooper, "The New Prod System: The Industry Experience," *Journal of Product Innovation Management* (June 1992), pp. 113–27.
15. Roger Calantone and Robert G. Cooper, "New Product Scenarios: Prospects for Success," *Journal of Marketing* (Spring 1981), p. 49.
16. Robert G. Cooper, "The Myth of the Better Mousetrap: What Makes a New Product a Success?" *Business Quarterly* (Spring 1981), pp. 71, 72.
17. Reported in Ann M. Morrison, "The General Mills Brand of Manager," *Fortune* (January 12, 1981), pp. 99–107; another interesting discussion appears in "Brand Management System Is Best, but Refinements Needed," *Marketing News* (July 9, 1982), p. 12.
18. Jacob M. Duker and Michael V. Laric, "The Product Manager: No Longer on Trial," in *The Changing Marketing Environment: New Theories and Applications*, eds. Kenneth Bernhardt et al. (Chicago: American Marketing Association, 1981), pp. 93–96; and Peter S. Howsam and G. David Hughes, "Product Management System Suffers from Insufficient Experience, Poor Communication," *Marketing News* (June 26, 1981), p. 8.
19. Adapted from John R. Rockwell and Marc C. Particelli, "New Product Strategy: How the Pros Do It," *Industrial Marketing* (May 1982), p. 50.
20. Rockwell and Particelli, "New Product Strategy," p. 50.
21. Quoted in Mary McCabe English, "Marketers: Better than a Coin Flip," *Advertising Age* (February 9, 1981), p. S-15. Copyright 1981 by Crain Communications, Inc.
22. Dylan Landis, "Durable Goods for a Test?" *Advertising Age* (February 9, 1981), pp. S-18, S-19.
23. Everett M. Rogers, *Diffusion of Innovations*, 4th ed. (New York: Free Press, 1995), pp. 243–51.

24. For a discussion of the characteristics of early adopters, see Jagish N. Sheth, Banwari Mittal, and Bruce I. Newman, *Customer Behaviour* (Orlando, FL: Harcourt Brace, 1999), pp. 320–22, and Frank Alpert, "Innovator Buying Behaviour Over Time: The Innovator Buying Cycle and the Cumulative Effects of Innovations," *Journal of Product and Brand Management* 3:2 (1994), pp. 50–62.

25. Ronald Marks and Eugene Hughes, "Profiling the Consumer Innovator," in *Evolving Marketing Thought for 1980*, eds. John H. Summey and Ronald D. Taylor (New Orleans: Southern Marketing Association, 1980), pp. 115–18; Elizabeth Hirschman, "Innovativeness, Novelty Seeking and Consumer Creativity," *Journal of Consumer Research* (December 1980), pp. 283–95; and Richard W. Olshavsky, "Time and the Rate of Adoption of Innovations," *Journal of Consumer Research* (March 1980), pp. 425–28.

26. For a more thorough discussion of the speed of the adoption process, see Everett M. Rogers, *Diffusion of Innovations*, 4th ed.

## Chapter 12

1. Christine Roy, *The Services Industries and Trade in Services*, Statistics Canada, 63F0002X1B No. 36, August 2001.

2. World Trade Organization, *International Trade Statistics, 2001*, http://www.wto.org/english/res_e/statis_e/its2001_e/chp_4_e.pdf.

3. L. Berry, "Services Marketing Is Different," in *Marketing Management and Strategy: A Reader*, eds. P. Kotler and K.K. Cox (Englewood Cliffs, NJ: Prentice-Hall, 1988), p. 278.

4. A. Rushton and D. Carson, "The Marketing of Services: Managing the Intangibles," *European Journal of Marketing* (1989), p. 31.

5. J. Bateson, "Do We Need Services Marketing?" in *Marketing Management and Strategy*, eds. Kotler and Cox, pp. 278–86.

6. Valarie A. Zeithaml, A. Parasuraman, and Leonard L. Berry, "Problems and Strategies in Services Marketing," *Journal of Marketing* (Spring 1985), p. 33.

7. Theodore Levitt, "The Industrialization of Service," *Harvard Business Review* (September–October 1976), pp. 63–74.

8. L. Berry, "Services Marketing Is Different," p. 281.

9. L. Berry, "Services Marketing Is Different," p. 281.

10. Christian Grönroos, *Service Management and Marketing*, 2nd edition (Toronto: John Wiley and Sons, Ltd., 2000), p. 331.

11. V.A. Zeithaml and M.J. Biotner, *Services Marketing*, 3rd ed. (Toronto: McGraw-Hill Irwin, 2003), p. 319.

12. G.L. Shostack, "Breaking Free from Product Marketing," *Journal of Marketing* (April 1977), pp. 73–80.

13. L. Berry, "Services Marketing Is Different," p. 281; and A. Rushton and D. Carson, "The Marketing of Services," p. 31.

14. A. Parasuraman, Valarie Zeithaml, and Leonard Berry, "A Conceptual Model of Service Quality and Its Implications for Future Research," *Journal of Marketing* 49 (Fall 1985), pp. 41–50.

## Chapter 13

1. Adapted from David J. Schwartz, *Marketing Today*, copyright © 1981 by Harcourt Brace Jovanovich, Inc.

2. This section is adapted from Edwin G. Dolan, *Basic Economics* (Toronto: Holt, Rinehart, and Winston, 1984), pp. 57–58; and Ross D. Eckert and Richard H. Leftwich, *Price System and Resource Allocation*, 10th ed. (Chicago: Dryden Press, 1988), pp. 55–58.

3. For a discussion of the application of price elasticity to a consumer service, see Steven J. Skinner, Terry L. Childers, and Wesley H. Jones, "Consumer Responsiveness to Price Differentials: A Case for Insurance Industry Deregulation," *Journal of Business Research* (December 1981), pp. 381–96.

4. Some problems of using economic models in practice are discussed in Kent B. Monroe and Albert J. Della Bitta, "Models of Pricing Decisions," *Journal of Marketing Research* (August 1978), pp. 413–28; see also Robert J. Dolan and Abel P. Jeuland, "Experience Curves and Dynamic Models: Implications for Optional Pricing Strategies," *Journal of Marketing* (Winter 1981), pp. 52–62.

5. See Mary Louise Hatten, "Don't Get Caught with Your Prices Down: Pricing in Inflationary Times," *Business Horizons* (March–April 1982), pp. 23–28.

## Chapter 14

1. See William J. Baumol, "On the Theory of Oligopoly," *Economica* (August 1958), pp. 187–98; see also William J. Baumol, *Business Behavior, Value, and Growth* (New York: Harcourt Brace and World, 1967).

2. An interesting discussion appears in Carl R. Frear and John E. Swan, "Marketing Managers' Motivation to Revise Their Market Share Goals: An Expectancy Theory Analysis," in *Southwestern Marketing Proceedings*, eds. Robert H. Ross, Frederic B. Kraft, and Charles H. Davis (Wichita, KS: 1981), pp. 13–16; see also William Brand, "Pricing Strategies for Profit," *Sales and Marketing Management in Canada* 27:11 (December 1986), pp. 30–31.

3. Walter J. Primeaux, Jr., "The Effect of Consumer Knowledge and Bargaining Strength on Final Selling Price: A Case Study," *Journal of Business* (October 1970), pp. 419–26; another excellent article is James R. Krum, "Variable Pricing as a Promotional Tool," *Atlanta Economic Review* (November–December 1977), pp. 47–50.

4. Bernie Faust et al., "Effective Retail Pricing Policy," *Purdue Retailer* (Lafayette, IN: Agricultural Economics, 1963), p. 2.

5. Karl A. Shilliff, "Determinants of Consumer Price Sensitivity for Selected Supermarket Products: An Empirical Investigation," *Akron Business and Economic Review* (Spring 1975), pp. 26–32.

6. John F. Willenborg and Robert E. Pitts, "Perceived Situational Effects on

Price Sensitivity," *Journal of Business Research* (March 1977), pp. 27–38.

7. Jack C. Horn, "The High-Class Nickel Discount," *Psychology Today* (September 1982).

8. See David M. Georgoff, "Price Illusion and the Effect of Odd–Even Retail Pricing," *Southern Journal of Business* (April 1969), pp. 95–103; see also Dik W. Twedt, "Does the '9 Fixation in Retailing Really Promote Sales?" *Journal of Marketing* (October 1965), pp. 54–55; Benson P. Shapiro, "The Psychology of Pricing," *Harvard Business Review* (July–August 1968), pp. 14–16; David M. Georgoff, *Odd–Even Retail Price Endings: Their Effects on Value Determination, Product Perception, and Buying Propensities* (East Lansing, MI: Michigan State University, 1972); and JoAnn Carmin, "Pricing Strategies for Menus: Magic or Myth?" *Cornell Hotel and Restaurant Administration Quarterly* 31:3 (November 1990), pp. 44–50.

9. See, for instance, I. Robert Andrews and Enzo R. Valenzi, "The Relationship between Price and Blind-Rated Quality for Margarines and Butter," *Journal of Marketing Research* (August 1970), pp. 393–95; Robert A. Peterson, "The Price–Perceived Quality Relationship: Experimental Evidence," *Journal of Marketing Research* (November 1970), pp. 525–28; David M. Gardner, "An Experimental Investigation of the Price/Quality Relationship," *Journal of Retailing* (Fall 1970), pp. 25–41; Arthur G. Bedelan, "Consumer Perception as an Indicator of Product Quality," *MSU Business Topics* (Summer 1971), pp. 59–65; and R.S. Mason, "Price and Product Quality Assessment," *European Journal of Marketing* (Spring 1974), pp. 29–41.

10. J. Douglass McConnell, "An Experimental Examination of the Price–Quality Relationship," *Journal of Business* (October 1968), pp. 439–44; see also J. Douglass McDonnell, "The Alphabet and Price as Independent Variables: A Note on the Price–Quality Question," *Journal of Business* (October 1970), pp. 448–51;

Jerry B. Gotlieb, "Effects of Price Advertisements on Perceived Quality and Purchase Intentions," *Journal of Business Research* 22:3 (May 1991), pp. 195–210; and William B. Dodds, "Effects of Price, Brand, and Store Information on Buyers' Product Evaluations," *Journal of Marketing Research* 28:3 (August 1991), pp. 307–19.

11. James H. Myers and William H. Reynolds, *Consumer Behavior and Marketing Management* (Boston: Houghton-Mifflin, 1967), p. 47.

12. See Kent B. Monroe and M. Venkatesan, "The Concepts of Price Limits and Psychophysical Measurement: A Laboratory Experiment," in *Marketing Involvement in Society and the Economy*, ed. Philip R. McDonald (Cincinnati: American Marketing Association, 1969), pp. 345–51.

13. *Market Spotlight* (Edmonton: Alberta Consumer and Corporate Affairs, March 1979).

14. J. Edward Russo, "The Value of Unit Price Information," *Journal of Marketing Research* (May 1977), pp. 193–201.

15. This is one of many important terms outlined in a publication called *INCOTERMS*, published in Paris in September 1999 by the International Chamber of Commerce.

## Chapter 15

1. Committee on Definitions, *Marketing Definitions: A Glossary of Marketing Terms* (Chicago: American Marketing Association, 1960), p. 10; some authors limit the definition to the route taken by the title to the goods, but this definition also includes agent wholesaling intermediaries who do not take title but who do serve as an important component of many channels.

2. This section is adapted from Louis W. Stern and Adel I. El-Ansary, *Marketing Channels*, 3rd ed. (Englewood Cliffs, NJ: Prentice-Hall, 1989), pp. 7–12.

3. The first five functions were developed in Wroe Alderson, "Factors Governing the Development of

Marketing Channels," in *Marketing Channels for Manufactured Products*, ed. Richard M. Clewitt (Homewood, IL: Irwin, 1954), pp. 5–22.

4. Donald A. Fuller, "Aluminum Beverage Container Recycling in Florida: A Commentary," *Atlanta Economic Review* (January–February 1977), p. 41.

5. Industry, Science and Technology Canada, *Wholesale Trade Industry Profile* (Ottawa, 1988), p. 7.

6. An interesting discussion of types of wholesaling appears in J. Howard Westing, "Wholesale Indifference," *The Courier* (Spring 1982), pp. 3, 8.

7. James R. Moore and Kendell A. Adams, "Functional Wholesaler Sales Trends and Analysis," in *Combined Proceedings*, ed. Edward M. Mazze (Chicago: American Marketing Association, 1976), pp. 402–405.

8. Lawson A.W. Hunter, "Buying Groups," *Agriculture Canada: Food Market Commentary* 5:4, p. 15.

9. Downloaded from Francon Canada Web site at http://www.francon.com/CDNFACTS.htm.

10. Combines Investigation Act, Part IV.1, 31.4, 1976.

## Chapter 16

1. "Canuck," *Pen Pictures of Early Pioneer Life in Upper Canada* (Toronto: Coles, 1972), pp. 80–82.

2. Interesting discussions include Sak Onkvisit and John J. Shaw, "Modifying the Retail Classification System for More Timely Marketing Strategies," *Journal of the Academy of Marketing Science* (Fall 1981), pp. 436–53; and Bobby C. Vaught, L. Lyn Judd, and Jack M. Starling, "The Perceived Importance of Retailing Strategies and Their Relationships to Four Indexes of Retailing Success," in *Progress in Marketing: Theory and Practice*, eds. Ronald D. Taylor, John J. Bennen, and John H. Summey (Carbondale, IL: Southern Marketing Association, 1981), pp. 25–28.

3. A good discussion appears in Mary Carolyn Harrison and Alvin C. Burns, "A Case for Departmentalizing Target Market Strategy in Department

Stores," in *Progress in Marketing: Theory and Practice*, eds. Taylor, Bennen, and Summey, pp. 21–24.

4. Clayton Sinclair, "The New Priorities for Shopping Centres," *The Financial Times of Canada* (March 21, 1983).

5. The following discussion of Reilly and Huff's work is adapted from Joseph Barry Mason and Morris Lehman Mayer, *Modern Retailing: Theory and Practice*, 5th ed. (Homewood, IL: BPI/Irwin, 1990), pp. 679–81.

6. Retail images are discussed in a variety of articles, for example, Pradeep K. Korgaonbar and Kamal M. El Sheshai, "Assessing Retail Competition with Multidimensional Scaling," *Business* (April–June 1982), pp. 30–33; Jack K. Kasulis and Robert F. Lush, "Validating the Retail Store Image Concept," *Journal of the Academy of Marketing Science* (Fall 1981), pp. 419–35; and Julie Baker, "The Influence of Store Environment on Quality Inferences and Store Image," *Journal of the Academy of Marketing Science* 22:4 (Fall 1994), pp. 328–39.

7. This section is based on Avijit Ghosh, *Retail Management*, 2nd ed. (Fort Worth, TX: Dryden Press, 1994), pp. 59–60.

8. Some of this section is based on Ken Jones, Wendy Evans, and Christine Smith, "New Formats in the Canadian Retail Economy," paper presented at the Retailing and Services Conference, Lake Louise, Alberta (May 7–10, 1994).

9. Superstores are discussed in Myron Gable and Ronald D. Michman, "Superstores—Revolutionizing Distribution," *Business* (March–April 1981), pp. 14–18.

10. This section is based on Tamsen Tilson, "Multilevel Marketing Sells Costly Dreams," *The Globe and Mail* (October 6, 1994).

11. Tyler Hamilton, "Sold on the Web," *The Globe and Mail* (March 11, 1999), p. T1.

12. Statistics Canada, *Vending Machine Operators, 1988*, Catalogue No. 63-213.

13. Jagdish N. Sheth, Rajendra S. Sisodia, in Jagdish N. Sheth, Abdoloreza Eshghi, and Balaji C. Krishnan, "Consumer Behavior in the Future," in *Internet Marketing* (Toronto: Thomson Learning, 2001), p. 78.

14. RBC Financial Group/Ipsos-Reid, "Canadian Families and the Internet," http://www.ipsos-reid.com/media/dsp_displaypr_us.cfm?id_to_view=1405 May 31, 2002.

15. NFO CFgroup, downloaded from http://www.nfocfgroup.com/news/01.06.12-corm.pdf, May 26, 2002.

16. Source: Industry Canada, "Electronic Commerce and Technology Survey," Statistics Canada: 2002-01-21.

17. Source: Industry Canada, "Electronic Commerce and Technology Survey," Statistics Canada: 2002-01-217.

18. Raymond Burke, "Do You See What I See? The Future of Virtual Shopping," p. 151 in Jagdish N. Sheth, Abdoloreza Eshghi, and Balaji C. Krishnan, *Internet Marketing*.

19. Robert A. Peterson, Sridhar Balasubramanian, and Bart J. Bronnenberg, 1997, "Exploring the Implications of the Internet for Consumer Marketing," *Journal of the Academy of Marketing Science* 25 (Fall) 1997.

20. This section is based on Industry Canada, "Canadian Internet Retailing Report," http:// strategis.ic.gc.ca/SSG/ir01582e.html, September 27, 1999.

## Chapter 17

1. Peter R. Dickson, *Marketing Management* (Fort Worth, TX: Dryden Press, 1997), p. 457.

2. Ram Ganeshan and Terry P. Harrison, *An Introduction to Supply Chain Management*, Penn State University. URL: http://silmaril.smeal.psu.edu/misc/supply_chain_intro.html

3. www.logistics.about.com, June 16, 2002.

4. The four pillars and their descriptions are based on John T. Landry, "Supply Chain Management: The Case for Alliances," *Harvard Business Review* 76 (November– December 1998), pp. 24–25.

5. Ibid.

6. Michael D. Hutt, Thomas W. Speh, *Business Marketing Management*, (Orlando: Harcourt, 2001), p. 154.

7. Sherry Butt, "Planning for Success," *Calgary Sun*, Resource and Supply Chain Management Supplement (January 1999), p. 2.

## Chapter 18

1. Don E. Schultz, "Integrated Marketing Communications: Maybe Definition Is in the Point of View," *Marketing News* (January 18, 1993), p. 17.

2. Similar communications processes are suggested in David K. Berlo, *The Process of Communications* (New York: Holt, Rinehart and Winston, 1960), pp. 23–38; and Thomas S. Robertson, *Innovative Behavior and Communication* (New York: Holt, Rinehart and Winston, 1971), p. 122; see also Claude Shannon and Warren Weaver, *The Mathematical Theory of Communication* (Urbana, IL: University of Illinois Press, 1978), p. 7; and Wilbur Schramm, "The Nature of Communication between Humans," in *The Process and Effects of Mass Communication*, rev. ed. (Urbana, IL: University of Illinois Press, 1971), pp. 3–53.

3. Wilbur Schramm, "The Nature of Communication between Humans," pp. 3–53.

4. S. Watson Dunn and Arnold M. Barban, *Advertising: Its Role in Modern Marketing*, 7th ed. (Chicago: Dryden Press, 1990), p. 9.

5. Committee on Definitions, *Marketing Definitions: A Glossary of Marketing Terms* (Chicago: American Marketing Association, 1960), p. 20.

6. Extrapolation based on "Dartnell's 30th Sales Force Compensation Survey" (Palm Beach Gardens, FL, 1999), p. 20.

7. Terrence V. O'Brien, "Psychologists Take a New Look at Today's Consumer," *Arizona Review* (August–September 1970), p. 2.

## Chapter 19

1. Canadian Media Directors' Council, *Media Digest, 1998–99*, p. 11. Publication can be accessed on-line at http:// www.marketingmag.ca.

2. This section follows in part the discussion in S. Watson Dunn and Arnold M. Barban, *Advertising: Its Role in Modern Marketing*, 7th ed. (Chicago: Dryden Press, 1990), pp. 16–19.

3. William M. Carley, "Gillette Co. Struggles as Its Rivals Slice at Fat Profit Margin," *Wall Street Journal* (February 2, 1972), p. 1.

4. Ralph B. Weller, C. Richard Roberts, and Colin Neuhaus, "A Longitudinal Study of the Effect of Erotic Content upon Advertising Brand Recall," *Current Issues and Research in Advertising* (1979), pp. 145–61.

5. Marina Strauss, "Ontario Judge Rules Pie Crust Ads Are Half-Baked," *The Globe and Mail* (October 14, 1994), p. B1.

6. Marina Strauss, "Vending Machines Get the Picture," *The Globe and Mail* (August 18, 1994), p. B6.

7. Rex Briggs, Jessica Sullivan, and Ian Webster, "Australian Online Advertising Effectiveness Study 2001," A.C. Nielsen Consultants, www.consult.com.au/adeffectivenes_jul_2001.shtml

8. www.doubleclick.com, June 26, 2002.

9. This section draws from Jim Steinhart, "Their Aim Is True," *The Globe and Mail* (February 15, 1994).

10. Ken Riddel, "New Study Shows Sales Promotion Spending May Be Inflated," *Marketing Magazine* (April 23, 1990), pp. 1, 3.

11. Walter A. Gaw, *Specialty Advertising* (Chicago: Specialty Advertising Association, 1970), p. 7.

12. Maurice Simms, "Retailers Pin Hope on Marketing Skill," *The Globe and Mail* (February 15, 1994), p. B28.

13. http://www.hbc.com/zellers

14. Terrance A. Shimp, *Advertising, Promotion, and Supplemental Aspects of Integrated Marketing Communications* (Fort Worth, TX: Dryden Press, 1997), p. 554.

15. Johanna Powell, "Mascot Maker Finds Success Is Little More than Child's Play," *Financial Post* (September 11, 1989).

## Chapter 20

1. All prices quoted in U.S. dollars.

2. http://www.economist.com/Story_ID=1098872, 5/12/2002

3. This section is adapted from "About the WTO: The Case for Open Trade," World Trade Organization, http://www.wto.org/wto/about/facts3.htm, June 21, 1999.

4. Warren Keegan, *Global Marketing Management* (New York: McGraw-Hill, 1989), pp. 31–33.

5. Philip R. Cateara and John L. Graham, *International Marketing* (Boston: Irwin/McGraw-Hill, 1999), p. 331.

6. Robert L. Kohls, *Survival Kit for Overseas Living*, (Chicago: Intercultural ZPress, 1979), p. 3.

7. George P. Mundak, "The Common Denominator of Cultures," in *The Science of Man in the World*, ed. Ralph Linton (New York: Columbia University Press, 1945), 123–142.

8. Edward T. Hall, "The Silent Language of Overseas Business," *Harvard Business Review* 38, May–June 1960, p. 87–96.

9. www.culturalsavvy.com, July 27, 2002.

10. "Northern Telecom: Mastering the International Market," *Business to Business Marketing* 94:13 (March 27, 1989), p. B12.

11. This paragraph is adapted from "About the WTO: Summary," World Trade Organization, http://www.wto.org/wto/about/facts0.htm, June 21, 1999.

12. These five principles are excerpted from "About the WTO: Principles of the Trading System," World Trade Organization, http://www.wto.org/about/facts2.htm, June 21, 1999.

## Chapter 21

1. Also referred to as "not-for-profit" organizations; we will use the two terms interchangeably in this chapter.

2. Philip Kotler, *Marketing for Nonprofit Organizations* (Englewood Cliffs, NJ: Prentice-Hall, 1982), p. 9.

3. These differences and others are outlined in Harvey W. Wallender, III, "Managing Not-for-Profit Enterprises," *Academy of Management Review* (January 1978), p. 26; Cecily

Cannon Selby, "Better Performance for 'Nonprofits,'" *Harvard Business Review* (September–October 1978), pp. 93–95; see also John M. Gwin, "Constituent Analysis: A Paradigm for Marketing Effectiveness in the Not-for-Profit Organization," *European Journal of Marketing* 24:7 (1990), pp. 43–48; and Katherine Gallagher, "Coping with Success: New Challenges for Nonprofit Marketing," *Sloan Management Review* 33:1 (Fall 1991), pp. 27–42.

4. Kotler, *Marketing for Nonprofit Organizations*, p. 482.

5. Alan R. Andreason, *Marketing Social Change: Changing Behaviour to Promote Health, Social Development and the Environment* (San Francisco: Jossey-Bass, 1995), p. 7.

6. David J. Rachman and Elaine Romano, *Modern Marketing* (Hinsdale, IL: Dryden Press, 1980), p. 576; the delineation of person, social, and organization marketing is proposed by Professors Rachman and Romano.

7. James M. Stearns, John R. Kerr, and Robert R. McGrath, "Advances of Marketing for Functional Public Policy Administration," in *Proceedings of the Southern Marketing Association*, eds. Robert S. Franz, Robert M. Hopkins, and Alfred G. Toma (Atlanta, GA: November 1979), pp. 140–43.

8. This section is based on Philip Kotler, *Marketing for Nonprofit Organizations*, pp. 306–309; see also Chris T. Allen, "Self-Perception Based Strategies for Stimulating Energy Conservation," *Journal of Consumer Research* (March 1982), pp. 381–90.

9. Michael L. Rothschild, "Marketing Communications in Nonbusiness Situations or Why It's So Hard to Sell Brotherhood Like Soap," *Journal of Marketing* (Spring 1979), pp. 11–20.

**ABSOLUTE ADVANTAGE** A nation has an absolute advantage in the marketing of a product if it is the sole producer or can produce a product for less than anyone else.

**ACCELERATOR PRINCIPLE** The disproportionate impact that changes in consumer demand have on business market demand.

**ACCESSORY EQUIPMENT** Second-level capital items that are used in the production of products and services but are usually less expensive and shorter-lived than installations.

**ADOPTION PROCESS** A series of stages consumers go through, from learning of a new product to trying it and deciding to purchase it regularly or to reject it.

**ADVERTISING** Paid nonpersonal communication through various media by business firms, nonprofit organizations, and individuals who are in some way identified with the advertising message and who hope to inform or persuade members of a particular audience.

**ADVERTISING AGENCY** A marketing specialist firm that assists the advertiser in planning and preparing its advertisements.

**AFFECTIVE COMPONENT** One's feelings or emotional reactions.

**AGENT** A wholesaling intermediary that differs from the typical wholesaler in that the agent does not take title to the goods.

**AIO STATEMENTS** Statements about activities, interests, and opinions that are used in developing psychographic profiles.

**APPROACH** The initial contact between the salesperson and the prospective customer.

**ASCH PHENOMENON** The impact that groups and group norms can exhibit on individual behaviour.

**ASPIRATIONAL GROUP** A type of reference group with which individuals wish to associate.

**ATTITUDES** A person's enduring favourable or unfavourable evaluations of some object or idea.

**AUCTION HOUSE** An agent wholesaling intermediary that brings buyers and sellers together in one location and allows potential buyers to inspect the merchandise before purchasing through a public bidding process.

**AVERAGE COST** Obtained by dividing total cost by the quantity associated with this cost.

**AVERAGE VARIABLE COST** The total variable cost divided by the related quantity.

**BALANCE OF PAYMENTS** The flow of money into or out of a country.

**BALANCE OF TRADE** The relationship between a country's exports and its imports.

**B2B E-COMMERCE** Doing business online through Internet-enabled marketplaces.

**BCG GROWTH-SHARE MATRIX** Plots market share relative to the market share of the largest competitor, against market growth rate.

**BENCHMARKING** The comparison of performance with industry best practices.

**BENEFIT SEGMENTATION** Depends on advanced marketing research techniques that focus on benefits the consumer expects to derive from a product.

**BIDS** Price quotations from potential suppliers.

**BOTTOM LINE** The overall-profitability measure of performance.

**BRAND** A name, term, sign, symbol, or design (or some combination of these) used to identify the products of one firm and to differentiate them from competitive offerings.

**BRAND ARCHITECTURE** The relationship between a company's products, brands, and sub-brands.

**BRAND EQUITY** Represents the value customers (and the stock markets) place on the sum of the history the customer has had with a brand.

**BRAND EXTENSION** The decision to use a popular brand name for a new product entry in an unrelated product category.

**BRAND FAMILIARITY** The first stage of brand loyalty, when a firm has developed enough publicity for a brand that its name is familiar to consumers.

**BRAND INSISTENCE** The ultimate stage of brand loyalty, when consumers will accept no alternatives and will search extensively for the product.

**BRAND NAME** Words, letters, or symbols that make up a name used to identify and distinguish the firm's offerings from those of its competitors.

**BRAND PREFERENCE** The second stage of brand loyalty, when, based on previous experience, consumers will choose a product rather than one of its competitors—if it is available.

**BREAK-BULK WAREHOUSE** Receives consolidated shipments from a central distribution centre, and then distributes them in smaller shipments to individual customers in more limited areas.

**BREAK-EVEN ANALYSIS** A means of determining the number of goods or services that must be sold at a given price in order to generate sufficient revenue to cover total costs.

**BROKER** An agent wholesaling intermediary that brings buyers and sellers together; operates in industries with a large number of small suppliers and purchasers.

**BUSINESS-TO-BUSINESS MARKET** Firms that produce or acquire goods and services to be used, directly or indirectly, in the production of other goods and services or to be resold.

**BUYING CENTRE** The key individuals who participate in a buying decision.

**BUZZ MARKETING** Giving a significant person in a social system a product to use in the hope that others will see and want to buy the product.

**CANNIBALIZING** Situation involving one product taking sales from another offering in a product line.

**CAPITAL ITEMS** Long-lived business assets that must be depreciated over time.

**CARTEL** The monopolistic organization of a group of firms.

**CASH-AND-CARRY WHOLESALER** Limited-function merchant wholesaler that performs most wholesaling functions except financing and delivery.

**CASH DISCOUNT** Reduction in price that is given for prompt payment of a bill.

**CATALOGUE RETAILER** Retailer that mails catalogues to its customers and operates from a showroom displaying samples of its products.

**CELEBRITY MARKETING** Having celebrities lend their name and influence to the promotion of a product.

**CENSUS** A collection of marketing data from all possible sources.

**CHAIN STORE** Group of retail stores that are centrally owned and managed and that handle the same lines of products.

**CHANNEL CAPTAIN** The most dominant member of the distribution channel.

**CHANNEL CONFLICT** Rivalry and conflict between channel members because of sometimes different objectives and needs.

**CLOSING** The act of asking the prospect for an order.

**CLUSTER SAMPLE** A probability sample that is generated by randomly choosing one or more areas or population clusters and then surveying all members in the chosen cluster(s).

**COGNITIVE COMPONENT** The knowledge and beliefs one has about an object or concept.

**COGNITIVE DISSONANCE** The postpurchase anxiety that occurs when there is a discrepancy between a person's knowledge and beliefs (cognitions).

**COMMISSION MERCHANT** An agent wholesaling intermediary that takes possession when the producer ships goods to a central market for sale.

**COMMON CARRIER** Transportation carrier that provides service to the general public, and is subject to regulatory authority including fee setting.

**COMMON MARKET** A customs union that also allows factors of production such as labour, capital, and technology to flow freely among members.

**COMMUNICATION** Personal selling, advertising, sales promotion, and publicity.

**COMPANY ELASTICITY** Refers to the sensitivity to changes in price that a particular company or brand faces.

**COMPARATIVE ADVANTAGE** A nation has a comparative advantage if it can produce a given product more efficiently per unit of output than it can produce other products.

**COMPARATIVE ADVERTISING** Advertising that makes direct promotional comparisons with competitive brands.

**COMPETITIVE BIDDING** A process by which buyers request potential suppliers to make price quotations on a proposed purchase or contract.

**COMPETITIVE ENVIRONMENT** The interactive process that occurs in the marketplace in which different organizations seek to satisfy similar markets.

**COMPONENT PARTS AND MATERIALS** Finished business-to-business goods that actually become part of the final product.

**CONATIVE COMPONENT** The way one tends to act or behave.

**CONCEPT TESTING** A marketing research project that attempts to measure consumer attitudes and perceptions relevant to a new-product idea.

**CONSUMER BEHAVIOUR** The activities of individuals in obtaining, using, and disposing of goods and services, including the decision processes that precede and follow these actions.

**CONSUMER GOODS** Those products and services purchased by the ultimate consumer for personal use.

**CONSUMER INNOVATORS** The first purchasers—those who buy a product at the beginning of its life cycle.

**CONTAINERIZATION** Combining several unitized loads.

**CONTRACT CARRIER** Transportation carrier that serves only customers it has contracts with. Contracts include rates to be charged.

**CONVENIENCE PRODUCTS** Products that are lowest in terms of both effort and risk.

**CONVENIENCE SAMPLE** A nonprobability sample based on the selection of readily available respondents.

**COOPERATIVE ADVERTISING** The sharing of advertising costs between the retailer and the manufacturer.

**CORPORATE STRATEGY** The overall purpose and direction of the organization that is established in the light of the challenges and opportunities found in the environment, as well as available organizational resources.

**COST-PLUS PRICING** Pricing technique using base cost figure per unit to which is added a markup to cover unassigned costs and to provide a profit.

**COST TRADEOFFS** Approach that assumes that some functional areas of the firm will experience cost increases while others will have cost decreases.

**CREATIVE SELLING** Selling that involves making the buyer see the worth of the item.

**CREDENCE QUALITIES** Qualities for which, even after purchasing, the buyer must simply trust that the supplier has performed the correct service.

**CRM SOFTWARE** Software designed to analyze a customer database and determine customer needs and characteristics.

**CUE** Any object existing in the environment that determines the nature of the response to a drive.

**CULTURE** An integrated system of learned behaviour patterns that are distinguishing characteristics of the members of any given society.

**CUSTOMER RELATIONSHIP MARKETING (CRM)** Identifying and establishing, maintaining and enhancing, and, when necessary, also terminating relationships with customers and other stakeholders so that the objectives of all parties involved are met, through a mutual exchange and fulfillment of promises.

**CUSTOMER SATISFACTION MANAGEMENT (CSM)** A program that focuses on identifying key performance areas to meet or exceed the average customer's expectations.

**CUSTOMS UNION** Agreement among two or more nations that establishes a free trade area, plus a uniform tariff for trade with nonmember nations.

**DATABASE MARKETING** Creation of a marketing plan based on the use of database technology to define the characteristics and needs of customers.

**DEMAND VARIABILITY** In the business market, the impact of derived demand on the demand for interrelated products used in producing consumer goods.

**DEMARKETING** The process of cutting consumer demand for a product, because the demand exceeds the level that can reasonably be supplied by the firm or because doing so will create a more favourable corporate image.

**DEMOGRAPHIC SEGMENTATION** Dividing an overall market on the basis of characteristics such as age, gender, and income level.

**DEMONSTRATION** Actions that supplement, support, and reinforce what the salesperson has already told the prospect.

**DEPARTMENT STORE** Large retailer that handles a variety of merchandise.

**DEPRECIATION** The accounting concept of charging a portion of the cost of a capital item as a deduction against the company's annual revenue for purposes of determining its net income.

**DERIVED DEMAND** Demand for a product used by business derived from (or linked to) demand for a consumer good.

**DEVALUATION** Situation in which a nation reduces the value of its currency in relation to gold or some other currency.

**DIFFERENTIATION TRIANGLE** Differentiation of a retail store from competitors in the same strategic group through price, location, and store atmosphere and service.

**DIFFUSION PROCESS** The filtering and acceptance of new products and services by the members of a community or social system.

**DIRECT INTERNATIONAL TRADE** Exporting directly to markets and/or importing directly from suppliers in other countries.

**DIRECT INVESTMENT** The ownership and management of production and/or marketing facilities in a foreign country.

**DIRECT RESPONSE MARKETING** An interactive system of marketing that uses one or more advertising media to effect a measurable response directly to the advertiser.

**DIRECT-RESPONSE WHOLESALER** Limited-function merchant wholesaler that relies on catalogues rather than on a sales force to contact retail, industrial, and institutional customers.

**DIRECT-SALES RESULTS TEST** A test that attempts to ascertain for each dollar of promotional outlay the corresponding increase in revenue.

**DISASSOCIATIVE GROUP** A type of reference group with which an individual does not want to be identified.

**DISCOUNT HOUSE** Retailer that, in exchange for reduced prices, does not offer such traditional retail services as credit, sales assistance by clerks, and delivery.

**DISTRIBUTION** The selection and management of marketing channels and the physical distribution of goods.

**DISTRIBUTION CHANNELS** The paths that goods—and title to these goods—follow from producer to consumer.

**DISTRIBUTION WAREHOUSE** Designed to assemble and then redistribute products.

**DRIVE** Any strong stimulus that impels action.

**DROP SHIPPER** Limited-function merchant wholesaler that takes orders from customers and places them with producers, which then ship directly to the customers.

**DUMPING** Practice of selling products at significantly lower prices in a foreign market than in a nation's own domestic market.

**DYNAMIC BREAK-EVEN ANALYSIS** Combines the traditional break-even analysis model with an evaluation of consumer demand.

**E-COMMERCE** Commerce conducted via the Internet.

**ECONOMIC ENVIRONMENT** The factors in a region or country that affect the production, distribution, and consumption of its wealth. Key elements are monetary

resources, inflation, employment, and productive capacity.

**ECONOMIC ORDER QUANTITY (EOQ)** A model that emphasizes a cost tradeoff between inventory holding costs and order costs.

**ECONOMIC UNION** A common market that also requires members to harmonize monetary policies, taxation, and government spending. In addition, a common currency is used by members.

**ELASTICITY** A measure of the responsiveness of purchasers and suppliers to changes in price.

**ELECTRONIC EXCHANGE** An organized group of buyers and sellers from a specific industry linked together electronically.

**ELECTRONIC EXCHANGE NETWORK** A single point of access to suppliers and customers through the Internet.

**EMBARGO** A complete ban on importing a particular product.

**ENGEL'S LAWS** As family income increases, (1) a smaller percentage goes for food, (2) the percentage spent on housing and household operations and clothing will remain constant, and (3) the percentage spent on other items will increase.

**ENVIRONMENTAL SCANNING** The process by which the marketing manager gathers and sorts information about the marketing environment.

**ESCALATOR CLAUSE** Allows the seller to adjust the final price based on changes in the costs of the product's ingredients between the placement of the order and the completion of construction or delivery of the product.

**E-TAILING** Retailing via the Internet.

**ETHNOCENTRIC COMPANY** Firm that assumes that its way of doing business in its home market is the proper way to operate, and tries to replicate this in foreign markets.

**EVALUATIVE CRITERIA** Features the consumer considers in making a choice among alternatives.

**EVOKED SET** The number of brands that a consumer actually considers in making a purchase decision.

**EXCHANGE CONTROL** Requirement that firms gaining foreign exchange by exporting must sell their foreign exchange to the central bank or agency, and importers must buy foreign exchange from the same organization.

**EXCHANGE PROCESS** The means by which two or more parties give something of value to one another to satisfy felt needs.

**EXCHANGE RATE** The rate at which a nation's currency can be exchanged for other currencies or gold.

**EXCHANGE RISK** The risk of negotiating a price in another nation's currency and finding upon delivery of the product that the currency's value has dropped in relation to your country's currency.

**EXCLUSIVE DEALING** An arrangement whereby a supplier prohibits a marketing intermediary (either a wholesaler or, more typically, a retailer) from handling competing products.

**EXCLUSIVE DISTRIBUTION** The granting of exclusive rights by manufacturers to a wholesaler or retailer to sell in a geographic region.

**EXPENSE ITEMS** Products and services that are used within a short period of time.

**EXPERIENCE QUALITIES** Characteristics of products that can be assessed mainly through using them.

**EXPLORATORY RESEARCH** Learning about the problem area and beginning to focus on specific areas of study by discussing the problem with informed sources within the firm (a process often called situation analysis) and with knowledgeable others outside the firm (the informal investigation).

**FACILITATING AGENCY** An agency that provides specialized assistance for regular channel members (such as producers, wholesalers, and retailers) in moving products from producer to consumer.

**FADS** Fashions with abbreviated life cycles.

**FAMILY BRAND** Brand name used for several related products.

**FAMILY LIFE CYCLE** The process of family formation, development, and dissolution.

**FASHIONS** Currently popular products that tend to follow recurring life cycles.

**FISCAL POLICY** The receipts and expenditures of government.

**FLEXIBLE PRICING** A variable price policy.

**FOB PLANT** The buyer must pay all the freight charges.

**FOLLOW-UP** The post-sales activities that often determine whether a person will become a repeat customer.

**FRANCHISE** An agreement whereby one firm (franchisee) agrees to meet the operating requirements of a successful business (franchisor) in return for the right to carry the name and products of the franchisor.

**FREE TRADE AGREEMENT (FTA)** The agreement establishing a free trade area between Canada and the United States that preceded NAFTA.

**FREE TRADE AREA** Area established by agreement among two or more nations within which participants agree to free trade of goods and services among themselves.

**FREIGHT ABSORPTION** The seller permits the buyer to subtract transportation expenses from the bill.

**FREIGHT FORWARDER** Wholesaling intermediary that specializes in international logistics.

**FRIENDSHIP, COMMERCE, AND NAVIGATION (FCN) TREATIES** Treaties that address many aspects of commercial relations with other countries; such treaties constitute international law.

**GE BUSINESS SCREEN** A process using a 3 x 3 matrix that considers business strengths and industry attractiveness.

**GENERIC NAME** A brand name over which the original owner has lost exclusive claim because all offerings in the associated class of products have become generally known by the brand name (usually that of first or leading brand in that product class).

**GENERIC PRODUCTS** Food and household staples characterized by plain labels, little or no advertising, and no brand names.

**GEOCENTRIC COMPANY** Firm that develops a marketing mix that meets the needs of target consumers in all markets.

**GEOGRAPHIC SEGMENTATION** Dividing an overall market into homogeneous groups based on population location.

**HAZARDOUS PRODUCTS ACT** A major piece of legislation that consolidated previous legislation and set significant new standards for product safety; defines a hazardous product as any product that is included in a list (called a schedule) compiled by Consumer and Corporate Affairs Canada or Health and Welfare Canada.

**HIGH-INVOLVEMENT PRODUCTS** Products for which the purchaser is highly involved in making the purchase decision.

**HOUSE-TO-HOUSE RETAILER** Retailer that sells products by direct contact between the retailer–seller and the customer at the home of the customer.

**HYPERMARKET** Mass merchandiser that operates on a low-price, self-service basis and carries lines of soft goods, hard goods, and groceries.

**HYPOTHESIS** A tentative explanation about the relationship between variables as a starting point for further testing.

**IMPLEMENTATION AND CONTROL** Consist of putting the marketing plan into action as well as doing ongoing monitoring and gathering feedback on how well the plan is accomplishing the stated marketing objectives.

**IMPORT QUOTA** A limit set on the amount of products that may be imported in a certain category.

**INDIRECT INTERNATIONAL TRADE** Exporting and/or importing only through other domestic companies that trade internationally.

**INDIVIDUAL BRAND** Brand that is known by its own brand name rather than by the name of the company producing it or an umbrella name covering similar items.

**INDIVIDUAL OFFERING** Single product within a product line.

**INDUSTRIAL DISTRIBUTOR** A wholesaler that operates in the business goods market and typically handles small accessory equipment and operating supplies.

**INDUSTRIAL GOODS** Those products purchased to be used, either directly or indirectly, in the production of other goods or for resale.

**INDUSTRY OR MARKET ELASTICITY** Refers to changes in total demand resulting from general changes in price across the industry.

**INFLATION** A rising price level that results in reduced purchasing power for the consumer.

**INFORMATIVE PRODUCT ADVERTISING** Advertising that seeks to develop demand through presenting factual information on the attributes of a product or service.

**INSEPARABILITY** A characteristic of services in which the product is produced and consumed simultaneously.

**INSTALLATIONS** Major capital assets that are used to produce products and services.

**INSTITUTIONAL ADVERTISING** Promoting a concept, idea, or philosophy, or the goodwill of an industry, company, or organization.

**INTANGIBLE ATTRIBUTES** Those attributes that cannot be experienced by the physical senses.

**INTEGRATED MARKETING COMMUNICATIONS (IMC)** A comprehensive marketing communications plan that takes into consideration all the communication disciplines being used and combines them to provide clarity, consistency, and maximum communications impact.

**INTENSIVE DISTRIBUTION** A form of distribution that attempts to provide saturation coverage of the potential market.

**INTERACTIVE MARKETING** Term used to describe the interrelationship between the employee and the customer.

**INTERNAL MARKETING** A marketing effort aimed at those who provide the service so that they will feel better about their task and therefore produce a better product.

**INTERNATIONAL PRICING** Setting prices to be charged to buyers in other countries taking into consideration exchange risk, price escalation through multiplication of channels, and transportation.

**INVENTORY ADJUSTMENTS** Changes in the amounts of materials a manufacturer keeps on hand.

**JOINT DEMAND** Demand for an industrial product that is related to the demand for other industrial goods.

**JOINT VENTURE** A partnership of firms from different countries, often to set up a local business in a country that is foreign to one of the partners.

**JUDGEMENT SAMPLE** A nonprobability sample of people with a specific attribute.

**JUST IN TIME (JIT)** An approach to minimizing inventory costs through identifying minimal inventory levels and arranging with suppliers to replenish stocks just in time to be used in production.

**LABEL** The part of a package that contains (1) the brand name or symbol, (2) the name and address of the manufacturer or distributor, (3) information about product composition and size, and (4) information about recommended uses of the product.

**LARGE-FORMAT SPECIALTY STORE** Large, warehouse-type retail store that specializes in selling a great variety of one category of merchandise at very low prices.

**LAW OF RETAIL GRAVITATION** Principle that delineates the retail trade area of a potential site on the basis of distance between alternative locations and relative populations.

**LEARNING** Changes in knowledge, attitudes, and behaviour, as a result of experience.

**LICENSING** Granting authority to produce and sell a product developed in one country in another.

**LIFESTYLE** The mode of living.

**LIFETIME-CUSTOMER VALUE (LCV)** The sum of all future-customer revenue streams minus product and servicing costs, acquisition costs, and remarketing costs.

**LIMITED-LINE STORE** Retailer that offers a large assortment of a single line of products or a few related lines of products.

**LINE EXTENSION** The development of individual offerings that appeal to different market segments but are closely related to the existing product line.

**LIQUIDATOR** Specialty retailer that either comes into a bankrupt store and handles

the closeout, or buys the entire lot and sells it in its own stores.

**LIST PRICE** The rate normally quoted to potential buyers.

**LOCAL CONTENT LAWS** Laws specifying the portion of a product that must come from domestic sources.

**LOGISTICS** That part of the supply chain process that plans, implements, and controls the efficient, effective forward and reverse flow and storage of goods, services, and related information between the point of origin and the point of consumption in order to meet customers' requirements.

**LOGISTICS CONCEPT** The integration of the total-cost approach, the avoidance of suboptimization, and the use of cast trade-offs.

**LOSS LEADER** Goods priced below cost to attract customers.

**LOW-INVOLVEMENT PRODUCTS** Products with little significance, either materially or emotionally, that a consumer may purchase first and evaluate later (while using them).

**LOYALTY PROGRAM** A program that gives rewards, such as points or free air miles, with each purchase in order to stimulate repeat business.

**MAIL-ORDER MERCHANDISER** Retailer that offers its customers the option of placing merchandise orders by mail, by telephone, or by visiting the mail-order desk of a retail store.

**MANUFACTURERS' AGENT** An independent salesperson who works for a number of manufacturers of related but noncompeting products.

**MARGINAL COST** The change in total cost that results from producing an additional unit of output.

**MARKDOWN** A reduction in the price of an item.

**MARKET** People with the willingness, purchasing power, and authority to buy.

**MARKET DEVELOPMENT STRATEGY** Finding new markets for existing products.

**MARKET ORIENTATION** A focus on understanding customer needs and objectives, then making the business serve the interests of the customer rather than trying to make the customer buy what the business wants to produce.

**MARKET PRICE** The amount that a consumer pays.

**MARKET RESTRICTION** An arrangement whereby suppliers restrict the geographic territories for each of their distributors.

**MARKET SEGMENTATION** Grouping people according to their similarity in one or more dimensions related to a particular product category.

**MARKET SHARE OBJECTIVE** To control a specific portion of the market for the firm's product.

**MARKETING** The process of planning and executing the conception, pricing, promotion, and distribution of ideas, goods, and services to create exchanges that satisfy individual and organizational objectives.

**MARKETING AUDIT** A comprehensive appraisal of the organization's marketing activities. It involves a systematic assessment of marketing plans, objectives, strategies, programs, activities, organizational structure, and personnel.

**MARKETING CHANNELS** The steps or handling organizations that a good or service goes through from producer to final consumer.

**MARKETING COMMUNICATIONS** All activities and messages that inform, persuade, and influence the consumer in making a purchase decision.

**MARKETING COMMUNICATIONS MIX** The blend of personal selling and nonpersonal communication (including advertising, sales promotion, public relations, sponsorship marketing, and point-of-purchase communications) by marketers in an attempt to accomplish information and persuasion objectives.

**MARKETING CONCEPT** An organization-wide philosophy that holds that the best route to organizational success is to find an unserved or underserved need in society and meet that need better than anyone else, while still meeting long-term organizational objectives.

**MARKETING FUNCTIONS** Buying, selling, transporting, storing, grading, financing, risk taking, and information collecting and disseminating.

**MARKETING INFORMATION SYSTEM** A set of routine procedures to continuously collect, monitor, and present internal and external information on company performance and opportunities in the marketplace.

**MARKETING INTERMEDIARY** A business firm operating between the producer and the consumer or business purchaser.

**MARKETING MIX** The blending of the four elements of marketing to satisfy chosen consumer segments.

**MARKETING OBJECTIVES AND STRATEGY** Flow from the situation analysis. They are a statement of what the organization intends to accomplish with its marketing program and the general strategic approach it will take.

**MARKETING PLAN** A specific detailed statement of how the marketing mix will be used to realize the marketing strategy.

**MARKETING RESEARCH** The systematic gathering, recording, and analyzing of data about problems relating to the marketing of goods and services.

**MARKETING STRATEGY** A strategy that focuses on developing a unique long-run competitive position in the market by assessing consumer needs and the firm's potential for gaining competitive advantage.

**MARKUP** The amount a producer or channel member adds to cost in order to determine the selling price.

**MASS CUSTOMIZATION** Organizing to make production of products more flexible to meet specifically stated customer requirements.

**MASS MERCHANDISER** Retailer that concentrates on high turnover of items, emphasizes lower prices than department stores, and offers reduced services.

**MEMBERSHIP AND WAREHOUSE CLUB** Very large, warehouse-type retail store that offers low prices because of its no-frill format and paid membership requirement.

**MEMBERSHIP GROUP** A type of reference group to which individuals actually belong.

**MERCHANDISE MART** Permanent exhibition at which manufacturers rent showcases for their product offerings.

**MERCHANT WHOLESALER** A wholesaler who takes title to the products carried.

**MICROCULTURE** A subgroup with its own distinguishing modes of behaviour.

**MISSIONARY SELLING** Selling that emphasizes selling the firm's goodwill and providing customers with technical or operational assistance.

**MODIFIED REBUY** A situation in which purchasers are willing to reevaluate their available options.

**MONETARY POLICY** The manipulation of the money supply and market rates of interest.

**MONOPOLISTIC COMPETITION** A market structure with a large number of buyers and sellers where heterogeneity in good and/or service and usually geographical differentiation allow the marketer some control over price.

**MONOPOLY** A market structure with only one seller of a product with no close substitutes.

**MOTIVE** An inner state that directs us toward the goal of satisfying a felt need.

**MRO ITEMS** Business-to-business supplies, so called because they can be categorized as maintenance items, repair items, and operating supplies.

**MULTILEVEL MARKETING** The development of a network among consumers to sell and deliver from one level of consumers to another using social obligation, personal influence, and motivational techniques.

**MULTINATIONAL CORPORATION (MNC)** A corporation that produces and markets goods and services in several countries.

**MULTI-OFFER STRATEGY** The attempt to satisfy several segments of the market very well with specialized products and unique marketing programs aimed at each segment.

**NATIONAL BRAND (MANUFACTURER'S BRAND)** A brand promoted and distributed by a manufacturer.

**NEED** The perceived difference between the current state and a desired state.

**NEGOTIATED CONTRACT** The terms of the contract are set through talks between the buyer and the seller.

**NEW TASK BUYING** First-time or unique purchase situations that require considerable effort on the part of the decision makers.

**NONPROBABILITY SAMPLE** A sample chosen in an arbitrary fashion so that each member of the population does not have a representative chance of being selected.

**NONPROFIT ORGANIZATION (NPO)** Organization whose primary objective is something other than returning a profit to its owners.

**NORTH AMERICAN FREE TRADE AGREEMENT (NAFTA)** The agreement establishing a free trade area among Canada, the United States, and Mexico that followed the FTA.

**NORTH AMERICAN INDUSTRIAL CLASSIFICATION SYSTEM (NAICS)** A coding system used to categorize different types of businesses and products (formerly the Standard Industrial Classification, or SIC).

**OBJECTION** Reveals a customer's interest in a product and can be used as a cue to provide additional information.

**ODD PRICING** Prices are set ending in some amount just below the next rounded number.

**OFF-PRICE RETAILER** Retailer that specializes in selling manufacturers' excess stocks of brand-name merchandise at a discount.

**OLIGOPOLY** A market structure in which there are relatively few sellers.

**OLIGOPSONY** A market in which there are only a few buyers.

**OPINION LEADERS** Trendsetters—individuals who are more likely to purchase new products early and to serve as information sources for others in a given group.

**ORDER PROCESSING** Selling at the wholesale and retail levels; involves identifying customer needs, pointing out these needs to the customer, and completing the order.

**ORGANIZATION MARKETING** Attempts to influence others to accept the goals of, receive the services of, or contribute in some way to an organization.

**PENETRATION PRICING** An entry price for a product that is lower than what is estimated to be the long-term price.

**PERCEPTION** The meaning that each person attributes to incoming stimuli received through the five senses.

**PERCEPTUAL SCREEN** The filter through which messages must pass.

**PERFORMANCE GAP** The difference between the company's performance and that of the best of the best.

**PERSON MARKETING** Efforts designed to cultivate the attention, interest, and preference of a target market toward a person.

**PERSONAL SELLING** A seller's promotional presentation conducted on a person-to-person basis with the buyer.

**PERSUASIVE PRODUCT ADVERTISING** Advertising that emphasizes using words or images to try to create an image for a product and to influence attitudes about it.

**PLANNED SHOPPING CENTRE** Group of retail stores planned, coordinated, and marketed as a unit to shoppers in a particular geographic trade area.

**POINT-OF-PURCHASE ADVERTISING** Displays and demonstrations that seek to promote the product at a time and place closely associated with the actual decision to buy.

**POINT-OF-PURCHASE COMMUNICATIONS** Materials designed to influence buying decisions at the point of purchase.

**POLITICAL–LEGAL ENVIRONMENT** The laws and interpretation of laws that require firms to operate under competitive conditions and to protect consumer rights.

**POLYCENTRIC COMPANY** Firm that assumes that every country is different and that a specific marketing approach should be developed for each separate country.

**POPULATION OR UNIVERSE** The total group that the researcher wants to study.

**POSITIONING** Shaping the product and developing a marketing program in such a way that the product is perceived to be (and actually is) different from competitors' products.

**POSITIONING ANALYSIS** Identifying brands in each segment and how they differ from each other.

**POST-TESTING** The assessment of advertising copy after it has been used.

**POWER NODE** Groupings of two or more large-format retailers that result in large customer drawing power.

**PREFERENCE PRODUCTS** Products that are slightly higher on the effort dimension and much higher on risk than convenience products.

**PRESENTATION** The act of giving the sales message to a prospective customer.

**PRESTIGE OBJECTIVES** Establishing relatively high prices in order to develop and maintain an image of quality and exclusiveness.

**PRETESTING** The assessment of an advertisement's effectiveness before it is actually used.

**PRICE** The value that a buyer exchanges for a good or service.

**PRICE ESCALATION** The increase in final price in a foreign market over a domestic price because of having to pay for the services of additional channel members to get the product to that market.

**PRICE LIMITS** Limits within which product quality perception varies directly with price.

**PRICE LINING** The practice of marketing merchandise at a limited number of prices.

**PRICE STRUCTURE** An outline of the selling price and the various discounts offered to intermediaries.

**PRICING** The methods of setting competitive, profitable, and justified prices.

**PRICING POLICY** A general guideline based on pricing objectives that is intended for use in specific pricing decisions.

**PRIMARY DATA** Data being collected for the first time.

**PRIVATE BRAND** A brand promoted and distributed by a wholesaler or retailer.

**PRIVATE CARRIER** Transportation carrier that provides transportation services for a particular firm and may not solicit other transportation business.

**PROBABILITY SAMPLE** A sample in which every member of the population has a known chance of being selected.

**PRODUCERS** Those who transform goods and services through production into other goods and services.

**PRODUCT ADVERTISING** Nonpersonal selling of a particular good or service.

**PRODUCT DEVELOPMENT STRATEGY** Introducing new products into identifiable or established markets.

**PRODUCT DIVERSIFICATION STRATEGY** The development of new products for new markets.

**PRODUCT IMPROVEMENT STRATEGY** A modification in existing products.

**PRODUCT LIFE CYCLE** A product's progress through introduction, growth, maturity, and decline stages.

**PRODUCT LINE** A series of related products.

**PRODUCT MANAGEMENT** Decisions about what kind of product is needed, its uses, package design, branding, trademarks, warranties, guarantees, product life cycles, and new product development.

**PRODUCT MANAGERS (BRAND MANAGERS)** Individuals assigned one product or product line and given responsibility for determining its objectives and marketing strategies.

**PRODUCT MIX** The assortment of product lines and individual offerings available from a company.

**PRODUCT ORIENTATION** A focus on the product itself rather than on the consumer's needs.

**PRODUCT PORTFOLIO** The complete collection of products or services that a company produces.

**PROFIT CENTRE** Any part of the organization to which revenue and controllable costs can be assigned, such as a department.

**PROFIT MAXIMIZATION** The point where the addition to total revenue is just balanced by an increase in total cost.

**PROMOTIONAL ALLOWANCE** Extra discount offered to retailers so that they will advertise the manufacturer along with the retailer.

**PROMOTIONAL PRICE** A lower-than-normal price used as an ingredient in a firm's selling strategy.

**PROSPECTING** Identifying potential customers.

**PSYCHOGRAPHIC SEGMENTATION** Uses behavioural profiles developed from analyses of the activities, opinions, interests, and lifestyles of consumers in identifying market segments.

**PSYCHOGRAPHICS** The use of psychological attributes, lifestyles, attitudes, and demographics in determining the behavioural profiles of different consumers.

**PSYCHOLOGICAL PRICING** The use of prices to suggest values of a product or attributes of a product/price offering.

**PSYTE** A geodemographic classification system that identifies lifestyle cluster profiles across Canada.

**PUBLIC RELATIONS** A component of marketing communications that focuses on creating favourable attention and word of mouth among various publics.

**PUBLIC WAREHOUSE** Independently owned storage facility.

**PUBLICITY** Normally unpaid communication that disseminates positive information about company activities and products.

**PULLING STRATEGY** A promotional effort by the seller to stimulate final-user demand, which then exerts pressure on the distribution channel.

**PURE COMPETITION** A market structure in which there is such a large number of buyers and sellers that no one of them has a significant influence on price.

**PUSHING STRATEGY** The promotion of the product first to the members of the marketing channel, who then participate in its promotion to the final user.

**QUALIFYING** Determining that the prospect is really a potential customer.

**QUANTITY DISCOUNT** Price reduction granted for large purchases.

**QUOTA SAMPLE** A nonprobability sample that is divided so that different segments or groups are represented in the total sample.

**RACK JOBBER** Wholesaler that provides the racks, stocks the merchandise, prices the

goods, and makes regular visits to refill the shelves.

**RAW MATERIALS** Farm products (such as cattle, wool, eggs, milk, pigs, and canola) and natural products (such as coal, copper, iron ore, and lumber).

**REBATE** Refund by the seller of a portion of the purchase price.

**RECIPROCITY** Extending purchasing preference to suppliers who are also customers.

**RECYCLED MERCHANDISE RETAILER** Retailer that sells castoff clothes, furniture, and other products.

**REFERENCE GROUP** A group whose value structures and standards influence a person's behaviour.

**REGIOCENTRIC COMPANY** Firm that recognizes that countries with similar cultures and economic conditions can be served with a similar marketing mix.

**REINFORCEMENT** The reduction in drive that results from a proper response.

**RELATIONSHIP MARKETING** Identifying and establishing, maintaining and enhancing, and, when necessary, also terminating relationships with customers and other stakeholders, at a profit, so that the objectives of all parties involved are met, through a mutual exchange and fulfillment of promises.

**REMINDER-ORIENTED PRODUCT ADVERTISING** Advertising whose goal is to reinforce previous promotional activity by keeping the product or service name in front of the public.

**RESEARCH DESIGN** A series of advance decisions that, taken together, make up a master plan or model for conducting the investigation.

**RESPONSE** The individual's reaction to the cues and drives.

**RETAIL IMAGE** The consumer's perception of a store and of the shopping experience it provides.

**RETAIL TRADE AREA ANALYSIS** Studies that assess the relative drawing power of alternative retail locations.

**RETAILER** A store that sells products purchased by individuals for their own use and not for resale.

**RETAILING** All the activities involved in selling goods and services to the ultimate consumer.

**REVALUATION** Situation in which a country adjusts the value of its currency upward.

**REVERSE CHANNELS** The paths goods follow from consumer to manufacturer or to marketing intermediaries.

**RFP (REQUEST FOR PROPOSAL) OR RFQ (REQUEST FOR QUOTATION)** Common procedures used by firms to get information on alternatives or prices.

**ROLE** The rights and duties expected of an individual in a group by other members of the group.

**ROLE MODEL MARKETING** Marketing technique that associates a product with the positive perception of a type of individual or a role.

**SALES BRANCH** Manufacturer-owned facility that carries inventory and processes orders to customers from available stock.

**SALES MANAGEMENT** Securing, maintaining, motivating, supervising, evaluating, and controlling the field sales force.

**SALES MAXIMIZATION** The pricing philosophy analyzed by economist William J. Baumol. Baumol believes that many firms attempt to maximize sales within a profit constraint.

**SALES ORIENTATION** A focus on developing a strong sales force to convince consumers to buy whatever the firm produces.

**SALES PROMOTION** Those marketing activities, other than personal selling, mass media advertising, and publicity, that stimulate consumer purchasing and dealer effectiveness.

**SCRAMBLED MERCHANDISING** The retail practice of carrying dissimilar lines to generate added sales volume.

**SEARCH QUALITIES** Physical qualities that enable products to be examined and compared. This eases the task of choosing among them.

**SECONDARY DATA** Previously published matter.

**SEGMENT ELASTICITY** Refers to the sensitivity to changes in price that a particular market segment exhibits.

**SELECTIVE DISTRIBUTION** The selection of a small number of retailers to handle the firm's product line.

**SELLING AGENT** An agent wholesaling intermediary that is responsible for the total marketing program for a firm's product line.

**SERVICE** A product without physical characteristics—a bundle of performance and symbolic attributes designed to produce consumer want satisfaction.

**SHAPING** The process of applying a series of rewards and reinforcement so that more complex behaviour can evolve over time.

**SHOPPING PRODUCTS** Products that are usually purchased only after the consumer has compared competing products.

**SIMPLE RANDOM SAMPLE** A probability sample in which every item in the relevant universe has an equal opportunity of being selected.

**SINGLE-OFFER STRATEGY** The attempt to satisfy a large or a small market with one product and a single marketing program.

**SITUATION ANALYSIS** Considers the internal circumstances of the organization or product, the external environment, competitive activity, and characteristics of the customer that may be relevant to the marketing plan.

**SKIMMING PRICING** Choosing a high entry price; to sell first to consumers who are willing to pay the highest price, and then reduce the price.

**SOCIAL CLASS** The relatively permanent divisions in a society into which individuals or families are categorized based on prestige and community status.

**SOCIAL MARKETING** The analysis, planning, execution, and evaluation of programs designed to influence the voluntary behaviour of target audiences in order to improve their personal welfare and that of society.

**SOCIETAL MARKETING CONCEPT** An organization-wide philosophy that holds that the best route to organizational success is to find an unserved or underserved need in society and meet that need better than anyone else, while still meeting long-term organizational objectives and also considering the long-term impact on society.

**SOCIOCULTURAL ENVIRONMENT** The mosaic of societal and cultural components that are relevant to the organization's business decisions.

**SORTING** The process that alleviates discrepancies in assortment by reallocating the outputs of various producers into assortments desired by individual purchasers.

**SPECIALTY ADVERTISING** Sales promotion medium that uses useful articles to carry the advertiser's name, address, and advertising message.

**SPECIALTY PRODUCTS** Products that are highest in both effort and risk, due to some unique characteristics that cause the buyer to prize that particular brand.

**SPECIALTY STORE** Retailer that handles only part of a single line of products.

**SPECIFICATIONS** A specific description of a needed item or job that the buyer wishes to acquire.

**SPONSORSHIP MARKETING** The practice of promoting the interests of a company by associating the company or a brand with a specific event.

**SSWDs** Single, separated, widowed, or divorced people.

**STAGFLATION** High unemployment and a rising price level at the same time.

**STATUS** Relative position in a group.

**STATUS QUO OBJECTIVES** Objectives based on maintaining stable prices.

**STOCK TURNOVER** The number of times the average inventory is sold annually.

**STORAGE WAREHOUSE** Stores products for moderate to long periods of time in an attempt to balance supply and demand for producers and purchasers.

**STRAIGHT REBUY** A recurring purchase decision involving an item that has performed satisfactorily and is therefore purchased again by a customer.

**SUBLIMINAL PERCEPTION** A subconscious level of awareness.

**SUBOPTIMIZATION** A condition in which the manager of each logistics function attempts to minimize costs, but due to the impact of one logistics task on the others, the results are less than optimal.

**SUPERMARKET** Large-scale, departmentalized retail store offering a large variety of food products such as meats, produce, dairy products, canned goods, and frozen foods in addition to various nonfood items.

**SUPPLIES** Regular expense items necessary in the daily operation of a firm, but not part of its final product.

**SUPPLY CHAIN** A network of facilities and distribution options that performs the functions of procurement of materials, transformation of these materials into intermediate and finished products, and the distribution of these finished products to customers.

**SUPPLY CHAIN MANAGEMENT (SCM)** The systematic, strategic coordination of the traditional business functions and the tactics across these business functions within a particular company and across businesses within the supply chain for the purposes of improving the long-term performance of the individual companies and the supply chain as a whole.

**SUPPLY CURVE** The marginal cost curve above its intersection with average variable cost.

**SWOT ANALYSIS** The combined summary of the internal analysis and the environmental analysis. Stands for *strengths, weaknesses, opportunities*, and *threats*.

**SYSTEMATIC SAMPLE** A probability sample that takes every nth item on a list, after a random start.

**TANGIBLE ATTRIBUTES** Those attributes that can be experienced by the physical senses, such as sight, touch, and smell.

**TARGET MARKET** A market segment that a company chooses to serve.

**TARGET MARKET DECISION ANALYSIS** The evaluation of potential market segments.

**TARGET RETURN OBJECTIVES** Either short-run or long-run goals, usually stated as a percentage of sales or investment.

**TARIFF** A tax levied against products imported from abroad.

**TASK-OBJECTIVE METHOD** A sequential approach to allocating marketing communications budgets that involves two steps: (1) defining the realistic communication goals the firm wants the marketing communications mix to accomplish, and (2) determining the amount and type of marketing communications activity required to accomplish each of these objectives.

**TECHNOLOGICAL ENVIRONMENT** The applications of knowledge based on scientific discoveries, inventions, and innovations.

**TEST MARKETING** Selecting areas considered reasonably typical of the total market, and introducing a new product to these areas with a total marketing campaign to determine consumer response before marketing the product nationally.

**THIRD-PARTY LOGISTICS PROVIDER** Specialist firm that performs virtually all of the logistical tasks that manufacturers or other channel members would normally perform themselves.

**TIED SELLING** An arrangement whereby a supplier forces a dealer who wishes to handle a product to also carry other products from the supplier or to refrain from using or distributing someone else's product.

**TOTAL-COST APPROACH** Holds that all relevant factors in physically moving and storing products should be considered as a whole and not individually.

**TOTAL CUSTOMER SATISFACTION** Providing a good or service that fully and without reservation conforms to the customer's requirements.

**TOTAL PRODUCT** A total bundle of physical, service, and symbolic characteristics designed to produce customer want satisfaction.

**TRADE DISCOUNT** Payment to channel members or buyers for performing some marketing function normally required of the manufacturer.

**TRADE FAIRS** Periodic shows at which manufacturers in a particular industry display their wares for visiting retail and wholesale buyers.

**TRADE INDUSTRIES** Organizations, such as retailers and wholesalers, that purchase for resale to others.

**TRADE SHOW** An organized exhibition of products based on a central theme.

**TRADE-IN** Deduction from an item's price of an amount for the customer's old item that is being replaced.

**TRADEMARK** A brand that has been given legal protection and has been granted solely to its owner.

**TRANSFER PRICE** The price for sending goods from one company profit centre to another.

**TRUCK WHOLESALER** Limited-function merchant wholesaler that markets products that require frequent replenishment.

**UNIFORM DELIVERED PRICE** The same price (including transportation expenses) is quoted to all buyers.

**UNIT PRICING** Stating prices in terms of some recognized unit of measurement (such as grams or litres) or a standard numerical count.

**UNITIZATION** Combining as many packages as possible into one load.

**UNIVERSAL PRODUCT CODE** A code readable by optical scanners that can print the name of the item and the price on the cash register receipt.

**USAGE RATE** Divides the market by the amount of product consumed, and/or the degree of brand loyalty.

**UTILITY** The want-satisfying power of a product or service.

**VALUE** A subjective term that is defined by the customer; part of customer expectations, which are a combination of cost, time, quantity, quality, and human factors.

**VALUE ADDED** The increase in value of input material when transformed into semifinished or finished goods.

**VARIETY STORE** Retailer that offers an extensive range and assortment of low-priced merchandise.

**VENTURE-TEAM CONCEPT** An organizational strategy for developing new products through combining the management resources of marketing, technology, capital, and management expertise in a team.

**VERTICAL MARKETING SYSTEM** A network of channel intermediaries organized and centrally managed to produce the maximum competitive impact.

**VERTICAL WEB COMMUNITY** A site that acts as a comprehensive source of information and dialogue for a particular vertical market.

**WARRANTY** A guarantee to the buyer that the supplier will replace a defective product (or part of a product) or refund its purchase price during a specified period of time.

**WEBER'S LAW** The higher the initial intensity of a stimulus, the greater the amount of the change in intensity that is necessary in order for a difference to be noticed.

**WHEEL OF RETAILING** Hypothesized process of change in retailing, which suggests that new types of retailers gain a competitive foothold by offering lower prices through the reduction or elimination of services; but once established, they add more services and their prices gradually rise, so that they then become vulnerable to a new low-price retailer with minimum services—and the wheel turns.

**WHOLESALERS** Wholesaling intermediaries who take title to the products they handle.

**WHOLESALING** The activities of intermediaries who sell to retailers, other wholesalers, and business users but not in significant amounts to ultimate consumers.

**WHOLESALING INTERMEDIARIES** Intermediaries who assume title, as well as agents and brokers who perform important wholesaling activities without taking title to the products.

**WORLD TRADE ORGANIZATION (WTO)** The international body that deals with the rules of trade between nations.

**ZONE PRICING** The market is divided into different zones and a price is established within each.

# Company and Organization Index

# Subject Index

inventory adjustments in, 222
joint demand in, 222
market demand, 222–223
numbers of buyers, 219
Business-to-business markets, 62
defined, 218
e-commerce, 236
electronic exchange, 238
features of, 219
geographic concentration, 219
Internet, 236
number of buyers, 219
purchase decision process, 219
scope of, 220–221
types of, 219
Buy or lease, 328
Buyers, 229, 412
Buyer's remorse, 210
Buying centres, 227–228
Buying specialists, 370
Buzz marketing, 481

Canada Year Book, 151
Canada–U.S. Free Trade Agreement
(FTA), 529
Canadian Social Trends, 151
CANSIM, 151, 167
Capital items
defined, 223
purchasing, 224–225
Carriers
common, 439
contract, 439
private, 439
water, 439–440
Cartels, 520
Cash cows (products), 94, 95
Cash discounts, 355
Cash-and-carry wholesalers, 382
Catalogue retailers, 416
Category killers, 414–415
Celebrity marketing, 480–481
Census data, 151
Census, in marketing research, 157
Chain stores, 402
Chambers of commerce, 168
Channels, distribution, 365
*See also* Distribution channels
Charter of Rights, 36
Chase mania, 104
Children, consumer behaviour and, 194,
196–197
Civil damages, 33
Climate, marketing and, 49
Closing, in the sales process, 499

Clothing, marketing research publications, 172
Cluster sample, in marketing research, 158
Cognitive components, of attitudes, 202,
203
Cognitive dissonance, 209–210
Combines Investigation Act, 32
Commission merchants, 382
Common knowledge, 203
Common markets, 529
Communication(s)
defined, 106
generalized process, 449–451
international marketing, 524–525
marketing. *See* Marketing communications
nonpersonal, 452
point-of-purchase, 453
Community shopping centre, 424
Companies
approaches to international marketing,
513
business orientation, 8–12
ethnocentric, 513
geocentric, 514
international, 12
international marketing by, 515
marketing and, 13
multinational, 515
polycentric, 513
profit-oriented, 101–102
regiocentric, 513
strategic export planning, 515
Company elasticity, 325
Comparative advantage, principle of,
511–512
Comparative advertising, 479–480
Competition
alternative-gratification, 23
among brands, 254–255
analysis of, 99–100
direct, 23
economic conditions and, 163
indirect, 23
intelligence generation and, 10–11
international, 103, 348
inter-product, 23
intertype, 103
marketing communications and, 453
marketing concept and, 12
monopolistic, 321
new-product offerings, 24
product-substitute, 23
pure, 321
retailing, 401

total-dollar, 23
types of, 23
value and, 126
Competition Act, 9, 31, 32–37, 351, 353,
392, 520
Competition Bureau of Industry Canada,
32
Competitive bidding, 333
Competitive environment, 22–24
Component parts and materials, 266
Computers
marketing, in, 25, 163–164
marketing research publications,
172–173
Conative components, of attitudes, 202,
204
Concept testing, 290
Consumer, 293
Consumer analysis, pricing and, 342
Consumer and Corporate Affairs Canada,
32
Consumer behaviour
attitudes and, 202–204
cultural influences, 185–188
defined, 184
environmental factors, 184–197
family influences, 193–197
individual factors, 197–206
inflation and, 30
learning and, 204–206
lifestages and, 194
lifestyles and, 191–193
perceptions in, 200–202
psychological processes, 197–206
social classes and, 190–193
social influences, 189–193
unemployment and, 30–31
Consumer decision process, 207–210
alternative evaluation in, 208
classification of, 210
information search in, 208
postpurchase evaluation, 209–210
problem recognition in, 207
purchase act, 208
purchase decision, 208
Consumer goods, 43
distribution channels, 369–371
Consumer innovators, 293–294
Consumer products, characteristics, 260
Consumer response, 450
Consumerism, 29
Consumption, production and, 305–307
Containerization, 442
Contests, in sales promotion, 494
Contingency theory, 103

# Photo Credits

Page 2: Courtesy of TELUS Mobility; Page 4: © 1995-2002 FedEx. All rights reserved; Page 6: Courtesy of MasterCard Canada; Page 9: Courtesy of Target Corporation; Page 10: Courtesy of Rogers AT & T Wireless and Scotiabank, photography by Hasin Dattu, creative department MacLaren McCann, Toronto; Page 15: Courtesy of Toronto Zoo. Ad produced by Roche Macaulay Advertising; Page 20: © Rob Lewine/ CORBIS/Magma; Page 24: Reproduced under permission of Lever Pond's. © 1999 all rights reserved. ® Registered trade-marks of U L Canada Inc.; Page 25: Courtesy of Minolta Canada Inc.; Page 26: Courtesy of Amazon.com, Inc.; Page 28: Courtesy of Council for Bio-technology Information; Page 40: Courtesy of Sing Tao Newspaper (Canada 1998) Ltd.; Page 44: Courtesy of Goodyear Canada Inc.; Page 53: Courtesy of La Coupe and Centura Brants Inc.; Page 60: Courtesy of Parmalat Canada; Page 68: Courtesy of Reitman's (Canada) Ltd.; Page 71: Courtesy of Procter & Gamble Inc.; Page 78: Courtesy of Teen People Magazine; Page 84: "Coca-Cola" trademarks appear courtesy of Coca-Cola Ltd.; Page 88: Courtesy of Air Canada; Page 93: Dick Hemingway; Page 100: Courtesy of Zellers; Page 102: Courtesy of Procter & Gamble Inc.; Page 103: Courtesy of W Network; Page 115: Courtesy of Marsh Technologies Inc.; Page 116: Courtesy of Hard Rock Café; Page 120: Courtesy of Canada Post; Page 121: Reprinted by permission of General Motors of Canada Ltd. (Saturn); Page 122: Courtesy of Shell Canada Products; Page 124: Courtesy of Intel of Canada Ltd.; Page 127: Courtesy of Ford Motor Company; Page 134: Courtesy of Delta Hotels; Page 136: Courtesy of Indigo Books and Music Inc.; Page 142: KEL-LOGG'S®, KELLOGG'S FROSTED FLAKES®, TONY THE TIGER® and T H E Y ' R E GR-R-REAT® are registered trademarks of Kellogg Company, © 2002 Kellogg Company; Page 146: Courtesy of The Gillette Company; Page 156: Courtesy of Campbell Soup Company Ltd.; Page 158: Courtesy of IKEA Canada; Page 182: © Gail Mooney/CORBIS/Magma; Page 189: Courtesy of Benetton USA Corp.; Page 194: Courtesy of Bombardier Recreational Products; Page 195: Courtesy of YTV, Corus Entertainment; Page 197: Courtesy of GlaxoSmithKline; Page 200: Trademark reproduced with the permission of Hudson's Bay Company; Page 201: Courtesy of Sun-Rype Products Ltd.; Courtesy of Bozell Worldwide; Page 209: Courtesy of ROOTS Canada; Page 211: Courtesy of The Toronto Star Syndicate; Page 216: Courtesy of Intrinsyc Software, Inc., Vancouver, Canada; Page 218: "Access Granted" Ad. Copyright © 2002 Novell, Inc. All Rights Reserved. Reprinted and used with permission of Novell, Inc.; Page 220: Courtesy of Toronto Hydro Energy Services; Page 223: Courtesy of STAPLES Business Depot; Page 235: Courtesy of RBC Financial Group; Page 237: Courtesy of Microsoft Canada; Page 244: Courtesy of Ford Motor Company of Canada, Limited; Page 250: "Coca-Cola" trademarks appear courtesy of The Coca-Cola Company and Coca-Cola Ltd.; Page 253: Thomson Nelson photo; Page 254: Courtesy of Victorinox-Switzerland; Page 257: Thomson Nelson photo; Page 259: "Coca-Cola" trademarks appear courtesy of The Coca-Cola Company and Coca-Cola Ltd; Page 260: Courtesy of Ocean Spray Cranberries, Inc.; Page 265: © 2002 MINI Canada, a division of BMW Canada Inc. All rights reserved. The MINI trademark and logo are registered trademarks. Reproduced with the permission of MINI Canada for educational and non-commercial pur-poses only.; Page 270: Courtesy of Creative Labs, Inc.; Page 273: Courtesy of Procter & Gamble Inc.; Page 276: Courtesy of Nokia Products Limited; Page 285: Courtesy of Procter & Gamble Inc.; Page 286: SKI-DOO®, SEA-DOO®, BOMBARDIER® ATV, MX Z®, REV™, XP® and DS650™ are trademarks of Bombardier Inc. or its subsidiaries; Page 301: Rudi Von Briel/IndexStock; Page 303: Courtesy of State Farm Life Insurance Company; Page 304: Courtesy of Pacific National Exhibition; Page 306: Courtesy of Canadian Broadcasting Corporation; Page 318: Courtesy of Sony Computer Entertainment America Inc.; Page 322: Courtesy of DaimlerChrysler; Page 323: Courtesy of Samsung Electronics Canada; Page 326: Courtesy of STM; Page 335: © David Pollack/CORBIS/Magma; Page 341: Courtesy of Air Canada; Page 354: Used with permission of Inter IKEA Systems B.V.; Page 357: Reprinted with permis-sion from Realm: Creating Work You Want™, published by YES Canada-BC. Available online at http://realm.net and in print by calling (604) 412-4142. For more information, Phone: (604) 412-4144 Email: info@realm.net; Page 363: Courtesy of Flanagan Foodservice Inc.; Page 365: Courtesy of Carlos Redig, Marketing Director of Pitbull North America, Inc.; Page 370: Courtesy of The Globe and Mail; Page 374: Courtesy of Jetsgo Corporation; Page 376: Courtesy of Kulin Enterprises; Page 385: Courtesy of Cara Operations Limited, Harvey's; Page 391: PORSCHE, 911, CARRERA and the Porsche Crest are registered trademarks and distinctive shapes of PORSCHE automobiles are trade dress of Dr. Ing. h.c.F. Porsche AG. Used with permission of Porsche Cars North America, Inc.; Page 399: Courtesy of La Senza; Page 402: Courtesy of Home Depot and The Richards Group; Page 403: Courtesy of Wendy's International Inc.; Page 406: Shaun Best/Reuters News Picture Service; Page 412: Courtesy of Holt Renfrew; Page 413: Courtesy of JustWhiteShirts.com; Page 421: Courtesy of Blaney's Travel; Page 425: Courtesy of

West Edmonton Mall; Page 430: © Tom Wagner/CORBIS SABA/Magma; Page 433: Courtesy of Demand Solutions; Page 435: Courtesy of Canadian Professional Logistics Institute; Page 440: Courtesy of Canadian National Railway; Page 447: Courtesy of TBWA\CHIAT\ DAY and the Infiniti Division of Nissan Canada Inc.; Page 452: One of a Kind Show and Sale, a Merchandise Mart Properties Canada Inc. Show; Page 465: Courtesy of Ryerson University; Page 470: Courtesy of Canadian Magazine Publishers Association; Page 474: Courtesy of Harry Rosen Inc.; Page 478: Courtesy of LCBO; Page 486: Courtesy of Nike Canada; Page 488: Courtesy of Scotiabank; Page 492: Courtesy of Canada Post; Page 503: Courtesy of Fuji Photo Film Canada Inc.; Page 504: Courtesy of Acadian Seaplants Limited; Page 511: Courtesy of Toyota Canada Inc.; Page 522: Courtesy of McDonald's Restaurants of Canada Limited; Page 527: Courtesy of Export Development Canada; Page 536: left, AP/CP Picture Archive; right, © Reuters New Media Inc./CORBIS/Magma; Page 540: Courtesy of United Way of Greater Toronto; Page 542: Courtesy of Works & Emergency Services, City of Toronto; Page 546: Courtesy of MADD Canada; Page 548: Courtesy of Palmer Jarvis DDB, Vancouver.